MARIE-A[...]

John Hardman is one of the world's [...]
and the author of several distinguish[...]

Further praise for *Marie-Antoinette*:

'Insightful ... The impressive depth of Hardman's knowledge of the old regime's factional court politics makes it essential reading for anyone who wants to know more about the decision-making that led France into revolution – decisions in which the queen played an active part.' Marisa Linton, *BBC History Magazine*

'Presents [Marie-Antoinette] as much more than a symbol whose meaning is in the eye of her beholder. In Hardman's telling she is neither martyr nor voluptuary but rather a serious participant in politics.' Lynn Hunt, *New York Review of Books*

'It is worth making time for John Hardman's *Marie-Antoinette* ... [This] is a well written and sympathetic life of a woman out of her depth in the world of politics, and a good companion piece to the same author's life of her husband Louis XVI.' Jonathan Sumption, *Spectator* Books of the Year

'Hardman is far more than a biographer: his works are key to understanding the politics of the reign of Louis XVI. Steeped in the original sources and well able to decode the plots and schemes of the factions, this is both an entertaining and convincing new interpretation of the tragic queen.' Peter Campbell, author of *Power and Politics in Old Regime France*

'Superb. Hardman draws upon his vast knowledge of the period to present a new, deeply researched and compelling portrait of a much-maligned queen.' Julian Swann, author of *Exile, Imprisonment, or Death*

'A fresh perspective grounded in robust scholarship, *Marie-Antoinette* offers readers new insight into the political role of the last Queen of France.' Will Bashor, author of *Marie Antoinette's Darkest Days*

MARIE-ANTOINETTE

The Making of a French Queen

John Hardman

YALE UNIVERSITY PRESS
NEW HAVEN AND LONDON

Published with assistance from the Annie Burr Lewis Fund.

For information about this and other Yale University Press publications, please contact:
U.S. Office: sales.press@yale.edu   yalebooks.com
Europe Office: sales@yaleup.co.uk   yalebooks.co.uk

Set in Minion Pro by IDSUK (DataConnection) Ltd
Printed in Great Britain by Clays Ltd, Elcograf S.p.A

Library of Congress Control Number: 2019941055

ISBN 978-0-300-24308-6 (hbk)
ISBN 978-0-300-26094-6 (pbk)

A catalogue record for this book is available from the British Library.

10 9 8 7 6 5 4 3 2

This book is dedicated to those who helped me recover from serious injury, especially Gill Alcock, Chris Fishburne, Rod Fishburne, Mr Chris Armistead, Jane Hardman, Dr Meg Hardman, Dr Richard Hardman, Colonel Robert Hardman, Sheila Hardman, Joy Jones, Patrick Jones, Pam Lamb, Sheryl Millington, Jacqui Moore, Alan Peachment, Jane Platt, Professor Harry Procter, Jane Procter, Hazel Todhunter, Peter Todhunter and Barbara Wyatt.

CONTENTS

❖

ILLUSTRATIONS

✤

PRINCIPAL CHARACTERS

Some of the following classifications are somewhat schematic. There were over-laps: for instance, Marie-Antoinette's social group, the Polignacs, were also the king's political supporters often in opposition to the queen. I have placed Robespierre among the republicans but as late as 1791 he thought the declaration of republic would be aristocratic. Lafayette and the Girondins were doctrinaire republicans but when it came to the crunch tried to save the monarchy – ineffectively, because their heart wasn't in it.

THE AUSTRIAN ROYAL FAMILY

Francis I, Holy Roman Emperor 1745–65.

Maria-Theresa, his wife, queen of Bohemia and Hungary in her own right, 1740–80.

Joseph I, their eldest son, Holy Roman Emperor 1765–90 and co-ruler with his mother.

Leopold II, their second son, grand duke of Tuscany then Holy Roman Emperor 1790–2.

Marie-Antoinette, their youngest daughter, b. 1755, archduchess of Austria, then dauphine of France 1770–4 and queen of France 1774–92.

THE FRENCH ROYAL FAMILY

Louis XV, king of France 1715–74.

Maria Leszcyńska, his wife, d. 1768.

Madame de Pompadour, his *maîtresse-en-titre*, d. 1764.

Madame du Barry, his *maîtresse-en-titre* 1768–74.

Louis-Ferdinand, his only son, the 'old dauphin', d. 1765.

Adélaïde and Victoire, his daughters, known as Mesdames Tantes under Louis XVI.

Louis-Auguste, eldest surviving son of Louis-Ferdinand: dauphin 1765–74, king of France 1774–92.

Louis Stanislas Xavier, his next brother, comte de Provence, known as 'Monsieur', then Louis XVIII 1813–24.

Charles-Philippe, the next brother, comte d'Artois then Charles X 1824–30.

Elizabeth of France, their sister, known as Madame Elizabeth, guillotined 1794.

THE CHILDREN OF LOUIS XVI AND MARIE-ANTOINETTE

Louis-Joseph, the 'first dauphin' 1781–9.

Louis-Charles, the 'second dauphin' 1785–95, sometimes called Louis XVII 1793–5.

Marie-Thérèse-Charlotte, Madame Royale 1778–1854, their eldest child.

Sophie, 1786–7.

MARIE-ANTOINETTE'S SOCIAL CIRCLE, THE POLIGNAC SET

Yolande de Polastron, comtesse then duchesse de Polignac, governess of the royal children 1782–9.

Armand, comte then duc de Polignac, Yolande's husband, *Surintendant des postes*.

Diane de Polignac, Armand's sister, the brains behind the group.

Vaudreuil, Joseph Hyacinthe, comte de, lover of Madame de Polignac.

Adhémar, Jean-Balthazar, comte d', ambassador to the Court of Saint-James, 1783–7.

Calonne, Charles-Alexandre de, finance minister 1783–7.

Artois, Charles-Philippe, comte d'.

MARIE-ANTOINETTE'S POLITICAL CIRCLE

Breteuil, Louis Auguste, baron de, minister of the household 1783–8, head of the 'ministry of the hundred hours' 12–14 July 1789.

Castries, Charles-Eugène, marquis de, minister of the Marine, 1780–7.

Choiseul, Étienne-François, duc de, foreign minister 1757–61, dominant minister in the 1760s, arranged Marie-Antoinette's marriage to the dauphin.

Guines, Adrien-Louis, comte then duc de, ambassador to London 1770–6.

Ségur, Philippe Henri, marquis de, minister for war 1780–7.

Loménie de Brienne, Étienne-Charles de, Archbishop of Toulouse, prime minister 1787–8.

Mercy-Argenteau, Florimond, comte de, Austrian ambassador, 1766–89.

Necker, Jacques, finance minister 1776–81, de facto prime minister 1788–9.
Vermond, Jacques-Mathieu, abbé de, Marie-Antoinette's tutor.

THE KING'S PARTY

Calonne, Charles-Alexandre de, finance minister 1783–7.
Maurepas, Frédéric comte de, minister for the household 1718–23, minister for the Marine 1723–49, de facto prime minister 1774–81.
Montmorin, Armand Marc, comte de, foreign secretary 1787–91.
Vergennes, Charles Gravier, comte de, foreign secretary 1774–87.
And the Polignac set in general, as above.

REVOLUTIONARY LEADERS

Constitutional Monarchists
Barnave, Antoine, deputy in the Constituent Assembly.
Duport, Adrien, *parlementaire* then deputy in the Constituent Assembly.
Lameth, Alexandre comte de, courtier then deputy in the Constituent Assembly.
The above three known as 'the triumvirs'.
Duport de Tertre, Marguerite-Louis-François, minister of justice, 1790–2. The conduit for the implementation of Marie-Antoinette and Barnave's policy in 1791.
Lafayette, Gilles, marquis de, commander of the Parisian National Guard, determined enemy of Marie-Antoinette whom he blamed for stiffening the king's resistance to the Revolution.
Mirabeau, Honoré Gabriel, comte de, journalist, deputy in the Constituent Assembly, secret adviser to Marie-Antoinette.
Mounier, Jean Joseph, deputy in the Constituent Assembly. Supported a strong constitutional monarchy and seceded from the National Assembly in protest at the October Days.
Malouet, Pierre Victoire, deputy in the Constituent Assembly. Supported a strong constitutional monarchy.
Narbonne, Louis comte de, minister of war 1791–2. Lover of Madame de Staël, advocated war.

Republicans
Pétion, Jérôme, deputy, mayor of Paris.
Robespierre, Maximilien, deputy, member of the Committee of Public Safety. It was his influence which sent Marie-Antoinette before the Revolutionary Tribunal.

PRINCIPAL CHARACTERS

David, Jacques-Louis, painter, deputy, member of the Committee of General Security.

Hébert, René, editor of *Le Père Duchesne*, official in the Commune of Paris.

Danton, Georges, deputy, member of the 'first' Committee of Public Safety.

Brissot, Jean-Pierre, deputy, the leader of the war party 1791–2.

Vergniaud, Pierre, deputy, Girondin associate of Brissot.

Fouquier-Tinville, Antoine Quentin, public prosecutor of the Revolutionary Tribunal which tried Marie-Antoinette.

Herman, Armand-Joseph, president of the Revolutionary Tribunal.

OTHER CHARACTERS

D'Aiguillon, Emmanuel, duc, foreign secretary under Louis XV, and Marie-Antoinette's first 'scalp' on becoming queen.

Fersen, Axel von, Swedish nobleman in the service of France, reputed lover of Marie-Antoinette.

Guéméné, Victoire-Armande, princesse de, governess of the royal children 1778–82. Marie-Antoinette once told her, 'I will love you to my dying day', but had her dismissed after the spectacular bankruptcy of her husband.

Kaunitz, Wenzel Anton, prince von, Austrian chancellor 1753–92. Kaunitz discounted Marie-Antoinette's utility to Austria, calling her a 'bad payer'.

Lamballe, Marie Thérèse Louise of Savoy, princesse de, *surintendant* of the queen's household. An early favourite, she returned to France at Marie-Antoinette's request in 1791 and was killed in the September Massacres the next year.

Lamoignon, Chrétien-François de, president in the Parlement, justice minister 1787–8. Lamoignon organized the acquittal of Cardinal Rohan by the Parlement but Marie-Antoinette had to work closely with him a year later.

La Motte-Valois, Jeanne, mastermind of the heist known as the Diamond Necklace Affair.

Noailles, Anne comtesse de, *dame d'honneur* (no. 2) in the queen's household. Dubbed 'Madame Etiquette' by Marie-Antoinette, who also thought the power of the Noailles had become too entrenched.

Ossun, Geneviève de Gramont, comtesse de. Marie-Antoinette attended her salon when relations with Madame de Polignac became strained in 1787. Guillotined in 1794.

Rohan, Louis, cardinal de, ambassador to Vienna 1772–4, Grand Almoner 1777–86, hated by Marie-Antoinette and the dupe in the Diamond Necklace Affair.

Staël, Germaine, Madame de, daughter of Necker, lover of Narbonne, she published an anonymous defence of Marie-Antoinette when she learned she was to be tried.

Turgot, Anne-Robert-Jacques, distinguished economist and finance minister 1774–6. Marie-Antoinette threatened to have him thrown in the Bastille but her role in his downfall has been exaggerated.

PREFACE

hroughout her life Marie-Antoinette was haunted by the spectre of death, and her days were riddled by destructive ennui. Her beloved father Francis I, duke of Lorraine and Holy Roman Emperor, had died in 1765 when she was ten; in adult life she would go on to lose two of her four children; and as queen, half expecting to be killed, she would pore over David Hume's recently published account of the English Civil War along with her husband the king, who hoped thereby to dodge the fate of Charles I.[1] In the grounds of her Versailles pleasure villa, the Petit Trianon, there stood a tomb inscribed with a French translation of *Et in arcadia ego*, 'I, death, am present even in Arcadia'. The tomb was fake, as was the rustic simplicity Marie-Antoinette affected, but the shudder it must have evoked was genuine.

During her early years as queen Marie-Antoinette moved between listlessness and hedonistic activity, seeking out pleasure in the form of balls and gambling for high stakes with her court favourite, Madame de Polignac, by her side. Her periods of unpredictable and rash activity following her arrival at the French court in 1770 oscillated with periods of inertia – she was, from birth, a pawn in others' strategies. Nonetheless, Marie-Antoinette also intervened to a degree politically – and her interventions escalated so that, particularly in the six years preceding her death, she would play a significant part in determining the course of her own life, and that of her country. In 1788, before the Revolution was properly under way, she wrote, 'My fate is to bring misfortune'. The contrast first highlighted by Madame de Staël between her glittering beginning and tragic fall was really present throughout.

Six months after the birth of Marie-Antoinette, her Austrian mother Maria-Theresa, wife of Francis I but de facto ruler, worked to ensure that she be pledged as wife to the dauphin, thereby sealing the Austrian-French alliance. Initially a passive player exploited by her mother and brother, Joseph II, Marie-Antoinette would in her later years come to assert her independence. As queen of France she would play a decisive role in the unfolding of events, try to make the constitutional monarchy succeed and strive to turn the tide of revolutionary fervour, albeit with limited success.

The scene of the French court into which Marie-Antoinette arrived as the young dauphine was marked by an atmosphere of ossified tradition, severe formality reinforced by the entrenched power and influence of certain long-established noble families, rivalry between different groups with vested interests, and distrust and hatred of the mistresses of Louis XV who had sown seeds of division, past (Madame de Pompadour) and present (Madame du Barry). It was also a court presiding over a country in dire financial straits, and badly in need of reform. France had recently emerged from the Seven Years War in which she had been trounced on land and sea, losing Canada and her influence in India to England, accumulated debt, and become involved in internecine disputes with the political judges sitting in the Parlement whom Louis XV considered to be 'republicans'. Many in France attributed France's defeats to a one-sided commitment to her new ally, Austria. Marie-Antoinette would have to be careful, particularly in resisting her family's attempts to enlist her in their striving for territorial expansion.

This life of Marie-Antoinette looks at the extent of her power and influence, and the political role she played, prior to and during the French Revolution. This influence only became marked when the king's morale collapsed after the Assembly of Notables rejected his comprehensive reform programme in 1787 – the first in an unbroken chain of events which led to revolution. Then the king turned to her in his distress, but she came to the task largely unprepared as he had hitherto excluded her from matters of state. She had, as she told Antoine Barnave in 1791, some 'experience derived from following politics silently [sic] for 17 years'. But would it be enough?

This biography will demonstrate how before the Revolution Marie-Antoinette's favouritism, notably for the Polignac circle, was not just driven by a desire for constant amusement but was also an ambitious attempt to rebalance the Court and diminish the power of established families. In this, she sought to emulate her mother. Maria-Theresa had slackened the rigid, gloomy and austere Spanish etiquette that her father the emperor Charles VI had introduced to the Austrian court, and had managed to achieve the difficult balance between informality and familiarity. But where the mother had succeeded, the daughter's rebalancing was seen as capricious favouritism and only served to deepen her unpopularity.

During the revolutionary period, Marie-Antoinette's stance was markedly less 'reactionary' than is generally thought. Nor at first was she wholly opposed to the growing demands of the Third Estate in 1788–9. In the aftermath of the royal family's flight to Varennes and their forced return to Paris, it will be argued that Marie-Antoinette made sincere and concerted efforts to make the constitutional monarchy work during the last year of its life, between July 1791 and January 1792. The full significance of the exchange of letters between the queen and Barnave during this period will be brought out. An early leader of the Revolution, by autumn 1790 Barnave had come to the conclusion that a strong constitutional monarchy was necessary in order to 'stop the Revolution' before it descended into barbarism and an attack on property. In the closing months of 1791 Marie-Antoinette and Barnave governed France by secret correspondence. Their letters (forty-four apiece) show how policy was hammered out in detail between them. Their correspondence was published in 1913 but has never been fully exploited. At first many considered it a forgery because it presented Barnave as a 'traitor' but when in 1934 handwriting expertise showed it was undoubtedly genuine, another obstacle arose: the correspondence was worthless because Marie-Antoinette was palpably insincere, stringing Barnave along until her Austrian relatives saved her. I argue that the queen was sincere as long as there was a chance of success, but in order to bring their policy alive one needs to know how it was implemented. This can be done via the correspondence between two insiders,[2] which shows how the policy agreed by Marie-Antoinette and Barnave was given via the justice minister Duport du Tertre to a cabinet committee sitting in a specially designated room in the Tuileries. It was then rubber stamped by the Conseil d'Etat for executive action. This, Marie-Antoinette's most serious essay in government, necessarily sheds light on one of the most obscure and under-investigated aspects of the Revolution: the ministerial politics of the constitutional monarchy.

But the queen's intervention in politics came at a price. There wasn't supposed to be any politicking in a theoretically absolute monarchy like France; and even if, in practice, the king was obliged to spend some of his time on it, the queen certainly wasn't. In 1788, Marie-Antoinette 'sighed, and said there has been no more happiness for me since they turned me into an intriguer', claiming that in entering the political arena she was 'yielding to necessity [the king's depression] and my unfortunate fate'. But who had 'turned Marie-Antoinette into an intriguer'? Or was she merely being self-indulgent, something of which she was capable? It was not her Austrian relatives: Maria-Theresa and Joseph both urged her to stay clear of internal politics given its precarious nature and keep her powder dry to aid their foreign policy. The Austrian ambassador, however, Florimond Mercy-Argenteau, off his own bat plugged the candidacy of Loménie de Brienne, the archbishop of Toulouse, to be prime minister and, after he had played the role of leader of the opposition in the Notables, Marie-Antoinette was indeed instrumental in making him prime minister and then supporting him heart and soul during his disastrous eighteen months in office. I have called the chapter devoted to this period, 'The Ascendancy of Marie-Antoinette'. Her association with the hated premier completed her dangerous unpopularity, which had already deepened as a result of the Diamond Necklace Affair of 1785–6.

Who else dragged a not always unwilling queen into politics? Yolande, comtesse then duchesse de Polignac, was one of the seminal friends of Marie-Antoinette, the other two being Axel von Fersen and the revolutionary leader he was madly jealous of, Barnave. Marie-Antoinette was accused, in the scurrilous pamphlets that abounded, of sleeping with all three, especially Madame de Polignac.[3] But a well-informed observer considered that by 1785 the king was fonder of Yolande than the queen was.[4] She was prettier than the queen, though it was said that contemporary portraits did justice to neither. But that was not the main reason for the king's interest.

Madame de Polignac was 'planted' at court by her relative, the king's chief minister, the comte de Maurepas, to neutralize what he considered the queen's dangerous influence, particularly on foreign policy, and to keep a watchful eye over the Austrian fifth columnist. Maurepas was the young king's Mentor, but Louis needed no encouragement to keep his wife out of foreign policy: as she was Austrian, he considered excluding her from affairs of state essential to prevent the alliance from becoming unbalanced. On two recorded occasions he shouted at her at the top of his voice and on one of them the row could be heard through the bedroom doors. Louis used Madame de Polignac to calm his wife after such episodes.

Naturally Louis raised no objections when Marie-Antoinette asked him to shower the favourite and the Polignac circle with more offices, pensions and lands than any of Louis XV's mistresses acquired. The Polignacs, to preserve their position, then sought to influence ministerial appointments. And here, as with foreign policy, they served the king rather than the queen, so that although they were the queen's social set they formed an important part of the king's political society. This inevitably led to tensions culminating in the ministry of Charles Alexandre de Calonne, whom Madame de Polignac supported, and 'for whom ... [Marie-Antoinette] had a violent aversion'. Calonne's measures sparked off the Revolution. His fall led to an estrangement between the queen and her best friend, who was exiled to Bath ostensibly to take the waters. Returned to favour, in June 1789 Madame de Polignac disastrously turned Marie-Antoinette from her policy of supporting the pretensions of the Third

Estate against the nobility – for once uniting the king's and queen's policies, which only magnified the catastrophe.

A fringe member of the Polignac set was Axel von Fersen. He was a favourite of Gustavus III of Sweden. Sweden was France's oldest ally and Gustavus was a frequent visitor to Versailles. It has been suggested recently that Madame de Polignac, who certainly knew about Marie-Antoinette's liaison with Fersen, was blackmailing her and that this accounted for much of their wealth.[5] But this cannot be proved and depends on the assumption that Fersen and the queen slept together. This cannot be proved either though it is likely that they did from 1786 onwards, after Marie-Antoinette had provided the king with an heir and, since he was sickly, one to spare.

Until the Revolution Fersen's friendship with the queen was purely disinterested – he received little financial reward and did not involve himself in politics, though he gave some advice on the dispute between France's two allies Austria and the Dutch Republic in 1785. But he became a violent supporter of Counter-Revolution, organising the Paris end of the royal family's attempted escape, which culminated in recapture at Varennes in 1791. This event was a turning point in that it greatly enhanced popular hostility towards the institution of the monarchy as well as towards the king and queen themselves. Fersen did not help matters when, after the catastrophe, he engaged in futile attempts to secure a second escape or foreign intervention. In part his hardliner stance was motivated by sexual jealousy of another of Marie-Antoinette's friendships, that with Barnave with whom, as said, she experimented in a form of epistolary government. In fact, because of Barnave's security concerns, he and Marie-Antoinette seldom met in person, to her expressed regret and despite a side door to the Tuileries manned in readiness.

Marie-Antoinette's origins also made it easy for her to be cast in the role of 'intriguer', and her precarious position in France was not just down to her intervention in politics, and the distrust with which she was viewed as a result, but also owed something to the fact that she was seen and reviled as 'l'Autrichienne', as her enemies referred to her. However, Marie-Antoinette was as much French as anything and her father was duke of Lorraine. In this book she will be presented as French rather than Austrian. She left Austria when she was fourteen and by 1778 needed German lessons, which she abandoned. This point shouldn't need labouring. However, since its publication in the mid-nineteenth century the correspondence between Versailles (Marie-Antoinette and the Austrian ambassador Mercy-Argenteau) and Vienna (Maria-Theresa, Joseph II, Leopold II and the chancellor, Count von Kaunitz) has formed the bedrock of all the numerous biographies of Marie-Antoinette, and one can see why. The material is detailed – Maria-Theresa loved gossip – and both she and Joseph took an interest prurient as well as dynastic in the sexual relations between Marie-Antoinette and the dauphin, later Louis XVI. They were chatty people and provide material for chatty biographies. But the Austrians' correspondence is skewed by the idée fixe that Marie-Antoinette should promote their aggressive foreign policy, something which the queen herself did not prioritize. It is further distorted by distance. There is moreover plenty of French source material available, including from before the Revolution: the manuscript diary of Marie-Antoinette's protégé the marquis de Castries (naval minister 1780–7), and the published and unpublished diary of the abbé de Véri, best friend and chronicler of Maurepas, who was Louis XVI's Mentor but Marie-Antoinette's adversary. I have adopted a similar approach to the queen in the Revolution. It was, after all, the *French* Revolution. Her attempts to secure foreign intervention were nebulous, confused, sterile and unrewarding, partly because of her 'profound ignorance' (her phrase) of what exactly her brother the emperor wanted. So the key source for this period is the aforementioned correspondence between Marie-Antoinette and Barnave. Marie-Antoinette only knew Barnave for the last six months of 1791 and, as with Fersen, their letters were crucial. Given Barnave's place in Marie-Antoinette's story, I have placed extracts from his brilliant *Introduction à la Révolution française* at the appropriate places in the narrative, starting with his verdict on Louis XV. This makes it possible to trace a measure of convergence in the thinking of these two unlikely partners in government.

❧

This book has benefited greatly from the editing of Marika Lysandrou at Yale University Press, Richard Mason, a freelance copy-editor, and proofreader Lucy Isenberg. I am also indebted to the advice and encouragement of three historians in particular: Munro Price, Ambrogio Caiani and Peter Campbell. Finally I would like to thank Lucy Buchan for facilitating small but essential changes to the paperback edition which is now the definitive one.

ONE

FROM ARCHDUCHESS TO DAUPHINE

*M*arie-Antoinette was born on 2 November 1755, at a time when the balance of power on mainland Europe was precarious and a monarch's strength was dependent on their ability to gain – and retain – territories. Maria-Theresa's brave and decisive actions as a ruler in this theatre of war would be held up as a model to her daughter in the years to come.

Marie-Antoinette was, at least on her father's side, as much French as anything. Her father, Francis, had been duke of Lorraine and her grandmother was the sister of the duc d'Orléans, regent for Louis XV. Francis spoke French and refused to learn German when he married her mother, Maria-Theresa, daughter of the Habsburg Holy Roman Emperor, Charles VI. A host of Lorrainer nobles had flocked to Vienna in the wake of Francis as they would to Paris in the wake of his young daughter. The Habsburg court, as became a polyglot empire, was trilingual or even quadrilingual: Spanish because the Habsburgs had ruled that country and Charles had tried to get it back; Italian because they had possessions in the peninsula; German because that was what the natives spoke; and French because it was the universal language. Marie-Antoinette spoke French as her first language but with a German accent and many Germanisms.

Francis Stephen had lost his duchy in a complicated swap at the end of the War of Polish Succession (1733–5) fought to restore Louis XV's father-in-law Stanislas Leszcyński to the Polish throne from which he had been evicted by Augustus the Strong, Elector of Saxony and father of Louis XVI's mother. Stanislas was compensated with Lorraine and on his death in 1766 the duchy was incorporated into France as stipulated in the treaty. Francis received the Grand Duchy of Tuscany (Florence) whose ruling dynasty, the Medici, had conveniently died out (1737). But more importantly, France and all the major European powers recognized the Pragmatic Sanction of 1713 allowing Maria-Theresa to succeed to Charles VI's dominions of Bohemia, Hungary, Austria and modern Belgium. Succession in some of these dominions was (as in France)

1

confined to men. But there was a stronger impediment: the electors of Bavaria and Saxony had married the daughters of Charles VI's elder brother and predecessor, Joseph I. By the Pact of Mutual Succession (1703), Joseph had left his territories to his brother Charles but with reversion to his own daughters should Charles not have a male heir.

After Charles VI died, in 1740, Charles of Bavaria claimed the Habsburg dominions and in 1742 was crowned Holy Roman Emperor as Charles VII. The Prussian king Frederick II seized the rich province of Silesia. The twenty-three-year-old Maria-Theresa fought back and recovered everything but Silesia, which was retained by 'the monster' as she called Frederick, otherwise called 'the Great'. Maria-Theresa has been called 'the one great monarch of the Austrian line',[1] though Charles V and Leopold I would also be candidates. On Charles VII's death in 1745, Maria-Theresa's husband was elected Holy Roman Emperor with the title Francis I. Women could not become emperors, but Maria-Theresa, courtesy empress but de jure queen of Bohemia and Hungary, ruled her husband. Her daring exploits in salvaging her territories became legendary. Echoing, albeit faintly, Elizabeth of England's Tilbury speech, she said and proved that though she had the frame of a woman she had the heart of a king. One story in particular still resonated for Marie-Antoinette during her own troubles. It was of her mother, on horseback and holding her baby son Joseph in her arms, haranguing the Magyar nobility in Budapest. Years later Mirabeau was to say it was time to see what could be achieved by a woman on a horse holding her son in her arms.

Joseph, born in 1741, fourteen years her senior, would be Marie-Antoinette's favourite brother, but his restless territorial aggression would be a source of her misfortunes. By the time Marie-Antoinette was born, Maria-Theresa had given birth to four sons and ten daughters, most of them surviving. A final child, Maximilian, was born in 1756. The day before Marie-Antoinette's birth, 1 November 1755 (All Saints' Day), was also the day of the earthquake that shattered Lisbon and (with Voltaire's help) shook the Christian religion. To this extent the superstitious linking of the two events has some validity. But what really had a decisive impact on the course of Marie-Antoinette's life occurred six months after her birth, the signing of the First Treaty of Versailles on 1 May 1756 between France and Austria. It has become known in English as 'the diplomatic revolution', though in France it has the more modest but also more descriptive title of *la renversement des alliances*. For centuries France and the Habsburgs had been enemies, as they had during the War of the Austrian Succession that had just ended (1748). But slowly the recognition was dawning on Maria-Theresa and her chancellor Kaunitz, and on Madame de Pompadour and, with less conviction, her lover Louis XV, that they were less threatened by each other than by the emergent powers of England (which was struggling with France for empire in India, North America and the West Indies) and Prussia (which had seized and so far kept Silesia).

The significance of Marie-Antoinette, which was not realized at the time of her birth, was that she happened to be just the right age for the man who in 1765 became dauphin of France, the heir to the French throne. Louis XV would have preferred Marie-Antoinette's older sister Marie-Caroline to marry his grandson, had their ages been right.[2] 'The diplomatic revolution' had been disastrous for France. Over-committed to Austria by the second Treaty of Versailles (1757), she had lost Canada to England and, more importantly, the chance to control India; whilst at Rossbach, Frederick had inflicted on France the worst military defeat since Agincourt. Austria had done no better – for Frederick kept Silesia. Nevertheless, Maria-Theresa was desperate to maintain the alliance, despite its unpopularity with the French, and saw in a marriage between the dauphin and Marie-Antoinette the 'pledge' of its continuation.

Marriage of course was usually an instrument of policy for all the dynasties of Europe but especially that of the House of Austria whose old motto was 'Bella gerant alii, tu Felix Austria nube' ('Other nations prosper by warfare, thou Austria by marriage'). And in the fifteenth and sixteenth centuries marriage had brought the Habsburgs Bohemia, Hungary and the Low Countries, half of Italy, Spain and Spanish America. The motto meant the strict application of the arranged marriage, even though the results might be the inbreeding of the Spanish branch that ended in the decrepit Charles II, or the heartless cynicism of Maria-Theresa and her great chancellor Kaunitz. If the marriage brought territory that was an end in itself; otherwise it must be made to serve what was termed the 'August Service'; it must, in Kaunitz's word, be made to 'pay'. If it did not pay through territory it must pay through services which, according to Joseph II, meant helping Austria to acquire territory. Kaunitz would consider Marie-Antoinette 'a bad payer'. He argued that given her ineffectiveness it was best to assume Marie-Antoinette's role in France was the same as that of a queen in every other country – nothing – and that he should 'extract all we can from a bad payer'.[3]

At the time of her birth Marie-Antoinette had no special place on this dynastic chessboard. The future Louis XVI only became the ultimate heir on the death of his elder brother in 1761 and next in line (dauphin) on the premature death of his father, the old dauphin, in 1765. This means that we know very little about Marie-Antoinette, or Antoine (Antoinette within the family) as she was known: ever since the time of the Emperor Leopold I all the archduchesses were called Marie-something. Her tragic destiny also means that this little is embroidered by hearsay and pure invention. We know that, like the rest of the family, she spent her winters at the Hofburg palace in Vienna and the summers and autumns at Schönbrunn, a miniature Versailles five miles from the centre and rebuilt after it had been destroyed by the Turks during the siege of Vienna in 1683. But talk of sleigh rides and heron shoots is embroidered out of gossamer. If, like her sisters, she had married bottom-drawer Bourbons like the semi-imbecile king of Naples or the fully imbecile and degenerate duke of Parma, we would not be regaled with such stories. The king of Naples was married to Marie-Antoinette's favourite sister Marie-Caroline. Maria-Theresa wrote with typically heartless cynicism: 'So long as she fulfils her duty towards God and her husband and earns her salvation, even if she is unhappy I will be satisfied'.[4] Maria-Theresa's favourite children were Leopold, who succeeded his brother Joseph as emperor in 1790 and whose stance on the French Revolution would be critical, and Maria-Christina, but she did not really have the time to be fond of any of them. As Maria-Christina wrote: 'you know the manner in which she loved her children. Mixed in with her love there was always a dose of mistrust and a coldness palpable.'[5]

Two stories relating to Marie-Antoinette's undocumented early childhood are often told. One has her mother on her birthing bed (a sort of chaise longue) having a tooth out and signing state papers so as not to waste time during her delivery. If she had had a tooth pulled with every confinement she would have needed wooden replacements like George Washington. Another has her father turning back from his journey to the wedding of his second son Leopold of Tuscany in order to give Marie-Antoinette a last embrace, having a presentiment that he would not see her again. The memorandum he left behind and enjoined his children to read twice a year did, however, contain this prophetic warning for his youngest daughter: 'Friendship is one of the sweets of life; but one must be careful on whom one bestows it and not be too prodigal with it.' He also warned against gambling.[6] He would have turned in his grave if he had known the extent to which his daughter would go on to ignore his advice.

Francis I died of apoplexy in 1765 in the arms of his son Joseph, who was elected Holy Roman Emperor and gradually began to share the burdens of office with his mother. Maria-Theresa had been hurt by her husband's multiple infidelities but thought it was a wife's duty to accept them: she would tell Marie-Antoinette to do the same in the (unlikely) event of Louis XVI taking a mistress. She donned the widow's cap and wore it for the remaining fifteen years of her life, as can be seen in the 'Maria-Theresa thalers' modern currency in Arab countries to this day, still bearing the date 1780.

4

The main reliable source for Marie-Antoinette's early years – and that only from the age of thirteen – are the letters written by her tutor and confessor the abbé Vermond to the Austrian ambassador to Versailles, the comte de Mercy-Argenteau.[7] Most of Mercy's estates lay in what is now Belgium, but one was in Lorraine, an additional link with Marie-Antoinette. Once it became certain that the marriage between Marie-Antoinette and the dauphin would go ahead, Vermond had been sent from France to finish or, as it transpired, begin her education. Maria-Theresa had been keen on a French marriage from as early as 1765 when the old dauphin died. When Louis XV's wife died in 1768, Maria-Theresa seriously considered a match between the sixty-year-old king and her daughter Maria-Elizabeth. But apart from the fact that the once beautiful Maria-Elizabeth had been marked by an attack of smallpox, which touched several members of the imperial family including Marie-Antoinette, Louis had found a new mistress, Madame du Barry, whom he soon made his *maîtresse-en-titre* (official mistress), a title unknown at the Viennese court. Nor was Louis particularly keen on an Austrian match for his heir; and that heir's mother, Marie-Josèphe of Saxony, wanted a Saxon match and was well aware that according to the normal rules of heredity her own family had a better claim to the Austrian dominions than did Marie-Theresa. Marie-Josèphe's death in 1767 removed one obstacle.

Louis, however, still dithered – he had his own secret diplomacy, *le Secret du roi*, in order to mitigate the effects of the Austrian alliance. If his previous *maîtresse-en-titre*, Madame de Pompadour, had still been alive, the match would have faced fewer obstacles, but she had died in 1764. Her successor as de facto prime minister, the duc de Choiseul, strove valiantly for the match and secured it just in time before his fall from grace on Christmas Eve 1770. Choiseul's father had worked in the small diplomatic service of Marie-Antoinette's father whilst Francis was still duke of Lorraine. Louis XV formally gave his consent to the marriage on 13 June 1769. Choiseul provided Vermond as Marie-Antoinette's tutor on the recommendation of Loménie de Brienne, archbishop of Toulouse, whose *grand vicaire* (deputy) Vermond had been before taking up his post as librarian at the Bibliothèque Mazarin, housed in the beautiful domed building one can see facing the Louvre. A man of humble birth, Vermond, like the nobility, added 'de' before his surname – Mathieu-Jacques de Vermond – and was a doctor of the Sorbonne. Marie-Antoinette trusted him implicitly and these three men – Choiseul, Brienne and Vermond – were to play a major part in her story.

The duc de la Vauguyon, the dauphin's governor with overall responsibility for his education, wrote to Maria-Theresa urging her to reconsider the choice of Vermond. He had two objections to the abbé. First his modest social standing as 'an ordinary college librarian'. More importantly, he was 'one of the greatest supporters of the Encyclopédie [the bible of the *philosophes*] in all Paris'. La Vauguyon pointed out that the dauphin had been brought up as a devout catholic opposed to all that the Enlightenment stood for.[8] This was not strictly true: the dauphin had bought some of the volumes of the *Encyclopédie* out of his allowance. But the dauphin's dead father had hated the philosophes, Choiseul and 'the diplomatic revolution', and would undoubtedly have opposed an Austrian marriage for his son. And La Vauguyon had made the new dauphin stand before a portrait of his sainted father and meditate on one of his virtues every day. Actually the old dauphin was a hypocrite, unfaithful to his wife, morbid and *dévot* rather than devout. But enough of his prejudices had rubbed off on his son to give him a lifelong suspicion of Austria, a simmering suspicion that would occasionally boil over in his dealings with Marie-Antoinette.

Years later Marie-Antoinette told her brother Joseph, 'the King's natural distrust was confirmed in the first place by his governor before my marriage. M. de La Vauguyon had frightened him about the empire his wife would want to exercise over him and his black mind took a pleasure in frightening his pupil with all the bogies invented about the House of Austria.'[9] Louis, however, did not want to rupture the alliance, merely contain it. The dévot party and the Choiseulistes were opposed across the whole range of public issues. The dévots were pro-Jesuit (Choiseul had had the Society expelled from France); anti-Parlement (Choiseul had ruled in conjunction with them); anti-philosophe (Choiseul corresponded with Voltaire); and above all anti-Austrian. For them the match between Louis Auguste and Marie-Antoinette was a marriage of inconvenience and they would try to make it one for the couple too. And unfortunately for Marie-Antoinette this party was about to come to power. Not for a year, though, and Maria-Theresa told La Vauguyon to mind his own business. Vermond arrived and she would place her trust in him.

Vermond, then aged thirty-five, was appalled at the state of his pupil's ignorance. Her education, he told Mercy, had really only begun at the age of twelve when her lax if beloved governess Brandis had been replaced by the ailing but strict Lerchenfeld. She spoke French of a sort: pure French was 'impossible in a country where everyone speaks three languages [French, German and Italian]', but she couldn't write it. Her handwriting was babyish, her orthography appalling, and she wrote 'painfully slowly'. Vermond and necessity would turn Marie-Antoinette into a prolific letter-writer during the Revolution. He was only allotted one hour a day's formal instruction with the archduchess, though they had educational chats that he spiced up for her. Vermond was also admitted to the card games of the imperial family and every Saturday morning he reported to Maria-Theresa, now that her daughter's education had become a matter of moment. He told her that although he was her daughter's confessor he did not like hearing confessions. Maria-Theresa talked him round and he heard Marie-Antoinette's Christmas confession. When he accompanied Marie-Antoinette to France he became Maria-Theresa's confessor-spy. In reporting to Mercy and therefore to Maria-Theresa, he did not violate the secrecy of the confessional but everything else. Vermond's general conclusion about his pupil was that she was quick on the uptake but bad at retention – the opposite of her husband-to-be.

Vermond did not consider his charge an obvious beauty – 'one can find features more conventionally pretty' – but she had poise and charm. He was most worried by her short stature, which he mentions three times, regarding it as the only obstacle to her appearing regal. The dauphin, on the other hand, had outgrown the strength he would later have, inherited from his Saxon grandfather Augustus the Strong, and was nearly six foot tall. So Vermond was pleased to report on 14 October 1769 that 'between 13 February and 5 October she had grown 15 *lignes* in French measurements'. Marie-Antoinette had an oval face, a slight Habsburg jaw, brilliant blue eyes and a porcelain complexion. Opinion varies as to the colour of her hair. The historians Paul and Pierrette Girault de Coursac called it 'ruddy brown with deep streaks of agate',[10] whereas later portraits show it to be blonde. Auburn is nearest.

Her teeth needed straightening, which was done before she left for France. She had one shoulder slightly higher than the other but not that you would notice. Nevertheless Maria-Theresa insisted she wear a corset to correct the minor deformity, bullying her in dozens of letters on the subject. Vermond got to know his pupil well, noting that she teased people and that 'even more energetic than her sallies was the look in her eyes at once gay and malicious'.

Vermond's reports tell us much about what aspects of government would interest Marie-Antoinette as queen. This is not precocity but predilection. He notes that 'she sometimes amuses herself with the military establishment. I am sure that shortly after her marriage she will know all the colonels by name and will be able to differentiate the regiments by the colour and number of their uniforms'. Military appointments were to become her speciality as soon as she became queen. She broke one minister (the prince de Montbarrey) for resisting her meddling. She was even taxed with it at her trial in 1793. And she would exchange long and heated letters with Barnave over the design of the uniform of the king's Constitutional Guard, its recruitment and the personnel of its general staff.

Marie-Antoinette and Vermond had long discussions about French history, though they did not go back much before the reign of Henri IV (1589–1610), the first king of the Bourbon branch of the Capetian dynasty. They spent a lot of time on the reign of the current king, Louis XV, which may have been difficult territory for a young girl. Where a king had encountered problems, Vermond pressed his pupil to say what she would have done. He 'was pleased to be able to report that she often took the right course'. Vermond stressed the role of French queens and of those who had been Habsburgs. In fact there had only been one, Anne of Austria, the mother of and regent for Louis XIV. Did she later see herself in that role if anything happened to Louis XVI? An interest in history was one of the few things she had in common with her future husband, and Vermond considered she 'didn't just rely on memorizing facts but reasoned'. One day Maria-Theresa descended on them and Marie-Antoinette held her own with her mother on historical topics for two hours. An important part of her discussions with Vermond was his 'stress' on 'the great French families and above all those who occupy positions at court'. She would in due course initiate her own court revolution.

Vermond talks of his pupil's 'légèreté' (frivolity) – a word many will apply to her. One observer thought her unpopularity in 1787 undeserved since all she could be taxed with was 'légèreté'. In the context I translate it as 'flightiness', perhaps mingled with a certain insouciance that led to the invention of the let-them-eat-cake story. But the Coursacs find a deeper meaning in the word 'légèreté'. They equate it with 'a nervous almost pathological instability' and detect it in her sisters Amelia and Caroline.[11] 'Frenetic' is a closer translation and we shall observe that trait in the almost desperate pleasure-seeking that characterized her first years as queen.

At the same time, Vermond provided Mercy with a pen-portrait of the dauphin: thin, pale, slightly bow-legged, blonde hair, high forehead, a large but not disproportionate nose. Like everyone else he commented on the dauphin's eyes – not their colour, which was a fine deep blue, but that they 'blinked' and, like his personality, lacked 'lustre'; people speculated that he was short-sighted, though from the extreme convexity of his eyes in the portraits the fault would rather seem to lie in the other direction. Vermond commented, perceptively, that the dauphin's smile suggested 'kindnesses' rather than 'gaiety' and that this, coupled with the lack of animation in the eyes and a certain nonchalance, gave an appearance of stupidity. This portrait does not resemble the familiar ones of him as king, plump and kindly, but it was the face that was to appear on his coinage, unchanged until 1791, and thus the one that was known by the millions of his subjects who never saw him in the flesh. The dauphin, according to Vermond, 'had no liking for the arts and a special loathing of music' – despite or perhaps because of harpsichord lessons; and because of his clumsiness, his dancing and fencing lessons were similarly counterproductive. 'The navy,' Vermond continued, 'is his favourite study and on this subject he possesses as much knowledge as can be acquired without having gone to sea.' He had no 'love of luxury even that associated with his station in life'. Finally he was possessed of 'firmness or, if you prefer, stubbornness' – all in all a very perceptive portrait.[12]

The marriage contract between archduchess and dauphin was signed on 4 April 1770. Maria-Theresa gave her daughter a dowry of 200,000 gold florins and the same value in jewellery. Louis XV thought this insufficient – 'Viennese dowries are lightweight' – but gave her an annual income of 20,000 gold écus and 200,000 gold écus of jewellery.[13] Actually there weren't any gold écus around – the French mint paid too much for silver and the English one too much for gold; so the écus of six livres (or francs as they were beginning to be called) were of silver. Although 'livre' means 'pound', there were 24 livres to the pound sterling. Forgetting this makes Marie-Antoinette's expenditure as queen seem even more prodigal than it actually was.

On 19 April the couple were married by proxy in Vienna, Marie-Antoinette's brother Ferdinand standing in for the dauphin. On 21 April, Marie-Antoinette left Vienna on a stately progress to France. Typically it took ten days to get from Vienna to Versailles. This journey took twenty-four days to allow for formal receptions along the way. At Nancy she paid a reverential visit to the convent of the Cordeliers where her ancestors the dukes of Lorraine were buried, their monuments surmounted by a closed crown, symbolizing that they had been sovereign rulers. At last, on Monday 14 May she met the dauphin in the forest of Compiègne. He embraced her. His laconic diary entry reads, 'Meeting with Madame la dauphine'. He would continue to address his wife as 'Madame' for the rest of their lives. Finally, on 16 May the gilded grilles of Versailles were opened to receive the royal party and the next day the couple were married. Neither the dauphin nor the dauphine gave an account of the wedding night – and why should they? – but this has led to speculation about what precisely happened. We do, however, know that the next day a bad-tempered bridegroom abandoned his new wife to go hunting. As the duc de Croÿ relates, the dauphine 'dined alone, M. le dauphin and the king having gone hunting. It was very soon to have left her.'[14] Marie-Antoinette herself confessed to Vermond that 'since their meeting in the forest of Compiègne M. le dauphin had not repeated the embrace and had not even touched her hand a single time'.[15]

This is unusual conduct by any standards and it has been used to challenge the accepted view that Louis would not or could not consummate the marriage, though a natural interpretation would be that the dauphin was ashamed and angry at not having done what was expected of him. If she did withhold her favours, a natural explanation would be that she was barely adolescent, having only just had her first period. Louis XV told his grandson the duke of Parma, 'the dauphine is charming but very childlike'.[16] It could also have been that Choiseul and Vermond (to whom Louis refused to speak until 1780) had turned the girl's head against her future husband. Choiseul told Louis XV that La Vauguyon had given the dauphin so bad an education that if things were not rectified 'he would become the horror of the nation'.[17]

Choiseul was not objective. However there is other corroborating evidence. Recent reassessments of Louis XVI show that before his nervous breakdown in 1787 he was a capable and vigorous ruler. His sufferings after 1787 humanized him and Marie-Antoinette warmed to this new Louis. This was the reverse side of the coin. But maybe there was a reverse side to the pre-1787 king. There is evidence of his cruelty to animals. The comte de Montmorin, who had been a *menin* or official playfellow of the dauphin and was to stand by him to the end (his own), related 'that the King is by nature cruel and base. An instance of his cruelty, among others, was that he used to spit and roast live cats'.[18] He certainly had it in for cats. At night Louis would chase them from the roofs of Versailles and on one occasion he shot the pet Angora cat belonging to Mme de Maurepas, the wife of his chief minister. Fortunately Louis was able to source an identical replacement for the animal.[19] He also disliked dogs. Marie-Antoinette adored them and they roamed all over the place; but they were banned from Louis' private quarters.

A relative of another *menin*, the comte d'Angiviller, thought Louis' cruelty extended to humans, telling the American ambassador Gouverneur Morris, 'that he is very brutal and nasty, which she attributes chiefly to a bad education. His brutality once led him so far, while Dauphin, as to beat his wife, for which he was exiled for four days by his grandfather Louis XV. Until very lately he used always to spit in his hand, as being more convenient'.[20] Whilst the accusation of wife-beating seems far-fetched, Louis could be callous and insensitive. In 1783, after the finance minister Henri Lefèvre d'Ormesson had apologized for a hurriedly prepared report because he had been up all night nursing his dying son, Louis replied brutally: 'C'est fâcheux!' ('What a bore!') – leaving it in doubt whether he was referring to the father's lack of preparation or the boy's plight: 'une réponse brusque du Roi', d'Ormesson writes in the margin.[21] Another minister, Marie-Antoinette's protégé, Castries, accusing him of a basic lack of courtesy, confided to his diary that 'it would be too distasteful to serve such a master if one were serving him alone and not the state as well'.[22]

To these moral failings one of Marie-Antoinette's intimates, the prince de Ligne, adds physical ones: 'I can demonstrate that . . . [after] her wedding to the best but also the ugliest and most repulsive of all men, I never saw her pass an entire day of unclouded happiness'.[23] Even allowing for exaggeration – and Choiseul's detestation of the dauphin was fully reciprocated – these epithets from those close to Marie-Antoinette suggest that she recoiled in 'horror' from her husband quite as much as he (for whatever reason) shrank from her.

THE FALL OF CHOISEUL

Revolution was an overworked word before it acquired its capital R in 1789. Two earlier usages played a part in Marie-Antoinette's story: the 'diplomatic revolution' of 1756 of which she was the 'pledge' and the 'revolution of 1771', which occurred six months after her arrival in France. Both were heavily influenced by a mistress of Louis XV: the 'diplomatic revolution' by Madame de Pompadour and the 'revolution of 1771', the attack on the political appeal court known as the Parlement de Paris, by Madame du Barry. At first Marie-Antoinette did not know what Madame du Barry was 'for' and was told that she was there to please the king. The mistress was not so noticeable in the vast palace of Versailles, but hardly had Marie-Antoinette arrived there than the Court embarked on its carefully scheduled series of progresses around the smaller royal châteaux that ringed Versailles. These removals, remarked Mercy, 'resembled the march of an army' and were almost as expensive.[24] These costly displacements, unlike the royal progresses of old, were not designed to get a better knowledge of the country for they were always the same: Marly, La Muette, Compiègne, Choisy and Fontainebleau. Louis XVI would add Rambouillet and Marie-Antoinette would add Saint-Cloud. The objective of these 'voyages', as they were known, was purely to seek pleasure in variety. The palaces chosen (in January) varied from year to year but the royal couple always ended up in the autumn at Fontainebleau for the hunting and to fix departmental spending (seldom adhered to). Some of the châteaux, such as Marly, were cramped, so Marie-Antoinette would see the new mistress at table. Choiseul braved the king's wrath by asking permission for all the ladies of his family to withdraw from court. He did not need to add that it was so they would not be contaminated by contact with Madame du Barry. The dauphin, who hunted for pleasure and for health, asked the king whether he could attend the suppers that followed, at which Madame du Barry presided.

When they were all at the château of Compiègne the dauphin and Marie-Antoinette first began to exchange confidences and he told his new wife exactly what the role of Madame du Barry was. He also told her that his governor, La Vauguyon, was one of her most servile flatterers, constantly paying her court, and that he, Louis, despised the man, adding that La Vauguyon had given him a rotten education; and now that La Vauguyon's official role had ended with the dauphin's marriage, Louis would seek to supplement it by private study. Marie-Antoinette, who had been led by Vermond and Mercy to believe that the dauphin was in thrall to his governor, ventured to ask whether Madame du Barry was behind all the intrigues to have Choiseul dismissed. But at the mention of Choiseul, the dauphin's face clouded over and he was amazed that she didn't know that Choiseul had come to power in exactly the same way as Choiseul's enemies were plotting. What do you mean? her raised eyebrow enquired. Did Louis need to add, through the previous mistress, Madame de Pompadour? And he might have known, because he was being taught diplomacy by the abbé de La Ville, *premier commis* at the Foreign Ministry, that Maria-Theresa had stooped as low as addressing the Pompadour as 'ma soeur' – a form used only between reigning monarchs. He might also have known that La Ville was about to play a key role in bringing down Choiseul, after which he would run the Foreign Minstry until a new foreign minister was appointed. Marie-Antoinette decided to probe her husband no further – or she would have learned of Choiseul's blazing row with the dauphin's beloved father. She merely observed that Choiseul enjoyed a high reputation in Europe and that there was a big difference between Madame de Pompadour and Madame du Barry, as indeed there was.[25]

Choiseul meanwhile sought to bolster his position by having a long audience with the dauphine, which Mercy arranged. Coached by Mercy and Vermond, Choiseul told the dauphine to charm the king and keep good relations with his unmarried daughters without being dominated by them. Afterwards he told Mercy how impressed he had been: 'I didn't know Madame la Dauphine until today . . . I've never seen anything like it in one so young . . . when you get an opportunity, tell her that I am at her service for ever and that she can dispose of me as she chooses.'[26] The powerful but threatened *parti Choiseul* saw Marie-Antoinette not just as a present help in time of trouble but, assuming that she would dominate her lacklustre husband, as the 'reversionary interest' (to borrow a phrase from Hanoverian England) when the dauphin succeeded a king prematurely aged by his life of sad hedonism.

Ironically, this may have strengthened the enemies of Choiseul to act whilst there was still time. Choiseul was vulnerable on two fronts: relations between Crown and Parlement and foreign policy. There were thirteen parlements, of which the most important covering half the country was that of Paris. Their primary role was that of appeal courts, but the kings had given them the additional role of registering royal legislation to which they gave what Louis XVI would call 'simulated consent'. Real consent would have come from the only national representative institution, the Estates-General, but these did not meet between 1614 and 1789. In their absence the kings used the parlements to 'sell' unpopular measures such as taxation or to give royal loans their endorsement, in other words assurance that the money was needed and could be repaid. In normal times it suited both Crown and Parlement to cooperate – it was in both their interests to have the incompetent (in both senses) Estates-General meddling with government. But under Louis XV the system had broken down as divisive religious issues (Jansenists versus Jesuits) and financial ones (taxation of the nobility – the *parlementaires* were nobles, *noblesse de robe* after the red robes they loved to wear on ceremonial occasions) arose. The 1750s and 1760s had been punctuated by judicial strikes followed by exiles, and Choiseul was rightly perceived to be hand in glove with the *parlementaires*, buying peace at home so he could get the money to build up the navy and have a war of revanche against England. The latest quarrel was over the Parlement's declaring that the duc d'Aiguillon, the military commandant of Brittany, had forfeited his peerage over his conduct in that province. D'Aiguillon and Madame du Barry were thick as thieves. Meanwhile Choiseul's sister, the duchesse de Gramont, had been touring the Midi encouraging the local parlements to resist the government.

Equally alarming was Choiseul's attempt to make himself indispensable by involving France in the quarrel between England and Spain over possession of the Falkland Islands – Argentina was a Spanish colony and claimed Las Malvinas then as now. Even a political ally like Mercy said, 'I have little doubt that the duc de Choiseul thought that war would strengthen his position and make his presence in the ministry necessary.' The family compact between France and Spain obliged either country to provide eighteen warships on demand. But Louis XV was determined on peace because he could not afford war and it would make him dependent on the Parlement for wartime taxation. Finance and foreign policy are always linked but never more so than in *ancien régime* France because, in the absence of the Estates-General, the king was perpetually short of money, whereas the English king in Parliament was flush. With René de Maupeou, the chancellor, denouncing Choiseul for betraying royal sovereignty to the Parlement, Madame du Barry piled on the pressure by summoning La Ville, who told the king that the other courts of Europe would not miss Choiseul (Maria-Theresa didn't, as we shall see), and that Choiseul had been stirring up the quarrel between Spain and England. The king told Choiseul, 'Monsieur I have told you that I DO NOT WANT WAR.'

On Christmas Eve 1770 the duc de La Vrillière, the minister for the Maison du Roi, called on Choiseul with a *lettre de cachet*. These 'letters under the king's

13

signet ring' signified internal exile at the king's pleasure – the further from the king the deeper the disgrace. The portly La Vrillière's record for the number of *lettres de cachet* delivered stood unbroken when the practice was discontinued in 1789. His beady little eyes glinting with malign pleasure, La Vrillière delivered Choiseul the order to leave Versailles in two hours, clear his Paris town house in twenty-four hours, and proceed to his estate at Chanteloup in the Tourraine. As an extra twist of malice, the king's note to La Vrillière added, 'But for Madame de Choiseul, I would have sent the husband further afield; but he will only see his family and those I permit to go there.'[27] The king was disobeyed on that count: so many flocked to Chanteloup that Choiseul raised a column in the grounds where their names were dutifully inscribed. D'Aiguillon became foreign secretary and treated Marie-Antoinette, whom he called 'the coquette', with barely concealed contempt. D'Aiguillon had been close to the dauphin's late and revered father Louis Fedinand and the dauphin respected his legacy. In January 1771 the 'revolution' occurred when the Parlement was dissolved and its members were sent into exile to disagreeable spots, one of which was so obscure that it could not be found on the map. The Grand Conseil, an offshoot of the king's council, became the new Parlement, quickly dubbed 'le Parlement Maupeou' which, according to its many enemies, paved the way for unbridled despotism. For years the king's effigy on the coins had remained unchanged as a man of thirty, the most handsome man in his kingdom. In 1771 it was updated so that he now appeared as a grim old tyrant.

Where did that leave Marie-Antoinette? Maria-Theresa worried that her daughter was now left without a protector. Choiseul, who had made her match, was in internal exile at Chanteloup, and her husband had accompanied Louis XV to punish the Parlement and wrote on his copy of the disciplinary edict, 'that is the correct public law; I am absolutely delighted with M. le Chancelier'.[28] Marie-Antoinette seemed to support him: most of the princes of the Blood boycotted the ceremony installing the new Parlement and signed a letter of protest, yet Marie-Antoinette not only attended but called the princes' letter of protest 'impertinent'. She particularly blamed the conduct of the prince de Condé for making his son, 'a lad who is not yet fifteen', sign the protest.[29] This either shows naiveté or a brilliant realization that the two exiles, of Choiseul and of the Parlement, were not necessarily connected. Four years later, her husband would show her that this precisely was the case. And is it fanciful to see an implied rebuke of her mother in Marie-Antoinette's protest at a boy of her age being treated as a political pawn?

The dauphin now stopped going to the hunt suppers where Madame du Barry presided, even though he had himself asked to attend. His change of heart was due to his aunts, who told him his salvation was being threatened by his association with a former prostitute; but Louis XV blamed the dauphine's influence. The aunts had tolerated Madame du Barry as an instrument in the downfall of the hated Choiseul, but once this had been accomplished they were free to display their true prudish colours. In a loveless family, the dauphin was the favourite of the dominant aunt, Adélaïde. She told him to be himself, smash her Dresden and Sèvres china, and make a noise – be noticed. Maria-Theresa had advised her daughter to take her cue from the aunts, who (as she imagined) were upright souls. She soon changed her tune when she realized, too late, that they were threatening her foreign policy. In their hatred of Madame du Barry, dauphin and dauphine were united in adolescent prudery. At last they had something in common.

It has been suggested that the jealousy of the dauphin's younger brother, the comte de Provence, who did much to destabilize the reign of Louis XVI, was inflamed by Madame du Barry's faction. Certainly he had reservations about Austria, writing to Gustavus III of Sweden, 'I do not greatly approve of our alliance with Austria; on the contrary I think Cardinal Richelieu was very right to want to destroy this hydra.'[30] Provence married soon after the dauphin and their youngest brother the comte d'Artois soon after that, each to sisters from the House of Savoy. The household of the new comtesse de Provence was filled with women from the now reigning faction, who did everything to poison relations between the brothers. Marie-Antoinette's household had been formed during the last months of Choiseul's ascendancy and its members were chosen to suit – though that did not prevent Marie-Antoinette finding fault with their stuffiness, especially its head the comtesse de Noailles, whom she christened Madame Etiquette. One of the Marie-Antoinette stories has her falling off her donkey and joking that they had better send for the comtesse to find out what the etiquette was for a dauphine falling off such an animal. Vermond was concerned that Marie-Antoinette, 'who by her own confession disliked [Noailles] nevertheless gave her more signs of friendship than was necessary'. Should she subsequently break with her *dame d'honneur*, principal lady-in-waiting to the queen, he added prophetically, 'all the caresses that she presently lavishes on her will be taken for falseness, which will create a very bad impression.'[31]

Louis XV blamed Marie-Antoinette because, like everyone else, he thought she was dominating her husband. But the king was too embarrassed to speak in anything but circumlocutions that no one understood. He talked about Marie-Antoinette's over-familiarity particularly in hunting parties, but what he wanted to say was: why does the chit insist on cutting dead the woman I have chosen to spend my few remaining years with?

Meanwhile, as if liberated, the very day that he exiled Choiseul, the king put Madame du Barry in Madame de Pompadour's apartments. Squeezed into the eaves of Versailles, they were connected with his own private apartments by one cast-iron spiral staircase. The narrow staircase is hard to climb – I've done it – so from the king's library a secret passage was installed that didn't involve any climbing. These rooms, a rival centre of power to her own, would cloud Marie-Antoinette's life for the next ten years. Madame du Barry's rooms were furnished in the latest 'transitional' taste, more classical than the rococo the king still preferred. But some rococo features were included, notably an enormous ormoulou clock by Jean-Joseph de Saint Germain with a cupid arrow pointing to the hour. The walls were decorated with Flemish paintings by such artists as David Teniers. And for grand receptions the king gave his mistress the elegant white marble château of Louveciennes. Marie-Antoinette had to make do with hand-me-downs: the old furniture that had belonged to Louis XV's neglected queen. She felt slighted, patronized, treated like a child. In her turn Marie-Antoinette 'was bored in the king's company and didn't always bother hiding the fact'. The king tried to be nice to her, 'but his attempts were often met with respect yet at the same time with a frigidity that embarrassed and surely was not acceptable to him'.[32]

The stand-off between Marie-Antoinette and Madame du Barry lasted until 1 January 1772. It was ended by the intervention of Mercy and Maria-Theresa, who needed the dauphine to neutralize French opposition to their plans to share in the Partition of Poland. Frederick of Prussia and Catherine of Russia had long intended to carve up Poland, a large but weak state. Maria-Theresa thought it was immoral but her scruples were overcome when she was awarded the biggest slice of the Paczki (Polish cake), as appeared in contemporary cartoons. France was the traditional defender of the Polish Republic as, with its elective monarchy, it was called. Indeed Louis XV's secret diplomacy, *le Secret du roi*, had originally been designed to put a French prince on the Polish throne. Mercy had a long talk with the comte de Broglie, head of the *Secret*, and gave him to understand that if Marie-Antoinette would be nice or at least civil to Madame du Barry then Louis XV would raise no objection to the Partition.

Maria-Theresa told her daughter that her one duty was to obey the king. Mercy did not stress Poland, for Marie-Antoinette was already beginning to think of herself as French. Instead he explained the danger Marie-Antoinette ran by alienating the desperate gang, men like d'Aiguillon who crowded under Madame du Barry's skirts for protection. The king 'was not old in virtue of his years but he was in virtue of his lifestyle; he was growing weaker and could pop off at any moment'. Anyone could see that Marie-Antoinette would dominate the new king. She had announced no quarter, so Madame du Barry's faction must give her none: end the alliance with Austria; have her sent back there (she hadn't provided an heir); even poison her. Madame du Barry herself was not vengeful, she just wanted recognition. One word from the dauphine would do.

And on New Year's Day 1772 she got it. Indeed a whole sentence: 'There are a lot of people at Versailles today.' Everyone relaxed – except the king's daughters, who never forgave the traitor Marie-Antoinette. Marie-Antoinette told Mercy afterwards: 'I have spoken once but I am absolutely determined to leave it at that; this woman will never again hear the sound of my voice.' Under pressure from Mercy she also persuaded the dauphin to resume going to the king's hunting suppers presided over by the favourite. But she didn't get much thanks either from Mercy or his principal, the chancellor Kaunitz. Mercy told him, 'If only Madame la dauphine were more considered, less obstinate in her conduct towards the favourite I would have more room for manoeuvre'; whilst the cynical old chancellor summed up Marie-Antoinette: 'I regard Madame la dauphine as a bad payer from whom we must be content to get what we can.'[33] Maria-Theresa was just as brutal in pressing Mercy to get Marie-Antoinette to 'align herself with the current situation and with my interests'. The whole future relations between Marie-Antoinette and her Austrian family are summed up in those chilling words from the noble Maria-Theresa and Kaunitz, the valetudinarian old man who would bury them all. Austria got its thick slice of Poland, but that was all it ever got from the French alliance.

Whilst pressure was being put on Marie-Antoinette, her husband the dauphin was receiving expert instruction in foreign affairs from the abbé de la Ville, a defender of traditional French diplomacy. Marie-Antoinette later said the seeds of Austrophobia had been planted by the dauphin's governor La Vauguyon. But though La Vauguyon had peddled prejudice, La Ville conferred such expertise on his pupil that when he ascended the throne at the age of twenty he came to his task fully armed like Pallas Athena. Louis XVI was still harbouring resentment at Austria's role in the Partition of Poland when five years later, in 1777, he brought it up directly before Marie-Antoinette, whilst Austria was trying to annex Bavaria: 'the ambition of your relatives is going to upset everything. They began with [the Partition of] Poland. Now Bavaria is the second volume. I am sorry for your sake.'[34]

Perhaps it is wrong to see this episode in terms of personalities: Louis XV selling out Poland for some commonplace words addressed by the dauphine to the royal mistress. But even if it was not so – after all Poland was unstable and great powers abhor a vacuum – that is how it seemed to the actors. Furthermore, Mercy had talked of reprisals from Madame du Barry's faction to persuade the dauphine to be civil to her. But these were merely a paper tiger: the real reprisals were those of Marie-Antoinette when she came into her own and these were so severe against d'Aiguillon that they damaged her reputation. And Marie-Antoinette had judged the king and found him wanting. She refused to address a single word to d'Aiguillon. She found her mother's solicitations more imperial than tender. As Mercy wrote to the queen-empress: 'Madame l'Archiduchesse is only too aware of certain things.' Finally, if Marie-Antoinette had been civil to Madame du Barry (that was all that was required), Maria-Theresa would not have been able to use her to put pressure on Louis XV and he may just possibly have opposed the Partition of which he told Marie-Antoinette he disapproved. And this might just possibly have stirred the empress-queen's conscience. As Frederick wrote: 'The empress Catherine and I are two brigands but how does that religious bigot of a queen-empress square it with her confessor?' Moreover, the ministers whom the royal mistress supported were carrying out necessary reforms however brutally implemented. Joseph-Marie Terray, the finance minister, with his forcible reduction in the rate of interest paid on royal loans and other measures to end tax evasion by the nobility, may have prolonged the life of the regime by a generation; whilst Maupeou, the chancellor, freed the Crown from the obstreperous opposition of the Parlements.

Madame du Barry and d'Aiguillon made one last attempt to win over not just Marie-Antoinette but the whole royal family, who were almost as hostile to her. Madame Adélaïde was ruled by her *dame d'honneur* the comtesse de Narbonne, so d'Aiguillon offered her inducements to win over Adélaïde and with her the royal family: the king's daughters, the dauphin's brothers Provence and Artois, and the dauphin and dauphine. The attempt failed and according to the well-informed duc de Croÿ, 'Madame la dauphine rules all these domestic matters.' Then in 1773, d'Aiguillon was made minister of war. Military appointments, the biggest source of patronage, were now in his gift and, despite continuing to 'entertain for the duke a horror which passes all bounds', Marie-Antoinette shamelessly put pressure on him to promote her friends. Desperate to win her favour, d'Aiguillon obliged, appointing 'the brother of one of her almoners within 24 hours'. But, as he explained to Mercy, an ally now after the minister's complaisance over Poland, he wanted the dauphine to make a distinction between the favours 'in which she took a real interest' and those 'where she was yielding to the importunities of her coterie'. This would enable d'Aiguillon to 'satisfy . . . [her] wishes without too much prejudice either to justice or the good of the service'.[35]

Leaving aside the cynicism, even falsity, of the dauphine in seeking favours from a man she was determined to destroy when she came into her own, we have here an early example of a dangerous tendency she would display as queen, one that would alienate half the Court. Already as dauphine she had an 'importunate coterie'; as queen, in the Polignac set, her *société intime*, she would have an insatiable one. Vermond also confessed that the dauphine's 'weakness of character has reached such a point that it can only be supported by those who exploit it'. He picked up this theme in 1776: 'happily it is the case that the queen's affections are diffused and they lose in force that which they gain in extent and I have always regarded it as essential for this august princess that she should not be dominated by a single person.'[36]

Neither d'Aiguillon nor Marie-Antoinette could know that within a year she would have her chance. The Austrian sources stress that Louis XV was old for his years, worn out by his sexual excesses. But his love-making, though indiscriminate, was not immoderate. What killed him was smallpox, of the virulent 'black' strain. The king felt indisposed on 27 April 1774, had a headache and hunted from a calèche, a light low-wheeled carriage. Madame du Barry had wanted to keep him at the Petit Trianon so she could control events, but the senior doctor told Louis sententiously, 'Sire, Versailles is the place to be ill.' As the nature of the king's illness became apparent the factions circled like vultures around his bed.

Madame du Barry was well aware of the position – if the king was deemed in need of the last sacraments no priest would administer them unless she was banished. Likewise the concern of her faction headed by d'Aiguillon and his rival Maupeou was to persuade the king that he was not seriously ill. (They were aided in this by Louis' belief that he had already had smallpox in 1728.) Bleeding was the only remedy offered by the doctors and three bleedings were considered necessary. Since, however, a third bleeding was usually accompanied by the last rites, d'Aiguillon persuaded the doctors to make do with a copious second bleeding.

The adherents of the duc de Choiseul – still exiled to his estates at Chanteloup – rejoiced indecently and said the king should make his confession so he could get to heaven quickly. One of their number, the duc de Liancourt, even mocked the king's daughters for selflessly attending the king's deathbed knowing full well the risk of contracting the disease, which they did, albeit in a mild form. The main reason, Liancourt said, why three-quarters of people were not touched by this action 'was the object of their sacrifice. The king was so degraded, so despised, above all despised, that nothing that anyone did for him had any claim on public sympathy.'[37] Such was the public indifference at Paris and Versailles, even inside the palace, the duc de Croÿ noted, that 'a foreigner would not have been able to tell that they were losing their king'.

Croÿ gives a graphic description of the king's face as the pustules coalesced to form a solid mass. He beheld, lit up by the priests' white candles, 'a bronze mask enlarged by the crusts . . . the mouth open without however any disfigurement of his face . . . in short it looked like a Moor's face, a negro's, coppered and inflated'.[38] The windows had to be kept open and the stench from the king's putrid body polluted the Cour de Marbre below. By this time the king knew his condition and made his confession; du Barry was sent away and the grand-almoner announced to the courtiers: 'Messieurs, the king has asked me to tell you that he asks God's forgiveness for having offended him and for the scandalous example he has given his people. That if God restores him to health, he will devote himself to penitence, the support of religion and lightening the taxation [*soulagement*] of his people.'

The dauphin and his brothers were not allowed near the king for fear of contagion – the nearest he could get was the first step of the staircase leading to the king's chamber. Marie-Antoinette, however, had already had smallpox. Having acquired immunity she could have attended the king, but given the stench and the fact that she was not fond of the old man one can hardly blame her for declining. Precise as always, the dauphin's diary notes: '10 [May]: Death of the King at two in the afternoon.' The king had retained full consciousness to the last. At a pause in the death rattle, his confessor asked him whether he was in much pain. 'Ah! Ah! Ah! Beaucoup,' Louis replied. 'As long as I live,' the abbé recalled, 'those three Ahs! will stick in my memory.' A valet snuffed out a candle that had been placed in a window to signal the king's passing. Immediately there was a mighty roar, like a thunder roll, or the crashing of a series of mighty waves. It was the stamp of courtiers' feet as they rushed headlong from the king's ante-chamber to those of the dauphin – the sound of power escaping from a vacuum. For as the Great Chamberlain announced in the salon of the Oeil-de-Boeuf, 'Messieurs, le roi est mort! Vive le Roi.'

There are several accounts of how the new king and queen received the news. The most celebrated has Louis and Marie-Antoinette falling to their knees, saying 'May God guide and protect us for we are too young to reign.' Louis' brother Provence has the new king throwing himself into the arms of Marie-Antoinette and saying 'what a burden but you will help me to bear it'.[39] The duc de Croÿ, who was there, notes that Louis XVI 'let out a great cry' and said he was 'devastated to be king so young and with so little experience'. Marie-Antoinette's reaction is expressed in a letter to her mother 'Though God caused me to be born to the rank I hold today, I cannot refrain from admiring the workings of Providence which has chosen me, the youngest of your children, to occupy the finest throne in Europe. I am more than ever aware of what I owe to the tenderness of my august mother who has expended so much worry and hard work to procure this fine establishment for me.'[40] There is a certain smugness here – Marie-Antoinette had not got on with the old king – coupled with a sly observation that her mother was an accomplished matchmaker – as Mercy had noted, 'Madame l'Archiduchesse is only too aware of certain things.'

Louis XV has found a few panegyrists, notably Pierre Gaxotte and Michel Antoine. But, among his contemporaries and historians, they are few and far between. Most stress the moral degradation and 'despotism' of his last few years, those of du Barry and Maupeou whose coup d'état demonstrated that the regime did not offer sufficient safeguards and the king could tax and imprison at will. Therefore recourse was had to the Estates-General. These two verdicts on Louis XV – moral degradation and despotism – were synthesized by Barnave, the early radical who came to think that 'it was necessary to stop the Revolution'. Writing of the earlier 'revolution' – for contemporaries so qualified Maupeou's coup –Barnave said, 'Frenchmen combined such submissiveness with such contempt for their master that they seemed ready to suffer everything.' He added that, all love and respect for the monarchy having evaporated, it ruled only by 'mechanical means',[41] in other words a superb administrative machine that could keep running for a while without essential maintenance. The only way the political structures of the *ancien régime* could have endured, he argued, would have been to occupy the existing institutions with men taken from the Third Estate. This essentially is what the early Bourbons had done, drafting new men into their civil service to create a new regime. True, these men were enno- bled but that was how arrival was marked – similarly all Napoleon's prefects became barons and all his councillors of state counts. And by the Third Estate, Barnave did not mean plebeians but men whose wealth and education were the equal of the nobility's – men like himself and the other Third Estate deputies to the Estates-General. An argument *pro domo sua* perhaps. Barnave would see Marie-Antoinette as the key to achieving this, and set his sights on doing a deal with the queen.

TWO

THE COURT UNDER LOUIS XVI AND MARIE-ANTOINETTE

THE PARAMETERS OF THE NEW REIGN

*T*he diary entry of the new king is succinct:

> 10 [May 1774]: Death of the King at two in the afternoon and departure for Choisy.

This château was 9 kilometres to the south of Paris. Infection hung about Versailles and the royal family lost no time getting out. By 4 o'clock, just two hours after the king's death, Louis XVI, Marie-Antoinette, his brothers the counts of Provence and Artois and their wives all found themselves in one coach en route for the smaller château. Their baggage and the rest of the Court followed after. At first the occupants of the coach were solemn, but a flippant comment by the comtesse d'Artois broke the ice and they all started giggling. Only the new king had loved the old one. Marie-Antoinette was not to return to Versailles for nearly six months.

Marie-Antoinette's chief concern during these months in 1774 was personal vengeance against those she considered to have wronged her during her unhappy time as dauphine, namely Madame du Barry, the duc d'Aiguillon and the comtesse de Noailles; and an attempt to reward the exiled Choiseul who had assisted her mother and Providence in placing her on the 'finest throne in Europe'. We will look at these personal interventions in the next chapter. She played no part, indeed took no interest, in the major decisions of this year: the appointment of the comte de Maurepas as personal adviser to the young king and of Anne-Robert Turgot to the Finance Ministry, and the recall of the old Parlement.

The appointment or rather recall of Maurepas (for he was given no official position) took Mercy-Argenteau and Marie-Antoinette by surprise. Mercy asked her whether Maurepas had been recalled as a prime minister. She replied 'that such an eventuality was not on the table and that he was there merely to give the technical advice and advice on protocol of which he stood in great need'.[1]

Maurepas had been a naval minister (1723–49) and Louis XVI, who was passionate about the navy, wanted to build it up: at his accession there was only one battleship in service. La Vauguyon had also turned to Maurepas to suggest tutors for his charge. He had been dismissed and exiled to his estates in 1749 for circulating scurrilous verses about Madame de Pompadour. This gave him a hatred of Louis XV and all his works (including his reform of the Parlement) and an abiding mistrust of women meddling in politics, be they king's mistress or king's wife. This was emphatically demonstrated by his own installation in Madame du Barry's apartments. His fall had preceded Choiseul's rise but both were due to the Pompadour, and Maurepas was determined to block Marie-Antoinette's attempts to restore Choiseul to favour. Maurepas had hinted that the new king should make him prime minister, and though Louis did not take the hint Maurepas gradually became an informal one. Mercy was of the belief that the political influence of prime ministers and queens was mutually exclusive. It might depend on whether the king went up the stairs to see Maurepas or along the passage to see his wife. This triangular relationship would be the matrix for Marie-Antoinette's political activity until Maurepas' death in 1781.

Marie-Antoinette had nothing to do with the appointment of Turgot as finance minister in August 1774, though her brother welcomed the appointment of one of the greatest economists of the age. But he thwarted one of her protégés, the comte de Guines, ambassador to London, and she swore to have Guines made a duc and Turgot thrown into the Bastille on the same day. Her early interventions were not subtle.

Turgot was an honourable man but at the outset of his ministerial career he made a Faustian bargain that would undermine his attempts to reform the monarchy. Out of gratitude, one supposes, to Maurepas for getting him the Finance Ministry, he agreed, against his better judgement, to support Maurepas' attempts to persuade the king, against his better judgement also, to recall the old Parlement. Maurepas had left the ministry before the internecine struggles between Crown and Parlement that had culminated in Maupeou's coup d'état. And Maurepas' father, the chancellor Pontchartrain, had instilled in him the slogan 'no parlement no monarchy'; by which he meant that the parlements properly managed could sell royal policies, especially the high taxation needed to fund both land and sea wars, without an appearance of despotism. So Maurepas wanted a return to the golden age of the monarchy and of his youth under the premiership of Cardinal Fleury before Louis XV's reign was tainted by the rule of the mistresses. The trouble was that the regime could only be reformed over the dead bodies of the Parlement, who as well as being judges were also noble landowners determined to preserve their tax privileges. The brief period of Marie-Antoinette's ascendancy, 1787–8, which was also her political apprenticeship, would be dominated by a fight to the death with the Parlement.

Yet in 1774, Marie-Antoinette was completely ignorant of the issues involved. On 21 November, Louis XVI restored the old Parlement, with certain restrictions such as forbidding the judges to go on strike, which had the potential to bring such a litigious society to its knees. Four days earlier Mercy had written to Maria-Theresa:

> Her Majesty spoke a lot about the possible outcome of this event. I took the opportunity to give her some idea about a topic on which hitherto she had had no desire whatsoever to inform herself, always saying that the matter was too difficult for her to understand a word of it. I foresaw that she would say something similar to Your Majesty. I repeatedly stressed that without getting involved in a matter so complicated and so serious, it was nonetheless necessary that she acquire enough knowledge to understand the core of the matter and to be able to reply to the king's questions.[2]

The main point of this, Mercy argued, was to dispel the notion that Marie-Antoinette had no influence over major policy matters. If she had understood the issues involved, Marie-Antoinette would have known that her mother favoured the Parlement Maupeou and found the restoration of the old rebellious Parlement 'incomprehensible'.

THE COURT

Louis XIV had gathered all the higher nobility at Versailles because as the adage went: when they were not at court they were in rebellion. He kept an eye on them but they in turn kept an eye on him and not just (as he flattered himself and was flattered) as the cynosure. Maurepas' chronicler the abbé de Véri called them all jumped-up valets because their ceremonial roles – such as handing the king his shirt at his *levée* and his nightgown at his *coucher* – were essentially menial as their titles suggested: first groom of the chamber, master of the wardrobe, etc. But they fought to obtain these posts because they had been led to believe that they were prestigious and they needed them to defray some of the cost of representation at court. The king and queen were at the point of intersection between the Court and the government, two circles that hitherto had touched but scarcely overlapped. All that changed with the advent of Marie-Antoinette. Charles-Alexandre de Calonne, finance minister from 1783 to 1787, and Marie-Antoinette's nemesis as she was his, described the change she had brought about:

> Hitherto [he is writing in 1781] the royal family, surrounded by a stiff etiquette, did not discuss affairs of state with those who formed the Court. Even in the most intimate recesses of their society, there was no discussion of anything relating to the administration. The late king and the late queen did not permit even their most cherished courtiers to address them on affairs of state nor to give an opinion on the performance of ministers: none of them would have dared.
>
> The genteel charm that nowadays tempers the harsh brilliance of the throne has rendered it more accessible . . . [the rulers] are no longer strangers to the delights of society . . . but it has also had the consequence that when people who have most access to the royal family concert action to make a view prevail, they flatter themselves that they can carry their influence even to the operations of government and that society judges the ministers.[3]

Calonne is not here talking about the influence of the Court in general, which remained excluded from affairs. Rather, he is referring to the queen's *société intime*, as it was called, the Polignac set, and especially the queen's favourite, Yolande de Polignac, and her coterie (the main subject of this chapter). Calonne realized that if he were to achieve his ambition of becoming finance minister and retaining a post that had a rapid turnover, he would have to join the group.

The comte de Provence also talked about the stiff etiquette of Louis XV's court, which, he said, was 'serious and even a bit sad'. When Marie-Antoinette became queen, her household was essentially that of Louis XV's queen who had died in 1768. Marie-Antoinette had witnessed how her mother had slackened the rigid, gloomy and essentially Spanish etiquette which her father, the emperor Charles VI, had introduced as compensation for failing to conquer the throne of that country in the War of the Spanish Succession. And Marie-Antoinette thought she could do the same. But Maria-Theresa had managed to achieve the difficult balance between informality and familiarity. Whilst seeing Maria-Theresa as a 'friend', the Austrians never forgot that she was also their 'sovereign'. When Marie-Antoinette mingled with the courtiers, however, the French saw little difference between her and Louis XV's mistresses.[4]

Informality was the watchword at the Petit Trianon, which Louis XVI now gave to Marie-Antoinette, having exiled Madame du Barry. Marie-Antoinette would drive herself there in a cabriolet or walk the mile from the château attended only by a footman. Attendance was by invitation only: no one was there solely by virtue of their court office. When the First Gentleman of the Bedchamber insisted on his right to organize the amateur theatricals Marie-Antoinette staged (one of the few pleasures she shared with the king), she told him curtly, 'I don't hold court there. I live as a private individual.'[5]

Marie-Antoinette's love of the informal even extended to her clothes. Increasingly she discarded the rich silks of court costume for flowing white muslins. Muslin was cheaper than silk, but rather than being praised for economy she was accused of ruining the Lyon silk business, for Marie-Antoinette set the fashion for what soon became known as a *chemise à la reine*. Moreover, muslin was mainly imported from India, and India had been dominated by the English since the Seven Years War. It was also considered unbecoming for a queen of France, since hitherto muslin was mostly used for underwear. It was also diaphanous. Elisabeth Vigée-Lebrun's portrait of the queen wearing muslin was exhibited in a Paris salon in 1783 but had to be withdrawn. Vigée-Lebrun had first painted the queen in 1778; until then Marie-Antoinette had complained that no one had been able to 'catch her likeness'. Muslin was worn by planters' wives, but it was thought that the queen was patronizingly aping peasant dress to fit in with her model village in the grounds of the Trianon, complete with its Norman farmhouse, dairy (also one at Rambouillet), a real peasant, his wife and real farmyard animals – when a goat died Marie-Antoinette insisted that the replacement must be white to match.

Marie-Antoinette thought that the old-timers had run the Court for too long, their power increasing and becoming entrenched since the death of the old queen. Rich and poor alike were alienated (albeit to a degree that has been exaggerated). Marie-Antoinette felt herself 'besieged by these *femmes titrées* [as duchesses were styled] who watched her all the time' with a critical eye. The court offices had been monopolized by the Noailles and Rohan families. Marie-Antoinette would alienate them both, not carelessly as is usually implied but deliberately and with twin goals. To 'take them [the Noailles] down a peg or two', as she put it, as well as to find places for her own court faction, the Polignacs. The Court had become ossified; new posts were not created though old ones could be revived or existing ones divided (Marie-Antoinette resorted to both), so it was essentially a zero sum gain: the Polignacs could only rise to the extent that the established clans fell.

There were four active factions at court under Louis XVI and Marie-Antoinette: the Noailles, the Rohan, the Choiseul and the 'parvenu'[6] Polignacs. Other important families trod water. The La Rochefoucauld were protected by

Louis XVI's chief minister, the comte de Maurepas, who was proud of his (distant) relationship to the family. The Montmorency were needed whenever the prestige of an 800-year-old name was required for an appointment. It has been argued that Marie-Antoinette and, to the extent that he permitted it, Louis XVI, abandoned the sage policies of divide and rule, or balance between the factions, practised by Louis XIV and Louis XV.[7] This is questionable: surely it is better to have a harmonious rather than a divided court and a 'harmonious ministry' such as that sought by Louis' Mentor, Maurepas. The maintenance of division or the inability to impose unity is a sign of weakness.

Be that as it may, the main losers from Marie-Antoinette's policy were the Noailles family, who had held the most court offices in the previous reign. The Noailles had provided a minister during Louis XV's minority, and generals and bishops, but they were not essentially a political family; they were generally non-descript placemen. They were, however, related to a vain, grandstanding malcontent who will bulk large in Marie-Antoinette's story: Gilles du Motier, better known as the marquis de Lafayette. As she told her mother, Marie Antoinette was determined to demote this 'tribe with too much power here'.[8] It was an act of rebalancing.

At the start of Louis XVI's reign the tribe's standard-bearer was the comtesse de Noailles, *dame d'honneur* or principal lady-in-waiting to the queen, the one on whom Marie-Antoinette had lavished supererogatory affection. She effectively ran the queen's household because the post above hers, the Surintendance de la Maison de la Reine, was in abeyance following the death of Louis XV's queen in 1768. The Surintendance denoted a grand and ancient office with the right to order expenditure off one's own bat (*en commandement*). Marie-Antoinette revived the post in favour of her current favourite the princesse de Lamballe, a decision criticized at the time and soon regretted by Marie-Antoinette herself, who found the princess dull. This put the comtesse de Noailles in the shade or rather she took umbrage and resigned.

The Rohan were distantly related to the semi-sovereign dukes of Brittany, whose last duchess had brought the territory to Charles VIII as a dowry in 1491. As such they managed to enjoy a rank between that of the dukes and the princes of the blood. Their motto was: 'Roi ne puis, duc je daigne, Rohan suis' ('I cannot be king but despise the title duc; I am a Rohan'). Male members of the family were automatically invested with the Order of the Saint-Esprit on reaching their majority. The Rohan, like the Noailles, were not or had ceased to be a political family,[9] though one of them, the prince Louis de Rohan, coadjutor[10] bishop of Strasbourg, ludicrously aspired to be prime minister. And this hopeless ambition, coupled with Marie-Antoinette's hatred for him, was to culminate in the most destructive scandal of the reign, the infamous Diamond Necklace Affair.

Whilst he was ambassador to Vienna, Rohan sent the foreign secretary d'Aiguillon a dispatch in which he painted Maria-Theresa 'in a very unfavourable light', accusing her of 'hypocrisy' in weeping over the Partition of Poland whilst taking the lion's share of the booty – like the walrus and the oysters, 'with tears and sighs, she sorted out those of the largest size'. D'Aiguillon 'was imprudent enough to divulge the contents of the dispatch to ... Mercy-Argenteau, who of course went straight to the dauphine with it'. Provence, who relates this episode, censures d'Aiguillon rather than Rohan, who was merely doing his duty. But Marie-Antoinette blamed Rohan even more than d'Aiguillon.[11] According to the baron de Besenval, d'Aiguillon, in letters not dispatches, had also called Marie-Antoinette herself a 'coquette' available to all comers.[12]

Louis XV had promised the Rohan that their great hope, Prince Louis, would be made Grand Almoner to the king (the highest ecclesiastical appointment at Versailles) on the death of the incumbent, the Cardinal de La Roche-Aymon. Besieged by his Rohan ex-governess Madame de Marsan, Louis XVI had renewed this promise but Marie-Antoinette, egged on by the Choiseul faction, persuaded him to renege on it. When, however, the cardinal died in 1777, Louis, influenced by Maurepas with his 'puerile'[13] fear of Choiseul and for that matter of Marie-Antoinette also, appointed Rohan. To save face it was only to be for a year, but the condition was never applied and, moreover, Rohan was shortly afterwards made a cardinal, an honour that tended to go with the post of almoner. What Rohan was too stupid to realize was that being made a cardinal disqualified him in Louis' eyes from ever becoming a minister, because 'his eminence' would automatically have pre-eminence in the Council of State. Another disqualification, apart from Marie-Antoinette's loathing of him, was Rohan's scandalous lifestyle. Although the following anecdote may be apocryphal it was also characteristic. Seeing a young priest with Rohan in his carriage, the innocent king is said to have exclaimed to his brother Artois, 'if he was wearing rouge, I'd have sworn he was a woman'. The already debauched Artois explained that it was indeed a woman – Louis XV's bastard daughter, who had married Madame de Pompadour's brother.[14]

Things continued to go well with the Rohan, though their pride was teetering on classical hubris. In the same year that the prince Louis de Rohan was made Grand Almoner, his cousin, the prince de Rohan-Guéméné, already since 1775, Lord Chamberlain, was invested with substantial fiefs in Alsace by the king; and in the Parlement, ever the friend of the Rohan, Guéméné won his lawsuit against the Crown that put him in possession of all the port of L'Orient and its surrounding territory. The year 1778 saw the birth of Marie-Antoinette's first child, Marie-Thérèse-Charlotte, and the post of Gouvernante des Enfants de France was given to the princesse de Guéméné. Although she detested the Rohan in general, Marie-Antoinette made an exception of the princess to whom she once wrote, 'I will love you to my dying day'. Fine words. The symbolic high point for the Rohan was on 22 December 1781 when the governess, her train carried by Madame Adélaïde, presented the newly born dauphin to an adoring crowd.

One year later, to the day, indeed to the hour, the governess left Versailles in disgrace, abandoned by her bosom friend Marie-Antoinette with the cruel remark, 'it is not appropriate for the future King of France to have the wife of a bankrupt as his teacher'.[15] The bankruptcy of the prince was spectacular and, as a friend said, 'would have been so even for the richest and greatest potentate in Europe'. And the same friend likened the fall to that of a king –François I who was captured at the Battle of Pavia in 1525, adding that at least François kept his honour. The sum owed was 30 million francs – almost the entire cost of the Court for a year, or nearly half the yield of the main tax, the *taille* payable only by the peasantry and more than the *vingtième* paid by everyone but the Church. Two thousand creditors lost everything; they came from every walk of life from dukes to domestics, porters to Breton sailors. The police minister, Jean-Charles-Pierre Lenoir, an ally of the family as we shall see, advised the prince not to venture into Paris if he valued his life. The tactlessness of Cardinal de Rohan compounded the crime: 'Only a king or a Rohan could make such a spectacular bankruptcy'; and the marquis de Villette called it 'the most sublime of bankruptcies'. But this was just bravado.

For so powerful was family honour to the Rohan, that all the members of the clan, though most of them were in debt themselves, forked out to try to mitigate the loss to creditors. And they expected the king to chip in too! And he did. With gritted teeth. Cardinal Rohan – who else? – negotiated the sale of the city of L'Orient and its enclave to the king, and to achieve an inflated price he argued that everyone needed to make sacrifices and that it was in no one's interest for the leading non-royal family in France to go under. Too big to fail. Initially the cardinal asked for a twenty-five-year annuity of 700,000 francs plus an estate for Madame de Marsan in return for the sale of L'Orient and its enclave. Eventually 480,000 was agreed.[16] The sale was master-minded by the foreign secretary Vergennes, who as Chef du Conseil royal des finances ran the finance committee that made the decision. Vergennes would both block Marie-Antoinette's attempts to further Austrian interests and (discreetly) help Rohan in the Diamond Necklace Affair.

The king stumped up but otherwise he and Marie-Antoinette meted out punishments whose severity shocked the Court. Guéméné and his princesse held 'the two finest offices in the kingdom', lord chamberlain and governess to the royal children. They lost both. Dismissing Guémené, Louis told him not to appear at Court until his debts were discharged – an impossible feat since the sale of L'Orient would only have allowed him to pay 8/- in the pound. Louis had a horror of bankruptcy. Had he declared one himself as many advised, there may not have been a French Revolution. Guémené was told to go into exile to Navarre, on the Spanish border – as usual the distance from the king marked the depth of disgrace. His wife was exiled to Pontoise north-west of Paris, where the kings sometimes exiled refractory parlements. Not as cruel a separation as it appeared – they had lived apart for years, though the prince's long-time mistress had recently died of tuberculosis in Naples.

The royal governess was unceremoniously stripped of her post. Marie-Antoinette treated her former friend with 'pitiless harshness'. Madame de Guémené herself had enormous debts, owing 60,000 francs to her shoemaker, 16,000 for wallpaper, and the rest in proportion. But that is not why she lost her post: Marie-Antoinette wanted it for her favourite, Madame de Polignac, whose career, ironically, had been launched by Maurepas in Madame de Guémené's salon. When Madame de Marsan, who normally rode roughshod over opposition, came up with the cock-and-bull story that Madame de Guémené had only resigned on condition that she, Marsan, succeed her, Marie-Antoinette refused even to see her.

The Guémené bankruptcy has been called the death knell of the aristocracy, and likewise the Diamond Necklace Affair with another Rohan, the cardinal, at its centre, that of the monarchy three years later. In fact, the death of both would be caused by a Thucydidean struggle between aristocracy and monarchy in the *révolte nobiliaire* of 1787–8.

The deadly rivals of the Rohan were the Choiseul. Originally from Lorraine, a title in itself to Marie-Antoinette's favour since her father had been its duke, the Choiseul were not great aristocrats but Choiseul and his cousin César Gabriel Choiseul-Praslin, brought in by Madame de Pompadour, had dominated the ministry in the 1760s, when Choiseul had arranged the marriage of Marie-Antoinette. As we have seen, his family fell from grace shortly after the arrival of the young Marie-Antoinette in France, an unlucky conjunction that she tried in vain to redress. Their fall was brought about by Maupeou and d'Aiguillon, to Marie-Antoinette mere creatures of Madame du Barry. D'Aiguillon cancelled the appointment as ambassador to Vienna of Choiseul's protégé the baron de Breteuil, who had already packed his bags. The future cardinal de Rohan was sent instead.

Although the two categories obviously overlapped, the Choiseul were politicians rather than courtiers – as such when out of office they had to be kept in internal exile to sever their contacts and prevent their return to power. So although Marie-Antoinette sought to renew the social complexion of court life by favouring the Polignacs, in political terms she sought a return to the 1760s. But she could never get it into her head that though the king was happy to oblige her in little if expensive ways (military and ecclesiastic appointments were her speciality, plus diplomatic posts for the Polignac set), there was never the slightest chance that he would reappoint Choiseul. His reasons were personal and political. Louis, persuaded against his better judgement by Maurepas, had come to accept the recall of the Parlement as a pacifying synthesis of the warring creeds that had rent his grandfather's kingdom, but to reappoint one of the protagonists, Choiseul, would upset the balance completely and represent a denial of everything that he and his father had stood for. Louis' father's quarrel with Choiseul had been fierce and open. Choiseul even had the effrontery to tell the dauphin to his face that 'though he would have the misfortune to be his subject he would never have that of serving him' – an explosion that reverberated around the Court. Yet so brazen was Choiseul that he seriously expected to 'serve' the dauphin's son Louis XVI as a minister! Louis feared that Choiseul's reappointment, coupled with his marriage to an Austrian, would unbalance his alliance with that country.

MADAME DE POLIGNAC

Choiseul and his disciples, men such as Breteuil, Guines, Castries, Loménie de Brienne, would form the queen's political party – some in the 1780s became 'her' ministers, Brienne even her prime minister. But her social set, the Polignacs, was something different and, curiously, was usually opposed to her political party. Friendship was necessary to Marie-Antoinette but difficult. Monarchs cannot have friendships among equals – they live abroad. So the ones they cultivate often bear the derogatory epithet of favourite. Marie-Antoinette only had two intense friendships in her life and neither came from the ranks of the high nobility crowded together at Versailles. One was Axel von Fersen, a Swedish nobleman attached to the French court; the other was Yolande de Polastron, comtesse and later duchesse de Polignac. A third, perhaps, was Antoine Barnave, the Revolutionary politician with whom she directed the government of France in the last months of 1791.

Both the Polastron and Polignac families were ancient but poor. 'The House of Polignac,' wrote Jean-Louis Soulavie at the time, 'possessed ... the barony of that name in the Languedoc; but it was still vegetating there in 1774 in circumstances which scarcely allowed it to enjoy even the comforts of the bonne bourgeoisie, with an income of barely 8,000 livres [£300] a year.'[17] There had been a cardinal in the family, who was also a man of letters, but that had been the solitary example of distinction in five hundred years of genteel mediocrity. The others 'lived lives so obscure that we don't even know when and where they ended'. But they always lived beyond their means, 'in needy magnificence'[18] – a tradition Madame de Polignac preserved in good times and bad. Their family, as Mercy put it, 'had never had a position at court and their connections were not sufficient for them to appear at Versailles'.[19] In 1775, however, the comte de Polignac's clever if 'spiteful and ugly'[20] sister Diane obtained a place as lady-in-waiting to the wife of the king's youngest brother, the comte d'Artois, who was to become a mainstay of the Polignac set, what became known as the 'society' or what Joseph II called 'the so-called society of the queen'.

For Soulavie, Diane 'ruled' Madame de Polignac, 'and just as the duchesse was seductive and pretty, so Diane was malicious and ugly. Born with a superior mind and fertile in expedients, she was the author of the fortunes of her House, which she directed with authority, every morning giving her orders and the agenda for the day', like a modern political 'grid'.[21] Ugly, wanton and scheming Diane may have been but she imparted to the queen's society a quality, joie de vivre, which contrasted with its other more habitual and equally untranslatable quality, ennui. Fersen noted that members of French society had a depressing habit of saying 'je suis ennuyé'. There was a frenetic quality of pleasure-seeking in Marie-Antoinette, a kind of mirthless laughter that cannot be totally explained by the delayed onset of motherhood. It was in the apartments of the comtesse d'Artois, in 1775, that the queen 'saw [Yolande], was smitten by her beauty, loved her and spontaneously gave her confidence, which caused a malicious public to say that passion played a greater part in the matter than reflection'.[22]

Shortly after she first encountered Madame de Polignac, Marie-Antoinette found her an apartment almost adjacent to her own, at the top of the marble staircase in the old wing of the château of Versailles. It had formerly belonged to Louis XIV's second (secret) wife, Madame de Maintenon. The apartment was tiny but Marie-Antoinette had it enlarged, prior to her moving into a spacious set of rooms as Gouvernante des Enfants de France in 1782. These enlargements were necessary because of the curious inversion in the social arrangements between queen and favourite. As Provence put it: 'The natural result of the new liaison would have been that the comtesse was admitted into the queen's social circle. Instead of that it was the queen who was sucked into the circle of the comtesse.' Marie-Antoinette, he continued, was 'wrong to allow herself to be swept along like this but she loved and saw that her love was returned; this society entertained her'.[23] That is perhaps the clue: the easily bored young queen found a ready-made circle of friends who were entertaining, witty and, above all, musical.

The arrival of Mme de Polignac at court takes some explaining. My guess is she was 'planted' there by Louis XVI's chief minister the comte de Maurepas in the hope that she would neutralize the growing and, so he thought, dangerous influence of Marie-Antoinette on the new king – an influence that could only be exercised at his expense. Madame de Polignac was a country cousin of Maurepas'. Mercy calls her 'niece' and elsewhere 'cousin under an obligation' to Maurepas,[24] and adds that she is 'clearly . . . led by M. de Maurepas . . . [and] ventured to hint that it would be in the queen's interest to persuade the king to appoint . . . Maurepas prime minister; she tells [him] everything, however insignificant, that she learns from the queen.'[25] Nevertheless, Mercy also thought Madame de Polignac capable of playing a double game between queen and minister, 'which could have unfortunate consequences'.[26] Very few of Maurepas' letters survive from this period, but on 20 May 1776 he wrote to Cardinal Bernis, French ambassador to the Holy See, asking him to further a petition of the Polignacs' to the Pope. 'The object' of this petition, Maurepas explains, 'is all the more important because it is a question of restoring their finances which are in a pretty bad way and this is the only way of salvaging them'.[27] I don't know the basis of the Polignacs' petition – perhaps the services of Cardinal de Polignac (d. 1742) whom Bernis would have known as a young man. Nor the sum involved, which must have been considerable. At this stage, Maurepas had no idea that the queen would shower her new favourite with gold: hitherto her favour had been fickle. Maurepas needed a way of financing her stay at court.

What did Marie-Antoinette see in Yolande, a woman six years her senior? All witnesses agree that even the genius of Madame Vigée-Lebrun, painter to Marie-Antoinette and to the Polignac set, could not capture the beauty of the favourite. She was small – her friend the Duchess of Devonshire called her 'Little Po' – but perfectly formed, petite then, with that seductive combination of a brunette with gentle blue eyes. The duc de Lévis, a fringe member of the set, wrote: 'She had the most celestial face you could see. Her look, her smile, all her features were angelic. She had a head such as those where Raphael manages to combine a spiritual expression with infinite gentleness.'[28] Her one blemish was a slightly retroussé nose. She had an excellent singing voice and many of her set catered for Marie-Antoinette's love of music. She was lazy and her reluctance to accept the post of governess of the king's children– 'the finest that the King could bestow in favour of a woman' as Provence put it[29] – was probably genuine.

That word 'probably' introduces a note of uncertainty about Little Po. Faux-naif springs to mind. Over the course of ten years she obtained without seeming to try a whole series of court sinecures, pensions, dowries, gifts of land for herself, her family and all her friends. The list is impressive and to many was shocking, given the state of the royal finances: she was Gouvernante des Enfants de France; her husband was First Equerry to the Queen and (in 1780) duc de Polignac; her son-in-law was made duc de Guiche and captain of the Guards; her friend the comte d'Adhémar was made ambassador to London, where his ambassadorial bedroom was adorned with a picture of Madame de Polignac – Marie-Antoinette's was relegated to a corridor.[30] In 1782 she was given the *baronnie* of Fenestrange worth 1,200,000 francs.

Her sister-in-law, Diane de Polignac, thought she was an angel. Soulavie thought she was a fraud: 'Madame de Polignac . . . had a rare talent. She knew how to turn on the emotional tap, to . . . [feign] naiveté; she could blush at the drop of a hat.' 'She worked for the fortune of each individual member of a large and insatiable family. Intrigue and circumstances made them dukes, *surinten-dants* and governesses . . . whilst parallel intrigues debased and stripped . . . [their distinguished holders] of these same posts . . . She wished to obtain everything by surprise because she could lose everything by accident and the resentment of powerful enemies who were dying of envy.'[31]

A smash-and-grab raid, then. Yolande would not mind losing the queen's favour, did not even strive to retain it (which only served to intensify Marie-Antoinette's love for her), because she and her coterie were materially provided for. After 1787 she did indeed lose all her political influence with the queen (though it returned with disastrous consequences in 1789), but she never lost the queen's affection and returned it to the end of her life. As Provence says, 'I am convinced that their love for each other was equal in so far as it can be between one who is lively and the other poised to the point of indolence.'[32]

However, as we have suggested, Marie-Antoinette's promotion of the Polignacs was not merely a matter of friendship. On 14 September 1776 she told Maria-Theresa that she had 'taken it upon herself' to appoint as successor to the comte de Tessé, her First Equerry, the comte de Polignac, 'a man from a very good family. He is married to a woman whom I love unreservedly.' The appointment gave Madame de Polignac an income but there was more to it than that. Tessé's relatives, the Noailles, 'the most numerous and the most powerful of all those at court', had expected the succession for one of theirs so, Marie-Antoinette continues, 'I wanted once more to forestall the demands of the Noailles, a tribe with too much power here.'[33] Her 'once more' refers to her causing the comtesse de Noailles, 'Madame Etiquette', to resign as *dame d'honneur*. It may be said in passing that the comtesse de Tessé was the favourite aunt of Lafayette's wife Adrienne. Although Marie-Antoinette and Maurepas, as alternative prime ministers, were generally at odds, the Mentor supported her over this appointment because the Polignacs were his protégés too. Mercy told Maria-Theresa that Maurepas 'had been one of the principal agents' in getting M. de Polignac his post.[34] Apart from obliging his niece, Madame de Polignac, Maurepas also bore a deep grudge against all those favoured by Louis XV who had sent him into twenty-five years of exile. The comte de Polignac and Tessé exchanged angry letters that nearly culminated in a duel.[35]

Marie-Antoinette feels it necessary to say that M. de Polignac is 'of very good family' because the whole point of the exercise was that he wasn't. The queen was deliberately replacing the high nobility, the 'grands', the duchesses, with a nobility from a 'subaltern' layer. Instead of those hyper-critical old bats, those relics of the old court where, as dauphine, she had never been at her ease, where even the kindly Louis XV had secretly disapproved of her manners, instead of these, 'the queen needed a confidante, a woman who owed her existence to her, whom she had raised from nothing'. Marie-Antoinette, in Soulavie's words, 'affected to put herself at the head of an opposition [to the high nobility] by giving herself to the parvenus'. Later she would find that virtue could be discovered even further down the social scale. In her smaller way, Marie-Antoinette was doing with her court what Louis XIV had done with his government. Saint-Simon was exaggerating when he called Louis' ministers 'base bourgeois' – they were men recently ennobled by judicial office (*noblesse de robe*) rather than men of ancient military families. Similarly, the Polignacs were not 'nothing' but they were nothing at Court. Marie-Antoinette's hostility towards the old court was spurred on by Madame de Polignac, who had reasons of her own to hate the top tier of the nobility: Provence tells how 'circumstances which it would be too long to relate had from childhood up inspired in her an aversion to the Court of Louis XV, an aversion which extended to its very usages'. It is a pity that Provence could not spare the time to explain this 'aversion' – he had just proclaimed himself king after the boy Louis XVII's death.

A conversation between Maurepas and the king, recorded by the abbé de Véri, shows that the decision to slacken Court etiquette was not just a whim of Marie-Antoinette's but was fully supported by Maurepas, Louis XVI and Madame de Polignac from the very outset of the new reign. The First Gentleman of the Bedchamber had asked the king for a new codification of precedence for the various noble dynasties such as 'Lorraine, Rohan, Bouillon' when presented at Court. Maurepas told the king: 'the nation is not affected by decisions of this kind. Precedence is in the king's absolute gift without the citizens suffering from it. It is of little matter to the king whether families have or have not precedence over each other at court.' The king took all this on board when replying to the First Gentleman 'with astonishing . . . precision'. The king told him that the code was abolished and that in future the king would judge each case on its merits; 'he would take into consideration ancient titles of nobility but it would not be the sole basis of his decision'.[36] In other words the king was the sole fount of honour. Under Louis XV dukes were becoming ministers (Belle-Isle, Choiseul, d'Aiguillon); so Louis XV made a minister a duke (La Vrillière). The dukes looked down on Madame de Polignac's husband; so Louis XV made him a duke too.

Much was made at the time and has been since by historians of the damage that Marie-Antoinette's spurning of the upper nobility did to her and to the regime itself. Soulavie observed, 'a revolution was the result of the contempt she affected for the Court . . . and this revolution manifested itself both against the queen and against the Polignac women'.[37] He added that 'the queen could never understand that one needed the friendship of enemies', a failing which extended into the Revolution when, in particular, on two key occasions she spurned the offer of Lafayette (the grandson of the duc de Noailles) to save the monarchy. The Court became deserted, the old court nobles performed their official duties and formal ceremonies mechanically but preferred to spend their time in Paris, where they and the bulk of their wealth essentially resided and where they wrote and circulated scurrilous verses, songs and pamphlets about Marie-Antoinette, and the secret delights of her supposed lesbian relationship with her favourite. Circulated at first in manuscript, they soon found their way into the gutter of the underground press.

At first this undermined the prestige of monarchy in a general way: Provence notes that Marie-Antoinette was beginning to lose her popularity as early as 1776, just two years into the reign. Later it took on a political complexion, the point of flexion being the Diamond Necklace Affair of 1785–6. Daniel Wick argued that Marie-Antoinette's practice (or rather her policy) of concentrating her favours on a small coterie, by alienating those excluded, was a factor in the *révolte nobiliaire* of 1787–9 when, as the Revolution approached, they formed a steering committee to promote liberal policies; this was the so-called 'Committee of Thirty', though its membership was over fifty and dominated by the upper echelons of the court nobility, not one of whom, significantly, held a household appointment. The Committee, the Assembly of Notables and the Estates-General gave these members the institutional basis that, since the reign of Louis XIV, they had lacked as individual courtiers. All three of the Lameth brothers, Alexandre, Théodore and Victor, were members of the Committee. They were the recipients of some court patronage: the three brothers and their mother drew 60,000 livres (£2,500). But their mother was a Broglie and the

Broglie had been staunch opponents of the Austrian alliance.[38] They were Barnave's friends and associates in the French Revolution: he 'lodged' with and 'loved' them. This explains his curious (in view of his open-access beliefs) observation: 'Louis XV's profoundly corrupt court was succeeded by a young court which displayed a lack of foresight. It [i.e. Marie-Antoinette] played with abolishing all etiquette and pulling down all prominent people.'[39] Disgruntled courtiers the Lameths may have been, but in 1791 they would join Marie-Antoinette and Barnave in their attempt to restore monarchical authority.

If Madame de Polignac had enjoyed a deep relationship only with her lover Vaudreuil and Marie-Antoinette, we should not have learned so much about her; and in particular she and her set would not have accumulated the wealth that made them hated by court and nation. For the source of their wealth was of course the king. The marquis de Bombelles, diplomat and fringe member of the Polignac set, noted in his diary, 'of the king and queen it is the king who really loves Madame de Polignac the more'.[40] This was written on 15 November 1785 and the relationship took a while to develop. It had twin bases: social and political.

Before Madame de Polignac's arrival, the queen had frequented the salons of Mesdames de Lamballe and Guéméné where gambling for high stakes at the card game of Faro was the norm. Louis never set foot in either. Yolande also introduced gentler pastimes, especially amateur theatricals – Louis had a keen interest in the theatre, especially the Comédie française and the Comédie italienne, and he always applauded his wife's performances warmly; though Mercy complained that learning her roles took up time that could be better employed furthering the 'august service'. Louis as well as Marie-Antoinette found more congenial companions in the Polignac set than among the staid courtiers. It has been argued that the atmosphere was similar to the one the king enjoyed at his private suppers. In Lent 1780 – the most critical year in the American War of Independence – the party played forfeits with the forfeit being some 'bizarre' religious penance. Louis, Mercy was scandalized to note, entered into the spirit of this.[41] This was not a frequent occurrence: the king was not a party animal and though he would sometimes come to their soirées he was somewhat ill at ease, particularly when the participants gambled for high stakes. Indeed he could act as a dampener on proceedings; so, knowing he was a man who lived by his precision clocks, retiring for the night promptly at 11 o'clock, they often advanced the hour on the magnificent ormoulou timepiece in Madame de Polignac's apartments to get rid of him.

For it was individual encounters with Madame de Polignac the king enjoyed, either in the queen's company or tête-à-tête. When in 1780, Yolande went to Paris for a confinement for a child by Vaudreuil, Louis moved his entire court to the nearby château of La Muette so the queen could visit her easily. This he also did himself; he even notes it and the time, 'in the morning', in his diary: it was the only private house in Paris he ever visited. Calling on her caused a scandal among the dukes. Not because M. de Polignac was not the father of the child – no rarity among court circles – but because the mother was not of sufficient rank for such an exceptional honour. Louis rectified the situation to his satisfaction at least by making the cuckolded comte de Polignac himself a duke after the visit; and to put a stop to the rumours, Louis XVI took the step of standing godfather to the child.

Louis had a political alliance with Madame de Polignac as well as the deep friendship that followed on from it. Maurepas was Louis' Mentor. The Polignacs were his puppets. Their purpose was to neutralize the queen's influence where it conflicted with the king's and this purpose continued after Maurepas' death in 1781, when Louis XVI's personal rule began. The king's favourite ministers the comte de Vergennes and Calonne both worked with and for the Polignacs, Vergennes getting d'Adhémar the English embassy, for which he was unqualified, and Calonne heaping them with spoils. Louis mainly needed to contain the queen's influence on foreign policy, which was his chief task before the Revolution.

When Yolande was on leave of absence from her arduous task of entertaining the queen, Louis often summoned her back: as Mercy notes, 'when she is absent from Versailles the monarch is careful to write alerting her to the times when her presence might be most necessary or agreeable to the queen'. Whether this was when Marie-Antoinette was trying to meddle in foreign policy or when she was unhappy, or both, cannot be said. In 1778 at the height of the Bavarian crisis (see Chapter 3), Louis wrote to Yolande asking her to return to court after a well-deserved absence to keep the queen company and deter her from plugging her brother Joseph's Bavarian claim. In 1783, when Austria and Russia were threatening France's ally the Ottoman Empire, the king berated his wife: 'Now that you have given birth to a dauphin it is not fitting that you should subordinate his inheritance to the interests of the House of Austria.' He shouted so loud that his words could clearly be heard through the doors of the queen's bedroom. Two days later he asked Madame de Polignac, 'Is she still in a mood?' Yolande took Marie-Antoinette into a window embrasure and signalled to the king that 'with a bit of patience the queen would come round and see reason'.[42]

The height of the Polignacs' influence came when Calonne was finance minister. It culminated in his attempt with their support and the king's, but Marie-Antoinette's opposition, to reform the regime via the programme presented to the Assembly of Notables in 1787.

THE COMTE DE VAUDREUIL

The leading member of the Polignac set, apart from Yolande herself, was her lover, Joseph Hyacinthe de Rigaud, comte de Vaudreuil, whom Marie-Antoinette detested. Vaudreuil was Yolande's cousin as well as her lover. Family tradition has it that he was destined for her, but glimpsing her as a teenager in a convent he found her insufficiently attractive. If so, he soon changed his tune, and with his cousin married to the colourless M. de Polignac, foreswore marriage for himself. Vaudreuil was born in Saint-Domingue, the son of the marquis de Vaudreuil, a rich planter who was also governor of the island. His mother was a rich Creole of little birth. A valetudinarian aesthete given to temper tantrums, Vaudreuil often coughed blood and his face had been ruined by smallpox. Nevertheless memorialists said that he had the art of charming women lost with the Revolution and was one of the last exponents of the old French art of conversation. And despite his sickly mien, he lived until 1817, dying at the age of seventy-six as governor of the Tuileries under the restored Louis XVIII. There was a sickly quality to others in the set: Yolande was often ill and died young. So, to an extent, was Marie-Antoinette, whose family was not a healthy one: her father had died young and her brothers Joseph and Leopold would die before her.

Vaudreuil lived double though not secret lives. His twin centres were the salons of Madame de Polignac at Versailles and of the painter Elisabeth Vigée-Lebrun in Paris. In Pierre de Nolhac's words, 'As soon as he had discharged the duties of lover and courtier, he fled this futile life as quickly as possible to rediscover the life of the intellect at Paris.' There the immense wealth he derived from the French sugar plantations enabled him to play the role of Mycenas. 'His passionate soul took an interest in the whole spectrum of the arts of his time.'[43] He patronized the writers of the day, notably the poet Lebrun and Beaumarchais – he was the moving force behind the production of the *Marriage of Figaro* at Versailles, with himself playing the role of Almavida. But his forte was the visual arts and he amassed a spectacular collection of fine paintings and tapestries. The only post he wanted, and probably the only one he could execute efficiently, was that of Director of the King's Buildings – no sinecure at this time, with Louis XVI acquiring and renovating palaces as if there was no tomorrow, which in a sense there wasn't. However, the comte d'Angiviller, the king's childhood friend, was firmly ensconced in that post. Vaudreuil's hopes of becoming Gouverneur des Enfants de France (at the age of six the boys progressed from a governess to a governor) were not taken seriously.

As it was, the only post Vaudreuil obtained was that of Grand Falconer, with 3,000 livres a year and negligible duties: hawking was out of fashion so the

Falconer's duties were limited to solemnly taking possession of Icelandic falcons from the king of Denmark and their Mediterranean cousins from the Knights of St John at Malta. He was also invested with the Saint-Esprit, the highest order of chivalry, and to celebrate the honour Vigée-Lebrun painted him twice in 1784, once wearing the star of the Order, the other time its *cordon bleu*.

As the queen gradually woke up to the rapacity of her entourage and, more importantly, the fact that they often served to thwart her policies, the Polignacs moved beyond merely seeking positions and pensions and sought to influence the appointment and dismissal of ministers. Cynics said that this was merely to further line their pockets by going straight to the source, the finance minister or the king himself, rather than using Marie-Antoinette as an intermediary. This may have been largely a question of money, but they and the king came to share important political views.

It has recently been suggested that Madame de Polignac's continuing favour with Marie-Antoinette, despite their political differences and the queen's detestation of the favourite's lover, Vaudreuil, and despite the queen's growing concern at the rapacity of the set – indeed the continuing success of that rapacity – can best be explained by the assumption that Yolande was blackmailing Marie-Antoinette over her relationship with Axel von Fersen. This was possible because Madame de Polignac, according to Mercy, 'is the repository of all . . . [the queen's] thoughts and I very much doubt whether there is a single exception to these unreserved confidences'.[44]

AXEL VON FERSEN

Madame de Polignac was in a position to observe both sides of the relationship between Marie-Antoinette and Fersen, because he was a fringe member of the Polignac set whom, the comte de Saint-Priest observes, 'they tolerated because they saw no threat from this foreigner'.[45] Possible blackmail aside, Fersen was jealous of, and spiteful about, the queen's surely platonic friendship with Yolande, though our evidence for this emerges only *après le déluge*. I say 'surely platonic' because of the rumours that Marie-Antoinette, in addition to a string of male lovers, had a lesbian relationship with Madame de Polignac.

Fersen was not just a wealthy young foreign aristocrat who happened to drop into Versailles as part of his Grand Tour. He was the son of the leading magnate in Sweden and he and his brother Fabian were both romantically, possibly sexually, involved with the wife of Gustavus III's brother, later Charles XIII of Sweden.[46] Sweden, as Gustavus reminded Marie-Antoinette, was France's oldest ally. The two countries had defeated the Habsburgs in the Thirty Years

War and were co-guarantors of the Westphalian treaties which ended that conflict in 1648. Sweden had been a great power then,[47] in possession of modern Estonia, Latvia, Pomerania and Finland, and considered that its manifest destiny was control of the Baltic – *dominium maris Baltici*. But Peter the Great had defeated Sweden in the Great Northern War and stripped her of most of her possessions. There was another link between Fersen and France. Fersen's father had been close friends with Breteuil, who had been ambassador to Sweden from 1763 to 1777. He acted as an alter-pater to the son during his sojourns in Paris.[48] Breteuil was a protégé of Marie-Antoinette's and in 1783 minister of the household. Later he and Fersen would cooperate closely on the Flight to Varennes and would try to salvage something from that royal disaster.

Fersen was born on 4 September 1755, the year of Marie-Antoinette's birth, the son of Field-Marshal-Senator Frederick Fersen, a leading light in the Swedish 'Hat' party. The Hats favoured a weak monarchy and so were backed by Russia which, having dismembered the Swedish empire of Charles XII, aimed to keep it as weak as Poland to prevent any chance of revanche. Their opponents, the 'Caps', favoured a strong monarchy. In 1772, with French encouragement and inspired by Louis XV's coup d'état against the parlements, the young king Gustavus III had reasserted royal authority, helped by the peasants who formed a separate Fourth Estate in the Riksdaag. (Significantly there was no peasants' chamber in the French equivalent of the Riksdaag, the Estates-General.) Gustavus was a regular visitor to Versailles and recipient of a French subsidy. Mindful of this, he was the only sovereign prepared to put himself out to help Louis XVI and Marie-Antoinette in their hour of need.

Despite the political stance of the Field-Marshal, his son found favour with the young king, who appreciated good-looking men. With the backing of his court and his father's eminence, in 1773, aged eighteen, Axel Fersen set off on a very grand Grand Tour, being introduced to the royal families of all the countries he visited. His first stop naturally was France. On 10 January 1774 he notes, 'I went at three o'clock to the ball of Madame la Dauphine'. On 30 January he went to the masked ball at the opera at 1 a.m. Marie-Antoinette and the younger members of the royal family dropped in for half an hour. But being *in maschera* Fersen did not recognize the dauphine, who chatted with him for some time before revealing her identity. These masked balls were somewhat risqué – Joseph II thought 'all the riff-raff of Paris' turned up, 'libertines, prostitutes, foreigners'. He chided his little sister and saw danger where she saw opportunity in the whole rationale of the masked ball: the ability to say what you wanted to whomever you wanted.[49] In May, Fersen crossed the Channel and noted that since George III had only three or four topics of conversation he kept his voice down so no one would spot that he was repeating himself – a trick Louis XVI could have used to advantage.

In 1775, Fersen returned to Sweden, joined the army, and was in constant attendance on his king. But there was no role for a soldier in peacetime and the Swedish court, though glittering, was small. So in 1778 he resumed his travels staying for three months in England where he came to an 'understanding' with the fabulously rich heiress of a Swedish immigrant. In August he returned to France, now at war with England, and on the 26th was presented to the royal family. Marie-Antoinette remembered him: 'Ah here is an old acquaintance. The rest of the family did not say a word to me.' The equerry who presented Fersen to the queen noticed that 'her hand trembled with visible emotion.'[50] Fersen found the queen 'the prettiest and most amiable princess that I know'. He also noted in his diary that the queen was 'heavily pregnant'. She asked Gustav Creutz, the Swedish ambassador, why Fersen did not attend her Sunday card parties; he said that he had turned up one day and found no one there. Marie-Antoinette apologized and he became a regular attendee. She also asked him to attend her in her private apartments dressed in his Swedish uniform, which her expert eye considered the equal of French versions.

Over the next eighteen months they fell in love. On 10 April 1780, Creutz told Gustavus III, 'the queen could not take her eyes off him these last days; looking at him they were full of tears.'[51] An attempt to diminish the import of this dispatch has not succeeded.[52] A key moment in their relationship seems to have been a performance of Purcell's *Dido and Aeneas*. It was performed at Paris and Marie-Antoinette sung arias from it at the Trianon. In 1805 the opera was staged at the Swedish court and Fersen wrote in his diary, 'how many memories and excruciating regrets for my heart this performance brought me'.[53] Perhaps Marie-Antoinette had sung the famous lament 'Remember me' for him. Shortly afterwards, Fersen left for America to join the French troops, Marie-Antoinette having secured him a post as aide-de-camp to General Rochambeau.[54] This involved abandoning his suit of the Anglo-Swedish heiress, who went on to marry Lord De La Warr. Did Fersen flee to escape her clutches, a match his father had urged upon him? The natural and generally accepted explanation for his departure was to avoid compromising Marie-Antoinette.

Evelyn Farr has suggested that in this year, when Marie-Antoinette's love for Fersen was becoming obvious, Polignac 'made an outrageous demand for the county of Bitche in Lorraine – worth 100,000 livres a year – as an outright gift'. She concludes that 'the stench of blackmail simply reeks off the pages of these [Mercy's] ancient dispatches'.[55] At this stage, however, the relationship between Marie-Antoinette and Fersen must be taken as innocent: she could not risk producing a male bastard before a dauphin had been born – a dauphin, incidentally, born when Fersen was safely in America, and who, Gustavus III observed in 1786, 'is very tall and resembles his father the king'.[56]

In 1783, Abraham-Louis Breguet, the greatest watchmaker of the age, perhaps of all time, received a commission to make a watch incorporating all the latest developments in horology and be virtually self-winding. No expense was to be spared and the parts were to be of gold not brass, the jewelling of sapphires and the back case of rock crystal so that the complicated movement could be admired. It is sometimes referred to as the 'Breguet no. 1160 grande complication' (in horology each additional extra feature is known as a 'complication' and this included them all) or alternatively the 'Marie-Antoinette', for it was commissioned for her. Abiding legend has it that it was commissioned by Fersen. This is nonsense – he had no interest in watches and he could not have afforded this one. Although the Breguet ledgers do not mention the commissioner it was obviously the king, a known expert on and patron of horology. Perhaps it was to celebrate the Peace of Paris of that year. The century after 1660 had been the golden age of English clockmaking, culminating in John Harrison's chronometers that had made it possible to calculate longitude at sea. French clocks were and still are prized for their ormoulou sculptural cases rather than their movements. Louis sought horological as well as naval parity with France's foe. Sadly, Breguet's watch never reached Marie-Antoinette. He worked on it until his death in 1824 and his son completed the commission in 1827.

THREE

A QUEEN IN SEARCH OF A ROLE

1774–1781

MAUREPAS AND MARIE-ANTOINETTE

*J*n jottings of 1788, Mercy-Argenteau wrote: 'Reflexions on the advantages and disadvantages of having a prime minister . . . she [the queen] should reserve this position for herself.'[1] Mercy's rationale for this, outlined to Maria-Theresa on 17 May 1774 right at the start of the reign, was that 'the métier of a prime minister in France has always been to intercept and destroy the credit of the queens'.[2] This was not an abstract statement. He was referring to Jean-Frédéric Phélypeaux, comte de Maurepas, whom the young king had just summoned to him to supplement his inexperience 'with . . . advice and understanding'.[3] 'Intercept' is an important word here. For the key to power is access. Maurepas did not have a key to Louis XVI's private apartments but then he didn't need one. Louis installed him in Madame du Barry's old suite, crammed into the eaves of the palace above his own. It is still there untouched, as is Louis' suite with its enormous plain mahogany desk. The mob never penetrated up the narrow winding cast-iron stairway. To get there from her own apartments the queen had to pass either through a crowded room or the apartments of the king's busybody aunts, Adélaïde and Victoire, Mesdames Tantes as they were known. In 1775, Mercy arranged for the construction of a secret passage connecting the king's apartments to the queen's, though he complained that she did not make sufficient use of it.[4] This passage was later to save her life.

Mercy went on to tell Maria-Theresa that 'history is full of these striking examples' of prime ministers neutralizing the influence of queens and added 'the queen knows the truth of this'. Since no queen of France had exerted any political influence for over one hundred years,[5] and since the first prime minister, Cardinal Dubois, was appointed in 1722, Mercy was inventing a role for Marie-Antoinette fitted to present not past circumstances. This was possible because she was different from the colourless queens her predecessors. Louis XVI never took a mistress, and, after a shaky start, came to love his wife as one; although previous queens had exercised little influence, royal mistresses had. Madame de Pompadour was in some senses Louis XV's prime minister as well as his mistress (though not concurrently). And the woman who had blighted his career cannot have been far from Maurepas' mind as he observed his dazzling young rival. Moreover, the Pompadour and Maurepas had this in common: neither had an official position (*maîtresse-en-titre* was not a political office) and they depended for their power on intimate access to the king. Nor for that matter was queen a political post: that is why Mercy wanted to create a role for her along the lines of Madame de Pompadour, who had brokered the Austrian alliance. With Maurepas ensconced in the mistress's quarters, and the king and queen not enjoying conjugal relations, one can see why Mercy was so keen for Marie-Antoinette to use her 'secret' passage to the king's private suite.

Maurepas was aided in his task of excluding the queen from policy-making by the fact that this was also Louis XVI's aim. The king declared: 'I have absolutely no intention of letting women have any influence on my reign or affairs of state.'[6] But his 'absolutely' – a word used frequently by him and by other vacillating men – applied mainly to the conduct of foreign policy. If Marie-Antoinette did interfere in foreign policy he feared that the Austrian alliance would run out of control as it had in the Seven Years War, the consequence of which, the diminution of French prestige, had darkened his childhood and adolescence. Another reason why Louis was able to exclude his queen from matters of foreign policy was that he knew exactly what he wanted to do in the field: build up the navy almost from scratch, deal with England as an equal, and avoid being inveigled into continental wars by Austria. Moreover, Louis' objectives were shared by the bulk of the nation. And he was equipped to execute them having been trained by the accomplished diplomat and Austro-sceptic, the abbé de la Ville.

Louis, however, had had next to no training in domestic policy – Louis XV had not even allowed his heir to attend the Council of State. Moreover, the past thirty years had been times of experimental reform (free trade in grain, more equal taxation between classes and provinces) followed by reaction – all mediated through disputes with the Parlement, and the young king was somewhat at sea, as was the country. These issues divided the nation: for or against the Parlement Maupeou, regulation or control of the grain trade (and much else) or free trade, centralization versus devolution, etc. Home affairs were complex and the nation divided, but foreign policy was simple because most people shared the king's vision, including his suspicion of Austria. For this reason – and also because the conduct of foreign policy, *la politique* as it was called, was the *métier des rois* – Louis spent most of his time on foreign affairs, to judge by his surviving correspondence.[7]

This gave Marie-Antoinette an opening to influence domestic affairs though she did not know exactly how to set about it, being herself a woman more exploited than exploiting. Besides, Louis did not want her to interfere in major matters like ministerial appointments. Unfortunately for Marie-Antoinette the reappointment of Choiseul for which she strove (against the advice of her Austrian relatives) involved both ministerial appointments and foreign policy, for Choiseul had been not only foreign secretary but one of the architects of the Austrian alliance. The only major political tension between Louis and Marie-Antoinette concerned foreign policy and her related attempts to have Choiseul reinstated.

But whereas Mercy wanted Marie-Antoinette to play a major, even the major role in domestic affairs, Joseph wanted his sister to keep her powder dry in order to help him achieve his great goal of acquiring Bavaria by hook or by crook in order to round off his territories in Germany and make up for the 'rape of Silesia' by Frederick of Prussia in 1740 – the act that had sparked off a series of wars. The queen, he urged, should not dissipate her credit by getting lucrative pensions for her friends or interfering in ministerial politics. Maria-Theresa thought the same. Her advice was that her daughter should not get involved in the internal politics of a monarchy so 'broken down' as that of France. 'If the state of this monarchy,' she told Mercy, 'should get even worse I would prefer some minister to take the blame rather than my daughter.'[8]

In the struggle for the king's ear between Maurepas and Marie-Antoinette, the advantage lay almost entirely in favour of Maurepas. Such, however, was his fear of her influence – a fear that 'bordered on the puerile'[9] – that he believed it was the queen's ultimate intention to replace him with the duc de Choiseul, and the other ministers with a 'shadow' ministry of Choiseulistes. The reality was that there was a group of ministerial aspirants who knew that Maurepas would block their careers – men such as the marquis de Castries, a mildly successful general in the Seven Years War who believed that soldiers rather than lawyers should hold the service ministries; the baron de Breteuil, the well-connected ambassador to Vienna who wanted to be foreign minister; and the comte de Guines, an accomplished flautist (he commissioned a concerto from Mozart without paying for it) who was ambassador to London. They had been associated with Choiseul when he had patronage at his disposal, but now, as the abbé de Véri put it, 'if any of them became a minister, assuredly he would not work for Choiseul's return.'[10] Increasingly they looked for protection not to Choiseul but to the queen herself and in the course of the reign they were transformed into what could be called a 'Queen's Party'. But that was a long way off in 1774.

MARIE-ANTOINETTE'S EARLY POLITICAL INTERVENTIONS

Marie-Antoinette had been rather cowed as dauphine. The faction that had brought about her marriage had fallen and been replaced by one owing much of its position to Madame du Barry. Louis XV had treated Marie-Antoinette like the child she still was and bullied her into acknowledging the existence of his mistress. Now she was queen she immediately started throwing her weight around. So it was no surprise that the first to feel the new queen's displeasure was Madame du Barry. Indeed, even before Louis XV was dead, to be precise after he had received the last rites but before he had expired, Marie-Antoinette dashed off a letter to her mother rejoicing that 'the creature' had been exiled. She asked Mercy to expedite the letter but he, thinking it tasteless, delayed sending it. He was right. Maria-Theresa, who pitied 'poor' Madame du Barry, was shocked that her daughter had called her a 'creature'.[11]

The new king, 'out of consideration for the memory of the [late] King', granted Madame du Barry a pension – but she had to spend her time in a convent. Later she would be guillotined. The mistress had been wont to call the dauphine 'the little redhead' – though not to her face because Marie-Antoinette refused to speak to her. Marie-Antoinette wrote to her mother: 'the king has restricted himself to sending the creature to a convent and banishing from court all who bear her scandalous name'. But Marie-Antoinette's vengeance was only part of the story. Louis gave the deeper reason for du Barry's exile to La Vrillière, the agent of exiles: 'since she knows too much she must be confined sooner rather than later. Send her a *lettre de cachet*[12] to enter a provincial convent and command her to see nobody.'[13] A year later Louis relented and allowed her to go to one of her properties, and in June 1776 he gave her back Louveciennes in the great park of Versailles and her pensions totalling 155,000 livres a year. All she lost was the Petit Trianon, which went to Marie-Antoinette.

Next in line was the duc d'Aiguillon, who had called the dauphine a 'coquette' and was notoriously linked to Madame du Barry. On 2 June he resigned in anticipation of being dismissed from his two ministries of foreign affairs and war. He hoped that by resigning he could escape the lot of disgraced or even ex-ministers – internal exile. His relative Maurepas told the king: 'I will only act as his kinsman in seeking to obtain from you some relaxation in the *traitements de rigueur*' (i.e. to moderate the depth and duration of d'Aiguillon's exile).[14] He succeeded: d'Aiguillon was sent only as far as his estate at Veuvret in the

Tourraine (Loire Valley). He was also spared the indignity of a *lettre de cachet*; instead he was put on his honour to stay there.

Maria-Theresa and Mercy were appalled by Marie-Antoinette's intervention – d'Aiguillon had deplored but permitted the partition of France's traditional ally Poland, though it can be argued that Louis, without Marie-Antoinette's prompting, had already decided to dismiss him for this reason.[15] Maria-Theresa was equally shocked that her daughter cared only about revenge and took no interest in influencing the appointment of d'Aiguillon's replacements. Marie-Antoinette should have tried harder since d'Aiguillon's successor the comte de Vergennes was to prove an implacable obstacle to her brother Joseph's territorial ambitions and she would find herself bawling at the minister like a fishwife.

Marie-Antoinette, however, had not done with d'Aiguillon. She considered he had shown bias in what became known as the 'Guines Affair'. This affair, like the later Diamond Necklace Affair, was very convoluted. The comte de Guines was ambassador to the Court of Saint-James, that is England. He was a protégé of Choiseul's and as such dear to Marie-Antoinette. Since 1770 he had been engaged in a lawsuit against his secretary, appropriately called Tort. Tort had speculated on the futures market that English stocks would fall if the country became involved in a war with Spain over the Falklands – his patron Choiseul had been dismissed for trying to bring this about. Choiseul's fall meant peace; English stock rose and Tort had to honour his obligations. But he claimed that he had only been acting as Guines' agent and sued Guines to recover his losses. Why, Guines retorted, would he speculate against English stocks when he knew, as ambassador, that war would be averted? But how, one might ask, did he know that war would be averted when it was only averted by Choiseul's disgrace? Guines also claimed that d'Aiguillon, as foreign secretary, had intervened on Tort's behalf.

Tort v. Guines took place at the Châtelet, the central criminal court in Paris, and Guines sought Marie-Antoinette's assistance in producing evidence for the defence. First Guines wanted access to copies of letters from d'Aiguillon in the possession of Jean-Charles-Pierre Lenoir, the police minister, which he claimed would demonstrate d'Aiguillon's bias. Louis doubted that d'Aiguillon had shown bias,[16] but he gave way to Marie-Antoinette and asked Lenoir to produce the letters. Lenoir never forgave her and would later act against her in the Diamond Necklace Affair. Vergennes was furious and told the king so, albeit in courtly language: 'I was not surprised that the queen should ask M. Lenoir for copies of such letters as may have been sent to M. d'Aiguillon. It is the product of the kindness she shows in M. de Guines and the interest she takes in him; but I was thunderstruck that he should have sought the protection of the queen over a matter that I could have obtained for him without importuning Your Majesty.'[17] Of course it was the queen who was importuning His Majesty.

Guines also wanted to gain European support for his case by getting permission to publish extracts of his diplomatic dispatches. Vergennes did not conceal his horror from the king. First of all, Vergennes did not want the public of France let alone Europe prying into state secrets. He distrusted public opinion, though he also sought to manipulate it. Equally, he argued, if diplomats' conversations when relaxing over a glass of wine were liable to be published, tongues would be locked in their heads.

Guines won his case on 7 June and resumed his embassy in triumph. Not content with this, Marie-Antoinette insisted that the *secrétaire d'ambassade* at London, whose evidence in the case had not supported Guines' claims, be recalled. She told Vergennes, 'I persist and insist on this.' Vergennes did not dare reply but got Mercy to make her desist.[18] But Marie-Antoinette, encouraged by the baron de Besenval, colonel of the Swiss Guards, sought to inflict further punishment on d'Aiguillon. Besenval, an ageing roué with an elegant pen and a devoted Choiseuliste, had considerable influence on the queen in the first eighteen months of the reign. Later, he would be the field commander in Paris at the time of the fall of the Bastille. Besenval advised Marie-Antoinette that the proximity of Veuvret 'would make it easy for [d'Aiguillon] to maintain his faction . . . and remain as formidable as if he were in Paris'; but if he were sent to his seat at d'Aiguillon in the south-west, it would 'make it impossible for him to continue his intrigues whose thread, once broken, could not easily be mended'.[19] Marie-Antoinette was convinced that d'Aiguillon was behind the spate of scurrilous pamphlets about her supposedly hedonistic life, which were already circulating around court and capital.

She wrote to Count Rosenberg, a childhood friend:

This [d'Aiguillon's] departure is all my doing. The cup was overflowing; this evil man was conducting all sorts of espionage and spreading slander. He had tried to brave my wrath more than once in the Guines affair. As soon as judgment had been given in the case I asked the king to send him away. It is true that I did not want to employ a *lettre de cachet* but nothing has been lost since instead of remaining in the Tourraine, as he wanted, he has been told to continue his journey as far as Aiguillon, which is in Gascony.[20]

D'Aiguillon was not popular, but the way he had been shunted around the country to satisfy Marie-Antoinette's vengeance caused an outcry. Besenval notes that 'we heard talk of nothing but, *tyranny, hard justice, liberty of the citizen* and *legality*'. Maurepas ostentatiously feted d'Aiguillon at his estate at Pontchartrain, on his way to internal exile – the dumbest insolence available to him. Joseph also berated her: 'what are you playing at, exiling a minister to his estates!'[21] Later, d'Aiguillon snubbed Marie-Antoinette by refusing to return to Paris whilst he was forbidden to appear at court.[22]

Marie-Antoinette's next intervention coincided with the coronation of the king in Rheims Cathedral on 11 June 1775. Queens of France, unlike queens of England, were not crowned. The French for coronation is *sacre*, though sometimes *couronnement* is used. In fact both applied to the king but not the queen. The *sacre* invested the king with all the minor orders up to but not including the priesthood, though many regarded him still as a sacred figure, and Louis XVI touched 2,400 people for the king's evil after the coronation. As a modern man, however, who had been vaccinated against smallpox, he made sure that the touching was not mentioned in any of the official organs, since it was an obsolete superstition.

The queen, as a woman, could not receive this first part of the ceremony, though Marie de Medicis, Henri IV's second wife, had been simply crowned. None of the succeeding kings had been married at the time of the coronation and no one thought of crowning the women they later married, as Henry VIII had Anne Boleyn. Mercy wanted Marie-Antoinette to be crowned to bolster her status since she had not yet produced an heir. Louis thought not, perhaps since it was nearly two hundred years since Marie de Medicis had been crowned. Marie-Antoinette was observed to be weeping during the ceremony, but there were various conjectures as to the cause.

'Gratitude' and 'ingratitude' were important words for Louis XVI and Marie-Antoinette. She decided to use the coronation festivities to make a show of support for Choiseul, and to thank him for making her queen of 'the finest realm in Europe'[23] by giving him a long audience. Knowing the king's dislike of Choiseul, she thought it necessary and possible to trick him into giving permission for the audience by employing a device regularly made use of by parents to get their offspring to do something against their will, give them an illusory choice. Afterwards she boasted to Count Rosenberg, in the following terms:

> You will never guess the artifice I employed in seeming to ask for the [king's] permission. I told . . . [him] that I wanted to see M. de Choiseul and that the only problem was finding the right day. I succeeded so well that the poor man himself arranged the time which suited me best to see him. I think that I have made a suitable use of a woman's prerogative on this occasion – I bet old Maurepas can't sleep in his bed tonight.[24]

Rosenberg showed this letter to Maria-Theresa, who wrote a stinging letter to her daughter, accusing her of behaving like a Pompadour or a du Barry rather than a Habsburg. Marie-Antoinette was mortified that her own mother should compare her to two courtesans and told her so, explaining, weakly, that Rosenberg, who knew Versailles, would understand the tone of badinage she had employed. But Maria-Theresa was even more forthright with Mercy: 'What a tone! What a way to think! This only serves to confirm my fear that she is rushing headlong to her perdition. She will be lucky if she even preserves the virtues accompanying her rank. If Choiseul returned to the government she would be lost. He would treat her no better than he did the Pompadour to whom he owed his elevation and he was the first to traduce.'[25]

Marie-Antoinette got her meeting with Choiseul, but when, after the coronation, Choiseul's turn came to kiss the king's hand, he withdrew it and averted his gaze, not bothering to control 'a terrifying grimace'. Seeing no point in remaining at court, Choiseul departed for his estate at Chanteloup, turning an involuntary exile into a voluntary one, a variant on John of Gaunt's encouragement of Bolingbroke: 'Think not the king did banish thee but thou the king.'[26]

In supporting Choiseul, Marie-Antoinette had ignored the advice of Austria. Maria-Theresa thought his exile should be ended but the idea of his return to office filled her with alarm. She felt that if he had been in office in 1772 he would have grabbed the Austrian Netherlands as a quid pro quo for the Partition of Poland.[27] Chancellor Kaunitz considered that 'Choiseul is the man least suited to our purposes'.[28] When Joseph visited Versailles in 1777 he sedulously avoided Choiseul and told the king that his recall would have thrown the kingdom into confusion. He added that Louis had had 'a wise and tranquil ministry at the start of his reign', but left it in doubt whether he was referring to Maupeou or Maurepas. The king was pleased with these observations but Marie-Antoinette was 'displeased'.[29]

Maurepas had skipped the coronation, pleading his age, and instead relaxed at Pontchartrain. Marie-Antoinette came back from Rheims full of herself and fatuously told Maurepas that 'after the coronation the king will devote himself entirely to his royal calling, the economy and public order'.[30] Her next target was La Vrillière, minister of the royal household, who had organized the coronation. She must have remembered the callous way La Vrillière had delivered a *lettre de cachet* to Choiseul's cousin, Choiseul-Praslin: 'the duc de la Vrillière came to Paris to see the duc de Praslin and gave him his *lettre de cachet*, which was very frosty and exiled him to his estates. Praslin replied that he was ill and would not budge; he had been sick of his job for a long time but it was unfair to exile him.' Nevertheless, 'he was given until the end of the week to pack his bags, ill though he was and much as he detested both his wife and country life'.[31] Marie-Antoinette now took her revenge, telling Rosenberg: 'At last we are going to get rid of La Vrillière. Although he is hard of hearing he finally got the message that it is time for him to go if he doesn't want to get his nose trapped in the door.'[32]

Turgot, the finance minister, wanted La Vrillière to be replaced by Malesherbes, the reforming head of the excise court,[33] in order to cut down on court expenditure. But Marie-Antoinette informed Maurepas that if he wanted good relations with her, Antoine de Sartine must be moved from the ministry of the Marine to be minister for the Maison du Roi and a Choiseuliste called the comte d'Ennery must replace Sartine at the Marine. Marie-Antoinette had not taken the elementary precaution of asking Sartine whether he actually wanted to swap ministries. He didn't. With a naval war on the horizon and a navy-mad king on the throne, who gave him an extra 40 million livres – a tenth of the royal budget – to rebuild the navy, he was looking forward to becoming 'the important man in the ministry'. But the vacancy at the Maison du Roi still had to be filled: 'The capital point,' Maurepas told Véri, 'is not to allow the Queen to choose ministers or direct major affairs.'[34] He needn't have worried: he managed to install Malesherbes even though Malesherbes regarded his appointment as 'next to a fatal illness the worst thing that could befall me', and the king told Maurepas 'He [Malesherbes] is too dangerous an Encyclopaedist – don't mention him for anything.'

Marie-Antoinette's Austrian advisers on the spot had become alarmed at her scatter-gun interventions. Her tutor and confessor the abbé Vermond privately told Turgot, 'M. de Maurepas must not give way to her on this occasion. The issue is of too great a consequence for the state.'[35] Instead, he and Mercy sought to detach the Choiseulistes from the unacceptable Choiseul and forge them for the future into a genuinely queen's party of ministerial calibre headed by Vermond's close friend Loménie de Brienne. This group had a distinct quality, a synthesis of the various strands of which it was composed. From Choiseul himself they inherited a pro-philosophe stance, though (except for Brienne) without the intellectual pretension of the man who had corresponded with Voltaire. The deeper reaches of *Philosophie* were obviously beyond Marie-Antoinette, though she may have caught a whiff of the enlightened despotism practised by her brothers Joseph and Leopold. Many from this incipient party, however, such as Castries, were advocates of an extension of aristocratic power through revived provincial and general estates. This she would fight.

Joseph, too, was critical of his sister's inept interventions. He drafted a long letter to her which, perhaps on Maria-Theresa's advice, was never sent. 'You are meddling in a multitude of matters that don't concern you and on behalf of factions which flatter you and know how to arouse your amour propre or desire to shine; they even inculcate in you a certain hatred or rancour which leads you to make one intervention after another which will trouble your happiness.' Such conduct, he continued, 'by diminishing the king's friendship and respect for you', will also diminish the 'stunning popularity you have so far achieved'. He then moved on to particulars: 'My dear sister what do you think you are doing ousting ministers [La Vrillière], dispatching another to his estates [d'Aiguillon], giving this department to one and that to another [she had actually failed to do this], helping another to win his suit [Guines], creating a new and ruinous court position [*surintendant* of the queen's household, revived for her early favourite, Madame de Lamballe]?'[36]

But Marie-Antoinette continued on her course. In September 1775 she demanded that another Choiseuliste, Castries, replace the war minister the comte du Muy, who had died following surgery to remove a gallstone – the operation was a success but the prolonged pain endured with military stoicism killed the patient. Maria-Theresa was appalled that 'you dare to busy yourself with matters of state, with the choice of ministers'. Nor had Marie-Antoinette even been successful. So far her tally had been two dismissals, those of d'Aiguillon and La Vrillière (who may have departed without her intervention), and no appointments.

She also claimed the scalp of Turgot, dismissed as finance minister in May 1776. Many think he was on course to save the regime, so Marie-Antoinette's role in his downfall needs to be re-evaluated. Turgot's reputation rests on what he might have achieved rather than on the measures he actually introduced, which were both controversial and limited in extent. He scrupled to take advantage of the king's youth to propose measures that would have reduced his authority, such as devolved administrations for the provinces, which would then have co-opted a National Assembly. The main measure he actually introduced, in September 1774, was the abolition of most of the restrictions concerning the grain trade. Grain products formed the staple diet of 26 million out of the 28 million inhabitants of France and there was a continuing debate as to whether the grain trade should be regarded as social/police policy (in which case you made farmers offer grain to the local community and forbade export to another province even if there was a glut) or as a matter of economics requiring deregulation. The first favoured the consumer, the second the producer. Turgot was a great economist almost the equal of Adam Smith, whose *Wealth of Nations* was published in 1776 and who may have been indebted to Turgot for some of his ideas. Like Smith, Turgot advocated free trade.

Unfortunately, free trade in grain was only workable in eighteenth-century France when the harvests were bountiful, as they had been in the 1760s, for until the completion of the railway network across all *départements* in the 1870s, there were insuperable problems of distribution and a national market did not exist. The peasantry had an almost superstitious dread of allowing grain to leave their district.

The harvest of 1774 was poor; the price of bread almost doubled and in April–May 1775 the government had to face riots. These, known as the Flour War, were more serious than any for half a century, causing the king temporarily to lose control of the Isle de France and four adjacent provinces. The risings were put down with brutality – 25,000 troops were deployed and two men were hanged on a high gallows as an example. Mercy advised Marie-Antoinette that at a time when people were short of food, her extravagance was doing her damage. Her gambling in the salon of Mesdames de Lamballe and Guéméné went on until the small hours and bankers who ran the Parisian casinos were brought in. She doubled the number of horses in her stables from the 150 of the former queen to 300.[37] The Intendant of Minor Pleasures noted on 25 March 1775, 'I have been going over the accounts of the queen's balls. I am much grieved at the expenditure [for the month] which exceeds 100,000 livres, because of the quantity of gold embroidery which was used for the gowns and quadrilles'.[38]

Turgot had already crossed Marie-Antoinette when, with the king's backing, he had refused to revive Choiseul's costly sinecure of *surintendant de postes* for one of her favourites. Marie-Antoinette refused to speak to him at his next audience; now Turgot put himself forward in the second phase of the Guines Affair. In its first phase, Vergennes had been the one who had braved Marie-Antoinette's wrath, as was proper – he was the foreign secretary. In the second phase he was joined by Turgot. This was really none of his business and his extra-departmental interference was the primary reason for his fall. Maurepas and the king resented his trying to 'run all the departments', which was really the coordinating role belonging to a prime minister or (in his absence) the king. That is why Louis, who had given enthusiastic support to his reforming minister, finally concluded, 'M. Turgot wants to be me and I don't want him to be me.'[39]

Ever since Guines won his case, the ministers had sought a pretext to cashier him and at the same time to fire a warning shot across the queen's bows. Guines soon obliged them by offering the English foreign secretary, Henry, Lord Suffolk, mutual neutrality in the Spanish-Portuguese dispute over the boundaries of Brazil (the subject of the film *The Mission*). He made this proposal without authorization and Vergennes only found out about it when a letter from the Spanish ambassador to England was intercepted. Fearful of braving the wrath of the queen, Vergennes then put up Turgot, 'who was not afraid to affront the queen and importune the king', until Guines was recalled.[40] Louis further told Marie-Antoinette that Guines' diplomatic career must be considered to be finished: 'I have made it abundantly clear to the queen,' he told Vergennes, 'that . . . [Guines] could not serve either in England or in any other embassy.'[41]

Marie-Antoinette responded by seconding Guines' request that he should have it out in a disputation with Vergennes and Maurepas before the king and queen. Vergennes threatened resignation and starkly exposed the issues to the king:

> If Your Majesty deigns to remember that it was at his direct command that I informed . . . [Guines] of his recall, he will realize that the only explanation I could give him is to tell him that quite frankly he was dismissed because Your Majesty ordered me to dismiss him. There would be no harm in Your Majesty informing the queen of the reasons for your decision, but to submit them for discussion with Guines would not so much compromise the character of your ministry as to undermine your own supreme authority.[42]

This draft letter is much stronger than the one Vergennes ultimately sent the king. It also makes it clear that Guines is not acting alone. He says that Guines' 'fanatical supporters' – the parti Choiseul and the queen – are not so much interested in Guines' justification as in bringing the ministry down.

Quite independently of the Guines Affair, the ministry was divided over the latest instalment of Turgot's reforms, the famous Six Edicts, which included the abolition of the craft guilds that Turgot considered to be monopolies in restraint of trade; and the commutation of the *corvée* (enforced labour by the peasants to build and maintain the king's highway) into a money tax payable by all classes. Miromesnil, the justice minister, saw this as the thin end of the wedge: if the nobility were forced to pay the *corvée* the next stage would be to make them pay the *taille* also, hitting their honour as well as their pockets. And we know that Turgot was only waiting for the king to have gained enough experience before presenting him with proposals to abolish the feudal system as well as devolved assemblies elected by all classes, the only qualification being possession of a certain amount of land. These assemblies or 'municipalities' would elect a central body that would fill the gap left by the Estates-General of the kingdom, which had not met since 1614. Miromesnil was secretly working with the leaders in the Parlement, which had to register royal edicts, to have Turgot's legislation thrown out. The king forcibly registered the edicts by *lit de justice*, but was worried. Maurepas was jealous that Turgot was usurping his functions and, as said, so was the king. So Marie-Antoinette, with her (rather silly) boast that she would have Guines made a duke and Turgot thrown in the Bastille on the same day, was not the decisive factor in Turgot's fall from grace two months after the *lit de justice*. Admittedly, a year later, she did manage to get Guines a dukedom. Marie-Antoinette informed her mother of Turgot's fall, conceding that she was 'not displeased', but adding (truthfully) 'I had no hand in it'.[43]

So ended the frenetic period of Marie-Antoinette's immature political interventions. They were largely generated by 'rancour', as Joseph had said, and by an exaggerated sense of loyalty to Choiseul and his friends. Mercy may have believed that these could be welded into a queen's party, but there is no evidence that Marie-Antoinette thought so strategically at this stage. It is noteworthy that she played no part in the key events of the start of the reign: the dismissal of Louis XV's ministers (except for d'Aiguillon) or the restoration of the old Parlement, which Maria-Theresa thought was 'incomprehensible' and which would be a thorn in her daughter's side during her period of ascendancy (1787–8).

A cod psychologist might say that Marie-Antoinette's period of frenetic political activity 1774–6 was displacement activity to make up for her lack of sex and motherhood. He would point to the period of relative political stability that followed and attribute it to Joseph II's sex counselling during his visit in 1777 and the birth of Marie-Antoinette's daughter the following year. The psychologist may well be right, but we must also be aware of the post hoc propter hoc fallacy. It is equally possible to attribute the calm period 1776–80 to a concordat between the queen and Maurepas brokered by Madame de Polignac, whereby in return for not interfering in ministerial politics, the queen would be given carte blanche in court, ecclesiastical and above all military appointments. The first fruit of the concordat was the appointment of the princesse de Lamballe as *surintendant* of the queen's household. Madame de Polignac's family was not elevated enough for her to have this post, or even the one below it, *dame d'honneur*; but after Madame Etiquette had resigned from this post, not being used to having anyone over her, Madame de Polignac got the third-tier post of *dame d'atours* (responsible for the queen's wardrobe and dressing her). At the same time she tried the (over-ambitious step) of persuading Marie-Antoinette to tell the king that things would run smoother if Maurepas was made official prime minister. This never happened but, after the dismissal of Turgot, a rival centre of power, Maurepas was made *chef du conseil des finances*, the post held by Choiseul-Praslin before he was exiled into rural and domestic discord. It was Maurepas who in 1776 obtained for Madame de Polignac's husband the promised succession (*survivance*) as First Equerry to the Queen. In 1779 the queen and the finance minister, Necker, worked out the size of the Polignacs' remuneration. Judging the sum to be inadequate, they went direct to Maurepas, 'who lent his support to the full extent of their greed': the modest arrangement of the queen and Necker was torn up.[44] But we are entering into the period alluded to above when the Polignacs became a force independent of the queen and, in his last year, of Maurepas their other patron.

Another explanation for Marie-Antoinette's more measured behaviour after 1776 is that Mercy, who had a more strategic sense, told her that, given the king's confidence in Maurepas, nothing could be attempted whilst he lived. But, as he told Maria-Theresa in 1780, when Maurepas dies or retires, 'it is of the utmost importance that the successor be chosen by the queen and become her creature'.[45] In these calmer years also Jacques Necker, finance minister between 1776 and 1781, whom the king had personally appointed without Maurepas' advice, chose to adopt Marie-Antoinette as his patron.

MOTHERHOOD AND ITS REPERCUSSIONS

In 1777, Joseph II paid a long-expected visit to France and it is generally accepted that after and probably because of his visit, Marie-Antoinette became pregnant as a result of the marriage guidance her brother gave the king and queen. The notion is now discounted that Louis suffered some physical malformation such as phimosis or a tight foreskin, which made erections painful: the numerous medical examinations ordered by an anxious Louis XV, worried about the continuation of his dynasty, revealed nothing abnormal about his heir. Instead most people put the couple's problems down to a combination of coldness towards her husband amounting almost to frigidity on Marie-Antoinette's part and a staggering lack of technical knowledge on the part of Louis.

Accounts of Joseph's intervention generally stress his advice to his brother-in-law, which has become celebrated, but his catechizing his sister may have played an equal part:

> Are you ... tender when you are together? ... Are you not cold, distracted when he caresses and talks to you? Do you appear bored, even disgusted? In that case how do you expect a man who is himself cold to come close and finally love you? ... Don't lose heart and throughout your life sustain him in the hope that he may still have children.[46]

Joseph offered his brother Leopold his analysis of Louis' problems:

Here is the mystery of the conjugal bed. There are strong erections ... he introduces his penis, leaves it there for maybe two minutes without agitating it, takes it out, still hard, without ever ejaculating and says goodnight. This is incomprehensible since he has spontaneous emissions alone ... He says frankly that he is satisfied and that he only does it out of duty and takes no pleasure in it. Ah! If I could have been present just once I could have sorted it out. He should be whipped like a donkey to make him ejaculate out of anger![47]

Surely, however, Louis would only have acted as Joseph described if he had been trying to *avoid* his wife's pregnancy rather than desperately trying to sire an heir. One also has to bear in mind that Louis XVI and Joseph II detested and despised each other, Louis regarding his brother-in-law as an international brigand. At all events, on 20 December 1777, Marie-Antoinette was able to write to Joseph: 'I had great hopes, my dear brother, of telling you this time that I was pregnant. My hopes have once again receded but I have great confidence that it will not be long, since the king is living with me in the fullest sense, especially since our return from Fontainebleau when he has hunted less.' She had not long to wait: on 20 March 1778, Marie-Antoinette invited the American delegates Silas Deane, Arthur Lee and Benjamin Franklin to her game of cards and that night, in so far as these things can be calculated precisely, she conceived her first child.[48]

The American delegates had just been formally presented to the king following the signing of two treaties (a commercial and a secret, military one) between France and the American colonies that had declared their independence from the British Crown on 4 July 1776. For some time Vergennes had been pressing the king to enter the war on the American side to recover the diplomatic prestige lost in the Seven Years War. Louis, warned by Turgot that to enter the war would scupper the chances of reforming the regime 'for ten years perhaps forever', had been dragging his feet. What may finally have decided him was the death of the Elector of Bavaria without a direct heir. Louis knew what would happen next: Joseph II would claim Bavaria on the spurious grounds that it was a lapsed imperial fief; Frederick of Prussia would mobilize to stop him and Joseph would bully Marie-Antoinette into getting France to support his claim with troops. Louis felt that if he was already committed to an overseas war he could tell Marie-Antoinette that the country could not afford to fight a war on two fronts. Given rampant tax evasion and privileged exemption, the tax base of France was insufficient to support a first-rank army and a first-rank navy – none of the other powers did. Yet France had long land and sea borders. The young Maurepas when naval minister had tried piracy instead of a decent navy, *la guerre de corse*. But it was not a long-term solution and somehow unbecoming one of the two ancient monarchies of Europe. The other one, England, certainly thought so and in 1763 had insisted on having a commissioner stationed at Dunkirk, the nest of pirates.

For the presentation the wily Franklin had exchanged the fur cap and homespun coat he affected for a velvet one and silk stockings. Louis wore his ordinary brown coat and had not bothered to do his hair, which hung down lopsidedly.[49] Arthur Lee felt insulted. But Marie-Antoinette did Franklin the honour of letting him stand behind her chair as she played faro – a card game whose tediousness could only be mitigated by playing for high stakes. Marie-Antoinette lost 180,000 francs that year alone – a sum that would have taken a skilled artisan 360 years to earn.[50]

As expected there was a military standoff between Joseph II and Frederick of Prussia. And, as expected, Joseph exploited Marie-Antoinette's pregnancy mercilessly. Although the succession was already assured by the birth of two sons to the comte d'Artois, the duc d'Angoulême and the duc de Berry, if she should give birth to a dauphin her position would be immeasurably strengthened, within the country and within the family. Maria-Theresa hedged her bets; she told Mercy that the comte de Provence as the next heir and his wife, though 'great intriguers', should be treated well in case Marie-Antoinette did not produce a son. Indeed in 1780, Artois' elder son swapped his governess for a governor two years early, which designated him as the ultimate heir.[51]

A confident Marie-Antoinette, however, began to throw her weight around, summoning Maurepas and Vergennes to her presence and, as she told Maria-Theresa, addressing them 'quite strongly'. But Maurepas was adamant. The urbane old man was worked up to fever pitch. He stated quite simply that if the queen pressed for intervention in Germany he would resign and was driven to a final elaboration of his system of regulating the king's contacts. He could hardly insist that the queen only talk to the king in his presence but he did insist that the queen only talk to him, Maurepas, in the king's presence, which apart from being humiliating was also insulting to the queen because its sole purpose was to prevent her from pretending to Louis that Maurepas had made her concessions.[52] Louis confided to Vergennes – 'this is for you alone' – that the queen had just had a letter from her mother saying that she had been 'abandoned by her allies' and that 'having had glory all her life it had been reserved for her old age to know humiliation'.[53] Even the queen's *accoucheur* (obstetrician) weighed in, telling Louis how dangerous it would be to quarrel with a pregnant woman. 'I hear you,' Louis replied, 'but the queen must not ask me for what I cannot give her.' The *accoucheur* was Vermond's brother.

In view of her condition, and because he was becoming genuinely fond of his wife as they came together physically, Louis generally treated her gently if firmly and silently. He did not consult her on his decision to liaise with Prussia and, Marie-Antoinette told her mother, 'I could not hide from the king the pain his silence caused me . . . over a matter of such importance to me . . . [but] I was disarmed by the tone he adopted. He told me, "You see that I have so many faults that I don't have a word to say in reply"' – an elegant evasion.[54] On one occasion, however, he couldn't control his exasperation with his wife's meddling. Frederick had mobilized his forces on the border of the Habsburg kingdom of Bohemia and Joseph allowed him to enter it so he could activate his defensive treaty with France. Marie-Antoinette cornered her husband and asked him to support his ally with 30,000 troops. She blamed Vergennes, who bore the brunt of her wrath, for not stopping the conflict between the two Germanic powers. But Louis rounded on her: 'It is the ambition of your relatives which is going to upset everything. They began with [the Partition of] Poland. Now Bavaria is the second volume. I am sorry for your sake. – But you can't deny, Monsieur that you were fully informed and in agreement on this Bavarian matter. – So far was I from agreement that I have just ordered all the French diplomats to make known to the courts where they are resident that this dismemberment is done against our wishes and that we disapprove of it.'[55]

Joseph's attempted manipulation of his sister was all the more cynical because he knew it would gain her unpopularity. Advising Mercy that he was sending 12,000 men to occupy Lower Bavaria, he wrote, 'This will not go down well where you are', but added that France wouldn't interfere because it was about to go to war with England.[56] It is from the Bavarian crisis that Marie-Antoinette acquired her soubriquet of 'l'Autrichienne'. In view of Louis' dressing down of his wife, Mercy's reply to Joseph seems, to say the least, over-optimistic:

The queen's ascendancy over her husband has dramatically increased and nothing could resist her influence if she wanted to make a more considered use of it and one better adapted to the circumstances. The queen has nocturnal conversations with the king in which she brings up all sorts of matters, from grave to frivolous, bringing him round to her point of view on every one.[57]

The cynical Maria-Theresa was more realistic: 'Although I am glad that my daughter is beginning to further the interest of her House [Austria], I cannot refrain from repeating that I would prefer her to act with more circumspection so as not to compromise herself without achieving any material gain.'[58]

The way Louis used Madame de Polignac to neutralize the queen's actions at critical times is given in a dispatch of Mercy's, though the queen's minder seems oblivious to the king's ploy. Yolande had gone to the country to stay with relatives, but the king, 'seeing the chagrin and anxiety the invasion of Bohemia by the enemy army had given the queen, sent an express letter telling the comtesse de Polignac to return to court immediately', so as to comfort her friend.[59]

The stand-off between Austria and Prussia didn't develop into war because none of the so-called powers could afford to fight each other without a subsidy from what Frederick consequently called the only two great powers, France and England. And both France and England were waking up to this. So the others had to confine their attentions to dismembering the sick men of Europe, the Ottoman Empire and Poland. The logical solution was an alliance between France and England, as had happened under Cardinal Fleury and Robert Walpole in the 1720s and would be contemplated by Vergennes and the Earl of Shelburne after the American War of Independence. The trouble was that France and England were both rivals for the same bits of empire – India and the West Indies.

In the end, after French and Russian mediation at the Congress of Teschen (13 May 1779), Joseph had to content himself with a scrap of territory. The French representative was the ambassador to Vienna, the baron de Breteuil. Marie-Antoinette did not thank Breteuil for his role in the Austrian humiliation but he soon became her protégé. His success gave him an exaggerated notion of what a congress could achieve and coloured his and Marie-Antoinette's plans for dealing with the French Revolution. Vergennes warned Breteuil that he would not be well received in Vienna, where resentment at French mediation rankled and there was talk of reverting to the traditional alliance or at least hoping England would win in America. 'Wounded pride,' Vergennes advised him, 'is a dangerous counsellor and the progressive restoration of our prestige is a slow poison which will ultimately destroy the basis of the alliance.'[60] But a simulacrum of the alliance had to be maintained because, in the case of Austria, neutrality was not an option: it was either alliance or war; and because the emperor's sister was the king's wife.

Although he sought to exploit her mercilessly for dynastic gain, there is no doubt that Joseph dearly loved his sister. After their meeting at Versailles in 1777 he told their mother: 'She is amiable and charming. I spent hours on end with her, not noticing how the time flew by . . . She was deeply moved when we parted . . . it required all my strength to get up and go.'[61]

Marie-Antoinette had an easy pregnancy but a difficult (thirteen hours) delivery. July and August were stiflingly hot. She would take the night air with

Madame de Polignac and a few friends, the ladies all dressed in the fashionable flowing muslins. A select gathering. Soon music was incorporated and those excluded from these *soirées musicales* felt their exclusion. Rumours grew that these occasions were flirtatious. And during the Diamond Necklace Affair, Cardinal de Rohan was able to base his defence on the grounds that a reasonable man could conclude that the queen of France could give him a midnight assignation on the balcony or among the citrus-tree planters beneath. The king consulted Maurepas about the damage to the queen's reputation, since 'the wife of Caesar must be above suspicion'. Maurepas, who 'deep down believed that he was eternally damned,'[62] specialized in marriage guidance of a Mephistophelean kind, as Jean-Louis Soulavie relates: 'M. de Maurepas stirred up quarrels between Louis XVI and his wife . . . in 1774, 1775 and 1776, on the pretext of her inappropriate conduct. M. de Maurepas had a taste for meddling in family matters between husband and wife. The intermediaries he employed did the queen great disservice.'[63]

Madame Campan took a similar view. So when the king consulted his Mentor about the queen's conduct, 'the old minister had the cruel stratagem of replying . . . that she must be allowed to get on with it; that she was intelligent and that her friends were ambitious and wanted to see here dabbling in politics and that there was no harm in letting her acquire a reputation for frivolity'.[64] He didn't say 'give her enough rope', but that was his intention, seconded, Madame Campan adds plausibly, by Vergennes, his ultimate political heir. Both considered they had legitimate cause to 'destroy her public reputation', because they thought (with some exaggeration) that she sought to bend French foreign policy to Austrian advantage.

The hot summer was followed by a cold winter; the windows in the room where the queen was due to give birth were sealed with paper to keep the heat in. The *accoucheur* announced: 'The queen is about to give birth.' This was the traditional signal for anyone to enter. The crowd rushed in, including two men from Savoy who climbed onto the furniture to get a better view. The room was stifling and the queen passed out. She haemorrhaged; the *accoucheur* called for hot water; it didn't arrive. Louis used all his strength to force open the airtight windows. The queen was unconscious for some time and lost some of her hair (which led to a change in the fashion for hats). She was not informed of the sex of the child for an hour and a quarter and then she wept, whether from pain or from having failed to produce a dauphin is open to conjecture. Maria-Theresa wrote to congratulate her daughter on being 'more solidly established for the future'; but ever suspicious, she thought Marie-Antoinette had been deliberately injured to prevent her for from having more children.[65] This was ridiculous: the *accoucheur* was still Vermond's brother, the same who had tried to use the queen's pregnancy as a means to get Louis to support Joseph II over his Bavarian claims.

Louis invested the clumsy, political *accoucheur* with the Order of Saint-Michael. Despite his disappointment at not producing a son, the king ordered festivities at Versailles that cost 100,000 livres. The girl, born on 19 December 1778, was christened Marie-Thérèse-Charlotte: Marie-Thérèse because the empress insisted that the first-born daughter of all her many children be named after her, and Charlotte after the godfather, Charles III of Spain. Madame Campan has the queen addressing her baby: 'Poor little mite, you were not wanted but you will be none the less dear to me; a son would have belonged to the state, but you will be mine; you will have all my attention; you will share my happiness and lighten my sufferings'; famous words, doubtless 'polished and re-polished' like one of Voltaire's gems. Marie-Antoinette was not particularly fond of her (for the family) exceptionally healthy and (physically) precocious daughter, early to teethe and walk.

Marie-Antoinette was confined to her bed for eighteen days. Then in February the king and queen went to Notre-Dame to give thanks for the safe delivery. Their reception by the Parisians was cool, with a sprinkling of hired cheers that did not fool the queen, then or later during the Revolution. The abbé de Véri notes: 'The queen has known for some time that the people of Paris don't like her. And I don't see any signs of this knowledge making any difference to her lifestyle: her scandalous gambling, excessive [spending on] costume and jewellery and her pleasure seeking.'[66] The public 'censure', Véri, continues, 'did not redound to the king except for his weakness in tolerating the whims of his wife'.

Véri links this observation to some speculation on the conjugal relations of the king and queen. He observes that Louis had not slept with Marie-Antoinette even during the early stages of her pregnancy. 'This stunning coldness in a man of twenty-four could be explained if there was the slightest suspicion of a mistress.' Véri was sure that Louis did not have a mistress 'for the present'. But suspicion fell on the duchesse de Bourbon. Maria-Theresa, who had had to tolerate her husband Francis's multiple infidelities, callously advised Mercy: 'My rule of thumb is that the woman must just patiently endure her husband's lapses. There is no point in making an issue of it.' Marie-Antoinette, if Mercy is to be believed, went round telling all and sundry that she wouldn't mind the king taking a mistress, if it gave him 'more verve and energy'.[67] On 4 June, Louis told his wife 'that he loved her with his whole being and he could swear that he had never felt physical or emotional attraction for any other woman'. Marie-Antoinette concluded from this that Louis was aware of the rumours.[68] The truth of the matter was that the king did not need a mistress because, in Madame de Polignac, he already had a platonic one.

If Louis did not have a mistress, then the explanation must surely be that Marie-Antoinette had a lover. Rumours abounded that the father of the little girl was the duc de Coigny or (even worse) the king's brother, Artois. Further to muddy the waters, the Coigny had some physical resemblance to the king: the duc's brother impersonated the king as part of the deception needed for his flight on 20 June 1791. Further credence was given to the story when, the following April, the queen spent three weeks in the Petit Trianon with Coigny, the newly minted duc de Guines, count Esterhazy and the elderly roué Besenval. Marie-Antoinette had gone down with a bad attack of measles and since the king had not had the disease she put herself under quarantine. The king watched fondly through a telescope from his balcony – out of fondness not suspicion. Suspicion also rested on Fersen, who had joined her card table during the last stages of her pregnancy and after her confinement.

In fact, Marie-Antoinette complained of stomach pains after her delivery and after Vermond had bled her without hot water to hand. Louis did not press her. Both were somewhat under-sexed. Both by temperament and principle (words applied by Joseph to his sister), neither needed an extramarital affair. And there was an even stronger reason for their fidelity. Provence may have been behind some of the rumours concerning the paternity of Marie-Thérèse-Charlotte: he was, after all, the heir presumptive to the Crown. The question of paternity had occurred twice already in the history of the House of France: that of Charles VII (1422–61) and that of the Grand Condé who, until the birth of the future Louis XIII in 1601, was the heir to Henri IV. Still the question had not arisen – since girls could not inherit the throne or pass on a title to it. And in any case marital relations between king and queen resumed: Marie-Antoinette had a miscarriage in the summer of 1779.

THE AMERICAN WAR OF INDEPENDENCE, NECKER AND MARIE-ANTOINETTE

The king was in no hurry to enter the American War of Independence. On 18 October 1776, Louis told Vergennes that the British recapture of New York meant that 'they would not have war at least for some time'. The capture, Louis argued, strengthened the hands of a friendly administration, that of Lord North, and at the same time drew England deeper into a conflict they could only win at the expense of destroying their own finances and those of their colony. At the same time the king was determined to build up the French navy, which at his accession had only one warship in service. But Turgot had warned him (with some exaggeration) that rearmament was worse than war because the Parlement would resist a tax increase in time of peace. Turgot fell, and during the brief tenure of the Finance Ministry held by his successor, Jean de Clugny, his reforms were reversed. Clugny died in office, the only one to do so since Jean-Baptiste Colbert (who died in 1683).

Although Turgot had fallen, some of his lessons remained with the king: no new taxes, no loans and no bankruptcy. Louis adhered to the first and third items in the slogan. But it was impossible to observe all three with current rearmament and with war in the offing. That left loans. And this explains a very unusual appointment and one that would affect the destiny of Marie-Antoinette. She had no hand in the appointment of Jacques Necker, a Genevan banker, as finance minister in September 1776.[69] But she would become his patron and he her nemesis. The king had entered into a correspondence with Necker, who suggested ways of financing war without increasing taxes. Necker bounced Maurepas into accepting his appointment by telling him that the king had already accepted his plans.

To be fair to Necker, his system of loans with no collateral from extra taxes would have worked if the government's gamble of a one-campaign war had come off. Marie-Antoinette was not the only member of the family to gamble for high stakes. Louis, with a divided cabinet, took two major gambles whose combined effects would bring down the *régime*. In 1787 he gambled that an assembly composed of the privileged classes (the Assembly of Notables) would vote for an end to privilege. In 1778 he gambled that, with the element of surprise and a local equality, perhaps superiority, of forces in North America, he could knock England out of the war in a single campaign. France could recruit quickly from a system of naval reserves (*classes*) whereas England had to wait for returning merchantmen to crew the Royal Navy; so in 1778, France and England would have sixty warships apiece. If Admiral d'Estaing had reached America on time he could have pulled off a land-and-sea pincer movement like the one that succeeded at Yorktown three long and expensive years later. But he didn't, and so for the campaign of 1779, France would have about seventy ships to England's ninety.

Vergennes' solution was to rope Spain into the war. It was no accident that Charles III was made godfather to Marie-Thérèse-Charlotte. Spain's fifty warships added to France's seventy would give the allies parity with the Royal Navy. Spain's fifty ships would be necessary to avert disaster – what Vergennes characterized to Louis as 'the ruin of the navy and even ... [the] finances'.[70] Spain, however, had no interest in setting a precedent for independence to her own colonies in North as well as South America (she was still expanding in

California). A reluctant Spain was exigent. France had to agree to terms that were almost impossible to fulfil: no peace without Britain ceding Gibraltar to Spain. Since Gibraltar was impregnable an equivalent would have to be seized: London was selected; then, slightly less ambitiously, Portsmouth. As a result the whole of 1779 was taken up with an attempted invasion of England – an armada, less celebrated but no more successful than that of 1588. As Véri put it on 23 August 1780: 'This is the third campaign rendered totally useless either by waiting for Spain's alliance or as a consequence of its conclusion.'[71] The siege of Gibraltar (1779–83) was still in progress. It failed despite the use of fireships and the presence of Artois and Vaudreuil. Artois' 'sumptuous excursion' to the Rock cost 4 million francs. Vergennes, whose son had married a Noailles, had badgered the king to let 'the vicomte of this name' go as well, but the marquis de Ségur, as minister of war, complained at being bypassed. His *patronne* the queen, no friend to the Noailles, 'informed of these arrangements, got the king to revoke them on the grounds that two officers with better claims had been denied'. She then summoned Vergennes for a dressing down and he weakly defended himself by saying that the king of Spain had particularly asked for Noailles' participation.[72]

The year 1780 was critical for the French government. Spain was threatening to make a separate peace with England; Maurepas was tempted to do the same. Vergennes said he would only follow this up with the king's orders in writing, which brought him round. Necker was negotiating with England secretly through intermediaries and Joseph II was fishing in troubled waters by suggesting mediation by Austria and Russia (so long as Prussia was excluded), and he roped in Marie-Antoinette to press this on the king. She did 'two or three times', but Louis, who thought Austria was more likely to favour her natural and traditional ally, England, told her to mind her own business.[73] With no new taxes, the French finances were also in crisis and, appropriately in a naval war, the point of flexion occurred in the ministry of the Marine. Marie-Antoinette's role in ministerial appointments (hitherto it had been confined to dismissals) was initiated by a quarrel over the naval estimates between Necker and the naval minister, Antoine de Sartine. In 1779, Necker had allocated 120,000,000 francs for the campaign of 1780. Judging this to be inadequate, Sartine secretly opened a loan of 20,000,000 on the treasury of the Marine, which drew subscribers from Necker's much more extensive loans. When, in 1780, Sartine announced that he could only put sixty warships to sea with the funds Necker had allocated, Necker threatened to resign unless Sartine were replaced.

Maurepas, laid up in Paris with an unusually severe bout of gout, received the following note from the king: 'Shall we dismiss Necker, or shall we dismiss

Sartine? I am not displeased with the latter. I think Necker is more useful to us.'
At this point Madame de Polignac's set stepped in. Hitherto they had supported
Maurepas at nearly every juncture, particularly in his quarrels with Marie-
Antoinette. But by 1780 it was clear that Maurepas' health was failing and the
Polignacs like everyone else had to look to the future. They concluded that if
their own careers were not to come to an end they needed someone in the
ministry. Ideally, the comte de Vaudreuil would have preferred the marquis de
Vaudreuil, the head of the dynasty, to replace Sartine. But Necker's choice was
the marquis de Castries, who had promised to hand over to him the treasury of
the navy, and Vaudreuil and the Polignacs' set fell in with this option. All this
put Marie-Antoinette in an embarrassing situation. She detested Vaudreuil and
had no desire to see his cousin promoted and him given patronage of his own.
Castries, on the other hand, was a Choiseuliste and she had tried to get him the
War Ministry in September 1775. But, as we have seen, she also regarded Sartine
as her protégé. And Maurepas suspected that Sartine was requesting an audience with the queen to seek her protection. Madame de Polignac and Vaudreuil
suggested that Marie-Antoinette make the best of what was becoming a fait
accompli by summoning Castries 'to inform him that she was taking him under
her protection and to make him aware that he would owe his appointment to
Her Majesty'.[74]

This tactic nevertheless conflicted with the strategy of her Austrian minders,
Mercy and Vermond. They advised the queen that to provoke the resignation of
Maurepas at this juncture would be disastrous since, having failed to produce a
dauphin, she would have little chance of influencing the choice of his successor.
Maria-Theresa told Mercy that she would have preferred a prime minister
devoted to the queen, but the main thing was to prevent Maurepas' Prussophile
brother-in-law, the duc de Nivernais, obtaining such a position. She instructed
Mercy to do anything to prevent this, 'even if it means employing the comtesse
de Polignac to this end'.[75] The force of 'even' is that Mercy had consistently
blackened Yolande's name; and the assumption of the queen-empress was that
the favourite was open to the highest bidder. Two typical examples of Austrian
realpolitik. Accordingly, Mercy and Vermond advised Marie-Antoinette to
confine her attention to securing the cordon bleu of the Saint-Esprit for the
man they ultimately wanted to head the ministry, Vermond's former boss,
Loménie de Brienne, archbishop of Toulouse. So Marie-Antoinette merely told
Madame de Polignac that she would mention Castries' name to the king.

With communications between the king and Maurepas severed by the
latter's illness, Necker was able to profit from the confusion to dupe everyone.
Just as, in the prelude to his appointment in 1776, he had told Maurepas that the

king had already approved his financial projects, so now he profited from Maurepas' isolation to tell him that the queen had obtained the king's positive word to replace Sartine with Castries. Necker and the Polignacs had duped them all and the manoeuvre was so subtle that even that astute observer the abbé de Véri was taken in: 'Here is the first step we have seen the queen take, with the king's consent, to meddle in ministerial appointments.'[76] Maurepas applauded what he mistakenly took to be a fait accompli.[77] Subsequently it suited both Marie-Antoinette and Castries to preserve the fiction that it was her patronage which had secured him his post.

The next in the firing line was the minister of war, the prince de Montbarrey. He had the rare distinction for a war minister of having opposed entering a war. But Marie-Antoinette wanted to get rid of him, despite or because of his being Maurepas' relative. She had had several run-ins with Montbarrey on account of her interference in military promotion, as he relates in his memoirs. After one of these, he ran to the king's apartments, trusting that his superior speed would outweigh the queen's advantage of the secret passage. Outstripping her, he was the recipient of elaborate advice from the king:

> No one knows better than I [her husband] . . . what you have gone through; calm yourself; I will take it on myself to speak to the Queen of the matter. But for some time avoid seeing her; *and as for the matters of which you are accustomed to give her an account*, I will undertake them, and I will tell you when you may and when you ought to present yourself before her. For this await my positive orders. Moreover, rest assured about the possible consequences of this affair; I will take you under my protection and you have nothing to fear.

It was six weeks before Louis judged it right for Montbarrey to see the queen. The italicized sentence suggests that Marie-Antoinette had her own *travail* or working session with Montbarrey to discuss military appointments.

She told Joseph, 'M. de Montbarrey has been dismissed but out of respect for his relative M. de Maurepas he has been permitted to give in his resignation. It was way time because his private life and the graft he at least tolerated in his department . . . meant he could do no good. The king has not nominated a successor. I believe it will be M. de Ségur, a respected lieutenant-general.'[78] Her reference to Montbarrey's 'private life' concerns his decision not to take a conventional mistress (who would take up too much time, demand favours, and embarrass his wife) but to ask Lenoir, the police minister, to procure him a prostitute and arrange for her to be spied upon to prevent her causing trouble. He had informed the king who, 'without exactly approving, agreed with me that this course of action was the least subject to drawbacks'.[79] Marie-Antoinette was less indulgent, for contrary to popular myth she was prudish rather than libertine.

Marie-Antoinette's 'I believe it will be M. de Ségur' was coy: the marquis de Ségur, who had left an arm on the field of Krefeld, and supported a stick with the other, was her candidate. But not that of the Polignacs. They wanted one of their set, the comte d'Adhémar, appointed. To have got their hands on military promotions would indeed have been a major coup for the Polignacs. But military promotions were Marie-Antoinette's domain. So she blocked d'Adhémar's appointment and her own candidate, Ségur, was duly appointed. Suddenly, and somewhat fortuitously, Marie-Antoinette was in a very strong political position. Ségur really was her appointee and he was to display an exaggerated deference to her in making military promotions. Presumably she had a *travail* with him too. Castries looked to her as his patronne and Necker was now seeking her protection. In 1780, Maria-Theresa sent her compliments to Necker and his wife, sentiments that Mercy endorsed, adding, 'of all the king's ministers ... Necker is the one of whom the queen had the best opinion and who has the most of her esteem'.[80]

Ségur's name is coupled with the Ordonnance of 1781, which restricted commissioned entry to the army to those with four generations of nobility on their father's side. Rightly or wrongly, it was regarded as the symbol of an aristocratic reaction. 'Because a corrupt government [Louis XV's] had abased the aristocracy,' Barnave wrote, 'it was thought that a paternal one ought to raise it up ... the parlements were restored ... the third estate was progressively excluded from a military career.' He was thinking of his grandfather's blocked career and his brother's had he lived. Yet 'if there had been any way to prevent the explosion of popular power it would have been to associate it with the government as then established and to open all careers to the third estate. Instead they did the complete opposite.'[81]

Maria-Theresa did not live to see this 'explosion', which both she and Joseph had in a way predicted. She died of dropsy on 29 November 1780, aged sixty-three. The news took a week to reach Versailles. Louis didn't want to break the news to Marie-Antoinette. So he got Vermond to do it. Vermond had arrived at court with Marie-Antoinette in 1770, but in the ten intervening years Louis had not addressed a single word to him, probably regarding him as an Austrian stooge or possibly blaming him for poisoning her mind against her new husband. As we shall see, he made clear his feelings about Vermond a year later. For the moment, however, he made up for lost time by thanking him effusively for performing a task he could not face himself.

Maria-Theresa had manipulated her daughter heartlessly and cynically in the interests of their dynasty. What made it worse was that, unlike Joseph, she had no illusions as to Marie-Antoinette's effectiveness or even willingness to be an Austrian pawn. If any one person (apart from herself) was responsible for Marie-Antoinette's unpopularity it was the queen-empress. Nevertheless, on 10 December, Marie-Antoinette wrote to Joseph: 'Devastated by this awful misfortune, I write to you in tears. Oh! My brother! Oh! My friend. Look after yourself . . . I can no longer see what I am writing for tears'. She kept to her rooms until 9 December and in her letter next day thanked Joseph for a gift for Madame de Polignac, 'which has touched her and me too, above all at a time when I have needed her friendship'.[82] It is in the same letter that Marie-Antoinette told Joseph that her candidate, not Madame de Polignac's, had been made war minister. Nothing better illustrates the gap between her social and political circles. As for Maurepas, he felt Ségur's appointment as the deadliest blow he ever received, compounded by the role Marie-Antoinette had played in it. In the twilight of his life he had lost control over the composition of the ministry.

But the fates would allow the aged Maurepas, like Simeon, his 'Nunc dimittis'. In 1781, France entered the fourth year of her war. It was England's sixth and Vergennes began to wonder whether the two European great powers would survive intact, leaving only isolationist China and no one to check the predatory rapacity of Frederick II, Catherine II and Joseph II, which for the first two has been rewarded with the soubriquet 'the Great'. Four years of war and still taxes had not been raised, though one due to expire in 1780 had been extended until 1790. People began to wonder whether the 400,000,000 francs of loans raised by Necker were safe investments. Interest rates crept up then soared. Necker claimed that the economies he had made in the royal household and financial offices (with Marie-Antoinette's backing) were enough to cover the interest on the loans. In the famous/infamous *Compte rendu au Roi*, published in February 1780, he asserted that the 'ordinary' budget enjoyed a surplus of 10,000,000 francs. To arrive at this figure he had omitted the cost of buying out the offices, most of which had been purchased and, more importantly, the cost of the war, to date roughly the same as the amount he had borrowed, 500,000 francs – rather like omitting mortgage repayment from a modern family's budgeting but listing scrupulously every packet of crisps bought. Technically, Necker was correct: the state of war, though common, was not 'ordinary', but this was semantics not accountancy.

Without actually accusing Necker of dishonesty, Barnave said 'he hid the problem'. He also, rather sniffily, said that Necker as a banker employed the techniques of 'his personal profession', implying that the habits of the counting house were no way to run a great nation. 'He based the finances on credit, and credit on the moral character of the minister, thus rendering himself indispensable.'[83]

The *Compte* was published with blue wrappers, as were fairy tales at the time, so Maurepas called it the *Conte bleu*, a witticism that shot around court and capital. The Polignac set, and particularly the comte d'Artois, feeling their income threatened by Necker's incremental reforms, now abandoned their temporary alliance with Necker. Artois' treasurer, Antoine Bourboulon, wrote a scathing pamphlet against Necker, and signed it. Vaudreuil's friend Charles-Alexandre de Calonne, the Intendant of Flanders, who wanted to succeed Necker, wrote a better one, but didn't sign it. In 1788, Marie-Antoinette referred to the 'infernal machinations which had caused . . . [Necker] to fail'.[84] It seems from the context that she was referring to the Polignac set.

To boost his position, Necker now asked for what were termed 'external marks of confidence' from the king – 'external' because they didn't necessarily relate to what the king actually thought. He asked for a range of such 'marks': his principal demand was to be made a *ministre d'état*, that is one who has the right to sit in the Council rather than just the ministerial committees that prepared the ground for it. Maurepas said that the Fundamental Laws, or unwritten constitution, confined entry to Catholics. Then Necker twice asked the queen to back his demand, but she refused.

Thwarted, Necker came up with an alternative mark of confidence. On 15 May he gave Maurepas a memorandum to present to Louis, requesting that control of the treasuries of the Marine and war ministries should be entrusted to him at least for the duration of the war. Next day Castries went to Marly and told the king that he was ready to relinquish the treasury of the Marine. The initial reaction of the king, who had to consider the long-term integrity of the naval department, was 'but this separation is impossible'; Castries then went to see the queen but was told that she was in bed, though Maurepas was present and in the half hour Castries waited outside, Louis entered her chamber three times. When Castries finally managed to see the queen she warned him that if Necker's demands were met, he would become 'the most powerful man at Versailles' and 'it is pretty certain that you will not keep your place and that, once degraded [by losing control of its treasury] it will be given to an *homme de robe* and you are against that'. He in turn accused her of privately giving Necker encouragement but declining to make this public. The king and queen were angered by Castries' importunity.[85] Because of his association with Necker relations between Louis XVI and Castries remained tense for the next six years.

Finally, Maurepas offered Necker the *grandes entrées* (which conferred the right to sit in the king's closet rather than having to stand in the ante-chamber) and the king's assurance that provincial administrations would be set up in all the provinces. There was a near consensus in the royal bureaucracy that the regime would be strengthened by devolving some powers to provincial assemblies. Necker had set up two pilot assemblies but their general adoption had been deferred by the onset of war. According to Castries, Necker was tempted to accept but Maurepas, desperately wanting a refusal that he would not fail to distort, diluted and belittled the concessions. Madame Campan plausibly suggests that Maurepas substituted 'and' for 'or' in Necker's various demands. Necker then gave his letter of resignation to Maurepas to present to the king but he, as if to emphasize the withdrawal of any residual element of protection, refused to hand it to Louis, telling Necker 'if he did not want to address the king directly' he would have to give it to the queen, which he did on 19 May.[86]

Soulavie considered that Necker's letter of resignation to the king was 'truly republican' – because it presumed to make conditions – and insulting, being written 'carelessly on a scrap of paper three and a half inches long by two and a half wide'.[87] The king, weary of Necker's demanding conditional marks of confidence, like an English minister, did not press Necker to stay though he blamed him for going, regarding it as a dereliction of duty in the middle of a war still in stalemate. Necker was not dismissed but resigned 'voluntarily', as the king would remember. When Maurepas told Necker of the king's verdict, he was so shaken that he could not find the door-handle to leave Maurepas' apartments. The triumphant old man told a lackey to 'see M. Necker out'. Nunc dimittis, indeed, thought Maurepas, though no Messiah was on the horizon.

The above account, based on Castries' contemporary diary, suggests that Marie-Antoinette's support for Necker had been lukewarm. The queen, who supported Necker's general position – Maria-Theresa and Joseph had come under Necker's spell – disliked the Genevan's importunity and above all his timing. She felt that Necker should follow her example and patiently await Maurepas' death as the king was fond of the old man; then there could be major changes in the government. She probably had in mind Necker serving as finance minister under the archbishop of Toulouse. It would be her administration. Joseph II, who took the view that the *Compte rendu* was very impressive if it was true, asked Mercy to try to lure Necker to Vienna to work for him.[88] The convention was that ex-ministers, even if they were not exiled, should keep a low profile so as not to embarrass their successors. Necker did the opposite, doing everything, in Vergennes' words, to 'nourish his faction'. Marie-Antoinette, according to Madame Campan, was displeased:

The interest that the queen had taken in M. Necker vanished after his resignation and even changed into dislike. He wrote too much on the policies he would have implemented and the good that would have resulted for the state. The ministers who succeeded him thought that their measures were undermined by the care that M. Necker and his partisans took to interest the public in his plans; his friends were too hot: the queen deplored the partisan spirit that had entered society and she ranged herself entirely with his enemies.[89]

Marie-Antoinette may have felt some of that. Nevertheless, as we will see, in 1783 she tried to bring him back into the ministry.

Maurepas had said of Necker that 'the irreplaceable man was yet to be born'. And it was true: his successor, the *conseiller d'état* Joly de Fleury, used his powerful family contacts in the Parlement to secure a tax increase and was able to tell the king that funds were assured for 1781, 1782, and that even for 1783 'His Majesty could make whatever military dispositions he needed'.[90] And suddenly things started to go well for France.

The proclamation announcing the birth of Louis' daughter had included the words, 'this visible mark of Providence makes me hope for the complete accomplishment of my desires and those of my people by the birth of a dauphin'.[91] Finally, after a miscarriage and when people were beginning to doubt whether she would ever produce an heir, on 22 October 1781 the queen at last gave birth to a dauphin. There was no overcrowding this time – only ten people attended the birth. Her ladies-in-waiting controlled their features and Marie-Antoinette believed it was a girl until 'the king . . . said to her with tears in his eye "M. Le Dauphin requests permission to enter."' Another version has it that Louis approached the bed and told Marie-Antoinette, 'Madame, you have fulfilled my desires and those of France; you are the mother of a dauphin.' She in turn, handing the boy over to his governess, still Madame de Guéméné, said, 'take him he belongs to the state but I will have my daughter back'.[92] In his joy the king burst the narrow confines allotted for the day in his diary with minute details of the confinement. The boy was given the same names as Louis' long-dead elder brother, the duc de Bourgogne. Joseph II, who had doubted it would ever happen, felt unfeigned delight at a new pledge of the alliance and the happiness of his sister. He told Mercy on 29 October, 'I thought I was no longer capable of feeling a young man's joy', and ordered all the theatres in Vienna to be open free of charge.[93]

Three days before the birth of the dauphin, though the news took a month to reach Versailles, the combined Franco-American forces had pulled off an improbable but decisive victory in Virginia. In 1780, 5,000 French troops under Rochambeau arrived at Rhode Island off New York and in the summer of 1781 dispatches came from Versailles indicating that Admiral de Grasse, commanding the main French fleet in the West Indies, would be available for combined operations against the English either for a siege of New York or in Chesapeake Bay, Virginia, where Lord Cornwallis had been ordered to create a deep-water harbour at the end of the Yorktown peninsula.

Rochambeau told de Grasse that he would prefer an attack on Cornwallis from Chesapeake. De Grasse obliged and the Spanish fleet in the West Indies offered to protect French shipping so that de Grasse could deploy his whole fleet of twenty-eight battleships carrying 3,000 soldiers to North America. In September de Grasse arrived at Chesapeake Bay where he defeated a British fleet sent to relieve Cornwallis and prevented him from escaping by sea, whilst the Franco-American forces proceeded to Yorktown by forced marches, having deceived Henry Clinton into believing that a siege of New York was intended. On 14 October they invested Yorktown and five days later Cornwallis, outnumbered and cut off, surrendered with 10,000 men.

Meanwhile Maurepas lay dying. Shortly after the birth of the dauphin he had his most serious attack of gout yet and this time there seemed no hope of recovery. As Maurepas lay on his deathbed news reached Versailles of the victory that might end the war. Louis, who did not see dying ministers, though he did cancel his hunting, was thoughtful enough to send the duc de Lauzun to tell Maurepas the good news. Lauzun ran through the list of prisoners, 214 cannon, and 22 standards taken. Maurepas ticked off each item with a crisp 'Good, good', but then, turning to Lauzun, he said: 'I am dying and I don't know whom I have the honour of addressing.'

Marie-Antoinette had performed her primary role – she was mother of a dauphin; her most determined antagonist was dead. She already had two protégés in the ministry. Surely the next premier must be her creature.

— FOUR —

GROWING UNPOPULARITY

1781–1785

This was the moment Marie-Antoinette, Mercy-Argenteau and the abbé de Vermond had been waiting for. Surely the death of the Mentor and the birth of a dauphin must change everything: all the pieces seemed to be in place to propel the archbishop of Toulouse towards becoming not just prime minister, but her prime minister. Brienne, who had been at college with Vermond, Turgot and Véri, was one of a band of 'administrator prelates' who ruled the secular as well as the spiritual life of the Midi. Brienne was an atheist or at least a deist and in refusing to translate him from Toulouse to Paris, Louis uttered one of his few *bon mots*: 'But an Archbishop of Paris must at least believe in God.'

Shortly after Maurepas' death the queen, at the instigation of Vermond, proposed that Brienne should enter the Council as a preliminary to his becoming chief minister. But they had forgotten one thing: Louis, now twenty-seven, intended to be his own prime minister. The birth of a dauphin certainly strengthened Marie-Antoinette's position but it also strengthened the king's, as had the events of Yorktown. Louis was winning a war to which Marie-Antoinette's only contribution had been to further her brother's clumsy attempts to broker a premature and humiliating peace.

Nor did Louis want the queen's nominee in the Council, especially if he were a priest. Priests should attend their flock. Jean-Charles-Pierre Lenoir, the police minister, was in the apartments of the king's aunt, Mme Sophie, when Louis burst in 'in a towering rage' and declared that 'the one [Brienne] must be confined to his diocese, and have his revenues confiscated and the other [Vermond] must be sent away from the Queen'.[1] Louis' rage subsided but, though thwarted, the ambitions of Brienne did not. After Maurepas' death, Mercy grudgingly admitted that the king did not need a prime minister for the conduct of foreign policy, but such an appointment for internal affairs was inevitable given the inveterate corruption in the system and the difficulties with the Parlement.[2]

Meanwhile the American War of Independence finally came to an end, both sides exhausted and indebted. Admiral Rodney's victory at The Saints, a group of islands off Guadeloupe, on 12 April 1782, made peace easier by salvaging England's pride and showing France the risks of prolonging the conflict. It also made it easier for the new finance minister, Joly de Fleury, to persuade the Parlement to register a third *vingtième* tax to last for the continuation of the war and three years thereafter. The disaster at The Saints was mitigated by the comte de Vaudreuil's cousin the marquis, who after the capture of Admiral de Grasse's flagship took command and limited the losses to seven ships. Like Admiral Byng, he was court-martialled *pour encourager les autres.* Vaudreuil tried to intercede with the marquis de Castries. But Castries, disliking his imperious tone, replied: 'But you seem to forget, Monsieur, that you are addressing a marshal of France and a minister of the king.' 'I am not likely to forget it,' Vaudreuil is said to have replied, 'since you owe them both to me; so it should be you who is doing the remembering.'[3]

The defeated fleet had been planning to seize Jamaica in exchange for Gibraltar, 'the great siege' by Franco-Spanish forces having failed. The treaty of Aranjuez had stipulated no peace without Gibraltar, and the Spanish king Charles III insisted on his pound of flesh in a dispatch that arrived on 25 December 1782 and must have ruined Louis' Christmas; for if the French fleet had set out in 1783 to try to take Jamaica again, it could well have led to a naval, financial and even regime disaster. Then Spain relented, satisfying herself with Florida and Minorca. They were the biggest gainers from the war. France surrendered most of her conquests in the West Indies and India and had to content herself with the removal of the English commissioner at Dunkirk, a slight improvement of French fishing rights off Newfoundland, and an enlargement of her colony of Pondicherry. France did not have the productive capacity to supply the needs of England's now independent colonies, which continued as before to conduct most of their trade with the mother country.

The cost of the war was some 1.5 billion francs. An internal inquiry revealed that Necker's *Compte rendu* was a fraud and that half of current revenue was needed to service the debt.[4] His successor Joly de Fleury set up a *Comité des finances* in February 1782. Its principal purpose was to coordinate departmental expenditure and in particular rein in the budget of the army and particularly the navy. Castries had not wanted to sign a peace treaty with England, hoped to resume the conflict as 'an avenue to glory', and intended to maintain the navy on a wartime footing. But it was a secondary purpose of the Committee that alarmed the Polignacs: to rein in and regularize court pensions. Their ally and candidate for the Finance Ministry, Charles-Alexandre de Calonne, went around saying that the Committee would be 'le tombeau des graces'. The Polignacs organized amateur theatricals with their children as players and invited the king, who presided over the Committee, on the days when it was due to meet. Joly de Fleury wrote a letter to Louis complaining of such behaviour, which the Polignacs 'presented as a resignation, which was accepted'. The king, however, did not appoint Calonne to the Finance Ministry, but Henri Lefèvre d'Ormesson, a personal choice. Calonne printed a pamphlet *Démocrite contre M. d'Ormesson*, ridiculing not only him but his wife,[5] whilst the Polignacs did all they could to undermine his administration.

D'Ormesson in fact treated the Polignacs fairly. His diary notes 'at this time the Polignac family and its hangers-on who formed the queen's habitual circle and thought that it gave them the right to every possible perk, had been wearing the ministry down for a long time'. However, he recognized that 'it was only fair to compensate this family which was scarcely rich and already considerably indebted by the expense incurred by the queen and a part of the royal family who had for some time been accustomed to eat and live off them every day'. The form that compensation had taken hitherto was unsatisfactory, consisting as it did of grants of royal estates and other favours which, being hard to evaluate, messed up d'Ormesson's accounting; so he proposed to give them a large annual pension instead, based on 'their own assessment of their annual expenditure at Court'. D'Ormesson worked out the proposal together with the comte de Vergennes and showed it to the queen, who seemed to approve. M. de Polignac, a modest man who was fully conscious of his good fortune, asked for 380,000 a year, but d'Ormesson offered him 400,000 on the grounds that ministers spent 300,000 a year entertaining less exalted members of the Court. M. and Madame de Polignac were perfectly satisfied with this arrangement. Vaudreuil, however, d'Ormesson notes, 'was secretly intriguing in favour of his worthy and long-time friend M. de Calonne, hoping with good reason . . . to get more out of him for himself and his society and from that moment the Polignacs ceased calling on me. Personally I was glad of it, but I realized that they were looking to have me replaced as soon as possible.'[6]

D'Ormesson also alienated Marie-Antoinette. She wanted to buy the château of Saint-Cloud, now in the suburbs of Paris, from the duc d'Orléans. The queen wanted a palace of her own, in her own name, and the lordship of the manor as well so she could be something in her own right, not just the consort of the king and mother of the dauphin. The manor would require a separate deal with the archbishop of Paris, who was also duc de Saint-Cloud. According to the comte de Provence, the seigneurie was more important than the château – why else, he argued, did she spend so much effort 'acquiring something which added very little to the enjoyment of the château'? Marie-Antoinette wanted to play the 'lady of the manor and personally benefit her vassals'.[7] Provence did not accuse her of wanting to play Lady Bountiful, but we can. Since these 'vassals' were ordinary villagers, her motives were on a par with those that prompted her to create her model village in the grounds of the Trianon. Saint-Cloud was on a bigger scale than Trianon and in a sense 'real' and different from her normal patronage: instead of getting regiments or embassies for courtiers she would be providing seed corn for villagers. We don't know if any of this happened.

The king was ready to oblige the queen over the Saint-Cloud purchase, but d'Ormesson told Vergennes to inform Louis that he was ready to resign over the issue and would raise it during his Sunday tête-à-tête (*travail*) with the king. 'On the king's reply,' d'Ormesson notes in his diary, 'hung my resignation if the king persisted in his acquisition projects.' On Sunday, d'Ormesson told the king 'very coldly that he saw no mention in his budget forecasts[8] of any funds allocated to his plans for acquisitions [of palaces, he had already bought Rambouillet] ... which were the talk of Fontainebleau [where the Court was residing] and Paris'. The king blustered, saying that nothing had been decided and d'Ormesson would be consulted. 'Being unable to insist for the present after such a reply which had obviously been prepared and discussed in advance', d'Ormesson left his resignation in his pocket and said 'coldly to the king that since His Majesty was giving me ulterior orders over the matter I would await them'.[9] The purchase of Saint-Cloud was shelved for the moment.

Having alienated the queen and the most powerful faction at Court, d'Ormesson completed his hat trick by trying to block Vergennes' sale of feudal rights attached to his estates in the east of the country at an inflated price. Since Louis had given Vergennes the property in the first place he was not pleased with his foreign secretary. As if that were not enough and whilst nerves were still frayed from a run on the Discount Bank in August, d'Ormesson embarked on a risky reform, the abolition of tax farming. The product of the indirect taxes (roughly half of royal revenue) was sold to the General Farm, a syndicate of tax Farmers, on a six-yearly contract. They made a handsome profit but they paid in advance (always a boon to a chronically cash-strapped monarchy) and, in times of crisis, they were ready to offer the king their personal credit, which was better than his own. As such, Louis XVI called them 'one of the pillars of the state', and now d'Ormesson was playing Samson.

That is not quite fair. D'Ormesson proposed a transitional arrangement, so there would be no cliff-edge. The remaining three years of the Farmers' contract would be converted into a *régie intéressée* (i.e. the Farmers would be paid a fixed salary plus a proportion of the amount collected over an agreed figure) with effect from 1 January. There would be no immediate saving since the existing Farmers would become the *régisseurs* and their profits would remain the same, because the money that they had advanced to the king against them (some 60–70 million livres) could not be repaid, but the exercise would make for an easy transition to a rational system of indirect taxation in 1787. However, the Farmers did not want an end to farming. D'Ormesson had now alienated the queen, the Court, the financiers and the head of the ministry (Vergennes had been given Maurepas' title of *Chef du Conseil royal des finances* in return for a semi-glorious peace). D'Ormesson presented his proposals to the king on Friday 23 October. Louis 'hesitated for an instant' before ordering the Farmers' lease to be rescinded.[10] The Farmers promissory notes depreciated dramatically and they demanded the impossible repayment of their advance to support them.

It was a dilemma. Do you attack vested interests or buy time by pandering to them? Or both – clearly not concurrently but consecutively, as Calonne was contemplating. There were two candidates to succeed an obviously doomed d'Ormesson: one backed by the queen (Necker) and the other by her 'society', the Polignacs (Calonne). On Friday, 31 October 1783, 'there was a committee in the queen's apartments to discuss Necker' – namely, his return to power.[11] As we have seen, Marie-Antoinette had adopted Necker and acted as his patron. She had tried to persuade him not to resign in 1781. Necker was waiting to exploit the financial crisis that seemed to be impending. But on the evening of Saturday 1 November, Marie-Antoinette, having held her salon and dined with the king, fell ill during the night and was bled twice. Next day, her twenty-eighth birthday, she experienced sharp birth pangs and was in labour all day. At crack of dawn on the Monday morning she miscarried of a deformed foetus conceived in July[12] and remained in bed for several days.[13]

Evelyn Farr speculates that this unborn child was Axel von Fersen's and states unambiguously 'in the summer of 1783 the two became lovers'.[14] On 28 June, Fersen had finally returned to Paris, apparently having avoided any of the fighting in America but being rewarded with the Order of Cincinnatus, presumably because his command of English gave him a role in negotiating General Cornwallis' surrender at Yorktown. In September pressure from Gustavus III on a visit to Versailles secured Fersen the Royal Swedish (French) Regiment with an income of 20,000 francs a year, reduced to 13,000 during the economic reforms of 1788 and naturally stopped in 1791 after his role in organizing the king's escape from Paris. Marie-Antoinette herself informed Gustavus of the appointment, but her role in military appointments was already well established. This was the only emolument that Fersen, whom Saint-Priest called Marie-Antoinette's '*ami-en-titre*', the male version of a *maîtresse-en-titre*, ever received. Saint-Priest contrasts this with the millions heaped on the Polignacs.[15]

On 31 July, Fersen wrote to his sister and confidante, Sophie Piper, 'I have made my decision, I don't want the ties of marriage, which are against nature. I cannot marry [*être à*] the only person I would want to, the only one who really loves me, so I can be no one's.'[16] This seems an unambiguous statement of forbidden love for Marie-Antoinette, though it has been argued that he used the pretext of his devotion to Marie-Antoinette as a means of avoiding entanglement with his numerous mistresses, including some in America of whom he wrote: 'I am having a great time here with lots to do. The women are pretty, amiable and available [*coquette*], that's all that I need.'[17]

However, in order to please his father, he toyed with the idea of marrying the finance minister Necker's rich and bluestocking only child with an annual income of 500,000; but he decided that another Swede, his friend Erik Magnus de Staël, would make a better fist of it. Fersen even believed that Pitt the Younger was in the running! On the strength of the marriage Staël soon became the Swedish ambassador to France, but as the Revolution approached his ideas, taken from his father-in-law, became too liberal for Fersen and Gustavus, who limited his role. We will see Madame de Staël playing a part in the ministerial politics of the constitutional monarchy through her lover the comte de Narbonne. Fersen described the famous bluestocking in a letter to his father: 'I've only seen her once in passing and I don't remember her face. I only recall that there is nothing disagreeable about her and she isn't deformed.'[18]

For Evelyn Farr, certain that Fersen and Marie-Antoinette became lovers that summer, the only question was 'where this long-awaited consummation took place'. Was it at the Petit Trianon? Or was it in the tiny apartments above her main ones connected by a secret staircase (a parallel arrangement to the king's)? These were a series of rabbit warrens on three stories enlarged after the birth of the dauphin in 1781, known to very few and mostly pulled down when Versailles was turned into a museum in the 1830s.[19] A straw in the wind: a locksmith sent in a bill in 1784 for 'locks and system of movement made in the château in the [two] bedrooms of the queen so that she can open and close the doors from her bed at will'. Maybe the queen was just lazy, but it has been suggested that the arrangement was connected with Fersen's visits.[20]

Finally, however, Farr opts for the Trianon because crowded Versailles with its lack of proper sanitation was insalubrious in the summer.[21] The king's diary shows that, exceptionally, the Court spent most of that summer at Versailles.[22] As Farr observes, relations between the king and queen were strained that summer because her brother Joseph II in alliance with Russia planned a dismemberment of France's traditional ally Turkey. Madame de Polignac naturally sided with the king.[23]

The marquis de Bombelles, however, diplomat, right-hand man of the queen's protégé Breteuil, minister for the royal household, thought this was 'a calumny'. Bombelles, when his not very onerous duties as ambassador to Portugal allowed, accompanied Marie-Antoinette at the piano during Madame de Polignac's *soirées musicales*. He adduces an interesting fact in favour of the relationship being innocent. The marquis de Ségur, minister of war, despite owing his appointment to the queen and despite her known interest in military promotions, tried to block Fersen's appointment as colonel of the Royal Swedish. Would he have done so had he known of the queen's special interest in the Swede? Breteuil, new in his job and not wanting to alienate a colleague, asked Vaudreuil to further Fersen's cause. Moreover, Bombelles, a keen observer of these things, noted on 9 October 1783 that she 'looked as if she had been pregnant for six months' – in other words beginning three months before Fersen's return from America.[24]

Farr's best argument in the absence of any concrete proof – the restored letters reveal passion but not sexual passion, nor would one expect them to – is that whereas Marie-Antoinette's pregnancies had been spasmodic up to 1783, they became regular thereafter at least until 1786: a miscarriage in November 1783, the birth of the duc de Normandie, Louis-Charles, on 27 March 1785, and Sophie on 9 July 1786. Farr notes that none of Fersen's numerous mistresses seems to have borne him a child and concludes that he knew how to take precautions, though one might equally conclude that Fersen was sterile. But Farr observes, the dates of Marie-Antoinette's three conceptions coincide with those of Fersen's returns after long absences.[25] So perhaps in the joy of their reunion, Dionysus rather than Artemis gained the upper hand. Except this is out of character for both of them.

Fersen was not there to comfort or advise Marie-Antoinette after her miscarriage, having left Paris on 23 September 1783 to join his regiment at Valenciennes, and with Marie-Antoinette *hors de combat*, it was left to Castries (on his own and the queen's behalf) to take up cudgels for his friend Necker. Castries wrote to the king saying that 'any [ministerial] change is bad in itself' but that if d'Ormesson had to go he should be replaced by Necker. Louis told him 'formally that neither M. Necker nor his friends must dream of his ever returning to office; that provided M. Necker kept a low profile and his friends did not get him talked about, I would leave him alone. But that if . . . he undermined the operations of the government, I should regard it as a personal attack and then I would send him back to Geneva never to return to France.'[26] The king repeated that 'in view of the generous way [*sic*] I treated M. Necker and the way he left me voluntarily he must think no more of return to office'.[27] There was also a suspicion that Necker had organized the run on the Discount Bank 'to make himself necessary'.[28] That left the way clear for Calonne. Many witnesses and her own ex-post facto remarks suggest that Marie-Antoinette was implacably opposed to Calonne's appointment, but we follow Castries in saying she was neutral – enmity came, and came with good reason, only after his appointment.

Meanwhile, the opposing party mounted its engine and put pressure on the king. The Polignacs acted in conjunction with 'Calonne's uncle, [Jean Daniel de] Bourgade, the Intendant of the Royal Treasury and [Joseph Micault] d'Harvelai its keeper, his intimate friend' and complaisant husband of his mistress whom he later married, a woman whose fabulous wealth enabled Calonne to subsidize the Counter-Revolution, continuing thereby to be a thorn in Marie-Antoinette's side. These men, rich bankers in their own right, did not just run the treasury but at a time when public and private were mixed, helped to finance it. They were hand in glove with the tax Farmers threatened by d'Ormesson's measure.

On 31 October, d'Harvelai sent the king 'a letter which terrified me', as he confessed to Vergennes.[29] It said that unless the Farmers' lease was restored and d'Ormesson dismissed, d'Harvelai could not answer for the consequences. Calonne was suggested as the ideal man to restore credit. Vergennes wanted to get rid of d'Ormesson but he was not keen on Calonne, telling d'Harvelai 'formally that he would never dare to take it upon himself to propose him to the king'. 'Very well,' replied d'Harvelai, 'don't propose him then; all I ask is that you don't oppose him otherwise I will resign on the 10th of the month.' D'Harvelai ran to Madame de Polignac and told her not to rely on Vergennes' support but to enlist that of the queen's protégé Breteuil, recently appointed minister of the royal household. Breteuil went straight up with Madame de Polignac to see the queen. He found her hostile to Calonne but she put them off until the next day, Saturday, when after 'long debates, they obtained from their majesties a nomination which would lead one day first to the total destruction of their kingdom and then to their own on the scaffold'.[30]

D'Ormesson refused to resign and insisted for the sake of his honour that the king should both sack him and say that he retained his 'esteem'. So on Sunday 3 November, Louis did just that, writing, 'that the situation of my affairs demanded your resignation but you retain my esteem and my protection'.[31] Louis instructs Vergennes to 'summon Calonne to Fontainebleau and explain what I want him to do', in other words restore credit. He adds, cynically or naively, 'I don't know whether he is at Paris [intriguing] or in Flanders [doing his job].' Louis told Marie-Antoinette, philosophically, 'there is not much to choose between the rival candidates but . . . [Calonne] at least has the financiers on his side'.[32] Fear of financial collapse was henceforth an idée fixe with the king.

We have looked in depth at the circumstances of Calonne's appointment because he was to become one of Marie-Antoinette's seminal enemies, the others being d'Aiguillon, Cardinal de Rohan and Lafayette. Jacques-Mathieu Augeard, Marie-Antoinette's chief financial officer (*secrétaire de commande-ments*), thought, as we have seen, that Calonne's appointment led (indirectly) to the scaffold for the queen, but so, for that matter, did the reappointment of Necker through her influence in August 1788. Those with a taste for counter-factual history might speculate that if Marie-Antoinette had not had a miscar-riage Necker might have been reappointed in 1783 and the regime saved. They would be wasting their time: Louis was not yet that hard up.

When Calonne was sworn in at the Chambre des Comptes (Audit Office) he made what Augeard called a noble and ridiculous speech in which he said, 'As soon as I have completed the arduous task of discharging the war debt, I will apply my mind to the execution of plans of general reform which . . . reveal that the true secret of lightening taxation lies in the proportionate equality of its assessment and in the simplification of its collection'. No one took him seri-ously; he was a playboy after all, a sybarite. But like his friend Vaudreuil, he was an intellectual. Besides, the urgency of reform and even the timing of it was in the logic of the situation. D'Ormesson had also outlined similar reforms to the king and had put a date to them, 1 January 1787, since the lease of the General Farm and wartime taxation expired at that time.[33] D'Ormesson had also commissioned budget forecasts for the period ending 1 January 1787. Something was likely to happen then but first, in Louis Blanc's poetic words, Calonne intended 'to give *les grands* a moment of happiness' and so confront them with the need for reform. Or, as Barnave had it, 'he was prodigal by character, by complaisance and by design'. By administering 'quack medicine' to a patient too weak to diet he hastened on the French Revolution and became 'its evil genius'.[34]

VAUDREUIL AND MARIE-ANTOINETTE

Vaudreuil had played a part in Calonne's appointment and he was the major stumbling block in the friendship between his mistress Madame de Polignac and her friend Marie-Antoinette. Marie-Antoinette wanted to monopolize her favourite's love and was jealous of Vaudreuil's claims. But the association of the Polignac set with Calonne and the increasing politicization of the comte d'Artois elevated a lovers' tiff to the level of national politics, just before and during the

Revolution. Calonne's appointment was the culmination of the Polignacs' quest for power and wealth. Vaudreuil probably got to know Calonne through another of his sinecures, governor ad honorem, of the citadel of Lille, with income of 6,000 livres a year. Lille was the seat of government of the Intendancy of Flanders, the second most highly paid of the thirty key administrative units into which France was divided, where Calonne had been stationed since 1778. The two men were bound to get on: Vaudreuil was an intellectual for whom paying court was a tedious necessity; Calonne had won all the prizes for Classics at university and claimed that the only plaudits he ever desired were academic ones.[35] Later they would share a deep friendship with Elisabeth Vigée-Lebrun – her portrait of Calonne in the Queen's Collection has a claim to be considered her masterpiece. Both men were rumoured to be her lover. Both were in a sense outsiders. Vaudreuil was a Creole whose mother was not considered quite *du bon ton*. Calonne was a provincial *noblesse de robe* of very recent vintage, his father having been ennobled. Yet both had more polished court manners than many to the château born.

Calonne's appointment to the Finance Minstry led to Vaudreuil's tapping the state for serious sums of money. The value of his sinecures was negligible, but already in 1779, four years before Calonne's appointment, through his mistress's good offices Vaudreuil had been granted a pension of 30,000 livres for the duration of the war, which cut him off from his West Indian revenue stream. He then exchanged this pension for a landed estate in France. Then in 1784 he found himself in dire financial straits. The reasons are not clear but were probably due to his extravagant lifestyle, his theatre in the country, banquets such as only the rich financiers who backed Calonne could give. Whatever the cause the king, through Calonne's intermediary, bailed him out with an advance of 1,200,000 livres. When this did not suffice he was obliged to sell part of his collection of paintings and the king bought some of them at an inflated price to help him out. Two years later, being unable to get a stay of execution for the repayment of a loan of 600,000 livres, Calonne sought the backing of Artois before forwarding Vaudreuil the money.[36] It had been Artois who had negotiated the exchange of his pension for the duration of the war for a landed estate.

Artois was Vaudreuil's best friend. They were together at the unsuccessful siege of Gibraltar in 1782 and, separated during the Counter-Revolution, conducted a voluminous correspondence. It may seem an unlikely friendship, for Artois was no intellectual, to put it mildly, but then neither was Madame de Polignac. Artois was anchored into the Polignac set by his love for the wife of Madame de Polignac's brother, M. de Polastron, and she weaned him off his addiction to Parisian actresses and began the process of turning him into the *dévot* and political reactionary he was to become as Charles X. Like Marie-Antoinette, he was more dangerous when serious than when frivolous. But it was the addition of Artois and Calonne to Vaudreuil and Madame de Polignac that gave the group what was termed *consistance*, a rare commodity in an increasingly shifting world. They were now a power in the land, especially as they had the backing of the king – why else should he, no lover of the fine arts, buy Vaudreuil's art collection? The set thought they could do without Marie-Antoinette.

THE SAINT-CLOUD PURCHASE

The seeds of enmity between Marie-Antoinette and Calonne were soon sown. If she thought that replacing d'Ormesson with Calonne would facilitate the purchase of Saint-Cloud she was quickly disabused; for like his predecessor, Calonne took a departmental, 'treasury' line. As d'Ormesson had informed the king, future revenues were mortgaged up to 1 January 1787. To compound matters, Calonne was not informed about the early stages of the negotiation with the duc d'Orléans, who was forced to sell, adding further friction between Marie-Antoinette and the first prince of the blood. And Marie-Antoinette's personal involvement was emphasized by the fact that these negotiations were carried out by Vermond, and the archbishop of Toulouse, which suggested that her plans to make him prime minister had only been postponed. We learn this from Castries, who refutes the common misapprehension that Breteuil was the chief negotiator.[37] Breteuil, the new minister for the royal household, would have been the relevant minister and he made great play of wanting 'to make the queen reign' (*faire règner la reine*). But although he passed for her protégé and would play a significant role as such in the Revolution, her feelings towards him were always ambivalent.

It was agreed to pay the duc d'Orléans 6 million livres for Saint-Cloud, plus 100,000 pin money for his daughter-in-law. Augeard, Marie-Antoinette's treasurer, criticized the sum as a poor bargain – he thought the château could have been got for 3 million – but didn't blame the king for indulging his wife: 'what private individual with 447,000 livres a year would not spend 6/9000 on diamonds for his wife?' Multiply by a thousand and 'the proportion was the same'. The details of the contract were handled by Marie-Antoinette's officers: the marquis de Paulmy, her chancellor, acted as her plenipotentiary, and Augeard as her *secrétaire des commandements* had to sign off the transaction to give it executive effect.

The king, however, was putting up the money, so at this stage Calonne had to be told since the funds would come from his department. Summoned by the queen, he told her coldly that he would 'take the king's orders'. He went straight round to Louis and, as Augeard has it, 'in words full of pathos and exaggeration' convinced him that he couldn't afford the purchase. The sale was cancelled, but a furious Marie-Antoinette summoned Calonne once more and employed blackmail to make him change his mind. Since Calonne had 'used the situation of the treasury as a pretext', she would furnish the king with 'a very detailed account . . . of the immense sums you have given to the Princes of the Blood and my brothers-in-law to bolster your support with the king and poured into the pockets of the court grandees in order to surround the king with men daily singing your praises'.

All this was true: one of Calonne's first acts on becoming finance minister was to have the treasury undertake to service Artois' 14,000,000 livres of debts; in 1785, Provence was given over 7 million livres and an annuity of 500,000, though in a complicated arrangement he bought L'Isle-Adam from the indebted prince de Conti and gave it to Marie-Antoinette's second son, the duc de Normandie. When Marie-Antoinette accuses Calonne of 'lining the pockets of les grands de la Cour' she is perhaps blaming him for reversing her policy of humbling the ducal families; for although in 1784 Calonne increased the Polignac family's income by 100,000 livres, the Rohan, Montmorency and Talleyrand families in particular were also his beneficiaries. Marie-Antoinette concluded her diatribe with the threat: 'Do as you like, but if I don't have Saint-Cloud, I forbid you my presence and in particular to go to Madame de Polignac's when I am there.'[38]

Calonne told the king that they would have to give in but that he 'would draft the letters patent so cleverly that she will think she has Saint-Cloud but won't actually have it'. Having given Paulmy a financial inducement, Calonne told him, 'here are draft letters patent to annex to your plenipotential powers'. When Paulmy raised a quizzical eyebrow, Calonne explained: 'Do you want the Emperor to have a piece of France should the queen die without issue?' Castries put it less crudely but just as emphatically: 'It is said that it is the first time that it has been a question of giving a property to a Queen of France because it is for her and not M. le Dauphin that the queen wants Saint-Cloud.'[39] Calonne was being hysterical – Saint-Cloud would not have been inherited by a Habsburg in any circumstances, but the episode contributed to the perception not only with the public but with ministers such as Vergennes, Castries and Calonne, and indeed the king himself, that Marie-Antoinette was, in its pejorative sense, *L'Autrichienne*. Paulmy gave Augeard the letters patent of Calonne's to enact, but Augeard pointed out the substitution to the queen, who called Calonne a 'rascal' and a 'chancer' and rounded on her chancellor:

You have given M. Augeard draft letters patent. I cannot even begin to contemplate using an instrument so ill befitting the dignity of my person and my interests. Here are replacements which I trust you will see are more appropriate. M. Augeard will read them to you ... How do you find them. – Much better, but I fear their registration will encounter opposition in the Parlement.

Letters patent had to be registered in the Parlement to have force of law, and opposition from that quarter was likely on the grounds that giving the queen a property would violate the Fundamental Laws or unwritten constitution of the kingdom. The public prosecutor of the Parlement pondered the matter and the firebrand counsellor Jean-Jacques d'Éprémesnil said, 'it is impolitic and immoral to see palaces belonging to a queen of France'.[40] But the queen's friends still had sufficient clout there to get the transaction registered.

Calonne thought that the acquisition of Saint-Cloud was 'a silly idea that had been put into the queen's head'.[41] Why did she want it, apart from wanting to play lady of the manor? Versailles had become 'the seat of boredom' for her and for the courtiers, who, partly as a result of her policy, were spending more and more of their time in Paris, only performing their ceremonial duties at Versailles where 'the sight of the same old faces nauseated Marie-Antoinette'. She could not herself go and live in Paris. When she was forced to on 6 October 1789 the whole point of Louis XIV's moving from the Louvre to Versailles – his 'powerful political reasons' – was rediscovered. So the next best thing was to have a château 'at the gates of Paris'. She hoped thereby, apart from having the entertainment of the capital at hand, to rejuvenate attendance at court, but this was the wrong way round: just as, according to Provence, the queen 'was sucked into the circle of Madame de Polignac' rather than vice versa, so now she was courting the courtiers in Paris.

Madame Campan had a different take on the purchase of Saint-Cloud. Versailles, now one hundred years old, needed major repairs. Indeed, Louis XVI did plan to modernize the whole Paris side of the château, the neo-classical replacing the baroque. Funds did not permit of a quick fix, so the king contemplated staggering the rebuilding over ten years, well into the 1790s. The machinery of government would remain at Versailles in the Cour des Ministres, as would the all-important stables, but the royal family would move to Saint-Cloud for the duration. The original plan was to swap La Muette and Choisy for Saint-Cloud, which would also save the cost of a governor for each. This fell through but one part of the plan survived: there would be no governor for Saint-Cloud: the queen would do the job herself. Accordingly, the servants would wear her livery and orders be given in her name, 'de par la reine', just like at Trianon. Trianon, though, was a private, subsidiary part of the Versailles complex, not open to the Parisian public, which swarmed round Saint-Cloud. The new regime at Saint-Cloud raised eyebrows, which hurt the queen: 'Is the use of my name out of place in my own gardens? Can I not give orders there without infringing the rights of the State?'[42]

The purchase revived neither her prestige with courtiers nor her popularity with Parisians: there was insufficient accommodation and the courtiers had to lodge in the village, which caused resentment. This led to the rumour that she was going to pull down the château and build another Versailles in the grounds. Instead, ordinary Parisians came. They were used to going to see the duc d'Orléans' fountains. Now there was an additional reason: 'All along the route from the capital the Parisians said, "we are going to Saint-Cloud to see the fountains and l'Autrichienne."' 'Only M. Lenoir,' the police chief Soulavie adds, 'knew how much it cost to get them to utter the banal cry of Vive la reine' instead.[43]

In the event, though, Saint-Cloud turned out to be value for money. The other châteaux that ringed Paris – whether the newly acquired Rambouillet and L'Isle Adam or the hallowed royal seats of Fontainebleau and Compiègne, with their 'ancient forests and their fairy-like quality' – were seldom visited as the Revolutionary crisis developed from 1787 onwards. But Saint-Cloud was used for five weeks in the summer of 1788 and it was the only palace the royal family were allowed to inhabit during the Revolution. In 1790 they were there from 4 June to 30 October.

THE DUTCH AFFAIR

Marie-Antoinette's clumsy intervention in the Austro-Dutch dispute of 1784–6 was responsible for a myth that would be dredged up at her trial: that she was siphoning off money to send to Joseph II. In 1784, her brother decided to improve his Belgian territories by opening the Scheldt to shipping. Dutch pressure had inserted a clause in the Westphalian treaties closing the Scheldt to prevent Antwerp from becoming a rival to Amsterdam. On 8 October an Austrian ship set off from Antwerp amidst applause, intending to sail down the Scheldt and buy wine in France. It was soon intercepted by Dutch frigates, one of which fired across her bows and forced her to head back. Joseph II demanded reparations for the insult to his flag, the cession of the key fortress of Maastricht, and asked what help his French ally proposed to give. Meanwhile he assembled his troops for an invasion of Holland. France, however, was preparing to sign a treaty of alliance with the Republic and readied troops to defend the Dutch. Vergennes drafted a sharp note reminding Joseph that the Scheldt was closed by an international treaty of which France was the guarantor. Louis showed the note to Marie-Antoinette, who complained that it would destroy the alliance and set her two families at loggerheads. Louis palmed her off with a five-day delay before the note was sent: 'That's all I could obtain,' she told her brother.[44]

Joseph announced that he would drop his claims against the Dutch provided the French would allow the Bavarian exchange to proceed – he was putting pressure on the next heir to forfeit his claim in return for being put in sovereign possession of most of the Austrian Netherlands. Marie-Antoinette thought she had squared with Louis on this exchange, writing to her brother on 2 December:

> As soon as I received your letters I went together with M. de Mercy to show the King one of your two letters and the plan for the exchange. Whether he did not want to commit himself on the spur of the moment or whether, because of a very confused recollection of what had been said to him about the exchange at the time of the Peace of Teschen, he did not at first take to this proposal, I have to say that before he had seen M. de Vergennes, further thought had already brought him round to it.

Louis was merely stalling whilst he assembled the Council, which advised that the Austrian overture be rejected. Vergennes pulled his punches, leaving it to the others to reject the plan outright. On 31 December, Marie-Antoinette wrote to Joseph: 'M. de Vergennes has communicated to all the minsters of the council his report on the proposals for the exchange. I do not know whether this is a new trick on his part but, according to what the King told me afterwards, his report is more conciliatory than the opinion of several other ministers.' To Marie-Antoinette's supposed protégé Breteuil is reserved the role of attacking the exchange outright, including a scathing personal attack on Joseph: 'He seems to think that the man who annexes the most territory will go down as the greatest prince in history.'[45]

The Council decided that the king should write the emperor a letter in which 'without for the moment dwelling on its conformity with my interests' he said he would consider only the effects of the proposed exchange on the German Empire and in particular on the king of Prussia – a cynical manoeuvre in view of the predictability of Prussia's response. The formulation of this letter caused Louis a great deal of distress because of pressure from Marie-Antoinette. In November 1784, Castries noted that the king was silent and abstracted. On 5 January 1785 he wrote to Vergennes: 'You were right to remind me, Monsieur, of your courier [for the letter]; I hadn't forgotten it but for two days I have not been in a fit state to concentrate.'[46]

The letter was difficult to write because Louis had to perform a delicate balancing act – hence the length of the letter. He could not yield to the emperor on essentials and although he had not 'dwelt on his interests' he realized that if the emperor gained Bavaria with its control of the Upper Danube, Alsace would be wide open to an Austrian invasion should Austria revert to her natural alliance with England. Moreover, public opinion was whispering that completion of the purchase of Saint-Cloud for the queen, which occurred in October 1784, was designed to divert funds away from sending troops to support the Dutch. Marie-Antoinette compounded Louis' worries, making a rational decision in France's best interest more difficult. That is the drawback to dynastic alliances.

On 27 November the queen had hurled abuse at Vergennes in Louis' presence, accusing him of manipulating the Council. Vergennes offered his resignation on the spot. Louis tried to calm her down and reiterated his confidence in his minister. She withdrew her accusations and told the Swedish ambassador that in future 'I will not meddle with anything once a decision has been reached and in any case, much as I love the emperor, I will never forget that [first and foremost] I am Queen of France and mother of the dauphin'.[47] Torn between two loyalties, she received advice from another Swede – Axel von Fersen – during the critical phase of the crisis. His abbreviated register of letters to 'Josephine', i.e. Marie-Antoinette, mentions 'spoke about Dutch affairs' (26 November 1784) and 'very detailed letter on current affairs' (22 January 1785). Unlike Madame de Polignac, Fersen had hitherto refrained from 'speaking about current affairs'. Mercy noted an increased 'dexterity' in the queen but assumed it would be put in the service of the emperor.[48]

Indeed, she now proceeded to bombard Vergennes with a series of notes, one of them complaining that the Dutch had opened their dykes to flood the Austrian troops and demanding that Vergennes have them closed.[49] Louis wearily wrote to Vergennes, 'I have given your notes to the queen, who made little objection to them. I hope the matter will end there.' It did not and both the queen and her relatives worked openly for Vergennes' disgrace. Her brother Joseph told Mercy, 'I am absolutely of your opinion that there should be a change in the ministry to benefit the queen ... in important matters we cannot count on M. de Vergennes'.[50] Marie-Antoinette's accusation in her tirade that Louis was the 'plaything' of his ministers wasn't true – rather he hid behind them. But for his wife's sake he had to be as polite to the emperor as possible, whilst not giving way on fundamentals. Hence the care he took to tone down the asperity of his letter.

Frederick of Prussia blocked the exchange as expected; and the heir of Bavaria the Duke of Zweibrucken, his resistance to the bullying Joseph stiffened by French encouragement, rejected the exchange. Joseph then resurrected his grievances against the Dutch, but this time Marie-Antoinette hinted darkly to her brother: 'your troops would make short work of the Dutch', but 'would they be alone?'[51] – that is, France would intervene on the Dutch side. Joseph, all the while protesting that he did not want to take his brother-in-law's money given the state of French finances, was induced to settle for the payment of 6 million florins, some of it provided by France herself. It was this transaction that gave rise to the myth in the French Revolution that Marie-Antoinette was secretly sending funds to her brother.

Stories shot the rounds that have come down to us as anecdotes. One has a prostitute asking one of Marie-Antoinette's favourites, the duc de Coigny, whether it was true that the queen had sent 200 million francs to her brother. 'All of that and we're not there yet,' replied the duke. His irony was lost on the woman, but again there was a grain of truth: the 6 million florins were to be paid in instalments. A fake letter from Joseph to Breteuil circulated in which the emperor asked for 50 million. 'Just add it to the current account deficit . . . and slap on a new tax . . . if not declare a bankruptcy. The queen will sing, Monsieur will groan, Artois will laugh, the good king will cry' – but will pay up. 'It's all one to me so long as I have the French people's money.'[52] These words, 'deficit', 'new tax', 'bankruptcy', already part of the political lexicon, in less than two years would dominate it.

For his part, Joseph came to the conclusion that Chancellor Kaunitz was right – his sister was indeed a 'bad payer' and no more could be expected from his nominal ally. He even thought that Louis and Vergennes were ready to ditch the Austrian alliance for a Prussian one. They were wrong: when Frederick's brother, Prince Henry of Prussia, visited Versailles he was greeted coolly by the French government but in Paris he was adulated, partly as a snub to Marie-Antoinette. These things would be worked out in the next few years.

MARIE-ANTOINETTE AND HER CHILDREN

'The fashion for looking after your own children had not yet arrived. In my childhood the very opposite was the case.' So wrote Talleyrand, born the year before Marie-Antoinette. His parents had 'left him for several years with a woman from a Faubourg in Paris', and he was still there when aged four he fell off a commode and hurt his foot. This was not noticed until he was sent to live with his great-grandmother in their ancestral province of Périgord, by which time it was too late to correct a permanent limp. Thus disqualified for military service 'or at least shining' in that profession, he was forced into a career in the Church for which he had no calling.[53]

Talleyrand was writing about royal and aristocratic families. But even here, partly under the influence of Rousseau's educational novel *Émile*, fashions were changing by the time Marie-Antoinette's first child, Marie-Thérèse-Charlotte, was born in 1778. But it was the abrupt dismissal of Madame de Guéméné as governess of the royal children on 22 December 1782 that was the main reason for Marie-Antoinette's developing a 'hands-on' approach to the upbringing of her own children. At this date she had, apart from her four-year-old daughter, the dauphin, a year-old baby. During the gubernatorial interregnum between the dismissal of Guéméné and the appointment of Madame de Polignac, she got into the habit of spending time with her children. One doesn't want to exaggerate: the queen spent only 'a portion of the morning alone with her daughter without the sub-governesses'. Nevertheless these and the bevy of those in subaltern positions worried that if 'Her Majesty determined to bring up her daughter herself', many would lose their jobs.[54] Apart from the governess, sub-governesses, wet and dry nurses and a doctor, the household of each royal child had an army of *femmes-de-chambre* – ten for 'Madame Royale', as the oldest unmarried royal daughter (Marie-Thérèse-Charlotte) was always known. They were bourgeois, neither 'upstairs' nor 'downstairs' but, like the Duke of York in his 1793 campaign in Flanders, 'neither up nor down'. In addition the girl had two male *valets-de-chambre*, who were still with her in 1789. They were, in Marie-Antoinette's words, 'absolutely insignificant creatures but as they had nothing to do beyond their basic service after which they did not remain in the room, that too was insignificant'.[55]

The sub-governesses varied in number between two and four. At one stage no fewer than three of these were relatives of Bombelles, the most important being his mother-in-law Madame de Mackau. This means that his diary is a unique source for the upbringing of Marie-Antoinette's children. We know most about that of Marie-Thérèse-Charlotte, because the dauphin was sick too much of the time to receive 'the education fitting for a prince', and that of the second son, the duc de Normandie, born in 1785 was interrupted by the Revolution. In any case when the boys reached the age of six or seven they were transferred from a governess to a governor – 'put in the hands of men' as the expression went. The governess, however, was responsible for the royal girls until their marriage. That being so, Bombelles informs us, the governess did not bother much with the boys' education, catering mainly for their 'physical' needs. The last child,[56] Madame Sophie, died in infancy. Marie-Thérèse-Charlotte was styled 'Madame' but that was also the title of the wife of 'Monsieur, comte de Provence'. So the girl was often referred to as 'Madame Royale' or 'Madame fille de roi', though given the way she sometimes treated her mother, Little Madam might seem more appropriate. She was nicknamed Mousseline or Mousseline la Sérieuse, even though her sorrows had scarcely begun.

Madame de Polignac, as we have seen, was reluctant to become the next royal governess. It took the king's persuasion and only this prevented her from resigning in 1785 a post that in 1787 she temporarily abandoned. She was lazy and 'to lighten the burden which she entrusted to her friend [the queen], personally undertook the education' of her daughter, who was moved to apartments nearer her own.[57]

All her four children, in their different ways, caused Marie-Antoinette heartache. In 1783 the queen fell off her horse. Vermond joined her, together with Marie-Thérèse-Charlotte, who when told that her mother could have been badly injured replied:

'What's it to me?' – 'Madame doesn't understand what it means to break your head. The queen could have died.' – 'So what?' – 'But Madame surely doesn't know what death means.' – 'On the contrary M. l'abbé I know perfectly well what it means. You don't see dead people any more. I would not see the queen any more and . . . I could then do what I wanted.'

What shocked Bombelles and cut Marie-Antoinette to the quick was that this was not just a childish outburst: the girl had expressed 'this horrible way of thinking with such logic and discernment'. Reproaching her, a sub-governess told the girl that surely she loved her mother: 'No because she hampers me and pays me no attention. For example when she takes me to see my aunts, she walks straight ahead and doesn't even notice whether I am following whereas my father holds my hand and pays attention to me.' She was a daddy's girl whereas the boys were fonder of their mother.

The four-year-old Marie-Thérèse-Charlotte had to be punished. The queen ordered that for a fortnight she only be allowed one course at her supper because it had been noticed that she skipped the earlier courses in the hope of filling up on puddings:

'Did the queen also order me to go straight to bed?' 'Yes, Madame' – 'Is that all?' – 'Yes, Madame' – 'You are mistaken, Monsieur, I'm sure she ordered me to say my prayers first.'

Marie-Thérèse-Charlotte accompanied this 'with a mocking smile of an irritable woman of thirty'. When taxed with this episode, the girl told her mother that she said such things because she wanted to see the expression on the faces of her servants.[58] To lessen the girl's hauteur – Habsburg or Bourbon – she was made to serve poor children at table – a child's version of the maundy Thursday ritual. She also had to give away her toys.[59]

It was suspected that the bevy of *femmes de chambre*, twelve to sixteen in number, were spoiling the little girl in the hopes of future benefits when she came of age, in the same way that, higher up the social scale, Madame de Marsan had ruthlessly played on her position as governess to the boy Louis XVI. Marie-Antoinette thought that these women were stealing her daughter's affection so she had seven of them dismissed, 'women of excellent character whose families had served the royal family for centuries'. Although Bombelles conceded that many of the *femmes de chambre* were superfluous, including one paid 1,200 francs a year whose sole function was to fasten the princess's collar, he thought that the dismissals smacked of arbitrariness.[60]

Bombelles was beginning to think that Madame had no heart, but on 9 December 1785 he was 'delighted' to record 'the first occasion when .... [she] showed true emotion'. Hearing that her little brother the dauphin had fallen ill, 'her beautiful eyes filled with tears which she strove [in vain] to conceal'.[61]

That brother was the opposite of his sister; where she was sturdy rather than beautiful, he was beautiful but delicate: constantly wracked by fevers on top of the late-diagnosed tuberculosis that would kill him, as it had his namesake Louis-Joseph-Xavier, Louis XVI's elder brother. He was sweet-tempered whereas his sister simply had a temper like her father in his youth. Although he was heir to the throne, we hear little of his training; the main concern of Marie-Antoinette's letters on this subject is the losing battle to keep him alive. On 22 February 1788 she tells Joseph that the boy's spine is deformed, with vertebrae sticking out. He had tuberculosis of the spine, but misled by doctors whose flattery was equalled only by their incompetence, the poor queen tried to delude herself into thinking that his sufferings were the result of cutting his second set of teeth. She was on the right track, however, when she sent him to the nearby château of Meudon set on a high plateau and known for its health-giving air. This, she pointed out, was where Louis XVI, 'who had been very feeble and sickly' as a boy, had been sent – and look how robust he was now as befitted the grandson of Augustus the Strong of Saxony! The king had probably suffered from mild tuberculosis and the fresh air and hunting may have saved him. But it was too late to save his son.

What a contrast, she continued, between the sick boy 'and his younger brother. He has all the vitality and health his brother lacks. He's a real peasant's son, big, fresh-faced and chubby'.[62] Louis-Charles was clearly not 'a peasant's son'. No one ever accused her of stooping that low! But whose was he? We have concluded that he was indeed the king's. The only connection between Axel von Fersen with his delicate porcelain complexion and Augustus the Strong was the Meissen factory the latter founded. Louis-Charles (Charles after his godmother, Marie-Antoinette's favourite sister Maria-Carolina, queen of Naples) was born on Easter Day 1785. Marie-Antoinette's pregnancy had been so pronounced that Calonne, as Grand Treasurer of the King's (Chivalric) Orders, had ordered two blue cordons of the Saint-Esprit, in case there were twin boys.[63] The baby was immediately invested with the Order and created duke of Normandy. He was Marie-Antoinette's favourite child and she called him her '*chou d'amour*'. Literally 'love-cabbage', it moved by a series of associations to mean perhaps cream cake. 'Sweetie Pie' might be as near as we can get in English. Louis XVI's mother had called her first-born, the duc de Bourgogne, *chou d'amour*. When he died young she did not transfer the name to the future king.

When Madame de Tourzel succeeded Madame de Polignac on the latter's exile to Switzerland after the fall of the Bastille in July 1789, Marie-Antoinette gave the new governess a memorandum with a character sketch of her surviving children (Louis-Charles, now dauphin, and Madame), together with a summary of the personnel of their respective establishments and the principles she herself applied to the raising of her children.[64] 'My son is two days short of being four years and four months' – it was 24 July 1789. No need to describe his physical appearance – 'you only have to look at him' to see how big and strong he is. But he was late in teething and 'my son cannot read and is a bad learner but he is too scatter-brained to apply himself'. She nevertheless considered his tutor, the abbé d'Avaux, to be 'very good at teaching my son his letters', but the abbé displayed 'bad form' and had to be removed from teaching his sister. He was replaced by a trusted *femme de chambre*. Madame de Polignac had been particularly worried that he hung about the boy beyond the allotted hours of work.

Louis-Charles was of a nervous disposition and 'the slightest unexplained noise had an extraordinary effect on him. For example he was scared of dogs because he had heard one barking nearby.' He had a temper 'and the word pardon stuck in his throat'. But he was loving towards his big sister and wanted her to share his treats. He had 'amour-propre', which could stand him in good stead, but no 'hauteur', and 'long may this continue: our children will find out soon enough who they are.'

Marie-Antoinette was a fairly strict mother – 'my yes and no are irrevocable' – but she always gave her children a reason for her decisions 'appropriate to their age'. If they did wrong she acted more in sorrow than in anger. But whilst assuring the new governess that her male charge was basically a 'bon enfant', she touched on two character defects that would have tragic consequences for the queen: dissimulation and mendacity. 'Until he gets to know someone, he knows how to control himself and eat up his anger and impatience so as to appear gentle and loveable. He keeps his word but is very indiscreet. He has a tendency to repeat what he has heard and, without exactly lying he often embroiders it with what his imagination suggests.'

During the Revolution her children were Marie-Antoinette's consolation, as she told Madame de Polignac on 29 December 1789, in Paris: 'but for strong ties to my children . . . I should often wish to die'. 'The Chou d'Amour is charming and I love him to distraction. He loves me too in his fashion without making a fuss of it . . . I sometimes ask him if he remembers you and loves you: "Yes," he says [diplomatically] and then I give him an extra cuddle. He's getting stronger and no longer has tantrums.' His sister too, 'poor little mite', was now 'always marvellously sweet to me'.[65]

FIVE

THE DIAMOND NECKLACE AFFAIR

1785–1786

*T*he scarcely credible heist known as the Diamond Necklace Affair is made slightly more explicable by considering Marie-Antoinette's earlier forays into high-value jewellery. For when a gang of confidence tricksters claimed they were buying diamonds from the court jewellers, Boehmers, on credit for the queen, Boehmers remembered Marie-Antoinette's transactions in the period 1774–6. The sum was greater – 1,600,000 livres – but not so great as to be unbelievable, for in the earlier period Marie-Antoinette had bought a diamond bracelet and diamond earrings for over 500,000 livres. Moreover, the queen had not at first dared to tell the king, merely saying that she had exceeded her allowance and using monthly payments of 24,000 livres from him to satisfy Boehmers. In the end Charles Auguste Boehmer had gone to the king, who agreed to repay 300,000 livres over a six-year period. The rest was still outstanding and presumably Marie-Antoinette paid it off out of her allowance. She had burnt her fingers, however, and after 1776 did not buy any more diamonds, which should have alerted Boehmers. There was also, according to Mercy, some skullduggery even in the earlier period. In order to pay for the earrings Marie-Antoinette traded in some of her lesser jewels and her 'entours' – Mercy's code for the Polignacs – persuaded her to undersell the jewels to other, corrupt jewellers.[1] In 1791 she sent her jewels to Brussels to be used as collateral for a loan if the Flight to Varennes had succeeded. Ultimately they were returned to her daughter.

By the time of the Revolution, Marie-Antoinette had received about 5 million francs from the king, either in jewellery or money – in 1781 he gave her 300,000 francs. She had about 3 million francs' worth of jewellery, whether of diamonds or coloured stones. She had also appropriated a piece worth 135,000 francs belonging to the Crown Jewels. To be precise, she had borrowed it and added some stones of her own so that it was impossible to tell which were hers and which the Crown's. The king would lend some of the Crown Jewels to princes of the blood for ceremonial occasions and borrow some himself, but they had to be returned. Marie-Antoinette kept hers. In addition, when she arrived in France, Louis XV gave her all the jewellery belonging to the dauphin's mother, worth 1,700,000 francs. The Girault de Coursacs, who have dug out this information, argue that Marie-Antoinette was not interested in jewellery per se and didn't wear much but valued only its monetary worth, as collateral for hard times. But how does that explain the duchess of Northumberland's comment that she was 'covered in jewels'? The queen gave very little to charity, the king paid for the upkeep of the Trianon and she lived free of charge with the Polignacs whose pensions were paid for by the king.[2]

The Diamond Necklace Affair shed a lurid light on almost every aspect of the *ancien régime* establishment. An out-of-favour cardinal-archbishop accused of being a knave was idolized when he turned out merely to have been a fool. The press was scurrilous to an extent that even our kiss-and-tell age would find offensive. The Parlement was revealed as nakedly political and venal. Ministerial rivalries trumped any loyalty to a king, who appeared despotic, arbitrary and vengeful. And the biggest sufferer of all was Marie-Antoinette who, despite the French name of the scandal – 'l'affaire du collier de la Reine' (The Queen's Necklace Affair) – was the innocent victim. For the kernel of the highly complex Diamond Necklace Affair consisted in the successful attempt by a gang of confidence tricksters to convince cardinal de Rohan, bishop of Strasburg and Almoner to the king, that the queen's favour was returning and would be complete if he could negotiate the purchase of a 2,800-carat diamond necklace for her in secret and without the king's knowledge. It relied on the assumption that the queen could do such a thing. She could, she had, but in this case she didn't. In some senses – though this can be exaggerated – the Affair marked the true 'unraveling of the ancien régime'.[3]

The necklace wasn't really a necklace at all, rather a series of loops and chains that cascaded down the bodice – hence its alternative names of 'river' or 'slave necklace' because though it appeared to flow, it actually imprisoned its owner. Or would have, had it ever been worn. It had been created by Boehmers towards the end of the last reign out of 647 large diamonds and was spectacular for 'the size, whiteness, match and fire of the stones'.[4] It was valued at about 2 million francs (though the price came down) or 1/500th of the cost of the American War of Independence. Boehmers were hoping that Louis XV would present it to Madame du Barry, but they committed three mistakes: they made it 'on spec' without a commission and they banked on the longevity both of the king and of the style of the piece. Louis died suddenly before he could give it to his mistress. The piece was in the style to which Louis XV gave his name and was unsuited to the classicism to which Louis XVI gave his. Apart from Madame du Barry the only other possible candidate in France was Marie-Antoinette.

Although she was known to be fond of diamonds, it was almost a standing joke between queen and jeweller that Boehmer would drown himself if she did not take this expensive stock off his hands and save the firm from bankruptcy. She advised Boehmer to break up the necklace and sell the stones separately, which ironically became its fate. Louis himself is said to have considered presenting the necklace to Marie-Antoinette after the birth of the dauphin in 1781, and to have had it in his cabinet for four months before abandoning the project on receiving news the following year of the naval defeat at the Battle of the Saintes.[5] The queen herself proclaimed that the money would be better spent on a replacement battleship. The point to retain about Boehmer is that impending bankruptcy made him credulous. The key to the heist depended on the despair-induced credulity of the two victims – Boehmer and cardinal de Rohan.

Louis René Edouard, prince de Rohan-Guéméné, belonged to the same branch of his clan – or 'tribe' as their many enemies called it – as the bankrupt duke of the name. The family hoped that the cardinal would rescue its fortunes, but his extravagant lifestyle and a fire in one of his châteaux made this unlikely. His one hope was to become a minister, indeed a prime minister in the mould of cardinals Richelieu and Mazarin; but this route was blocked by Marie-Antoinette, whose resentments never faded. Many of her prejudices dated from her miserable time as dauphine. The fall of Choiseul had led to the cancellation of Breteuil's appointment as ambassador to Vienna in favour of Rohan, who was allied to du Barry and d'Aiguillon. That left Rohan with two disgruntled and self-reinforcing enemies, Marie-Antoinette and Breteuil. Marie-Theresa obsessively fed the fire of her daughter's resentment towards the cardinal whenever it seemed to be dying down. This was imprudent since the Rohan clan were still a power in the land, intermarried with the princes of the blood. When Louis XV's ministry was replaced in 1774, so was Rohan – by Breteuil, who became minister for the Maison du Roi in 1783. Since, as effectively minister for the interior, the Diamond Necklace Affair fell within his remit, he thought that at last he had his hated adversary within his grasp. But hatred distorts judgement.

Although Rohan had been Court Almoner since 1777, Marie-Antoinette never addressed a single word to the cardinal before the affair broke in 1785. When Rohan's relative the princesse de Guéméné had been obliged to tender her resignation as governess to the royal children, Rohan was deprived of a channel of communication to the queen. When his arch-enemy Breteuil formed a dynastic alliance with the new *gouvernante*, the duchesse de Polignac, Rohan felt that an 'iron ring' had been placed about the queen. He became 'obsessed by the threat posed to his political existence . . . by Breteuil' – and putty in the hands of Jeanne de Valois, the woman who became his nemesis.[6] By a strange irony, whereas the Rohan had only a tenuous link with the ducal house of Brittany, Jeanne was actually the tenth in line of descent from its last duchess.

For Jeanne de Valois, who masterminded the heist, was descended from an illegitimate but recognized son of Henri II (d. 1559), of the Valois dynasty that had preceded the Bourbons. Her improbable descent (recognized by the stickler court genealogist Pierre Hozier) was just about the only genuine thing about her. Jeanne, an orphan, grew up in utter destitution, begging for her bread with the plea, 'take pity on a poor orphan of the blood of the Valois'. She was taken in hand by a court lady and, having satisfied the court genealogist, received a small pension. At court she threw fainting fits in front of the king's sister, Madame Elizabeth, the duchesse d'Orléans, and the finance minister of the day. Each gave her money. One day her patron's carriage crossed that of cardinal de Rohan and an introduction was effected. They probably became lovers. Jeanne convinced Rohan that she had become intimate with Marie-Antoinette – who later claimed she had never even met Jeanne, though this is doubtful – and that she was beginning to soften the queen's hostility towards the cardinal.

Rohan asked Jeanne to give Marie-Antoinette a letter and Jeanne got her lover, a blond guardsman called Rétaux de Villette, to forge the queen's replies. Rohan treasured the ensuing correspondence of over one hundred letters. Now Rohan wanted to meet the queen. This request could have proved a stumbling block, but Jeanne plausibly argued that given the queen's public hostility to the cardinal, the meeting would have to be at night, in a grove of citrus trees the queen was known to frequent. Jeanne found a twenty-three-year-old shop-keeper who bore a passing resemblance to the queen – Habsburg lip, aquiline nose, fair complexion. She was called Leguay, but Jeanne, quite gratuitously since Leguay would be posing as Marie-Antoinette, gave her the name baronne d'Oliva – an anagram of Valois. At midnight in August 1784 the newly minted baroness, dressed in the flowing muslins Marie-Antoinette favoured, gave the cardinal a rose as a pre-arranged symbol of friendship. Then from the shadows Rétaux called out to be quick as the king's sisters-in-law were approaching. The fake queen then beat a hasty retreat and the cardinal was hooked.

Hitherto, Jeanne had merely extracted money from the cardinal, but now that he had swallowed the bait she raised her sights: she would get hold of the fabulous necklace by convincing Boehmer that the queen had commissioned Rohan to buy it on her behalf. Rohan was provided with a forged memorandum and forged letter purportedly from the queen saying she wanted to purchase the necklace but as she was temporarily short of funds, she was charging Rohan with handling the matter. She would be paying interest on the whole whilst she discharged the capital in four payments starting in July 1785. It was now January. If Boehmer and Rohan's judgements had not been affected by their different but equally parlous predicaments, they would have realized that the queen's signature, 'Marie-Antoinette de France', was not the one she used. She would have simply signed herself 'Marie-Antoinette' just as the king signed 'Louis'.

But Boehmer didn't just rush into it. He told Rohan that he would have to square it with the banker Baudard de Saint-James, treasurer of the Marine, from whom he had borrowed 800,000 francs to construct the jewel. No one knew, but Saint-James himself was teetering on the brink of a spectacular bankruptcy that would rock the financial system a year later. Saint-James – who like Rohan was in thrall to the charlatan Sicilian soothsayer Alessandro, count of Cagliostro (Giuseppe Balsamo) – raised no objection and Boehmer handed over the necklace to the cardinal, who bore it in his carriage to the tiny apartment at Versailles that had been granted to Jeanne. There Rétaux arrived, this time dressed in the queen's livery, to take the necklace, as Rohan supposed, straight to Marie-Antoinette.

As soon as the cardinal had left, Jeanne and her lover attacked the necklace with a kitchen knife, damaging some of the settings of the stones. Then Rétaux proceeded to sell some of the individual diamonds to the various Parisian diamond merchants and pawnbrokers. They were suspicious, however, because he was offering them way below value, and called the police. Rétaux was detained and hauled before Jean-Charles-Pierre Lenoir, the police minister himself. Rétaux told Lenoir that he was acting on behalf of a woman of standing at court, Madame la comtesse de La Motte-Valois (Jeanne had married a guardsman called La Motte who fabricated the title of comte). This was all technically true and since no robbery had been reported Rétaux was released without charge. Meanwhile the 'comte' de La Motte took the bulk of the diamonds to London to sell. The perfect crime. La Motte got 300,000 livres for the diamonds plus £8,000 in *objets de vertu* from jewellers in New Bond Street and Piccadilly. Jeanne sold over 100,000 livres worth.[7] This was a fortune for someone who had started life as a beggar. The La Mottes bought a substantial house in their province, filled it with bronzes and marbles, and entertained the local notables. Like many poor people who win the lottery, Jeanne had no idea of pacing her spending.

One cloud hovered on the horizon: Rohan asked himself why the queen was not wearing the necklace – not even on great feast days such as that of the Purification on 2 February or Pentecost on 24 May. Because she had not yet plucked up the courage to tell Louis, Jeanne plausibly assured him. But the deadline approached for the first payment. Jeanne then said that the queen now found the necklace too expensive and would return it unless she had a 200,000 livres reduction. Reluctantly Boehmer agreed, but Rohan further insisted that Boehmer should thank the queen. He wrote a note to this effect and found a chance of presenting it to her on 12 July when returning the diamond epaulettes Louis had ordered for her to mark the baptism of his nephew the duc d'Angoulême, which had needed repairs. She was about to read the note when the finance minster Calonne entered and Boehmer retired. After Calonne had gone she read the note, but it was riddled with obsequiousness and worry and the crucial reference to the necklace came at the end of the rambling missive. Mystified, Marie-Antoinette either crumpled it up (accounts differ) or lit it with her silver-gilt taper stick left burning on her desk, and refused Boehmer's insistent pleas to grant her another audience.

A crucial fortnight elapsed at the end of which the first instalment was due. The 'queen' now proposed that she would increase the first payment to 700,000 livres provided it could be paid on 1 October instead of 1 August. As a masterstroke Jeanne then came up with 30,000 livres from the sale of the stones to cover the lost interest. Handing the sum over to Boehmer on 31 July, Rohan egregiously lied in telling him that the queen herself personally had given him the 30,000 livres, which – a gratuitous embellishment – he said she had taken from a little porcelain secretaire by her fireplace. Rohan even specified that the porcelain was Sèvres.[8]

By now Rohan was getting suspicious. At the end of July he showed Cagliostro the contract for the acquisition of the necklace. Cagliostro may have claimed to have been born on the Nile some millennia ago and to have met Jesus Christ, but he saw through the contract: 'I'll lay money on its being a forgery,' he told Rohan and advised him to make a clean breast of it to the king. 'It's too late to go back,' he was told. The question arises: by the time Rohan gave Boehmer the 30,000 livres did he know that the contract was a forgery? If so, he was no longer merely a dupe – a line of inquiry that could have been fruitfully explored.

Jeanne now informed Boehmer's associate Paul Bassenge on 3 August that Rohan had discovered that the queen's signature was a forgery but that he would compensate the jewellers out of his immense fortune. Rohan was indeed prepared to do this to preserve his reputation, though it would have gone better with him if he had gone straight to the king and confessed. If Rohan had still had an immense fortune Jeanne's would have been the perfect hermetically sealed crime.

But Boehmer knew he didn't and went straight to see the queen. Still unable to see her, on Friday 5 August he told Mme Campan what he knew and from her he finally learned that the queen had never received the necklace. On Monday 8 August, Mme Campan told the queen and finally Marie-Antoinette contacted Boehmer but in a curious way, via her *valet-de-chambre*, who wrote a semi-literate note to the jeweller, informing him that the queen's *premier femme de chambre* (Madame Campan) 'has instructed me to write to you on the queen's behalf telling you to present yourself tomorrow morning, the 9th instant, at Trianon. Her Majesty wants you to attend to a diamond buckle whose stones have become loose. The best time would be between 9 and 10 in the morning.'[9] Coupled with the fact that the queen had fobbed Boehmer off for a fortnight, this pretext seems unnecessary if not actually suspicious. The queen told Boehmer to see Breteuil, who advised him to draw up a memorandum including the forged documents but omitting any reference to Jeanne de Valois: Breteuil wanted his enemy Rohan centre-stage; though he did, according to Castries, believe 'that the cardinal was guilty'. Breteuil gave this memorandum to the queen, who went to see the king. Louis' first reaction was to convene a council of the entire Rohan family. If Rohan had gone straight to the king, if the family council had been convened, the matter could have been kept within these bounds – like the Guéméné bankruptcy. But now it became a matter of high politics involving just about everyone of importance and one played out in public.

Monday 15 August was the feast of the Assumption of the Blessed Virgin – she was also the patron saint of the queen since they were both called Marie. There was to be a big service in the chapel royal and the first worshippers were assembling. As a man of importance, the king's ceremonial alter ego, Miromesnil, the Keeper of the Seals or justice minister, had already taken his place when a messenger summoned him to attend the king. Not realizing why Breteuil was closeted with the king, Miromesnil's legs turned to jelly – he thought he was about to be dismissed, for the minister for the Maison du Roi was the agent of exile. On this occasion, however, Miromesnil need not have worried. Breteuil was closeted with the king and queen, who had not even had time to have her hair done. Miromesnil arrived at 10 a.m. and Louis ordered Breteuil to read out Boehmer's memorandum, which as instructed made no mention of Jeanne. Miromesnil watched silently whilst Breteuil egged the queen on to seek a dramatic revenge for both of them: Rohan, he said, should be arrested in his full pontificals as he was accompanying the king down the aisle of the chapel. The queen and Breteuil had had five days to decide what to do and it is hard to resist the conclusion that they wanted to use the solemn occasion as a *coup de théâtre* to destroy their enemy.

This crisis, like the Dutch affair, found Axel von Fersen with his regiment at Valenciennes. There was no point in the queen turning to Madame de Polignac: 'her' minister, Calonne, would be working for Rohan or at least against Breteuil. So Marie-Antoinette bombarded Fersen with letters on 12, 14, 15 and 16 August. He must have accepted her conclusion that Rohan was a fraud and not merely a dupe, for that is what he told his father on 24 August, believing the crime to have been all the more heinous because Rohan was in receipt of pensions worth 150,000 livres a year. Fersen called it 'an abominable affair'.[10] Louis shared this opinion, writing to the comte de Vergennes on 16 August: 'You will surely have learned, Monsieur, that yesterday I had Cardinal Rohan arrested; from what he confessed and from the papers found on him, it is proved only too well that he has used the Queen's name by means of forged signatures to obtain from a jeweller diamonds to the value of 1,600,000 . . . It is the saddest and most horrible affair that I have ever seen.'[11] 'Horrible', 'abominable' – a common source in the queen.

Louis, however, still wanted further information. He sent for Rohan, who was waiting in the wings for the ceremony to start, and (this is Miromesnil's account) 'whilst they were going to find him, I said to the king "I have an obser-vation to make to you. You are going to perform the dual function of king and judge and I beseech you to forget that it is your wife that is compromised".' Then, in his recollection, he replaced the last words with 'that you are the queen's husband'.[12] Advice that should have been taken.

To cover his back, Breteuil sent a full transcript of Rohan's interrogation to his deputy, Louis de Crosne, the new *lieutenant de police* in Paris, Lenoir having been forced to resign in mysterious circumstances on 30 July just before the cardinal's arrest.[13] At 11 o'clock Rohan arrived in his full pontificals, scarlet soutane and white surplice of English make. The king asked him whether he had bought a diamond necklace in the queen's name. Rohan replied, 'Sire, it is true, I have been tricked.' Marie-Antoinette asked: 'How is it possible, Monsieur le Cardinal, that you could have believed that I would have employed you to conclude such a transaction when I haven't spoken to you these eight years?' It was eight years since Rohan had been made Court Almoner, and Marie-Antoinette had cut him ever since to show her displeasure at his appointment. Moreover, she added, 'the slightest reflection should have told you that this was not my writing which surely you recognized'. Rohan, shaking badly, 'did not answer her but turning to the king protested his innocence'. Louis told him to compose himself and 'write down this instant everything I need to know, anything you can find to justify yourself'. A fuller account, deriving from the queen, has Louis saying, 'It is natural that you should have some difficulty in explaining yourself; pull yourself together and to assist you in this, lest the queen's presence and my own trouble the calm you need, go into the room next door where you will be left alone. You'll find paper, pen and ink there.' The king and queen then retired to his adjoining library, 'leaving M. le cardinal alone in his cabinet so that he could write in peace'. Louis ordered the two ministers to join him in the library and there the four of them debated what to do.[14]

Miromesnil proposed delay for further investigation, but the queen continued to demand that Rohan be arrested forthwith. 'But,' objected the Keeper of the Seals, 'surely not in his pontifical robes – You are not Rohan's lackey,' replied the king.[15] Sometime later Rohan brought the king his statement, which introduced into the tale 'a woman called Valois' whose role Breteuil had carefully omitted. 'Where is this woman?' asked the king – 'Sire, I don't know,' lied Rohan, who had helped her to get out of Paris on 6 August and gain her native province. '"Have you got the necklace?" the king returned – "Sire it is in this woman's hands. I'll pay for the necklace?" The king told him to return to the cabinet and wait there.' 'Shortly afterwards the king and queen returned to the cabinet ... Their Majesties [plural] ordered' Breteuil and Miromesnil to join them. The king ordered Breteuil to read out Boehmer's statement to the cardinal and asked him about the queen's purported letters of authorization. Rohan said, 'I have them; they are forgeries.' 'That I can well believe,' said the king acidly and concluded, 'Monsieur in the circumstances I have no choice but to place seals on your papers and assure myself of your person. The queen's name is precious to me. It is compromised. I must take every precaution.'

Rohan begged the king not to have him arrested in front of the whole Court: 'May Your Majesty deign to remember your affection for Mme de Marsan who looked over your childhood, the glory of the maréchal de Soubise [one of the most disastrous generals in French history], the brilliant name of my family.' 'The king replied: I will try to console them as far as I can; I hope you will be able to clear your name; I am doing what I have to do as a king and as a husband.' 'Afterwards the king was good enough to write to M. de Soubise and to Madame de Marsan.'

There were two strands in what Louis said to Rohan. 1: I hope you can prove your innocence i.e. that you were a dupe not a criminal, but 2: you have compromised the queen, taken her name in vain. These two strands got conflated so that no one really knew what was at issue in the trial. So even if it proved that Rohan was merely a dupe, that, as far as Louis and Marie-Antoinette were concerned, would not be the end of the matter – a sort of double jeopardy. This report to the police minister shows Louis acting more in sorrow than in anger, as does his letter to Vergennes with its conclusion, 'It is the saddest and most horrible affair that I have ever seen.'[16] Marie-Antoinette, however, was merely angry.

The king then told Rohan to leave his cabinet and the baron de Breteuil to follow him out and arrest him. Breteuil caught up with the cardinal in the Oeil-de-Boeuf and told him he was arresting him: 'But we can't remain stationary here! Can't you guard me as we are walking along?' And with that he proceeded along the gallery. 'Fearing perhaps that he would escape' – disguised as a cardinal? – Breteuil summoned an officer of the Guard and ordered him 'in the name of the king to arrest M. Le Cardinal and answer for his person'. Besides, Breteuil had a more important task: to go to Rohan's house and put seals on his papers. But he was dilatory and Rohan for once thought quickly. He asked the officer whether it was in order for him to write a note – 'Good Lord! Do as you like.' Rohan scribbled four lines in code telling his secretary the abbé Georgel to burn his papers. When he was escorted to his apartments at Versailles he gave this to a servant together with a code and instructions to rush to Rohan's hotel. The story goes that the servant made such speed that his horse dropped dead on arrival. Certainly he arrived well before Breteuil. But the cardinal had been too foolish by half: the letters that were burnt – his extensive correspondence with the 'queen' – would have shown that he was a fool not a knave.

Rohan was moved to the Bastille, but it was in a luxurious annex of the grim fortress and he was attended by a suite of servants and entertained his many visitors with oysters and champagne. Nevertheless, his supporters wore the colours of red and yellow to symbolize the cardinal in his red robes lying on a bed of yellow straw. Under questioning he admitted that he had given the necklace to Jeanne, who was arrested at Bar-sur-Aube. Before that she had lived in such great state that she had dined at the château of the duc de Penthièvre, prince of the blood and Grand Admiral of France. She had turned up in a coach-and-six.

Rohan invited Castries and Vergennes to visit him in the Bastille. He didn't want Breteuil to come because that minister, in Castries' word, 'hated' Rohan. Rohan asked them whether they came as friends or ministers. If they came as friends, Castries observed, they would not be able to attend the cabinet committee that would decide his fate. It was this cabinet, held on 25 August 1785 with Vergennes, Castries and Calonne as well as Breteuil and Miromesnil present, that transformed the Diamond Necklace Affair from an episode of interest only to *la petite histoire* to a defining moment in the history of the regime. The Council met to decide whether the cardinal would be tried by administrative law by a panel of the *Conseil d'état* or by *justice réglée*, literally 'regular justice', the French equivalent of Common Law. If the latter it would be heard by the Parlement. Conciliar justice had come a long way since the Louis XIV period travestied by Alexandre Dumas when innocent men could be enclosed in an iron mask at the king's bidding. It was already on the way to being the modern *droit administratif* reserved for cases where the state was involved – and if the state was not involved in the Diamond Necklace Affair, when was it?

However, the queen, fully aware how unpopular she had become, wanted to avoid any appearance of the verdict being fixed: If Rohan could believe that she had authorized 'such a transaction', then a hostile public surely would. Marie-Antoinette had not attended cabinet before, but on this one personal issue she was able to insist that the ministers only speak to the king in her presence – which made her, in effect, a prime minister for the conduct of the Diamond Necklace Affair – and, as she told her brother Joseph, 'they have not been able to budge ... [the king] an inch'. She told the Council: 'I am implicated. The public assumes that I have received a necklace without paying for it. I want to know the truth behind a matter in which people have dared to employ my name. The cardinal's relatives want him to be tried by *justice réglée*; he appears to want this too. I want the affair to be judged by this process.'

After the queen had made her impassioned statement, 'a profound silence descended on everyone'. Without being asked, Castries broke it, arguing that since judicial proceedings in the case so far had been 'by exceptional justice' (*par voie extraordinaire*), they might as well continue as they had begun. Why not make Rohan and Jeanne de Valois face each other – after all, council decisions were meant to be taken adversarially. He drew a parallel with the special commission or War Council, which had been set up to answer the various claims and counterclaims arising from the defeat at the Battle of the Saintes, when the various parties had been made to have it out in this way. Rohan had told Castries in prison that he wanted such a confrontation. Castries came near to accusing his patroness the queen, influenced by Breteuil, of lying when he said, 'I think I can answer for it that the relatives [of Rohan], though they do not fear regular justice have not asked for it.' But Miromesnil observed that Rohan's office of Grand Almoner did not automatically entitle him to trial by the Parlement since it was not a great office of state like that of chancellor. He recommended that the king send him for trial at the Châtelet, Paris's criminal court, which was less of a theatre than the Parlement.[17] This court preserved its reputation for impartiality into the early stages of the Revolution, when the baron de Besenval, commander of the troops at the time of the fall of the Bastille, was acquitted.

Vergennes said little. He had links to the Rohan family and the queen was still trying to get him dismissed. But at this stage, he didn't know whether Rohan was an accomplice or not. He confided to the French ambassador to Vienna: 'I am delighted by this outcome [Rohan's being tried by the Parlement] which will dispense me from taking any further part in proceedings. I hope the judges will get to the bottom of the matter. As for me, the more I see of it the less I understand. What is inconceivable is how the cardinal could have been such an innocent dupe as he claims to have been.' So the queen, the de facto prime minister for the case, without taking a vote, took the decision: 'Very well! *My opinion is that the cardinal should be given the choice*, that he should convene all his family, that he should weigh everything and that he should make a decision, whether to take the path of administrative law or regular justice in the matter; that he should give the king his decision in writing; that the document should be signed by the whole family and that, whatever route is chosen, the matter should be dealt with swiftly because I am compromised.' 'The king said to M. de Castries: – You will go tomorrow with M. de Vergennes – and the baron de Breteuil will have to go as well – to bring this decision to the cardinal and in three days I will need his reply.'[18]

It is usually said that Rohan opted for trial by Parlement. He did, but only as a second choice. His formal letter to the king, countersigned by the principal members of his family, is explicit on this point: 'Sire, I had hoped by the confrontation [with Jeanne de Valois] to have proved conclusively to Your Majesty that I was the victim of a fraud and in that case I should have desired no other judges but your justice and beneficence. Since the refusal of this adversarial confrontation deprives me of this hope, I accept [trial by the Parlement].'[19] There is little doubt that if Louis had consented to Rohan's request, Marie-Antoinette would have participated too, as the comte de Guines had wanted after his recall. Perhaps that is why Louis turned him down as he had Guines.

When the ministers went to see Rohan in the Bastille to present him with his options, he exclaimed 'My God! If I were allowed to confront the woman I am sure I could discomfit her.' But they told him that instead of an informal confrontation in front of the king – not a trial at all – he had to choose between two formal trials, either by the Parlement or by a special commission of the Council, where he would have been allowed to cross-examine Jeanne.

According to Castries, easily the most reliable witness, Rohan was in a genuine quandary as to which of these second-best options to choose. It took him the full three days Louis had given him, whereupon he opted for trial by the Parlement. He chose as his defence counsel the celebrated advocate Gui-Jean-Baptiste Target – Louis was to ask for him at his own trial (but Target declined).

Castries notes that the charges in the letters patent sent to the Parlement and dated 'Saint-Cloud 5 September' contained the phrases 'criminal attempt' and 'the king's indignation that one had dared to compromise the name of his august wife and companion' – 'and they seemed too strong'. They were also too vague. Was there still a crime of *lèse-majesté*? Was Rohan being accused of it? The facts presented in the indictment were simply those we know: Boehmer had supplied a necklace to Rohan on the basis of a forged instruction from the queen and the cardinal had 'declared to us that he had been deceived by a woman named La Motte, called de Valois'. As Jean-Louis Soulavie observed, previous 'kings had run a mile rather than entrust . . . [the Parlement], the rival of royal authority, with any matter of a political complexion'.[20] This would be a political trial in the public gaze, an anatomical dissection of the political system by a hostile press. A forensic examination by a special commission of the Council would have raised the usual mutterings about ministerial despotism and the exile of the cardinal by *lettre de cachet* some more. But the dirty linen could have been bundled into a basket and incinerated. Castries realized all this but was ignored. Why?

The crucial early stages of the affair were decided by the king, the queen and Breteuil. Marie-Antoinette boasted of this to Joseph II in a letter of 22 August:

> Everything has been decided between the King and me; the ministers knew nothing about it until the moment when the King summoned the Cardinal and interrogated him in the presence of the Keeper of the Seals and the baron de Breteuil. I was also there and I was genuinely touched by the reason and force employed by the King in this harrowing session. The Cardinal begged not to be arrested but the King replied that he could not consent to this either as King or husband.[21]

The queen and Breteuil, whose ministerial department happened to be the relevant one, had persuaded Louis to arrest Rohan without making sufficient preliminary enquiries into the affair. Lenoir asked his successor as *lieutenant de police*, de Crosne, why he had not taken steps to arrest La Motte and seize the diamonds in order to discover whether Rohan were a dupe or an accomplice. Lenoir was told that de Crosne's superior, Breteuil, had not wanted the police bureaux to have anything to do with the affair but had personally given his orders to the senior police officers and the governor of the Bastille where Rohan was imprisoned.[22] As we have seen, Breteuil had previously advised Boehmer to draw up a memorandum including the forged documents but omitting any reference to Jeanne de Valois. By inculpating her he would be exculpating

Rohan. Lenoir, however, wanted to get to the bottom of the affair to clear Rohan, and inculpate Breteuil and the queen for whom he had no love.

Castries does not accuse Breteuil of doctoring the evidence, but of something subtler: not resisting the royal couple's precipitate behaviour: 'The baron de Breteuil put no obstacles in the way of the king's desire to have Rohan arrested which was confirmed', though Castries conceded that 'it would have taken a stronger man than he to oppose' the king's determination. But why give the cardinal the option of being heard by the Parlement? The comte de Provence thought that the queen, who at this stage 'did not know all the details of the affair but who did know how far public opinion had turned against her, wanted a resounding judgement to establish the truth'.[23]

Castries believed the business of pressure from the Rohan clan for trial by Parlement was a cock-and-bull story. Rohan also was clearly undecided about which path to choose – conviction by the Parlement meant imprisonment. But the apparently magnanimous gesture of Breteuil, in whose office the *lettres patentes* sending Rohan before the Parlement were drafted, can be explained by the fact that he clearly believed that he could sufficiently manage the Parlement in what was always going to be a political trial to secure Rohan's conviction. Rohan and his supposed partners in crime would be judged by the members of the Grande Chambre, senior judges several in receipt of royal patronage, and the Tournelle (criminal division) sitting together.

Breteuil was relying on the support of the 'ministerial party' in the Parlement, which Miromesnil had built up by means of a judicious use of sticks and carrots, including Étienne-François d'Aligre, the *premier président*, and Adrien Lefèvre d'Amécourt, the king's political agent. But it was not as easy as that: Calonne and Vergennes had their own faction in the Parlement and were secretly working for Rohan's acquittal, as was Vaudreuil. Vergennes had strong links to the Rohan clan; whilst Calonne was hoping that failure to have Rohan convicted would lead to his rival Breteuil's downfall and that of his ally d'Amécourt, who hoped to supplant Calonne as finance minister.

There is no evidence that Calonne wasted any sympathy on the plight of the House of Rohan; but Vergennes did. Whenever the clan was in trouble they turned to him. Vergennes, for example, had allowed Rohan-Guémené to sell the town and environs of L'Orient to the king so it could be used as a free port by the United States. He played some part in the proceedings in the Parlement and a number of the judges paid fulsome tributes to him.[24] But Vergennes' main contribution towards thwarting the queen was performed with such subtlety that the king seems not to have suspected him or at least not to have borne him any resentment, though the queen did both: Vergennes ensured that the witnesses who could prove Rohan's innocence were available. In particular the guardsman Rétaux de Villette, who had forged the queen's signature, was extradited from Geneva and, under threat of torture, confessed. He was the key witness – the others were window dressing of the kind used in the show trials during the Terror. It was more difficult to extradite the 'baronne d'Oliva', who had impersonated the queen on the terrace, because the local laws in Brussels forbade extradition without the consent of the party. In the end Vergennes sent a police inspector to Brussels to 'indoctrinate' – Vergennes' word – the woman (Leguay), so she would return voluntarily, which she did. What he promised her is not known, but at the trial she was acquitted, whilst Villette, whose crime was almost treasonable, was merely banished for life.

The case of Jeanne's husband, La Motte, who had gone to London, presented a different problem. The ambassador to London, the comte d'Adhémar, wrote to Vergennes, 'do not forget, I beg you, Monsieur that the Queen ardently desires that the Sieur de La Motte can be heard before the judgement'.[25] For he, like Jeanne, would have based his defence on the assertion that Rohan was working for himself and if the La Mottes had been acquitted, Rohan would have been convicted. Nevertheless, Vergennes, on the king's orders, tried unsuccessfully to have La Motte kidnapped.

Meanwhile Marie-Antoinette sought to influence the trial herself using Mercy-Argenteau, the Austrian ambassador, as an intermediary. Mercy had 'a long-standing relationship' with d'Aligre and, as he told Joseph II on 10 March, this enabled him to keep the magistrate 'on side'. At this stage Mercy was principally concerned to keep anything 'sordid' out of 'this strange affair'. He was worried that 'people were trying to muddy the water with extraneous incidents' – such as the 'sordid' nocturnal encounter of Rohan with the 'queen' – and 'sidetracking the main point'. He didn't say what this was. 'At his [d'Aligre's] request', and having consulted the queen, he put his ideas on paper. Not only did he give this, now lost, 'little document' to d'Aligre but to Joseph, 'because it contains a fact relating to his august sister'.[26] Using the Austrian ambassador was ill-advised of Marie-Antoinette.

These calculations were upset by the arrival of the forger Rétaux de Villette shortly afterwards, an event that changed the course of the trial. This was the moment that Breteuil had dreaded and Vergennes hastened. Hitherto it had been a question of claims and counter-claims by Jeanne de Valois and Rohan and no one, including the judges, really knew the truth. D'Aligre told Mercy that it looked black for Rohan; in particular, even after he had discovered that the queen's authorizations were forged, Rohan tried to get Saint-James to find the money, assuring him that he would gain the queen's favour. There had been a question of banishing Rohan for life, which would have involved the loss of all his ecclesiastical revenues and his ruin.[27] Now it was quite clear that Rohan had been the victim of a hoax and a wave of sympathy engulfed him. Not only were the queen's signatures false but Villette had also forged her letters, which had been burned on the cardinal's instructions.

At this point, in a modern trial, the judge would halt proceedings and instruct the jury to acquit Rohan and meanwhile prepare his apostrophe to *la femme La Motte* that society had earned a rest from her. Instead (and this is not generally realized) Marie-Antoinette, through Mercy, intervened. Mercy gave d'Aligre a draft of alternative charges that Joly de Fleury, the public prosecutor, should present against Rohan. Since Rohan had now clearly been duped, they must change tack and centre the accusation on the 'lack of respect for the sacred persons of the King and Queen, a monstrous abuse of the queen's name'. This draft was adopted by Joly de Fleury, who asked for a verdict of *hors de cour* (not proven) and/or that Rohan should apologize before the court for 'rashly' involving himself in the purchase of the necklace and 'even more rashly' participating in the nocturnal rendez-vous with the 'queen'. Marie-Antoinette and Breteuil were fully involved in the discussions. She wrote to Mercy, 'The baron [Breteuil] will tell you my thinking [on the trial]; above all nothing must be said about the [nocturnal] rendez-vous and the terrace (actually grove) and he will explain my reasons' –reasons which seem obvious to us.[28] Nevertheless the reference to the rendez-vous was retained.

Joly de Fleury further demanded that Rohan apologize to their Majesties, resign his office, abstain from appearing within a certain distance of the royal residences, and remain in prison until these conditions had been fulfilled.[29] Mercy fully realized that they were asking for 'a verdict which had no precedent in the registers [of the Parlement]'. And he fully realized the consequences for the cardinal. He would be marked with 'an indelible stain which would render him ineligible for any position'. The canons of Strasbourg would hardly tolerate having such a man as their bishop. Exile from the king's presence was 'the gravest sentence that can be inflicted on a subject', especially one of such eminence as the cardinal.

Joly de Fleury had not consulted his associate, the attorney-general Antoine-Louis Séguier, who accused him of disgracing the magistrature by kowtowing to the Court. Joly de Fleury retorted that it was no surprise that the attorney should support Rohan, given that they were both libertines. Séguier replied that 'he may sometimes have had recourse to prostitutes', but that was a private matter; 'and at least he had never basely sold his opinion'.[30] One can see Séguier's point. It was necessary and accepted that the king's ministers should liaise with the *premier président* and the law officers to assist the passage of royal legislation, the conversion of letters patent into edicts needed to have the force of law, but it was quite something else for the queen, through the Austrian ambassador, to intervene and do so with an 'unprecedented' proposal. According to Castries, 'these conclusions were so singularly biased, so evidently dictated by and for the Court that the Parlement reacting in the opposite sense did not pronounce a single word against the cardinal for his culpable credulity . . . and in short for all that he suspected and admitted it possible for the queen to have done'.[31]

The *grand dénouement* of the trial was on 30 July 1786. The accused had spent the previous night in the Conciergerie prison where, seven years later, Marie-Antoinette would spend her last weeks on earth. The session, combining both examination of the accused and the votes with speeches from the judges, lasted from 5.30 a.m. to 10.00 p.m. Jeanne de Valois appeared sumptuously dressed in black and grey silk with a velvet belt set off with cut steel pearls. She was indignant that the descendant of Henri II should be made to sit in the dock, but carefully arranged the pleats of her dress as if she had been sitting on a throne. She had a hard smile and gave a brazen, bravura display. When asked about a particular letter supposedly from the queen to Rohan she at first declined to reveal its contents out of respect for Her Majesty. Savouring every moment, her cross-examiner told her that it was her duty to reveal all, and with fake reluctance Jeanne revealed that she had seen 200 such letters in which the queen, instead of 'vous', had called Rohan by the familiar pronoun 'tu', which would become *de rigueur* during the Terror, and that several compromising assignations had been arranged. The judges let out hypocritical shouts of protest. For his appearance, Rohan wore the violet cardinals used for mourning and the seventeen members of his family attending wore black; after nine months of comfortable imprisonment, he looked a broken man and had tears in his eyes. Instead of the dock, he was allowed to sit in the area reserved for the junior members of the Parlement.

The cardinal was acquitted by twenty-six votes to twenty-three. What made it worse for Marie-Antoinette was that because of the pressure Louis or rather Marie-Antoinette personally had put on the public prosecutor to have Rohan at least censured, people said that 'they had lost their suit'. With what his biographer is compelled to call 'breathtaking hypocrisy', Vergennes informed Adhémar: 'People are generally surprised [at the verdict], and no one more so than I.'[32] His 'hypocrisy' was 'breathtaking' because if he had not had Villette extradited – and extradition was still in its infancy – Rohan would not have been fully exonerated.

Vergennes had very serious policy differences with Marie-Antoinette, stretching from the Guines to the Dutch Affairs, and, with Joseph egging her on, she was trying to get Louis to dismiss him. Foreign policy overlapped with domestic policy and Vergennes had inherited Maurepas' neurotic dread of a Choiseul return masterminded by Marie-Antoinette; even after Choiseul's death in 1785, Vergennes was haunted by his posthumous party, headed by Marie-Antoinette, Choiseul's political legatee, the only kind of legacy a bankrupt could give. Vergennes was tiring with only a year to live and Rohan's acquittal was personal as well as departmental revenge. But surely he realized that the damage to the queen's reputation would damage the monarchy he loved. Marie-Antoinette was fully aware of Vergennes' role in her discomfiture: Mercy notes that the queen accused Vergennes of 'displaying a partiality designed to save the prelate' at the expense of her reputation. He also noted that Vergennes and Calonne were 'decidedly against the queen and far from scotching the rumours . . . [against her] they rather took pleasure in stirring them up'.[33]

In the trial the decisive role of Calonne is evident. We know from a list of the votes compiled by d'Aligre at the conclusion that seven judges had been directly influenced by Calonne, who had a hold on four of them through suspending payment of their debts to the Crown.[34] This group was led by president Lamoignon, who controlled a further three judges.[35] In addition, Calonne's *ame damné* Lenoir used his influence in the Parlement, deriving from joint responsibility for law and order in the capital, to secure Rohan's acquittal. Lenoir had personal links to his cousin Oursin and professional ones with Lamoignon, who for years had been working on a reform of the criminal code. Lenoir had probably been dismissed by Breteuil to stop him from getting to the bottom of the Diamond Necklace Affair.

Calonne had used the funds of the Finance Ministry, that is of the Crown, to achieve ends diametrically opposed to that of the king. Calonne's motives were twofold. First, a passionate hatred of Marie-Antoinette, who had not wanted his appointment and whom he had been unable to win over subsequently: her *bon mot* that d'Ormesson, an honest fool, had been succeeded by a clever knave had done the rounds. As we have seen, Calonne had clashed bitterly with Marie-Antoinette over the purchase of Saint-Cloud. He had also replaced her protégé (and his deadly enemy) Necker's Geneva with Holland as a source for royal loans. A long list, on both sides. And if that were not enough, Vaudreuil, Calonne's friend and Madame de Polignac's lover, had promoted pro-Rohan pamphlets.

Calonne's reckless hatred of the wife of his sovereign was compounded by his detestation of 'her' minister Breteuil, who thought that Calonne was insufficiently grateful over his role in Calonne's appointment. They also had jurisdictional disputes over responsibility for policing Paris, with Lenoir in the crossfire.[36] Calonne, who never acted out of pure spite, had a practical reason for wanting to discomfit Breteuil. He calculated that the acquittal of Rohan would lead to Breteuil's dismissal and that he could take his job. As we saw when looking at d'Ormesson's brief ministry, a financial crisis in 1787 was likely and Calonne was pursuing alternative approaches to it. One was to make a virtue out of necessity and gamble on a comprehensive and therefore risky reform of the financial system with enormous political implications; the other was simply to cut and run by swapping ministries. But for that he had to bring down Breteuil by securing Rohan's acquittal. And for this he mobilized his faction in the Parlement.

Marie-Antoinette was fully aware that Calonne had orchestrated the acquittal of Rohan by the Parlement because the information on the voting we have presented comes from a dispatch of Mercy-Argenteau, who told her everything. The trial marks the beginning of her political education. Soulavie claims that she even went to the Palais de Justice to lobby judges and two years later she would be heavily involved in *parlementaire* politics, giving us the earliest information we have about royal preparations for the coup of 8 May 1788 against the Parlement. And, belying Soulavie's dictum that 'the queen could never understand that one needed the friendship of enemies', within a year she would be sitting in cabinet committees with Lamoignon, who had orchestrated the defence of Rohan in the Parlement.

The Parlement had acquitted Rohan of all charges, but his triumph was short-lived. The hybrid, not to say 'unprecedented' nature of the charges against Rohan was symbolized by his detention in the Bastille throughout the trial rather than in one of the prisons attached to the Parlement, such as the Conciergerie, which was usual for those appearing before that court. He was detained in the Bastille, 'because the king did not regard him as simply guilty before the law, but guilty as his subject and his household servant', to whom he would mete out justice whatever the Parlement decided. This was of doubtful legality even under the *ancien régime*, but Castries sympathized with the royal couple: 'They were all the more outraged by the judgement in that having declared that the queen's honour had been compromised, the king had a right to expect the Parlement to take this statement into consideration and at least pronounce a censure.'[37]

Accordingly, the day after the verdict, Louis wrote Breteuil the following letter, enclosing a *lettre de cachet*:

Monsieur, my Keeper of the Seals has just informed me of the Parlement's judgement in the necklace affair. Since the queen's name has been found to have been grievously compromised in this affair and since M. le Cardinal has taken part in it as well as Cagliostro, you will proceed to M. le Cardinal's residence; you will require him to relinquish his office of grand almoner and his sash as chevalier of my Orders.[38] I join herewith a *lettre de cachet* ordering him to leave within three days for his abbey at La Chaise Dieu where it is my intention that he see few people; from now until his departure he must only see his relatives and his legal advisers. Cagliostro will leave Paris within three days and my kingdom within three weeks.

Rohan had penned a letter of resignation that might have spared him exile, but it arrived too late. When Vergennes handed it to the king, Louis said, 'The deed is done.' But he added cryptically, 'they always move too fast'.[39] For the gods themselves cannot withdraw their curse. The implication of Louis' reservation is presumably that he had given Breteuil his orders without specifying when they were to be executed, but that Breteuil, in his eagerness to discomfit his enemy, had rushed in before Louis had time to change his mind, which he might have done on receipt of Rohan's letter. Perhaps Louis had wanted to show willing to Marie-Antoinette but not go through with 'the deed'. Provence, however, attested that he 'did not know the part she played' in Rohan's internal exile.[40]

Rohan was exiled to one of the remotest spots in the country: Chaise-Dieu is situated in the Puy-de-Dôme in the Auvergne at an altitude of 1,082 metres. This recalled Maupeou's treatment of exiled *parlementaires* in 1771 and even, to a public saturated in Roman history, the *relegatio ad insulas* practised by the Julio-Claudian emperors. Madame de Marsan, calling in exhausted favours as the king's *gouvernante* as a boy, beseeched Marie-Antoinette to have Rohan allowed to take the waters for his bad knee rather than be exiled to such a 'frightful and insanitary spot'. When the queen refused, Marsan drew herself up to the full height of her semi-princely dignity and declared that 'this was the last time she would have the honour of presenting herself before her'.[41] Rohan's progress to his remote abbey was a stately triumph: by speeding the cardinal on his way, the public could display their hostility to the queen. But for some, how to treat Rohan presented a dilemma. The bishop of Nevers jumped fully clothed into his bath to avoid displeasing the Court by receiving Rohan as he passed through his diocese on his way into exile.

After the trial, Marie-Antoinette sought to rebalance the court factions by elevating the Montmorency, the leading family in the Isle-de-France, which had been somewhat 'neglected', at the expense of the Rohan. Within a fortnight the cardinal's office of almoner was given to Louis-Joseph de Montmorency-Laval, the bishop of Metz, who was thought to have accepted with too great alacrity. It was said that, in recommending Montmorency-Laval to the king, the queen had also borne in mind that the bishop's long-term mistress was a Choiseul.[42]

A possible explanation of Louis' vindictiveness is that he remained convinced that Rohan had played a role in stealing the necklace as well as compromising the queen's good name. If we recall his first letter to Vergennes on the subject, he said 'from what he confessed and from the papers found on him, it is proved only too well that he has used the Queen's name by means of forged signatures to obtain from a jeweller diamonds to the value of 1,600,000'. The account that Louis asked Rohan to draw up has been lost, as were 'the papers found on him'. According to Madame Campan, writing long after the event, Louis consoled Marie-Antoinette by saying, 'in this affair people have only wanted to see the prince of the church and the prince de Rohan whilst in fact he is just a man strapped for cash (I am using the king's very words), and just saw this as a way of plugging the gap in his finances'. Jeanne de Valois, Louis added, had subsequently 'double-crossed him' and made off with the spoils. 'Nothing could be clearer and you don't have to be Alexander to cut this Gordian knot.'[43]

Jeanne de Valois was sentenced to a public flogging, stripped naked and tied by a rope, and branded on both shoulders with a V for *voleuse* (thief). Unfortunately, the public executioner, whom she bit, was so nervous that his hand slipped and Jeanne was branded below the left breast. What made it even worse (and attracted public sympathy) was that the execution of the sentence was delayed until the Parlement returned from its summer vacation, which began the day after the trial. 'The hungry judges soon the sentence sign / And wretches hang that jurymen may dine.'[44] Jeanne had been sentenced to life imprisonment but escaped under mysterious circumstances two years later and settled in London, where the publication of her memoirs created a sensation. Rétaux de Villette, who had forged Marie-Antoinette's letters, got off with life-time banishment, whilst the 'baronne' d'Oliva was acquitted. La Motte was sentenced in absentia to the galleys for life and to be branded with GAL, short for *gallères*. He quickly shot through his fortune and ended up in penury.

The popular belief was that Marie-Antoinette was in cahoots with the cardinal to obtain the necklace without paying for it. Soulavie is obliged to say he doubts this, though he hints darkly that there were secrets about the affair which may never be revealed and that Rohan went about saying that he was the only one who had spoken the truth but he was obliged not to speak the whole truth.[45] The *mot juste* on the affair was Castries': Marie-Antoinette wanted Rohan punished 'for all that he suspected and admitted it possible for the queen to have done'.[46] But the Parlement found that his 'suspicion' was justified. Had not the queen indulged her taste for diamonds in 1774–6? Had she not appeared on the terrace at night in mixed company in 1778? She was expiating the sins of her protracted youth. As always there was a grain of truth in the accusations against Marie-Antoinette.

In her misery, Marie-Antoinette could turn to Axel von Fersen, either in person or by letter. We left him at the end of 1783 when Gustavus had commanded Fersen to attend him on his travels and concluded that Fersen and the queen were not or not yet lovers. Fersen did not return to Versailles in the company of Gustavus III until 25 May 1784. The marquis de Bombelles dismisses the notion that these long absences were subtle ruses by the queen to throw people off the scent.[47] During these eight months Fersen addressed twenty-eight letters to 'Josephine', which Farr has demonstrated to be code for Marie-Antoinette. She had been christened 'Marie-Antoinette-Josèphe', after her great-uncle the emperor Joseph I, who was also grandfather to Louis XVI's mother, Marie-Josèphe. None of 'Josephine's' letters in reply has surfaced.[48] When Fersen was writing about official business, either in connection with his regiment or to Gustavus III, 'Josephine' is replaced by 'La Reine'.

In these years their love, rekindled in 1783, reached a new level. One can speculate why. Bombelles talks of 'the distressing fluctuation in the affections and opinions' of the queen. She was 'faithful in her deep love' for Madame de Polignac. But Yolande and her coterie excluded anyone with talent but 'lacked enough character to fix that of the queen'. So she was like a bird 'fluttering from branch to branch in search of amusement and direction. . . . Soon she came to the conclusion that men of merit no longer existed and gave up trying to look for them.' Bombelles compared her position to that of the king, left rudderless and surrounded by mediocrities after the death of Maurepas.[49] So she was looking for an anchor when Fersen returned from the wars. And increasingly he offered her political advice as well as love which, unlike Madame de Polignac's, was disinterested, if no wiser. He looked ten years older, having suffered a succession of tertian fevers in the West Indies where the French forces were picking up sugar islands from England, mostly returned after the peace. He had grown thinner and had also lost most of his hair and there were age grooves running vertically down his cheeks. But Marie-Antoinette was sensitive to suffering, her own and that of others.

Fersen's return makes it possible that he was the father of Marie-Antoinette's second son, Louis-Charles duc de Normandie, born on Easter Day 1785. Evelyn Farr considers that Louis' matter-of-fact diary entry points that way: 'The Queen was delivered of the duc de Normandie at 7.30. The arrangements were just the same as for my son [the dauphin].' But Louis doesn't write, 'just the same as if he had been my son'. Although Marie-Antoinette's sisters, the queen of Naples and the duchess of Parma, were known adulterers and the queen of Denmark had been imprisoned for no more, nothing in Marie-Antoinette's character or the French situation suggests that she would have risked producing a bastard, particularly as her elder son was sickly and her brothers-in-law were eagerly watching for any evidence that would have moved them nearer to the succession. On 4 April 1785 the comtesse d'Artois gave birth to a child said to have been fathered by one of her bodyguards. The child was spirited away and the mother was shunned by the royal family, only returning to favour in January 1786. 'She was rumoured to have defended herself by saying to the king, or the queen or the comtesse de Provence: "nevertheless my behaviour was the best of the three" – that is, of the three wives of the siblings Louis XVI, Provence and Artois.[50] Tittle tattle. The best evidence that Farr produces is a picture: there is a strong resemblance between Louis-Charles and Fersen's nephew at similar ages.

On 9 July 1786, shortly after Rohan's acquittal, Marie-Antoinette gave birth to what would prove to be her last child, Madame Sophie. Farr notes that Sophie was the name of Fersen's sister and heiress but concedes that it was also the name of the king's aunt. She also notes Louis' diary entry for 9 July 1786, 'the queen gave birth to my second daughter . . . there were no congratulations, no firework display and no Te Deum', and uses his 'indifference' as evidence that the girl was not his.[51] In fact, the king (perhaps wrongly) did not regard it as his job to order Te Deums and rather than indifference, his entry suggests pique that they had not materialized.

Marie-Antoinette had told Joseph that 'she was annoyed at being pregnant because she thought she had enough children'. Joseph sent her a scolding letter. It is now lost but its extraordinary content may be surmised from his covering letter to Mercy: 'I brought home to her the disastrous consequences of such a conduct if she ever wanted either for comfort or convenience to separate from the king in order to avoid having any more children.' Joseph clearly means separate beds rather than divorce, though he later said that in the latter eventuality she could always make her home with him. At the time of his 1777 visit he had joked that if she were not already married he would end his widowhood with her; and added that 'if she became a widow without having produced any children he wanted her to come back to live with . . . [her mother] and himself'.[52] Joseph now lamented that 'it was sadly the mode among young people these days to think that once they had produced one or two children they had satisfied their marital duties'.[53] O tempora! O mores!

I would suggest that Marie-Antoinette ignored her brother's advice and, having indeed 'satisfied her marital duties' by providing two daughters, an heir, the dauphin, born in 1781, and (horrible but useful word) a spare in the duc de Normandie, began an affair with Fersen after this with Louis XVI's consent. But not at first: Fersen spent ten months of 1786 in Sweden as captain of Gustavus III's bodyguard. He flirted with the king's sister-in-law, the duchess of Sodermanland, whom he called 'La Petite'. When Sophie told the duchess that Fersen belonged to Marie-Antoinette she was heartbroken. During this period Fersen's letters to 'Josephine' dwindled to one a month.[54]

On 6 November he was back in Paris and his affair with the queen may have begun then. Purely by chance of course, some gold coins, Louis d'or worth 24 francs, were minted in 1786 with a curl on the king's forehead that looked like the horn of a cuckold. Known as the *Louis à la corne*, the issue was soon withdrawn but not before it had been noticed. A strong piece of circumstantial evidence for an affair is that on 14 October 1787 an order of the queen's was sent for the installation of a stove 'in one of her inner cabinets with heating pipes to heat a small room next door'. On 8 October Fersen had sent the queen a letter, under her code name 'Josephine' asking her 'to arrange a niche for a stove'.[55] Many of Fersen's letters to the queen are lost, but the contents are referred to elliptically in his log book. The entry for 7 April 1787 contains, as well as a reference to the Assembly of Notables which he attended, 'plan to lodge upstairs'; and on 20 April 'what she needs to get me to live upstairs'.[56]

The fullest evidence that Louis became a 'complaisant' husband – an unfortunate word suggesting shame rather than generosity – comes from the memoirs of the comte de Saint-Priest. Saint-Priest had been ambassador to Turkey and the Austrian candidate to succeed Vergennes on his death in January 1787; he had been unsuccessful but was soon made a minister-without-portfolio and, after the fall of the Bastille, minister of the royal household and as such needed to know of Fersen's comings and goings. Not only this but Saint-Priest's young wife (who bore him a child in 1789) had a liaison of some kind with Fersen to whom she wrote a series of letters, seven of which have been published.[57] Saint-Priest writes that in 1788, the time of Marie-Antoinette's ascendancy, she told Louis of all the reports current concerning her relationship with Fersen, which she offered to end, though with the observation that given the disloyalty of most of the French courtiers, the services of a loyal foreigner might prove useful (as they did). Louis agreed, both as to Fersen's utility and the continuation of his wife's relations with him. With 'infinite tact' Louis would withdraw if he saw Fersen with the queen out of the corner of his eye; and 'she did not have to fear being surprised by him'. After this conversation Fersen 'rode out to meet Marie-Antoinette, also on horseback, in the park of the Trianon three or four times a week'. This caused a scandal despite the fact that Fersen was 'the most discreet of all the queen's friends'.[58]

With passion came risk. For his part, Fersen had always been serious and circumspect; now they both had to be. To avert suspicion he spent some time with his regiment at Valenciennes on the northern border. Dating a letter 'Versailles', he told his sister that when writing to anyone else he dated his letter 'Paris', and concluded, 'Farewell. I must go to the queen.' He avoided the Polignac set and saw the queen alone at Trianon in the evenings.

SIX

THE ASCENDANCY OF
MARIE-ANTOINETTE

1787–1788

T hree weeks after the miserable dénouement of the Necklace Affair, Louis XVI embarked on a tour of Normandy, his richest province. The focal point of the tour was a visit to Cherbourg to bless a giant cone, part of a massive dyke intended to create the biggest artificial harbour in the world, a safe space where a fleet could be assembled for an invasion of England should that prove necessary. Despite having just given birth, Marie-Antoinette repeatedly asked to accompany him – she too wanted to get out and rediscover popularity in the provinces. But it was man's work, a naval review, and he told her to stay at home. Still, he brought her back a basket of oranges that two children had presented to him on the heights above Honfleur and gave her 50,000 écus to celebrate their daughter's birth. The final stop was Rouen, capital of Normandy. News of the king's mingling familiarly with the population had travelled quickly and a vast crowd assembled consisting 'not just of the inhabitants to the town but those from the extremities of the province'. There Louis made a pledge it would have paid him to keep: 'that he would make up for his short visit by promising to return soon', and this time accompanied by the queen whom he could not wait to tell of his reception.[1]

The idea for the excursion came from the queen's protégé, Castries, in whose department all things naval lay. But the details that made the trip a success – updates on all the naval and civilian personnel so that the king could find an obliging word to say, and maybe the words themselves, were provided by the queen's by now deadly enemy, Calonne. Knowing that he was about to present to the king a dangerous course of action, he wanted to contrive a pleasant interlude for him.

The Parlement's acquittal of Rohan had not just been a matter of lobbying or even of justice, though it had been both. As Castries observed, the Parlement would not even censure Rohan, precisely because the king had asked them for it.[2] The Parlement was exacting revenge on the king for hurling bad-tempered invective at them on 23 December the previous year. Every year since he had come to office, Calonne had borrowed some 100 million livres, and the enabling legislation had to be registered in the Parlement. He said he had needed to borrow in order to 'constitute' the war debt, that is, to standardize repayment at intervals of the government's own choosing or, in modern parlance, extend the maturity of the debt. By 1786 the debt was 'constituted' but that did not mean it was discharged.

In 1787 royal revenue was 475 million livres, but roughly half of this went on servicing the debt. Moreover, this debt was increasing every year since there was an annual deficit that Calonne put at 115 million and his successor at 140 million. There were two root causes of the debt: first, since she had last enjoyed a surplus in 1738, France had been engaged in three expensive world wars, in Europe and in the overseas struggle for empire with Britain; and, second, the tax base was skewed with the peasants paying too much and the nobility, clergy and even the bourgeoisie paying too little. The government could tell the Parlement about the second cause and indeed had been going on about it since at least 1748 when limited taxation of the nobility (but not the clergy) had been introduced, but the *parlementaires* were noble themselves and resisted further measures of equality. The government was not obliged to tell them about the first cause because in contrast to England there was no system of public accounting and royal finances were considered part of the *arcana imperii*. Although this secrecy was an integral part of the theoretically absolute monarchy it was also part of the problem: the transparency of English finances meant that George III could borrow at 2 per cent less than Louis XVI. This goes some way to explaining why there was no revolution in England.

To reveal the state of the finances would be a royal derogation, but it would also have led to financial collapse unless, as Calonne argued, a remedy was provided simultaneously. Necker with his *Compte rendu* of 1781 had attempted to square the circle in a fraudulent way: seeming to publish the accounts but, by omitting the cost of the war, giving the impression there was a surplus. Calonne could not tell the Parlement any of this. It suited them to believe that Necker's *Compte* was genuine and they couldn't understand why, after three years of peace, the king should be coming back for more money, on this occasion 80 million livres. So they accompanied their registration of the loan with a rubric, that they had done it 'at the king's express command', that is not freely which was, Louis thought, calculated to deter subscribers. An angry king summoned a delegation from the Parlement to Versailles.

These events were of great concern to the Polignac set because some of the money had gone on them: with the advent of Calonne they had come to power and also into money. Calonne was their man and he had lavished money on them. Whether the amount he had spent on them and on prime pumping the economy encouraging trade and industry was a major factor in the Crown's serious indebtedness is a matter of debate. I am inclined to think that the root cause was Necker's paying for the war by borrowing at exorbitant rates of interest without increasing taxes, which was the normal way to pay for the war. But others point out[3] that the war was over by the time of Calonne's appointment and that he should have economized as William Pitt was doing across the Channel, dealing with a financial situation equally acute because of involvement in the same war.

Be that as it may, on the night of 22 December 1785 the Polignac group was greatly agitated. The duc de Polignac, 'pacing up and down', neglected his guests; 'the duchess only arrived when supper was served. M. de Vaudreuil collared her immediately; anger flashed from the eyes of this outspoken friend of the controller-general'.[4] When the Parlement arrived for the audience, Louis deliberately snubbed the deputation by only opening one of the double doors to his audience chamber. The king began chastizing the *parlementaires* for publishing remonstrances intended for his own and not public consumption, and for abusing his kindness to the point of 'criticizing my administration at all times and all places'. He emphasized, 'in short, I want you to know that I am contented with my Controller-general'. He concluded: 'I am going to annul a decree which is as ill-considered as it is disrespectful.' Then he took a piece of paper out of his pocket and ordered the chief registrar to record everything he had just said. To make quite sure Louis repeated: 'Is that quite clear; the decree must be printed as it now stands?' – that is without the rubric 'at the king's express command', though now it was. For Louis this was the central event of the audience, as his diary entry makes clear: '23 December: audience with the Parlement to score out its registers.'

The above account is taken from the diary of the principal object of Louis' rage, his political agent in the Parlement, Lefèvre d'Amécourt, who was supposed to smooth the passage of royal legislation but whom Calonne accused of treating its clauses with 'sarcasm'. Louis dismissed d'Amécourt on the spot. Although the scene was played out in camera, it caused a sensation. D'Amécourt's mistress died of apoplexy and it was hard to find a suitable replacement as king's agent. And there was worse: Étienne-François d'Aligre, the *premier président*, who had kept together a ministerial party in the Parlement for the whole reign, was alienated – one product we have seen was his lukewarm defence of the queen's honour in the Diamond Necklace Affair. Alienated from the king, d'Aligre was barely on speaking terms with Calonne. Miromesnil, the justice minister, told Louis that d'Aligre's opposition to Calonne was 'implacable' and that Calonne was 'fully aware how disadvantageous it will be to have at the head of the Parlement a leader always disposed to undermine his legislation. He ardently desires that M. d'Aligre should go and I cannot blame him.' Calonne tried to force d'Aligre to resign by dragging up two unpaid debts of his to the Crown. Calonne had sat on this knowledge for some time, hoping to blackmail d'Aligre. When this failed he brought it up in the Council of State. The king detested financial dishonesty and a dishonoured d'Aligre was ready to resign, but Miromesnil persuaded him to stay on and told Louis a cock-and-bull story that it was impossible to force a *premier président* to resign without putting him on trial.

Impasse. When the head of the judiciary tells the king that the head of the Parlement is prepared to block the legislation of the finance minister and yet he cannot be dismissed, the days of the classical structure of the *ancien régime* polity, in which the king and the Parlement governed the country without reference to the truly representative institution, the Estates-General, are clearly numbered. So what was to happen next? The Parlement would refuse to register another loan and Calonne even told the king that it would be right to do so. So there were only two alternatives: either Calonne should resign and hope that someone else, which meant Necker, could get a loan registered, or he should stay and increase taxes.

The recall of Necker would have been Marie-Antoinette's preferred solution if Louis had consulted her or her protégé and Necker's advocate, Castries. But he had told Castries 'formally' in 1783, and repeated it to Marie-Antoinette in 1785, 'that neither M. Necker nor his friends must dream of his ever returning to office'. For some time Castries was reduced to writing the king letters on Necker's subject, knowing that Louis would not hear him out. If Necker had returned at this juncture, one critical enough for the king to allow him leeway but not yet so critical as to deny him the means of exercising it effectively, the result would probably have been a fairly swift transition from Bourbon semi-absolutism to an English-style aristocratic constitutional monarchy. Louis would have been George III, whom he liked, though Marie-Antoinette would never have been Queen Charlotte.

Instead, another course was chosen in which neither the queen was consulted nor her minister Castries, who told the king: 'Your Majesty has determined the most important event of his reign without deigning to test my loyalty.' Castries was not exaggerating: it was 'the most important event of the reign' at least so far: a major financial and administrative reform with political, social and constitutional implications, a truly royal revolution that would have achieved much of what the oppositional one did without the bloodshed. Because of the haphazard way that France had come together over the centuries, with provinces added by conquest or marriage, each clinging on to its privileges and distinctions, the country lacked, in a word, uniformity. That is what Calonne was trying to create and what the Revolution would create by smashing all the bits together.

In a celebrated passage from the *Précis d'un plan d'amélioration des finances*, which he gave to the king on 20 August,[5] Calonne lovingly delineates the defects of the system (if that is the right word). The fact that the passage can now only be understood with the aid of footnotes underlines the regime's remoteness from logical organization:

> I will demonstrate ... that a kingdom comprising *pays d'états*[6] and pays *d'élections*,[7] areas with provincial administrations[8] and hybrid forms of administration; one in which internal customs barriers separate and divide the subjects of the same sovereign;[9] in which some areas pay no duties[10] and the rest bear the whole weight; where the richest class contributes the least to taxation, where privileges distort everything; where it is impossible to have a fixed and common policy[11] is necessarily a very imperfect kingdom ...[12]

In this credo Calonne established the battlefield on which he and his opponents would meet: the question of uniformity. Against Calonne will be arrayed all the forces of particularism, whether regional or social; all with the same basis of legitimacy deriving from usage. It will be a battle of ideologies quite as much as of politics: utilitarian versus legitimist.

For Calonne uniformity had two aspects: standardization and equality. Standardization was not just a question of weights and measures – one of the dullest achievements of the Revolution – but the ability to pass general legislation for the whole country instead of having to do multiple deals with dozens of areas. Equality had a moral content as well as a practical one: the unequal distribution of taxation was unfair as well as inefficient. The main direct tax, the *taille*, bringing in some 80 million livres a year, was paid only by the peasants. The nobility and clergy were exempt. Everyone accepted it as a given that the peasants could not pay any more. This would have mattered less if the nobility was as small as in England – just peers and their relatives – but there were over 250,000 nobles in France and anyone with 250,000 livres to spare could buy an office conferring it. The nobility did pay the newer tax, the *vingtième*, introduced in 1748, and if it had yielded 1/20th of the nation's GDP as its name

126

suggested, that would have been enough, particularly as in time of war an extra one or even two *vingtièmes* could be imposed. But the nobility were able to overawe royal tax assessors so that the tax yielded only half of its potential. The clergy did not even pay the tax.

To end tax evasion Calonne planned to replace the two *vingtièmes* currently levied with a land tax payable by all equally and without exception, which would raise the yield from 55 to 105 million livres. To prevent the assessment from being rigged it was to be performed by an elected three-tier system of assemblies – parish, district and provincial – whose composition was determined exclusively by the possession of landed wealth. It was not an egalitarian system, since the rich would have more seats than the poor in the assemblies, but it was radical in completely ignoring the traditional division of political society into Orders. Calonne also explained to the king that the new assemblies would be a powerful weapon for royal propaganda, though the king was worried that they could acquire a life of their own.

Many regarded the other measures as window dressing. They included the establishment of a national bank, the abolition of internal customs barriers, and the phasing out of the hated salt tax, the *gabelle*. Less noticed was Calonne's plan to eliminate ministerial disunity by centralizing government on the treasury, which might have made him an English-style First Lord of that department. Fearing for his own independence, Louis was less enthusiastic about this.

The king did, however, see the grandeur of the project and that though radical it was only the logical extension of the centralizing mission of the monarchy; or, as Calonne put it, it would allow 'the king to have completed in three months all that his predecessors had desired (or should have desired) to do'. But Louis feared that the reforms would cause 'an insurrection of the clergy, the great landed proprietors and all those who have a vested interest in opposing them', placing him in the dilemma of yielding, which 'would compromise his sovereign dignity in the eyes of the whole of Europe' or 'having to put down eternal resistance'.[13] With the decision so finely balanced and Marie-Antoinette neutral at best, my guess is that the Polignacs, ardent supporters of Calonne and, as we saw, incensed by the Parlement's opposition to his policies, swung the balance in favour of Calonne's proposals. Viewed in this light, the project was not some madcap improvisation but the culmination both of the policies of the king's 'predecessors' and of his own twelve-year working relationship with Madame de Polignac. It also affords an insight into why she was so unpopular.

A programme of such magnitude could not be implemented by royal fiat. But the Parlement would have rejected it out of hand, especially coming from Calonne, whilst to convoke the Estates-General for the first time since 1614 (which some sources say Calonne proposed and Louis overruled) would have meant the end of Bourbon absolutism. So Calonne proposed a half-way house: an Assembly of Notables such as had last met in 1626. The king would nominate the members but they would be taken from the same categories as in 1626, leading ecclesiastics, *parlementaires*, *conseillers d'état*, etc. The assembly would need to have prestige because the idea was that its endorsement of Calonne's programme would enable the king to have it registered immediately, easily and simultaneously in all the *parlements* by *lit de justice* without creating an impression of 'despotism'.

On the same day that Calonne presented his *Précis* to the king, Mercy-Argenteau informed Joseph II that Calonne

> is now trying to enlist ... [the queen's] support for so-called reform projects which in all probability will serve only to procure him some new onerous taxes to support the pillage that has become beyond remedy under the present ministry. The most sensible portion of the public believes there has never been a more dangerous finance minister because they are convinced that he will exhaust every resource and will not leave office until he has made it untenable for his successor.

Mercy concluded: 'At such a delicate conjuncture, I am trying to impress upon the queen how important it is for her reputation to avoid being tricked into endorsing any disreputable schemes which would alienate public opinion and compromise her.'[14] Marie-Antoinette took Mercy's advice, though after Calonne's conduct in the Diamond Necklace Affair she couldn't have needed much persuading. We don't know what if any pressure she put on the king – she later claimed she had been 'neutral', and because of his links with Necker 'her' minister Castries was excluded from the committee of Calonne, Vergennes and Miromesnil in which the king, after four months of deliberation, finally decided to convoke the Assembly of Notables. Neutrality was probably the wisest course for Marie-Antoinette: Louis had set his heart on implementing Calonne's programme and if she had tried to interfere he would simply have told her to mind her own business, as he did in foreign affairs; he would never have forgiven her, particularly if the enterprise succeeded. But if the whole thing blew up; if, as Mercy warned, 'there could be some catastrophe which could overthrow the state', she would be there to pick up the pieces.

In any case at this discussion stage, the main opposition to Calonne came from one of the members of the committee, Miromesnil. He advanced the classic thin-end-of-the-wedge argument, which he had expressed most cogently in relation to Turgot's modest reforms: 'the privileges of the nobility and clergy are unjust in origin: agreed. The privileges of certain towns and corporations are in the same category. Agreed again. Eh bien! I believe we must respect them because they are linked to all the rest.'[15] But whereas Turgot's modest proposals had been the tip of the iceberg, Calonne's revealed its whole mass.

Louis deluded himself into thinking that Miromesnil had endorsed the reform programme and on Friday 29 December 1786 he simply told the Council that he was consulting an Assembly of Notables on 'extremely important measures designed to ease the lot of my peoples, to eliminate several abuses and to restore order to my finances'. To add insult to injury the king tossed this bombshell casually at his ministers right at the end of the Council when they were already closing their portfolios.[16] Castries felt his exclusion keenly: 'Your Majesty has determined the most important event of his reign without deigning to test my loyalty.' Marie-Antoinette feebly assured him 'that for eight days the king had been seeking an opportunity to impart his plans to him without being able to find one'.[17]

In choosing the Notables, Calonne and the king had to steer a delicate course. They wanted a compliant body but one with enough semblance of independence to silence *parlementaire* opposition. To pack or not to pack? Calonne tried to insert his allies from the Polignac set: in his initial list of candidates their representation is particularly strong: the duc de Polignac, the comte de Vaudreuil, the duc de Coigny and the prince de Robecq. Perhaps Calonne and/or the king felt that some of these choices smacked of cronyism, for the most flagrant examples, Polignac and Vaudreuil, were weeded out along with the duc de Coigny. Some names were, in Calonne's phrase, 'removed as possessing court offices'.[18] So the final composition of the Assembly to some extent represented the 'outs' rather than the 'ins' at court. Of the Polignac set only Robecq was finally chosen, though the comte d'Artois chaired one of the seven bureaux or working committees into which the Assembly was divided. Even so a famous cartoon represented the Notables as farmyard fowl – geese, hens and turkeys – with Calonne asking them with what sauce they want to be eaten. The birds spiritedly reply that 'they don't want to be eaten at all' and that was the problem: Calonne was asking the Notables to vote away their privileges, but turkeys don't vote early for Christmas.

The opening of the Assembly, originally scheduled for 29 January was postponed until 22 February 1787 because of the death in harness of Marie-Antoinette's old enemy Vergennes. Although Vergennes had tried to block all Austrian attempts at territorial expansion, Mercy had come to regard him as the devil he knew and he thought that Marie-Antoinette's hostility to him had become demeaning. A few months before he had written to Kaunitz:

> The queen, in showing . . . [him] a marked malevolence has inured him to it . . . such an approach diminishes a great princess who should never display her hatred without being able to follow it up. The queen might have sufficient credit to have . . . [him] dismissed if she were capable of following through her projects with consistency and energy but her total lack of these two qualities renders her influence doubtful whenever pacing and time are required.[19]

In the end Time did the job without Marie-Antoinette's assistance, though she was later suspected of having poisoned Vergennes;[20] but could she influence the succession? This was a golden opportunity for Austria and during Vergennes' final illness Mercy pressed upon the queen the necessity of her using her influence to get the comte de Saint-Priest appointed. Saint-Priest was the ambassador to the Ottoman Empire and Joseph II hoped he would not stand in the way of Austrian designs on those territories.

However, Mercy told Kaunitz that though Marie-Antoinette still retained 'a penchant for her native land, attachment to her blood and friendship for her brother', nevertheless she 'was suddenly possessed of a scruple [which Mercy thought 'bizarre'] that it was not right for the Court of Vienna to nominate the ministers of the Court of Versailles'. She 'defended this thesis with the strangest of arguments', which Mercy overcame to the extent that 'constrained rather than persuaded . . . [she] made feeble efforts on M. de Saint-Priest's behalf'; but as she admitted in a note to Mercy, she did not press the issue because 'you know my principles', which Mercy took to be her 'scruples'. Mercy feared that Joseph's intervention would do more harm than good 'because he did not have a perfect understanding of the twists in the character of his sister'. Of his entire output of dispatches, this is Mercy's most revealing: of the queen, of himself, of the project, of his despair of ever achieving it. In fact, Marie-Antoinette had always felt a scruple to which the Austrians had wilfully blinded themselves. In the end she sent Mercy the casual note: 'M. de Vergennes died tonight; his replacement is bound to be little Montmorin.'[21] Montmorin, small of stature indeed, had been a successful ambassador to Spain during the critical phases of the American War of Independence. A former *menin* or official playmate of the king when a boy, his appointment was Louis' personal choice and that choice, whatever Mercy said, did not 'depend' on the queen.

And she knew it. Marie-Antoinette's 'scruple' crystallized the moment when she ceased to be Austrian and became French. It had happened gradually, the natural consequence of time, distance and motherhood – a strong emotion with the queen. She now saw herself as the mother of a future king rather than the sister of the emperor. At her trial she proclaimed 'motherhood is the strongest relationship' and in 1785 she had said that French 'in the mouth of one's children is the finest language in the world'.[22] Her German was getting rusty. In 1782 she needed German lessons, but didn't want brother Joseph to know.[23] For a few years after her arrival in France, when she said 'my family' she meant the Habsburgs, but the death of Maria-Theresa broke the main tie to her birthplace. In any case, she had never been the Austrian pawn that her enemies thought her and her relatives wanted her to be. But she also knew that in a foreign-policy appointment she had no chance of influencing the king. And there were bigger stakes to play for as the drama of the Assembly of Notables unfolded.

Everyone knew, including the king and Calonne himself, that the project he had embarked upon was risky – a gamble in a word. Castries had told Calonne, 'perhaps you will be crushed by this colossus [the Assembly] but your fall will be *brilliant* and given the hole you are in you are equally sure of falling if you do nothing and you would remain obscure and blamed'.[24] Marie-Antoinette did not need to do anything at first. From the start the clergy and Necker's supporters made a dead-set at Calonne, 'falling on him', as Castries puts it, 'like a quarry they wanted to devour'; and they seemed likely to mangle the provincial assemblies beyond recognition and reject the land tax outright. In the ministry Castries attacked Calonne before the king, working for the recall of Necker. In the Assembly, Marie-Antoinette's long-time candidate to be prime minister, Loménie de Brienne, the archbishop of Toulouse, acted as the Leader of the Opposition. However, the real Leader of the Opposition *in absentia*, a sort of non-playing captain, for he was not a Notable, was Necker, who had a powerful following in the Assembly – a faction which Calonne called 'a powerful and fanatical sect'.[25] It was headed by three bishops, Bordeaux, Nevers and Toulouse himself who, as we shall see, wanted Necker to serve as finance minister under his premiership; and three Marshals of France, Beauveau, Broglie and Philippe de Noailles, duc de Mouchy and grandfather of Lafayette, who, though Louis thought him too young, had wangled a place in the Assembly with Castries' help.

It was the clerics who masterminded the attack on Calonne. It could not be a frontal one since after all Calonne's twin aims were popular: to secure a more equal distribution of taxes and a measure of devolution. And though the Society of Jesus had been expelled from France in 1764 the opposition's approach can only be described as Jesuitical. The archbishop of Toulouse drew a distinction between equality, which was undeniably good, and 'uniformity', which was bad.[26] The Notables' objections to the provincial assemblies were first that the 'confusion of ranks' was humiliating to the first two Orders who, according to Brienne, 'would not attend if they risked being presided over or even preceded by citizens of an inferior Order and that then the Assemblies would become tumultuous'; secondly, the Assemblies were too dependent on the king's agent the Intendant: 'democracy or despotism'.[27]

Their objections to the land tax occasionally followed an old path: that the priest should give the king his prayers, the nobleman his blood and the commoner his money.[28] Generally, however, the Notables shifted the ground from the basis of assessment (with which it was difficult to quarrel) to the very nature of the tax. They objected that the land tax was 'unconstitutional' because instead of its being related to a specific need, its duration and amount were open-ended. Their underlying objection was based on the concept of 'no taxation without representation', which had been enunciated by the American colonists.

After weeks of captious debate, the king and Calonne took a desperate gamble: on Saturday 1 April they published the *Avertissement* or warning to the Assembly, an appeal over its head to the people themselves, the supposed beneficiaries of his measures. The 'people', conditioned by the Notables' argument that royal despotism rather than equality was the issue, did not respond, and the 'appel au peuple', as Lafayette characterized it, served only to make Calonne desperate with the Assembly. From that point on they determined not just to reject Calonne's proposals but to drive him from office: 'only the king's amour propre', as Castries noted, keeps Calonne in place.

However, the king's *amour propre* was no trifling matter. The Assembly of Notables, despite the prestige it had acquired, could not force a resolute king to dismiss a minister. The king had created the Assembly out of nothing and could destroy his creation when he liked. No one challenged this. So the only way that the 'cabal'[29] who sought Calonne's downfall after the appearance of the *Avertissement* could prevail was by undermining the king's confidence in his minister. But how to get at him? Apart from Calonne, the only person with unfettered access to the king was the queen. Whilst the issue of the Assembly of Notables remained doubtful, Marie-Antoinette had followed the advice of her brother the emperor Joseph II to steer clear of politics during this difficult period. She had told Besenval that she had remained 'neutral', though her protégés Castries and Brienne were actively working for Calonne's fall. But when the publication of the *Avertissement* seemed to seal Calonne's fate, she threw her hat into the ring. 'The queen', in the archbishop of Toulouse's words, 'strongly disapproved of the *Avertissement*', though it was two or three days before she could make her opinions known to the king.[30] Marie-Antoinette also played on the king's recurrent nightmare of a credit crisis such as had brought Calonne to power:[31] Calonne complained of 'the false alarm instilled into the king by the incredible allegation that in a week there would not be a *sous* left in the royal treasury'.[32]

And, as so often with Marie-Antoinette, it became personal. Calonne relates that, having complained to the king that the queen was openly criticizing his projects, Louis summoned her on the spot and told her not to meddle in men's affairs. Then, to Calonne's amazement, he 'took her shoulders and frog-marched her out of the room like a naughty child'. Calonne was appalled and 'said to himself, "I am undone"'. As Calonne's biographer Robert Lacour-Gayet observes, Calonne 'had the misfortune to witness a scene such as no woman, let alone Marie-Antoinette, can forgive'. At the end of his life Calonne told Napoleon that he had been brought down by 'an abominable intrigue encouraged by the woman who should have been the first to defend my endeavours and promised to do so' –though she hadn't.[33] And Calonne would be a dangerous enemy to Marie-Antoinette, both before and (especially) during the Revolution. Even in smaller matters he was a thorn in her side. In 1788 Jeanne de la Motte-Valois, having escaped from prison, arrived in London where she published her own account of the Diamond Necklace Affair, necessarily but also with relish embellishing the story of Marie-Antoinette's dissolute morals. There is some evidence that Calonne revised the manuscript to remove any howlers due to Jeanne's 'complete ignorance of Court usages'.[34]

Given that Louis XVI was totally committed to the reform programme, there was only one line of attack open to the conspirators: to make a distinction between Calonne and the reforms. The only way of saving the reforms, they argued, was to jettison their author. Brienne persuaded Marie-Antoinette to forward to the king a memorandum making this distinction and hinting that the only way to get the Assembly to endorse the reforms was by Calonne's dismissal.[35] Brienne also persuaded Boisgelin, archbishop of Aix, to write another anonymous memoir and have it 'sent to the queen', though he didn't 'know if it went any further up'.[36] This gave a potted history of Calonne's policies since 1786: turning to the Notables because he knew the Parlement would not register a loan, 'still less did he dare to propose a tax'. Boisgelin concluded that the Assembly could do nothing for the king as long as Calonne remained in office. 'There is no middle way.' The placing of these memoranda was coordinated with interventions by Castries and Miromesnil with the king. Castries told Marie-Antoinette that Calonne 'had to be got rid of';[37] whilst Miromesnil wanted his bastard son François Le Camus de Néville to supplant him: Néville 'told the queen that he thought his appointment as finance minister was in the bag'.[38]

The dénouement happened in stages over three days. First, Calonne, threatened by a body acting like the English Parliament, asked the king for a united ministry under his direction of a unified treasury. The king agreed to dismiss Miromesnil after Calonne gave him police reports showing how he had conspired with the *parlementaire* members of the Assembly to undermine his measures and publish pamphlets against him. He also agreed that Miromesnil be replaced by *président* Lamoignon, who had orchestrated the acquittal of Rohan in the Parlement – one enemy Marie-Antoinette *would* have to work with. Then Calonne moved to Breteuil, his enemy though he had played no part in the revolt. At this point – the details of the drama vary slightly – the queen stepped in. According to the police minister Lenoir, Breteuil was 'dismissed momentarily', but the 'queen caused the order to be revoked'. Castries has the king, his 'pen raised' to do the deed, asking for time for reflection during which the queen persuaded him to dismiss Calonne instead of Breteuil. Brienne has Marie-Antoinette saying that 'as far as she was concerned he could dismiss the lot of them . . . even the baron de Breteuil but it was essential to dismiss the finance minister and this she obtained', though 'not without difficulty'.[39] The archbishop of Toulouse specifies that 'a deal was done between the king and the queen on the [Good] Friday' when 'the king spoke to the queen [about the dismissal of Miromesnil] and she agreed to it but at the same time asked for that of the finance minister'.[40] In 1789 Marie-Antoinette came to regret her decisive role in the dismissal of Calonne. She wanted to have him dismissed but came to think the timing, in the middle of a crisis, was ill-judged.[41]

Marie-Antoinette did not consult Madame de Polignac, 'only informing her of . . . [Calonne's] dismissal an hour afterwards'.[42] The sympathies of the Polignac set for Calonne were undimmed: virtually the only member of the Notables to champion Calonne unreservedly had been Artois, attacking the nobility for their intransigence, and his outspokenness had done more harm than good. After his dismissal Calonne remained at Versailles, ostensibly to brief his successor, who was none of the candidates we have mentioned but the councillor of state Bouvard de Fourqueux. He was an ally of Calonne's and indeed drafted much of his reform programme and many assumed that Calonne, in his own phrase, remained as 'the minister behind the curtain'.[43] The day after Calonne's dismissal, Brienne sourly notes, 'there was a vast gathering in his apartments and a big supper. Madame de Polignac came twice during the day. Today she was there at 10 o'clock. The [queen's] Society makes a public demonstration of its regret'.[44] It was an act of defiance or at least dumb insolence towards the queen. Although Marie-Antoinette loved Yolande as much as ever, and though it cost her more than it cost her insouciant friend, the act would not go unpunished.

Bouvard was a highly intelligent and enlightened civil servant, the friend and associate of Turgot. At sixty-eight he was old for the time but it was also a time for old ministers. However, the reason why the king had appointed him – his close identity with Calonne's reforms – was also the reason why he could not implement them. He wanted to dissolve the Assembly, realizing that he could not do a deal with it. The king was tempted and the ministry divided. But the stock market crashed; Louis' bugbear of a credit crisis was becoming a reality and he panicked.

Here, suddenly, was a major crisis. An enormous deficit had been revealed where six years ago people had been told there was a small surplus. The remedy proposed at the time of the revelation was in the process of being rejected by the body summoned to endorse it. The Parlement was alienated by being bypassed and said 'this step leads to the Estates-General'.[45] The solution suggested itself: appoint the Leader of the Opposition in the Assembly as chief minister. The Leader of the Opposition was Brienne; except behind him lay the real leader of the opposition, Necker. Why not appoint them both? Only the queen could effect the transaction and she tried, though she was hated in the country and Louis had hitherto sidelined her in major matters of policy. It was an inauspicious time to enter the fray, but as Louis' morale collapsed into what we would call a nervous breakdown, the queen had to do what her mother had done in 1740, when she harangued the Magyar nobility; though the time to see what could be achieved by a woman on a horse, in Mirabeau's phrase, was some years off.

Again the epistolary approach to the king was tried. Louis detested Brienne for his atheism and suspected him as an Austrian fifth columnist, so there was no question of an audience. Instead, through Marie-Antoinette, he sent the king a series of memoranda setting out how much of the reform programme he reckoned he could get the Assembly to endorse. He wrote his ideas on the right-hand side of the paper and Louis put his comments on the left. Together over several memoranda they thrashed out a deal. The sticking points were money and the organization of the provincial assemblies. Brienne weakened his position by recalibrating the size of the deficit upwards. Calonne, now exiled to his estates in Lorraine, ground his teeth at this incompetence. Whereas he had painstakingly established that the deficit was 112 million livres, allowing for a contingency fund of 12 million, Brienne put it at 140 million livres. He had to accept the king's minimum stipulation for 80 million from the land tax and proposed 60 million of economies, of which the war department would have to bear 15 million, but 'only' 40 millions could be effected immediately. This left a deficit of 25–30 million, to which the stamp tax would contribute some 15 million. The new land tax would be for a specific sum, not an open-ended percentage, but would be index-linked to the price of corn.

Louis gave way on the composition of the provincial assemblies: half the seats would be reserved for the nobility and clergy, who would also provide the president. A feature little remarked at the time was that votes were to be counted individually (*par tête*) rather than a bloc vote by each Order – clergy, nobility and third estate (commoners). Few could have guessed that a year later this would be the burning issue of the day. The king got his way over the powers of the assemblies. The guiding role of the Intendant remained intact and Brienne agreed that 'these assemblies must only have executive authority'.

The opinion of Pierre Chevallier, who published the negotiations between the king and Brienne, was that the archbishop's proposals were slipshod and dishonest in their optimism and that Louis quickly saw through them.[46] However, Brienne was banking on having Necker serve under him as finance minister whilst he enjoyed the co-coordinating role of *chef du conseil royal des finances*, the role enjoyed by Maurepas and Vergennes, the leading ministers of the reign to date. As the crisis deepened, Louis came to Marie-Antoinette's apartments in tears every day and she had gradually worn down his resistance to appointing Brienne in some capacity, maybe to have him in reserve as a minister-without-portfolio. But her first priority was to have Necker recalled.

Necker, however, was in exile. Just as there had been the joint dismissals of Calonne and Miromesnil, so there had been joint exiles, on the same day, 13 April, of Calonne and Necker. Necker had been exiled for defying the king's order, delivered through Castries, not to publish his defence against Calonne's refutation of the *Compte rendu*. The pamphlet carried neither author nor title but began, 'I was a minister of the crown for five years.' Necker had it printed but kept it under wraps. He read it in Madame de Buffon's salon and she advised delaying publication at least until the end of the Assembly.[47] But, such was Necker's hubris that he sent a copy also to the king and queen. Marie-Antoinette also received a letter blandly assuming that the king would not take this 'defence of his honour and reputation amiss'. She did not reply but she refused Louis' request to forbid Necker from publishing.[48] Then on 10 April, with incomparably bad timing, not realizing that Calonne's dismissal had been imminent, Necker actually published his defence. Only too late, as with his 1781 resignation, did he realize his mistake. 'M. Necker,' Brienne notes, 'is desolate that the disgrace of the minister should have preceded the publication . . . no one is more put out than me by the timing of M. de Calonne's dismissal.'[49] Castries was summoned to the royal presence and subjected to a series of outbursts: 'He has published his book without my orders. He has published a letter he wrote to me when it would have been common courtesy to notify even a private citizen . . . He has cast doubt on my justice when I told you I would look into the whole matter.' And the king's rebuke was equally aimed at Castries' patron and Necker's advocate, the queen.

The publication was not the only reason why Louis exiled Necker. The underlying reason was that Necker was the real Leader of the Opposition, albeit *in absentia*. This is clear from the diary of Castries, Necker's ally and 'openly the patron of the *frondeurs*'.[50] 'The truth of the matter is,' he notes, 'that there was enough momentum in the bureaux [of the Assembly] to give rise to the fear that they would demand the appointment of M. Necker.'[51] The king wanted Necker out of the way whilst the Notables were in session. This Louis admitted to Castries on 4 May when he agreed that Necker could return to Paris, 'when my business is finished'. When Castries looked quizzically at him, the king explained, 'after the Assembly'.[52] The king would not be pressurized by the Assembly into appointing the man who, he believed, had destabilized his government for the past six years. This motive was confirmed when on 4 June, a week after the end of the Assembly, and without informing Castries, Louis told Breteuil to notify Necker that he could return to Paris. Castries confided to his diary that 'it would be too distasteful to serve such a master if one were serving him alone and not the state as well'.[53]

Thwarted in her ambition to have Necker put in command, Marie-Antoinette fell back on the suggestion that he be placed under Brienne, which is what the latter wanted. Louis refused this also. But since the crisis was deepening, on 30 April Louis asked Brienne to be *chef du conseil des finances*, an overall co-coordinating role without departmental duties. Brienne asked for a day to consider. And one cannot blame him – the final entry in his diary before his ministerial duties absorbed all his energies was 'the Bourse goes from bad to worse'.[54]

Next day, in the queen's presence, Brienne accepted. According to the abbé de Véri, Brienne 'sought to model himself on Cardinals Richelieu and Mazarin rather than on his two predecessors as principal minister', Fleury and Maurepas.[55] That had always been Louis' fear if he appointed an archbishop. So when they discussed who should succeed Bouvard de Fourqueux to work under him as finance minister, Brienne was in for a disappointment. Brienne told the king 'in the most formal manner that his devotion to His Majesty and his sense of duty forbade him to propose anyone but M. Necker whose talents and skill far exceeded that of all the other contenders'. But Louis persisted in his refusal, adding graciously that with Brienne's talents he did not need Necker's.

This is the version of events sent by Mercy-Argenteau back to Vienna. Another version, not inconsistent with it, has Castries and Marie-Antoinette putting pressure on the king via a ministerial deputation of Lamoignon, Montmorin and Breteuil. They demanded Bouvard's replacement given the drift in the Assembly and the slide on the Bourse. According to Montmorin's account, the three ministers had at first pressed for the recall of Necker, a plan Montmorin had concerted with Necker, eventually wearing down the king's resistance to the point when, worn out rather than persuaded, he had finally said: 'Oh! Well, if there is nothing for it, we'll have to recall him.' But he said it so sadly and so irritably that Breteuil was able to get Brienne appointed instead. Necker's daughter, Madame de Staël, saw Breteuil as the villain of the piece, arguing that the king would be inconsistent if he appointed a man he had just exiled.[56]

Jacques-Mathieu Augeard had insights into Lamoignon's role in Brienne's appointment. Four days after Lamoignon's own appointment Augeard warned him:

> The queen doesn't like you; it was she who got Calonne dismissed and it was Calonne who proposed you to the king. The queen thinks you intrigued against her in the Cardinal's trial; she knows that those who acquitted him were all your followers ... granted you have the support of the queen's Society, who were the friends and flatterers of Calonne but be careful: the queen is beginning to tire of this Society and I advise you to consider getting the comte de Mercy and the abbé de Vermont on board.

Augeard was 'certain that this reflection determined him to work for the elevation of the Archbishop of Toulouse to the ministry'.[57]

'Here we have a prime minister,' rejoiced Archbishop Boisgelin, 'made so by circumstances, by the queen and I think even by the king, who wants to abandon affairs to him.'[58] And 'abandon affairs' sums up the king's position. The defeat and denigration of his cherished plans and the blows to his authority all wrought a profound change in the king. It is from this time that people note insouciance about affairs in him, an apathy often engendered by depression. His hunting increased perceptibly: in the fortnight after Calonne's fall he hunted on 11, 14, 16, 19, 21 and 24 April.[59] Mercy-Argenteau wrote to Joseph II on 14 August: 'Against such ills the King's low morale offers few resources and his physical habits diminish these more and more; he becomes stouter and his returns from hunting are followed by such immoderate meals that there are occasional lapses of reason and a kind of brusque thoughtlessness which is very painful for those who have to endure it.'

On 19 May, Mercy reported that Louis came to the queen's apartments every day and wept at the critical state of the kingdom. This is in marked contrast with Louis' extreme reluctance to discuss politics with Marie-Antoinette before 1787. Dependence is also frequently associated with depression. In short, most of the characteristics, good and bad, which are commonly attributed to Louis XVI – irresolution, dependence on Marie-Antoinette, sentimentality, kindness – emerge only after the Assembly of Notables, which marks the great watershed in his life and reign.

Two deaths also facilitated the rise of Marie-Antoinette's influence, those of Choiseul and Vergennes, one a friend the other an enemy. Marie-Antoinette herself realized that 'the death of M. de Choiseul had removed a great bugbear', which people used to persuade the king to exclude his (and her) acolytes.[60] Vergennes' death removed not only an enemy but the man of whom Louis said 'I have lost the only friend I could count on, the only minister who never deceived me.'[61] That left his wife.

But just as Louis turned to Marie-Antoinette for support, she needed someone to support her, especially after her infant daughter Sophie, who had never developed properly, died on 19 June 1787. Fersen and the queen met more frequently but still carefully, using the small attic rooms at Trianon or above the queen's private apartments at Versailles: on 14 August they started writing to each other in invisible ink or lemon juice.

It was a critical time for Marie-Antoinette to be putting her deep unpopularity at the service of the monarchy. Two days before Brienne's appointment, Boisgelin observed that he 'was master neither of his own bureau nor the Assembly'.[62] Brienne had wrested concessions from the king – the provincial assemblies would have a strong aristocratic component and the land tax they assessed would now be for a fixed sum and for a fixed period. But Louis' promised economies had been trifling, which mattered because, assuming that Necker's *Compte rendu* was accurate, it seemed to follow that Calonne, with the king's connivance or lack of supervision, had squandered a lot of money. They had uncovered evidence of where some of this money might have gone and how it could be concealed by 'exemptions from audit'. Money had gone on supporting the stock market and on buying or exchanging the estates of favourite courtiers such as the Polignacs or distressed ones such as the Rohan family. Larger sums had gone on paying the debts of the king's two brothers; palaces had been bought for the king and for the queen. A new road to Saint-Cloud cost 84,000 livres whilst the 'annual upkeep of the château, park and gardens of Saint-Cloud' came to 200,000 livres. All this had been revealed in the accounts for 1786 shown to the Assembly and almost immediately leaked to the press.[63] So to prevent a recurrence of such expenditure they demanded the institution of a finance council independent of the king's control and including lay members. Louis refused point blank.

Given the king's reluctance to make what they regarded as meaningful concessions, the Notables were equally reluctant to give unequivocal backing to his proposals, even though these had met many of their demands. As Castries put it, 'they enveloped their half-acceptance in so many words that those who refused and those who accepted are indistinguishable and one has to unravel their opinions in fifty pages of print'.[64] And this was likely to be insufficient to overawe the Parlement when the government came to present the measures for registration. The Assembly of Notables was dismissed on 25 May 1787. Axel von Fersen attended the closing ceremony.

Marie-Antoinette's decisive role both in the fall of Calonne and the elevation of Brienne had a big impact on her social life. For ten years Mercy, Vermond and Joseph II had tirelessly but in vain tried to undermine her reliance on the Polignac set. Now their man as well as hers, Brienne, was finally in place. He set out to persecute – the only word – both Calonne and the Polignacs. For her part, Madame de Polignac

detested ... [Brienne] and the abbé de Vermond; there was nothing that these two men did not do to turn the queen against her, without being able to succeed. However they did manage to get this princess to limit herself to displays of a sincere and constant friendship. But ... she no longer consulted her ... merely informed her of her faits accomplis. Inevitably such a manner of proceeding, after the unlimited confidence the two friends had hitherto enjoyed, led if not to coolness at least to an embarrassed reserve between the two ... all avenues were closed on this side.[65]

On 27 December 1787, Fersen told King Gustavus: 'Madame de Polignac continues to hold her position. She is still as well [placed] as she was but since M. de Calonne's departure, the individuals in her circle are nothing and have no influence at all. The queen is almost universally detested.'[66]

But it was not only politics that led to a cooling between the queen and her no longer docile favourite. Another problem was Madame de Polignac's lover Vaudreuil whom Marie-Antoinette detested both as a person and as her enemy in the Diamond Necklace Affair, and as her rival for Madame de Polignac's love. Marie-Antoinette went as far as telling Yolande that Vaudreuil was not welcome at their gatherings. To which the favourite replied haughtily: 'if your Majesty chooses to favour my salon with her presence, she has no right to exclude my friends'. Reporting this remark, Marie-Antoinette later confided, 'I don't blame Madame de Polignac for it; deep down she is good and she loves me, but her associates have subjugated her.' Swallowing her pride, Marie-Antoinette was forced to send a valet to enquire who would be attending Madame de Polignac's salon that evening, and if she disliked the company she would stay away.

This was humiliating and could not last, and eventually Marie-Antoinette ceased going to Madame de Polignac's apartments altogether. Then between 13 May and 29 June Madame de Polignac, her husband the duc and her lover Vaudreuil visited England, ostensibly to take the waters at Bath. An English politician noted, 'Among the news last week was Madame de Polignac's disgrace with the Queen of France and expected arrival in England to form a female treaty of opposition, I suppose, with the Duchess of Devonshire', who arranged for her to meet cabinet ministers in an attempt to boost Little Po's 'reputation in France'. Georgiana 'almost certainly' wrote to Marie-Antoinette on her friend's behalf.[67]

Mystery still attaches to Madame de Polignac's visit. Was she exiled? Internal exile was the norm for fallen ministers: her friend Calonne had been exiled to his estates in Lorraine, stripped of the Order of the Saint-Esprit, made the subject of an internal investigation under the chairmanship of d'Ormesson, who exonerated him, and finally put on trial (*in absentia*) by the Parlement. Not surprisingly, he fled first to Holland and then to England, taking with him archival material for the defence he published later that year. But Madame de Polignac was still governess of the royal children, including the sickly infant Madame Sophie. In releasing her temporarily from her duties, was Louis exiling her? It was very rare for Louis to order external exile, that is deportation – that of Cagliostro had been an exception – and soon he would wonder whether he had the right.[68] The editor of Vaudreuil's correspondence dismissed all the wild suppositions about the journey and put it down to 'the need for a long-dominant coterie to lie low'.[69] To save face Madame de Polignac asked whether she could be spared from her gubernatorial duties so that she could take the waters in Bath. Precedents were consulted and it was decided that this derogation could be permitted, given the uncertain state of the favourite's health. A solemn farce. Unfortunately, whilst Madame de Polignac was absent, the youngest of her charges, Madame Sophie, died. Marie-Antoinette, who had become a modern mother, had tended her and given up her pleasures, playing no music for the three weeks of her baby's agony.

On her return, Madame de Polignac took up her duties but seemed much more serious than before her trip to England, and many thought she had lost the queen's favour. The salon in her apartments as royal governess continued to function as before, but mechanically without Marie-Antoinette. There was a piano, a billiard table and a card table, to remind them of the favourite pastimes of the absent queen. But Marie-Antoinette needed to relax in an intimate group.[70] In 1780 she had chosen as a lady-in-waiting the comtesse d'Ossun, by birth a Choiseul and married to a former ambassador to Spain, now a minister-without-portfolio who slept through meetings of the Council of State. Marie-Antoinette gave her Madame de Polignac's old apartment when the favourite moved into her governess's apartment overlooking the Orangerie.

Although a woman of slender means, Madame d'Ossun asked for nothing and, such was the state of the royal finances, received little. She contrived to entertain the queen on a budget – dinner for four or five, occasional concerts as a substitute for the operas Marie-Antoinette no longer attended because of her unpopularity in Paris. The menfolk tended to be high-born foreigners: Mercy-Argenteau; the comte de La Marck, who during the Revolution would be her intermediary with Mirabeau; the Swedish ambassador Staël-Holstein; and, discreetly, Axel von Fersen. Indeed, it has been suggested that the main point of the exercise was to facilitate encounters with Fersen that would have led to gossip if held in the rival Polignac salon.[71]

The Polignacs' salon ridiculed that of its rival. On regular evenings there were just the old familiar faces, but on Sundays there was a grand reception for Versailles and Paris. The thing was that the courtiers, even with moistened fingers to it, 'were uncertain which way the wind was blowing because they witnessed the daily displays of affection from the queen towards the woman she still loved as an individual.'[72] The courtiers were not the only ones confused by Marie-Antoinette's ambiguous treatment of Madame de Polignac. The public 'attributed a portion of the [financial] disorders which tormented it' to the queen's favouring the 'rapine' of her society, and though she now saw them at their 'true worth' she could not dispense with them because, as Joseph said, she lacked the internal resources to stave off ennui. Mercy-Argenteau lamented the unfairness of the public's identifying the queen with Calonne, given that 'this princess consistently undermined the murderous administration of . . . Calonne and played the biggest part in getting him dismissed'.[73]

If Necker's accounts were accepted rather than Calonne's – and they were because this version suited the taxpayer – then it followed that in the space of three years Calonne had squandered 3 billion livres. Because royal accounts were secret, it was assumed that this money had been siphoned off by the queen to pay the Polignacs and her brother the emperor. In the summer of 1787 Marie-Antoinette began to be called Madame Déficit. That appellation 'Madame' had a sinister genealogy: Madame de Maintenon, Madame de Pompadour, Madame du Barry, Madame de Polignac and now Madame Déficit. A term of respect became one of abuse when applied to feisty women whose power was resented. 'Madame' is an ambivalent word, in English and in French. It could be addressed to a queen – that was how even a king, Louis XVI, addressed Marie-Antoinette – or used to describe a prostitute. The queen would soon be depicted in cartoons as a powerful prostitute or harpy.

Because Marie-Antoinette bent over backwards to spare her friend public humiliation, many thought Madame de Polignac and even Calonne would make a comeback. Madame de Polignac, no longer the shrinking violet whose subtle scent had first attracted the queen, *did* want to make a comeback. Courtiers were like iron filings attracted magnetically to those who had or would again wield power and therefore control the purse strings. In the heyday of the Bourbon monarchy dismissed ministers were never re-employed because this implied that the king had made a mistake in dismissing them. But first Choiseul, then Necker and now Calonne had changed this. Choiseul had died in 1785 but the debris of his party, liberal, aristocratic, found their magnet in Marie-Antoinette. But those who favoured the traditional Bourbon absolutism and had profited from his largesse looked towards Calonne, the prince across the water, backed by the prince on the spot, Artois, who, given the poor health of Marie-Antoinette's children, might and ultimately did succeed to the throne.

This is illustrated by a letter which the princesse de Robecq, one of the Polignac set, wrote to Calonne on 17 July 1787 arguing that a political come-back could easily be staged from exile. The letter details the pressure which the Polignac group was putting on Marie-Antoinette. The duchesse de Polignac, Robecq told Calonne, made a point of 'telling the queen whenever she hears news of you; it is her way of preserving the right to keep your name alive'. The comte de Vaudreuil, she added, was sending Calonne a letter. To keep him abreast of the rapidly developing situation she told him that Brienne was having difficulties with the Parlement that made Calonne's seem trivial: 'the Parlement will have him dismissed,' she gloated. Or, 'as Mgr. le comte d'Artois told me yesterday, the Archbishop of Toulouse is little occupied with M. de Calonne and greatly with his own predicament'.[74] Diane de Polignac, the most forceful of the set, badgered Marie-Antoinette and extracted the assurance that Calonne need not fear prosecution.[75] He was prosecuted by the Parlement but the government stopped the trial, transferring the case to the Council where it languished.

The Polignac faction consistently worked to undermine the administration of the archbishop of Toulouse and they played a role in bringing it down. Apart from ideological differences that should not be underestimated, there was sheer ill will on both sides. There is no doubt that Brienne was vindictive: Calonne had been exiled; but was there any need to strip him of the Order of the Saint-Esprit, a disgrace that, as he bitterly observed, was 'without precedent'? Again, Brienne, pursuing his twin goals of trying to force Calonne's modified programme through the Parlement and showing willing by effecting heroic economies, took a positive pleasure in putting the offices of the Polignac set first in the firing line. Vaudreuil's post of Grand Falconer was suppressed – history does not relate what happened to the birds. Vaudreuil was also affected by the bankruptcy of Saint-James, but when the duc de Polignac proposed that the king pay Vaudreuil's debts in return for acquiring his West Indian estates, leaving Vaudreuil the income for his life, Brienne, who had discovered in Calonne's papers that the minister had given Vaudreuil 900,000 livre, refused point blank.[76]

The duc de Polignac himself fared even worse. Marie-Antoinette, who set the example by making economies to the tune of 900,000 livres a year in her household, asked the duc to resign his office of *surintendant des postes*, the post horses for the royal mail. This, according to Mercy, had been hived off from the actual delivery of letters (the *messageries*) at an annual cost of 600,000 livres in order to give Polignac an income of 50,000.[77] Polignac asked Marie-Antoinette whether he could discuss the matter with Brienne in her presence. There, having according to Besenval reduced the archbishop to silence by a triumphant demonstration of the utility of separating the horses from the letters, 'he turned to the queen and said, Madame . . . the fact that you have hinted that I resign an office that I owe to your bounty is reason enough for me to give it back to you and herewith is my resignation. The queen accepted it, the while praising his nobility and honesty; which did not totally compensate him for the loss of 50,000 a year but did not affect his good humour . . . with the queen, which he never lost'.[78]

The duc de Coigny, another member of the Polignac set affected by the economies, did not display Polignac's equanimity. One of the most wasteful extravagances of the royal household was the vast number of horses used with two separate administrations known as the Great and Small Stables, though both were large. The two were amalgamated with an annual saving of 2,400,000 livres, but the Small Stables disappeared and with them Coigny's job. Coigny 'had an inkling of what was about to happen to him and sought a private talk with the queen but she refused even though . . . [he], then at Trianon, was dining and supping with her and spent the whole day there'. Finally, the thunderbolt arrived in the form of a ministerial letter saying that the two stables were being amalgamated but that he could keep his title and some of the emoluments that went with it. This was not enough: he lost his temper with the king and though Louis weakly said he sympathized, in a fit of pique Coigny resigned his office and the right of his son to succeed him. Marie-Antoinette was furious at the lack of respect he had shown the king, who had expressed sympathy. 'Madame,' Besenval replied when she told him the tale, 'he is losing too much to be satisfied with sympathy.' Then Besenval added, with the typical insolence that characterized him, 'indeed it is frightening to live in a country where one is not certain to possess in the morning what one had the day before. This only happens in Turkey.'[79] 'Turkey' was code at the time for 'despotism'. What made it worse was that Coigny was 'almost the king's favourite and very well treated by the queen'. If this could happen to him, who was safe?

Axel von Fersen backed the economies even though his income as colonel of the Royal Swedish regiment was reduced. He told his father: 'the consequence of this assembly [of Notables] are great reforms in the Princes' households, but they chiefly relate to abuses and ancient pomp ... which serve no useful purpose whatsoever and absorb a great deal of money'.[80]

The princes and court nobility had come to treat their sinecures almost as property, rather as their predecessors in the Middle Ages had been given grants of land (actually under Calonne this had happened too). Therefore, though the savings were worthwhile in themselves and, as Malesherbes pointed out, were useful propaganda, even so they alienated many whose support would be needed. Perhaps even more dangerous: Brienne's reforms also affected the central civil service and the army. The bureaucratic head of each ministerial department, the equivalent of the British Permanent Secretary, was the *premier commis*, literally first clerk, but he was more, just as a permanent secretary is more than a short-hand typist. The *premier commis* at the treasury was Achille Gojard. Gojard was a closet Calonne loyalist and had surreptitiously sent him documents to aid in his published defence of his administration. He would play a key role in bringing Brienne down. Above the *premier commis* were the Councillors of State, who had important functions administering the embryonic administrative law in cases where the state was involved. Brienne cut their salaries. These were already slender, though many had private incomes. The councillors were authoritarian absolutists, too cautious to support Calonne openly in the Notables but disquieted by his fall and ready to defend traditional monarchy. Mercy noted that Brienne was encountering insurmountable resistance from the 'top administration'.[81]

The army reforms imposed by the newly created War Council under Jacques, comte de Guibert, a published military theoretician inspired by Frederick the

Great's Prussia, achieved the worst of both worlds: for a saving of 9 or 10 million out of a budget of 114 million livres, the reforms managed to alienate the court nobility, the provincial nobility and the upper bourgeoisie! That Marie-Antoinette was au fait can be seen from her letter to Joseph of 22 February 1788, concerning the reform of the king's military household: 'we are continuing . . . with our economies and retrenchments. The Bodyguards are being reduced to four squadrons of 250 men each. That's only a total saving of 160, but we'll make some saving on the squadrons' horses which cost a lot and are only used for parades.' The Bodyguards literally guarded the sovereign's body and would save Marie-Antoinette's life when Versailles was invaded by a mob on the night of 5/6 October 1789. She continued: 'The abolition of the *gendarmerie* [élite heavy cavalry] is applauded [*sic*] by all the military. It is a very brilliant corps but since the rank of officer has been given to all the gendarmes it would have been difficult to integrate them into the army in time of war because of the multitude of horses and valets they would have to take with them. The saving from this retrenchment will be used to reinforce the regular cavalry regiments.'[82]

The colonel of the gendarmerie was Castries but his star in the queen's firmament was setting as Brienne's rose (as Louis XVI had predicted), and he was not able to save the regiment, which together with the Gendarmes de la Garde, the Gardes de la Porte and the Light Cavalry also disappeared. The abolition of the gendarmerie uniquely managed to alienate both the aristocracy and the bourgeoisie. Its full title was Gendarmerie de France and it was the one crack unit open to members of the upper bourgeoisie who made the Revolution of 1789. Following on from the infamous Ségur Ordonnance of 1781, which restricted commissioned entry to the army to those with four generations of nobility on the father's side, it now 'became obvious that no corps offering commoners a career would be allowed to exist.'[83] People noted that though the Bodyguard, whose abolition had been contemplated, was saved, the Gendarmerie was not. But that hardly lessened the resentment of the court nobility who, apart from seeing elite regiments reformed and the vast number of superior officers and their salaries reduced, saw their automatic right to reach the rank of colonel within a short period of time and with little training or experience severely curtailed. The effect of all this is hard to quantify since it concerned morale. But senior officers would soon be required to put down serious unrest in the provinces (in 1788) and in Paris (in 1789). Can one be surprised if their hearts were not in it?

The War Council set up two training camps to test the reforms, one at St-Ouen under the prince de Condé, the other at Metz under the duc de Broglie. These two disaffected men subverted the implementation. Condé, who was to become the general of the Counter-Revolution, called the members of the War Council 'charlatans'. Broglie 'refused to implement the ... ordinances of the War Council, which had the king's seal of approval, without calculating the danger of such an example [of insubordination] especially given the state of unrest' in the country.[84] In May 1788 Broglie refused to sit in the plenary court to which Lamoignon gave the parlements' political powers. 'In both these actions he was supported by all three of his nephews, the Lameth brothers.'[85]

This 'state of unrest', known as the noble revolt, the *révolte nobiliaire*, which led into the Revolution, lasted a long time: from the opening of the Assembly of Notables on 22 February 1787, to 5 December 1788, when the Parlement conceded that it was not competent to rule on the composition of the forth-coming Estates-General. The first phase of the revolt was that of the Assembly of Notables, where the nobility resisted the king's attempt to make them pay their fair share of taxation but also to make himself financially independent and so, they thought, despotic. The second phase was marked by the attempt by Marie-Antoinette, Brienne and Lamoignon to force a modified version of Calonne's reforms through the Parlement, and when that failed, to remodel that body in the coup d'état of 8 May 1788. This period may be called the *révolte parlementaire*.

THE REVOLT OF THE PARLEMENT

On 6 July the edict extending the stamp duty to bring in an extra 25 million livres was rejected by the Parlement, which demanded a statement of royal revenue and expenditure and declared that only the Estates-General were competent to grant a permanent tax. Even the qualification 'permanent' was removed when the modified land tax was presented in July.[86]

Many have found this demand by the Parlement for the Estates-General inexplicable – political suicide, since the Parlement exercised a fiduciary political role only in the absence of the Estates-General. Marie-Antoinette realized that the Estates-General would eclipse the Parlement and saw this as the sole advantage of convoking them. 'The clue to the enigma' is provided by Malesherbes, recalled as a minister-without-portfolio to give strategic advice. The *parlementaires*, he argued, thought the Estates-General would not be a threat to them because they were only summoned occasionally, had no standing committee when they were not in session, and had no legislative power, merely making requests that the king could either ignore or register in the Parlement. Moreover, as the only members of the nobility with political experience, the *parlementaires* could dominate the noble Order in the Estates-General, which in turn would dominate the whole body. Another explanation is simply spite. Louis XVI, by convoking the Notables, had unilaterally shaken the structures of the *ancien régime* and had created in the minds of the *parlementaires* a condition of doubt as to the continuance of their political role: if the king could summon the Notables, the Parlement could go one better and demand the Estates-General.

Brienne's response to the Parlement's defiance was to have it exiled to Troyes (15 August–20 September), but the government negotiated. A leading part in the negotiations was played by Lefèvre d'Amécourt, who was now rewarded by being restored as *rapporteur du roi*.[87] A compromise was hammered out whereby the king would abandon his new taxes in return for a massive loan of 500,000,000 livres staggered over a period of five years, at the end of which the Estates-General would meet. Malesherbes wrote scathingly in memoranda he gave to the king: 'The deal, by which the Parlement was allowed back . . . was no more to my taste than the authoritarian measures which had preceded it'; since in return for the prorogation of the unreformed *vingtièmes*, 'the Land Tax (which I have always regarded as being the only good measure in this field) was abandoned'. Marie-Antoinette was more worried about the promise to convoke the Estates-General – she told Joseph II on 23 November: 'What causes me a lot of distress is that the king has announced that he will hold the Estates-General five years from now. There was such a general clamour for this that it was thought better for the king to anticipate a direct demand and that by laying his plans . . . he could avoid the problems associated with these assemblies.'[88]

The compromise was to be solemnized in the Parlement on 19 November. Brienne thought he had secured enough support to allow a free vote (the best way to ensure the success of the loan), and indeed the queen believed that during the debate 'the majority of opinions was for registration'. But, she added, 'the king presides over the Parlement as he does over the Council without being obliged to abide by the majority', so 'without counting the votes, the king said '"I order the registration"'.[89] Marie-Antoinette was wrong on both counts here: the king did generally abide by the majority vote in the Council and though he could order the Parlement to register without a vote, the rubric would state that the registration had been 'at the king's express command', the formula for a *lit de justice*. He could command the Parlement to register his loan, but if he did he could not command the public to subscribe to it.

At this point the king's cousin, Philippe, duc d'Orléans, first prince of the blood and the richest man in France, stood up, hesitated a moment, then stammered out: 'Sire . . . this registration strikes me as illegal . . . it should be stated that this registration has been effected by the express command of Your Majesty.'

Louis, a little shaken, retorted: 'Think what you like, I don't care . . . yes, it is legal because I want it.'[90] Shortly afterwards the king left, but Marie-Antoinette noted that Orléans 'remained in the Parlement and – this is what proves his evil intentions – took a ready-made protest from his pocket. He could not get it all adopted but he managed to get a resolution passed declaring the form of the registration illegal.' 'The king,' she added, 'has exiled him to [his estate at] Villers-Cotterêts, without permission to see any but his family and members of his household.' He endured a five-month exile. Two *parlementaires* were also imprisoned. Marie-Antoinette told Joseph: 'it is disagreeable to have to resort to blows of authority; sadly they have become necessary and I hope that they work.'[91]

This looked like a re-run of the conclusion to the Diamond Necklace Affair: a *parlementaire* ruling ignored and harsh exiles imposed. It did not, as Vergennes had said on the previous occasion, 'play well in Paris'. Everyone knew of the queen's unswerving support for Brienne – and if they didn't he boasted of it. So in their remonstrances against the imprisonment of their colleagues, the *parlementaires* affected to say that the harsh measures could not have been inspired by the king's kind heart (in fact he hated the Parlement more than Marie-Antoinette did), but 'must come from some other source' – namely, the queen. From the bungled *séance royale* to a final confrontation with the Parlement was only a matter of time. The first clear details of the plan – and this is the measure of her new involvement in government – come in a letter of Marie-Antoinette to her brother Joseph of 24 April 1788:

> We are about to make great changes in the parlements . . . The idea is to confine them to the function of judges and to create another assembly which will have the right to register taxes and general laws for the [whole] kingdom. I think we have taken all the measures and precautions compatible with the necessary secrecy; but this very secrecy involves uncertainty about the attitude of large numbers of people who can make or break the operation . . .[92]

The idea of removing the judiciary from politics and conferring their powers on 'another assembly' (a plenary court) was radical: Maupeou had merely changed the personnel of the Parlement. It also, as Marie-Antoinette says, would have enabled the king 'to register taxes and general laws for the [whole] Kingdom' rather than see the twelve local parlements try to modify them in accordance with the local constitutions. Not only would the Parlement be confined to their judicial functions but even these would be reduced since the vast jurisdiction of the Parlement of Paris – nearly half of France – would be carved up and distributed among local *grand baillages*, which would make justice more accessible. It would also be cheaper since the *épices*, or gratuities that litigants were obliged to give the judges, were abolished.

Lamoignon, the justice minister, sought to diminish the parlements' hold over the people by confining the cases they dealt with to the rare civil cases involving sums of over 20,000 livres, criminal charges against nobles, and a few specialized cases. His reform of criminal procedure represented the work of a lifetime. He abolished the *question préalable* by which a condemned man was tortured to reveal his accomplices, and virtually abolished seigneurial justice by insisting that a manorial court be equipped with a strong prison and a graduate judge.[93]

On 6 May the members of the Parlement received *lettres de cachet* summoning them to Versailles for 8 May. There, after telling them that 'there was no transgression they had not committed over the past year', the king registered the edicts and ordered the Parlement, without protesting, to go on vacation until the new order had come into being. They complied. Paris remained calm. Indeed, on 26 May, Antoine de Gontaut, duc de Biron, colonel of the French Guards, complained to Breteuil of the excessive deployment of troops, 'considering the calm which obtains . . . throughout Paris'.[94] The king and Marie-Antoinette felt able to visit the Invalides, and Artois the royal gardens, and the royal family spent a few weeks at the newly acquired château of Saint-Cloud, on the outskirts of the capital.

In the provinces, however, the May Edicts led to a period of serious disorder. Some hardliners suggested that Louis put himself at the head of his troops and crush the disturbances in the worst-affected province, Brittany, 'without fearing the consequences of civil war',[95] a course Louis was consistently to reject. In July the Breton nobility sent a twelve-man deputation to Versailles to protest against the Edicts. They were arrested in the dead of night and conveyed to the Bastille.

They had been dining in the Marais at a reception given by their supporters. One of these was the comte de Boisgelin, brother of Archbishop Boisgelin who had sent Marie-Antoinette the memorandum denouncing Calonne. The comte was master of the wardrobe, a plum court office, which made his rebellion all the more heinous in the king's eyes. On 15 July, Louis took his revenge: 'Given your conduct over the past fortnight, it will come as no surprise that I am asking you to resign your office of Master of the Wardrobe . . . and that I forbid you to appear at Court. It is from those who are in closest attendance on me and serve my person that I am entitled to expect the greatest zeal and loyalty.'[96] He was replaced by the duc de La Rochefoucauld-Liancourt, who proved to be no more loyal.

Boisgelin was a Breton, as was another diner, the duc de Rohan-Chabot; but others with no connection to the province, such as the duc de Choiseul-Praslin, simply wanted to defy the government. Praslin's wife was stripped of her court appointment. Another of those at the reception was the ubiquitous Lafayette (who came from the Auvergne) – he kept his military rank but lost his command. The ambassador to Portugal, Bombelles, commented: 'As for M. de La Fayette, a lot of people are asking why he wants to be mixed up in everything, given that he is intrinsically nothing.'[97] Marie-Antoinette also wondered why an Auvergnat like Lafayette should have got involved. When this was reported to him, Lafayette made the sinister riposte that he was 'Breton in the same way that she was Austrian', in other words through his mother.[98]

Breteuil refused to sign the *lettres de cachet* committing the Breton deputies to the Bastille, and resigned (25 July). He no longer believed in the system he had played such a large part in undermining and had, for some time, been advocating a written constitution.[99] It may be that his resignation was designed to bring about the fall of the Brienne-Lamoignon duumvirate and his own elevation to Chef du Conseil royal. Certainly his friends were working for this.[100] Maybe he was just jealous of being supplanted by Brienne in the queen's political affections.

Marie-Antoinette was furious at what she rightly regarded as an act of disloyalty at a moment of crisis. Breteuil had wanted to inform the queen before formally handing in his resignation to the king. In a 'letter calculated to hurt' she refused to grant him an audience. Two days later she relented and sent him a kindly letter asking him to see her at the Petit-Trianon between one and two o'clock. She asked Breteuil to stay on as a minister-without-portfolio. He refused. The audience lasted only three minutes but the queen did say that if Breteuil ever wanted anything he had only to ask.[101]

Afterwards Breteuil gave a grand farewell reception. His acolyte, Bombelles, was rather offended to see that one of the guests was Marie-Antoinette's old bugbear Madame du Barry. In Bombelles' opinion, she 'was no longer beautiful; nor did she display the poise she was said to have acquired' to compensate. Another guest, significantly, was the duchesse de Praslin, who had been dismissed from her court post for attending the Breton gathering.[102]

It is hard to assess whether the provincial revolt extended much beyond Brittany and the towns boasting a parlement, especially Grenoble, the capital of Dauphiné, which asked for the restoration of its provincial estates. These were granted but when the government tried to impose conditions Barnave wrote a pamphlet arguing, 'God wishes that we should be faithful to the king . . . but when a good king is deceived by bad ministers, God wishes that the people should do all that it can to hinder the evils and they are working to enlighten the king.'[103] For such an original thinker as Barnave this was fairly conventional stuff and ignored the role of the queen, but the next step inspired by him and Mounier was not. The estates of Dauphiné decided that the Third Estate should have the same number of deputies as the other two Orders combined and that voting should be in common. This was already the case in the new provincial assemblies but to modify an existing institution was different and the Dauphiné model became a template for what the Third Estate required when the Estates-General should meet.

Meanwhile the king was told that 'the four corners of the kingdom were on fire' for, according to Bombelles, Louis was 'surrounded by a faction [Artois and the Polignacs], opposed to the Archbishop'.[104] Brienne wanted to exile the governor of Artois' two boys, but the prince said if that happened he would join them. Madame de Polignac assured Marie-Antoinette that she was not 'pushing any of her friends [Calonne] but merely wanted to rid the Court and the Nation of a man who had never had a settled strategy'.

Calonne backed this up by writing his *Lettre au Roi* from his English exile denouncing the coup d'état – a letter that is a milestone on his journey towards becoming prime minister of the Counter-Revolution. Brienne, he wrote, had made the king 'march his troops against his own subjects', exiled a 'prince of your blood' (Orléans), 'exiled three parlements . . . and shown his displeasure to them all' and 'filled the state prisons with the deputies of your provinces'. And why had he 'changed a key element in the ancient constitution of the kingdom? To make himself master of the registration [of edicts]'. Yet had not that been in effect the objective of Calonne's convocation of the Notables?[105] If Calonne's reaction to the May Edicts was surprising, the reaction of his enemy Miromesnil, whom Brienne sometimes consulted, was predictable: 'I would certainly not have advised him to create his plenary court or to employ any violence to introduce taxation.'[106]

However, whatever the Polignacs may have hoped, there was no chance of Calonne's return at this juncture – he was just too unpopular. And the only real alternative to Brienne was Necker – their deadly enemy who had been Marie-Antoinette's first choice to succeed Calonne. All the Polignacs could hope for was a suicidal revenge. And this attitude, together with its close relative the *politique du pire*, played a part in the outbreak of the Revolution. After all was not the Parlement, in calling for the Estates-General, also seeking a suicidal revenge?

But perhaps, already, the Polignacs had the baron de Breteuil in mind as they would the following April. He had been their ally until he found a better match for his granddaughter (her marriage to the son of the duc de Luxembourg was celebrated in June with enormous grandeur and at an enormous expense resented by the duc).[107] Breteuil's reasons for resigning as minister for the royal household remain mysterious to this day. Bombelles had his feet firmly planted in the Polignac and Breteuil camps and maybe acted as a go-between.

Bombelles, who had been 'permitted to attend her toilette', noted that Madame de Polignac, 'still the prettiest woman at court', was enjoying 'a return to the highest favour' with the queen as regards 'sterile external honours', but that 'it is still the Archbishop who governs absolutely'.[108] Nevertheless, Madame de Polignac's political influence was also beginning to reassert itself. Towards the end of July, Marie-Antoinette confided in Yolande, 'I only have two real friends in the world, you and the comte d'Esterhazy' – a favourite from happier days. She made no mention of Axel von Fersen. Walking in the Trianon gardens, the queen continued in the tragic vein that was now becoming habitual with her.

> How unfortunate she was to have chosen as principal minister a man who had enjoyed the reputation of eminent merit but who had rendered himself odious to the nation; how cruel it was to see herself hated when all she had wanted was the good of France; and at the same time to see her eldest son in such a parlous state and her brother humiliated in all his projects [Joseph's wars were going wrong and his peoples were in rebellion against reforms similar to the ones she was trying to impose]. 'Do you know a woman more to be pitied than me?'

Although he did pity her, Bombelles, who recounts these words, probably supplied by Madame de Polignac herself, thought Marie-Antoinette had only herself to blame because 'instead of remaining satisfied with the fine role of Queen of France, she wanted to be its king as well. Blinded by amour-propre and believing herself to be superior to the king her husband, she thought that this superiority would extend to events and the conduct of a machine too strong for her.' The abbé de Véri went as far as to say that 'people habitually referred to the queen's authority more than the king's'.[109]

As a diplomat, Bombelles also blamed her for trying to further her brother Joseph's expansionist ideas, and her mother Maria-Theresa for placing her brood of feisty daughters on half the thrones of Europe with the same aim in view.[110] But 'this vast enterprise could only have worked' if the empress-queen had been able 'to transmit to her children' all her qualities: constancy in adversity, wisdom, consistency, 'kindness to her subjects, and grace to foreigners'. If any one of these qualities was missing, Bombelles added with what we would call male chauvinism, a queen should stick to the 'gentle and tranquil virtues' associated with their sex. Needlework was suggested and, within that discipline, crochet: one day, passing through the Oeil-de-Boeuf having attended a ministerial committee with the king, she distinctly overheard a musician say, 'it is a queen's duty to stay in her apartments and do crochet work'.[111]

Instead, the Trianon was becoming an alternative seat of government. Bombelles noted on 19 July 1788:

> The Archbishop ... [Brienne] went to the Petit Trianon at 9 o'clock in the evening. The king followed closely, but whilst the principal minister was closeted with the queen in her cabinet, the king remained in the salon. When the queen joined him there it was clear that she had been crying. Sadly her vexations have further to go and her true servants believe that she is bringing new ones on herself by having herself admitted to cabinet committees because since the public know that she takes part in them she is held responsible for all the harsh decisions taken there.

She 'did not yet sit in the Conseil d'état', that would come, but people were 'getting used to her presence in the cabinet committees where affairs were discussed and therefore decided' before being submitted to the Council for a rubber stamp.[112] Not that Bombelles disagreed with the policies the queen was supporting: 'it is not the people who are in revolt ... The people are well aware that they are not being stirred up for the defence of their hearths and the scraps of comfort remaining to them. All the hostility comes from the seigneurs and the *parlementaires* who in a new regime would be made (by a fairer distribution of taxation) to pay the money they have always refused to give to the public treasury'.[113] One of the great enigmas of the period 1787–8 is why the government was unable to get this fairly simple message across despite 'as was commonly supposed sending emissaries to Brittany to stir up the people against the nobility'.[114] Somehow the 'seigneurs and magistrates' were able to convince the people, who nevertheless saw through them, that liberty was more important than equality. Soon that would change. They would want both and *fraternité* – being treated as a human being of equal worth.

Jean Egret argues that the Brienne ministry was ultimately brought down by a 'banal treasury crisis' – the failure to secure an advance against future receipts of taxation. But the crisis was far from banal: the treasury was empty, it was impossible to raise a voluntary loan, so on 16 August a forced one was imposed: all payments of government bonds (*rentes*) were suspended for a fortnight when they would be resumed, half in government paper bearing 5 per cent interest, half in coin. The crisis led to a concerted attack on the principal minister by the

Polignac-Calonne set. It was the suspension of payments that prompted Calonne to write the king the open letter quoted above, stressing that hitherto Louis had never allowed 'the slightest hint of bankruptcy, even indirect, partial or momentary to sully [his] reign'.[115]

Gojard, the Calonne loyalist in the treasury, had given Brienne to believe that the funds were assured until the following spring. He was dismissed on Necker's return, but Artois immediately made him his own treasurer. Artois, according to Brienne, was got up by the Polignacs to lead the attack: 'the moment the [suspension] decree ... was promulgated M. le comte d'Artois began to act against me, and from what the queen told me I have no doubt of this'. Artois warned Brienne he was going to tell the king that his very life was in danger if the crisis were further prolonged by Brienne's presence at the head of government. Artois read the king a memorandum along these lines[116] and, according to Besenval, 'despite his repugnance', asked the king to recall Necker for the good of the country. Brienne has a slightly different view of the matter:

> The idea of recalling M. Necker came to the queen; not just because M. de Mercy suggested it; not just because of her own desire to be seen to have been instrumental in a recall which public opinion rendered necessary; but also because she was keen to prevent the power and influence of M. le comte d'Artois who did not want M. Necker whom he feared almost as much as he feared me.[117]

Marie-Antoinette was instrumental in recalling Necker, widely regarded as the only man who could restore credit. She turned to Mercy-Argenteau to act as go-between. Jean-Louis Soulavie was shocked that the ambassador of a foreign power should have conducted such important negotiations. But his anti-Austrian paranoia blinded him to a change that had taken place in the relations between queen and would-be Mentor. Mercy had been sent by Vienna in the hope that Marie-Antoinette would further Austrian interests. He had failed in this, first because Louis was on his guard, later because the queen herself came to think that such intervention was inappropriate. But at the same time, and partly as a consequence, Marie-Antoinette turned to Mercy for advice on internal matters, so that during the years of her ascendancy, 1787–8, he is an important source for these concerns.

The recall of Necker was preceded by a bout of courtly shadow-boxing.[118] Brienne told Mercy that 'for some time' he had wanted Necker to serve as finance minister under him. Necker was reluctant or seemed so, first because he had (as Marie-Antoinette put it) been 'lacerated by the way the king had always treated him', and second because he didn't know the state of the finances – he sent Mercy the corrected proofs of his 'triumphant' refutation of Calonne's version of the deficit. The king did not want Necker back. The queen wanted Necker to know he owed his appointment to her. Necker did not want to serve under Brienne, who tried to stay on as *chef du conseil des finances* or even as a minister-without-portfolio, which the king, no friend to him, refused.[119]

So on 18 August, Marie-Antoinette told Mercy:

> I greatly fear that the Archbishop will be forced to disappear from the scene completely and then whom can we choose to have overall direction? Because we must have someone, especially with M. Necker. He needs to be restrained. The personage above me [the King] is in no fit state for this; as for me, whatever people say, I am only the second fiddle and despite the confidence of the first, he often makes me feel it . . . the king is extremely reluctant [to appoint Necker]; the only way to get his consent is to promise only to sound [Necker] out without making any commitment.

Necker made it quite clear to Mercy, though in a jocular way, that he was having nothing to do with having a prime minister over him: 'I presume there is no question of replacing his title of principal [minister] until we have seen what common sense can achieve.'[120] And the position of Mercy as chief negotiator was weakened by his own inside information that the state of the treasury was even worse than imagined – the archbishop himself was not fully informed how bad it was.

But what did Marie-Antoinette mean by saying that Louis 'was in no fit state to restrain' Necker? Was it just that Louis was too feeble? But he had had sufficient strength to thwart all her attempts to influence foreign policy for fourteen years and prevent Necker's return in 1783 and 1787. She was probably referring to Louis' mental and possibly physical state. A month later, on 27 September, Bombelles recounts an episode that was carefully hushed up – 'our best court bloodhounds will not get to the bottom of what goes on inside ours':

> Today, when the king was out hunting, he was brought a bundle of letters. He retired to a copse to read them and soon he was seen sitting on the ground with his face between his hands and his hands on his knees. His equerries and other people, hearing him sobbing, fetched M. de Lambesc [the Grand Equerry]. He approached the king. The king told him brusquely to go away but he insisted. Then the king, turning towards him a face bathed with tears repeated, but this time kindly, 'leave me alone'. Shortly afterwards His Majesty

needed to be lifted on to his horse, where he seemed to be suffering from some malady. A chair was brought for him to sit on, but he was ill a second time. Finally he returned to Versailles, having recovered his senses and external composure as well as his good health. This adventure has been kept secret but the secret will not be well kept with so many people in the know.

Bombelles did not know what the letters contained to have such an effect on the king: 'I am reporting a fact; a distressing fact. But I have no idea what caused it.'[121] Evelyn Farr speculates that this 'bundle of letters' may have been from Axel von Fersen, who had been recalled to Sweden for most of 1788, only returning to Paris on 6 November.[122] However, he and Marie-Antoinette employed trusted couriers rather than risking regular mail, because the Intendant des Postes, the comte d'Ogny, had a *cabinet noir* of twelve clerks employed in opening intercepted letters and showed Louis extracts from these on Sundays. Besides, as we have seen, Bombelles did not believe that Marie-Antoinette and Fersen were having an affair.

One hesitates to offer a medical diagnosis at this distance – was the king's malady psychosomatic? Maybe this is why he felt it necessary to address Marie-Antoinette's concern that he would not be able to 'restrain' Necker, by drafting a detailed set of instructions to be used by Mercy in negotiating Necker's return to the ministry. These are written in Marie-Antoinette's awful handwriting, and the details were probably thrashed out between the royal couple:

So far M. de M. [ercy] has only spoken to M. N[ecker] as if on his own initiative . . . but now he can tell him that the king has been informed of the negotiation and sanctions it; that he desires to put M. Necker at the head of the finances again; that he will have a seat in the Council [the point over which he had resigned in 1781] and will have carte blanche in his department; that the king thinks that after a disagreeable operation [the 8 May coup] but one that was necessary in the circumstances, whatever M. N. proposes can only be approved by the public and that he will restore confidence; that the king is firmly resolved to summon the Estates-General at the time indicated [May 1789] and to work with them on ways to end the deficit and make sure it doesn't recur. That the king cannot in advance undertake to restore the parlements, but that he will work on doing this at the end of their vacation, whilst at the same time preserving the benefits gained by the people from greater access to justice [the *grands baillages* carving up the Parlement's jurisdiction]. If M. N. can think of further economies [on top of Brienne's] he can rest assured that the king is ready for any personal sacrifice.[123]

Louis could not bear to negotiate directly with the man who had undermined his government for the past six years. As Necker had handed his 1781 resignation to Marie-Antoinette, so she handled his return, just as she had been the intermediary between the king and Brienne leading to his entry into the ministry.

On 25 August the king appointed Necker *Directeur-général des finances* and two days later vindicated his resignation in 1781 by granting him, as a *ministre d'état*, entrée to the Council, which was to enjoy a renaissance as a decision-making body during Necker's second ministry. Since the king had granted toleration to Protestants in 1787, the obstacle that in 1781 had debarred him from the Council had been removed. There was no one placed over him and, indeed, during his second ministry, Necker seems to have possessed the essential attribute of a prime minister under Louis XVI: that the other ministers had to apprise him of important matters before raising them with the king.[124] But Louis did it all with a bad grace, and the new attitude of cynical compliance noted when he appointed Brienne is encapsulated in his remark: 'I was forced to recall Necker; I didn't want to but they'll soon regret it. I'll do everything he tells me and we'll see what happens.'[125]

Brienne confessed that his 'character was not made for stormy times'. His parting advice to the king was not to surrender unconditionally to the Parlement. Riotous rejoicing greeted the news of Brienne's departure and Louis ordered Biron, colonel of the French Guards, to repel force by force. There were several deaths. Brienne left in secret with hired horses for the country seat attached to his new and lucrative see of Sens. Véri thought his translation ill-advised because Fontainebleau lay in his new diocese, which would be embarrassing if he fell from power.[126] On his way Brienne avoided Paris where his effigy was burnt. 'He proposed shortly,' Bombelles comments, 'to go to Pisa where perhaps he will run into M. de Calonne, and then they will have a good old laugh together over the public's madness and their own.' As a leaving present Marie-Antoinette gave Brienne a gold box with her portrait, studded with 'superb diamonds'.[127]

SEVEN

THE LAST YEAR AT VERSAILLES

THE QUEEN'S UNPOPULARITY DEEPENS

*M*arie-Antoinette had turned thirty in 1785, and between then and 1788 her long and careless youth finally came to an end. The years had witnessed the Saint-Cloud purchase, the Diamond Necklace Affair, the Assembly of Notables and the failure of 'her' prime minister. Her youth had been careless – insouciant – but not carefree. There had always been a frenetic quality to her gaiety, brittleness in her laughter. Now she was pensive, even melancholy. Her carelessness had made her unpopular and her unpopularity made her serious, not to appease public opinion but because it made her sad.

On 25 August, Marie-Antoinette confided to Mercy-Argenteau: 'I tremble (forgive my weakness) that I am bringing him [Necker] back. My fate is to bring misfortune. And if diabolical plots should cause him to fail again [as in 1781] or if he should surrender some of the royal authority, I will be detested even more.'[1] This is a locus classicus for Marie-Antoinette in two respects. First, she is aware that Necker is associated with a dilution of royal power both by inclination (in his first ministry) and by force of circumstances (the present crisis). Moreover, since she supported him in his first ministry (and his attempts to return) and was instrumental in his final return, she must be taken to be at least ambivalent (if also fearful) about that dilution. She was after all Choiseul's residual legatee. Second, she is aware not only that she is 'detested' but why: because of her perceived and actual involvement in home and foreign affairs.

Jeanne Arnaud-Bouteloup considers that Marie-Antoinette simply could not comprehend why she was 'detested', citing her famous rhetorical question to Madame Campan: 'What have I done to them then?' There is also her conversation with her page, the comte de Tilly. This took place during a visit to the Paris Opéra in 1782 – that is, just months after Louis had approached her birthing bed and announced 'Madame, you have fulfilled my desires and those of France; you are the mother of a dauphin' – that is fulfilled her primary role. After the performance at the opera, Marie-Antoinette asked Tilly, 'Why was I scarcely clapped?' When Tilly blustered that he wasn't aware of the slight, the queen interrupted him: 'How could you have failed to notice. Well . . . too bad for the people of Paris. It's not my fault.' When Tilly tried to play down the incident, Marie-Antoinette, 'tears rolling down her cheeks', said 'it was all the more painful since she had nothing with which to reproach herself'.[2] Arnaud-Bouteloup sympathizes with the queen's failure to grasp the causes of her unpopularity because it was out of all proportion to its object[3] – after all, what *had* she done to them? She was the scapegoat of an irrational age suffering a nervous collapse, the so-called rationality of the Enlightenment shot through with the charlatanism of a Mesmer, a Cagliostro and, for that matter, a Necker.

But the penny was beginning to drop. Marie-Antoinette took desperate steps to win back the love of the people: she mingled with the crowds at Saint-Cloud; she opened up the Trianon on Sundays, but people were disappointed not to find the fabled room paved with diamonds – it was obviously off limits rather than non-existent. She persevered in going to the capital until the police minister and his superior Breteuil told her it was counterproductive even dangerous. Like Louis, she was bad at propaganda and even disdained it. For example, her role in recalling Necker, the idol of the people, was unknown – Soulavie only discovered it through his privileged access to the ex-king's papers. On the other hand nearly every member of the royal family, especially Artois, queued up to inform the public of his or her role in the ministerial changes. What the public did know was how Marie-Antoinette, to repay what she conceived of as a debt of honour, got Brienne a cardinal's hat, lavished pensions on him and his relatives, some of them distant, after his resignation, as well as the inevitable diamond-studded *boîte à portrait*. An emblematic anecdote crystallizes the public's attitude at this juncture. Marie-Antoinette asks Necker to find a place in the Finance Ministry for one of her protégés; Necker replies that he needed a more qualified candidate. 'You are refusing me then but I esteem you none the less for it.' This reply was so flattering that M. Necker asked permission to speak of it. 'I consent, said the queen – but you will not be believed.'[4] In 1787 it was thought inadvisable to display in the salon the famous portrait of her with her children painted by Madame Vigée-Lebrun. No violence was yet done or threatened to her person, though the comtesse de Tessé was attacked by a mob in the mistaken belief that she was Madame de Polignac.

It is considered chic in some academic circles to intellectualize the scurrilous or the horrendous, the juxtaposition of incongruities being a hallmark of the intellectual. Such treatment of the scurrilous pamphlet literature concerning Marie-Antoinette and later her gruesome trial and death are cases in point. This literature did the queen some damage, though it is hard to quantify and at her trial, as Maximilien Robespierre realized, such accusations were counterproductive if not actually counter-revolutionary. We don't venture far down this road, except where it borders on the relationship between Marie-Antoinette and Madame de Polignac, a particular interest of the present study.

The calumnies are rebutted by the comte de Tilly, who prefaces his list of Marie-Antoinette's supposed lovers with the rhetorical lament: 'Must I be condemned to repeat this absurd list of lovers that numbers no less than that of the Great Mogul?' Thus self-'condemned', he joyfully proceeds to regale us with the fullest extant list: the duke of Dorset (English ambassador and one of the Polignac set whom Marie-Antoinette called 'a pretty woman'); Édouard Dillon; the duc de Liancourt, grand master of the wardrobe; the Grand Duke of Hesse-Darmstadt (married to the queen's sister); Du Roure (whose death elicited a tear from the queen); Lambertye, a Bodyguard; Saint-Paer; Count Romanov; Lord Hugh Seymour; the duc de Guines; and 'to complete this ridiculous list' Vaudreuil and the duc de Polignac, 'who could not have been further from her mind'.

Tilly treats in further detail the cases of the duc de Coigny and Axel von Fersen: Coigny, an older man such as the queen preferred and Fersen a man, like the queen, of a cold and proud exterior. Both realized that the queen was attracted to them; both realized the danger that this attraction posed for her and nobly took steps to remove themselves from the scene – Fersen even going as far as America to fight in its war of independence.[5] Both realized that the danger of causing her hurt and even offence by absenting themselves was less than that of damaging her reputation by remaining. But Fersen came back.

To top it all, the Diamond Necklace Affair would not lie down. Cardinal Rohan was elected to the Estates-General for Alsace. The king forbade him to take up his seat. Then the younger sister of Jeanne de Valois brought a case against the royal domain for the restitution of titles and lands, claiming to have discovered the ancient deeds to them among her sister's papers. The Crown stopped the case and it was assumed that the girl would be compensated out of her sister's confiscated properties. Unfair, wrote the *Correspondance secrète* – any proceeds should have gone to the cardinal: 'Thus injustice always goes side by side with arbitrary authority . . . even under the most just of despots' – like Louis XVI.[6]

NECKER

Necker was now in power and he had the queen's support, having been her first choice in 1787. But he was not confident. For a start the king detested him – even more than he had detested Brienne. Also the situation had deteriorated since his first ministry. Then he had been a good incremental reformer – perhaps the only kind the regime could sustain. He had made mistakes; delaying the introduction of wartime taxation for too long, though he like all the ministers had been gambling on a short war; above all by publishing his fraudulent *Comte rendu*, which made it impossible for anyone but him to run the system for long. And the situation had deteriorated even further since Marie-Antoinette had failed to get him reappointed in April 1787. And he knew it – hence his lament, 'If only I could have had the 18 months of the Archbishop of Toulouse.'

Necker now saw his job as a holding operation: keeping the state solvent until the forthcoming Estates-General could solve all the problems. He knew also that they would not solve them without requiring a diminution of the royal authority as the price of bailing out the profligate regime. Marie-Antoinette seems to have known this too, viz her fearful reference to the Estates-General at the time of the *séance royale* in November 1787 and her fear that Necker might 'surrender some of the royal authority'. Necker believed that the king had few cards left to play. He thought that by making strategic surrenders he could disguise this weakness and retain something for the monarchy. Malesherbes said the same at the time and to the king's face. The king, he said, should draw what we would call 'red lines' around those portions of the royal authority he could not surrender, but voluntarily surrender the rest.[7] Many, however, thought, even before the Estates-General met, that it was not for the king to draw up a programme. He had made a mess of things and must sit back and take whatever the nation as represented by the Estates was prepared to offer in the form of a written Constitution.

But would the Estates in fact represent the nation? That was the burning question in the autumn of 1788. It was a question of organization as well as representation and, at least at this stage, few doubted that it was for the king to settle. For there was a need for an honest broker, a referee, and the general belief was that however incompetent Louis had shown himself to be, he was at least fair. There was need for an umpire because, having achieved their victory over 'royal despotism' in the shape of Calonne and Brienne, the victors fell out over the spoils. The 'Third Estate', the commoners, though forming 95 per cent of the population of 28 milllion, had been very much the junior partners in the struggle. Indeed, Calonne had assumed that they would be on the side of the king as they had in all previous conflicts between king and nobility. *Le Roi et le tiers état*. Hence his *Avertissement*. But the Third Estate had not responded and for the most part had sat out the struggle. Brienne had also tried to enlist their support by his provocative proclamation of 5 July 1788, lifting press censorship and inviting information on all sides as to how the future Estates were to be organized. Miromesnil thought that this was a step towards 'introducing popular government to France'.[8]

For the proclamation implied that the traditional form of the Estates such as had obtained when they last met in 1614 was no longer appropriate given 'the rise of the bourgeoisie'. In 1614 the three Orders – clergy, nobility and the Third Estate – had sat in separate chambers. The Third Estate had slightly more than a third of the total number of seats, but this was irrelevant since there was bloc (*par Ordre*) rather than individual (*par tête*) voting. Brienne[9] and Malesherbes preferred a more modern system: a National Assembly co-opted from the new provincial assemblies without distinction of Orders or at least with voting by head rather than by Order. This Malesherbes called 'the plan of 1787', which had been derailed by *parlementaire* opposition.[10]

Louis did 'everything Necker told him to do'. He recalled the exiled Parlement – after all they had spearheaded the revolt that had led to Necker's triumphant but secretly worried return – and he did so unconditionally despite Brienne's warning. The king also, after dithering, dismissed Lamoignon and abandoned his reform of the judicial system. Like Brienne, Lamoignon was rewarded lavishly, with gifts including a silver wine-taster set with gold coins and inscribed 'don de royal amitié'. But the Parlement's first step was to wade into the debate about the future organization of the Estates-General and to do so in a way that threw Necker off course.

The Parlement declared that the forthcoming Estates should be 'regularly convoked and that according to the forms of 1614'. That meant with the three Orders sitting separately, in other words with the Third Estate in a permanent minority of one. (The Parlement had said much the same in 1787 but few had twigged.)[11] It was not just a question of fairness – why should the representatives of 95 per cent of the population have so little say – but of content, since the rights and privileges of the nobility and clergy were the key issues and as Calonne had found, turkeys don't vote early for Christmas. There was the unequal tax system that Calonne and Brienne had sought in vain to reform and also the whole feudal regime, a corner of which Lamoignon had sought to reform by virtually abolishing the manor courts – now restored. The feudal system was not as oppressive as it had been in medieval times – *pace The Marriage of Figaro* no lord still exercised the *droit de seigneur* over the maidenhead of every new bride in the village, if he ever had done. But there were still irksome and humiliating if not onerous exactions such as the requirement to have your grain milled by the lord and residual rights over land making true freehold or clear leasehold impossible in many areas. So although the government had received no support from the Third Estate, these issues had been agitated, indeed stirred up by both Calonne (the *Avertissement*) and Brienne (the proclamation of 5 July).

But the Parlement's pronouncement derailed Necker's plan, which was to convoke the Estates for 1 January 1789. It shouldn't have done. If he had been truly sensitive to the voice of his god, public opinion, he would have realized that the Parlement was a spent force. By its pronouncement it lost all its credibility. Instead of realizing this, and even with the king and queen's detestation of the Parlement, he still felt that he did not have sufficient authority to overrule the Parlement without the backing of the Assembly of Notables, which reconvened on 6 November. But the second Assembly of Notables (with almost the same personnel as the first) was no more willing to oblige Necker than it had been his enemy Calonne. Why should it? As Brienne wrote in his memoirs: 'I would never have reconvened the Notables composed of the privileged whose mentality I knew so well.'[12]

The only thing Necker asked the Assembly to advise on (apart from the number of deputies, which he could and should have decided himself) was whether the Third Estate should have a double representation (*doublement*) equal to that of the other two Orders combined. Necker tactfully or pusillanimously avoided the question, which would have rendered *doublement* meaningful: should voting be *par ordre* or *par tête*. But the Notables embarrassed him by placing it among their list of supplementary questions and favouring the former.[13] All but one of the Assembly's committees (Provence's by a majority of one) rejected *doublement*. Then on 5 December the Parlement 'interpreted' its previous ruling by stating that 'no law or fixed usage stipulated the respective number of deputies'. By now, however, the Parlement was irrelevant and the Notables would not be summoned again: both were by definition eclipsed by the Estates-General. It was the king in council who would decide. What mattered now was dissension within the royal family and within the wider Bourbon dynasty. For it too was at stake. Barnave realized this. Some renegade 'princes having stirred up the revolt of a few nobles against the general will, dragged the king into the nobles' party and presented him to the French people as the head of a faction'.[14]

Artois and the Polignac set, supported by five princes of the blood, had come to the conclusion that concessions to the Third Estate threatened the survival of the monarchy and that though the nobility and clergy had contested that authority in the *révolte nobiliaire* of 1787–8, *au fond* their interests and those of the monarchy were the same. The Polignacs had given the king and their ally Calonne strong support in the first Assembly of Notables and had quarrelled with the queen over this. By December 1788, though, they had realized that what had started the previous year as a necessary and desirable administrative and political royal revolution was fast becoming a social and constitutional one. This is made clear in two publications associated with the group, Calonne's *Lettre au Roi* (published in London) and the *Mémoire des Princes*, signed by five of the princes of the blood (not the comte de Provence or the duc d'Orléans), headed by the comte d'Artois, whose chancellor, Montyon, prepared the draft. The king reprimanded Artois for 'signing this fine production' and asked, 'when I paid your debts (several times over) whose money did I use, that of the nobility or that of the Third Estate?'[15] The *Correspondance secrète* observed that Calonne's *Lettre au Roi* 'took nine hours to read. This ex-minister has presumed too much on our monarch's leisure'. He was recommending despotism to the king and in his desire to return to office was playing a game of 'double or quits', risking being arrested by returning to Flanders in the hope of being elected to the Estates-General. The electoral college there told the prince de Robecq, who was presiding, that it would suspend its session unless Calonne departed. He returned to England.[16]

Calonne and Artois defended the consistency of their position: throughout they had stood for the maintenance of royal authority and equal taxation; Calonne had never attacked a single legitimate right – for abuses such as tax evasion were not rights; or, as Artois put it, 'all that was at issue was repairing not destroying'. Louis and Marie-Antoinette were not moved by such reasoning in December but, coming from a group that had provided political support (to the king) and friendship (to the queen), it sowed a seed of doubt, though the *révolte nobiliaire* had soured the soil in which it grew. This seed would grow and within six months lead to the fall both of the Polignacs and of the Bastille.

For the moment, though, it was *le Roi – et la Reine – et le tiers état*. Marie-Antoinette's *éminence gris*, the abbé de Vermont, having like her supported Brienne, now 'became a tribune of the people and an energetic advocate of the Third Estate'.[17] After hearing all the conflicting advice the question of *doublement* was decided in a marathon session of the Conseil d'état. It was not only Necker who had hitherto been excluded from the Council. Marie-Antoinette had been and this mattered because the Council still played a meaningful role in foreign policy, her principal concern. There were no leaks and no minutes so, as she confessed to Joseph, she had to pretend to ministers that she had gleaned half the story in the hope that they would supply the rest.[18] She had attended cabinet committees under Brienne but now she attended this crucial meeting of the Council.

It has justly been observed that 'never perhaps WAS a royal decision subjected to a more thorough scrutiny'.[19] Before the meeting the king presided over a series of cabinet committees consisting of the adversaries, Necker (for *doublement*) and Barentin, Lamoignon's successor (against), plus two further ministers. Since Barentin tells us that the latter two were different every time, we can calculate that the king wore out twenty pairs of ministers in sessions lasting from four to five hours each – maybe one hundred hours of discussion. 'His Majesty made frequent observations but it was impossible to divine his opinion.' Feeling he was losing the battle, Necker considered resigning. Marie-Antoinette dissuaded him, saying that she would personally attend the council to support him.

Finally, a double session of the Conseil des Dépêches was convened on 27 December. The queen did attend. Her protégé Saint-Priest, present as a minister-without-portfolio, notes that this was the first time that a queen-consort (as opposed to a queen-regent) had ever attended the Conseil d'état; and added that 'it did not happen again for several months'.[20] Louis, who was supposed to abide by a majority decision, kept taking the votes until he got the one he wanted. 'The Queen,' as Barentin sourly observes, 'maintained total silence; it was easy, however, to see that she did not disapprove double representation for the Third Estate . . . The King pronounced for *doublement*.' Two ministers changed their minds. Marie-Antoinette's enemy, the former police minister Lenoir, thought such a proceeding despotic.[21]

Marie-Antoinette's silent intervention may have been decisive since, according to his confidant, Malouet, Necker had his doubts about *doublement*: 'The *doublement* of the Third Estate was pronounced and I make no secret of the fact that I favoured it even against the opinion of M. Necker, who resisted it for a long time, foresaw the disadvantages and only yielded to the impression that the voice of public opinion always produced on him. No one outside his intimate circle knew how much he hesitated over the famous *Résultat du Conseil* or with what misgiving he promulgated it . . .'[22] Necker's ally, the archbishop of Bordeaux, saw a printed first report by Necker refusing *doublement* and merely giving the major towns some extra deputies.[23]

The decisions of the Council were published as the *Résultat du Conseil*, a curiously detached way of referring to such a contentious issue. It consists of five short paragraphs providing: (1) that there should be 'at least a thousand deputies' in the Estates; (2) that the electoral unit should be the *baillage*, the number of its deputies being determined by its population and taxation; (3) *doublement*. This is followed by Necker's lengthy report that had formed the basis of the Council's discussions. It was redrafted for popular consumption when the *Résultat* was published as a twenty-six-page pamphlet. The report emphasizes that by granting *doublement* there is no intention of prejudging the question of voting by head or by Order (which Necker seems to favour). In the last section Necker has the king thinking aloud with his ministers and promising to become a constitutional monarch. His pledges include regular meetings of the Estates, their consent to taxation and control over the budget (including the king's personal expenditure), and consultation with them on *lettres de cachet* and freedom of the press.

Necker included in the printed version some words he attributed to the queen to the effect that the king would make any personal sacrifices for the common good, and that 'our children will do likewise if they have any sense and if they don't the king will have fulfilled a duty in placing some restraint on them'. Condé went about saying that Necker had made up the queen's speech, but Marie-Antoinette stated in front of witnesses: 'I consented that my words be printed in the *Résultat du Conseil* . . . these are indeed my sentiments and that my esteem for M. Necker knows no bounds.'[24] Her once and future minister Breteuil, however, who had resigned in support of the *révolte nobiliaire*, considered that for a minister to publish proceedings of the Council was 'perfidious' and part and parcel of Necker's 'habitually illegal proceedings'.[25] His enemy Calonne lamented the dismemberment of royal authority and wrote prophetically: 'A revolution followed by a counter-revolution (*une révolution contraire*) is the worst calamity that can befall a nation.'[26]

But would the concessions be enough? At each stage of the complicated electoral process, lists of grievances (*Cahiers de doléances*) were drawn up. Formed into a general cahier for each Order, these were traditionally presented to the king in the hope rather than the expectation that some of them would be embodied in law. Mercy-Argenteau gave Joseph II a summary of how they were shaping up and he was alarmed at how 'eloquent [they were] against the royal authority'. Demands included 'in future a double oath for the army both to the king and to the nation'; a Civil List for the personal use of the king, who would not 'have the use of funds destined for state expenditure'; 'ministerial responsibility to the Estates-General'.[27] The Revolution was already accomplished in idea. The fall of the Bastille was indeed only symbolic. It took a foreigner like Mercy, a native of the Austrian Netherlands where these things had already started, to see it. And Marie-Antoinette was the recipient of his fears. They made her own vague sense of foreboding more specific.

Mercy told Joseph that in the *Résultat* Necker exhibited a confidence he did not feel. The financial crisis that gave him his authority within the government threatened to sink it also. The quarrels between the first two Orders and the Third Estate threatened to make the outcome of the Estates-General 'fruitless'. 'At such a critical juncture,' he continues, 'the queen has wisely and indeed necessarily decided to keep her own counsel; to avoid any semblance of favouring one party or the other. Such prudent navigation through rocky seas will only serve to enhance her credit when the time comes to make use of her influence when she knows the situation better and there is less risk involved.'[28] That is perhaps why the queen's intervention in the Council had been a silent if minatory one.

That was written on 6 January 1789. By the time Mercy wrote to Joseph again, on 22 February, the situation had deteriorated further and 'it depended on the queen to fill the gap' left by the king's 'disinclination to restore internal discipline' within 'the royal family', a disinclination that caused her chagrin. This important dispatch is somewhat obscure. Obviously the discipline needed does not just refer to the drunkenness of Provence's wife, though this 'has led to several disgusting scenes'. It refers to the sides taken by the members of the immediate royal family – Provence, Artois and their sister Madame Elizabeth in the developing political struggle.

As anyone could have foreseen the granting of double representation to the Third Estate only shifted the focus to what Mercy called 'the manner of voting in the Estates', by head or Order. 'The Clergy and Nobility feared the preponderance of the Third Estate [if voting was by head] and it is very probable that the latter will win the day.' This led to Mercy's and presumably the queen's dawning realization that the victory of the Third Estate would 'threaten the royal authority which has already been reduced to the point that it does not know how to resist the disorder which worsens every day'.

It was the devil or the deep blue sea. Back to the sixteenth or forward to the nineteenth century. The nobility sought to turn the clock back to the period of aristocratic ascendancy before the rise of Bourbon absolutism under Richelieu and Louis XIV. The Third Estate, who would soon call themselves the Commons, thereby rejecting the society of Orders altogether, were taking massive strides towards a more democratic and therefore more effective limitation of the royal authority. Artois, having backed Calonne's attempt to found a proto-Napoleonic despotism – equality without liberty – now fell back, for the present but with fingers crossed, towards throwing in his lot with his former opponents the aristocracy as the lesser of two evils. Provence had used his influence to get his committee in the Notables to recommend *doublement* but now he was havering. Although passing for a liberal, he also had an authoritarian streak, having tried to persuade his brother not to recall the Parlement in 1774.

In this at least Karl Marx was right: a regime only falls when its elite splinters. With the French Revolution this process is generally considered to have been marked by the *révolte nobiliaire* of 1787–8. But this misses the point, for the nobility and its values were never an integral part of the *ancien régime*, which was a relatively modern political structure grafted awkwardly on to a pre-existing social one based on the military aristocracy. The first true cracks in the *ancien régime* can be detected when the ministry began to divide over ideological issues around 1770, at the time of Maupeou's attack on the Parlement. But the defining moment was the split (again ideological) within the Bourbon dynasty (the Orléans versus the rest of the princes of the blood) and the immediate royal family (the king and queen versus Artois and Madame Elizabeth) dating from the end of 1788, continuing to the fall of the Bastille when Artois was forced to emigrate, and reviving as the Counter-Revolution.

For the moment Necker was the litmus test and for the moment Marie-Antoinette backed him both in rejecting a Russian alliance proposed by Joseph II with endorsement from Montmorin and Saint-Priest and in supporting the Third Estate in order 1. to moderate their pretension; and 2. to 'fill the coffers of the treasury'. Artois had called for Necker's return through gritted teeth; now he wanted the king to dismiss him. The Polignacs naturally supported Artois. This meant that the queen could not 'have recourse to them which left her even more isolated'. The 'public' knew about the internal debate within the royal family and expected the queen to act in support of Necker. Mercy is ambivalent about how much influence Marie-Antoinette had. Within the space of a single paragraph he writes of 'the public's injustice in thinking that she can supplement the king's deficiency', but that 'it depends on her to fill this void by dealing with the high matters to which her credit now stronger than ever' entitles her.[29]

Marie-Antoinette was still supporting the pretensions of the Third Estate. On 2 February 1789 the *Correspondance secrète* notes that the deputies for the Third Estate of Brittany had given the queen a memorandum complaining that the voting system in their province was rigged against them. The queen took it with her to read in the chapel and 'told the ladies who accompanied her "it is the memorandum of the Breton Third Estate; they are being treated very unfairly"'. When their deputies came to lobby at Versailles, the queen showed 'interest' in their cause.[30] It will be remembered that in the previous summer the Brienne government had sent Breton noble deputies to the Bastille. Now, having failed to get their way, the Breton nobility refused to send any deputies at all to the Estates-General. The Breton Third Estate deputies, however, would come to Versailles intending, as they put it, 'to do everything for the King, so to re-establish his authority that the nobility and the parlements could never damage it again'.[31] This was an avenue that should have been exploited.

At the beginning of April the comte de Provence, 'thinking that he had been led astray during the Assembly of Notables', came round to Artois' way of thinking and together with two princes of the blood, Condé and Conti, assured the king 'that they would oppose any attempts either by aristocracy or democracy to destroy the royal authority'.[32] They thus recognized that the king had to navigate between Scylla and Charybdis but at this stage offered no way of avoiding either peril. They recognized that Necker had steered too close to Charybdis but could not suggest a way of rectifying his course. As Machault, an octogenarian former minister put it, Necker was 'a man too dangerous to keep and too awkward to dismiss'. The Polignacs, as an alternative to both Breteuil and Necker, had suggested to the queen that Machault be made premier. They then put the proposition to the old man 'as coming from' the queen. Marie-Antoinette 'showed her annoyance at this singular proposal', which Machault in any case rejected. Miromesnil also was sounded out for some post but not the justice ministry.[33]

The next piece in the anti-Necker jigsaw was reconciliation between Breteuil and the Artois-Polignac set, who had always sided with Calonne in his bitter dispute with Breteuil. Their long-term aim remained to bring back Calonne and exploit any situation that could 'sooner or later restore him to office'.[34] But for the moment they gave Breteuil to understand that not only would they not propose Calonne's recall, but they would 'welcome' Breteuil back 'as being the only man capable of maintaining the rights of the crown'.[35]

This was a clever move on the Polignacs' part because Breteuil had been Marie-Antoinette's protégé. By now she had resumed going to Madame de Polignac's salon. On 16 February she sang duets with Madame de Polignac's daughter, accompanied on a new-fangled pianoforte by Bombelles. Bombelles then played dance music and to everyone's amazement Marie-Antoinette started waltzing with the chevalier de Roll, who must have brought the new dance from Vienna. Bombelles 'could have desired less spectators and the duchesse de Polignac agreed'.[36]

Madame de Polignac suggested that Breteuil should start attending the Council again or even be made foreign secretary. He would act as a break on Necker's attempts to undermine the royal authority. They soon went further suggesting that Necker be surrounded by a string of new ministers and be confined strictly to raising money. Louis replied that he was 'very happy with the members of his Council, that all, without exception, were serving him very well and above all were suited to the circumstances because of their gentle and prudent conduct'.[37] Louis also rejected the princes' request to enter the Council themselves. But the king and queen's resistance was crumbling and it was provisionally decided to dismiss Necker on 13 April. Then Marie-Antoinette changed her mind because the timing was 'inappropriate' and this was the occasion when she cited the example of the premature dismissal of Calonne. Saint-Priest implies that the king, who after all detested Necker, was ready to dismiss him but was dissuaded by the queen. Saint-Priest thought that this was bad advice because although the dismissal of the popular minister would have led to a 'commotion', at this stage firm leadership could have contained it.[38]

She may have also have been swayed by the reluctance of 'her' minister Breteuil to return and above all, because he made no secret of the fact that he did not know what to do. When Artois and Madame de Polignac asked his spokesman, Bombelles, what should be done, he replied 'Nothing'. Breteuil himself further elaborated: 'Nothing, except to keep calm, always remain faithfully attached to the King and to the country and to look to the tutelary genius of France for that which one can no longer expect from the sensible measures which should have been taken.'[39] This exchange between Artois and Breteuil occurred on 30 April. The Estates-General were due to open on 5 May, so this was a last-ditch attempt. The astute Miromesnil gained the impression that the plan was to see how Necker fared in the Estates-General before deciding whether to move against him[40] – which is what actually happened.

The king was working on the speech with which he would open the gathering. Bombelles noted, 'it is the king who is working by himself on his speech' and feared he would not give it sufficient 'dignity' to stem the tide. Bombelles, usually well informed, is wrong on this occasion. Louis' speech was a compilation of drafts by himself, five ministers, a civil servant and Marie-Antoinette.[41] Apart from Necker and Barentin (his main internal opponent – Louis both institutionally and personally needed to hear both sides of a question), the others (including Marie-Antoinette) had some expertise in foreign affairs. This perhaps bears out the Prussian ambassador's view that Louis' main reason for summoning the Estates was the collapse of foreign policy because of the collapse of the finances. The queen (unlike the others) merely adds or deletes odd phrases to the king's first draft rather than giving a full version of her own. But Louis incorporates her suggestions. These tend to remove anything controversial in the king's speech and reveal nothing of the evolution of her own views.

In his first draft Louis admits that 'despite the most severe economy in expenditure, I will be obliged for some time to ask the Nation for increased taxation, but a more equal assessment will lighten the burden for the poorest tax payers'. This is the only draft, including the speech he ultimately delivers, which states openly that the reason for convoking the Estates is to raise money. Louis also gives vent to his frustration at the opposition to his reforming plans in 1787–8: 'I have often been thwarted in my policies but my goal has never changed. I will be greatly in your debt, Messieurs, if you will give me your full support in accomplishing them.'

Louis then showed this draft to Marie-Antoinette, who advised him to omit the references to increased taxation and his having been thwarted in his reforming ambitions. She left in, however, the reference to the nobility and clergy renouncing their fiscal privileges and added that Louis was 'touched' by this gesture, which in fact only some of them had made. Louis includes all these changes in his second draft. The queen also adds: 'I hope that this assembly will maintain that submission which is necessary alike for the people's happiness and the preservation of the monarchy.' Louis, in his second draft, adds, after submission 'and the respect due to the laws', otherwise leaving the queen's sentence intact. Marie-Antoinette does not change Louis' statement, 'The burden of taxation and the indebtedness of the state, in combination with a spirit of anxiety and innovation, threaten the greatest misfortune if a prompt remedy is not brought to bear.'

Meanwhile the deputies were rolling in in droves – over 1,200 of them, more than a modern parliament, but then they were lords and commons together or separately as Necker would have liked. Why, he thought, not solve the voting problem by having two chambers, Lords and Commons, an idea he floated with several prominent Third-Estate deputies and 'everyone who had written in favour of an upper house'.[42] In such a system the opposing forces would be equally balanced 1:1 and the king could manoeuvre between them. Under the existing system either the aristocrats won (voting by Order conferred a permanent 2:1 majority) or the commoners did: under voting by head they would be bound to win adherents from the 'liberal' nobility and especially the clergy, since the country curates (heavily represented) had in entering the seminary merely exchanged their peasant smocks for the soutane. But here was an irony: the Third Estate deputation was heavily dominated by lawyers – there were few merchants and only one genuine peasant, Père Gérard, who was sometimes depicted in a smock but actually wore his Sunday best. So the officially styled First Order (the Clergy) was the only one to contain men of peasant origins. And though the Third Estate claimed to represent the 95 per cent of the population who were neither clergy nor nobles, an equal 95 per cent who lived in the countryside were best represented by the clergy and nobility who had country estates. These are not just clever historians' points – they were made at the time.

On 4 May, the day before the opening of the Estates-General, there was a procession and solemn Mass. Louis looked radiant but Marie-Antoinette's 'brow was troubled, her lips tight-set and she made vain attempts to hide her agitation'. Any cries of 'Vive la Reine', Bombelles noted, were stifled. He continued: 'Never has a Queen of France been less popular; and yet no act of wickedness can be laid at her door. We are decidedly unjust to her and far too severe in punishing

1 The imperial family. Painted in 1760 when she was five, the child seated in the background may be Marie-Antoinette. The emperor Francis I is seated on the left, Maria-Theresa to the right with Joseph on her right and Leopold on her left. Maria-Theresa treated Marie-Antoinette badly, ignoring her education until she became a valuable pawn on the international chessboard – one that could be and was sacrificed to imperial ambition.

2 Marie-Antoinette was miserable as dauphine: treated as a child by Louis XV, despising Madame
du Barry, ignored by her husband and at odds with the ministry which had ousted her protector,
Choiseul, she could only dream of vengeance when the time came. It came sooner than anyone
expected – a year after this portrait was painted.

3 Marie-Antoinette's brothers Joseph, emperor 1765–90, and Leopold, emperor 1790–2. The eldest son of Maria-Theresa and Francis, emperor and co-ruler with his mother after Francis's death in 1765, Joseph was close to Marie-Antoinette but his attempts to get her to support his expansionary policies only had the effect of making her unpopular. Right up to his sudden death Marie-Antoinette complained that Leopold maintained a 'profound silence' on his stance towards the Revolution.

4 This portrait does not compliment Louis XVI, Marie-Antoinette or her brother Maximilian Francis – they look like waxwork figures – and raises the question of whether the rest of the illustrations shown in my selection flattered them. Marie-Antoinette thought that only Vigée-Lebrun could catch her likeness.

5 Marie-Antoinette's in-laws. Clever Provence (left) subtly undermined Louis both before and during the Revolution but became a surprisingly effective king as Louis XVIII (1814–24). Artois and Marie-Antoinette were close in her early heedless years but they drifted apart as he aligned himself politically with the Polignac set and Calonne. He compromised her with his counter-revolutionary activities. Elizabeth stayed in France and looked after the children in prison until her own execution in 1794.

6 Madame de Polignac by Elisabeth Vigée-Lebrun, 1782. The relationship between Polignac and Marie-Antoinette was intense but not, as some suggested, lesbian. Politically she was aligned with the king, who used her to calm Marie-Antoinette down after her attempts to get French backing for her Austrian relatives. This took its toll on the friendship. Yolande's influence revived in 1789 and influenced the disastrous policies which culminated in the fall of the Bastille and the emigration of the Polignac set.

7 In 1784, the comte de Vaudreuil was invested with the Saint-Esprit, the highest order of chivalry, and to celebrate the honour Vigée-Lebrun painted him twice, once wearing the star of the Order and the other its *cordon bleu*. Marie-Antoinette detested Vaudreuil and this caused friction with Madame de Polignac who was his lover. Moreover, Vaudreuil's best friend was Artois, who was a thorn in Marie-Antoinette's side during the Revolution.

8 Marie-Antoinette first encountered Fersen briefly in 1774, just before she became queen. Despite – or maybe because of – long absences, the relationship deepened to the point where most authors now consider that they became lovers, the only question being: when? The years 1783, 1786 and 1792 are possibilities. Fersen increasingly gave Marie-Antoinette political advice; it was mostly bad advice, but he did organize the successful escape from Paris in 1791.

9 Vigée-Lebrun painted this family group in 1787 during Marie-Antoinette's brief political ascendancy. Marie-Thérèse-Charlotte stands on the left; the baby is the duc de Normandie, later Louis XVII. The 'first' dauphin, Louis-Joseph, stands on the right, pointing to the empty cradle of Marie-Antoinette's last child, Sophie, who had died in infancy that year. The dauphin was not as healthy as he looks here and would soon join Sophie.

10 This contemporary reimagining shows Benjamin Franklin (wearing a homespun coat instead of the silk he actually wore) about to be crowned with a laurel wreath by Diane de Polignac, whom Jean-Louis Soulavie considered to be the brains behind the Polignac set. Yolande de Polignac is on the left and the princesse de Lamballe, holding flowers, is next to her. The foreign secretary Vergennes, to the right of Franklin, thwarted all Marie-Antoinette's half-hearted attempts to further her brother Joseph's expansionary policies.

11 Appointed in 1783 while Marie-Antoinette suffered a miscarriage, Calonne tried to thwart her purchase of Saint-Cloud and successfully mobilized his faction to work for Rohan's acquittal. Once Calonne was wounded by the Notables' opposition to his comprehensive reform package, Marie-Antoinette delivered the coup de grâce. She came to regret her role in his fall as it marked the beginning of the revolutionary situation. The public was unaware of her hostility to the minister and at her trial Marie-Antoinette was criticized for her links with 'the execrable Calonne'.

12 This infamous necklace was created by Boehmers towards the end of the last reign out of 647 large diamonds and was spectacular for 'the size, whiteness, match and fire of the stones'. The heist relied on the assumption that the queen was capable of making a midnight assignation with a prince of the church to buy diamonds valued at 2 million francs without consulting the king. It marked a milestone in the unravelling of the regime.

13 On the mantelpiece of the council chamber stands a clock to the glory of Louis XIV, made for Louis XV in 1754. The two vases, known as the Mars and the Minerva, were made for this room in 1787. A year later Marie-Antoinette attended the council for the first time for the discussions which resulted in doubling the representation of the Third Estate.

14 Marie-Antoinette profited from the king's dejection after his defeat by the Notables to have Loménie de Brienne nominated principal minister in 1787. Marie-Antoinette started attending cabinet committees and Brienne's unpopularity increased hers. In July 1788 she lamented 'How unfortunate she was to have chosen as principal minister a man who had enjoyed the reputation of eminent merit but who had rendered himself odious to the nation; how cruel it was to see herself hated when all she had wanted was the good of France.'

15 After the séance of 23 June, the Third Estate simply refused to obey the king's order to 'disperse immediately'. To the Master of Ceremonies, Mirabeau addressed his famous apostrophe: 'Go tell your master that we will only move at the point of the bayonet!' But Mirabeau was a monarchist who dreamt of being the modern Richelieu. He gave Marie-Antoinette what she had been in search of – a political philosophy and a modus operandi.

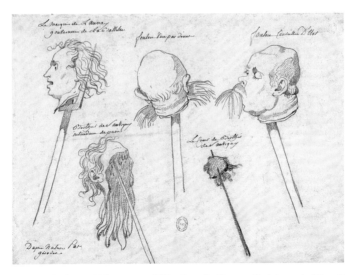

16 The centre-right deputy Malouet wrote: 'If the Court had been at Paris instead of Versailles, it would have been the ministers, the Princes who would have been slaughtered instead of Foulon [centre], his son-in-law Berthier [below and heart] and de Launay [left]. It was as the agents of the Government that they were pursued . . . here was a ferocious populace in search of victims and it would have taken them alike in the street or on the throne.' Barnave asked in the National Assembly: 'When all is said and done, was the blood which has just been shed all that pure?'

17 A Bodyguard is hacked down by the mob outside the queen's bedroom at dawn on 6 October 1789, but he is able to shout 'save the queen'. Marie-Antoinette finds safety by using a secret passage. Disappointed of their prey, the mob slash her bed to ribbons. Henceforth, death becomes Marie-Antoinette's familiar spirit, a corrosive fear which colours the rest of her life.

18 Bombelles commented: 'As for M. de La Fayette, a lot of people are asking why he wants to be mixed up in everything, given that he is intrinsically nothing.' That was in 1788. By 1789–90 Lafayette was almost everything: commander of the Parisian National Guard, he was the most important man in France. During the period of his pomp he bullied Marie-Antoinette whom he held responsible for stiffening the king's resistance to the Revolution. Consequently, she opposed his attempts in 1792 to rescue the monarchy.

19 Barnave was Marie-Antoinette's unlikely partner in government in 1791. In fact their positions had converged. Whilst never disavowing his role in the Revolution, Barnave now thought it must be 'stopped' before it descended into an attack on property. Marie-Antoinette saw in Barnave the living proof that talent and good manners were not the preserve of the nobility – nor should the plum appointments be. For three months they ruled the country by letter.

l'Homme du Peuple *l'Homme de la Cour*.

Tantot Froid tantot Chaud Tantot blanc tantot noir
A Droite maintenant mais autrefois a gauche
Je vous disoit bon jour, et je vous dis bon Soir

20 This 'Janus head' engraving mocks Barnave's change of course. The left-facing head is captioned 'the man of the people'; the right, 'the man of the court'. His right foot tramples 'The Rights of Man, Tennis Court Oath and "is this blood so pure"', and his left 'Patriotism, Liberty, and Virtue'. In his hand is a bag of gold with, left, 'Civil List' and right, 'opinion on the rights of negroes'. But as Lamartine wrote, 'Mirabeau sold himself, Barnave gave himself'.

21 An acolyte of Lafayette's, the justice minister du Tertre contemplated putting Marie-Antoinette on trial. But he soon changed his tune and was the ministerial conduit for the policies thrashed out between Barnave and the queen. Put on trial with Barnave, he told the Revolutionary Tribunal: 'You are going to kill me, posterity will try me.'

22 After the king abandoned the Tuileries on 10 August, the royal family took refuge in the Assembly where they were placed in the reporters' box (top right). Bachmann, the major of the Swiss Guards, had said 'If the king goes to the Assembly he is lost'. Marie-Antoinette had wanted to stay and fight: 'Nail me to these walls before I will consent to leave them.' Louis was suspended from his functions, not deposed as the mob here demands: his fate was to be decided by a new assembly, a National Convention, voted by manhood suffrage.

23 Despite the unpromising start to their marriage, the king and queen came to love each other in their way. This engraving of their farewells the night before the king was guillotined is not sentimental. The girl, Madame Royale, was the only one to survive the Revolution.

24 Pressed at her trial to answer the accusation of incest with the dauphin, Marie-Antoinette replied: 'If I did not respond, it was because it would be against nature for a mother to reply to such an accusation. On this I appeal to all the mothers who may be here.'

25 Jacques-Louis David was not just a great painter but a member of the Committee of General Security. In this capacity he accompanied Hébert when he questioned the dauphin over his relationship with his mother. It was thus a determined enemy who made this cruel sketch from a window as Marie-Antoinette passed in her tumbrel. However, though ravaged by illness and suffering, Marie-Antoinette, to paraphrase Milton, 'appeared not less than queen ruin'd and th' excess of glory obscur'd'.

26 Marie-Antoinette on her way to the guillotine depicted by Jacques-Louis David. Her hair, once golden, now white, is cropped for the guillotine. Her grim face shows pride but above all exhaustion and illness – she had been haemorrhaging for weeks and did so again the night before her execution.

her for, at most, a few examples of flightiness.'[43] And yet she had brought back the people's idol, Necker, supported *doublement* in the Council debate, and resisted pressure from her friends to have Necker dismissed. She looked anxious again during the opening ceremony on 5 May.

The ceremony was the final symbolic fling of the society of Orders soon to disappear even from memory. The nobility wore brightly coloured costumes with plumes in their hats. The clergy wore clothes of sombre magnificence. These first two Orders were allowed in first before the deputies for the Third Estate in regulation plain black clothes and plumeless hats were finally admitted. Famously, they were kept waiting in the rain. It was hoped/feared that Necker would throw some light on the two burning issues of the day: the division of power between king and Assembly, and voting arrangements within that body. Necker, whether deliberately or not, offered only obfuscation. The *Correspondance secrète* offers as hearsay (*on prétend*) a dialogue that probably did take place 'a few days' before the opening:

> M. Necker . . . being with the king in the presence of a throng of courtiers, His Majesty suddenly came out with: 'Monsieur Necker, will I be presenting a constitution to the Estates-General or will the Estates-General be presenting one to me?' M. Necker was a little embarrassed as to how to reply but he was even more so later that day when finding himself with the queen she asked him, 'whether the Estates-General will be the masters over the king or whether the king will remain the master of the nation'.

I say this exchange (or similar) probably did take place because Louis made these points when correcting the draft of Necker's speech: 'At the beginning I have added "at the request" of the Estates because . . . they cannot make law on their own'.[44] No previous Estates-General had. Louis probably wanted to give his subjects a constitution or at the very least to retain the initiative in legislation as the king of England did.

This was the heart of the matter, left unresolved, but it was temporarily obscured by wrangling in the Estates over whether voting should be by Order or by head. On this the government speeches said little either. It was difficult to disentangle from them any marked preference let alone a decision on one or the other. Barentin seemed to favour voting by Order, Necker a mixed system depending on the matter to be discussed. And he let on –inadvertently – that ultimately he favoured a two-chamber system, as in England. This was 'slipped in' (twice) and this time Louis did not remove it. Perhaps he hadn't noticed it – no one else did or has. Necker was leaving it to the Estates to sort out their own voting procedures. These, however, were essentially technical matters, if ones with political implications, which the king could and should have resolved before the Estates opened, though precedent and public opinion were against this. Saint-Priest thought Necker just did not want to delay the opening of the Estates.

The first seven weeks of the Estates (until 17 June) were occupied by procedural wrangles designed to pre-empt the question of voting by Order or head. The deputies of the Third Estate insisted that the credentials of all the deputies should be 'verified' in the third's chamber, refusing to constitute themselves as a separate Order as the nobility and clergy quickly did. The king offered a futile arbitration service and many suspected that the lack of a resolution would give him an excuse to dissolve the Estates-General.

At some point during this vast expanse of time, the still centre of the storm, Marie-Antoinette underwent a volte-face. Having originally supported the Third Estate, she was now vacillating between the king and Artois. A gap in her correspondence with Joseph II makes it difficult to speak with certainty about her views in May and June. This difficulty is compounded by the fact that since the fall of Brienne she had been extremely circumspect in her behaviour, 'imposing on herself the useful, even necessary expedient' of making herself forgotten in the hope that her unpopularity would die down.[45] We have pieced together evidence of a discrete support for the pretensions of the Third Estate, but Jeanne Arnaud-Bouteloup is 'uneasy' in attributing any policies to the queen in the entire period between August 1788 and June 1789,[46] when moreover she gave herself up to family life and tending to the dauphin who was dying before her eyes. But her watchword was caution.

This comes across strongly and with tragic overtones in a letter to Mercy of 27 February concerning foreign policy. Joseph wanted to draw France into the Austro-Russian alliance against Turkey. Marie-Antoinette told Mercy that this was frankly impossible. Turkey was a traditional ally of France and the combination proposed would make it hard for her to mediate in the struggle. But there was a further consideration: 'although the Estates-General ought not to meddle in questions of peace and war there would nevertheless be complaints and protests if they saw a new treaty which could lead to an increase of expenditure' – especially a treaty involving Austria, because 'of the prejudices against my brother'. Furthermore 'half the population is persuaded that I am sending millions to Germany' and this would make it 'inevitable that I should be held responsible for this treaty and that in the Estates-General the ministers should turn the blame for it on my apparent credit and influence. Imagine the odious role I should be made to play.'[47]

Marie-Antoinette, then, at the end of May was still exercising discretion both in home and foreign affairs, though discreetly supporting Necker. But in June, Necker's son-in-law, the baron de Staël, writes of Artois' confidence 'now that he has won over the Queen',[48] and Mercy describes her as having been momentarily 'swept along by the infernal plot directed against the Finance Minister'.[49] Hitherto, as we have seen, she had resisted this pressure.

We cannot know precisely what caused this volte-face but it occurred shortly after the long agony of the dauphin ended with his death on 4 June. In the vain hope that the bracing air would do the boy good, he had been moved from Versailles to the château of Meudon, on a hill 4 kilometres south of Paris. This meant that the king and queen had to make frequent visits to the dying boy when the political situation required their presence at Versailles. Marie-Antoinette attended his deathbed bathed in tears, but the boy's governor, the duc d'Harcourt, interposed himself between them so the dauphin would not see her crying. The dauphin noticed this and asked him to get out of the way, 'so that I may have the pleasure of seeing my mother crying'. The boy's mind was obviously wandering and he just meant he wanted to enjoy a last glimpse of his mother, but malicious courtiers gave this as an example of Bourbon depravity even in one so young.[50] Back at Versailles, the courtiers in black 'filed in a sort of slow procession' past a queen 'almost throttled by sobs'.[51] Lady Elizabeth Foster claimed that she told Marie-Antoinette she should have another son, to which the queen replied, 'And why? So the Duc d'Orléans can have him killed?'[52]

Fersen had been preparing to join his regiment at Valenciennes for the summer but he deferred his departure to comfort the queen and saw her on 6 June. He wrote to his father a clinical account of the boy's death: 'M. Le dauphin died on the night of the 3rd/4th. This event has not created much of a stir because it was long expected and his ill-health prevented him from receiving the education necessary for a prince.' What advice Fersen gave the queen we do not know. He saw her again on 13 June and the next day left for Valenciennes, because the royal family was leaving Marly that day.[53]

They stayed at Marly, a château 27 kilometres to the west of Paris, from 14 to 21 June. This unusual trip in the middle of a crisis was arranged by the comte d'Artois and Madame de Polignac ostensibly to allow the boys' parents a space to grieve, actually to isolate and convert them to their cause. Necker later wrote that 'the visit to Marly had been arranged to make it easier to surround the King and to work his mind against the plans of the Ministry'; Vaudreuil advised, 'let us make sure that nothing contrary to us reaches [the king and queen] and leads them to turn towards the nation either from prudence or from weakness'.[54]

Montjoie wrote: 'A vast silence reigned about the King; access to the throne was difficult.'[55]

At first Necker's enemies had not found the king receptive; one of their group, the comtesse d'Adhémar, writes:

We never ceased repeating to the king that the Third Estate would wreck everything and we were right. We begged him to restrain them, to impose his sovereign authority on party intrigue. The King replied: 'But it is not clear that the *tiers* are wrong. Different forms have been followed each time the Estates have been held. So why reject verification in common? I am for it.' The King, it has to be admitted, was then numbered among the revolutionaries: a strange fatality which can only be explained by detecting the hand of Providence.[56]

But the king's resistance and more easily that of the queen was broken by an act of flagrant defiance by the Third Estate. Tired of waiting for the other Orders to join them, on 17 June they unilaterally declared themselves to be the 'National Assembly'. Moreover, in d'Angiviller's penetrating analysis, 'it declared null and void all hitherto existing taxes and established the principle that even in the past, the tacit consent of the nation had not been sufficient to legitimize a tax, that its formal consent was necessary and that registration by the parlements had not been a substitute.'[57] The whole *ancien régime*, stretching from 1614 to 1789, had lacked legitimacy.

The king returned to Versailles to hold an emergency session of the Council. Even before the declaration of the National Assembly, Necker had finally come round to the view that it was time for royal intervention in what was still – and Marie-Antoinette long continued to call – the Estates. Necker proposed that the king should deploy the panoply of a *lit de justice* to command the first two Orders to join the third in discussing matters of general interest including the crucial one of the organization of future Estates, but that matters like the feudal and honorific privileges of the nobility should be voted by Order. Also that the king 'reserved to himself the full exercise of the executive power, especially the administration of the army'.[58] Necker wanted to 'pass over' in silence the declaration of a National Assembly in the hope that, once voting procedures had been settled, the problem would go away. The Council finished at 9.30 p.m. so a further meeting was arranged for 19 June, back at Marly, to finalize details for the *séance royale*. Necker thought that this was a mere formality but the *conseiller d'état* Vidaud de la Tour, who played a key role in drafting the final text, considered that Necker's memorandum was merely 'taken into consideration'. Vidaud's role was recognized in a satirical pamphlet where he was christened 'Le Sieur Astuce' (Sir Crafty).[59]

When Necker arrived at Marly the queen summoned him and tried to dissuade him from reading his memorandum, 'to which she was violently opposed' to the Council. She and Artois had another version in mind. Voting in common on matters of general interest would be retained, but the king would suggest that motions should only be carried by a two-thirds majority and insisted that the organization of future Estates should be decided by the Orders sitting separately. This perpetuated the key element of the old social order: division into Orders, rather than union of citizens. Otherwise the reaffirmation of the promises made in the *Résultat du Conseil* may have sufficed. Necker went ahead and read his memorandum to the Council where, he claimed, no substantive objections were raised. The king had remained silent but, according to Necker, was about to terminate the session by approving the proposals:

> and the portfolios were already closing when suddenly we saw an official in attendance enter; he approached the King's fauteuil, whispered to him and immediately His Majesty rose, instructing his ministers to remain where they were and await his return. This message, coming as the Council was about to finish, naturally surprised us all. M. de Montmorin, who was sitting next to me, told me straight out: 'Everything is undone; only the Queen could have allowed herself to interrupt the Conseil d'État; the Princes must have got round her and they want, by her intervention, to postpone the King's decision.'[60]

Saint-Priest, who also attended the Council, thought such an 'interruption' of its proceedings was 'without known precedent' and 'amazed all its participants'. The king was gone for 'nearly an hour' and 'on his return some change in his demeanour was noticed'. It was later learned that 'he had been subjected to a verbal mangling by the queen and the comte d'Artois and a lighter squeeze by Monsieur'. Louis reconvened the Council the next day at Versailles and the queen for the second time in her life attended it. The king said the final decision would be taken back at Marly.

Necker could not attend, being detained in Paris by the extremity of his sister-in-law, Madame de Germany, but, realizing the pressures the king would be under, he sent him an urgent note: 'Several drawbacks to a *séance royale* which I had missed have been pointed out to me and it is thought that a simple letter of invitation [to the Orders] would serve better.' But orders had already been given to the troops in preparation for the *séance royale* to bar entry to the hall in which the Assembly met. The *séance* was announced for 22 June, but crassly by wall posters, not even a royal message. The Assembly, wrongly concluding that the king intended dissolution of the Estates-General, took a further, decisive, step: repairing to an indoor real-tennis court, they took the famous oath not to separate until they had given France a constitution (20 June). Just them, not the king alone or even in conjunction with the Assembly.

And it was in this charged atmosphere that the Council met again at Marly. The chevalier de Coigny, one of the Polignac group, writes to the bishop of Soissons how the queen and Artois tried to persuade the king to adopt their version. Louis still vacillated, so Mme de Polignac wheeled in the royal children, and the queen

pushed them into the arms of their father, beseeching him to hesitate no further and to confound the plans of the enemies of the family. The king, touched by her tears and by so many representations, gave way and inti- mated his desire to hold a Council on the spot. The princes were sent for and the Council met immediately without summoning . . . [Necker] who knows nothing of this. Everything is settled: the King will issue a declaration which will satisfy the nation, will order the deputies to work in their respective Chambers and will severely punish the meddlers and intriguers. You may rest assured that he will not budge and a *séance royale* is announced; it is there that the plan that I tell you of will be unfolded . . .[61]

It was the Tennis Court Oath rather than the declaration of the National Assembly that enabled Marie-Antoinette to prevail. For Louis could not allow the Assembly to have unfettered legislative let alone constituent power. The *séance*, in which for the last time the king appeared in his full regalia, was a fiasco. The Third Estate simply refused to obey the king's order to 'disperse immediately and proceed tomorrow morning each to the Chamber allocated to his Order'. To the Master of Ceremonies, Mirabeau addressed his famous apos- trophe about only moving at the point of the bayonet. The versions of Louis' reactions to this are at total variance, ranging from 'No, not bayonets' and 'So they want to stay? Damn it let them' to 'Clear them out!' The very criers refused to proclaim the new laws, claiming that they had colds.

Something more must be said about the programme enunciated in the *séance royale*, because 'as necessarily modified by circumstances and events',[62] as Marie-Antoinette put it, it was to be the basis of her policy for the rest of her life and for the monarchy, whether in exile or restored, for the next forty years. Vidaud de la Tour, the councillor of state who drafted the final version, said that the differences between it and Necker's version 'were not considerable but essential'.[63] This is not surprising because this final version resembled the programme announced in the *Résultat du Conseil*, which had been drafted by Necker and endorsed by Marie-Antoinette. That programme had, according to the duc de Luxembourg, granted 'all that the Estates-General on bended knees would have dared to ask'. But the National Assembly was not asking for anything let alone on bended knees; it was not even consulting the king; it had by the Tennis Court Oath sworn unilaterally to provide France with a constitution. The king wanted to issue a constitutional charter such as 'La Charte' that Provence, now Louis XVIII, was to issue on his restoration in 1814. But the National Assembly would have none of it – whether it was Necker's version or Vidaud's. Necker's ally Saint-Priest admitted as much in a letter to the king two days before the *séance* when he conceded that the Third Estate 'in its present exalted state . . . might well take umbrage at the sovereign intervention of Your Majesty at this juncture'.[64]

At this stage of the Revolution at least there was not a great gap between what the king was prepared to grant and what the Assembly was determined to impose. But in a deeper sense it did matter which, because if the king issued a charter he was still sovereign whereas if the Assembly drafted a constitution it was. And if the king issued a charter he could withdraw or modify it. And if the Assembly did, it could also – and did in 1793, 1795 and 1799. Everyone, including Marie-Antoinette, knew this: the Third Estate deputies were mostly lawyers and the councillors of state who advised the king were essentially lawyers.

Necker had absented himself from the *séance*, which refurbished his fading popularity; which is ironic because, as Saint-Priest suggests, his version of the *séance royale* would probably have been rejected as well. Necker had not informed the king, who arrived at the ceremony to find the other ministers and state councillors in place but the finance minister's chair empty. Louis waited a little for him to arrive, looking round myopically, but Necker was sitting in his carriage He was in a quandary: to resign before the *séance* would have caused a riot. On the other hand to attend the *séance* would be to endorse policies of which he disapproved. So he sat in his carriage with the horses harnessed up and dithered until his daughter, the feisty Madame de Staël, told him it would be dishonourable to attend. Marie-Antoinette qualified Necker's absence as 'treason or criminal cowardice'.[65] Nevertheless she summoned him and for twenty minutes begged him not to resign. She needed to because with rumours of his resignation swirling through the streets of Versailles, a vast populace poured into the royal palace, reaching the doors of the royal apartments, where, on this occasion, the Bodyguards were able to halt them.

Necker agreed to stay on. The hardliners blamed Marie-Antoinette for her conciliatory tone, as Vaudreuil recounts:

'Dare I ask the Queen,' I said bowing respectfully, 'whether M. Necker accompanied the King to the Assembly?' 'No,' she replied with an air of surprise and annoyance, 'but why this question?' 'Just that if the principal minister is not put on trial today, tomorrow the monarchy will be destroyed.' Hardly had I pronounced these words when a severe gesture from the Sovereign ordered me to leave. I bowed even lower to show even greater respect: 'I am pained to see that I have incurred the Queen's displeasure but I will never hesitate between favour and duty.' After a third bow, even lower than the others, I retired and was not recalled.[66]

Necker was not able to get Louis to agree to form a ministry of Necker's choice but on 27 June the king commanded the nobility and clergy deputies to join what was now officially the National Assembly. According to Mercy, this was brought about by the 'moderation and wisdom of . . . [the queen's] counsels'.[67] It was equally likely that she was just scared. She knew she was hated, protected only by the king's gravity-defying popularity. On the previous Friday or Saturday, whilst the Council was discussing intervention, the dwellings of even moderate nobles, like the marquis de Ferrières, had been painted with a black 'P' for 'Proscribed'.

But Marie-Antoinette was only playing for time. 'Straight after . . . [the *séance royale*] she agreed with the king's brothers to overturn the ministry and form a new one.' Necker and Montmorin, the foreign secretary, would have to go, 'but the queen wanted to sound out my [Saint-Priest's] thinking and summoned me to her presence'. Saint-Priest advised that in the current volatile situation 'extreme measures would be dangerous' and that, whatever his failings, Necker had to be retained. 'Seeing that his advice had not found favour', Saint-Priest realized that his ministerial days were numbered.[68]

That number was about twenty days, the time it would take to bring troops up to Paris; for as long as the king controlled the army, and so long as the army remained loyal and could be paid, the Tennis Court Oath was only words. The first orders had been given on 22 June, the day Necker's version was finally jettisoned and the day before the *séance royale*: the troop build-up was an important concomitant of the *séance*. Louis signed the first order, for the Swiss Reinach regiment to leave Soissons and arrive at Paris on 26 June. On that day, the day before he ordered the nobility to sit in the National Assembly, further orders were given, so that by 14 July there were some 30,000 troops assembled in the

Paris region – far short of the 100,000 intended. They were put under the general command of the duc de Broglie with Marie-Antoinette's friend Besenval his field commander in Paris, though as a wag had it, he was more suited to the service of Venus than of Mars. The satirical pamphlet cited above took Broglie's measure when it dubbed him 'Marshal Rodomantade'.

But what were the troops summoned for? Most people at the time (and since) have assumed that the king's intention was to throw off the mask of conciliation, dissolve the National Assembly, and subdue Paris by force of arms. There is not a shred of evidence for this assumption. The correspondence between Broglie and Besenval contains no mention of offensive measures; even defensive ones are restricted. On 1 July, Broglie writes:

> The King consents that you assemble all the forces on which you can rely to safeguard the Royal Treasury and the Discount Bank and that you confine yourself to defending these two positions . . . at a time when we are unfortunately not in a position to look to everything. I shall authorize the marquis d'Autichamp to remain in his command at Sèvres and then, if it becomes necessary, to bring up the Salis Regiment as reinforcements to protect Versailles, falling back on the Palace if necessary.[69]

Defending 'the palace' was Marie-Antoinette's priority: the troops were ordered to guard the approaches to Versailles from Paris and to guard the royal palaces of Rambouillet, La Muette, Meudon and Marly. Fersen's register records several letters to and from Marie-Antoinette but not their content. However, we can guess at this from Fersen's correspondence with his father since, being away at Valenciennes, he probably relied on the queen for his information. Fersen told his father: 'approximately 10,000 to 15,000 men are being brought to the area surrounding Versailles, at La Muette and Meudon, but my regiment is not yet among' them. He needed to be there because 'one cannot rely on French soldiers and so it is necessary to employ foreigners as much as possible'. Again, was he repeating Marie-Antoinette's view of the situation? She was nervous and frightened: it was the first time she had raised her head above the parapet in nearly a year. Naturally she would want her lover to be there to guard her with the regiment she had procured for him. Whether spontaneously or in response to her request, he wrote to Marie-Antoinette both privately (addressed to 'Josephine') and formally (Madame), so this letter could be forwarded to the war minister asking that his regiment be sent to Versailles.[70] Events, however, moved too quickly for Fersen's regiment to be brought up.

There is no mention in Fersen's letters of Paris. Versailles did not want to attack Paris; rather the fear was that Paris would attack Versailles in support of the National Assembly. Similar concerns had induced Louis XIV to build Versailles in the first place. The troops were to hold the ring whilst the programme announced in the *séance royale* was implemented; to create a *cordon sanitaire* between Paris and Versailles or possibly, as the king suggested to the Assembly, translate it to Compiègne. For all this the dismissal of the Necker ministry was necessary and its replacement by another. It was headed by Breteuil. Marie-Antoinette had mixed feelings about him. His judgement in the Diamond Necklace Affair had been clouded by personal animosity towards Cardinal Rohan; his resignation from the Brienne ministry at a most critical time must have seemed, like Necker's absence from the *séance royale*, an act of treason or cowardice. And, as we have seen, he had no plan: he devoted his one hundred hours in office to organizing his secretariat. He was the sort of man who would keep summoning his *premier commis* (assuming he had time to appoint one) just to hear the flattering 'Oui, premier ministre' or, more correctly his *chef du conseil*, though that sounds a bit culinary.

Breteuil's appointment, or rather Necker's dismissal, led to the very 'general insurrection' Broglie had told Besenval they could not contain: 'If there is a general insurrection we cannot defend the whole of Paris and you must confine yourself to the plan for the defence of the Bourse, the Royal Treasury, the Bastille and the Invalides.' They couldn't even do that: the Invalides was invaded and the weapons seized there used to storm the Bastille. Everyone in Paris associated with the government was slaughtered. The centre-right deputy Malouet wrote: 'If the Court had been at Paris instead of Versailles, it would have been the ministers, the Princes who would have been slaughtered instead of Foulon [a minister in the new government], his son-in-law Berthier [Intendant of Paris] and de Launay [governor of the Bastille]. It was as the agents of the Government that they were pursued . . . here was a ferocious populace in search of victims and it would have taken them alike in the street or on the throne.'[71] Foulon's mouth was stuffed with grass for having allegedly said 'let them eat grass', which has no more authenticity than Marie-Antoinette's supposed 'let them eat cake' or 'brioche' in the less contemptuous French version. There can be little doubt that if Marie-Antoinette had been there she would have been killed and her corpse mutilated.

The 'assassination' as he called it, of Foulon and Berthier elicited a notorious rhetorical question from Barnave in the National Assembly: 'When all is said and done, was the blood which has just been shed all that pure?' In his *Introduction* Barnave expressed regret for his words but said they had to be placed in context. He was replying to Lally-Tollendal's speech calling for a proc-lamation condemning the lynchings, which is what they were. Lally had turned on the emotion, employing 'theatrical tricks'. Barnave had employed the 'you can't make an omelette without breaking eggs' argument, which would become a revolutionary trope, adding that the answer was not to condemn the Revolution but to reorganize municipal government.[72]

At first no one dared to tell the king about the events in Paris, but on the night of 15/16 July an emergency meeting of the Council was held at which Breteuil advocated flight to Metz, which had a strong citadel. Artois went down on both knees begging him to go. But as Louis later recounted, 'Monsieur himself begged me not to go and the maréchal de Broglie, the commander-in-chief, replied to me: "We can certainly go to Metz but what do we do when we get there?" I was abandoned by everyone.'[73] According to Madame Campan, Marie-Antoinette attended this Council and advocated flight escorted by the troops whom the king had ordered to return to their posts. She packed her jewels and burnt her papers.

The Council being divided, Louis was meant to decide but, as with the fateful decision to enter the American War of Independence, he didn't want to: 'So, Messieurs, we have to decide: Do I go or do I stay? I am ready for either.' In the end he stayed, obsessed as he was by the fear of civil war or of his cousin Orléans seizing a vacant throne. Whatever the grounds for the latter fear, Barentin, no less, told the royal historiographer, Moreau, at two o'clock on the morning of 16 July: 'I believe we must have recourse to another dynasty.'[74] The members of the short-lived ministry fled, Breteuil it is said disguised as a monk. He had been of little use, but Marie-Antoinette continued to put her faith in him and within a year she would be in communication with him on ways of resisting the onward march of the Revolution.

Madame de Polignac was so publicly identified with the Breteuil ministry that she too had to leave. There are various accounts of her departure. One has the king telling her, 'I have just ordered the comte d'Artois to leave. I now give you the same order. Pity me, but don't lose a moment. Take your family with you. You will always be able to count on me. I will not fill your offices.'[75] This leaves open whether the king was sending them away for their own safety or exiling them for political purposes. Diane de Polignac's contemporary account rings truest, particularly as it redounds to her own disadvantage. M. de Polignac persuaded his reluctant wife that they should leave. They went to Marie-Antoinette and told her they must go, 'because their presence acted as a pretext for all the horrible things that were being said about Her Majesty'. 'At the word "leave" the queen collapsed in tears. The king entered and Her Majesty told him "they want to go". Then the king squeezed . . . [Madame de Polignac's] hand and said to her, "All the decent people are abandoning us, then?" "No, Sire," replied my brother [M. de Polignac], "just give the word and we will stay if you think that we can be of use to Your Majesties" . . . We were thinking of the queen's safety and not our own.' The queen said 'wait a while', hoping things would calm down. When they didn't, at 8.0 p.m. on 16 July, the queen told them to leave as quickly as possible 'as secretly as possible'. The king gave the Polignacs a false passport in the name of a Swiss merchant called Etlinger of Basle. The whole family travelled to Switzerland in a large berline. They did not dare to stop for food and subsisted for three days on bread and wine and had to make do with two shirts apiece.[76]

The comte d'Artois, on the other hand, the scatter-brained companion of Marie-Antoinette's youth, and Condé had to be ordered to go. Louis told them that he feared for their safety, but Lafayette, commander of the newly formed National Guard, claimed that Louis forced the emigration of Artois and Condé, who 'shed tears of rage' at having to go.[77] With Artois went his mistress Madame de Polastron, his friend Vaudreuil, also the Bourbon-Condé – they all packed up and left the country. The emigration had begun.

Soulavie has this withering indictment of the Polignacs:

> In six years they managed to destroy the reputation of the queen, to make that princess the object of the hatred of the whole French nation. A revolution was the result of the contempt she affected for the Court . . . and this revolution manifested itself both against the queen and against the Polignac women, enveloped them indistinctly in the proscription of 1789 . . . They had taken six years to build their fortune, in six days they were the sport, I do not say of the Revolution only but of the whole of France.[78]

A letter from the duc de Polignac in 1791, written 'with a naiveté devoid of any irony', suggests the Polignacs had no idea of the damage they had caused the queen: 'I defy anyone to raise his voice to accuse either Madame de Polignac or myself of having harmed her.'[79] 'Six years to build their fortune' except they hadn't saved a penny, which, as Marie-Antoinette bitterly observed, 'was a long way from what people thought in Paris'. Yolande hadn't made a profit from royal munificence because she was obliged to entertain the queen at a great rate. It was the norm at court to live up to one's income (and beyond), not within one's means. The Polignacs had helped to impoverish the state without enriching themselves. So the queen gave her friend a purse of 500 gold louis d'or for her travelling expenses and told her to regard it as a loan to be repaid in happier times.[80]

Those times never returned; and after their tearful farewell the two friends, who were to die within a month of each other, never met again. They did, however, maintain a correspondence that increasingly had to be secret. 'Nearly all the people,' Droz writes, 'who had taken part in the projects which had been so speedily overthrown, emigrated or retired to the provinces.'[81] Their departure 'left the queen', in Saint-Priest's words, 'more isolated than ever. Only Fersen remained, who continued to enjoy free access to her apartments at Versailles and had frequent rendez-vous at the Trianon.'[82]

The friendship between Marie-Antoinette and Madame de Polignac gave rise to a flood of pamphlets. Up to the emigration those attacking the favourite tended to be respectful of the queen, even in 1789: 'virtuous princess whose faults though not in your nature are nevertheless real, save the remaining shreds of your popularity by getting rid of the favourite Polignac. "La princesse Priape", was "the evil genius of Marie-Antoinette". This, it has been argued, was scarcely more than what Mercy had been urging on Marie-Antoinette for years.[83] But when she did send her friend into exile (permanently this time), the abuse only intensified. One pamphlet dubs Yolande 'The French Messalina', a trope that would be transferred to Marie-Antoinette at her trial. The full title of the pamphlet in translation is: 'The French Messalina or the nights of the duchesse de Polignac together with the mysterious adventures of the princesse d'Hénin and the queen, being a useful course of instruction for would be young libertines, written by the abbé [Vermont] who escorted the duchesse de Polignac on her flight' – a bit of a mouthful but a fair synopsis of the contents. Lesbianism is the frequent theme, the initiative coming now from the Polignac now from the queen. One pamphlet has Marie-Antoinette descending to Hell and addressing Madame du Barry: 'you are going to replace my Polignac: I can already see my sweet Jules in you . . . There, come and kiss me.' In analysing this material, Hector Fleischmann, no fan of Madame de Polignac, observes: 'the romantic interest of these encounters is a little puerile but they are brilliantly realized'.[84]

On 29 July the king sent Madame de Polignac a letter by ordinary post to the Poste Restante at Basle under the name of Etlinger he had given her. In it he said that he was in good health 'but not in spirits' and added 'the allegory of Pandora's box is really appropriate'.[85] He and Calonne had opened that box with the Assembly of Notables two long years ago, with the support of Madame de Polignac and the hostility of Marie-Antoinette, who had opened a similar box herself in sending Rohan for trial before the Parlement.

On the Polignacs' arrival at Basle they encountered Necker and his son-in-law, Erik Magnus Staël. Madame de Polignac gave him a letter to give to the queen saying they were safe. Necker looked puzzled. He did not know what had happened; the king's courier asking him to return had not arrived. He got Madame de Polignac to fill him in. She told him of the fall of the Bastille, the lynchings, the king's planned visit to Paris and the queen's doubt whether he would ever return. 'He seemed concerned', which he was – he would have to sort out the mess. Diane de Polignac did not believe him; she thought he was revelling in his anticipated triumph.[86] The bizarre encounter between Necker and Madame de Polignac gave rise to two satirical pamphlets supposedly reconstructing their exchanges.[87]

So Necker returned to office together with Montmorin, and Saint-Priest, the latter now given a portfolio particularly relevant to Marie-Antoinette, that of minister for the royal household and Paris. Marie-Antoinette 'put on a brave face' when she saw them and 'urged them to show zeal for the royal service, an obligation strengthened by being recalled to office'. Montmorin and Saint-Priest, hardened courtiers both, swallowed their pride and bowed low. This was not Necker's style. He replied that 'zeal for the king's service went with the job but that nothing obliged him to show gratitude' – for indeed his would be a thankless task. The situation was beyond his capacities and probably beyond those of anyone. He really was 'concerned'.

No one really knew what would happen next; it was 'Pandora's box' indeed. The Bastille had been taken by storm. It meant that the assumption of sovereignty implicit in the Tennis Court Oath had become a reality. It had been only theoretical as long as the king had the ability and willpower to use the army to assert his own rival sovereignty. The army was the *ultima ratio regum*, the king's ultimate weapon. Louis XIV had engraved the motto on his canons – and never had to use them. Louis XVI had needed to but hadn't. And wouldn't. Nor apparently would have Marie-Antoinette. 'How could Mirabeau', the demagogue-royalist who would advise her, 'how could Mirabeau seriously contemplate civil war?' she asked rhetorically. Maybe *ultima ratio regum* should be translated as the 'last resort of kings', almost a confession of failure, with its connotations of despair. Yet Marie-Antoinette, observing 'royal authority decline from day to day' after 14 July, said to Saint-Priest sadly, 'so long as the king is allowed the disposition of the army – otherwise all is lost'.

And the army *was* needed. What had happened in Paris on 14 July 'was communicated like an electric shock' throughout the country.[88] In every city, town, village, hamlet, the sequence was replicated: the royal officials were replaced by elected ones, the inadequate royal police by local national guards: Lafayette became the commander of the Paris national guard, the comte d'Estaing of the smaller one in the town that had grown up to service Versailles. The towns had spoken. The countryside had yet to speak. What did the peasants care about voting by head or by Order – in Sweden they had their own separate Order and it had swung behind the king. Louis XVI had abolished servitude *personnelle* or serfdom on his Crown lands in 1779 together with *mainmorte*, which prevented the serf from transmitting his land to any but his children. Why did the National Assembly not do the same and more? Tired of waiting, the peasantry resorted to burning châteaux, destroying records of feudal dues and simply ceasing to pay them. Their Bastille was the château.

The Assembly did not like this: many of the rich bourgeois who sat in the Assembly, though not noble, owned manors. The obvious solution would have been to send in the army. But they feared that the king would then turn the troops on themselves. So they decided to put a brave face on it and pretend that they had planned to abolish the feudal system all along. They did this in a carefully orchestrated session of the Assembly on the night of 4/5 August. They arranged that the duc d'Aiguillon, son of Marie-Antoinette's enemy and one of the richest men in France, should speak first to start the ball rolling, but he was actually pipped to the post by the vicomte de Noailles, whom Vergennes had tried to send to the siege of Gibraltar only to be overruled by Marie-Antoinette. The ball rolled further than expected and became a wrecking one, smashing the whole *ancien régime*: the abolition of privilege in taxation, tithes, sale of office, and the different privileges of the towns and provinces of France. Marie-Antoinette told Mercy that a Te Deum to celebrate this was not necessarily bad but 'inopportune' given continuing unrest in Normandy and Brittany.[89]

Then the Assembly began to draft a new constitution – it would take two years – beginning with a Declaration of Rights heavily influenced by the American one. Louis with some exaggeration told Lafayette that it was *his*, Lafayette's, declaration. In fact, the first nine of the seventeen articles of the Declaration were his and he had presented a version to the Assembly as early as 11 July, that is, before the fall of the Bastille.[90] The Assembly then decided to give the king a suspensive veto (for two parliaments) over legislation but no say whatsoever in the framing of legislation or the drafting of the Constitution, each section of which was to be presented to him for his 'sanction'. In other words he could take it or leave it, which implied abdication. Barnave, on the centre left of the Assembly, criticized his Grenoble colleague Mounier on the centre right for trying to reassemble the broken bits of the *ancien régime* into a more liberal configuration, in other words, 'a transaction between a power [the Assembly] which was everything and a power [the monarchy] which no longer existed'.

But Barnave was inconsistent. He rejected the solution chosen by Parliament in the Glorious Revolution of changing the order of succession in order to demonstrate that the king now ruled by its permission. He did this because Louis XVI, unlike Charles I and James II, was no tyrant. Also because there was no suitable replacement – who would want Orléans or Lafayette? Moreover, Barnave thought that given a unitary legislature (Mounier wanted two chambers) it was essential that the king should have not only a veto but the right of dissolution, which latter was denied. When the Constitution was finally operational, in September 1791, we will see how stubbornly Barnave and Marie-Antoinette defended the king's right to apply his veto against pressure from republicans. For Barnave believed that if the king did not have a veto, France would be de facto a republic.[91]

Many moderate deputies thought that the Assembly had overplayed its hand, run ahead of the will of Frenchmen as expressed in the *Cahiers de doléances*, and was too intimidated by the continued threat from Paris. Alarmed, several deputies asked the king to withdraw to Compiègne and propose that the Assembly be transferred to nearby Soissons – Louis had himself proposed this to the Assembly on 12 July, when it had enraged these same deputies. At this point – probably at this point alone – the king could and should have made a stand. But now, on 30 August, Louis himself refused to move. The bishop of Langres asked Necker why and received the 'impatient' reply: 'Monsieur, if you want to know the truth understand that our role is very arduous. The King is good but difficult to persuade. His Majesty was tired . . . he slept through the Council – an affectation he used to "conceal his agitation".[92] We were for translating the Assembly but the King woke up, said "No" and withdrew.'[93] This, not 15 July, was the chance Louis should have taken. On 15 July he would not have had a party. But he had now demonstrated his willingness to compromise and shown his opponents to be intransigent. People would have flocked to Compiègne.

Having decided to stay put, what was Louis to do? What did Marie-Antoinette think of the business? There were two aspects: the content of what was presented to him and the agency. As regards the content he had objections only of detail: after all had he not already abolished the worst aspects of serfdom on his own estates and had not the abolition of fiscal privileges for social and geographical entities been the whole point of his own royal revolution in 1787? But he thought that those feudal dues, which were really just the equivalent of rent, should not be forcibly redeemed and he also thought that confiscation of the seigneurial rights of foreign princes with possessions in the former German province of Alsace, the 'princes possessionés', would lead to a diplomatic row. It did and Louis informed the Assembly that the princes had already lodged strong protests. Later Marie-Antoinette would urge the foreign powers to make this a pretext for intervention. As regards the Declaration of Rights, he thought it was a metaphysical farrago (but kept his counsel for two years), and in any case drafting the preamble before the body of the text was like putting the cart before the horse.

The king said all this. What he chose not to say was that he entirely rejected the notion of the Assembly rather than the king giving France a constitution. In his own Declaration of 1791 he said that, in accordance with the *Cahiers de doléances*, it should be done by himself and the legislature 'in conjunction'. Marie-Antoinette, however, thought the constitution should be issued by the king alone. It should be based on the provisions of the *séance royale* of 23 June 'as necessarily modified by circumstances and events'.[94] It was a question of sovereignty quite as much as content. The king's detailed criticisms of the legislation (let alone his concealed questioning of the whole process) led to impasse. Pressure from Paris would have to be brought to bear on the king.

Louis and Marie-Antoinette got wind of the Parisians' advance. In his 1791 manifesto Louis said he had had 'ample warning' to make his escape. In September, Madame de Tourzel, Madame de Polignac's replacement as governess to the royal children – Louis had not kept the position open as he had promised the exiled favourite – was told to make her charges ready. Of Marie-Antoinette's four children only two were now living: Madame Royale, now eleven, and the four-year-old new dauphin, Louis-Charles. But Tourzel was not told where they were going and in fact they stayed put.[95] As a precaution, however, Saint-Priest, minister both for the royal household and the interior, brought up the seemingly loyal Flanders Regiment to bolster the palace's defences. To preserve their loyalty the Royal Bodyguard gave them a banquet. It was reported that some drunken officers had trampled underfoot the tricolour cockade that had been adopted in July – red and blue for Paris, white for the dynasty – and even sported a black Habsburg one. The queen was present; the king out hunting. In 1793, Antoine Fouquier-Tinville, the public prosecutor, said that this banquet 'degenerated into a veritable orgy as she [the queen] intended'.[96] This was the pretext for the long-planned march on Versailles. One of those who 'protested loudest about the banquet given by the Bodyguard' was Adrien Duport, the guiding hand of the 'Comité des Trente', who had orchestrated the Third Estates' campaign in 1788 but was later an adviser, with Barnave, to the queen in 1791–2. She never liked him and the hostility may have dated to the incident of the banquet.

Since the opening of the Estates-General conspiracy theories had taken hold of otherwise rational men in this *soi-disant* Age of Reason, and none more than Lafayette. Just before the march on Versailles, Lafayette wrote a letter expressing his belief that there was a conspiracy afoot to dissolve the National Assembly, seize the duc d'Orléans, and 'immediately cut the throats of M. Bailly' and himself. 'The queen, M. d'Estaing and M. de Saint-Priest were in on the secret and they hoped to rope the king into the plot' – otherwise he too would be abducted.[97]

At about ten o'clock on 5 October, Saint-Priest received intelligence that an armed force had left Paris and was making for Versailles.[98] It was a motley crowd containing mainly women and demanding bread and the king's sanction to the Assembly's decrees. Saint-Priest sent a message to Marie-Antoinette to return to the palace from the model village at the Petit Trianon. The courier found her in the grotto, resting after feeding her ducks and goldfish, and she returned immediately. The king was out shooting nearby (not hunting as is generally assumed), so was quickly contacted and convened the Council at 1.30 p.m. There Saint-Priest proposed that the queen and the royal family should be sent for safety to the recently purchased château of Rambouillet where a loyal regiment was stationed, but that the king should personally command the troops to intercept the Parisians at the Pont de Sèvres. The Council was divided, so Louis adjourned it 'without coming to any decision wishing no doubt to consult the queen first'. 'The queen . . . who knew she was hated (however unjustly) by the people had convinced herself that her life would be in danger if she was separated from the king's person. She told him that she would not go to Rambouillet without him' and Saint-Priest's plan 'was not adopted'. Saint-Priest also blamed Marie-Antoinette for replacing a capable commander of the Bodyguard with the duc de Guiche, who had married Madame de Polignac's daughter.[99]

The sequel is well known. The Paris women arrived, followed by the National Guard. The queen agreed to flight now that the whole family was to go to Rambouillet and Saint-Priest sent his pregnant wife on ahead – but the stable lads cut the traces of the royal carriages. Under pressure and with tears in his eyes the king sanctioned the August decrees and the Declaration of Rights. Lafayette arrived. With his troops milling around the palace, his enemies shouted, 'Cromwell!' 'Cromwell,' he retorted, 'would not have entered the king's presence alone.' Mere sophistry – the troops were in the courtyard. Lafayette asked the king to install himself at Paris. Louis stone-walled. Having tried to soften Louis up, an exhausted Lafayette finally left the château at 5 a.m. and went to his grandfather Noailles' townhouse in Versailles. There he threw himself onto a sofa and fell into an exhausted sleep. In view of what happened next he was dubbed General Morpheus and accused of 'sleeping against the king'. But this is unfair: no one suspected what was about to happen. Louis went to bed at 2 a.m., Marie-Antoinette having already retired to her separate apartment with two ladies-in-waiting.

About half an hour after Lafayette's departure, daybreak on a misty autumn morning, a portion of the crowd broke into the royal palace, made for the queen's apartments, and outside the doors hacked down two of her Bodyguards, shouting 'We want to cut her head off, and fry her heart and liver and it won't stop there.' What more could they possibly imagine? One of the Bodyguards just had time to reach the queen's apartments and shout to a lady-in-waiting, 'Madame, save the queen, her life is in danger.' Then he was cut down and left for dead. Miraculously he survived. Behind the queen's bed, concealed in the panelling, was a door opening onto a secret passage leading to the king's apartments. Constructed in 1775 to preserve her political influence, now it preserved her life. Dressed only in her shift, Marie-Antoinette made for the king's apartments. Some accounts have the furious populace, disappointed of their prey, slashing the mattress of the queen's bed to ribbons. But she was not safe yet, for when she reached the king's apartments she found the door locked: for ten agonizing minutes the queen hammered on the door, whilst the mob pursued her from another direction through the Hall of Mirrors towards the Oeil-de-Boeuf, loyal guards closing the doors of the enfilade behind them. Finally, the whole family was reunited in the Oeil-de-Boeuf. That day Marie-Antoinette's blond hair went white at the temples.

Revolutionary crowds never go away empty-handed. Early in the morning they were back in the Marble Court to make the king appear on the balcony. Then they asked for the queen. She appeared with her children, surely for propaganda not protection, but the mob howled, 'No children! The Queen on the balcony alone!' She turned to Lafayette, who asked her, 'What do you really want to do? – I know the fate which attends me but it is my duty to die at the king's feet and in the arms of my children – Very well, Madame, come with me – What alone on the balcony? Have you not seen the gestures they have made me [and indeed they were terrifying] – Yes, Madame, let us go.' He then egregiously told the crowd that the queen had learned from her mistakes and the whole family appeared with him on the balcony as for a curtain call. Always gracious when appeased, the Parisians volleyed *Vive le général! Vive la reine!*[100]

But they were not to be diverted from their central aim: the royal family must go 'To Paris! To Paris!' Louis sat 'in a state of stupefaction' in an armchair: he knew his history; he knew why Louis XIV had transferred his seat of government to Versailles. But Saint-Priest 'took the liberty' – and liberty it was – 'of telling him that by not consenting to leave he was exposing himself and the royal family to the utmost danger; that he must regard himself as a prisoner, subject to the laws imposed on him'. Marie-Antoinette agreed: 'you couldn't make up your mind to go whilst there was still time; now we are prisoners ... As for me, I put myself in God's hands.' She put it rather differently to Saint-Priest: 'Why did we not go yesterday evening? – It was not my fault,' replied Saint-Priest, again 'taking a liberty'. 'I know it wasn't,' she replied, 'which proved to me that she did not count for nothing in yesterday's counter-order' about barring the Pont de Sèvres.[101] Marie-Antoinette turned to Necker's wife (the minister, like the king, had not uttered a word) and said in a horrified whisper, 'they want to force us, the king and me, to go to Paris with the heads of our bodyguards carried before us at the end of their pikes'.

And so they did, pikes and all. It took seven hours to cover the twelve miles from Versailles to Paris, during which time Louis did not utter a single word. Fishwives shouted abuse and gesticulated at Marie-Antoinette's window. Even that was not the end of it. On arrival in Paris they had to appear on the balcony of the Hôtel de Ville before finally, at 9 o'clock, being installed in the palace of the Tuileries. Fersen was waiting for them in the king's apartments. Saint-Priest told him to leave, for 'it is certain that if some wretch had pointed him out to the populace which was milling around, he could have been slaughtered'.[102] Lord Holland claimed that Madame Campan confided to him that 'Fersen was in a tête à tête with Her Majesty in her boudoir or bedroom on the famous night of 6 October 1789. He escaped . . . in a disguise procured for him by Madame Campan.'[103]

For Louis and Marie-Antoinette the point of no return was not 14 July but 6 October. After all, on that morning the queen had come within an ace not just of being killed but horribly mutilated, her head no doubt stuck on a pike like the Bodyguard who saved her, her coiffure reconfigured. On 6 October she overheard the baying crowd threatening to make cockades out of her entrails. And it wasn't just bravado. The *volonté punitive* of the Parisians was gruesome. When Louis was at last able to speak his mind he talked of the miracle that had stopped the French people being indelibly dishonoured.

That 6 October was the defining moment is clear from the letter that on 12 October 1789 Louis wrote to his Bourbon cousin, Charles IV of Spain. 'I have chosen Your Majesty, as the head of the second Branch, to place in your hands this solemn protest against my enforced sanction of all that has been done contrary to the royal authority since 15 July of this year and at the same time my intention to implement the promises which I made by my Declaration of the previous 23 June.'[104] It is significant that the letter was sent not after the fall of the Bastille but after 6 October and it introduces the key to both his and his wife's new attitude: force majeure invalidates promises. The October Days would come to be seen as the original sin of the Revolution that the death of the king compounded rather than expiated.

EIGHT

APPEASEMENT AND PLANS FOR RESISTANCE

THE TUILERIES AND SAINT-CLOUD

THE NEW SITUATION: THE LOCATION OF POWER IN 1790

*J*f Marie-Antoinette pursued a tortuous path it was because the Revolution itself was a maze. Or perhaps an apter image might be one of the complicated astronomical instruments of which the king was fond, maybe an orrery. Marie-Antoinette's confidant, the comte de La Marck, had another image, that of Cartesian vortices in perpetual collision. In normal times, he said, you could analyse a political faction: how it worked, its aims and its methods, and deal with it accordingly. But in Revolutionary France you had 24 million Daltonian atoms perpetually colliding (they underestimated the population because of tax evasion). A man could be a mere instrument one day and a leader the next.[1] The Revolution had introduced both social and political mobility. The underlying power was public opinion, which Necker had unleashed and which was stronger than any institution.

Since it was difficult to determine where real power lay, it was difficult for Marie-Antoinette to know whom to deal with, and in default of a disheartened king it was increasingly she who was doing the dealing. Much of this variable geometry concerned timing, which meant that by the time an early radical turned to the Court, his day was often done. In this volatile situation it was difficult to make promises stick; perhaps it was as dishonest to make them as to break them.

Theoretically, the National Assembly was the centre of everything since it had, in abbé de Siéyès' phrase, 'the dictatorship of constituent power'. It was the *fons et origo*, the God of Creation. In its early, heroic days, May–July 1789, the Assembly had spoken virtually with one voice as Jean-Jacques Rousseau, had he not died in 1778, would have wished. But by August the Assembly had split into several factions, though they would have eschewed a word that smacked of *ancien régime* intrigues. The main factions in the Assembly (from right to left) were: first, the 'noirs' or 'purs', who wanted a restoration of the *ancien régime* or as a minimum the Declaration of 23 June – some had emigrated, many would follow them; second, the *monarchiens*,[2] who favoured a strong constitutional monarchy based on England's; and third, what may be called the 'soft left', the logic of whose position was a republic, but who found it more comfortable and/or acceptable to keep Louis XVI as a figurehead deprived of any real power, executive or legislative.

These last were led by the 'triumvirate' of Adrien Duport, a former *parlementaire*, one of the few who had secured election to the Estates, Barnave and Alexandre de Lameth, one of the many disgruntled courtiers who were annoyed that Marie-Antoinette's favours went to the Polignacs rather than to them.[3] On the extreme left were men like Jérôme Pétion and Robespierre, though even as late as 1791 Robespierre said (darkly) that the declaration of a republic would be 'aristocratic'. He believed that the Declaration of Rights should be the litmus test for all policy. He was not yet influential but (until his nervous breakdown in the spring of 1794) he had a superb strategic sense. Hard to label was the maverick Mirabeau, who, for all his bombast was closest to the *monarchiens*. Marie-Antoinette would deal with all of these except for Robespierre, who truly was incorruptible, leaving no more than small change in his pockets when he was sent to the guillotine.

Nevertheless, the sovereign Assembly, divided as it was but armed with its 'dictatorship of constituent power', was able to remodel France. In its Versailles period the National Assembly had passed constructive legislation that had the support of the vast majority of the population: they established the career open to talent not birth, ended feudalism and the privileges of classes and regions in France – consummating, as Mirabeau rightly told Marie-Antoinette, the work of the previous Bourbon rulers. This was supported by a wide section of the deputies whether nobles or from the Third Estate; the gamut stretched all the way from Mounier and Malouet (Third Estate) through great nobles like Lameth, La Marck and Lafayette, *parlementaire* grandees such as Duport and lesser nobles like Mirabeau to Barnave who, with a *roturier* father and a noble mother, embodied synthesis.

But after the October Days and with its own removal to Paris on 9 November, the Assembly lost its way. It made irreversible mistakes and alienated half the population. The 'biggest single blunder' of the Assembly, according to Talleyrand, was its Civil Constitution of the Clergy, voted on 12 July 1790. The Civil Constitution introduced popular election of bishops and curés. This ended the apostolic succession of clergy and meant that Jews, Protestants and indeed atheists could choose their clergy. It was not this doctrinaire measure, though, that led to difficulties but the new bishoprics which were to be co-extensive with the *départements* that replaced the old provinces. As there were 135 old bishoprics and only 83 *départements*, some bishops would have to resign and others be assigned new sees. This change required papal institution. Pius VI was hostile both to the French Revolution in general and to the Civil Constitution in particular. Louis begged the Pope to find a compromise but he condemned it. The Assembly compounded its blunder on 27 November when it enforced an oath to observe its provisions on all clergy. Half the curés and all but four of the bishops refused, thereby destroying the 'magical unity' of 1789, establishing schism, and fatally alienating a king who was ready to sacrifice his prerogative but not his Christian conscience.

Louis' refusal to give immediate sanction to part of the Assembly's August legislation had been the pretext for the October Days. Thereafter he sanctioned everything willy-nilly. It has been argued that the queen persuaded him to do this in order to demonstrate that he was not free.[4] (Devious Marie-Antoinette or sulking king – take your pick.) Being free to reject the Civil Constitution (if indeed the king had the legal power to do so) would have validated his acceptance of all the other measures he had nodded through. But he would have asserted his right (as demanded by the *Cahiers de doléances*) to have a say in the framing of the Constitution with support in the country if not in Paris. However, his ministers, ineffectual in defending his powers, badgered him day and night to sign in order to safeguard theirs. Images of riots, the end of the monarchy, or at least of the summer vacation at Saint-Cloud, were brought before his myopic eyes.

The same argument applied to another measure Louis cannot have welcomed: the abolition of nobility on 19 June 1790. Nobles were obliged not just to abandon their coat of arms but to adopt their family rather than titular names: Mirabeau as Riquetti; Lafayette as Motier; why not Louis XVI as Capet,[5] as indeed he would soon be called. The measure gratuitously alienated 250,000 nobles. As Barnave said, the decree turned the Revolution from being 'an individual matter to one of caste and corporate consciousness'.[6] Indeed, it recreated a new corporate entity after the corporate organization of the *ancien régime* – parlements, gilds, village communes had been abolished. The Civil Constitution of the Clergy performed the same service for the refractory priests and when these two natural allies – aristocracy and Church – united in the Vendéen rising of 1793 the Revolution was in trouble. The decree created a new wave of émigrés, who, dishonoured in their own country, settled in new lands as 'colonists' or 'pilgrims', in Barnave's colourful words, and dreamt of returning as conquerors. The émigrés were a thorn in Marie-Antoinette's side because it was wrongly assumed that she was in league with them. The king also was affected. Although the monarch and the nobility had spent much of the previous centuries at odds (as Mirabeau and

Barnave observed and Marie-Antoinette conceded), yet they were obverse and reverse of the same coin. Louis XIV had proclaimed that he was *nec pluribus impar* ('not just first among equals') but was he really *sui generis* – how do you stand on top of a pyramid that has not so much crumbled as been mined? Why the decree abolishing nobility was passed has never satisfactorily been explained.

And notice that the above were all radical measures. When the Assembly tried to do anything for the king there were popular demonstrations inside and outside the chamber. Whatever the links between members of the Assembly and the Paris risings of 14 July and 5 October, it had been a Faustian bargain and now Paris exerted pressure on the Assembly as well as the king, especially when with some reluctance the Assembly itself joined the king in Paris. The popular movement was centred on the electoral unit known as the Section and was dominated not by the mob (who didn't have the leisure for the time-consuming pursuit of left-wing politics) but by skilled artisans who became known as the *sans-culottes* – originally a term of abuse (men who without the fashionable knee-breeches or *culottes* wore trousers instead). There were also two clubs, the Jacobins and the Cordeliers.

The point of intersection between the Assembly and the popular movement was the Jacobin Club, officially the Society of the Friends of the Constitution who met in the abandoned Dominican church of Saint-Jacques in the Rue Saint-Honoré. To begin with the Jacobins were dominated by centre-left deputies – Mirabeau, the triumvirs (Lafayette didn't bother to go), but a key moment occurred when Robespierre was elected president on 31 March 1790. He made the Club his instrument and within a year transformed it into the national pressure group whose workings Louis eloquently described in his 1791 manifesto:

> In nearly all the cities and even in several country towns and villages associations have been formed with the name Société des Amis de la constitution [Jacobin clubs]. In defiance of the laws, they do not permit the existence of any other clubs that are not affiliated to themselves, thus forming an immense corporation even more dangerous than any of those which previously existed.[7] Without authorization, nay in contempt of the laws, they deliberate on all aspects of government, correspond with each other on all subjects, make and receive denunciations, and post up their resolutions. They have assumed such predominance that all the administrative and judicial bodies, not excepting the National Assembly itself, nearly always obey their orders.

The Cordelier Club was not for deputies and was dominated by Danton – an up-and-coming lawyer who at this stage used the aristocratic apostrophe d'Anton. The king's Civil List was used to buy his support. Popular pressure on the Assemblies – the National Assembly, its successor the Legislative Assembly and finally the National Convention – lasted from the autumn of 1789 to the spring of 1794, when Robespierre crushed the popular movement and integrated its remnants into the machinery of government, emasculating its members by paying them a salary.

There remained armed force, the old (the royal army) and the new (the National Guard). Marie-Antoinette had said to Saint-Priest in August, 'so long as the king is allowed the disposition of the army – otherwise all is lost'.[8] In fact, most regiments of the royal army were in any case disintegrating fast and discipline was collapsing. But General Bouillé, based at Metz, was keeping his force in order – for the moment. Bouillé wanted a very strong but constitutional monarchy. He was slow to take the new oath to 'the Nation, the Law and the King' and this made him unpopular with the new Metz municipality, though he did eventually take the oath. Lafayette tried desperately to win Bouillé over but, failing, made Louis write him a letter recalling him to Paris. Louis, however, sent Bouillé a secret letter countermanding this and he stayed put.[9]

Lafayette headed the most important unit of a military force parallel to the troops of the line, the National Guard of Paris. Every municipality had its Guard but the most important naturally was that of Paris, and Lafayette was the most powerful individual in the country for a year after the October Days. He made and broke ministers, bullied the king and queen though usually with courtesy, organized grain supplies, saw to general matters of law and order. The king, trying to officialize his position, anchor it within the traditions of the monarchy, offered him the two most prestigious offices available: Constable or even Lieutenant-General of the kingdom, pre-Bourbon offices. He turned them down. What Lafayette really wanted went back beyond Bourbon days, beyond even the medieval and Renaissance period of the constables, back to the Dark Ages: he wanted to be a Mayor of the Palace, the man who had controlled the later Merovingian kings, the long-haired kings, the sacred puppets, the *rois fainéants*, the do-nothing kings. His rival Mirabeau expressly accused him of being a Mayor of the Palace.[10]

Lafayette turned down the king's offer because it came from the king. But what if another offer more legitimate in his eyes came from the National Assembly? Over dinner in November 1789 he told Gouverneur Morris, the American minister in Paris, 'that in a Fortnight ... [the Assembly] will be obliged to give him Authority which he has hitherto declined. I ask him what Authority. He says a Kind of Dictatorship such as Generalissimo. He does not know exactly what will be the Title . . . Here is vaulting Ambition, which o'erleaps itself.'[11] Lafayette's hero Washington had been generalissimo and president, but

Cromwell, who declined the crown because its scope had been circumscribed by law and battle, was both generalissimo and dictator. Cromwell, however, as Lafayette had insisted on 5 October, had not left his troops outside.

Sometime in December – his letter is merely dated 'This Monday' and the recipient is unknown – Lafayette recounted 'a long and useless conversation with the queen'. He tried to scare her into wholeheartedly supporting the Revolution because the counter-revolutionaries and the Orléanists both wanted to destroy 'the person of Louis XVI', and the Orléanists wanted to 'have the queen divorced or sent to the scaffold'. But Lafayette also contemplated having the queen divorced on grounds of adultery. Axel von Fersen came to see her 'almost every day' and Lafayette deliberately left the entrance he used unguarded 'so he could enter unobserved'. Saint-Priest wondered whether this was not due to 'some additional malice', namely, to catch her in the act of adultery.[12]

But these arrangements were not put in place for some months: the secret passages that had made life tolerable for the royal family at Versailles had still to be constructed. Marie-Antoinette's letter to Madame de Polignac of 29 December reveals that although she and Fersen saw each other practically 'every day' they were never alone and were effectively 'separated' for 'three months' by court etiquette. 'At last,' as Fersen told his sister, 'on the 24th [December] I spent the whole day with Her. It was the first. Imagine my joy.' Marie-Antoinette gave Madame de Polignac her account of the meeting: 'the personage [Fersen] is amiable like you. I saw him. Because after three months of separation, although in the same place the personage and I managed to see each other safely once. You know us both so you can judge of our happiness.'[13]

Lafayette accused the king of 'wanting to make the constitution fail by his own inertia' and he thought the only salvation was for himself, Montmorin, the king and queen to act in perfect good faith and union. He could easily choose all the ministers himself; but that would be risky for him so he 'would rather that M. de Montmorin appeared to be doing it than me'. He then made a perceptive point about Marie-Antoinette: that she 'would rather make a fine display of facing dangers than prevent them', adding 'she seemed both to hate me and esteem me and she thought that I needed the king's support to stay in power'. He told her brutally that he put the survival of the Revolution before that of the king.[14]

APPEASEMENT AND RESISTANCE

Nevertheless for a few months after the October Days, Marie-Antoinette tried to make the best of the new internal situation in the hopes that something would turn up. When the little dauphin complained about the Tuileries – 'It's very ugly here, Maman' – Marie Antoinette replied, 'Mon fils, Louis XIV lived here once and found it very comfortable.'[15] But it wasn't comfortable. It had last been occupied by the Court during the minority of Louis XV, from 1715 to 1722, And the royal family did nothing to make themselves more at home, not even bothering to furnish the place, deliberately giving the impression that they were camping out before returning to their proper home, Versailles, which (as Marie-Antoinette neglected to tell her son) had been built as a refuge from Paris and the Parisians. That they had not given up hope of returning is clear from the king's order in November 1789 for an iron grille to bar the approach to his private staircase.[16]

The day after their installation in the Tuileries and for some days afterwards Marie-Antoinette had to appear in the gardens. Sometimes she stared down her tormentors with the inbred Habsburg pride that both infuriated and silenced her enemies. Then they left her alone. But neither she nor Louis ventured beyond the palace for another four months. They were scared and wanted to show that they were scared and above all not free, hoping to raise doubts about the validity of the National Assembly's legislation because they had sanctioned it under duress.

Marie-Antoinette talked a lot about her courage, and on the great set-piece occasions of her life she certainly displayed a self-conscious courage – imitating her mother Maria-Theresa. But her dominant emotion during the Revolution was a gnawing, corrosive, health-destroying fear. This is not a contradiction in terms. The man who is without fear is abnormal and his heroism in a sense is devalued. Her heroism on the balcony on 6 October was paired (if Saint-Priest is correct) with her sabotage of the defense plans the previous day, because she feared to be removed from the aegis of the king. From the fall of Brienne in August 1788 until the middle of 1790 her principal concern was to make herself forgotten in the hope that Frenchmen could come to their senses about her in particular and the role of the monarchy in general. She had not even bothered to proclaim her decisive role in the recall of Necker or the doubling of the representation of the Third Estate. At the investigation into the October Days, she said with coy nobility that she spurned to accuse her husband's subjects.

The queen was scared. It was considered impolitic for her to see Mercy-Argenteau. On 6 October he had tried to see her but Saint-Priest had told him to leave Versailles as quickly as possible, as 'his presence could serve no purpose' and even be 'very counterproductive'. And Marie-Antoinette herself told him 'you would do well not to come here for a while'.[17] But Mercy had been in hiding since the fall of the Bastille and 'there is a strong hint of personal cowardice in . . . [his] behaviour during the Revolution'.[18] It may also be that he felt his advice to Marie-Antoinette (not just his support of Austria) but also his disinterested political advice, and notably his role in the recall of Necker, had turned out badly.

Marie-Antoinette did not even dare to contact her brother Joseph, who was dying of tuberculosis; she wrote to Mercy on 10 October: 'You will write to the Emperor for me; I think it is more prudent that I don't write to him at the present juncture, even just to tell him that I am alright.' And Joseph knew exactly why – the old canard of the millions sent into Germany. He told their brother Leopold: 'they still come back to the idea that my sister has secretly sent me millions; ... [whereas] I have never received a sou from France.'[19] As we have seen, this was not strictly true: France had contributed 4 million gold ducats towards buying off Joseph in his quarrel with the Dutch in 1784 and the episode marked the zenith of Marie-Antoinette's lobbying for her brother. At last on 6 January 1790 she wrote to Joseph, 'but I confine myself to speaking of his health and ours'.[20]

Fear was now added to the prudence that had caused her to lie low since the fall of Brienne. On 28 October she told Henri, baron de Flachslanden, an Alsatian deputy and secret adviser, of her reasoning, though 'perhaps you will find my fears puerile': 'Above all I need to be circumspect ... My present role is to stay strictly within my apartments [she kept her two children there too] and try by means of total inactivity to blot out every impression of me ... I must have no marked influence either in appointments or politics.' But she needed his advice in forming a longer-term strategy.

For slowly the realization was dawning on her that she was, in her own words, losing 'the propaganda war'.[21] So the king and queen changed tack in an effort to win over their enemies. Marie-Antoinette made strenuous efforts to woo the Parisians. 'I talk to the people,' she told Mercy on 7 October within twenty-four hours of the attempt on her life, 'soldiers, fishwives take my hand; I give them mine.'[22] She literally kissed babies – or at least one, a new arrival at the Foundling Hospital. And she wryly remarked that the people were far nicer when she came to them than when they came to her!

For his part Louis, under Necker's aegis, took several steps publicly to identify himself with the Revolution. On 4 February 1790 he went down to the Assembly and made a speech in which he 'placed himself at the head of the Revolution', swore to uphold the Constitution and, according to Elizabeth, the soul of the Counter-Revolution within the Tuileries, 'lost whatever crown was still left on his head'.[23] Of this proceeding, however, which amounted to a speech unaccompanied by a policy, it has justly been observed: 'If one merely utters sentimental phrases one obtains only fleeting applause ... Necker raised a peristyle which did not lead to any building.'[24] The king's request that the Assembly attend to the deficit was ignored. When Malouet, seeking to profit from the enthusiasm produced by the king's speech, asked the Assembly to confirm the king as head of the army and the administration, the Assembly did not even vote on his proposals. General Bouillé was so appalled that the king should have capitulated without a quid pro quo that he considered throwing in his command and emigrating.[25]

Lafayette told Gouverneur Morris that the king should be given some 'sugar plum' as a reward for his speech, to which Morris retorted that the Assembly 'had already parcelled out the executive authority in such a way that they cannot restore it to the monarch'.[26] Never has the situation been better summarized. In April, Lafayette submitted a programme to the king and undertook to implement it. It gave the king complete control of the executive, the judiciary and the army. Louis was tempted and signed his copy, though observing that the details were vague. The queen's long-time friend the Hungarian count Esterhazy had acted as an intermediary. He gained the impression that Lafayette had made verbal demands – such as relieving Bouillé of his command and remodelling the ministry – that Marie-Antoinette found unsatisfactory. In any case, when the question of choosing the personnel of the judiciary arose, the Assembly, with no objection from Lafayette, decided that they should be elected rather than appointed by the king. The queen decided that he could not deliver his side of the bargain and the concordat came to nothing.[27] Marie-Antoinette was not to be fobbed off with sweets.

And the king and queen were both 'very displeased' with Necker whose initiative had also come to nothing. 'Mécontente' was the strongest polite word in Louis' vocabulary. This was the background to Marie-Antoinette's approach, through intermediaries to Mirabeau. As early as her letter to Flachslanden of 28 October, Marie-Antoinette had come to the conclusion that 'it will perhaps be necessary to make use of people . . .'; she broke off on hearing of a decree annulling monastic vows, but evidently she would have continued '. . . of whom we disapprove'; and in a later letter to Flachslanden she articulated who she had in mind: Mirabeau. Mirabeau's 'immorality' filled her with 'horror'. But this 'horror' and dread of meeting in person the man whom she believed (wrongly) was responsible for the October Days had something of the theatrical quality never entirely absent from Marie-Antoinette, who had, after all, trodden the boards at the Trianon.

MIRABEAU

Mirabeau, the firebrand in June and July, was at heart a monarchist, albeit a constitutional one à l'anglaise – he had offered his services first to Calonne in 1786 and then to Necker at the start of the Estates-General, but Necker had turned him down. Mirabeau's ambition was to be a minster, to be the modern Richelieu, to create a new monarchy; but this ambition was known and the Assembly passed its 'fatal decree' of 7 November forbidding members of the Assembly to enter the ministry – *ad hominem* legislation that guaranteed war between the executive and legislative branches. So Mirabeau would have to work clandestinely and therefore ineffectively. It is often said that he worked for Marie-Antoinette rather than Louis. Some of the expressions employed by Mirabeau in his 'Notes for the Court' suggest that Louis was not meant to read them, for example, 'The Queen ... must have a clever agent about the King under her secret influence.'[28] But in fact his original intention was to offer his services to the king using their mutual friend d'Angiviller, director of the royal buildings, as intermediary; but in the end d'Angiviller pulled out because he believed that his dealings with Mirabeau would inevitably get out and undermine Mirabeau's effectiveness.

So Marie-Antoinette took up the challenge, using as her intermediary La Marck, a Belgian aristocrat with an estate in France. La Marck was trusted by both Marie-Antoinette and Mirabeau, who was to die in his arms. She also employed her old standby Mercy-Argenteau. Mercy did not want to compromise his diplomatic character, so there was much use of gardens, side gates and alcoves, as at Versailles. It was agreed that Mirabeau's debts would be paid off; he would have a pension of 5,000 francs a month and a million francs at the end of the session of the National Assembly if his conduct had been satisfactory. On the strength of this Mirabeau moved into a fine apartment in the fashionable new Chaussée d'Antin complex, which raised suspicious eyebrows.

Mirabeau developed his ideas in a series of fifty 'Notes for the Court' (actually for the queen), which he sent Marie-Antoinette over the next year – they only met in person once and in great secrecy. Considering her youthful backwardness in writing, the role of correspondence in Marie-Antoinette's policy (internal as well as, necessarily, foreign) is striking: the appointment of Brienne and Necker, Mirabeau (one way), and then running the government with Barnave. The National Assembly, Mirabeau argued, had achieved what the king had been seeking in 1787: the Revolution, properly understood, by destroying the *pouvoirs intermédiaires* 'facilitated the exercise of power' – notably, on 3 November 1789 the Assembly had 'buried alive' the parlements by indefinitely prolonging their summer vacation, finally abolishing them on 7 September 1790. 'Richelieu,' he adds, 'would have been pleased by the notion of forming just one class of citizens.' Mirabeau distinguished between the destruction of the corporate organization of the *ancien régime*, an irreversible achievement that could only strengthen monarchical authority, and the new Constitution that shackled it but could still be modified.[29]

Marie-Antoinette's meeting with Mirabeau was on 3 May in the grounds of Saint-Cloud, where the royal family had been allowed to spend the summer of 1790 to scotch the idea that they were the prisoners of Paris. The report that she had fainted on seeing the 'monster' is not credible. The meeting went well and Mirabeau proclaimed (prematurely) that the monarchy was saved. He was a thespian too: 'Go tell your master that we will only move at the point of the bayonet!' – the Revolution was much given to theatrical tableaux.

And for all her histrionic horror it was Mirabeau, for better or (as it turned out) for worse, who gave Marie-Antoinette what she had been looking for – a political philosophy and a modus operandi. Marie-Antoinette's understanding of French politics had made giant strides since her clumsy and pointless interventions motivated purely by personal likes and dislikes in the 1770s. Brienne's ministry had been her apprenticeship. One cannot learn from theory, whether peddled by Vermond, Mercy or Joseph – all, moreover, interested parties. Manuals on statecraft don't work, neither Machiavelli's *The Prince* nor Richelieu's *Political Testament*. Has anyone ever followed their advice or, if they have, profited by it? You have to learn on the job or from an old hand, as Louis had learned foreign policy from the abbé de la Ville. Mirabeau carried her understanding forward another step. The most tangible example of his influence was that, immediately after their meeting, she toyed with the idea of the king's asking the Assembly to allow its members to become ministers, by repealing the 'fatal decree' of 7 November.

Now Marie-Antoinette understood – in so far as anyone could, faced with the Cartesian vortices – what was happening. That the National Assembly was by degrees taking over not just the legislative but also the executive power by means of its committee system shadowing the ministers. Above everything Mirabeau persuaded her that Louis' and Necker's policy of passive acceptance of the Revolution was not working and was even being mocked by those who had benefited from it: Lameth famously jibed, 'the Executive Power is playing possum'.

After the meeting between Marie-Antoinette and Mirabeau, his influence on her increased, partly because with the decree on the Civil Constitution a month later, the political situation deteriorated. On 20 August she told Mercy that 'matters are becoming more difficult and more painful with every passing day'.[30] On 15 August she had asked Mercy, rhetorically, 'How could Mirabeau or any rational being think that we could ever but especially at this moment provoke civil war', and refused Mirabeau's request for a second meeting.[31] But the 'moment' was passing – just three days later she or Louis, or probably the two together, concocted a position paper that she dictated to Mercy to show Mirabeau and which is very equivocal on the subject of civil war. The key passage runs:

> One can never accept that civil war is necessary, but one can imagine the possibility that it becomes inevitable; [and] provided it comes about neither through the actions or [even] the wishes of the king, he will prepare himself to accept it, without fear or remorse; and it is in line with this thinking that he would like to see a plan worked out with the foresight, wisdom and the probability of success necessary in such critical circumstances.

This sophistical mindset had always been present in the king, but Marie-Antoinette was now affected by it too: much is made of Marie-Antoinette's influence on Louis, but one should not rule out a reciprocal influence. They must not provoke or even desire civil war, but (and this is the contradiction) they must get ready (*se préparer*) for it by taking appropriate measures for which they give Mirabeau an amber light. The paper also accepts Mirabeau's advice about mounting an elaborate propaganda and secret-service machine to prepare the country for the king's escape from Paris. Appeasement having failed, escape was now the queen's central objective. The only question in the various escape plans under consideration was whether the royal family should leave openly under armed escort, or secretly, at night, heavily disguised. Mirabeau strongly favoured the former as he told La Marck: 'Remember . . . that you must never under any pretext be an accomplice or even a confidant in a secret escape [*évasion*] and that a king must leave in broad daylight if he wants to remain king.'[32]

THE ESCAPE PLANS

All the escape plans centred on Bouillé. He had come to Louis' attention by dint of suppressing a serious mutiny – that of the garrison at Nancy in August 1790, just when the escape plans were being drawn up. One hundred were killed and forty were hanged as an example. There had been a protest riot in Paris that frightened Necker into resigning, after which the Assembly took complete control of the finances, rendering the king, in his own words, 'more of a stranger to that department which he understands than any other'. The king wrote to Bouillé, 'look after your popularity; it may be very useful to me and the

Kingdom; I regard it as the sheet-anchor which may one day be the means of restoring order.'[33]

Mirabeau wanted Bouillé to march on Paris and conduct the royal family in broad daylight to Compiègne, a château that figures time and time again in royal escape plans. Rouen, an earlier option, was no longer safe because being an open if loyal town it could experience a rising organized by the local Jacobin club. The *départements* (Mirabeau thought he had thirty-six lined up) would petition the king to dissolve the National Assembly on the grounds that it had exceeded its mandate and convoke a new one to Compiègne. The new Assembly, in consultation with the king, would frame a new constitution keeping the best bits of the one being drafted – abolition of feudalism, career open to talents, consent to taxation – but an absolute veto for the king, two chambers, royal initiative in legislation and complete control of the executive, army and foreign policy. It was hoped for a grand coalition of Mirabeau, Calonne and even (briefly) the comte d'Artois, then staying with his in-laws, the king of Sardinia-Piedmont, based in Turin. But Marie-Antoinette could never have worked with Calonne. Hopes of a 'Lafayette–Mirabeau–Bouillé coalition'[34] for internal affairs also foundered on the rock of mutual suspicions.

In September, Marie-Antoinette was offered a second plan drawn up by 'her' minister, Breteuil. From Switzerland he sent the king a memorandum stressing the 'urgency of adopting any plan whatsoever' rather than drifting, which 'inspired general mistrust in all parties' – exactly the point Mirabeau had been making. The best plan was for the king 'to leave Paris . . . in order to withdraw to a safe place within the Kingdom' and surround himself with the forces of General Bouillé.[35] Over the months the details were worked out. Louis asked Bouillé to propose a fortified town to which he could withdraw in safety with his family; Bouillé offered him Valenciennes, Besançon and Montmédy in Lorraine, which was ultimately chosen. Marie-Antoinette asked the emperor to assemble a body of some 8,000 troops on the Luxembourg frontier to give Bouillé a pretext for his own troop concentrations and as protection if the plan failed and they had to cross the border. What would happen next was never made clear. As Breteuil confessed to his friend Fersen as late as 29 May, 'I don't rightly know what His Majesty is planning to do.'[36] Fersen was heavily involved in the plans, and personally organized the escape from Paris.

The main differences between the two plans were that Breteuil's involved a clandestine escape instead of an open one; going to a fortress instead of a château, and the involvement of Austrian troops. But the differences were to some extent more apparent than real. The king planned, once things had settled down, to move his headquarters from Montmédy to Compiègne – he had even (counting his chickens) ordered furniture 'for the estates', *sic* for the Assembly;[37] whilst Marie-Antoinette claimed that her plan for foreign involvement actually came from Mirabeau. She told Mercy, 'It strikes me that another of the more reasonable points in Mirabeau's plan' is that Austria and Prussia 'on the pretext' of contagion from the French Revolution, and of 'the shoddy way the king is being treated', should put pressure on the Assembly to do something (unspecified) to bolster the king's position. But, key point, they must do this 'without invading arms in hand but as guarantors of all the treaties' that confirmed the feudal rights of German princes with possessions in Alsace and Lorraine.[38] This does, however, seem alien to Mirabeau's thinking and does not appear in any of his Notes for the Court. He may have alluded to it during their one and only meeting. The Breteuil and Mirabeau plans were considered in tandem until the sudden death of Mirabeau on 2 April 1791 put paid to his.

In November 1790 the king had sent Breteuil 'plenipotential powers and authorization vis-à-vis the different Powers with whom you may have to treat on my behalf', which concluded 'I approve of all you do to attain the aim I have set, which is the restoration of my legitimate authority and the happiness of my peoples.'[39] The Girault de Coursacs suggest that Marie-Antoinette and Fersen commissioned the forgery of these plenipotential powers. Their claim has been endorsed by the leading authority on Breteuil, who commissioned a handwriting expert.[40] However, the Coursacs make a further extravagant claim: the negotiations with Bouillé were conducted exclusively by Marie-Antoinette and Fersen. Marie-Antoinette kept everything from the king, whom she had originally planned to leave behind in Paris as an encumbrance. She would escape with the dauphin, who would be proclaimed king as Louis XVII with herself as regent. The king only resolved on flight after the royal family was prevented from going to Saint-Cloud in April 1791. Then he decided on flight in order to demonstrate that he was free and induce the nation to accept the reforms of the National Assembly. Only at this point, the Coursacs argue, did Louis contact Bouillé. For six months Bouillé had been working on the details of the queen's escape plan in the mistaken belief that the king was privy to it. Now he had to put the original plan to the king as something newly devised. However, in order to prevent the king from finding out what he had previously put his pen to, Bouillé caused the escape to miscarry by making sure Louis ended up in a cul-de-sac at Varennes!

Wild as this general thesis is, the Coursacs demonstrate from several lapses in Marie-Antoinette's correspondence – such as 'I' crossed out and replaced with 'the king' – that in speaking for the king, she is really putting forward her own ideas. That the queen wished to conceal matters from the king is clear from the following letter to Fersen: 'The Bishop [of Pamiers, Breteuil's agent] should have told you already about the problems of writing to me. Only today, M. La Porte, who shows everything to the King, gave him your packet.'[41] This packet contained a long memorandum of Fersen's on the general situation and some skeleton letters for the queen to write to foreign rulers. Clearly most of the correspondence concerning the Montmédy plan was conducted by the quartet of Marie-Antoinette, Fersen, Mercy and Bouillé.

To add to the conventional account of the escape plans and the fanciful one, there is a third account that deserves some credence because it is the account Marie-Antoinette herself gave to one of her most trusted advisers, who figures heavily in the Mirabeau and Mercy correspondences – François de Fontanges, archbishop of Toulouse. His publications *Fuite du Roi* and *Arrestation de la famille royale à Varennes* are essentially hers. Fontanges had been trying to persuade the queen to take advantage of their stay at Saint-Cloud to make good their escape. But Marie-Antoinette replied: 'What are you asking? Do you expect the king to go miles from Paris, without money, without the personal ascendancy to recall the army back to its allegiance, without knowing how to proceed, without advisers to supplement this deficiency; and on top of all this with his dread of civil war? Don't raise the subject again.'

But then came the further encroachment of the Assembly on the Executive following Necker's resignation in September and above all the Civil Constitution. So 'towards the end of 1790' the king decided on flight, using Mirabeau's plan that involved 'putting in motion a pretty complicated [bribery] machine whose first fruit would be to get the electoral sections of Paris to demand that the king be free to go to one of his châteaux'. A date of May or June 1791 was envisaged. Marie-Antoinette was still against this plan 'for the reasons given above' and 'not only did she not seek to strengthen . . . [the king's] determination to flee but she only turned her mind to it seriously after he had urged it many times when she became thoroughly convinced that his decision was inflexible'. The death of Mirabeau ended this plan and the 'Saint-Cloud Departure' (see below) convinced her that flight was necessary although she 'foresaw the misfortunes which could befall them'.

Then Marie-Antoinette threw herself into the plan and, together with Fersen, made all the arrangements to get the royal family out of Paris and as far as Châlons where Bouillé's command began. Fontanges reminded the queen of her previous doubts based on the king's reluctance to take decisive actions, 'but she replied with these exact words: "It's just a question of setting the king in motion; once he is I will answer for his keeping going." '[42] This account has a ring of truth: Marie-Antoinette had seen the king pledge to support a reforming minister – Turgot, Necker, Calonne – only to weaken under pressure. But once they had embarked on the escape there would be no going back. She had to be sure.

THE OBJECTIVES

There is no single document that 'fully explains in all its details' what the king intended to do if he reached Montmédy.[43] Hence the controversy that still surrounds the venture. But there seem to have been two strands to it. 1. Negotiation with the Assembly once the king had freedom and a force at his disposal. 2 A financial settlement involving restoring its lands to the Church and making the clergy responsible for redeeming the *assignats* at a discount. Fersen told Breteuil, 'The king thinks that the Church should get back its lands by purchasing the 1.2 billion *assignats* [new paper currency] in circulation at their current value of 20% below par, that is 1 billion payable in silver.' Those who had bought church lands would be reimbursed. This should be accompanied by a forcible reduction in the rate of interest paid to creditors of the national debt.

The clearest statement of Marie-Antoinette's ultimate objectives is to be found in her letter to Mercy of 3 February 1791:

> The King is busy now collecting together all the materials for the manifesto which he must necessarily issue as soon as we are out of Paris. It will be necessary first to explain his flight, pardon those who have merely been led astray, flatter them with expressions of love; to except from the pardon the revolutionary leaders [*les chefs des factieux*], the City of Paris unless it returns to the old dispensation, and everyone who has not laid down his arms by a certain date; restore the parlements as ordinary law courts without their ever being able to meddle with administration and finance. Finally, we have decided to take as a basis for the Constitution the Declaration of 23 June as necessarily modified by circumstances and events. Religion will be one of the great points to bring to the fore.

Apart from the reference to 'the Declaration of 23 June', little of this appears in the king's actual manifesto, which was left behind when they escaped. Louis does not mention pardons let alone punishments; also he would never have exploited the religious schism as Marie-Antoinette here proposes. His is essentially a negative critique of the Constitution the Assembly had almost completed and his virtual house arrest in Paris rather than a set of concrete proposals, though one can derive from it a constitution similar to the one in the Mirabeau plan.

Marie-Antoinette has some strange ideas about the international background to an escape. For example, some of the proposals for the cession of French territory to buy foreign support, revealed in her correspondence with Mercy-Argenteau, are not only treasonable but fanciful in the extreme. Their premise is that the post-1787 alliance of England, Prussia and Holland would not allow Austria to restore the power of the French monarchy. England, therefore, must be bought off by territorial concessions – the West Indian sugar islands or all the French possessions in India, leaving only trading counters, are suggested. Alternatively, an alliance of Spain, Sardinia and Denmark (!) must be formed, by means of similar concessions, to contain the Triple Alliance. Not surprisingly, the king is said to have been unhappy about these concessions. Bouillé had suggested the Indian surrenders.[44]

THE KING AND QUEEN DECIDE TO ESCAPE

What finally determined the king and queen to escape – Marie-Antoinette is explicit about this – was the episode that has come to be known as the 'Saint-Cloud Departure', which managed to combine the two key elements of the Civil Constitution and the king's lack of freedom. The royal family had spent most of the summer of 1790 at Saint-Cloud and they planned to spend Easter 1791 there, 'leaving on [Monday] 18 April and returning on Wednesday or Thursday week'.[45] Even under the *ancien régime* kings rarely left the seat of government at Easter – they spent much of the summer in their smaller châteaux and the autumn at Fontainebleau for the hunting and to set next year's budget; so this aroused suspicion.

It has long been assumed that the king wanted to go to Saint-Cloud to avoid having to receive Easter Communion at the hands of the abbé Poupart at Saint Germain l'Auxerrois, the local church. Poupart had been the king's confessor for fifteen years and he regarded his acceptance of the Civil Constitution as a betrayal. But the evidence suggests that the king had already made his communion secretly in his private chapel on 16 April, two days before he was due to leave for Saint-Cloud. This was against the advice of the bishop of Clermont, whom he consulted on his worthiness to receive the sacrament. Clermont, who had led the opposition to the Civil Constitution in the Assembly, told him that his sanction of the decrees 'has had the most disastrous consequences for religion'. The bishop understood that the king had yielded to duress, but added: 'Your Majesty knows that it was only resistance to force which produced the martyrs.' He concluded that the king should postpone making his communion that Easter.[46]

So if he had already made his communion (albeit not in a state of grace), why did he want to go to Saint-Cloud? He had been ill, coughing blood for some time, and daily bulletins were placed outside the gates of the Tuileries. Both Elizabeth and Marie-Antoinette believed that his recent illness, which lasted several weeks, was caused as much by mental as physical strain. Marie-Antoinette writes on 19 March: 'You already know how much I have been worried about the King's health; it was all the more disquieting because it is really the overflowing of his cup of sorrows which has made him ill.'[47]

This letter marks a new phase in Marie-Antoinette's unusual marriage to the king. There are no traces left of her adolescent mocking of him as 'the poor man' or the rude 'Vulcan' at his forge; of his lack of interest in her pleasures – dancing, music, clothes, pictures; or of her lack of interest in his pleasures – hunting, geography, finance, history. All were now immaterial. In protest against his 'imprisonment' in Paris he no longer hunted and she no longer danced or sang, believing that such pleasures were for happy people. Instead, they played billiards with Madame Elizabeth and devoted themselves to their children like their new bourgeois Parisian neighbours. And under Louis' guidance she had for some time been reading David Hume's *History of England*, with particular reference to Charles I – probably a bad thing for they both already had a streak of fatalism. Furthermore, instead of castigating the queen for her dealings with her Austrian relatives, in the new situation Louis turned a blind eye to them. The redemptive power of suffering had awoken in them a new kind of love that would endure to the end.

Whatever their motives for going to Saint-Cloud, the crowd that barred their passage on 18 April, whilst they sat in the coach ready to depart, thought that the journey was merely the first leg of one to the frontier or beyond. It has convincingly been argued that 'the religious issue' was merely a 'pretext'.[48] The short length of the royal couple's planned stay at Saint-Cloud is intriguing.

Despite the pleas of Lafayette and the mayor, Bailly, the National Guard mutinied and did nothing to drive back the crowd. Lafayette asked the king whether he should use force to allow the coach to proceed, to whom the king gave a typical response: 'it is up to you to do what you think necessary to enforce your constitution'.[49] This was passing the buck. Whilst they were detained in the coach the steward, who read the situation well, asked the queen what they would like for dinner. He was dragged off. The queen leant out of the carriage to order the crowd to release him because he was in the king's service, only to be greeted with 'there's a pretty c . . . who thinks she can give us orders'.[50] After two hours sitting in the carriage and seeing that Lafayette was powerless, Louis took his family back into the palace and they abandoned their plans. The crowd, led by the grenadiers of the National Guard, entered the vestibule of the palace and tried to follow Marie-Antoinette to her private apartments. But a furious king shouted: 'Grenadiers! Stop right there!' And, as Fersen relates, 'they all stopped dead in their tracks as if they had had their legs cut right off'. Next day Louis went down to the Assembly to complain and received a weazelly reply from the president: 'riots are inseparable from the progress of liberty'.

This was the point of no return: after all, if the guards had managed to reach Marie-Antoinette's apartments the work of 6 October could have been completed. As she said, 'the guard placed about us is our biggest threat'[51] – a continuing threat over and above the spasmodic one of popular irruptions. Spasmodic but still continuing; for La Marck advised Marie-Antoinette on 21 April: 'Unless public opinion shifts, I swear on my honour that the safety of the royal family depends on its taking communion without delay at the parish [of Saint-Germain].' La Marck asked Fontanges to put pressure on the queen, but he replied that he was 'terrified by the uproar', yet being a 'man of the [non-juring] cloth' he needed to think about it.[52] Think, that is, about advising the king, queen and Madame Elizabeth to endanger their immortal souls for temporal and only temporary safety. Escape would remove the dilemma, so on 20 April Marie-Antoinette told Mercy that 'the king wants it [to escape] even more than me'.

Madame Campan, however, thought that the king and queen were secretly pleased by the episode because it would serve to justify their flight.[53] Fersen also thought the 'Saint-Cloud Departure' would invalidate all the constitutional decrees the king had sanctioned by proving that the king's assent was forced.

INTRODUCING BARNAVE

On 23 April, Montmorin sent a circular letter to all the French ambassadors stating it was a calumny to say the king was not free. Montmorin did not want to send what he called a 'devil of a letter'[54] because the king himself had told the Assembly three days before that the National Guard had prevented him from going to Saint-Cloud and persisted in his desire to do so. But Montmorin told La Marck, 'Someone [*On*] puts great store by it', code for the king or queen or both. It has been claimed that the letter was written by Barnave on instructions from the king. And that it had twin goals: to stop the émigrés invading from the Midi and to facilitate the flight of the royal family by slackening security around the Tuileries.[55] These were indeed the goals of the letter. Following Fersen's advice, Marie-Antoinette said that they must lull suspicions by 'seeming to yield to everything right up to the moment when we can act'.[56] Barnave's authorship of the circular letter cannot be proved, but we have evidence of royal contact with the triumvirs and their allies before the flight to Varennes based on their realization that the Constitution was defective and the king's authority needed to be strengthened before the country disintegrated.

This realization by the centre-left had dawned some months before. The starting point had been Le Chapelier's proposal of 23 September 1790 that seven new members be added to the Assembly's Constitutional Committee to give a coherent final draft to a Constitution whose articles had been voted piecemeal over the past twelve months, and tweak the final product to enhance the king's power. Among the seven were Barnave, Lameth and Duport – the 'triumvirs' – who quickly established control over the Committee. By the autumn of 1790 they had come to the conclusion that, as Barnave later said, 'it is time to stop the Revolution' before it degenerated into an attack on property and even civilization.

Soon Mirabeau established contact with them. On 17 January 1791 he told the queen that he had had 'a very interesting conversation with Alexandre de Lameth', in which he detected that he and his colleagues were 'embarrassed' by the radical stance that they still had to keep up to perpetuate their popularity.[57] Duport had proposed in the Assembly that a king's commissioner should be present in criminal courts. But the key man was Barnave, whose close personal relationship with Marie-Antoinette will dominate the next chapters. The others, d'André, Lameth, Le Chapelier and Mirabeau, all met together in the apartments of Montmorin, who paid d'André for services to the monarchy. Montmorin was necessarily the only minister privy to the secret. But Mirabeau 'took the precaution with Barnave that he should never be present at Montmorin's with the others'. La Marck thought this precaution 'most striking' and explains it by inter-factional rivalry between these Revolutionary prima donnas.

La Marck charts the meteoric rise of 'this young man who had scarcely left college [Barnave was twenty-nine]' and who had risen from being 'an ordinary provincial lawyer' to being feted by high society: 'the ducs d'Aiguillon and de La Rochefoucauld, Laborde de Méréville, eldest son of the richest banker in France, the salon of the old duchesse d'Enville'. In short that fusion of birth and money, known as 'les grands', which characterized late *ancien régime* society. These men 'initiated him into all their pleasures and political intrigues'.

There was certainly a social gulf between La Marck, the son of a prince of the Holy Roman Empire, and Barnave, but the latter was far from being a provincial nobody, though his mixed origins may have acted as the grit in the oyster. His grandfather was an army captain who could progress no further because he was a *roturier*. His father held a judicial post that conferred 'personal', that is lifetime, nobility. But his mother belonged to an ancient noble family, the de Prest, which boasted senior army officers in its ranks. Barnave was also related to his future triumvir colleague, Adrien Duport, a judge in the Parlement, a post that conferred hereditary nobility. When Barnave was nine his mother chose to sit in an unoccupied theatre box reserved for a lackey of the governor. The management asked her to leave, which she did; but she made such a fuss that the rest of the audience left with her and did not return for some months. Nothing better illustrates Louis XVI's observation that the Revolution was all about 'bourgeois vanity'.[58]

Barnave was a brilliant student but he had had to be educated privately because the family were Protestant. His younger brother was even more precocious. A gifted mathematician, he was destined to be an artillery officer, like Carnot, also a bourgeois captain and later the 'organizer of victory' in the Committee of Public Safety. With so many army and noble connections it is not surprising that Barnave fought two duels in his short life – one against the right-wing deputy Cazalès and one in defence of his brother's honour. The brother died young in Paris, where Barnave nursed him for three months. He later wrote that whenever he had noble thoughts his brother's sweet and handsome features would float before him as he drifted off to sleep, but whenever he did anything dishonourable the vision left him, as one imagines it did when he asked 'Is their blood so pure?' of the murdered Foulon and Berthier.[59] A Protestant half-noble then – an explosive mixture barely contained in the tight-necked bottle of the *ancien régime*.

Barnave enjoyed mixing with dukes and bankers, but like Prince Hal he knew their worth and his. And 'before Mirabeau designated him to the Court as one of his auxiliaries', he had already decided to distance himself from his friends. He had 'seen M. de Montmorin alone' and Mirabeau wanted to keep it that way. Barnave impressed Montmorin 'which confirmed ... [Mirabeau] in his opinion that they could derive great benefits from an association with Barnave and therein lies the reason why he was going to be an isolated agent in Mirabeau's plan'.[60]

Marie-Antoinette, ironically in view of their future relationship, was less impressed with Barnave, as she explained to Mercy on 6 May 1791. The queen was in contact with the father of Barnave's friend Laborde de Méréville. Marie-Antoinette needed to raise enough money to sustain an army for two months at Montmédy until the situation resolved itself. Laborde wanted her to sell her diamonds and was so insistent that she had to pretend she had removed them from the Tuileries. 'Well, let me sell them from their new location,' he urged. But

Marie-Antoinette thought it better to keep them as collateral – they couldn't use the Crown Jewels because, as she said, they were now regarded as national property. Otherwise, as we have seen, she might well have done.

On this occasion, though, Laborde had not come about the diamonds but 'had been sent by his son and his associates Duport and Barnave to get her to identify herself with the Revolution which they regarded as "completed" ' – key word with Barnave. 'They were not so ill-disposed as she imagined and he sang the praises of . . . [Barnave] in particular with whom he seemed enchanted'. 'As you can imagine I went along with everything he said' – her habitual stance now that flight was imminent. Laborde was not privy to the exact details of the flight, but he had already liquidated some of her assets and sent them to England together with 2 million livres of his own money to be used as the occasion demanded. So, at the least, Laborde did not regard flight and working with Barnave as incompatible.

However, the question that was raised at the time by Robespierre, and in 1924 by the Robespierrist historian Georges Michon,[61] was how much did Barnave and his associates know. They couldn't possibly have known the precise details of the flight (only four people did). But Barnave, as Mirabeau's number two, must have known of the plan to get the king to Compiègne. Now Mirabeau was dead and Barnave was his legacy to the queen. Barnave probably also knew, through Laborde's son, that the idea of flight continued after Mirabeau's death.

Following his death the baton was taken up by what one may call Marie-Antoinette's kitchen cabinet. With some input from Montmorin, it consisted of La Marck and Archbishop François de Fontanges. They met and corresponded frequently until 10 May. Then there is a gap until 21 June, the day the royal family fled. Marie-Antoinette had told Fontanges to lie low in the country for a bit. She said no more but they all must have guessed something was afoot. The flight to Varennes, Fontanges told La Marck, cleared up the mystery of the previous two months.[62]

There had to be 'mystery' because there was no question of Marie-Antoinette's confiding the escape plan to her adherents, who would be compromised if it failed, and still less to the ministers, who would betray it. Montmorin was the only surviving minister, from before the Revolution and the queen behaved icily towards the man who was the king's personal friend, partly because she had opposed his appointment but mainly because he had followed Necker slavishly. But she was urged to be nice to Montmorin, to invite him to confer with her because he was too shy to ask.[63] This was necessary because most of the other ministers were hostile to the queen, especially the justice minister, Duport du Tertre, an acolyte of Lafayette's. La Marck told Mercy that he was 'a slave' to the deputies on the left. 'Of all the ills that M. de Lafayette had caused the hardest to forgive' was forcing the appointment of this minister 'who stated in open cabinet that he wanted her out of the way'. When Montmorin asked what he meant, du Tertre 'replied coldly that he would not personally lend himself to ... [having her assassinated] but that it would be a different matter if it was a question of putting her on trial'. To clarify, Montmorin asked whether as a minister of the Crown he would put her on trial, to which he replied yes, if that was the only way of getting rid of her.

A trial is what (according to La Marck) Duport du Tertre had in mind. Madame de la Motte-Valois was invited back to France to stir up trouble and the plan was to let her plead her case at the bar of the Assembly. She would state that Marie-Antoinette was the guilty party and demand a retrial. The queen herself would then be tried 'before the new tribunals which had just been set up with elective officials independent of, and hostile to, the Crown'. Another tack was this: with the confiscation of the church lands, which had been 'put at the disposal of the Nation' (Revolution-speak for confiscated), Cardinal Rohan had lost the income with which, as a gentleman, he had been repaying the court jewellers for the diamond necklace. Now there was a movement afoot to deduct the money from the Civil List, which the Assembly had granted the king in lieu of his crown lands, which, too, had been put at the disposal of the nation. The point of this manoeuvre was to establish that the queen herself had commissioned Rohan to get the necklace, which she had then sold – no doubt to give the proceeds to the emperor. If the words attributed to du Tertre were indeed his, then within the year we will see him make the biggest personal volte-face in the history of the Revolution. Mirabeau was so shocked by this plot to besmirch the queen that he stopped giving the radical speeches he judged necessary to preserve his popularity and 'redoubled his energy' in trying to save the monarchy: 'I will save this unfortunate queen from her butchers or die in the attempt.'[64] He did – on 2 April.

It was time for the royal family to get out.

NINE

THE FLIGHT TO VARENNES

*T*he royal party were to travel in disguise, with passports issued to one Baroness de Korff. Marie-Antoinette posed as the governess to her children, Amélie and Aglaé (the dauphin had to be dressed as a girl). Their real governess, Mme de Tourzel, reversed roles with Marie-Antoinette and posed as Madame de Korff. Madame Elizabeth wore the plain dress and cap of a maid. Louis was acting as Madame de Korff's steward, but he directed: 'you will put in the carriage box . . . the red coat with gold lace that I wore at Cherbourg'.

Madame de Korff was not just a *prêt-nom*. The Swedish widow of a Russian colonel, she was the focal point of the Swedish community in Paris. She had managed Axel von Fersen's finances in his absence and helped him buy his regiment. The carriage in which the royal family were to travel – large enough to accommodate seven people and known as a berline – had been ordered in Korff's name on 20 December 1790 but paid for by Fersen. It cost 3,944 livres or £165 – not an enormous sum;[1] certainly not enough to buy what the journalist Mercier called 'a miniature Versailles, lacking only a chapel and orchestra'. It was just a large carriage, dark green with a black undercarriage and yellow wheels, and it travelled at a respectable 7 miles per hour, 10 at a push.

Louis asked Bouillé for a route to Montmédy and Bouillé suggested the shortest one via Rheims and Stenay. Louis rejected Rheims because he had been crowned there and feared recognition. So Bouillé suggested entering Austrian Flanders via Chimay then crossing the Ardennes to reach Montmédy by the back way. Louis rejected this on the grounds that by leaving France even momentarily he would forfeit his crown according to the new Constitution. Marie-Antoinette, however, wanted to send at least the children in the care of their aunt Elizabeth via Flanders. But the king 'would never consent to separate his lot from that of his children'.[2] The comte de Provence and his wife, however, successfully followed this route.

So on the night of 20–21 June, the shortest night of the year, the king and queen, Mme Elizabeth, the royal children and their governess, Madame de Tourzel, left the Tuileries on foot – separately to avoid recognition. They were to reassemble at the Petit Carrousel, where Fersen was waiting with a two-horse carriage to drive them out of Paris. The queen left last; as she walked from the royal palace, Lafayette's carriage, with blazing torches, passed so close that she could touch it with her cane. She pressed herself against a wall and then continued but got lost in the maze of small streets around the Tuileries. Some say she even crossed the Seine by the Pont-Royal before finding her way back and arriving half an hour late. Louis had been more fortunate. A fortnight previously the chevalier de Coigny, who resembled the king, had left the royal palace at night wearing clothes similar to the ones Louis was to wear. Accordingly, the king, after chatting with Lafayette and Bailly at his *coucher*, was able to leave the royal palace by the grand staircase and the main entrance. 'So completely was he at ease,' he told the rest of the party, 'that his shoe having become undone, he put it right without attracting attention.' When the queen finally reached the waiting hackney carriage and was safely inside, the king 'took her in his arms, kissed her, and said over and over again "How glad I am to see you here!" They all kissed each other; all the Royal Family did me [Mme de Tourzel] the same honour.'[3]

Fersen then drove the carriage out of Paris to the Barrière Saint-Martin where he installed the party in the berline. Fersen conducted it as far as Bondy, where a relay of six post-horses was put in. Why he left at this point is not clear. He had planned to accompany the party and he had asked Bouillé to prepare a room for him at Montmédy. He even sought permission from Gustavus III to wear a Swedish uniform. But on 29 May he had informed Bouillé that he would not be accompanying the king, who 'didn't want me to'.[4] It has been suggested that Louis, who had hitherto been a complaisant husband, decided that the moment when he was about to reclaim his political authority should also be that to reclaim his wife. Marie-Antoinette 'cried a lot' on parting from Fersen. Why should she do that if they were only to have a short separation?[5] In fact (though neither could have known it), this was effectively the end of their affair, except for the twenty-four hours they were to spend alone together in the New Year. Perhaps Fersen (and Louis) simply did not want to lend weight to the suspicions that Fersen was having an affair with the queen. Certainly the king expressed no ill will towards the Swede. On the contrary, he told him a few hours before their departure, 'Monsieur de Fersen, whatever befalls, I will not forget everything you have done for me.'[6] Both Louis and Marie-Antoinette were aware that they were in his debt, literally. They both signed a note authorizing Mercy to pay Fersen 1,500,000 livres 'in compensation for all his losses'.

Fersen had rustled up 1,000,000 livres and sent the notes to Bouillé to pay the troops, borrowing 300,000 from Madame de Korff and her mother and another 300,000 from Eleanor Sullivan, who had started life as an Italian actress and who was to be his mistress for the next decade.[7]

He galloped off alone to Belgium with the Great Seal in his saddlebags, planning to take it to the king at Montmédy where a house, still standing, in the lower part of the town had been prepared for the royal family. At Bondy they were joined by two waiting-women in a yellow carriage that was to precede the berline. An ordinary postilion took Fersen's place, with two disguised Bodyguards sitting on either side in case of trouble. 'Adieu, Mme de Korff!' Fersen shouted to Madame de Tourzel.

At Meaux, 26 miles from Paris, the sun rose; and with it their spirits: 'Here I am,' remarked Louis, 'outside that town of Paris where I have experienced so much bitterness. You may be quite sure that once I am firmly seated in the saddle I shall be a very different person from the one you have seen hitherto.' They broke into the provisions Fersen had provided: *boeuf à la mode*, cold veal, a bottle of wine and five bottles of water. They had no cutlery or plates, which made it difficult to attack the *boeuf à la mode*, which is a casserole. At 8 a.m. Louis consulted his gold precision watch and observed, 'right now La Fayette will be in a pretty pickle'.

At Chantrix (90 miles from Paris) the post-master recognized the king but he was loyal and refused to accept payment for his service. Louis presented him with two silver *écuelles* (two-lugged broth bowls), which have been handed down in the family. But just outside the town one of the wheels of the carriage bumped against a bridge; the horses reared and their traces were broken. It took an hour to repair them and by the time they reached Châlons-sur-Marne it was 5 p.m.

At Châlons the king was recognized by at least one person; accounts differ, but it was a loyal town and the carriage was not stopped. 'When we have passed Châlons we shall have nothing further to fear,' said the king. 'At Pont de Sommevel we shall find the first detachment of troops and we shall be safe.' The area of Bouillé's command began at Châlons, and as Fontanges puts it, 'the arrangements made by the queen for the journey ended there and so far had happily succeeded'. But just after leaving Châlons a man in bourgeois clothing tapped on the window of the berline and said to Madame de Tourzel, 'your plans were badly laid, you will be stopped' and then disappeared. Marie-Antoinette was shaken.

Louis had insisted, against Bouillé's advice, on having detachments of cavalry placed in the towns between Pont de Sommevel and Montmédy. But when they reached Pont de Sommevel at six in the evening there were no troops to meet them. Louis turned white as a sheet and 'felt that the very ground was giving way beneath his feet'. The queen 'turned to Madame Elizabeth and told her that all was lost and that they would be stopped'.[8] The berline was two hours late and the duc de Choiseul, son of the former minister, after waiting until a quarter to six, concluded that the escape had been postponed and had withdrawn his forty hussars. The hussars were not the only absentees: Marie-Antoinette's hairdresser also failed to materialize. Choiseul had given him a note to tell the detachments further along the route that the escape had been cancelled. Some stayed put, some got drunk, some fraternized with the inhabitants, some were arrested, some ended up at Varennes.

When the berline reached Saint-Menehould at eight o'clock, the troops were there all right – forty dragoons under Captain d'Andoins – but their presence had aroused so much suspicion in this ultra-Revolutionary town that their captain had felt unable to use them: as luck would have it, the local peasants had just lost a lawsuit against their seigneur and they thought the troops had been sent to enforce judgment. D'Andoins 'rode up to the carriage for a moment and said to [Mme de Tourzel] in an undertone: "The arrangements have been badly made; I am going away in order not to arouse suspicion."' And he told the bodyguard posing as a postilion, 'Leave immediately; hurry or you are lost.' Furthermore, the king was again recognized and this time by an enemy – Drouet, the post-master at Saint-Menehould. He thought he recognized the king from his portrait on the new *assignats* – the one on the coins still portrayed him as young and slim. Drouet kept looking from the king to the *assignat* to make sure and Marie-Antoinette caught him doing this, 'which redoubled her anxiety'. But by the time Drouet had convinced the authorities and set off with a companion in pursuit, the royal family had a start of an hour and a half.

They thus safely reached Clermont at 9.30 p.m. Here again the relay of troops was present – a hundred dragoons under Colonel Damas – but again the town was seized by a panic-fear and would not let the troops leave with the carriage, as the king had asked Damas to do. Even more ominous, when Damas ordered his men to force their way out, the troops, who had been fraternizing with the inhabitants, refused to obey. He cried out, 'Who loves me follow me.' Only two or three did. Damas alone knew who was in the carriage, but one doubts whether this knowledge would have made the troops any more obedient.

Just outside Clermont, the king's party turned left off the main road, taking a minor road to Montmédy, via Varennes. They had been advised not to take the main road through the radical Verdun. Unfortunately, Drouet had asked at the posting-house at Clermont (where the horses had been changed) which route the berline was taking – otherwise he would naturally have shot past the turning and on to Verdun. By cutting across country, Drouet was able to reach Varennes at about the same time as the king.

Since Varennes did not boast a relay-station, Bouillé had made private arrangements for a change of horses, but they could not be found. In what must have been a state of blind panic, the king and queen went down the street knocking on doors. Varennes is in two halves, divided by the river Aire. The postilions could not be persuaded to continue their journey with tired horses, which had covered the last two stages at 10 miles per hour, but they finally agreed to drive over the river to see whether the relay was there. It was, and also another detachment of cavalry. But whilst Marie-Antoinette had been knocking on doors, Drouet had had time to assemble a small posse that stopped the berline under an arch in the town walls leading to the bridge. The use of force by the two Bodyguards would quite possibly have enabled the carriage to cross the river. Fersen would have tried. Passports were demanded and seemed in order. Nevertheless, the *procureur* of the town, a small grocer aptly named M. Sauce, asked the occupants to step into his house above the shop. They agreed. Marie-Antoinette 'placed herself where she could see all that was going on in the street'. As the crowd swelled she knew they had been recognized.

At first Louis insisted that he was not the king. There was an altercation, 'which increasingly passed the limits of respect'. Marie-Antoinette obtained silence by saying 'If you recognize him as your king then at least show him the respect to which he is due.' Then the king declared in a loud voice: 'Yes, I am your king; here is the Queen and the Royal Family. Surrounded by daggers and bayonets in the Capital, I have come to the provinces to find the liberty and peace you all enjoy in the midst of my faithful subjects: I could not live in Paris without perishing, my family and myself. I have come to live among you my children and I will not forsake you.' He was much moved and embraced everyone present. They too were moved. He said he only wanted to go to Montmédy and was prepared to be escorted there by the local National Guard. He just wanted 'to examine the Constitution thoroughly and discover what the people really wanted' and freely accept their views. His speech was a simplified version of his manifesto. He appealed to Sauce, but the *procureur* was scared.[9] He was a small man, standing in for the mayor who was away in Paris as a deputy to the National Assembly. The queen appealed to Madame Sauce, who wept but replied: 'What would you have me do, Madame? Your situation is very unfortunate; but you see that would expose M. Sauce; they would cut off his head.'[10]

Then Choiseul and François Goguelat, Bouillé's aide-de-camp, arrived with the forty hussars who should have been at Pont de Sommevel. The crowd outside was not yet large, but growing. Choiseul and Goguelat were able to go in and see the king. 'Right!' said Louis. 'When do we start?' 'Sire, we await your orders.' Choiseul suggested that the king mount up with the dauphin in his arms and the rest of the party mount up also. Then, surrounded by the hussars, they should try to break out. Marie-Antoinette was prepared to take the risk.[11] The king asked, 'But can you answer for it that in this unequal struggle a bullet will not hit the Queen, or my sister or my children?' The plan was abandoned. This if ever was the moment when Marie-Antoinette should have shown, in Mirabeau's words, what a woman could have done mounted on a horse with her little boy before her, like Maria-Theresa. At 5 o'clock in the morning another officer, Deslon, arrived with sixty dragoons, but there was now a crowd of 10,000 around the shop, summoned by the tocsin. Deslon was allowed in alone to see the king. He explained that his sixty men could do nothing but that Bouillé was on his way. Yet 'the king was in such a state of prostration that . . . [Deslon] feared that His Majesty had not heard him, though he repeated himself three times'. Finally he asked him what he should tell M. de Bouillé. 'You can tell him that I am a prisoner, that I fear he can do nothing for me, but that I ask him to do what he can.' Deslon then asked the king for his orders, but Louis bitterly replied: 'I am a prisoner and have none to give.'[12] Deslon then turned to Marie-Antoinette and, fearing he was being overheard, spoke in German. She complained of the 'harshness' of their treatment, complaining 'that they wouldn't even let them go to Verdun to rest'.

Bouillé was the last hope. Word had been sent to him at Stenay, less than 30 miles away but over mountains, with the Royal Allemand regiment. Louis played for time. But at 6 a.m., seven hours after the king's arrest, there arrived not Bouillé but Lafayette's aide-de-camp Jean-Louis Romeuf, with orders to intercept the king. Romeuf's orders did not say that Louis should be returned to Paris, but that is what the crowd were demanding. Louis read the order and placed it on the bed of his sleeping children and said, 'There is no longer a king in France.' Marie-Antoinette picked it up and flung it on the floor: 'I don't want it defiling my children.'

At 7.30 a.m. the berline headed on its mournful way back to Paris. Bouillé arrived at 9.30, but the horses were exhausted and the berline was in any case surrounded by 6,000 National Guards and an immense crowd. Even if Bouillé could have caught up with the king, his intervention would have provoked a general massacre. So he withdrew to Stenay and immediately crossed the border. Later he received an emotional letter from the king:

> You have done your duty, Monsieur; stop blaming yourself; you have dared all for me and my family and have not succeeded. God has permitted

circumstances which paralyzed your measures and your courage. Success depended on me; but civil war horrified me and I did not want to shed the blood of my subjects, whether deluded or faithful. My fate is bound up with that of the Nation and I do not want to rule by violence. You, Monsieur, have been courageous and loyal: I wanted to express my thanks; and perhaps one day it will be in my power to give you a mark of my personal satisfaction.[13]

'Success depended on me' – what a curious expression. All Louis had to do was sit in a carriage; 'but civil war horrified me' suggests that Louis didn't try very hard, was deliberately indecisive, if one can be. He said in his position paper for Mirabeau that he could 'accept' civil war, provided that it was handed to him on a plate, as it were. But Louis by his flight had initiated a chain of events whose likely outcome would have been civil war. That is why the National Assembly proclaimed that he had been 'abducted', though they knew that this was not true. But Louis might not even have been able to muster a civil war since the little town of Varennes – village really – became on 21–22 June a microcosm of France: if Louis couldn't pass through Varennes there was no point in passing it. The fact that Louis was stopped at Varennes suggests that his whole enterprise would have failed.

THE REACTION IN PARIS

Louis had miscalculated the timing of the journey, but he had estimated that of the reaction in Paris to a nicety. 'Around about 8 o'clock', as Louis had said consulting his watch, Lafayette was indeed in a pickle. But the first to be told, though Marie-Antoinette did not know 'by whom', was the influential deputy Antoine d'André. He was a *monarchien*, an advocate of a strong constitutional monarchy who 'had ended up by enlisting secretly for the king from whom he was receiving 1,000 écus a month via M. de Montmorin'. He informed Montmorin that the king had fled. Montmorin was incredulous but whilst he was still with d'André 'or on the point of leaving', he received a letter from the king saying simply that he had left and Montmorin was to await further instructions. The letter was sent by La Porte, the Intendant of the Civil List, which he had used to finance Mirabeau's 'complicated machine' of corruption. The sealed packet La Porte received also contained instructions to the other ministers not to transact any business until further orders, and also the king's manifesto that La Porte was ordered to read to the Assembly, which he bravely did. Marie-Antoinette explicitly says that the manifesto 'was entirely written in . . . [the king's] hand and composed by himself', though she had seen it.

The Assembly feigned outrage. But 'the vast majority, at least of those who had an independent opinion, regarded this event as lucky and secretly prayed that it would succeed, but for different reasons'. A few deputies on the extreme left, such as Jérôme Pétion, were glad because it might lead to a republic. But the entire right wing welcomed it, as did the centre left. This grouping, 'fairly numerous and influential through their talents, wanted a revolution but considered that this one had already gone too far'. The Constitution was 'defective in several important particulars' and vitiated by the fact that 'the king's acceptance was not freely given'. 'The king's flight if it succeeded would necessarily lead to a negotiation.' The reaction of Barnave and the other triumvirs to the king's recapture is epitomized by Alexandre de Lameth's lament: 'What a disaster! In my terror at the speed with which public order is disintegrating, I hoped that a negotiation with the King, from a position of demonstrable and complete independence, could, through reciprocal concessions, give France the rest for which I seek in vain except through such a conjuncture.'[14]

There was, however, a third grouping that was alarmed by the king's flight and it was led by Lafayette. He felt squeezed by an upper and nether grindstone. If the king turned on Paris with an army there was no knowing what form Marie-Antoinette's personal vengeance on her *bête noire* would take. Meanwhile the savage Parisian populace was blaming him for the escape for which, as the king's gaoler, he was responsible if not complicit. Under popular pressure the Assembly took steps to recapture the king that it might otherwise have neglected, but they did not know what route he had taken; indeed on the assumption (shared till recently by many historians) that Louis was trying to flee the country, Lafayette 'believed or seemed to believe that the king was heading for Valenciennes'. He told his aide-de-camp Romeuf, 'they have gained too much ground for us to reach them; but we must be seen to be doing something'. Romeuf discovered the route the royal family had taken but was almost lynched himself. So it took a further hour before commissioners were dispatched from the Assembly to find the king. The choice of commissioners was settled by a rare agreement between the triumvirs and the right, including Malouet and Cazalès.[15] They were Pétion, a republican, Latour-Maubourg, towards the right of the Assembly, and Barnave. They joined the royal party at Epernay.

MARIE-ANTOINETTE AND BARNAVE: THE START
OF A POLITICAL AFFAIR

The return to Paris was squalid and lasted eight days. The berline was surrounded by a crowd so dense that it raised a thick cloud of dust like a fog.

Although the sun was blistering, the occupants were not allowed to draw the blinds. Often the crowd compelled the berline to go at walking pace. Someone spat in the king's face. A priest who had ridden up to greet them was hacked to pieces in front of their eyes. A. M. de Dampierre came up to the carriage to pay his respects. The queen warned him to go away since they were after his life. 'He mounted his horse and at a distance of fifty paces he was shot down on the plain like a rabbit. When he had fallen to the ground he was butchered and they came back to the carriage with bloody hands and presented his severed head.' Marie-Antoinette spotted another man who looked hungrier for food than blood and she cupped her hand to offer him some *boeuf à la mode* but his companions told him to beware poison, so she ate some herself and offered the rest to the dauphin. Mme de Tourzel writes: 'It is impossible to give any idea of the sufferings of the Royal Family during this unfortunate journey – sufferings both moral and physical: they were spared nothing.'[16]

At Clermont and Sainte-Menehould they were subjected to officious insults. At Epernay the mayor presented the king with the keys to the town but said: 'You should be grateful to the town for presenting its keys to a fugitive king!' Only at Châlons were they treated well: they were housed in the former Intendance where twenty-one years before the young Archduchess Maria Antonia had been rapturously received on her way to wed the dauphin. At the little town of La Ferté-sous-Jouarre the wife of the mayor served the royal family herself, dressed as a servant. She knew that otherwise the king would invite her to join them and did not want to invade their momentary privacy. This little gesture, with its delicate respect for fallen majesty, is one of the most affecting of the whole journey.

Just outside Epernay the royal family were joined by the three commissioners from the National Assembly, Barnave, Pétion and Latour-Maubourg, who were to escort them back to Paris. Latour-Maubourg was the only one Marie-Antoinette knew and she seemed to want him to join her in the carriage. But he told her that she already had his loyalty and that the important thing was to win over Barnave 'whose influence in the Assembly was considerable'. Barnave at this time was 'rather the friend of those who wanted to reverse the Revolution than holding this opinion himself'. Or that is what he told the queen for much of the information that Marie-Antoinette gave to Fontanges presumably came from Barnave. Pétion and Elizabeth, who were of ample proportions, occupied the back seat, with Pétion between Elizabeth and Madame Royale. The handsome Barnave, 'who was fairly slim', sat between the king and queen in the front seat. The women took it in turns to have the dauphin on their knees. Maubourg and Madame de Tourzel travelled with the waiting-women in the other carriage.

Marie-Antoinette told Fersen that Maubourg and Barnave had behaved 'very well' but that 'Pétion was disrespectful'. That was putting it mildly: he taunted her with her liaison with Fersen. 'Pétion said that he knew all; that they had taken a hire-cab near to the château driven by a Swede called ... (he pretended not to know my name) and asked the queen to supply it; she replied: "I am not in the habit of knowing the names of cabbies."'[17] Pétion, a blond, big-nosed lawyer from Chartres, was consistently rude, talked of republics, and regretted that France was 'not yet ripe for one'. On his return he asked the National Assembly to put the king on trial.[18] He has left an account of the journey that is replete with naive presumption.[19] We are told that Madame Elizabeth was falling for his charms when he asked himself: 'What if this was a trick to buy me? Had Mme Elizabeth agreed to sacrifice her honour to make me sacrifice mine? Yes, at Court no price is too high, one is capable of anything; the Queen could have planned it.' Pétion's works were published in four volumes yet all one remembers of him is this egregious account of Madame Elizabeth's trying to seduce him away from the Revolution,[20] and his terrible end – his bones discovered in a cave, half-eaten by wolves as he hid from his former friend Robespierre.

Pétion's feelings were ones of forced contempt mixed with a good deal of superstitious awe for royalty. He was amazed that during the twelve hours it took them to reach Paris from Meaux none of the royal ladies had needed to relieve herself. Of Louis, he writes:

> The King tried to strike up a conversation ... He asked me if I was married,
> I said that I was; he asked me if I had any children. He wished to speak to me
> of the English, of their industry, of the commercial genius of that nation. He
> formulated one or two phrases, then became embarrassed, noticed it and
> blushed. [So] he applied himself greatly to following his maps and he would
> say: we are in such and such a *Département* or district or spot.

The royal family were clearly wasting their time with Pétion.

With Barnave, however, it was different. Whether he was converted on the road to Paris is doubtful. This mission, for which he had proposed himself in the Assembly, was, unlike Paul's, not one of persecution. As we have seen, the radical of 1789 had in any case for some months been convinced that the Revolution must be 'stopped', before it turned into an attack on property and that for this an entente with the Court was necessary. In his *Introduction to the French Revolution* Barnave denies that anything untoward happened on the return journey:[21] 'On the road there were never fewer than eight in the same carriage. In the houses where we broke our journey, the commissioners stayed together . . . The precautions we took to guard our consignment [the king] were very strict and did not permit anyone to get to him secretly.' The only political discourse came from the king when he told Barnave (in front of a fourth commissioner, Dumas) 'that he had never intended to leave France'. Barnave told Dumas, 'that short speech has saved the king'.[22]

Barnave put it rather differently in one of the series of forty-four secret letters he later sent to Marie-Antoinette. He had 'never known' her before the journey and it was only 'pure and noble sentiments' that had led him to take an interest in her. Their contact would have ended with the journey 'if the queen had not asked him to keep it up'.[23] But their relationship got off to a bad start when Barnave, thinking that one of the three Bodyguards sitting on top was Fersen, gave a sardonic smile. Marie-Antoinette disabused him by smoothly giving their names.[24] Thus began a dangerous rivalry between two men who aimed to save the queen; two men with a passing resemblance, though Fersen's features were more pinched.

So, whilst Pétion flirted with Madame Elizabeth, threw chicken bones out of the window, and teased the little dauphin, whilst Barnave did the honours of the chamber pot for the little boy and engaged in serious conversation with the king, the queen drew her veil down contemptuously and resolved never to utter a word to any of the commissioners. But she couldn't keep it up. She had been listening to every word and soon broke into the conversation. With shoulders, thighs, knees and possibly feet touching for hours on end, intimacy was almost incumbent on them and, as Fontanges relates, 'from that time dates the sort of confidence [in Barnave] that the queen had forever afterwards'.

Barnave was a gallant and handsome young man of middle height, well built, with a long face, upturned lips and husky voice. He was highly intelligent. His manner was cold but, according to a friend, he was 'burning inside'. The same could be said of Fersen and, to an extent, the queen also whose misfortunes undoubtedly awoke in Barnave a personal devotion. There was obviously some sexual attraction between the two and an intellectual one developed, though at the start of their six-month political affair Barnave told her that she was 'very frivolous, incapable of undertaking anything serious, incapable even of thinking logically'. Give a dog a bad name. No one – except the jealous Fersen – ever suggested that they were lovers. Marie-Antoinette was deeply in love with Fersen, whilst for Barnave the feeling was akin to knightly chivalry. As its great historian Norman Hampson was wont to say, the French Revolution was all about the nationalization of honour, which hitherto had been thought to descend through a noble blood line (though the majority of nobles had bought their nobility). Edmund Burke's *Reflections on the Revolution in France* had been published on 1 November 1790 and Louis and Barnave can be assumed to have read it – both read English and in any case the French translation appeared on 29 November. Two passages must have seized Barnave's attention. One was Burke's quotation from a French source referring to Barnave's infamous 'is their blood so pure' quip: 'M. Barnave laughing . . . when oceans of blood surrounded us'. Barnave was haunted by the memory of his sally and, as we have seen, devoted a chapter (and chapter heading) to explaining and apologizing for it.[25]

The second was the famous passage about Marie-Antoinette: 'I thought ten thousand swords must have leaped from their scabbards to avenge even a look that threatened her with insult – But the age of chivalry is gone.'[26] Barnave was offered an opportunity to show it hadn't when Marie-Antoinette noticed a priest being manhandled by the National Guard. She alerted Barnave who, in order to address the assailants, leaned out of the door of the coach so far that Madame Elizabeth, won over by his gallantry, grabbed his coat tails to stop him falling out! This astonished Marie-Antoinette, given that Elizabeth was a die-hard counter-revolutionary. From this indecorous position, Barnave harangued the mob: 'Tigers! Have you ceased to be French? Nation of heroes, have you become one of assassins?' The priest escaped with his life.[27]

At their first meal-stop after the commissioners had joined them (Fersen had only provided food for the voyage out) 'the king and queen noticed that the table had only been set for the royal family'. They asked the commissioners to join them; Barnave and Maubourg out of delicacy at first refused; Pétion was made of coarser stuff. During these long hours of conversation Marie-Antoinette and Barnave worked out a concordat based on common needs. As Marie-Antoinette's confidant, La Marck surmised, Barnave and his associates had twin fears – an invasion by the émigrés backed up by Austria and an attack on property at home. Marie-Antoinette could remove the first fear and a restored king the second. The National Assembly during the two years it had effectively or rather ineffectively governed France had not been able to stem a rising tide of lawlessness. Perhaps the king could: he had not been prepared to put down a political rising in 1789 perhaps because he felt he had not the right; but he had put down the Flour War in 1775 vigorously, even brutally. So the deal was briefly this: Barnave and his allies in the Assembly would try to revise the Constitution along the lines suggested in the king's memorandum. In return, first, the king would wholeheartedly accept it – why should he not if he could secure all he had aimed for by flight without civil war? And, second, Marie-Antoinette would ask her brother Leopold to mark his own acceptance of the Revolution by signing a new treaty of alliance with France. Deprived of the support of the emperor, the king's brothers and the émigrés, having no hope of overthrowing the Constitution, would return to France, particularly if the king ordered them to do so.

The first point involved not acting on or even taking advice from anyone but the triumvirs, and (as a true disciple of Mirabeau) Barnave suggested propaganda. For example, the king should ban the performance of royalist productions such as Grétry's opera *Richard Coeur de Lion*, an aria from which had been sung at the infamous banquet for the Flanders regiment that had triggered the October Days. Why, Barnave further asked her, had the king not bothered to furnish the Tuileries – camping out as if he intended his stay to be temporary? Why did he not resume his wonted pleasures, such as hunting, which he had abandoned as a protest against the October Days? The king should be more interested in the 'masses' (*sic*) than individuals and he should 'try to provide employment'.[28] (No wonder Marxist historians have regarded Barnave as a precursor.)

Paradoxically, Barnave argued, it would be easier for the queen to recapture her popularity than the king, 'because she has always been regarded as an enemy, she made open war, so to speak'. She could not be accused of duplicity (unlike the king he didn't need to say). Therefore, if she embarked on a 'pronounced' popular policy it would be easier to win back trust. 'The French people will soon get tired of hating.'[29] In the Revolutionary lexicon the frank foe was preferable to the false friend. This explains why, after the king's flight, there was some talk of offering the crown to the comte d'Artois, because his opposition to the Revolution was unambiguous and he was a known quantity. What they failed to grasp is that Marie-Antoinette had been in many instances 'a force for moderation', as Mercy put it in the critical days after 23 June 1789.

As for the second point – that Marie-Antoinette should persuade Leopold to recognize and legitimize international recognition of the Revolution 'by any act' – this was more than she could perform. Leopold had passed as a liberal when, as its grand duke, he had granted a constitution to Tuscany. He was a cautious pragmatist not an ideologue. The bulk of the evidence suggests that Leopold, Kaunitz and Mercy supported Barnave, at least until the end of 1791.[30] But he was too fine a player to declare his support openly. Barnave's request to get Leopold to acknowledge the Constitution openly embarrassed her and she took a while to reply. When she did she pointed out that she had not seen Leopold for fifteen years and had never been close to him in any case. He was a cold fish if a nimble one, having restored the damage done by Joseph's over-hasty reforms. Barnave wanted Leopold to renew the 1756 alliance and Marie-Antoinette to get the credit for it. But would there be any credit? Most people in France detested the Austrian alliance; it had been the root cause of Marie-Antoinette's unpopularity; would not its renewal further inflame an irritated nerve?

In his *Introduction à la Révolution française*, Barnave made a brilliant analysis of Austria's relationship to France and its Revolution. Austria was 'our natural rival on the Continent but our actual ally' (a similar point had been made by Vergennes). She did not need military assistance from France (that in the Seven Years War had been a bonus) but rather 'a guarantee of our inertia, which would enable her to deploy all her own forces' for her expansionist projects. France's 'demi-Révolution' suited Austria perfectly. She didn't want the restoration of 'despotism' because France's absolute monarchs had been a thorn in her side. But nor did she want the overthrow of the Bourbon dynasty on which depended 'the maintenance of our alliance'. She wanted, in short, a bourgeois revolution in which the 'martial' spirit of the aristocracy would be replaced by a 'mercantile' one.[31]

Both Barnave and Marie-Antoinette knew foreign affairs were crucial. They would settle the fate of the monarchy: its death (1792) and its resurrection (1814).The triumvirs, like most people in France, took the threat of a foreign invasion seriously – perhaps too seriously at this stage, manning the frontiers at great expense, for as La Marck observed, if the French 'ruined themselves for threats which were perhaps chimerical' they would 'have nothing left with which to counter real ones'.[32]

Marie-Antoinette told Barnave that she had become a bit closer to Leopold in the last year or so. Presumably she meant since the death of their brother Joseph. Or was she dropping her guard and referring to his involvement (or lack of it) in her escape plans? Leopold, in fact, had not lifted a finger to help his sister – perhaps because Mercy had filtered her requests to him. But then, when he believed the escape had succeeded, he suddenly promised her everything she wanted – money, troops, everything; he was entirely at her disposal. This was logical: he could do nothing for her as long as she was a prisoner. But it sticks out like a sore thumb from his other pronouncements and was probably an emotional aberration. Nevertheless Barnave thought, significantly, that Leopold had favoured 'the escape in 1791 and the camp at Montmédy' because all those involved in it, such as Bouillé, were advocates of a strong monarchy rather than advocates of a return to the *ancien régime*: 'All the indications relative to the king's escape in 1791 and the camp at Montmédy . . . prove that it was coordinated with Leopold and that its object was the establishment of a strong constitutional monarchy [*un système mixte*].'[33] I have translated '*système mixte*' as 'strong constitutional monarchy' because Barnave means that pre-Varennes France was effectively a republic with a decorative figurehead. For a proper monarchy the king and assembly had to be equal or 'mixed' powers. That is why he argued for the power of dissolution and the initiative in legislation to be vested in the king to counterbalance a unicameral legislature. The power of dissolution meant that it was always open to the king to appeal to the people against the legislature.

Barnave would have told the queen that when she returned she would be heavily guarded and held incommunicado and that he could not see her without risking both their lives. Neither minimized the high stakes at issue, yet over the coming months she repeatedly asked to see Barnave because there was a limit to what could be put in a letter. But letters it had to be. She dictated forty-four unsigned letters to be sent to Barnave and his associates. Barnave sent her an equal number back, elegantly worded. She used a simple code to refer to persons, A=1, B=2, etc. So Barnave, Ba, is 2:1, Duport is 415, Alexandre de Lameth is 112 and François Jarjayes, the loyalist go-between, is 10.

Marie-Antoinette used Madame Campan to get her letters to Jarjayes – Madame Campan partially conceals his identity as 'J . . .' When Marie-Antoinette explained that she was entering into relationships with Barnave, Duport and Alexandre de Lameth, Madame Campan was shocked and told her so. Marie-Antoinette replied that Barnave was 'full of intelligence and noble intentions'. She added, 'A sentiment of pride for which I cannot really blame him led him to applaud everything which opened up to him the path to honours and glory.' She even went as far to say that some of the nobility had been blocking posts 'often to the detriment of people from a lower Order among whom were to be found men of the highest talent'. So finally she accepted the notion of the *carrière ouverte aux talents* she had excised from the royal programme presented on 23 June 1789. She had told Mercy that there must be 'necessary modifications' to that programme. Well, here was the living proof.

Marie-Antoinette came to this conclusion from observing that Barnave's manners were just as gentlemanly as those of the nobles she had hitherto consorted with, and that he was better educated since the military aristocracy joined the army in their teens – the more educated army officers were concentrated in the less prestigious artillery where nobility was not a prerequisite. He later explained this process in his *Introduction à la Révolution française*: 'Just as the arts, commerce and luxury goods enriched the industrious part of the people, impoverished the great landed proprietors and made the financial position of the classes more equal, in the same way the sciences and education made their manners more alike.'[34]

The people she really blamed were those nobles who had received her benefits and repaid them by siding with the Revolution. This may explain why

Marie-Antoinette never really warmed to Lameth (a court noble who had received her benefits) and Duport (a *parlementaire* noble). We have seen in her letter to Mercy outlining her objectives in flight that there would be punishment meted out. Not to Barnave, however: 'Barnave's pardon is already engraved on our hearts.'[35]

In her correspondence Marie-Antoinette refers to the triumvirs and their allies as 'ces Messieurs', sometimes with a touch of irony. She bound the letters together and wrote on the packet: 'An exact copy of all that I have written to 2:1 by the intermediary of 1:0 and his replies . . . I shall number each sheet. Mine are always brought back to me, and to the "agent" I employ I dictate my replies. Thus I avoid the danger of my handwriting being recognized in case the papers are discovered.'[36] As the net closed, she would tactlessly entrust the packet to Fersen, and for a century it lay undiscovered in the castle belonging to his beloved sister and heir, Sophie.

REVISION AND ACCEPTANCE OF THE CONSTITUTION

The coach arrived back in Paris at eight o'clock in the evening of Saturday 25 June. The Champs-Elysées was densely packed, but there was total silence. Everywhere placards sententiously proclaimed: 'Whoever applauds the King will be thrashed; whoever insults him will be hanged.' Everyone left their hats on. Doubtless those who didn't usually wear a hat acquired one. The arms of the National Guard were reversed, as for a funeral, drums gratuitously rolled – ritual humiliation. On their arrival at the Tuileries, the vicomte de Noailles rushed to give the queen her arm; regarding him as a traitor, she brusquely rejected it.[37] The king and queen were placed under the strictest house arrest. A few minutes later, Pétion went into the king's bedroom: 'Already all the valets had preceded him there in their usual costume. It seemed as though the King were returning from a hunting-party; they did his toilet. Seeing the King, contemplating him, you never could have guessed all that had just happened: he was just as phlegmatic, just as tranquil, as if nothing had happened. He immediately put himself on show.'

'He put himself on show', externally and internally; that is the clue. It was partly a matter of conditioning, the life on display he had known since a small child, partly a way of holding himself together. The flight to Varennes appears in his diary as an 'ordinary voyage', his name for pre-Revolutionary visits to his various palaces. The detail is meticulous: there was no *coucher* at Dormans because there was no bed. He had slept in a *fauteuil*. Soon, too, Barnave was referring to the Flight to Varennes as a 'voyage' rather than the ridiculous official version of a 'kidnapping' (*enlèvement*) or the embarrassing truth of a flight. Indeed, both Louis and Marie-Antoinette treated it as a voyage, a voyage of discovery. Marie-Antoinette confessed to Fersen on 31 October that her journey had convinced her that 'there is not a single town, not a regiment on which we can rely'.

Written across Louis' diary for the month of July are the words: 'Rien de tout le mois: la messe dans la Galérie.' For August: 'Tout le mois a été comme celui de juillet.' He seems to be saying: 'What a boring month!' In fact, he had been suspended from his functions and was kept under such close surveillance that the family were not even not allowed to go to the chapel to hear Mass. The king's sanction was no longer required for bills to become law: the minister of justice applied the seal on the instructions of the Assembly. This showed that the king was a decorative irrelevance: the Constituent Assembly had not created 'un système mixte'. This was a more eloquent demonstration of why the king had fled than his long and repetitive manifesto. The only form of exercise that could be taken was indoors. Marie-Antoinette had played billiards with Madame de Polignac; now she made Louis join her 'after the *diner* so that he might get some exercise'. Louis kept a record of his games against his wife and sister between July 1791 and July 1792.[38] It provides an interesting parallel chronicle to the political events for, though he usually won, in moments of crisis his game tended to fall away.

But strictly guarded as they were, with guards sleeping in Marie-Antoinette's bedroom, chimney sweeps preventing an escape via the roofs, she somehow managed to smuggle out a letter of reassurance to Fersen who, like Leopold, had heard conflicting accounts, including one that the royal family had been rescued at Varennes and escorted to Luxembourg or Flanders. Her note to Fersen is curiously dated 'Du 28 Juin 1791'; she would normally write either 'ce 28me' (for short) or '28 Juin 1791'. It runs: 'Don't worry about us. We are alive. The leaders of the Assembly seem to want to treat us gently. Speak to my relatives about pos[sible] outside help.' Next day she wrote him a longer note, the recently reconstituted passages are in italic:

I exist *my beloved and [it is] to adore you.* I pray this letter may reach you. Don't write, it would compromise us and above all don't return here under any pretext. They know that it was you who got us out of here; you would be lost if you turned up. We are guarded day and night. Rest assured nothing will happen to us, the Assembly wants to treat us gently. *Calm yourself if you can. Look after yourself for me.* I won't be able to write to you anymore. *But nothing in this world can stop me adoring you until I die.*[39]

She was right: the Assembly did want to 'treat us gently'. When the king and queen had been brought back, commissioners from the Assembly helped them to make prepared statements in which the king said that his *voyage* had revealed to him the extent of support for the Constitution in the country. And to make absolutely sure that the royal couple should have time to prepare their 'story', it was arranged that the queen should be in the bath when the commissioners arrived – she gave them her statement the following day. To emphasize the reversal of positions, she sardonically offered them a *fauteuil* and sat on an ordinary chair herself.

The truth was that the Assembly needed the king as much as the king, after Varennes, needed the Assembly. They had designed a constitution with the king as the keystone, ornamental yet load-bearing. They did not know whether without it the edifice would stand. We saw how the previous December, Lafayette had ridiculed Marie-Antoinette's belief that he needed the king to maintain his, Lafayette's, authority; and after the discovery of the king's flight Lafayette toyed with declaring a republic, perhaps to deflect criticism of his suspected collusion in the escape. A meeting of deputies was hastily assembled at the house of his friend the duc de La Rochefoucauld, but its sense was decidedly against such a move. The reason is embedded in Fersen's diary, kept in note form: 'The 19th [July], Arrived at Spa 9.0 A.M. Alex. Lameth, Barnave, Lafayette, Duport, [Laborde] de Méréville in coalition, have broken with the Jacobins; have made overtures to Mercy through Laborde père to get the king to come to an understanding with them. Mercy replied that he had not had any communication with the king; told them some home truths.'[40]

Another entry, that for 21 September, is revealing: 'It is said that the queen sleeps with Barnave and lets herself be led by him.'[41] The sexual jealousy Fersen continued to feel for Barnave (who never slept with the queen) would distort his judgement of Barnave's policies and cause Marie-Antoinette to belittle them to spare Fersen's feelings. But in early July, Marie-Antoinette was herself having second thoughts about joining with the constitutional monarchists. She liked and trusted Barnave; but she did not like Duport and she detested Lafayette. Indeed, Fersen's diary entry for 12 June, when he was seeing the king and queen every day to finalize the details of the flight, runs: 'The journey is put off till the 20th. The reason is a [suspect] chambermaid. *Planned trial of Lafayette changed to a court martial.*'[42]

The triumvirs had been asking the impossible: that Marie-Antoinette should get Leopold openly to back the Constitution (he actually did but privately). She notes: 'After receiving this [Leopold's] reply, I let several days pass before writing. 2:1 asked if I had no news to give them. The two friends [Barnave and

Lameth] did not attempt to conceal that they thought me very frivolous, incapable of undertaking anything serious, incapable even of thinking logically. 2.1 himself sent a short note which I have burned containing the assurance that affairs are looking better.'[43] Frivolous indeed! How could anyone be after what she had been through? Frivolous – in the 1770s maybe. It was during this anxious period of waiting that the triumvirs and their allies contacted Mercy to get the king (i.e. the queen) to come to an arrangement. But soon she resumed the correspondence.

Marie-Antoinette had no news of Fersen until late September. Mercy held back her letters, hoping to further her negotiations with Barnave, which it suited him and Leopold to accept at face value. Fersen and Gustavus wanted military intervention, which was the last thing Mercy and Leopold – and Marie-Antoinette at this stage – wanted. On 9 July she wrote Fersen an important letter that has only recently been decoded and published. Amid protestations of love, she tells him to lie low, entertain Gustavus, 'and . . . to appear as little as possible in all this'; not to try to seek armed intervention – 'force will only do harm . . . there would be no time to rescue us'. 'We must yield to the storm.' Above all he must not judge her present actions until she is able to explain them to him. The crux comes at the end: 'The Lameths and their associates give the appearance of wanting to serve us in good faith. I am profiting by it but will trust them only in so far as is necessary. Adieu.'[44] Here, and in the rest of their correspondence, Marie-Antoinette never once mentions Barnave by name. It is always the Lameths, the *enragés* (fanatics), etc. She is aware of Fersen's sexual jealousy and bitterness at being sidelined after all his efforts and the success of his part in the Varennes adventure (getting the royal family out of Paris).

On 31 July, Marie-Antoinette wrote to Mercy: 'I have reason to be fairly satisfied with ... Duport, [Alexandre de] Lameth and Barnave. Right now I have a sort of correspondence with the last two which no one knows about, even their friends. I have to do them justice. Although they always stick to their opinions I have always found in them great openness, strength and a true desire to restore order and consequently royal authority.'[45]

The next stage in the royal rehabilitation was for the Assembly to prepare what Marie-Antoinette called its 'grand report' on the fate of the monarchy. This was settled on 13 July when Barnave made a celebrated speech: 'Are we going to terminate the Revolution or are we going to start it up again? What you have accomplished so far is good for liberty and equality. But if the Revolution takes a further step, it cannot do so without danger. The next step towards further liberty could entail the destruction of the monarchy and the one after that – a lurch towards equality – would involve an attack on property.' Barnave's speech had not prevented the king from being suspended from his functions but it could have been worse: the extreme left, led by Robespierre, Pétion and François Buzot, had wanted even sterner treatment for the king, ranging from trial (Pétion) through presumed abdication (Vadier) to a referendum (Robespierre).

The whitewashing of the king, as they saw it, was greeted with fury by Parisian radicals. The Cordelier Club got up a republican petition and on 17 July took it to the Champ de Mars to collect signatures. But the municipality replied to the petition by declaring martial law, in token of which Bailly, the mayor, Lafayette and the National Guard arrived on the scene accompanied by a red flag. Now and for the rest of his life, Lafayette, having flirted with the republicanism that remained his ideal, was committed to saving the monarchy, though always on his terms.

The National Guard advanced. One shot was fired from the crowd and Lafayette ordered his men to open fire, killing some fifty of the petitioners. The popular leaders, men like Danton, Camille Desmoulins and the brewer Santerre, went into hiding and popular politics was dead for some months. All but a handful of the deputies in the Jacobin Club seceded and joined the more moderate Feuillant Club. Robespierre stayed in the Jacobins and dominated it for the rest of his and its life. The Massacre of the Champ de Mars, as it became known, was a watershed. The National Guard had fired on the people for the first time and in defence of, not against, the king. The dividing line now was between Parisian popular politics and the Assembly backed up by the essentially bourgeois National Guard. La Marck believed that the National Guard had fired on the people 'less to repel them than in self-defence' – in other words if the gathering had not been dispersed it would have marched on the Assembly and forced it to declare the republic.[46]

Having thus cleared the decks and with the popular movement cowed but not broken, the Feuillants, as they began to be called after their anti-Jacobin club, set about performing Barnave's half of the bargain with the queen: revising the Constitution in the light of the king's manifesto and the statement he had made on his return. The statement countersigned by La Porte had been presented to the committee with 'a simple and noble account [of the king's return journey] without any commentary'.[47] The Constitutional Committee made the manifesto the basis of its operations.[48] The original plan was to give Louis the right of dissolution and the initiation of legislation; there was also to have been a bicameral parliament. The tragedy is that, pursuing their disastrous *politique du pire*, the 250 members of the right refused to endorse measures that would have brought the king and queen into genuine harmony with the

Revolution. Marie-Antoinette exercised what influence on them she could in her seclusion, but the right-wing deputies preferred, in Ferrières' words, 'to risk their own destruction and that of the monarchy rather than surrender the hope of restoring the Ancien Regime'.

The Committee had to content itself with the support of fifty from the moderate right led by Malouet and Cazalès, with whom Barnave had previously fought a duel. This was insufficient for a frontal revision of the Constitution and the Committee had to employ the expedient of reclassifying certain constitutional decrees as ordinary unentrenched legislation subject to repeal. The Civil Constitution of the Clergy was put in this category, which meant that the king could in good conscience swear to uphold the Constitution but not the ecclesiastical settlement that everyone knew he detested; so also was the abolition of the king's prerogative of mercy on which Louis had also dwelt at length in his Declaration. But without the support of the right wing, the Committee was not able to have these decrees simply repealed, nor did it even manage to reclassify the decrees forbidding the king to command the army in person or move more than twenty leagues from Paris.

The Committee was, however, successful in obtaining for the king a Bodyguard of his choice, 1,200 infantry and 600 cavalry, whose purpose, the debates made clear, was to protect him from insurrections such as the October Days and Saint-Cloud Departure. The Committee also managed to introduce a clause allowing ministers to appear before, though not to be members of, the Assembly (a generous concession, Robespierre considered). On 26 August the Committee's proposal to the Assembly to restore the fiscal initiative to the ministers was rejected. Finally, the king was declared 'hereditary representative of the Nation' instead of merely its 'first functionary', which went some way to placing his theoretical authority on a par with that of the Assembly. On 13 August, Barnave told the Assembly that the previous evening the Committee had discussed whether it should resign in view of the Assembly's recent decrees, such as abolishing all the Orders of Chivalry except that of Saint-Louis.

Barnave played down the extent of his failure to Marie-Antoinette, who was not fooled – even though, as she told him, she was 'isolated, unable to see anyone, receiving no news from any one, writing even less, I only learn the news on the day from the press'. On 16 August she told Mercy that 'the leaders . . . for the last eight days have realized that they are absolutely beaten'. Realizing that things were going wrong she asked (in vain) to see 'ces Messieurs' because she had insights to offer; not 'knowledge – I don't flatter myself that I possess that commodity'. But at least she could offer them her 'experience derived from following politics silently [sic] for 17 years'. She only wanted peace and to give the king sufficient authority to make his people happy, and she meant all the people not just the privileged.[49]

On 28 August, Barnave tried to highlight the powers still remaining to the king in the Constitution he would shortly be asked to accept: although most of the executive agents are to be elected rather than chosen by the king, that could change when the king has won the people's trust. Many of the things he mentioned in his manifesto have been addressed and provision is made at the beginning of the Constitution for revision if it proves necessary. Barnave's refrain in italics is that *the Constitution is very monarchical*, with the exception of the decree forbidding ministers to be members of the Assembly, which a later legislature could repeal.[50] He is clearly protesting too much and Marie-Antoinette knew it: 'the Queen is amazed: These gentlemen say that "the Constitution is very monarchical"; I confess that I have need of enlightenment on this point . . .'[51] She told Mercy that the Constitution remained 'a tissue of absurdities'.[52]

Moreover, a last hope that the revision of the Constitution could be modified, by observations from the king prior to his acceptance, was dashed by Robespierre's withering speech of 3 September warning the triumvirs against attempting such a move and accusing them of wanting to become ministers. The triumvirs failed to defend themselves, whilst the right wing laughed. There was truth in Robespierre's accusation. Barnave, like Mirabeau, wanted to repeal the 'fatal decree' and would have liked to be a minister himself, but so what? People were so used to decrying 'ministerial despotism' under the *ancien régime* that they thought ministers were ipso facto wicked. Even more important for Barnave would have been to repeal Robespierre's 'self-denying ordinance' forbidding members of the Constituent from being elected to the Legislative Assembly or at least to prolong the session of the former to bed in the Constitution.

Louis made himself ill with indecision about what to do, though the only alternative to acceptance was abdication, and as Mirabeau had said (of both king and queen), to lose the crown meant they would also lose their heads. To give the illusion that the king's acceptance was free he was allowed to travel the seven miles down the Seine to Saint-Cloud to ponder his decision. But the dauphin was kept in Paris as a hostage. The only thing to consider was the drafting of the king's letter of acceptance. Montmorin wrote a long-winded effort of some fifty pages, which the queen thought lacked nobility. He and Marie-Antoinette had both contributed to drafting the king's speech opening the Estates-General way back (as it seemed) in 1789. Marie-Antoinette realized Montmorin's draft would not do, though bits could be incorporated. She asked

Barnave to supply something shorter and nobler than Montmorin's. It must not apologize for what was now officially the 'voyage' to Varennes. She and the king would then make a compilation as was usual. She told Barnave not to tell Montmorin (with whom he had been in contact since the beginning of the year) that she had rejected his draft or indeed was in contact with Barnave at all. So in a sense, for these months, Barnave was her minister and Montmorin, loyal but out of his depth, the king's.

Louis' letter was sent on 13 September. It was not just cobbled together but represented a synthesis of all the advice that had gone into forming Marie-Antoinette's political philosophy at the time: 'I have tried as much as I can to listen to those of both sides and it is from these that I have formed my own version,' she told Mercy. One of the inputs into the speech did come from Montmorin, 'though in fact,' she added, 'it is by Pelin' (*sic* for Pellenc, Mirabeau's secretary). His input she considered to be 'detestable'.[53] There is some dramatic irony here: the man whose name Marie-Antoinette got wrong was actually Mercy's source not just of information (because of his close links to the triumvirs) but of judgement. He sang Pellenc's praises to Kaunitz.[54]

Cut off from news from abroad the queen had not been influenced by Provence and Artois, whom she despised and feared, or by Leopold, whose policies given his 'profound silence' remained an enigma. By 'both sides' we should understand centre right (La Marck, Montmorin) and centre left (Barnave and the triumvirs), and this compromise represented her 'whole soul', that is to say it was a policy statement not just an ephemeral document to dodge the rocks around the Flight to Varennes. She had been trying to do what her mother would have done, and her eyes were blinded with tears as she wrote.[55] She would 'courageously' follow her 'long and perilous path' to the end 'not for her sake but for that of her child'. Sentiment aside, she was trying to create a 'space which she could inhabit with honour'. I have translated her word '*milieu*' as 'space'; but there is also perhaps a suggestion of *juste milieu*, the right middle ground between die-hard radicals and diehard ultras.[56]

The final draft of the king's letter was a skilful document highlighting the improvements to the Constitution made since his flight, to which, it was insinuated, they were attributable. 'You have shown a desire to restore order,' the deputies were told, 'you have considered the lack of discipline in the army; you have recognized the necessity for curbing the licence of the press.' He ended with a flash of candour: 'I should, however, be telling less than the truth if I said I perceived in the executive and administrative resources sufficient vigour to activate and preserve unity in all the parts of so vast an empire; but since opinions are at present divided on these matters, I consent that experience alone shall decide.'[57]

Jeanne Arnaud-Bouteloup considered that Marie-Antoinette wanted the king's letter of acceptance to show enough doubt about his acceptance of the Constitution to convince her brother Leopold that Louis' acceptance had not been free, but sufficient enthusiasm for it to get by Barnave's scrutiny. Arnaud-Bouteloup argues that the king merely promised to defend the Constitution '*with the powers delegated to me*' and no more. This is not a natural reading and one refuted by the long letter the king sent his brothers explaining that his acceptance had been free. A key passsage is this:

> I know that my émigré subjects flatter themselves that there has been a great change in people's attitudes. I myself for a long time thought that this was happening but I am now undeceived. The Nation likes the Constitution because the word recalls to the lower portion of the people only the indepen-dence in which it has lived for the last two years and to the class above [the bourgeoisie] equality. The lower portion of the people see only that they are reckoned with; the bourgeoisie sees nothing above them. Vanity is satis-fied. This new possession has made them forget everything else ... The completion of the Constitution was all that stood between them and perfect happiness; ... time will teach them how mistaken they were, but their error is nonetheless profound ... One can never govern a people against its incli-nations. This maxim is as true at Constantinople as in a republic; the present inclinations of this nation are for the Rights of Man, however senseless they are.

His line will be that if he sincerely works within the Constitution its defects will be revealed as in a controlled experiment and the people themselves will see the need to rectify it. For good measure, a duplicate was sent to Leopold so that Provence and Artois could not pretend they had not received it – Leopold tripped them up on that one: 'Not only do I believe that my brother-in-law the King has genuinely [*sérieusement*] accepted the Constitution, and is against [*répugne*] any idea of counter-revolution, but I have positive proof. So do Your Royal Highnesses: he has communicated his real intentions to you in a secret memorandum which contains arguments for the decision he has taken which outweigh those advanced against.'[58]

Crucially, as Munro Price first observed, this duplicate was sent to the emperor not by the king but by Marie-Antoinette herself via Mercy.[59] So obvi-ously she endorses its sentiments and wants Leopold to know that she does. And the king's memorandum paraphrases the caveat in the king's letter accepting the Constitution that Marie-Antoinette had helped to draft: 'I realize all the difficulties of governing a large nation in this way – indeed I will say that I realize that it is impossible.' Had she played a part in drafting the memorandum too?

However, the queen sent Mercy a covering letter that on the face of it seems to contradict the enclosure, for it is here that she adumbrates the notion of a 'Congress at Aix-la-Chapelle of all the Powers with an interest in the survival of the French monarchy'. She may have got the idea of a congress from Mirabeau[60] or from Breteuil, who had participated in the one at Teschen in 1779. The 'fear of an external force' – elsewhere she calls it 'not war but the threat of war' – would enable the king to act as mediator, neatly buying off an artificial threat with the restoration of his authority. Clearly Marie-Antoinette does not think that the two policies are incompatible – allowing the people to come to their senses and forcing them to do so, a rather Rousseauesque notion. And it is the resolution of this dichotomy that provides a clue to the accusation that the queen was playing Barnave false or playing him along by appearing to support his plans for a constitutional monarchy whilst at the same time working for an 'armed congress'.

A further clue, even a reconciliation, is provided by Marie-Antoinette's response to the Declaration of Pillnitz of 27 August from the emperor and the king of Prussia, which stipulated that, provided the other great powers assisted, 'then and in that case' (*alors et dans ce cas*) the co-signatories would intervene to restore the king of France to his rightful position. The emperor knew full well that English determination to remain neutral removed any obligation on his part to intervene in France. He wrote to Kaunitz: 'then and in that case is with me the law and the prophets. If England fails us the case is non-existent.'[61] But the qualification 'then and in that case' was lost on most Frenchmen, who assumed the Declaration had been requested by the king. When she read the signatures of Provence and Artois at the bottom of the Declaration, Marie-Antoinette uttered one word: 'Cain'.[62] But Marie-Antoinette saw through the Declaration: 'I don't see that foreign help is that imminent particularly by the Declaration of Pillnitz,' she told Fersen on 26 September; and she added, 'perhaps it is fortunate because the more we proceed the more these wretches will recognize their misfortune; *they may even come to want foreign intervention themselves.*'[63] Indeed, by January 1792 two of the triumvirs (Alexandre de Lameth and Duport), if not Barnave, had themselves come to recognize the need for 'foreign intervention'.[64]

On 14 September, as king of the French rather than king of France and Navarre, wearing the red cordon of the Saint-Louis, the only Order left, Louis XVI took the oath to the Constitution before the Assembly; he was standing while they, with the solitary exception of Malouet, were seated with their hats on.[65] Both Louis and (watching in a box) Marie-Antoinette were mortified, especially as the king had not been provided with a throne – just an ordinary chair albeit one covered with blue velvet strewn with the lilies of the old France. Back home at the Tuileries a tearful Louis apologized to the queen for the degradation he had brought to a Habsburg archduchess. She complained to Barnave, who tried to brush it off; it didn't really matter – chairs, thrones, sitting, standing, hats on, hats off were only symbolic. Yet he knew the value of symbols. The crowds had cheered them back to the Tuileries, but a cynical Marie-Antoinette was not fooled: 'I know how to reckon that; most of the time it is paid for.' Happiness was gone forever; she lived only for her son. Her hair had gone white at the temples on 6 October. But when she took her bonnet off after the return from Varennes, she revealed to Madame Campan 'hair as white as a woman of seventy'.[66] Acceptance of the Constitution meant a kind of liberty but with it came different problems: 'I am reduced to fearing the moment when they will seem to be giving us a kind of liberty. At least in our present state of total nullity, we have nothing with which to reproach ourselves.' Nevertheless, in the following months she would be more actively engaged in government than at any time in her life.

TEN

'MARIE-ANTOINETTE WILL BECOME QUEEN OF FRANCE AGAIN'

GOVERNMENT BY LETTER

*I*f the Roman Republic was the textbook for the French Revolution, we should not be surprised to encounter the 'duumvirate' of Brienne and Lamoignon and the triumvirate of Barnave, Duport and Alexandre de Lameth, pale comparisons to the triumvirate of Octavius, Mark Antony and Lepidus. But we are concerned here with an unnoticed duumvirate, that of Barnave and Marie-Antoinette, exercised in the period between the king's acceptance of the Constitution and Barnave's withdrawal to his native Grenoble in January 1792. In this four-month period the king was virtually *hors de combat*. Louis XVI, sunk in depressive apathy, lived in the bowels of his palace, rarely on display. All those with a personal concern for him – Montmorin, Mirabeau, Pellenc, their secretary, and La Marck – realized that the queen would have to act in his place. Gustavus III was not embarrassed to advise her 'to use all the ascendancy you have acquired over his [the king's] mind'.[1] La Marck wrote:

> This system is based on the personal character of the king . . . over the past two years. As long as the queen is not the focal point of affairs . . . there will be big mistakes and dangers. For there is no getting round the fact that the king is incapable of ruling and only the queen, with suitable backing, can supplement this deficiency. Even this will not be enough: the queen must learn how to apply herself methodically and consistently to politics. She must prescribe for herself the rule of not giving half-confidences to several people and to give her whole confidence to the man she had chosen to help her.

La Marck had in mind a minister, a modern Richelieu à la Mirabeau. A man moreover with whom the king was comfortable. That man would be Barnave. For the moment they had to rely on the king's personal friend, Montmorin, to stop Louis from slipping free from the queen's control. But he was a stop-gap, and after four years in the firing line Montmorin wanted to retire.

But did the queen give Barnave 'her whole confidence'? In the previous chapter we addressed the oft-made accusation that Marie-Antoinette played him false, pursuing a secret conflicting policy. The stock argument uses her words to Fersen, who was worried that she had thrown in her lot with the Feuillants: 'Rest assured,' she wrote, 'I am not carried away by the fanatics (*enragés*) and if I find myself in treaty with some of them it is only to use them.'[2] But we have seen that in another letter to Fersen she said that the king could not go back on what had been done unless the nation saw the necessity. Fersen advised Marie-Antoinette 'you will never win over *les factieux* [his word for the triumvirs]. They are too aware of their faults to expect forgiveness.' But had not Marie-Antoinette said: 'Barnave's pardon is already engraved on our hearts'?[3] Above all she had to avoid hurting Fersen's feelings given the intensity of his personal animosity stemming from sexual jealousy of Barnave.

The trouble was that after the Flight to Varennes, Marie-Antoinette did not stand down the team with which she had worked to prepare it. And, perhaps to compensate for their failure, Fersen and Breteuil now adopted a more hard-line stance than Marie-Antoinette and certainly the king would have tolerated in the event of success. Indeed, to judge from the Breteuil memorandum discovered by Munro Price, Breteuil was already even before the Varennes fiasco – and in contrast to his previous liberal stance – arguing for the dissolution of (rather than negotiation with) the National Assembly, a possible end to representative government itself, and no commitment even to the *séance royale* of 23 June 1789.[4] The removal from the team of Bouillé, a constitutional monarchist, served to intensify the reaction of the remaining members. Fersen felt 'marginalized' and poorly repaid – even by Marie-Antoinette – for all his efforts. He now relied on help from his own king, Gustavus of Sweden, who favoured an approach closely akin to Louis XVI's brothers and the émigrés, which was anathema to Marie-Antoinette.

She kept the old team intact as reinsurance, to give her a fallback position if things went wrong. She had frankly warned Barnave of this possibility on 31 August: 'Despite the decrees, the Constitution and the oaths, who can guarantee that [the next legislature] will not want to change everything and that the republican party will not regain the upper hand? If that happens, where is the force to prevent it?' This uncannily accurate prediction was not a complete shot in the dark. Primary assemblies for elections to the successor Assembly had already begun when the royal family escaped from Paris and the final round was due to start on 5 July, and in his manifesto Louis gloomily noted, 'if one can detect any disposition on the part ... [of the primary assemblies] to go back on anything it is in order to destroy the remains of the monarchy and set up a metaphysical and doctrinaire form of government [a republic] which would not work'. The final result of the elections, delayed as intended by the Flight, was just as bad as Louis and Marie-Antoinette had feared.

Nevertheless the forces of monarchy and republicanism were evenly matched. The issue could go either way and whilst there was still a chance the queen intended to make the best fist possible of French politics. Besides, she did not expect her brother to intervene – he was so embarrassed by her requests that he did not write to her between 20 August and 31 January 1792, by which time the picture had changed for all concerned. The new assembly, the Legislative, which met on 1 October, was more radical than its predecessor. The aristocratic right wing entirely disappeared, many to join the king's brothers the comtes de Provence and d'Artois at Coblenz, and there were only about twenty nobles in the entire Assembly. The new right was made up of the constitutional monarchists, whether followers of Lafayette or of the triumvirs. Of the new deputies, 264 joined the Feuillant Club, to be joined by a further seventy by the end of the year.

The left wing was numerically inferior – 136 joined the Jacobin Club – but they tended to include the more eloquent and forceful speakers, notably a group of lawyers from the *département* of the Gironde headed by Pierre Vergniaud; they were allied with Jacques-Pierre Brissot and the former Constituents Jérôme Pétion and François Buzot. Barnave said bluntly that Brissot 'only wanted to become a deputy the better to destroy the Constitution' – exactly the point Marie-Antoinette had made.[5] Some were republicans, all wanted to capture the government. A smaller group including Georges Danton, Georges Couthon and Louis Antoine de Saint-Just were to acquire the name Montagnards because they sat on the extreme left of the Assembly where the seats banked steeply; they were suspicious of everyone else.

The king had made no bones about the Constitution's imperfections but had 'consented that experience alone should decide'. Bertrand de Molleville, before his appointment as minister for the Marine on 1 October, said he needed to know the king's personal position on the Constitution before deciding whether he could serve him. Louis replied, 'I have sworn to maintain it, such as it is and I am determined ... to be strictly faithful to my oath. For it is my opinion that the literal execution of the Constitution is the best way of making the Nation see the alterations to which it is susceptible'. Bertrand felt comfortable with this approach, but these days ministers needed to know whether this was also the queen's view. 'Yes,' Louis said, 'and she will tell you this herself.' And she did: 'surely the only plan ... [the king] has to follow is to adhere to his oath? Allons;

be of good cheer M. Bertrand. With a little patience, firmness and consistent conduct I hope you will find that all is not yet lost.'[6] Marie-Antoinette's attitude was more positive than Louis' – influenced by Barnave she seemed to think there was a sporting chance of making the Constitution work.

In a monarchical system the king rules through the ministers, his agents of execution. But Barnave thought that, given the poor quality and dubious loyalty of the government, a distinction should be made between it and the king and queen: 'In our opinion, the path of government and the personal course of the king and queen are two different things. Each must be pursued as well as possible; but when the steps of the government falter it is more than ever important that the personal side should hold good, that they should not be charged with the shortcoming of the government.'[7] Back in August, Barnave had told Marie-Antoinette that during the *ancien régime* the ministers had ruled; now 'Marie-Antoinette will become Queen of France again.' Ministers were in hoc to the Legislative Assembly as they had been to its predecessor and had to be disciplined by Barnave working through the queen. And to minimize these shortcomings, Barnave devised a method of control. A minister trusted by both himself and the queen – he suggested the comte de Ségur – might succeed Montmorin, who was desperate to retire, and this minister should 'transmit' his advice, '*after laying it before the queen by letter* . . . openly to the king and Council'.[8]

In fact, they chose Duport du Tertre, the minister of justice and former enemy of the queen, who had mellowed and was, according to Molleville, now 'attached to the Constitution more by gratitude for raising him from being a lowly clerk to the most prestigious post in the kingdom after the king'. 'Lowly clerk' was a slight exaggeration: prior to being made justice minister on 20 September 1790 after the collapse of the Necker administration, du Tertre had been deputy mayor and public prosecutor of the Commune. He had enjoyed the backing of Lafayette and the left in the first Assembly. Quite likely his hostility to Marie-Antoinette (no doubt exaggerated by La Marck) was merely a reflection of his patron Lafayette's. Even after the dissolution of that Assembly, Bertrand added, du Tertre 'continued in intimacy with some of those who had composed it; namely the Lameths, Barnave and Adrien Duport, who were every day at his home: he did nothing without consulting them.'[9] Du Tertre was characterized by Claude de Lessart as 'the senior minister and in some respect the chief of the Council' – 'chef du Conseil', an echo of its *ancien régime* namesake.[10] He became Barnave and Marie-Antoinette's conduit to the ministers, the mechanism being: letters between Barnave and the queen to thrash out a policy; transmission to du Tertre to be finalized in the committee; thence to the king in his Council for a rubber stamp.

In the Versailles phase of Louis XVI's reign, the king had always presided over the committees that prepared the work of the Council.[11] In the constitutional phase these committees met without the king, either in the residence of Duport du Tertre or in a room in the Tuileries specially set aside for them. Furthermore, the king followed the advice of the committee. For example, Bertrand de Molleville wanted the king to take action against an article in Brissot's *Patriote française* and sent Louis a letter on the subject. But Louis observed that the matter lay in the department of du Tertre as minister of justice and added 'I shall await the determination of the committee.'[12] This procedure – first, an epistolary discussion between Marie-Antoinette and Barnave, second, committee, and third, transfer by Du Tertre to the Council – was adopted over important decisions during this period: the formation of the king's constitutional guard and its uniform, and the Assembly's punitive legislation against the émigrés and refractory priests.

Jean-Joachim Pellenc analysed the modus operandi of what he called 'les Lameths', namely, the triumvirate of Alexandre de Lameth, Duport and Barnave. The ministers, he said, were 'evidently and almost publicly' directed by them. They also directed the Feuillant Club. The result was that the king (who followed the ministers' 'impulsion'), the right wing of the Assembly and the triumvirs 'formed a single party, a single army'. They also mounted a propaganda/corruption machine similar to the one that had operated in the period before the Flight to Varennes. Mirabeau's machine had embraced Paris and the provinces. On his death its activities under Antoine-Omer Talon were restricted to Paris. The Flight to Varennes had achieved something – the partial revision of the Constitution – but something also had been lost: the civil-list money to finance the machine during the king's suspension. On his reinstatement it had to be reconstituted. Bertrand de Molleville tells us that it was restarted by Alexandre de Lameth and continued first by Montmorin and finally by himself.[13] Talon put in an expenses claim that was found in the *armoire de fer*. He ends his letter by asking the king 'to get Her Majesty the Queen to cast a favourable eye over this memorandum',[14] which suggests her involvement, particularly when we remember that in May 1790 she had lamented that she was losing the propaganda war.

Pellenc thought that the above analysis of the Feuillant party's modus operandi was a 'given' that one needed to grasp in order to understand the political situation. On paper it was a formidable grouping and Bertrand adds: 'It has been remarked that the last months of the year 1791 formed the only period, perhaps, of the Revolution in which the king and Council adopted the tone which became them with the Assembly.'[15] He attributed it to the decision of the ministers to deal directly with the Assembly, bypassing the committees that shadowed their own ministries – an informal and dangerous institution, he observed, not mentioned in the Constitution. The Constituent Assembly had seven such committees but the Legislative Assembly had twenty-three. Yet the main reason for the improved 'tone' was the entente between Barnave and Marie-Antoinette. However, the combination mentioned by Pellenc was a silent majority and as Edmund Burke observed, 'The only thing necessary for the triumph of evil is for good men to do nothing.' Or as Barnave put it, 'The portion of the nation which desires the maintenance of order and the laws is almost totally passive and not involved in politics, whereas the active minority [is] composed mostly of dissidents.'[16]

Because from the outset the Girondins sought a confrontation with the king: by introducing savage legislation against the émigrés and the refractory priests and by seeking war with the queen's brother the emperor Leopold II, they aimed to manoeuvre Louis either into appointing a Girondin government or appearing as a traitor. On 9 November they had a decree passed enjoining all émigrés to return to France within two months upon pain of being considered suspect of conspiracy, having their lands confiscated and being punishable by death. On 29 November another decree declared that priests not taking an oath to the Constitution within eight days were to be 'considered suspect of revolt against the law and of evil intentions towards the Patrie'. They were to be stripped of their pensions and held responsible for all religious disturbances in their neighbourhood.

The idea behind the legislation was to make the king unpopular by exercising his veto. Exercising the veto against bad legislation was of theoretical as well as practical importance. As we have seen, Barnave believed that a monarchy without a veto was really a republic – especially with a unicameral legislature in which ministers were debarred from sitting. When Marie-Antoinette had asked Barnave what would happen if despite the Constitution the republicans gained the upper hand she perhaps meant by trying to deprive the king of this essential attribute of a functioning constitutional monarchy, though she could not have known that the exercise of the veto would be the main battleground in domestic politics for the rest of the life of the monarchy.

In order to make the king's veto acceptable Marie-Antoinette decided that the émigrés must be dealt with; she sought to dissuade them from raising a loan of 40 million livres on their estates to pay for the Counter-Revolution or invading France on their own, which would ruin both themselves and the king. This was a key point for both the queen and Barnave. They both wanted the émigrés in general and Provence in particular to return. They failed in this but

Marie-Antoinette did persuade Madame de Lamballe to return and, again on Barnave's advice, they went to the opera together. Lamballe even resumed her salon, which had been eclipsed by that of Madame de Polignac.

The return of the émigrés would both remove the principal stick the republicans used to beat the monarchy and swell the ranks of the royalist party. Indeed, Pellenc thought that the main objective of the decree against the émigrés was to put them on their honour *not* to return. He told La Marck that the decree was not one of those spontaneous outbursts that characterized the Revolution but had been 'carefully prepared in the committees' of the Assembly, who were frightened that the returning nobles, joining forces with the refractory clergy in the countryside, 'would give greater force to an embarrassing resistance'.[17] The queen made the same point to Barnave.

They decided that the king should veto the decree. The negativity of the veto suited Louis' personality and, as Barnave observed, there was little difference between the old system where 'ministers drafted laws that were vetoed by the parlements' and the new one where the Assembly made the laws and the king had the veto. There was something in that because for much of his reign Louis' role had been negative; indeed, one insider, to show that the king did play a part, had said 'but if you could see the negatives I have seen'. The veto was Louis' natural instrument of government – provided he was allowed to use it. He had 'played dead' whilst the Constitution was being drafted. But now that the Constitution was operative he insisted on his right to exercise his veto whenever his conscience or his interests were involved. This was the negative role that suited him. Veto, meaning 'I forbid', is a negative.

Barnave argued that if the king sanctioned a decree sentencing his two brothers to death if they did not return by 1 January, it would prove to Europe that he was not free. But the veto must be accompanied by an order to the king's brothers to return. To organize this he would get the ministers to ask the king for an emergency cabinet that night. This happened but Marie-Antoinette wanted to water down the order somewhat lest, again, it would not be believed. So there was another ministerial committee. In the margin of a 'bullet point' note by the foreign secretary, the king has written: 'agenda for a ministerial committee concerted with MM Alexandre Lameth and Barnave'. The agenda is: king's veto; further letter to the king's brothers, which must be 'fraternal and royal'; further proclamation to the émigrés; and a new letter to the foreign courts not to shelter émigrés.[18] This shows the mechanism by which the 'triumvirate' transmitted policy through the queen (who had softened the approach to the king's brothers so that it was 'fraternal' as well as 'royal') to the ministers for executive action. This note would later incriminate all of them.

The next matter was the organization of the king's constitutional guard. Barnave wanted it to be organized along patriotic lines, notably by getting the departmental directorates to nominate 500 or 600 out of the total of 1,500 from their local National Guard. The patronage would also weld the departmental administrations to the regime. Marie-Antoinette agreed but was worried that, if their choice of deputies to the Legislative was anything to go by, the *départements* would send radicals for a body whose primary purpose was to afford the royal family protection against another 5 October rather than fraternizing with the assailants.[19] She was proved right – the moderate *départements* sent moderate men, the radical *départements* sent *enragés* who immediately joined the Jacobin Club and denounced the Constitutional Guard itself as counter-revolutionary.[20] All these measures, thrashed out in letters between Barnave and Marie-Antoinette, came to pass.

The only difficulty concerned the uniform of the new guard. Barnave thought that it should comprise the three national colours of the Revolution, red, white and blue. So if the body of the uniform were white, the collar and facings should be blue and red. Moreover, the blue should be dark blue, *bleu de roi* after Louis' dark blue eyes, which also gave a new colour to the Sèvres porcelain palette. Sky blue would remind the people of foreign regiments. Marie-Antoinette didn't like this idea and she came up with a compromise – why not choose the colours of the former grenadiers who had had an illustrious career – surely, she said, 'that would be very French' and the main colour was indeed *bleu de roi*. 'The points made by *ces messieurs* are fair and have been incorporated. So it will be like the former grenadiers of France.' However, she omitted to say that the facings of this uniform would be yellow and Barnave observed that *ventre-de-biche*, doeskin, was used by the émigrés at Coblenz.

That may well be the case, replied Marie-Antoinette, but my facings will be daffodil yellow. She added that it was too late to change the order, which had already gone out to the suppliers. 'The inconvenience of sky blue having been avoided, no one could object to jonquil facings which everyone recognized as the colours of the grenadiers.' Also her proposal would be cheaper. And the guard could wear the national cockade in their hats. But Barnave persisted: 'the three colours will unite the people against the Jacobins. Yellow will unite the people with the Jacobins against the king.' Marie-Antoinette caved in, even thanking Barnave for his 'persistence'. She would try to change the order without arousing suspicion that the change had been dictated by secret advisers, 'this matter having been already definitively settled'. But it was too late to change the order and Barnave sulked: 'since the matter has been settled there is no point raising it again'.[21]

Trivial perhaps, the gradations between sky blue and *bleu de roi* – Marie-Antoinette and Barnave were not colourists when all was said and done, though in fact she was the patronne of Madame Vigée-Lebrun and he had studied painting as a boy.[22] And the stomach of a roe deer bore scant resemblance to a daffodil. But these were symbols in an age of symbolism. After all did not Artois' grandson (Henri V to his adherents) turn down the offer of the crown because he would not surrender the white flag for the tricolour? As Barnave told the queen, 'the French can be led by ribbons'; and protested 'a kingdom for a uniform'! This heated haggling over colours, replicated over more important matters, is perhaps the best indication of Marie-Antoinette's sincerity in her dealings with Barnave: would she have argued the toss over a constitutional uniform if she had been banking on a foreign intervention to restore the insignia of old France?

More important than the uniform was to have good relations between the king's Bodyguard and the Parisian National Guard. Marie-Antoinette had got off to a bad start by having the king appoint the duc de Cossé-Brissac as the commander of his guard. Barnave told her that everyone was retailing the story that when interviewing recruits he had asked them if they were patriots. When they inevitably said yes, the commander had replied, 'in that case your place is at the front; the king has no need of patriots in his guard'. Marie-Antoinette replied that if he had used these words it was indeed blameworthy but it was unlikely that he had been so stupid. Indeed.

The next question that Barnave and Marie-Antoinette had to sort out was the decree punishing refractory priests. Marie-Antoinette was adamant that the king must veto the measure on the grounds that 'the constitution itself . . . establishes liberty for all opinions'. Barnave agreed that the measure was illiberal but observed that the oath did not oblige priests to swear to uphold the *Civil* Constitution. Why therefore, observed the queen, was Pierre-Edouard Lemontey's amendment rejected, which would have permitted priests to preface their oath with a statement that it did not prejudice their views on the Civil Constitution?

Barnave gave way and got the *département* of Paris to ask the king to veto the measure. The *département's* address was written by Duport and Barnave[23] and they also got du Tertre to withdraw his opposition, thereby bringing his patron Lafayette on side. Marie-Antoinette thought they should waste no time in applying the veto, on 11 December, but Barnave wanted it to be accompanied by a letter denouncing the émigrés and further concessions on the king's guard. It did not matter because the Assembly claimed that it was unconstitutional for the king to explain the reasons for his exercise of the veto: as he wrote on the projected speech to be given by Duport du Tertre: 'They did not want to hear it.'[24] Nevertheless the debate on the veto, whose length worried Barnave, passed off without incident.

Barnave wanted to remodel the government: de Lessart to replace Montmorin as foreign secretary, comte Louis de Narbonne to replace Louis de Duportail as minister of war, and Louis-Antoine Garnier to be minister of the interior (as the government for the Maison du Roi had become). Narbonne, one of Louis XV's many natural children, had the advantage, Barnave thought, of being familiar with the Court. Marie-Antoinette had been casting about for a foreign minister to replace Montmorin, and was happy to have the reliable de Lessart. He was a capable and loyal man who before becoming foreign secretary had been minister of the interior under Necker. The queen regarded Garnier as 'clever' if lacking in character, but he declined to be a minister. Marie-Antoinette was worried that his refusal 'is particularly important because it throws fresh discredit on the Ministers and shows the unpopularity of their functions'. Barnave then suggested Bon-Claude Cahier de Gerville. He was at heart a republican and affected to be insulted when the king gave him 'permission' to read a report. Marie-Antoinette could not be expected to know all these former ministerial clerks with funny names. *Cahiers de doléances*? He certainly had a chip on his shoulder: Madame de Tourzel wrote that the king had to be very careful 'not to wound his self-love which was combined with a truly revolutionary vulgarity'.[25] The queen did not think that 'he has the required qualities'. She called him 'a small-time lawyer earning only 700 livres a year'.[26] Nevertheless he was appointed on 17 November.

The problem, and ultimately the cause of the collapse of Barnave and the queen's system, was comte Louis de Narbonne, the lover of Necker's celebrated daughter, Madame de Staël. The king thought he was entirely unsuitable for the government. He was right but ignored. The queen thought that Narbonne was good in his present post of major general but was not of ministerial calibre. She put it to him more tactfully and Narbonne let Madame de Staël broadcast the queen's praise without her reservation. Barnave joked about this with Marie-Antoinette: Madame de Staël was even better at publicity than her father, indeed 'thousand-tongued fame was not her equal'. He added 'however little fitted M. de Narbonne may appear for the post he wishes, the queen will see, no doubt', that he must be humoured to avoid causing resentment in his circle 'at this critical time when it is necessary to gain over anyone who has a finger in the popular movement'. The queen must also say nothing of reconciliation with Lafayette, which Barnave had urged on her because Narbonne's circle hated Lafayette's. He added: 'M. de Lafayette is the only man in France who could get into the saddle and find himself at the head of a party against the king.'[27] In the end Marie-Antoinette concluded: 'If M. de Narbonne must be appointed minister of war, it should be done swiftly.' She added, 'It is important to have a safe pair of hands [*sic*!] in that post.'[28]

On another occasion Narbonne told Marie-Antoinette that the critical situation required a prime minister. She mischievously explained that 'by the Constitution His Majesty has not the right to appoint a *prime* minister. He is obliged to name six, each of whom must have the full direction of his own department' – in order, she did not add, to be able to attach criminal responsibility. Narbonne thought he could persuade the Assembly to overlook this provision; and at this point announced that he had himself in mind. The queen, bursting into laughter, merely replied 'Are you mad M. de Narbonne?' Then Narbonne 'fell on his knees and entreated her, with tears, to consider his conduct with indulgence'. Marie-Antoinette then repeated the tale to Bertrand the next day, but he reserved it for his memoirs.[29]

There then followed an important royal initiative that Barnave thought was either due to the queen's 'lack of confidence' in him or 'a simple misunderstanding'. The Assembly had been clamouring for further action against the émigrés, so on 14 December Duport du Tertre told the Assembly that the king would summon the Elector of Trier, on pain of war, to disperse the émigré formations before 15 January 1792; and, to reinforce this ultimatum, Narbonne announced the formation of three armies under Luckner, Rochambeau and Lafayette, who had relinquished his command of the National Guard to run as mayor. (He was defeated by Pétion. Marie-Antoinette, who detested both men, secretly backed Pétion,[30] because if Lafayette combined the mayoralty with his residual influence on the National Guard, his declining influence would have revived.)

Barnave considered that before this speech, 'which was put into the king's mouth', the Girondins 'scarcely even dared to speak openly of war', but the speech 'seemed to announce war to the nation and seemed to push public opinion in that direction'. War with the queen's brother Leopold was incompatible with Barnave's system that relied on alliance with him. By introducing the possibility of war the government seemed to sanction it, or put the idea into peoples' heads. Marie-Antoinette blustered that the speech Barnave wanted delivered had only arrived at 5 p.m. and 'de Lessart and the king had only got it 5 minutes before the Council was due to open'. She 'never saw the king either in Council or when he was with the ministers'. Besides, she had assumed that the triumvirs would already have conveyed their thinking to de Lessart in advance, or, she could have added, to du Tertre, their normal ministerial conduit. Adrien Duport was probably cognizant of the speech and this led to a cooling between him and Barnave.

Du Tertre had not forgotten his old allegiance to Lafayette, whilst Narbonne, Lafayette and the Girondins in temporary alliance all wanted war but of different scope and for different ends: Narbonne to strengthen the monarchy,[31] the Girondins to capture or (that failing) destroy it. They all assembled in the apartments of Narbonne's mistress, Madame de Staël, to agree on their action. Another explanation is that the king took a rare initiative: it was his personal agent Bigot de la Croix who went to Germany to settle the matter, and in the short term the king's initiative did dampen down war fever.

However, as Barnave argued, the king's initiative had admitted the Girondins into a space from which the Constitution barred them: the king's right to conduct foreign policy. They needed war because on many counts the constitutional monarchy was succeeding. 'The king's acceptance of the Constitution had brought about a big change in his favour among the majority of Parisians.' This was replicated in the provinces; all in all 'the king was more popular now than before the flight to Varennes'.[32] But as so often, disintegration began at the centre: the disintegration of Marie-Antoinette and Barnave's system began when the government through which they ruled was disrupted by Narbonne, a man whom Barnave, albeit with some misgivings, had thrust upon a reluctant queen. For Narbonne was moving towards an alliance of convenience with the Girondins and they were determined to wreck the constitutional monarchy. The Girondins wanted to secure an understanding with Prussia and isolate Austria – a move that many in France had wanted since the moment Marie-Antoinette had crossed the border in 1770. De Lessart explained the king's true position in a private letter to Emmanuel, marquis de Noailles, the French ambassador to Vienna, dated 16 January: 'As you can well believe, the King is at the head of those who are against it [war]; his excellent mind, in conformity with his heart, seeks to reject the very idea. Even were it to be successful, he regards it as a calamity for the Kingdom and a scourge for humanity.'[33]

However, Narbonne became the most powerful man in the government and he wanted war, albeit a limited one. Narbonne's plan was to secure the benevolent neutrality of Prussia, thereby isolating Austria and enabling France to conduct a military promenade through the territories of the Electors of Mainz and Trier, who were accused of harbouring concentrations of émigré troops. The victorious French army would then be used to close the Jacobin Club and restore monarchical authority. When the matter was discussed in the Council on 9 December, Louis left after twenty minutes during which he had not opened his mouth.[34]

Louis' personal policy – note the distinction between the king and the ministers Barnave had drawn – was actually the same as Barnave's. The king, queen and Barnave all wanted the émigré formations dispersed but without further inflaming the situation. That is why Louis sent Bigot de Sainte-Croix to Trier to make sure the Elector did comply with the summons and so avert war. It so happened that the Elector himself wanted to be rid of the émigrés for, as Bigot told de Lessart, 'the French émigrés are now the masters of the Electorate'.[35] Accordingly, the Elector immediately complied with the French ultimatum. Bigot was relieved for he realized what damage the émigrés were doing to the king's cause. For, he considered, the emigration achieved the dual purpose of creating both 'an imaginary connivance [on the king's part] with those who aspired to save the king' and 'the external threat which was necessary in order to propagate terror at home'.[36] Having supervised the evacuation of the electorate by the émigrés, Bigot wanted to return home, but de Lessart told him to stay put to give the lie to any Girondin claims that the émigrés had returned. Barnave had the grace to compliment the queen on the happy outcome.[37]

That should have been the end of the matter; but on 17 December the Austrian chancellor, Kaunitz, handed the French ambassador a gratuitously provocative note to the effect that if France attacked the Elector's territories the emperor would defend them with his own troops. Hitherto Kaunitz had been even more pacific than Leopold: he observed that the new Constitution rendered France less of a danger than it had been and that 'if it was bad, it was bad only for France'.[38] And Leopold had found it convenient to take Louis' acceptance of the new Constitution at face value. He had ignored Marie-Antoinette's pleas. But perhaps at last he had woken up to what she termed 'the shame and reproach before the whole universe of having allowed his sister and nephew [no mention of his niece, ever the dynastic imperative] and ally to be dragged through the mud when he could have rescued them'.[39] Perhaps the drip drip drip of her pleas had at last worn a pathway into his stony heart. Indeed, he now championed her idea of an armed congress, 'not war but the threat of war', which for months he and Kaunitz had ridiculed. And he based his demands on the violation of the feudal rights of the *princes possessionés* in Alsace, as she had suggested way back in the summer of 1790. But that was a minor contributory cause of his new attitude, although one picked up by the Girondins and instinctively (they had no evidence) attributed to Marie-Antoinette. On 17 January 1792 they passed a decree stating that 'any Frenchman who participated in a congress designed to modify the Constitution shall be declared a traitor'. But the congress was for Leopold merely a side issue and he would only have summoned one at the request of the French people.

For the key to an understanding of foreign affairs in 1792 – and one vouchsafed to none of the parties in France – is that Austria and Prussia, for fifty years mortal enemies, had come to a solid understanding that was ratified by a treaty of alliance on 7 February 1792. The Girondins' gamble of detaching Prussia and isolating an indebted Austria with half of her provinces only precariously pacified after Joseph's hasty reforms was a pipe dream. Not only this but Frederick William II of Prussia was actually far more interested in attacking France than was Leopold. And it was Frederick William rather than Leopold who wanted to annex French territory on the pretext of paying for the cost of the campaign. So the Girondins and Marie-Antoinette both misread the Prussian situation: the Girondins in thinking they could keep Prussia out of the war in order to achieve an easy victory, and Marie-Antoinette in wanting to involve Prussia in order to restrain her brother from annexing Alsace or Lorraine. If that happened it would only be because Frederick William wanted to incorporate Julich and Berg and needed to give Leopold compensation in France.

This, however, was not the limit of the territorial ambitions of Frederick William, who equalled his uncle Frederick the Great only in his acquisitiveness. In 1791 he gave Leopold to understand that he would no longer oppose the Bavarian exchange provided Leopold would allow him to pick up Danzig (Gdansk) in a second partition of Poland. This meant that Leopold could no longer overlook the trouble being fomented by French revolutionary emissaries in Belgium, since the Elector of Bavaria could hardly be expected to swap his country for one in turmoil. Leopold believed that there could be no permanent pacification of the province until the revolutionary ferment in France itself had been bottled up. Accordingly, by January 1792 he had decided on armed intervention in France, delaying only to conclude his alliance with Prussia and for the campaigning season to begin.[40]

Just as France misread the international situation, so Austria completely misread the French one. She believed that the bluff of Pillnitz had frightened the National Assembly into restoring Louis XVI and revising the Constitution in his favour. She now believed that similar threats would see off the Girondins' incursions against his restored throne.[41] The Austrians were cut off from the information normally supplied by an ambassador because Mercy-Argenteau had been in Brussels since October 1790. Mercy relied for his information on Pellenc, who relied for his on the Feuillants, who were losing control of the situation, and on Marie-Antoinette who wasn't sure what she wanted. At the risk of stating the obvious, countries only go to war when they think they can win, and for it to come about all parties must share this illusion. So Louis XVI told Frederick William that the French army would not hold up for more than half a campaign and the Girondins thought or hoped they would only be fighting an enfeebled Austria. In fact, France would sustain over twenty campaigns and only Austria would face her in all of them until England took over after the Battle of Wagram in July 1809.

Kaunitz's bellicose statement enlarged the scope of the conflict and enabled the Girondins, who favoured an ideological War of Nations, to persuade Narbonne to raise his sights from the Elector to the emperor himself. In the Assembly, Armand Gensonné questioned whether the emperor's declaration was compatible with the 1756 alliance, and on 25 January the Assembly asked Leopold to clarify this point before 1 March; otherwise France would be obliged to go to war. The Girondins wanted war in order to smoke out the queen's presumed treason when confronted with war with her brother. As Brissot put it in December 1791, 'I have only one fear; it is that we won't be betrayed. We need great treasons; our salvation lies there, because there are still strong doses of poison in France and strong emetics are needed to expel them.'[42]

The Girondins used Narbonne as a dispensable Trojan horse to enable them to storm the government by exploiting internal quarrels in the existing Feuillant one. The *casus belli* (metaphorical this time) was a quarrel between Narbonne and Bertrand over an article Narbonne sent to Brissot's *Patriote française* claiming (rightly) that Bertrand did not like the Constitution and was enforcing it to the letter rather than in the spirit. The triumvirs who now regretted urging Narbonne since their system was based on alliance not war with Leopold, sought to use this incident as a pretext to get the king to dismiss Narbonne.[43] Narbonne, spurred on by Madame de Staël, responded by getting the three generals Lafayette, Rochambeau and Luckner to write Narbonne a letter saying that his resignation would be a disaster with a war on the horizon. They came to Paris to make this point and (quite unconstitutionally) attended both the Council and the ministerial committees. The king was furious but Lafayette told du Tertre: 'we shall see which of us, the king or I, has the majority in the kingdom'.[44] Neither had – Lafayette's star was setting and du Tertre, once his client, did not support him as Bertrand's letter to the king shows:

> The Ministers [minus Narbonne] assembled last night in Committee and debated until three in the morning upon [Narbonne's letter to the *Patriote français*]. His conduct being highly disapproved of by all they intended to propose that your Majesty dismiss him; but as the dangerous woman who governs him [Madame de Staël] might exploit the present crisis to excite an insurrection on pretext that a patriotic Minister is dismissed for having criticized an aristocratic one [Bertrand should resign straight after Narbonne had been dismissed].[45]

This solution had been suggested to the king by de Lessart, who also stressed that the queen should be involved at every stage. Barnave thought that the 'brusque' dismissal of Narbonne on 9 March was a tactical mistake, given his popularity. And that the government was blowing hot and cold about war. He thought that Narbonne was the first minister under the new Constitution to seek to build a ministerial party in the Assembly.[46] What he meant is probably this: whereas Molleville blamed Narbonne for working with the select committees in the Assembly that shadowed the ministries, this was actually the best way to achieve effective government. However, Barnave also suspected that Narbonne was coming round to the Girondins' view that the Austrian alliance should be ditched for the Prussian one and that this would 'weaken the position of the queen and draw her to them'.

But Barnave was no longer there to advise the queen, having returned to Grenoble. He later wrote, 'I was detained in Paris [in December 1791] for six weeks longer than planned, for reasons totally unconnected with politics.' On 5 January he sent her his last letter. On it Marie-Antoinette writes: 'End of the correspondence with 2: 1 [Barnave] who left the same day. It is 4:15 [Duport] who will carry on the correspondence.' Before he left Marie-Antoinette told him: 'I know that M. Barnave is going away soon and I am aware of the powerful motives that have decided him. I count on his not forgetting the end of our last conversation.'

Does this emotional 'last conversation', as relayed by Madame Campan, throw any light on the reasons for Barnave's departure? Barnave urged her not to give up on the constitutional monarchists: their 'flag was tattered, but the word "constitution" on it was still legible'. And people would rally to it if the king would give it his backing; then the authors of the Constitution, 'recognizing their own errors', would make the necessary changes. Theirs was the only national party – all the others, the princes, the foreign powers would dismember France – Marie-Antoinette's own chief fear. Austrian foreign policy was driven by realpolitik not 'consanguinity' – again something that haunted Marie-Antoinette and she stated so explicitly. Realpolitik *avant la lettre*, for French was still the language of diplomacy, even for the Austrian Kaunitz whose cynicism epitomized it.

Barnave's last piece of advice concerned the king's constitutional guard. His predictions about its reactionary general staff were coming true. There was talk in the Assembly of halting the formation of the guard. Barnave told Marie-Antoinette that they should replace the general staff with men who whilst appearing to be Jacobins had actually come round to his way of thinking. He had a list of such people to hand and their appointment would give a breathing space of perhaps a fortnight before the Assembly rumbled the ploy. This interval should be used to get the royal family out of Paris escorted by the 1,500-strong guard. This was the first time Barnave had admitted the need for flight, though as Mirabeau's lieutenant he must have considered it. But, as a constitutional monarchist, flight would have been within the twenty leagues' circle the king was permitted to travel, though Barnave had tried to have this stipulation removed. The flight would probably have been to what was becoming the hoary old chestnut of constitutional resistance, Compiègne.[47] That was the place Duport favoured. Barnave told the queen that staying in Paris hoping to be rescued by an invading army would be hopeless:

> You are too far from help; you would be lost before it reached you. I sincerely hope that my gloomy prediction is wrong; but I am convinced that I will pay with my head for the interest that your misfortune awoke in me and the services which I have wanted to perform for you. All I ask for in recompense is to be able to kiss your hand. The queen granted this favour, her eyes bathed in tears. And she kept the most favourable judgement of the high and noble sentiments of this deputy. Madame Elizabeth shared it, and the two princesses often talked of Barnave with lively interest.[48]

Barnave had been asking Marie-Antoinette what was going on in Leopold's head. On 3 January 1792 she told him, in her last letter, that not having heard from her brother she could only guess. She presumed that Leopold originally had considered that the Constitution gave the king sufficient powers to govern and saw no occasion to interfere; but that recently the Assembly had insulted the European powers without the king's being able to do anything about it, so Leopold had changed his stance.[49] He said much the same when he finally wrote to the queen on 31 January,[50] and it meant that instead of the entente with Austria, the lynch pin of Barnave's system, all sides were moving towards a war that would destroy the fragile basis of the constitutional monarchy. Barnave didn't blame Marie-Antoinette for this: his final letter recalled 'the last words of the queen during our second conversation. I have all the more reason to believe them because all that has happened since has confirmed her constant resolution. So I am full of confidence in her courage and sincerity.'[51] Over their six-month relationship each had needed reassurance, like any *physical* lovers, especially clandestine ones. He had suspected her of hedging her bets; she had thought he had overestimated their chance of success. There was some truth in both doubts. But their positions had converged, as we will see, in those of the remaining two triumvirs after Barnave's departure.

So it was not an inner conviction of Marie-Antoinette's bad faith that caused Barnave to depart. He had to sort out a legacy from his uncle, but is this adequate explanation for such an important step? The most natural explanation is his realization that war would revolutionize a Revolution which he had tried to 'stop'. Maybe a turning point had been the bellicose summoning of the Elector on 14 December for which he (wrongly) blamed Marie-Antoinette. On the other hand we have his (later) statement, 'I was detained in Paris for six weeks longer than planned, for reasons totally unconnected with politics.' And his comment that he had to be persuaded to address the Feuillant Club in the autumn and only went because it was 'borne upon me, and my friends, that in refusing to go there we would throw into question the perseverance of our opinions and our political character'.[52]

Did it occur to him that he was doing precisely that in leaving? He later realized that the system he had operated with Marie-Antoinette had ended with his departure when he wrote 'all might have been well if the ministers having decided amongst themselves these [salutary] measures, had sent a résumé of them to the king, bolstered by the opinion of the [remaining] two former deputies [Lameth and Duport]', a variant on the mechanism by which he and Marie-Antoinette had governed.[53] 'It is 4:15 [Duport] who will carry on the correspondence,' the queen had written, but Barnave implies that Duport and Lameth would not continue with the system of transmitting strategy agreed with her to the Feuillant government. Therefore, he urges the queen herself to emerge into the open and 'see the ministers often to impress upon them the force of her decisions and the solidity of her character'.[54] We don't know whether this happened, but it is unlikely that Marie-Antoinette ran the government in the way she had with Barnave, and in any case all contact with the ministers ended with the appointment of the Girondin government. Alexandre de Lameth, though, was certainly in regular contact with the king who, just before the sack of the Tuileries, smuggled out 'a great amount of correspondence' with the triumvir, but this may have concerned Alexandre's running of the propaganda machine started by Mirabeau.[55]

A month after Barnave's departure, Axel von Fersen, his rival in affection and policy, made a secret visit to the Tuileries to sound out the king and queen on Gustavus' madcap schemes for a royal escape. Barnave's and Fersen's paths never crossed but Marie-Antoinette, curiously, would give Fersen a permanent reminder of her association with Barnave. Marie-Antoinette warned Fersen that it would be too dangerous to come: he was proscribed as one who had assisted the 'abduction' of the king on 20 June. So he came disguised as a Swedish courier carrying messages for the Portuguese court. One escape plan envisaged an invasion of Normandy but this collapsed when Spain backed out; another was for the king to escape separately, but the king ruled this out because Marie-Antoinette and the dauphin would be used as hostages. There were alternative plans for a congress of the great powers. Gustavus was the only ruler prepared to stick out his neck for the king and queen, but his plans were impractical and Sweden was no longer the great power she had been in the seventeenth century.

Fersen stayed in a safe house belonging to Quentin Crawfurd, a wealthy Scot, where he kept his mistress Mrs Sullivan. Crawfurd and Marie-Antoinette were just about the only people who did not know that Mrs Sullivan was also Fersen's long-standing mistress. His sister Sophie warned him that their liaison was becoming common knowledge and that if it reached the queen – always referred to as 'Elle' in their correspondence – it would deal her a 'mortal blow'. 'Think of unhappy Elle and spare her the most deadly pain imaginable.'[56]

Having dumped his things Fersen proceeded to the Tuileries, dodged the National Guard, and entered the queen's apartments by 'my usual route . . . Got to her lodgings perfectly. Did not see the king [one word heavily crossed out]. Stayed there'[57] – presumably for the night. He did not see the king until twenty-three hours later. Fersen generally used the phrase 'Resté là' as code for spending the night with one of his many mistresses, but too much should not be made of this, though the crossing out may be significant. Many consider that even if Marie-Antoinette and Fersen had not made love before, they did this time when they both knew they would never have another chance. On the other hand, as Antonia Fraser rightly observes, if they hadn't made love at 'the free and easy Trianon' they were hardly likely to do so when they could be interrupted at any moment. Maybe, she suggests, this was 'a nostalgic fling' and one 'rather hopes so'.[58] I share this view and this wish, believing that their affair started in 1786. But this question can no more be settled than that of the origins of the French Revolution.

Marie-Antoinette told Fersen that 'she was seeing Alex. Lameth and Duport, that they repeatedly told her that the only remedy was the intervention of foreign troops; otherwise all was lost; that the present situation could not go on'. They also told her 'that they had been forced to go further than they had wanted [in the way of the Revolution] because of the folly of the aristocrats' and lack of support from the Court. Marie-Antoinette's attitude was 'now they tell me'. Embittered herself, she put their change of heart down to their own bitterness and their hatred of the Legislative Assembly 'in which they had no influence' and '*fear* [her stress] because they saw that all this must change and wanted to be in credit with the victors'.[59] This was unworthy of Marie-Antoinette. As we shall see, Duport was to risk his life in a last-ditch effort to save the monarchy. Moreover, their hatred of the Legislative Assembly was not just sour grapes. True, 'they had no influence', but equally the Feuillants in the Assembly, though in a large majority, did not have the guts to stand up to the Girondins. Fersen did not see the king until 6 p.m. the following day, when Louis refused all escape plans, said the best opportunity had been the proposed flight to Metz on 15 July 1789, and authorized Fersen to tell the European rulers to discount any pronouncements he made under duress.

Fersen told Marie-Antoinette that he was going to Spain but instead he spent another week with his mistress and left Paris on 21 February without ever seeing the queen again. Had she offended him? Before he left, Marie-Antoinette gave him her correspondence with Barnave with the enigmatic comment, 'you shall judge of it yourself, for I am keeping it all for you'. She had told him earlier that she was 'keeping a very interesting volume of correspondence for when we meet in happier times; it is all the more interesting because one must give their due to those who have taken part in it. No one suspects its existence or if they have spoken about it it falls into the same category as the thousand and one stupidities which are bandied about every day'.[60]

On the face of it, giving this correspondence to Fersen seems tactless. There appear to be two possible explanations. One, that having heard of his affair with Mrs Sullivan, Marie-Antoinette wanted to punish or bring him closer. The second and more likely explanation is that she wanted to demonstrate to Fersen that she had not simply 'sold out' to Barnave. She had told Barnave at the outset of their correspondence that she must be free to speak her mind. And she had. She had argued the toss on every issue however small, such as the uniform of the Constitutional Guard; had conceded some things but held her ground on others, such as the veto on the decree against the refractory priests, on which she had won him round and which he came to see as the turning of the tide in the battle between the monarchy and the Legislative Assembly.

That Marie-Antoinette kept the Barnave correspondence shows what store she set by it. Giving it to Fersen must have aroused some jealousy on his part, but it was the only way she could smuggle it out. And it would serve as an *apologia pro vita sua* for the by now explicitly counter-revolutionary Swede. So important was this correspondence to the queen that she made another copy. Shortly before the storming of the Tuileries she instructed Madame Campan to give François Jarjayes 'her family letters and several correspondences which she thought important to keep for the history of the Revolution, and particularly Barnave's letters and her replies, of which she had made copies . . . M. de J . . . was not able to preserve this archive, it was burnt'.[61]

Marie-Antoinette was becoming a historian: undeservedly unpopular she wanted to be able to give an account of the Revolution from her point of view. Fersen, as his journal shows, was jealous of Barnave: he was younger, just as good looking, and above all much more intelligent: Fersen hated Barnave so much that when Barnave was arrested in August 1792 he wrote, 'I really hope he will be executed. No one will have more richly deserved it.'[62] Marie-Antoinette, as a sensitive lover, in her letters to Fersen, played down her relations with Barnave, indeed never mentioned him by name, but when they had ended she felt compelled to give Fersen the evidence that for four months the two of them had directed the government of France.

WAR

The Girondins threw their weight behind Narbonne and, though he was not reinstated, they were able to bring down the Feuillant government by impeaching de Lessart and having him sent before the National High Court at Orléans to stand trial for the crime of *lèse-nation*, which had replaced that of *lèse-majesté*. Terrified, the remaining Feuillant ministers – Duport du Tertre, Tarbé and Cahier – 'all gave in their resignations between the 15th and the 20th of March', leaving the field to the Girondins and the war party.[63] Alexandre de Lameth noted: 'The king has abandoned de Lessart and appointed Dumouriez. If he knows his history of England [which he knew Louis did] he would not have sacrificed his minister' – a reference to Charles I's allowing the execution of the earl of Strafford. Lameth advised his correspondent to sell his *assignats*, which would depreciate by 30 per cent.[64] Du Tertre took up the lucrative post of public prosecutor of the central criminal court, which Robespierre vacated on 10 April. Their tenures were equally brief: for du Tertre the court was too radical, for Robespierre not radical enough. Barnave asked Theodore de Lameth to lobby for du Tertre's appointment as governor to the dauphin – an important role as there was increasing talk of the king's abdication or dethronement. But du Tertre sought safety in retirement, making the same mistake as Barnave and later Danton of believing that it was possible to retire from the Revolution. Its pension was death.

Reviewing the French situation, Breteuil said wearily to Mercy-Argenteau in Brussels that doubtless there would be yet another imperial declaration, another empty threat. Mercy replied: 'A declaration, Sir! It's no longer declarations we need; the emperor has realized it and has at last changed systems.' Then, seizing the pommel of his sword, the pacific septuagenarian ambassador added: 'This is what we need; the emperor is determined on it and soon you will see the results.'[65] Goaded, as Marie-Antoinette had told Barnave, by French provocation by word and deed (the formation of three massive armies on his borders), the emperor had apparently decided on war. But at the same time Mercy gave Kaunitz an analysis of just what foreign intervention could and could not achieve.

Mercy told Kaunitz that there were three scenarios which would unite the whole French nation. First, 'If the Court committed a grave error, such as a new plan for the king's flight'. That, Mercy implies, would be the end of the monarchy. Second, any attempt to impose a counter-revolution especially by, third, the émigrés. The émigrés, composed of nobles, parlementaires, *privilégiés* of all sorts, were by definition 'opposed to the general interest'. Moreover, a 'crusade' on their part would lead to insurrection in the allied armies and in their states and enable 'the French Revolution to romp over Europe in six months'. So, *divide et impera*, divide and rule, was the only option for the emperor if he wanted to intervene.[66] Therefore, the sword Mercy unsheathed was more like a foil.

Barnave also in his *Introduction à la Révolution française* amplifies why Leopold had 'changed systems'. Before the Revolution, Leopold and Joseph II, like Louis XVI, had seen the aristocracy as the enemy. Now, with the Girondins propagating international revolution, they forged a guarded alliance with their former foes. This also occurred with the other European rulers who, seeing 'democracy' as the common enemy, also dropped their inter-state rivalry and became 'allies in their terror'.[67]

So the emperor was not the only one who, stung by the reckless wrecking tactics of the Girondins, had 'changed systems': all of Europe had, except England where monarchy and aristocracy were already united. The most important player to 'change systems' was Louis XVI himself, albeit with the qualifications typical of the man. Louis had originally decided to give the Constitution a go if only to prove that it needed modifying. But on 3 December he wrote to Frederick William II of Prussia, advocating an armed congress 'at the moment when, despite my acceptance of the new Constitution, the men of faction openly display their aim of completely destroying the remains of the monarchy' – a reference to the decrees on the émigrés and the priests, which had been deliberately introduced to force him to depopularize himself by using the veto.

It has been claimed that this letter, the only extant one by the king on the subject – the rest all being written by Marie-Antoinette – is a forgery. But this is not the case. Not only has a handwriting expert pronounced it to be genuine,[68] but it contains a sentence entirely characteristic of Louis' sophistry: 'there remains war if it becomes inevitable', a stance similar to that with which he had 'prepared himself' for the possibility of civil war in 1790 – provided he had not worked for either eventuality. This comes over most clearly in a rare letter to Breteuil: 'Instead of a civil war, it would be a foreign war and things will be all the better for it. The physical and moral state of France makes it impossible that she should support even a half-year's campaign. It is not I who wanted war . . . my conduct must be such that in its misfortune the Nation sees no other resource than to throw itself into my hands' – as mediator.[69]

This may explain why Louis XVI took the extraordinary step of appointing a Girondin government in the certain knowledge that it would advise him to declare war on the emperor. Pellenc believed that given the likely defeat of the French armies, the appointment of a 'Jacobin ministry with the king declaring that he would always abide by its majority decisions' was a 'one in ten thousand chance' of salvation for the Court. (Actually, Louis was merely restating the convention that the king should abide by the majority vote in the Council.) War was inevitable, but if it was declared by a Feuillant government its members would soon follow de Lessart to the High Court at Orléans. There were other equally compelling reasons for what has always seemed a puzzling and fatal decision. The very day that Louis replaced de Lessart with Dumouriez, Pétion, the Girondin mayor, withdrew his opposition to the formation of the king's constitutional guard and it was immediately activated. Pellenc considered that this would cover the departure of the Court to Fontainebleau.[70]

At the same time Brissot's journal scotched the idea that Marie-Antoinette was going to be put on trial. This had seemed a real possibility. Vergniaud, the most eloquent of the Girondin deputies, having told the Assembly that 'presumption [of guilt] is sufficient to ground a decree of accusation', went on to make a scarcely veiled threat to Marie-Antoinette: 'All the inhabitants [of the Tuileries] should be aware that only the person of the king is inviolable.' Since the queen was not 'inviolable', a committee was held at the house of the mathematician Nicolas de Condorcet, now a leading Girondin, to discuss sending the queen herself to the High Court at Orléans on twenty-three trumped-up charges. Among those present were Lafayette, Pétion, Brissot, Narbonne and Siéyès – a wide spectrum of enemies. A rumour was spread that she should appear before the Assembly and ask for leave to retire to Germany.[71] There had also been a move afoot to send du Tertre as well as de Lessart to the High Court – if du Tertre had been tried, his links with Marie-Antoinette and Barnave's system of government might have come to light; and there was talk of denouncing Alexandre de Lameth together with the queen.[72] The hounds were temporarily called off.

According to Madame Campan, Dumouriez told Marie-Antoinette that he had merely 'pulled a red cap of liberty down to his ears' in order to disguise his real intention of serving the monarchy and Marie-Antoinette should believe him when he said 'let me save you'.[73] The king was in a desperate state, 'praying all day long, preparing for everything with a desolating and resigned despair'.

All in all, Pellenc concluded that the change of government 'was likely to turn to the profit of the personal safety of the king and queen'. 'The three new ministers have already given fairly satisfactory assurances on this.' The whole transaction was arranged by the outgoing minister of the interior Cahier de Gerville – 'there was no other influence'.[74]

At the same time, however, Louis informed the Assembly that the former ministers had 'earned the respect of public opinion for their honourable conduct', whilst their replacements were only 'accredited by popular opinion', a neat distinction. Barnave thought that by sending this message the king had played into the hands of those who wanted to drive a wedge between him and the nation. Barnave thought that the Girondins were mainly interested in 'money and ambition'. Since the king had not the power to prevent their appointment he should allow them to discredit themselves by displaying their venality. They were the only ones with the energy to govern, and this energy could be channelled in defence of a constitution the Feuillants no longer had the 'strength' to save, as Barnave put it.[75]

He might have added 'or desire'. For the Feuillants no longer wanted to save the Constitution, at least in its present form. Within a day of the appointment of the Jacobin government, the leading constitutional monarchists (Fayettist and Feuillant) met at Adrien Duport's to discuss radical changes to the Constitution. Or rather Duport, the Lameth brothers and Laborde *fils* (Laborde de Méréville) pressed for changes, most of which Lafayette resisted. Both sides agreed that there should be a second chamber, but Duport wanted an hereditary peerage, which was a red line for Lafayette. Indeed, Lafayette claimed that the time to have made changes to the Constitution was during the revision after the Flight to Varennes. Duport, the Lameth brothers and Dumas wanted the Legislative Assembly to be dissolved prematurely. Lafayette accused them of being 'counter-revolutionaries', the whole meeting broke up, and 'those who had proposed it lost face'. Pellenc concludes, smugly, 'Some regret was shown that I wasn't invited. I would have refused.'[76] This report is important since it shows that both wings of the constitutional monarchists contemplated radical changes to the Constitution earlier than is usually supposed and this in direct response to the formation of a Jacobin government. It also highlights the differences between the two wings which, as we shall see, were never resolved, and (joined with Marie-Antoinette's opposition) it doomed last-ditch attempts to save the monarchy. For at heart Lafayette was a republican and told Thomas Jefferson that he expected France to be a republic in about twenty years.[77]

The Lameths, though practically 'flat on their backs, were trying everything to prevent war'. And if war came they did not want the king to propose it but to throw the responsibility onto the Assembly, which itself wanted to evade it. The Girondins for all their bravado and the king for all his pessimism (the French army would not last 'a half-campaign') both knew that the coming war was risky – though no one imagined it would last twenty-three years at a cost of millions of lives and billions of livres. No one that is except Pellenc who wrote on 14 January 1792: 'There has never been a more remarkable moment in history. If the war begins, whatever its outcome, it is going to decide the destiny of mankind.'[78] So each side tried to throw responsibility for the declaration of war onto the other. Just before his arrest, de Lessart had told the king that the Assembly wanted war, 'but at the same time they were all for leaving to the King the whole burden of this great decision. They said that the King should make full use of his initiative and that the National Assembly should take no part and that it was better to risk everything [not going to war?] than explain itself on this particular.'[79] But the Lameths wanted to leave it to the Assembly to declare war and the king to veto it. Or, having obtained the installation of the Constitutional Guard, the king should dismiss the new government.

The Lameth brothers and other 'members of the former [Constituent] Assembly' were exploiting divisions within the new government to prevent the country from going to war with the emperor whom they regarded as a political ally. 'M. de Grave [war minister] does not want war and is even prepared to resign over the issue. Dumouriez says he doesn't want it either. Clavière [finance minister] hesitates. La Coste is neutral and Roland is a fool.' Dumouriez, like most of the war party, had been banking on Prussian neutrality or even assistance; but he had learned of the Austro-Prussian alliance and sat on the information. Pellenc continues: 'There is much intriguing around the ministry on this question [war]'; and he adds, cryptically, 'they [the Lameths] want to establish a majority and a minority on this issue and this issue alone.'[80]

The king, however, was having none of it. If the government was split, he would have to decide; but if it was united he could blame them for the decision. The Girondin deputies could not under the Constitution be ministers, so Louis had to make sure that the ministers he appointed were clearly identified with that party, thereby throwing responsibility for the consequent declaration of war squarely onto them. His agent Radix de Saint-Foy thought the king should appoint the radical comte de Kersaint as naval minister rather than the more moderate Élie Lacoste to make this clear, 'since this is a kind of gamble which is being proposed to the King and the praise or blame for it [war?] must necessarily redound to its prime movers'.[81] In the Council, Louis, according to Madame Roland, 'delayed the decision for a long time' and only yielded to 'the unanimity of his Council'.[82] Moreover, he insisted on obtaining the signed, holograph opinion of the individual ministers and had them published by the Imprimerie Royale together with his own précis of Dumouriez' position paper.[83]

If the foregoing is convoluted, it is because the motives of those who would decide peace or a war, which would determine 'the destiny of mankind', were convoluted also. And many individuals (like the king) were conflicted. So war, like the French Revolution itself, was not inevitable. Both depended on the shake of the kaleidoscope. The Jacobin Club was divided: Robespierre was urging the affiliated societies to petition the Assembly for peace. He thought war was playing into the hands of 'the queen who was the moving force behind the [European] Powers'.[84] His obvious enemies, the Feuillants, also wanted peace, whereas his erstwhile allies the Girondins wanted war. Most of the generals, usually the beneficiaries of war, wanted peace because they feared insubordination in their troops. But Lafayette wanted war to restore his waning influence. Louis spent all day asking for divine guidance, 'aware of the dangers surrounding me, I submit my fate to the Sovereign Master of the Universe'.[85] As for Marie-Antoinette, her attitude was 'vous l'avez voulu Georges Dandin' ('You asked for it').

And got it: on 20 April 1792, as prescribed by the Constitution, the king went to the Assembly to propose war on the king of Bohemia and Hungary, Francis II, son of the Emperor Leopold, who had died suddenly and mysteriously in March. Marie-Antoinette believed he had been poisoned by French emissaries.[86] In Vienna an actor interrupted his performance to inform the audience; there was silence with a thin sprinkling of applause. Emperor Leopold had not been loved. An autopsy revealed no traces of poison. Two days before France declared war, the Austrian council of state decided on an offensive war against France. They did it reluctantly and in case further delay caused Prussia to withdraw its offer of assistance.[87]

The king's proposals were ecstatically accepted, with only seven dissenters. Louis was pale and stammered; there were tears in his eyes; he delivered his speech in a monotone, 'in the same tone of voice as if he had been proposing the most insignificant decree in the world'; as if to distance himself from his words, as in a modern 'speech from the throne'. And the words themselves were impersonal: 'I have come in the name of the Constitution formally to propose war.' On 3 August he was to tell the Assembly that 'my former ministers know what efforts I made to avoid war'. In this warlike atmosphere it was said in March that Louis, surely ironically, had dubbed the dauphin a knight and that, asked to choose a lady to champion, the boy had selected his mother: 'I swear to die in defence of your rights against all the world.'[88]

ELEVEN

THE FALL OF THE MONARCHY

ith the appointment of a ministry responsible to the Girondin faction in the Legislative Assembly, that assembly, as Bigot de Saint-Croix observed, had usurped the last remaining prerogative of the king: the conduct of foreign policy. Louis took no further part in government, merely reading the newspapers in the Council and translating the English-language journals for the ministers if required. One prerogative, however, remained; and in June he would use it not, as in the previous winter, to shield the émigrés and priests, but quite simply to save his palace, his family and his throne.

Marie-Antoinette's interesting experiment in government had diminished with the departure of Barnave and ended with that of Bertrand de Molleville. Her sole interest now was care of her two children and contact with the world outside France, though this was made difficult by the increasingly tight surveil-lance and by spies within the palace: her letters now are few and sparse. Her first choice had been the armed congress – not war but the threat of war – in order that her husband should be the natural solution, as mediator, to an artificial crisis manufactured by herself. It was never going to work. The next best thing was war but it posed many dangers. The most obvious one (as Barnave had predicted) was that the palace would be stormed before the allies reached her, but she thought that their role as hostages would save their lives. It never occurred to her that the French army could win or turn the invaders back. But she told Madame de Tourzel: 'My brother does not understand France; by declaring war against the Jacobins, he puts us and our faithful servants under the axe.'[1] Presumably she meant by this that the emperor should have concen-trated on purely foreign-policy concerns – the rights of the *princes possessionés* and the annexation by France of the papal enclave of Avignon.

Her next fear was that even if the allies reached the Tuileries, the émigrés would hold the king in tutelage and put her on trial. In doing the latter, Jules Michelet thought the comte de Provence, as regent of the kingdom, 'would satisfy his personal hatred and that of the nation'.[2] Marie-Antoinette was at least able to ensure that the small ill-equipped émigré army was kept at the back of the invading queue. Her third fear (of which she needed no reminder from Barnave) was that Austria would seize French territory – Alsace and/or Lorraine. Alexandre de Lameth also expressed this fear in a letter from the front to Barnave of 13 April.[3] She thought that Prussia, who had thwarted Joseph's attempts to alter the balance of power within Germany by acquiring Bavaria, would act as a check on Austrian ambitions without wanting a share in the spoils. As we have seen she was wrong on this: Prussia certainly wanted a share in the spoils, though her main interests lay to the East – in a second partition of Poland – rather than the Rhine. Ostensibly, Frederick William confined his demands to asking that the expenses of the campaign be met by Louis XVI. Marie-Antoinette had been dragging her heels about paying for the invasion. On 17 April, Mercy-Argenteau told Kaunitz: 'I have once again made strong representations about a reply to [a request to meet both Austrian and Prussian expense]; I observed how misplaced the silence of the Tuileries on this point was.'[4]

Axel von Fersen wrote to Marie-Antoinette on 21 June:

> The Emperor plans a dismemberment [of France] . . . but there is perhaps a way of preventing it; it is to give the King of Prussia a written undertaking for the payment [of his expenses]: he wants it but the King's signature is necessary. I still have one blank seal left which I have not mentioned to the B.[aron de Breteuil]. Do you want me to make use of it if it might be of use in assuring us of the King of Prussia's opposition to any dismemberment? . . . It would be good to have three more [blank seals].

On 3 July the queen bit the bullet and sent the seals.[5] This is a moral maze: the queen of France was arranging for the king to subsidize the invasion of his own country in order to prevent the dismemberment of the same. But Marie-Antoinette would not have seen it this way nor her more celebrated betrayal of the French war plans. In the *ancien régime* there had been the vague crime of *lèse majesté* – Marie-Antoinette and Breteuil had tried to pin this on Cardinal Rohan but it would not stick. The National Assembly changed *lèse majesté* to *lèse nation* – a gratuitous insult to the king, separating him from his people, where the neutral 'treason' would have been more appropriate. Naturally, Marie-Antoinette did not accept the change and since by definition a ruler cannot commit *lèse majesté*, she saw nothing wrong in sending Mercy and Fersen the French plan of campaign. In any case, as Talleyrand observed to Tsar Alexander after Napoleon's fall, treason is only a matter of dates.[6]

On 26 March, before the declaration of war, the queen had given Mercy a résumé of the campaign: 'Dumouriez plans a preemptive strike on Savoy and another one via Liège, the latter being conducted by Lafayette's army. That was decided in the Council yesterday. It is worth knowing this proposal so as to be on one's guard and take the necessary measures.. This apparently will be soon.'[7] Marie-Antoinette had told Barnave that she did not attend the Council, so Louis must have given her the details. Whether he knew she would pass them on cannot be known. Rumours were rife. Pellenc notes that it was said that the king 'kept the war directives in his pockets for six hours and sent out couriers [to the enemy] before' they were sent to the French generals. 'A portion of the Parisians believed for some hours that M. Dumouriez made the queen cry by showing her one of these directives.'[8]

On 5 June, Marie-Antoinette wrote to Fersen: 'Luckner's army has been ordered to attack immediately; he is against this but the Ministry wants it. The troops are lacking in everything and in the greatest disorder.' On 23 June she wrote again to Fersen: 'Dumouriez leaves tomorrow for Luckner's army; he has promised to rouse Brabant to rebellion.' 'Rousing Brabant' worried her because it would prevent the Bavarian exchange and the emperor would be all the more eager to seize Alsace or her father's patrimony of Lorraine in compensation. Marie-Antoinette's position was complicated: she wanted the allied invasion to succeed in order that Louis XVI's authority could be restored – though Fersen in February had difficulty in convincing the king that it could ever be restored to its pre-1789 level. But she did not want to surrender any French territory in the process. So in pre-1789 terms she was a patriot and in post-1789 ones a traitor. Two rival legitimacies to be settled by the sword.

Louis gambled that the appointment of Girondin ministers would make them responsible, following Mirabeau's dictum that a Jacobin minister was not the same as a Jacobin in the ministry. He was disappointed in this hope because the new ministers fitted instead into another pattern, noted by Soulavie for the whole reign, that of ministers acting in government like an opposition. So the new ministers sponsored further measures to embarrass the king: between 27 May and 8 June decrees were introduced to disband his Constitutional Guard, to form an armed camp of 20,000 provincial national guards (*fédérés*) in Paris, and to deport the non-juring priests. According to Madame Campan, Louis was ready to give way and sign the decrees, but Marie-Antoinette stiffened his resistance.[9] However, none of his ministers was prepared to countersign his veto of the decree abolishing his Constitutional Guard, so he was obliged to give his sanction.[10] By forcing him to disband his guard, the Girondin ministers had reneged on the principal element of the concordat that had brought them to power. Thus disarmed, however, Louis did not intend to deliver himself up to the mercies of the *fédérés*; nor had he any intention of sanctioning the deportation of what he regarded as the only Catholic clergy in France.

Exploiting a split that had developed within the Ministry, on 12 June, Louis dismissed the most intransigent ministers, Jean-Marie Roland (interior), Joseph Servan (war) and Etienne Clavière (finance), retaining Dumouriez, Antoine Duranthon, the Keeper of the Seals, and Lacoste at the Marine. Dumouriez may have suggested this manoeuvre – he had not been informed about the camp of *fédérés* and drew his sword on Servan in the Council. But when Dumouriez himself pressed the king to sanction the decrees, Louis dismissed him too on 16 June – Louis' diary specifically refers to a dismissal (*'renvoi'*). Barnave, still in Dauphiné and no longer advising the queen, thought that the dismissal of the Jacobin ministry was a mistake: they should have been made to carry the can for the military defeats that punctuated the summer. He considered that the Feuillant ministry the king now formed 'was perhaps the worst for the circumstances. This sort of anti-Jacobin revolution existed only in the Council of ministers, not in the nation, circumstances or the majority of the Assembly.'[11] The views of Barnave and Duport now diverged for, as Mercy told Kaunitz, the new ministry 'in its entirety was formed under the influence of M. Duport . . . [who] has maintained a correspondence with the king and was able to influence his choice of the new ministers'. Mercy, however, also told Kaunitz that this correspondence was with the queen.[12] Pellenc, who shared Barnave's viewpoint, was nevertheless hoping to be made cabinet secretary, but did not get the job.[13] Dumouriez was shocked by his dismissal – he didn't know Louis had it in him but the king said, 'don't imagine you can frighten me with threats, I have made up my mind'.[14] Dumouriez left to take up a command at the Front.

The dismissal of the Girondin ministers, amid a growing conviction that the king was planning to seize control of Paris before the arrival of émigré or allied troops, provoked a similar reaction to that caused by the dismissal of Necker in 1789. A petition was due to be presented to the king asking him to withdraw his veto to the two decrees on 20 June, the double anniversary of the Tennis Court Oath and the Flight to Varennes. Apprehensively, Louis wrote to his confessor, M. Hébert, on 19 June: 'Come and see me; I have never stood in so great a need of your consolations. I have finished with men; I look to Heaven. Great misfortunes are expected tomorrow; I shall have courage.'[15]

The orderly presentation of a petition degenerated into the occupation of the Tuileries for five hours by a mob drawn from the electoral Sections. During this ordeal Louis stood on a window-seat with nothing between him and the mob but a table and a handful of grenadiers. Before him were paraded the bleeding heart of a calf with the inscription 'heart of an aristocrat' and blood-thirsty, misspelled placards, such as 'tremble tyrant your hour has come' and 'down with Monsieur Veto and his wife'. Louis humoured the crowd by wearing a cap of liberty but he would not give his sanction to the decrees. 'I am your king. I have never swerved from the Constitution,' Louis said. 'We'll come back every day until he sanctions the decrees', was heard from the crowd. Madame Elizabeth stood in the next window embrasure with the tip of a sword pressed against her throat. Some of the rioters thought she was Marie-Antoinette and she did not disabuse them, thinking to draw their fire.

Marie-Antoinette had wanted to stay with the king: 'What can they do to me? Kill me, today is as good as tomorrow. What more can they do?' Instead Marie-Antoinette, the dauphin and Madame Royale were shuffled from room to room and ended up in the council chamber. She barricaded herself behind its great velvet topped table. A doll dressed in her likeness dangling from a model lamppost with the caption 'Marie-Antoinette à la lanterne' was wafted before her. She was given a cap of liberty, which she accepted but declined to wear. The dauphin was made to don a cap of liberty but it was way too big for him and since he was suffocating he was allowed to hold it. Madame Roland, wife of the man whose dismissal had caused the invasion of the palace, wished she could have been there. 'What wouldn't I have given to witness her long humiliation? How much her pride must have suffered?'[16] Marie-Antoinette was not around to witness Madame Roland's own journey to the guillotine in November 1793 when, as the tumbrel passed the enormous statue of liberty, she uttered her famous cry: 'Oh Liberty! What crimes are committed in thy name!'

The authorities – Pétion, the mayor, and Santerre of the National Guard – let it go on for hours. Arriving on the scene, Pétion said, 'Sire, I have just this minute learned of the situation you are in', to which the king replied, 'That is very surprising, this has been going on for two hours.' The crowd finally left at eight in the evening. 'Pétion is my enemy,' Louis had told Dumouriez, and when next day Pétion tried to justify his conduct, Louis told him to 'shut up; go and do your duty; I will hold you personally to account for good order in Paris. Goodbye.' Then Louis turned his back on him. Marie-Antoinette feared that this would do the king damage.[17] She herself smuggled out a message to Fersen written in sympathetic ink: 'I am still alive but it is a miracle. The *journée* of the 20th was appalling. I am no longer their main target; it is the life of the king himself they seek. He displayed firmness and courage which overawed them for the present, but the danger can recur at any time.'[18]

The duke of Brunswick, generalissimo of the Prussian army, aggravated the situation by issuing a manifesto on 25 July that threatened Paris with total destruction if the royal family were harmed or the Tuileries invaded again. Marie-Antoinette had been pressing for such a declaration and Fersen had a hand in drafting a document that was not only counter-revolutionary but counter-productive.[19]

'The *journée* of 20 June forebodes another,'[20] noted Marie Antoinette, so she and the king had to decide what to do with their papers. They wanted to satisfy two conflicting requirements: first, to assemble the archival material necessary for them or their adherents to give a history of the Revolution from their point of view, but second, to destroy anything that might incriminate them if they were put on trial. Louis was coming to the conclusion that this rather than assassination would be the approved method. Madame Campan burned 'almost all of the queen's papers' – a fact corroborated by Madame de Tourzel.[21] She burned them in batches so there would not be too much charred paper for the many spy-servitors in the palace to discover, saving only a copy of the Barnave correspondence.

Louis had already ordered an entire edition of Madame de la Motte-Valois' memoirs to be incinerated in the kilns of the Sèvres porcelain manufactory. Marie-Antoinette had heard of the edition but said she had scorned to take action when she had been in a position to do so and would not now. At her trial Marie-Antoinette said she had only been informed of the event.[22] Louis indeed had not consulted her, but when the queen confronted him about it she noticed that his head was bent shamefacedly over his dinner plate. They dined now as four: the king, the queen, Madame Elizabeth and Madame Royale, who at fourteen was judged old enough to join them; the little dauphin – or Prince Royal as he was now called after 'Dauphiné' was abolished – had his nursery tea. Dining in public, which had been embarrassing, would now have been dangerous. Looking up from his empty plate, the king confessed that he had ordered the conflagration whatever its effect on the next batches of porcelain. To avert suspicion, the king even had to repeat this confession to the Legislative Assembly.[23] At the end of May 1792 the episode received a new lease of life when the Girondins 'spread a rumour throughout Paris that the papers burnt ... [in the fire] were copies of a proclamation tending to justify the assassination of a certain number of deputies that the court wanted to get rid of. I [Pellenc] am assured that the queen personally will be denounced over this.'[24]

The king, meanwhile, busied himself with constructing an iron safe that he concealed in a trompe-l'oeil panelling simulating marble. Both he and Marie-Antoinette already had small safes in the fall-front *secrétaires* they favoured,[25] but Louis wanted something larger. Marie-Antoinette warned him that his assistant, the locksmith Gamain with whom he had practised his art over the years, was a dangerous Jacobin. To humour her he extracted the most dangerous items and put them into a portfolio that he entrusted to Madame Campan. It proved too heavy for her to lift, so Louis carried it up to her apartments. Marie-Antoinette told her not to leave the palace even on her days off and Madame Campan guessed that this was because the portfolio contained the pre-Revolutionary Great Seals with the legend 'Louis XVI by the grace of God King of France and Navarre', which she presumed would be used if there were a 'counter-revolution'. Louis told Madame Campan that the queen would tell her what else the portfolio contained. Marie-Antoinette told her that it contained papers that would prove 'fatal for the king if they went so far as to put him on trial'. But the main item was something which, she thought, would exculpate him: 'the minutes of a meeting of the Conseil d'état in which the king gave his opinion against going to war. He made the entire ministry sign it and in the eventuality of a trial he was counting on this document being of great utility.'

Madame Campan ended up entrusting the portfolio to M. Gougenot, a senior tax collector, with instructions to use his discretion over what to burn and what to keep. He chucked the seals into the Seine, as James II had chucked his in the Thames, kept the minutes of the Council meeting, and burnt the rest. He did, however, note the names of the correspondents: '20 letters from Monsieur, 18 or 19 from the comte d'Artois, 17 from Madame Adélaïde, 18 from Madame Victoire, a lot of letters from Alexandre de Lameth, a lot from M. de Malesherbes, with their accompanying memoranda etc.' Gougenot gave the council minutes to Malesherbes, the king's counsel at his trial, but for some reason they were not used.[26]

Louis' passive courage temporarily rekindled support for the monarchy. Petitions expressing outrage flowed in from provincial authorities including that of Varennes. A petition condemning the *journée* was signed by 20,000 Parisians, each one of whom would be defined as a 'suspect' under the law of that name in 1793. A judicial inquiry censured Pétion, who was suspended from his functions on 6 July. Baffled, the Girondins now had either to accept defeat or to overthrow the king. Even at this stage the fall of the monarchy was not inevitable. Paris was equally divided, the Legislative Assembly was discredited even in the eyes of many of its members, and a majority of the *départements* favoured the king. But the king's supporters were timid and paralyzed by his own timidity and above all his fatalism. Marie-Antoinette told Madame Campan that the king

is frightened to give orders and more than anything he fears to address a gathering ... in the present circumstances a few well-articulated words addressed to the Parisians who are loyal to him would centuple the strength of our party. But he won't say them. For my part I could be well content to mount a horse if need be. But if I acted it would only serve to give ammunition to the king's enemies. Clamours against l'Autrichienne, and the domination of a woman would be heard throughout France. Moreover I would unman the king by putting myself forward. A queen who is not a regent must in these circumstances do nothing and prepare herself for death.[27]

Where the royalists were faint-hearted, the opposition from Parisian popular politics and the nationwide network of Jacobin clubs was well organized and intrepid, though Robespierre himself spent the *journée* of 10 August in hiding. To break the gridlock in early July an orchestrated campaign for Louis' dethronement (*déchéance*) was launched: the Assembly was flooded with petitions from Clubs, Sections, from town and country. Vergniaud explored the constitutional possibility of overriding the royal veto if 'the Patrie was in danger', which it was proclaimed to be on 11 July when Pétion's suspension was lifted.

The 'Patrie en danger' decree had several important consequences. It called up for national service everyone capable of bearing arms. On the same day the Commune decreed that everyone with a pike could enter the National Guard. Hitherto entry had been restricted to 'active citizens', those who had the vote. Now 'passive citizens' could enter and this changed the tone of the National Guard, which lost its bourgeois and (constitutional) monarchist character. Administrative authorities were ordered to be *en permanence*, that is, to meet daily. On 25 July the Legislative, under pressure from the electoral Sections, decreed that the permanence be applied to Sectional meetings and that in this emergency 'passive citizens' could participate. The *journée* of 10 August was made by 'passive citizens'.

On 31 July the Mauconseil Section declared that it withdrew its allegiance from the king. On 27 July, Louis entered in his diary: 'alert the whole day'. Marie-Antoinette was so exhausted that she slept through one of these alerts. She was angry that she had not been at the king's side, but he said that it was a false alarm and that she was going to need her sleep. Attacks of nerves, she said, were the luxury of the frivolous and happy. She had long ceased to be either. She thought that the king would be put on trial, but 'they will assassinate me, a foreigner'.[28] With half the denizens of the Tuileries being spies and after a suspected assassinated attempt, Marie-Antoinette was reduced to having a little dog by her bedside. She ordered two protective gilets of taffeta, twenty layers thick, one for herself and the other for the king.

The tension inside the Tuileries was unbearable. As the royal family passed along the gallery to the chapel on the Sunday before 10 August, half the soldiers of the National Guard shouted '*Vive le roi*' whilst the other half shouted 'No king! Down with the veto.' At Vespers it was worse. During the chanting of the Magnificat 'the singers . . . tripled the sound of their voices with frightening effect when they came to "*Deposuit potentes de sede*" – he shall cast down the mighty from their seat'. But the royalist choristers, shocked by this display, added three times 'et reginam' after '*Domine salvum fac regem*' ('God save the King'),[29] the motto inscribed on the edge of pre-Revolution silver écus. Unable even to enjoy their devotions in peace the royal family did not always go to the chapel. There is a haunting, primitive painting of them kneeling on simple *prie-dieux* to receive the sacrament that conveys their anguish and their stupefaction. Things were so bad that the king and queen had to take it in turns to sleep, so one of them could guard against assassination.

Meanwhile the royal family had to endure another of those interminable festivals that for them commemorated a defeat: the third anniversary of the storming of the Bastille. The celebrations lasted from 10 a.m. to 7 p.m. and the royal family all had their roles assigned for this ritual humiliation. But provocatively, or more like tactlessly, the royal carriage was preceded and followed by ones containing the *crème de la crème* of the court nobility still remaining in France. This highlighted the fact that Louis had ignored Barnave's advice to fill the vacancies caused by emigration with Revolutionary notables with the exclamation that it would never do for the queen to be attended by the likes of Madame Pétion and Madame Condorcet, though the latter was a marquise. Madame de Tourzel faithfully records the occupants of the coaches: 'In the carriage preceding that of His Majesty were MM. de Saint-Priest, de Fleurieu, de Poix, de Tourzel, de Broglie, de Montmorin, the Governor of Fontainebleau . . . and de Nantouillet.' The carriage immediately following the king contained the court ladies, again lovingly listed: 'Madame d'Ossun, Lady of the Bedchamber, to the queen, Mesdames de Tarente, de Maillé and de la Roche-Aymon, lady attendants and Madame de Serène, Lady of Honour to Madame Elizabeth.'[30]

Marie-Antoinette was placed some distance from the king as he swore to uphold the Constitution on a raised altar. She nervously watched through a telescope 'his powdered head bobbing up in the midst of those black-haired heads; his clothes, still braided as formerly, contrasted with the costume of the populace who pressed around him.'[31] *Fédérés* had come from all over France to join in the celebrations, after which they were supposed to head for the Front. But Robespierre's Jacobins persuaded them (with offers of free hospitality) to stay on to lend a hand in bringing down the monarchy.

Faced with the imminence of a second rising this time to dethrone him (the first had merely been orchestrated to bring the Girondins back into the ministry), the king had two choices. One was to try to hold out in Paris until the Prussians arrived (Marie-Antoinette had their itinerary; by the end of August they reached Verdun, the last fortress between them and Paris). This plan would involve doing some kind of a deal with the Girondins (themselves engulfed in a wider movement they could no longer control), spending money lavishly on buying support in Paris, and putting the Tuileries in some sort of defensive posture. The other choice was for the king to put his trust in Lafayette, 'the only man', as Madame Elizabeth had put it, 'who by placing himself on a horse can give the King an army'.

Relations between the queen and Lafayette continued desperate, but by the summer, Molleville notes, the king's mistrust of Lafayette 'had largely been dispelled'. Lafayette in turn believed that the king's technical adherence to the Constitution was sufficient, since it allowed him only 'the exercise of a very limited and scarcely dangerous power'.[32] In this frame of mind, Lafayette made two attempts to save the constitutional monarchy on his own terms. First, on 28 June, he left his army and appeared before the Assembly to denounce the *journée* of 20 June. Next day, according to Louis' diary, 'there was to have been a review of the 2nd Legion [of the National Guard] in the Champs Elysées'. Lafayette planned to review this loyal legion with the king, harangue it, and march with it to close down the Jacobins. Lafayette claims that the queen told Pétion, as mayor of Paris, to countermand orders for the review. She said 'M. de La Fayette wants to save us but who will save us from M. de La Fayette.'[33]

A coup d'état in Paris having been rejected by the king and queen, Lafayette came up with a detailed plan to get the royal family out of Paris. It had been arranged with the minister of war, d'Abancourt, that Lafayette's Army of the Rhine and Luckner's Army of Flanders should exchange positions. Their armies would cross at Compiègne, which was within the *rayon constitutionel*, the circle of twenty leagues' radius in which the Constitution confined the king.[34] Lafayette was to arrive in Paris and announce to the Assembly that the king was going to his palace of Compiègne, as was his entitlement under the Constitution. They would leave under the escort of the Swiss and loyal units of National Guards.

At first both the king and queen accepted the proposal. But when Lafayette's aide-de-camp Guillaume La Combe arrived at the Tuileries to finalize details, the king had changed his mind. He said that he wanted to avoid civil war and that Lafayette's best plan was to strengthen his position with his own army, as Bouillé had done with his. He feared also that if he abandoned Paris before the Prussians arrived, they might put his brothers forward. Lafayette has him saying: 'I do not want to fall foul of my brothers by going to Compiègne.' He stayed put as he had in 1789, when he feared that the duc d'Orléans would seize a vacant throne. As Lafayette said: 'He feared the victor whoever it was.'[35]

These reservations might have been overcome but for pressure from Marie-Antoinette, as can be seen from Louis' concluding remark to La Combe: 'go and see the queen'. 'M. de La Combe found the queen even more opposed [than the king] to the plan which had initially delighted her.' Adrien Duport, 'who had been of such service to the king and queen after Varennes, which she appreciated', rushed to the queen and on bended knees urged her to reconsider. All in vain. She had been dissuaded by men 'who were prepared to sacrifice the individual fates of the royal family if that was the price to be paid for the restoration of the *ancien régime*'. Such is the account of Théodore de Lameth, Duport's collaborator in this venture.[36]

Marie-Antoinette's sparer contemporary account accords with Lameth's. On 11 July she wrote to Fersen: 'The Const.[itutionalists] [Duport and the Lameth brothers] in conjunction with La Fayette and Luckner want to conduct the King to Compiègne the day after the Federation [15 July]. For this purpose the two generals are going to arrive there. The King [to whom the plan was given by the Minister of Justice on 9 July] is disposed to lend himself to this project; the Queen is against it. The outcome of this great venture which I am far from approving is still in doubt.' It was 'still in doubt' whilst Duport pleaded with her to have a care for France if she had none for herself. The problem was Lafayette. We know what Marie-Antoinette had in store for him: a court martial. But what did he have in store for her? She said to La Combe: 'We are very grateful to your general but it would be better for us to be imprisoned for two months in a tower.'

Lafayette noted her fixation with towers: 'Shortly before his death Mirabeau had warned her that if it came to war, Lafayette would want to hold the king prisoner in his tent.' She said, 'it would be too trying for us to owe our lives to him twice'.[37] Fersen had urged Marie-Antoinette to stay put in Paris, but 'if you do [risk flight] you must never summon La Fayette, but the neighbouring Départements'.[38] Théodore de Lameth considered that Marie-Antoinette could never forgive Lafayette for flaunting his power over the king and queen 'in the period of his pomp'. To win the queen over and demonstrate that the king was not his prisoner, Lafayette had agreed (under pressure from Duport?) that none of the general staff of the 15,000 men at Compiègne would belong to his adherents and that the commanding officer would be an ally (and relative) of the queen's, the comte de Lignéville.

But were 'the Const.[itutionalists] in conjunction with La Fayette'? Disjunction, rather. We saw back in March that a meeting between them and Lafayette broke up in rancour. Their differences had not lessened. Lafayette would have kept Louis as a *roi fainéant* as he had in 1789–90, though he claimed that he would reestablish his Constitutional Guard. By February, Duport believed that force, even foreign force, was needed to change the Constitution. With some exaggeration Robespierre's brilliant advocate, Georges Michon, in his study of Adrien Duport, claims several times that Duport now wanted to establish 'a royal dictatorship'. What Michon means is that there would be a transitional period between the dissolution of the Legislative Assembly and the meeting of its successor (stuffed with ex-Constituants), and that the new Assembly would not sit permanently but have sessions and vacations like the English Parliament – more, perhaps, than any other factor the permanence of the French assemblies had made the king subservient to them.

Indeed, what Duport was after was not a 'royal dictatorship' – if so, why would not Marie-Antoinette have bid him rise from his bended knees and accept the plan – but an English-style constitutional monarchy with a bicameral Parliament, an absolute veto, the right of dissolution, and the restoration of a titled nobility without material privileges. The king would mediate peace with Austria. After pleading with Marie-Antoinette, Duport sent an envoy to Mercy-Argenteau in Belgium to enlist his support. Mercy's reaction was favourable. The points he made chimed with Duport's ideas, as we know from coded letters from the envoy found on Duport after his arrest. Mercy stressed that the 'invalid', namely the king, must 'choose a healthy place for himself on his estates – he has plenty to choose from – but the airiest and most exposed to the north wind [? Lille, Rouen] would be best'. His accommodation must be able to allow for 'a spare room', in other words a second chamber, and his restoration to health would be aided by 'Swiss herbs', that is, the Swiss Guard. The 'American elixir', in other words the National Guard, could not be relied on nor could family members (Artois and Provence) who are led by 'charlatans' (Calonne).[39]

Michon considered that Mercy's response to Duport's envoy, Saint-Amand, amounted to a refusal; Munro Price comes to a similar conclusion.[40] They may be right. But Mercy told Kaunitz that his main concern was not the plan itself, which 'suited the general convenience of Europe pretty well', but that 'the Lameth party lacked the strength to implement it'.[41] Nor need Mercy's approval of the plan surprise us. Jules Flammermont back in the 1880s demonstrated that the advice Mercy gave to Marie-Antoinette came mainly from Pellenc.[42] Pellenc's sympathies lay with his main informants who were Barnave, Duport and the Lameths, though Marie-Antoinette never understood this. Mercy and Leopold had always displayed benevolent neutrality towards the Feuillants. Mercy's opinion, as rendered in code by Saint-Amand, does not look like a refusal: it includes escape by means of the Swiss Guard; doubts about a congress; nothing until the king was unequivocally free; distrust of Prussia – following his old mistress Maria-Theresa rather than a new diplomatic revolution of alliance with Prussia; distrust of the king's brothers, who were backed by Prussia. Given the Feuillants' weakness, Mercy inclines to thinking that the royal family should stay put, though he worries that the Prussians would reach Paris first as the Austrian army had not pressed home its early advantages. And the Prussians had a timetable, though they also had one in 1914.

The final plan to save the monarchy was devised by the duc de la Rochefoucauld-Liancourt, who 'answered for the fidelity of his regiment which was in garrison at Rouen. He offered to escort the king thither and told Lafayette that there was not a moment to lose in assuring himself of his own army.' If things went wrong, the royal family could embark at Le Havre for England, which was neutral at the time. But the king's intelligence service informed him that neither the city of Rouen nor its surrounding *département* could sufficiently be relied upon. Nevertheless in just over a year, Normandy would be in rebellion against the National Convention. This plan was discussed in a committee at the Tuileries on 4 August, with the king and queen, Bertrand de Molleville, Montmorin and Malouet in attendance. The king backed it but changed his mind the next day under pressure from Marie-Antoinette, who detested La Rochefoucauld-Liancourt.[43]

We do not know what if any part Barnave played in these plans, but shortly afterwards he wrote: 'In the month of July 1792 I resolved to defend not just the monarchy but the person of Louis XVI.'[44] Presumably any action would have been coordinated with his friends and colleagues Duport and the Lameth brothers.

Having rejected all the escape plans, the king and queen had to secure their position in Paris as best they could. The king had 7 million livres in cash from his Civil List and borrowed another million. Laporte distributed money lavishly, spending 377,000 francs on 16 June alone: the roll call would have brought a blush to several patriotic faces – Danton and Santerre and probably Pétion.[45]

The Girondin deputy Marguerite-Elie Guadet haughtily refused to take the money but he and his colleagues Gensonné and Vergniaud did negotiate with the king through the Court painter Joseph Boze and the Keeper of the Seals, Étienne Dejoly. They wanted him to enlarge his Council with patriotic ex-deputies and personally arrange a truce. Louis pointed out that 'we owe the declaration of war entirely to the self-styled patriot ministers' and concluded that a ceasefire must be left to official diplomacy. Dejoly considered that the reply 'would not satisfy either a friend of liberty or a man of ambition. It is dry and negative.'[46] Barnave had been partially right: the Girondins were motivated by ambition but not money.

They held several secret meetings as a 'Commission of 12' between 3 and 6 August to decide how to proceed. The Mauconseil Section had demanded the king's dethronement. But the Girondin leaders thought that it was bad to give way to a motley group of Sections and *fédérés*. Dethronement should be regularly proposed by the Assembly and 9 August was pencilled in. They then considered options for dealing with the ex-king. They ranged from exile, imprisonment at Rambouillet as a hostage, to pushing him outside unarmed for the mob to assassinate. The last was Condorcet's idea. He was more lenient towards Marie-Antoinette. Forgetting that the Revolution had abolished them, he thought she should be put in a convent and separated from the dauphin, whose education he, the famous mathematician, would undertake.[47]

But 9 August passed and the king still sat on his tottering throne. Flirting with and cajoling the king was the Girondins' style[48] – they were essentially an oppositional party and could not handle power. Three times they staved off the impending insurrection before it broke with the dawn on 10 August.[49] At 5 p.m. the day before, the recently installed foreign minister, Bigot de Saint-Croix, was given a paper outlining a plan to put Marie-Antoinette in an iron cage and parade her through the streets before taking her to the La Force prison in Paris. A milder fate awaited the king – imprisonment in the Temple. Bigot proposed to read the plan to the troops, circulate multiple copies, and attack the invaders under cover of darkness. Nothing came of it.[50] Two ministers had asked the Assembly to send members to give the king moral support, but the Legislative ignored them and instead doggedly continued its discussion of the Negro rebellion on Saint-Domingue.[51]

At midnight on 9 August the bells of the Paris churches began to ring out their tocsin one by one and everyone in the Tuileries rushed to the windows to pick out the distinctive tones of each and its patron saint – Saint-Laurence, Saint-Roche, Saint-Eustache, Saint-Germain des Près, Saint-Etienne-du-Mont – until the whole sky was filled with their noise. Louis snatched a few hours' sleep; Marie-Antoinette did not go to bed.[52] At 4 a.m. Madame Elizabeth brought her to the window to see the dawn. At 5 o'clock Marie-Antoinette had the children woken and told them that bad men were about to attack the royal palace.[53]

Forewarned, the palace was also forearmed. The 1,000 Swiss Guards, absolutely loyal, had been brought back from their barracks at Rueil and Courbevoie, and there were 1,000 mounted police and 2,000 National Guards. However, they were short of cartridges and 'the king and queen refused to commandeer any by force'.[54] Nevertheless, these troops, Marcel Reinhard considers, were 'enough to contain the insurrection, perhaps to crush it'. Provided the National

Guard remained loyal. They had forced the royal family out of Versailles in 1789 and prevented them from going to Saint-Cloud in 1791; but they had fired on the crowd later that year, therefore would they do so again? Their loyalties, the individuals who comprised the Guard, were divided, and the balance was tipped when the Municipality, from which the National Guard took its orders, was replaced during the night by an 'insurrectionary Commune' comprising delegates from the Sections, which gave the orders to march on the Tuileries next day. The marquis de Mandat, the loyal commander of the National Guard, having been summoned to confer with the old municipality, was murdered by the new one.

Even so, Marie-Antoinette would have put up a fight and maybe won. After all, it had been her decision to remain in Paris rather than accept the shelter of Lafayette's tent. But it was the king not the queen who gave the orders, and as she observed, 'he fears above everything else speaking to assembled men'. He could find no rousing words for the troops. The most loyal troops had been placed nearest the Palace – they shouted '*Vive le Roi!*' – but as he progressed, his reception became cooler. 'My God, they are booing the King!' shouted a minister. 'What the devil is he doing down there? Let's go and fetch him quickly.' He was brought back. Pierre-Louis Roederer, of the *département* of Paris, advised that resistance was impossible and that the royal family should take refuge in the Assembly. He had devised this as a contingency measure after the invasion of 20 June and had planted this seed in the exhausted soil of the king's mind.[55] Nicolas Franz Bachmann, the major of the Swiss Guards, said 'If the king goes to the Assembly he is lost.' Marie-Antoinette, her face blotched red and white with passion, exclaimed, 'Nail me to these walls before I will consent to leave them.'[56] But the king looked at his ministers and for the first time not waiting for their advice said, 'Come, gentlemen, there is nothing more to be done here', and, raising his hand, 'let us go and make this last sacrifice to the Nation.' Louis said to the Maréchal de Mailly, whom he had put in charge of the Tuileries, 'We shall be back – once calm has been restored.'

Roederer led the little procession, the royal family, the ministers, the departmental officials, along a double hedge of soldiers to the Assembly. From the king's bedroom Madame de Tourzel's daughter saw this sad procession pass on its way: 'The idea of a funeral procession came to mind; it was indeed the cortège of the monarchy.' In the night there had been a fall of leaves and the gardeners had put them in piles along the route taken by the procession. The dauphin kicked them carelessly. 'The leaves are falling early this year,' Louis said to Roederer. It had been predicted in a radical journal that the monarchy would fall with the leaves. On leaving the royal palace, Louis had omitted to countermand the orders to defend it. This the Swiss Guards did, killing or seriously wounding about three hundred insurgents. When Louis, at about 10 o'clock, finally gave orders to the Swiss Guards to stop firing, they were butchered almost to a man.

The Assembly prevaricated. Louis was suspended from his functions, not deposed: his fate was to be decided by a new assembly, a National Convention, voted by manhood suffrage. Barnave was full of contempt for the Assembly, 'whose despicable feebleness had given a fistful of men the audacity to subjugate it and make a great revolution in the state by means of a popular riot'.[57] This 'great revolution in the state' was the 'second Revolution' he had striven to prevent.

The royal family spent the day crowded together in the reporters' box. At two in the morning they were transferred to the neighbouring Convent of the Feuillants, where they remained for three days. There was a dispute between the Assembly and the Commune over the final destination of the royal family, the Assembly preferring the Luxembourg, former home of Provence, the Commune preferring the Temple, which had belonged to the comte d'Artois. He lived in more modern quarters but in its grounds still stood the massive central tower: with its pointed roof, walls nine feet thick and mere slits of windows it looked like a prison. This grim building had been the medieval habitation of the former Knights Templar, before Philip the Fair dissolved the Order. On her visits to Paris the tower had cast its spell over Marie-Antoinette and she had begged Artois to demolish it. The Commune, not the thoroughly discredited Legislative Assembly, was now the real power in the land and it got its way.

On 13 August, at 6 o'clock in the evening, Pétion called to take the royal family away. There were nine in the carriage and someone wondered whether they would be too squashed. 'Not at all,' the king said with a wry smile. 'M. Pétion knows full well that I can endure a longer journey in cramped conditions.'[58] The royal family were driven at a snail's pace through immense hostile crowds, to the Temple. Night was falling when the party reached their destination, where they were met by the officials of the Commune who had assumed responsibility for their custody. Hats on head, they delighted in addressing the king as 'Monsieur', not 'Sire'.[59]

TWELVE

IMPRISONMENT IN A TOWER

*T*he first three weeks in prison had a soothingly monotonous quality. At 9 o'clock the family came up to the king's room for breakfast, which would consist of coffee, chocolate, fruit, bread and milk foods. At about 10 o'clock they all went up to the queen's room on the third floor, where the ladies sewed whilst Louis instructed his son, mainly in Latin and geography.[1] At noon they all walked outside to give the children some air and exercise, returning at 2 o'clock for their *diner*, which was quite an elaborate affair with two main courses and dessert, red and white wine. The king usually drank half a bottle of champagne and a glass of liqueur with the dessert. Marie-Antoinette followed the example of her mother in not touching alcohol. This food cost 80,000 livres a month and was provided by two chefs and eleven sous-chefs taken straight from the Bouche or kitchen of the Tuileries.[2] After their *diner*, Louis and Marie-Antoinette would play piquet or backgammon until 4 o'clock, when the king had a nap. At 6 p.m. Louis gave his son more lessons or played games with him. After supper, at 9 o'clock, the king retired to his study and read until midnight.

One of the members of the Bouche who continued in service was Louis-François Turgy. He claimed to have been the one who closed the door behind Marie-Antoinette as she fled to join the king on 6 October 1789. Now he was to perform an equally valuable and dangerous role in conveying information from the outside world to the royal family. On the night of 19/20 August they were deprived of Madame de Tourzel and the Princesse de Lamballe. They were imprisoned in La Force. On 2 September, Louis' valet François Hüe was arrested. Soon the prisoners were left with only the king's valet Jean-Baptiste Cléry. The queen and Madame Elizabeth mended the king's clothes whilst Marie-Antoinette asked Cléry to teach her daughter how to do her own hair, finding this preferable to being attended by the wives and relatives of municipal officers.[3]

There was no need to smuggle in information about the September Massacres: it was brought brutally to their door or rather window. The guiding hand in both the massacres and in the trial of Marie-Antoinette was Robespierre. With the Legislative Assembly discredited in the period between the fall of the monarchy and the meeting of the National Convention (10 August–21 September), effective power was seized by the insurrectionary Commune of Paris, which had made the *journée* of 10 August. Robespierre had not been a member of the Commune on 10 August, but on 12 August he was elected to it and quickly seized control. He then, until the meeting of the Convention, exercised the only real dictatorship of his life, but one in the classical Roman sense – short and total.

His influence led to the removal of the royal family to the Temple under guard of the Commune. One of his adherents among the guards of whom we will have more to say was the cobbler, Henri Simon, who was guillotined with him on 28 July 1794. But the royal family was not Robespierre's immediate concern. This was to employ terror to influence the elections to the National Convention and (since his electoral success was confined to Paris where his adherents won all twenty-four seats) to have his Girondin opponents killed to prevent them exploiting a likely majority in the Convention. He especially wanted the scalp of Brissot whose *Patriote française* was easily the most popular journal.

Events played into Robespierre's hands. On 23 August the fortress of Longwy fell to the invading Prussians and on 1 September news reached Paris that Verdun, the last fortress between the invaders and Paris, would not be able to hold out. On 2 September began the September Massacres. They lasted until 6 September, by which time some 1,300 prisoners had been murdered. The official explanation, perpetuated by French neo-Jacobin historians, is that this was a spontaneous panic reaction to prevent the prisoners escaping and murdering the Parisians left defenceless with their menfolk away at the Front. In fact, the massacres were directed by the Commune's surveillance committee on which Robespierre sat, and coincided with the election of the Parisian deputation to the Convention. On the night of 2 September the surveillance committee ordered the arrest of Brissot, Roland, and up to thirty leading Girondins (accounts vary). If the order had been carried out, they would all have perished.

But the order was countermanded by Danton, now minister of justice and working alongside the reinstated Girondin ministers. Danton, though a Montagnard and elected as one of the Paris deputation to the Convention, remained a moderating influence: Marie-Antoinette's fate would be decided when Robespierre wrested control of the government from Danton.

Hüe and Madame de Tourzel survived the Massacres to write their memoirs, but Madame de Lamballe did not. The mob brought her corpse to the Temple. Presumably their intention was to show it to the queen before murdering the prisoners. This did not suit the purposes of the authorities. With the Prussians at the gate it would have been impolitic. Instead an official, having strung a tricolour ribbon across the entrance, parleyed with the mob. 'Two men were dragging a headless corpse along the ground with the stomach slashed open as far as the chest.' To show that they had not lost all sense of propriety, these two men 'laid the corpse down with elaborate ceremony and arranged its members with some artistry', which, the official noted, 'opened up a vast field to philosophical speculation'. Less delicate, another man pressed Madame de Lamballe's entrails against the official's chest whilst another brandished her head at the end of a pike, as was now traditional. The tricolour being of such symbolic significance, the mob paused, and it was agreed that a small deputation be allowed to present the remains of Madame de Lamballe to the ex-queen. Madame de Staël has Marie-Antoinette 'struggling to make out the bloody features' of her friend.[4] Pétion, still mayor, arrived on the scene – late as usual. 'He seemed desperate that we had not stopped Marie-Antoinette from having to kiss the head of the Lamballe.' 'The magistrates,' he said, 'should never have countenanced such a horror.'[5]

In fact, they hadn't. The delegation had lifted the princess's head aloft on the end of its pike so that it was visible from the Tower. A dispute arose between the municipal officers and the National Guard as to whether the royal family should show themselves at the windows. Louis asked a guard what was going on and received the brutal reply: 'Very well, Monsieur, if you really want to know, it's the head of Mme de Lamballe they want to show you. I advise you to show yourselves unless you want the people to come up.' The queen fainted. The king replied: 'We were ready for everything, Monsieur; but you could have dispensed with telling the Queen this appalling news.'[6] It was especially painful for Marie-Antoinette because she had persuaded Madame de Lamballe to return to France – she was the biggest trophy of the policy the queen had pursued with Barnave of bringing leading émigrés back.

On 21 September the Convention met and one of its first acts was to declare that France was now a republic. The guards were now justified in calling Louis 'Monsieur' not 'sire' – Marie-Antoinette was not affected since she had always been called 'Madame' even by her husband. On 22 September, Dumouriez, after brilliant manoeuvres, checked the Prussians at Valmy, very near Varennes, and allowed them to retreat – they had one eye on a second partition of Poland. He then turned on the Austrians in Belgium, defeated them at Jemappes, near

Mons, on 6 November, and a week later entered Brussels. These victories robbed Louis of his status as a valuable hostage, and though Dumouriez personally favoured a restoration of the monarchy, this only served further to endanger the life of the king.

Then, on 20 November, Jean-Marie Roland, the minister of the interior, made his dramatic announcement to the Convention concerning the discovery of the 'iron safe', the *armoire de fer*. Marie-Antoinette had been right to warn Louis that the locksmith Gamain was not to be trusted. However, he did take her advice on removing the most incriminating items. The documents found in ordinary desks and cupboards during the sack of the Tuileries were actually more incriminating than those in the safe as they showed that the king had continued paying his Bodyguards even after they had emigrated and joined the prince de Condé at Coblenz. They showed also that Louis had subsidized the Feuillant Club and the *Logographe*, the journal of the Legislative Assembly. The new discoveries did not provide any proof of dealings with the foreign powers since Louis and Marie-Antoinette systematically burned such papers – that proof came only when the papers of their correspondents became available. What the documents in the iron safe – and those captured in the sack of the Tuileries – do demonstrate is Louis' relations with Mirabeau, Lafayette, Dumouriez, and also his spending considerable sums of money to win over public support at the level of popular politics and through subsidizing the royalist press. In short Louis XVI, who was familiar with English politics, was using his Civil List as George III did his to buy political support. Given the drama of the discovery, that was enough.

The discovery of the iron safe meant that the Girondins could no longer prevaricate about bringing Louis to judgment – the very minimum that their opponents to the left, the Montagnards, would accept. The Montagnards' preferred line, as outlined by Robespierre and Saint-Just, was that Louis had already been 'judged' by the *journée* of 10 August and should be put to death without more ado. The trial can best be seen as an impeachment, as in contemporary England and modern America. Purely political. The only difference was that those two countries had a bicameral system. The National Convention was prosecutor, judge and jury, but otherwise the normal procedures of a trial were observed.

The trial began with a preliminary hearing on 11 December. At 11 o'clock in the morning Louis was instructing the dauphin as usual when two municipal officers entered and took the boy away without explanation – as 'co-conspirators', his family were to be denied access to him. On 15 December he was told that he could see his children but only on condition that neither saw their mother or Madame Elizabeth so long as the trial lasted. Naturally Louis refused. He was particularly upset that he was not allowed to see his daughter on her fourteenth birthday.

The indictment consisted of thirty-two composite charges, some of them going back to 1789, leading to the general accusation of 'conspiring against liberty and an attempt against the safety of the State'. The general accusation was virtually meaningless, certainly not susceptible of legal proof or disproof. Louis did not follow the example of Charles I in challenging the competence of the court but offered a defence based on the laws in force at the various times when he was supposed to have committed the crimes. On 26 December, Louis made his second and final appearance before the Convention, but it did not proceed immediately to a vote. For a fortnight the parties manoeuvred. Many of the Girondins, obscurely aware that the king's death would enlarge the conflict, at home and abroad, devised ways of saving his life.

Finally, between 14 and 20 January 1793, the Convention voted on four motions and they did it by *appel nominal*, which meant that individual votes were recorded. This obviously favoured those who wanted to kill the king and was soon used as a basis for proscription. The first motion was phrased: 'Is Louis Capet, former King of the French, guilty of conspiring against liberty and an attempt against the safety of the State? Yes or no.' Some 691 voted 'yes', with 27 abstentions. No one dared vote against the motion. The second motion, proposed on 15 January, concerned the appeal to the people. The voting was 287 for, 424 against, with twelve abstentions. The third motion was on Louis' punishment – death, deportation, imprisonment or whatever. The voting lasted thirty-six hours and could not have been closer: out of 721 voters, only 361 voted unconditionally for death – a majority of one. Given the closeness of this vote, a fourth motion was put, whether there should be a reprieve, but this was rejected by a majority of seventy. The Convention decreed that Louis should be notified 'within the day' and executed twenty-four hours after this notification. The Convention rose at 3 o'clock on the morning of 20 January 1793.

At two in the afternoon Joseph Garat, the minister of justice, informed Louis of the sentence. Louis produced a document from his portfolio. In it he requested 'a three-day stay of execution to prepare myself to appear before the presence of God'; the right to see a priest of his choice and to see his family 'without witnesses'.[7] The Convention rejected the first but granted the other two requests. Louis also asked that his family should be freed. Garat replied with Revolutionary grandilo-quence, 'that the nation, always magnanimous, always just, would consider the fate of the family'.[8] The king conferred with his confessor until half-past-eight, when the abbé withdrew to one of the side-turrets so as not to alarm Louis' family, who were now admitted for the first time in six weeks. He placed a glass of water on the table in case the queen should pass out.[9]

Madame Royale has left this account of their meeting:

> We found him greatly changed. He wept for our grief but not for his death. He told my mother about his trial, excusing the scoundrels who were bringing about his death. He repeated to my mother that people had wanted the Primary Assemblies but that he had not because that would have disturbed France. Then he gave sound religious teachings to my brother; above all he commanded him to pardon those who were about to cause his death. He gave his blessing to my brother and myself. My mother desperately wanted us to spend the night with my father. He refused, having need of tranquillity.[10]

As they parted from the king, their screams could be heard on the staircase, through the massive doors. His daughter was carried out fainting. Cléry, who witnessed the scene through a glass door, noted, 'it was easy to see from their gestures that ... [the king] himself had told them of his sentence'.

In the morning, just before 9 o'clock, Louis left the Temple with the commander of the National Guard, Antoine Joseph Santerre, and his confessor the abbé Edgeworth, who was permitted to accompany the king to the scaffold. He asked for his will to be given to the queen – 'to my wife', he corrected.[11] He was taken to the place of his execution – the former Place Louis XV – not in a tumbrel but in a bottle-green carriage belonging to the minister of finance, a security measure perhaps but one that helped the king to die with dignity.[12]

Louis had promised to see his family again but he feared it would shake his composure and theirs. They learned of his execution via the accompanying thunder of cannon. 'The monsters are happy now', said Madame Elizabeth. Marie-Antoinette bowed before her little boy whom she now recognized as Louis XVII. He was placed at the head of the table, which told against his mother. She now took over the boy's education from the late king: history, travel books and novels. Marie-Antoinette was even given use of a pianoforte. She asked the municipal officer on duty to provide mourning wear for the whole family – 'the simplest available', she added. It arrived two days later. There was no change in the situation of the family for another six months. But the new Republic was entering a critical phase.

The conquest of Belgium followed quickly after the Battle of Jemappes (6 November 1792), but the Convention made mistakes. On 19 November it declared that it would give armed assistance to any peoples wanting to throw off the yoke of monarchy. It was now an ideological war. Then, on 31 January, against Dumouriez's advice, the Convention ordered him to invade Holland. This brought England into the war since she could not allow a major European power to occupy harbours ideal for an invasion fleet. Soon France was at war with all the great powers save only canny Catherine the Great's Russia.

The Convention also ordered the confiscation of all ecclesiastical and feudal property in the occupied territories including the Rhineland, Savoy and Belgium in order to prop up the *assignat* that had lost half its value; the paper currency was imposed on those territories. These unpopular measures enabled Austria to knock out the garrisons Dumouriez had left behind in Belgium and on 18 and 21 March they defeated him at Neeerwinden and Louvain. He then signed an armistice with a view to marching on Paris and proclaiming Louis XVII – hadn't he said to Marie-Antoinette, 'Allow me to help you'? Her liberation was a condition of the armistice. But the army refused to follow him and he emigrated with his general staff, including his second-in-command, the young son of the duc d'Orléans, later Louis-Philippe, king of the French.

On top of this, in March the *département* of La Vendée rose for throne and altar and soon the whole of the Catholic West was in revolt and Paris itself threatened. With the sugar islands in revolt there was a shortage of that commodity and riots broke out in Paris on 23–24 February. Robespierre was disgusted that people should revolt for what he considered a luxury item – his own weakness was for oranges.

In response to the many-faceted crisis, the Committee of Public Safety (CPS) was formed. It was technically not the government – there were still ministries though they would be abolished a year later – just a committee of the Convention. But it was the de facto government, though in rivalry with an older, police committee of the Convention, known as the Committee of General Security (CGS). The 'first' CPS, as it was called, was dominated by Danton. Robespierre refused to join it because, as he frankly admitted, he would not have commanded a majority there. Danton would have liked (when the time was right) to end the war. But the Austrians wanted less the liberation of Marie-Antoinette than the annexation of Alsace and Lorraine, as she had always feared. Besides, Danton's immediate concern was to end the internecine struggle between the Montagnards and the Girondins. The Girondins rejected concilia-tion – after all, as Madame Roland had said, 'Robespierre holds a knife at our throats' during the September Massacres. The result was a popular demonstra-tion on 31 May and 2 June, on which date the Convention ordered the house arrest of twenty-nine Girondin leaders and two ministers. Seventy-three Girondin backbenchers who protested were imprisoned but not executed. Some of the twenty-nine broke bail and raised the provinces against Paris. Throughout the summer the four corners of the country were on fire: royalists in the west; Girondins in the Midi, Bordeaux and Normandy; Toulon handed over to the English fleet.

Naturally, the prisoners in the tower wanted to know what was going on. They wanted contact with the outside world less in order to escape – though several people devised escape plans on their behalf, some more promising than others – but rather in order to learn their fate. What did the CGS have in store for them? Would they be deported? There was talk of deporting Marie-Antoinette and keeping the dauphin and his sister as hostages at Choisy. Would they be put on trial – surely not the children, though one fourteen-year-old boy was guillotined in 1794. Would the allied powers try to buy their freedom? Fat chance. How was the war going? Madame Elizabeth, curiously, wanted to know whether Switzerland had joined the allies. Just as inconsequently, Marie-Antoinette before Varennes had wanted to know the stance of Denmark. They knew England had joined the war. But what was the fate of the fine navy that her brother the king had built from scratch – was it still operational after so many officers had deserted; where was it stationed, if indeed it was at sea at all and not laid up? What were the king's brothers doing? In September 1793, Elizabeth asked: 'Yesterday we saw a journal which talks of Saumur and Angers as if they are still in the hands of the R[epublic]. What does this mean? Is Marat really dead? Has it led to rioting?' 'What do you mean by saying things are going well? ... Has there been a change in the public mood?' 'Has anyone we know been executed?'[13]

The royal family were kept strictly *au secret*, that is incommunicado, to prevent them from 'conspiring'. Conspiring would be the buzz word for the next two years. But despite elaborate precautions, guards in every room, search upon search, confiscation of the dauphin's algebra homework because that branch of mathematics uses symbols, despite all this, the royal family ran rings round their jailors.

Their mastermind was Madame Elizabeth and she used loyal servitors like Turgy and Commune officials like François Adrien Toulan, who was given the code name of Fidèle. Turgy had legitimate contact with the outside world in getting food for the prisoners and he could arrange to have criers shout news outside the walls of the tower. But he also saw the marquise de Sérent who provided him with news of the people Elizabeth was interested in – Edgworth her confessor and her friend Madame de Bombelles, who had emigrated.

Elizabeth and Marie-Antoinette devised a series of signals: 'If the Austrians were winning in Belgium, place the second finger of the right hand on the right eye.' More specifically, 'if they were invading via Lille, the second finger as above, if by Mayence, the third'. Keeping the finger in place would indicate the importance of the engagement. If the great powers spoke of the royal family it was fingers on the hair, if they were 15 leagues from Paris, the mouth. Everything to do with the Convention: left hand; the Powers: right, etc.

Actual messages were conveyed in screwed-up balls of paper placed as stoppers for decanters and carafes. In England glass stoppers had been long in use, but for some reason screwed-up paper was the norm in France and these could easily be substituted. Or lead shot could be included and the missile sent through a window or into a fauteuil. The queen and Elizabeth found ways of indicating whether they wanted to reply.[14]

The royal family were left in comparative peace until 3 July when the dauphin was separated from them and placed in the king's former quarters. The municipality acted in accordance with a decree of the CPS dated 1 July. The Committee had got wind of a plan by General Dillon – le beau Dillon of Marie-Antoinette's youth – to stage a coup d'état and have the little boy proclaimed king as Louis XVII in the Convention. The official report notes that 'la veuve Capet', in other words Marie-Antoinette, finally gave way after a show of resistance and that the boy was put into the hands of Henri Simon. The minutes note sententiously that the whole operation was conducted 'with all the sensitivity to be expected in the circumstance, in which the magistrates of the people showed all the consideration compatible with the severity of their functions'.[15]

Simon was charged with the boy's education – a difficult task because Simon was barely literate: an example of his chaotic orthography survives. But this was not the main charge levelled against him. He turned the boy against his family. One of the guards was playing carpet *boules* with the boy one day when they heard chairs being moved around in the room above occupied by the rest of the family: 'Haven't those f . . . whores been guillotined yet,' the boy exclaimed. The official didn't want to hear any more and 'abandoned the game and the place'.[16] He was a bright boy – his sister said he was much cleverer than she was – and he could read without any help from Simon. So Simon, according to what he told an English spy, 'gave him the most obscene books to read for his amusement . . . and that nothing was omitted in order to corrupt him'.

He was taught to swear and blaspheme and consume strong liquors.[17] Simon said that he had tried to prevent this. The spy did not believe him but it seems that the inspiration for corrupting the boy came from Jacques Hébert, editor of the foul-mouthed *Père Duchesne* in which Marie-Antoinette was variously dubbed 'the Austrian she-wolf', 'the crowned whore', etc. Hébert, a blond, blue-eyed and withal mild-mannered man, despite the violence of his journal, was the deputy prosecutor of the Commune and its guiding spirit after Robespierre had left to pursue his parliamentary career. Hébert, who aspired to be minister of the interior, had two aims in corrupting the boy. The first was so to degrade him and undermine his health that he would never be fit to rule; and the second was to get him to testify against his mother.

THE QUEEN'S TRIAL

On 1 August, Bertrand Barère, the honey-tongued spokesman for the CPS, made a series of proposals. One (Article 11) was that on the first anniversary of the attack on the Tuileries, the long line of royal tombs at Saint-Denis should be smashed – fragments still turn up on the market today: in 2017 two marble lions no more than 18 inches in height from the tomb of Charles V (r. 1364–80) fetched £8.2 million, a record for any medieval work of art at auction. Another article was that the food given to the royal prisoners should be cut down to the bare essentials for survival. They had been used to elaborate dishes served on silver plates and cutlery (silver-gilt for fruit to prevent corrosion). Now, suddenly (the prisoners got no wind of this) their commons was reduced to a single dish of *bouillon* with a small piece of meat floating on it and a chunk of bread chucked in, no doubt served on pewter plates, and eaten with pewter spoons and horn-handled knives.

Halfway through Barère's lengthy report was Article 6: 'Marie-Antoinette is to appear before the Revolutionary Tribunal; she will be immediately transferred to the Conciergerie.' The Conciergerie was the prison attached to the Palais de Justice where the *ci-devant* Parlement had presided. Cardinal de Rohan had spent some time there before his appearance in the Diamond Necklace Affair seven years before. Other members of the Bourbon dynasty were to be deported except those due to appear before the Tribunal (the duc d'Orléans). Exceptions were made for the dauphin and his sister. Madame Elizabeth would be deported providing the trial of Marie-Antoinette did not throw up incriminating evidence against her. Marie-Antoinette left the Temple for the Conciergerie in the night of 1/2 August. She banged into a lintel and was asked whether she was hurt: 'Nothing can hurt me now.' During the two months she was to spend in her new prison, alone of the inmates she was not allowed to take exercise. She did not see the sky again until the day of her death.

The Convention's decree prompted Madame de Staël to rush out an anonymous pamphlet defending the queen. Entitled *Réflexions sur le procès de la reine par une femme* and written by a feminist *avant le lettre*, it has inevitably led to a discussion as to whether it is a feminist defence of the queen; and whether it was legitimate for a woman in eighteenth-century France to play a part in government – a question Marie-Antoinette herself considered and answered in the negative.[18] Most commentators have concluded that Madame de Staël's defence of the woman and the mother could cut no ice with accusers who prioritized her malign political influence symbolized by her soubriquets of 'l'Autrichienne', 'Madame Deficit' and 'Madame Veto'. De Staël 'minimizes the queen's role in the fall of successive ministers and her attempts to favour the Austrian court'.[19]

Actually, de Staël gives an accurate insider picture. She inhabited the political purple, daughter of a leading minister, Jacques Necker, lover of a minister (Narbonne) and wife of a diplomat. Necker was Marie-Antoinette's protégé. De Staël makes the point we have made and which Marie-Antoinette made herself: leaving Austria at the age 'of 13 [*sic* for 14]' and a subordinate position in that country, she came to be queen of 'the French whose grace and gaiety were so analogous with her own'. All she wanted was to preserve amity between the two countries. But most important, de Staël makes the point that we, following the comte de Provence and the weight of evidence, have also made, that 'her first influence on public affairs' was the dismissal of Calonne and the appointment of Brienne.[20] I would make a minor quibble with this, in that she played an, almost accidental, part in ministerial appointments from 1780; but endorse de Staël's view that she played no part in the dismissals of Turgot and Necker. These were the work of Maurepas, who 'from the very start of the reign of Louis XVI showed himself against the queen resenting her young influence on a young king and managing to exclude her from affairs thereby reinforcing her youthful lack of interest in them'. Vergennes continued this system. As did Calonne 'for whom she had a violent aversion'.

Madame de Staël also points out, as we have, that 'Brienne pitted the commons against the parlements, the nobility and clergy' and Brienne's later stance revealed democratic tendencies. She adds, cautiously, 'I don't know how far the queen was in on his secret' but concludes that 'when the only period of her influence coincided with the first stirring of democratic principles . . . can one accuse her of being the enemy of liberty?'

Barère was just the spokesman for the CPS. He was a trimmer, having in 1791 joined the Feuillant Club. When the Jacobin regime collapsed he was due to be deported to Guyana – called the dry guillotine because very few survived the conditions. But the boat had taken advantage of a favourable tide before he arrived and Barère was allowed to stay. It was the only tide he ever missed, as the wags had it. The real driving force in the CPS was now Robespierre. Danton and four colleagues had been voted off the CPS on 10 July after a series of setbacks, notably the fall of Saumur to the royalists on 9 June. Robespierre was voted in on 27 July, joining his soulmates Couthon and Saint-Just. Thereafter the composition of the CPS remained unchanged for exactly one year: 27 July 1794 was 9 thermidor year II in the new Revolutionary calendar.

It was the replacement of the 'first' or Dantonist CPS by the Robespierrist or Great CPS that ensured that Marie-Antoinette would be tried. Robespierre did not reach total dominance until the following spring but his personnel already controlled the Revolutionary Tribunal, an institution 'chosen to vary the form of assassination and make it more enjoyable'.[21] It was Danton, however, who had proposed the creation of the Revolutionary Tribunal, which was decreed on 13 March 1793. His rationale is illuminating: 'there is nothing more difficult than defining a political crime ... I see no middle way between the ordinary law courts and a revolutionary tribunal. We must be pitiless to dispense the people from being so.'[22] The September Massacres had, for many, blotted the Revolution's scutcheon. Blood must henceforth flow along official channels. Danton had talked of a 'political crime', rightly blurring the distinction in a revolution. But in so far as the two can be separated, the king's trial had been political, that of Marie-Antoinette was criminal. She was charged with breaking chapters, clauses and sub-clauses of the criminal code. In her last testament she specifically denied that she was a criminal. And, perhaps for this reason, the trial of Marie-Antoinette observed the forms of justice in a way that of the king had not. Instead of the legislators being prosecutors, judge and jury, for the queen's trial there were judges, jurors and witnesses theoretically independent of the government.

Marie-Antoinette's general line of defence was in conformity with that expected of a woman in eighteenth-century France: she obeyed her husband, the king. Feisty was the last thing she wanted to appear. But whereas Louis had mostly confined his replies to bored monosyllables, Marie-Antoinette entered into the spirit of the game and argued her case with some verve and ingenuity, lying where necessary. She may, even, have hoped to 'get off': for example, she asked her counsel whether one of her replies had been too forceful.

Another difference between the two trials was that there was no documentary evidence produced against Marie-Antoinette. One witness claimed to have seen a note signed by her giving Madame de Polignac 80,000 livres, but it got lost amidst the paperwork of the burgeoning bureaucracy of the Republic.[23] So the public prosecutor, Antoine Fouquier-Tinville, badgered the CPS to get him the evidence left over from the king's trial.

An interesting feature of Marie-Antoinette's trial was that fourteen of the forty-one witnesses were subsequently guillotined, plus one stabbing and two suicides. Some, like Jean-Sylvain Bailly, were already under arrest and were summoned from their cells to give evidence in the hope that they would incriminate themselves as well as the queen. Of the jurors five were guillotined, and four died in Guyana. Many of these jurors were adherents of Robespierre's. His private notebooks show us how he conceived of his brainchild, the Revolutionary Tribunal.

The first mention in his political notebook (*carnet*) was, 'Nomination of the members of the Revolutionary Tribunal', which was reorganized on 3 September 1793 and filled with his personal adherents: Martial Herman, the presiding judge, headed his list of 'Patriots with more or less talent' – the men he would appoint to key positions. Robespierre describes him as 'Enlightened, honest, capable of the highest office' – he ended up as head of the civil service. Herman, thirty-four, good looking, son of the registrar of the estates of Artois, had known Robespierre from childhood. They practised law in the same circuit. Other Robespierre adherents who participated in Marie-Antoinette's trial were Pierre Coffinhal and Marie-Joseph Lanne, judges, and Léopold Nicolas (Robespierre's printer), Joseph Souberbielle, his doctor, Léopold Renaudin, Jean Nicolas Lumière, François Trinchard and Claude Louis Châtelet (jurors).[24] Coffinhal, thirty-one, a giant of a man, was to lead 2,200 of Robespierre's troops against the Convention on 9 thermidor but failed to press home his advantage, perhaps because he was drunk. Nicolas printed the bulletin of the Revolutionary Tribunal from property belonging to the joiner Maurice Duplay with whom Robespierre lodged, on the Rue Saint-Honoré.

Dr Souberbielle was the Duplay family's doctor and treated Robespierre for ulcers in his upstairs room reached by a simple outside staircase. Souberbielle, who was a distinguished practitioner, was renowned for his treatment of gallstones but, as a juror, he was invaluable in detecting women who had falsely claimed to be pregnant in order to cheat the guillotine. He had also attended Marie-Antoinette and the children in the Temple – she perhaps for the haemorrhages from which she certainly suffered in her last weeks, the boy perhaps for the tuberculosis he later displayed, and Marie-Thérèse-Charlotte, who was strong as an ox, doubtless for some children's disease. Because he had known the ex-queen, Souberbielle asked to be excused jury service, but Herman told him to pull himself together and do his duty. Souberbielle lived on to the age of ninety. In his old age he persisted in considering that Marie-Antoinette had committed not just 'faults' but 'crimes'. Nevertheless, had he been judging her today, he told a friend, he would not have condemned her.[25]

Another juror was known to her, but one who reminded her of happier times. Claude Châtelet, forty, was a painter. In 1781, Marie-Antoinette had commissioned him to produce an album of the fetes held at the Trianon. *Et in*

Arcadia ego. Herman accused her of being the 'goddess' of these fetes. Now Châtelet heaped his incense on another deity and formed one of the bodyguards who escorted Robespierre from his lodgings to the Jacobin Club.[26]

Fouquier-Tinville, the public prosecutor, was not an adherent of Robespierre's, considering that his primary duty lay with the police committee, the CSG, which had conducted the first interrogation of Marie-Antoinette. Robespierre had to pull him up short for stinting his reports to the CPS. Consequently, he was not guillotined with Robespierre's adherents. Nor was Herman, who deserted him at the last moment. However, the following year, after a lengthy and fair trial, they were both condemned, despite Fouquier's claim 'I had orders; I obeyed' or, more picturesquely, 'I was only the Convention's axe and you can't blame an axe.' Neither Fouquier-Tinville nor Herman showed any repentance, Fouquier mouthing obscenities when he was condemned to death, Herman throwing a book at the jurors.

Robespierre conceived of the Tribunal as explicitly political – defeated generals, like the comte de Custine, should appear before the Tribunal rather than a court martial. What Herman and Robespierre called 'legal niceties' (*arguties du palais* [*de Justice*]) should be ignored. They belonged to the *ancien régime* system headed by the parlements. Rather, the judges and jurors should be guided by their patriotic instinct. Patriotism rather than skill was the criterion, and not just in the Tribunal. Generals should be appointed on this basis – Jean-Antoine Rossignol, for example, a goldsmith with no military experience, was put in charge of the war in the Vendée, with the results we have seen. The predictable consequence was the conviction of innocent men by the Tribunal and military catastrophe. Luckily for France there were men in the CPS who tempered this trend: Barère, for example, wanted to accede to General Custine's request to be court-martialled; he failed, but Lazare Carnot, 'the organizer of victory', was able to run the war along rational lines and, more than any one man, was responsible for ending Robespierre's reign on 9 thermidor.

The trial of Marie-Antoinette took place on 14–15 October 1793. Prior to that there had been two preliminary interrogations, one by the stony-hearted Jean-Pierre-André Amar of the CSG, the other by Herman and Fouquier-Tinville for the Revolutionary Tribunal. The first interrogation, by the police committee, chiefly concerned the affair of the carnation – an incident whose importance was magnified at the time and in subsequent historiography. In the Temple, Marie-Antoinette had been kept secluded; but in the Conciergerie the governor, Jean-Baptiste Michonis, charged members of the public to see the captive. One of the visitors, the chevalier de Rougeville, dropped a carnation at the ex-queen's feet. It contained a message saying that the chevalier had men and money at his disposal to rescue her – whether an escape was viable is extremely doubtful. Her writing materials having been confiscated, Marie-Antoinette laboriously pricked out a reply on a bit of paper. It was spotted and though Rougeville escaped, the incident may have hastened the queen's trial. Too much has been made of 'this incident which is only a prison intrigue', as Herman himself told the jurors, 'and has no place in an accusation of such magnitude'.[27]

The second interrogation on 12 October consisted like the first in a series of questions and answers. Marie-Antoinette was asked about sending money to her brother the emperor Joseph II. She said that she was well aware of that hoary old chestnut but that her brother did not need any money and that she loved her husband too much to want to impoverish his subjects. When accused of deceiving the people, she replied, magnificently: 'Certainly the people have been deceived and cruelly so but neither by my husband nor myself but by those who had an interest in doing it.'[28]

At the trial itself Fouquier-Tinville, forty-six, massive, thin-lipped, pock-marked, boiled down the accusations against Marie-Antoinette to just three:

1. 'Of having, in concert with the king's brothers and the execrable Calonne, dilapidated the French finances in a terrible way and having sent incalculable sums to the emperor ...'

2. 'of having informed the enemies of France of the plans of campaign and attack drawn up in the Council'

3. 'of having set alight civil war in various parts of the republic, contrary to section 2 of the penal code and article 2 cap 1 of the first section'.[29]

On the first charge, in the *interrogatoire* Herman had accused her of lavishing money on 'the construction and embellishment of the Petit Trianon, where you gave fetes in which you were always the goddess'. Marie-Antoinette conceded, and it was her only concession: 'It is possible that the Petit Trianon cost immense sums, perhaps more than I could have wished. I was dragged into expenses little by little.'[30]

She was accused of colluding with the 'infamous Calonne' to exhaust the treasury; she must have smiled bitterly since Calonne had been an enemy whose appointment, but for a miscarriage, she might have prevented. Fouquier-Tinville also accused her of being both the friend and persecutor of Madame La Motte-Valois – a myth that ironically Calonne may have helped to propagate. 'Was she not,' Herman added, 'your victim in the famous necklace affair?'[31] She was accused, with some fairness, of interfering in ministerial and army appointments – the assumption being (which she privately acknowledged) that such was not the proper role of a queen of France.

But all these blackenings merely served as hors d'oeuvres for the pre-Revolution entrée: sending millions to her brother Joseph, just the old canard going back to buying Joseph off the back of France's Dutch ally in 1785. The prostitute whom Coigny had strung along with this tale now appeared as a witness 'whose precision and integrity has been noted' in order to repeat the story as fact.[32] But Herman was dangerously near the truth when he asked Marie-Antoinette, 'Did you not get Vergennes to give . . . [the Emperor] six millions?' – the exact sum he obtained.[33] Interestingly, Marie-Antoinette was not accused of treason with Prussia, at once the more dangerous enemy but also the one with which many in the Convention, as in the *ancien régime*, wanted to do a deal.

On the second charge, she was clearly guilty. This accusation was so accurate that it must have come from a leak from one of the ministers. But these were Girondins, themselves dead, in hiding, about to be tried or (in the case of Dumouriez, the most likely source of the information) no longer in the country, so their evidence could not be used. A subsidiary charge was that Marie-Antoinette wanted Austria to annex Lorraine.[34] In fact, the main purpose of her international 'armed congress' was precisely to prevent this happening. She had also been accused in the interrogation of financing the invasion. Although she did not actually give the allies money, she had promised to meet the king of Prussia's expenses. We have the proof of all this, the Tribunal did not. The acid test of the Rule of Law is to acquit for lack of evidence even though you are morally certain that the accused is guilty. *Pace* Robespierre, this is not a mere 'legal nicety'.

The third charge was ridiculous because she was in prison when the expulsion of the Girondins sparked the civil war. Not only this but the Girondins were her deadly enemies who had thwarted her attempt with Barnave to stop the Revolution.

At the trial Marie-Antoinette, a fortnight from her thirty-eighth birthday but looking much older, appeared in the black mourning dress she had worn since the king's death. No one seems to have minded this form of dumb *lèse nation*, though the authorities would draw the line at her wearing black to the scaffold. She also, according to one account, wore a pair of shoes dating from grander times with red high heels, the hated *talons rouges* of the aristocracy. Perhaps she wanted to seem taller – a preoccupation dating to her Vienna days. If indeed she wore them, it is perhaps this that elicited the exclamation 'God she's proud' from one of the audience – for this was a show as well as a show trial. Another spectator thought it 'pride without an objective', though the objective was surely to help her to hold herself together through two days under pressure without sleep. One of the attendant guards had been at Versailles. Instinctively he doffed his hat. He was put on trial but acquitted when he put his gesture down to the unseasonably hot weather. In this spring time of the Terror there were almost as many acquittals as convictions – at least of the lesser fry.

Forty-one witnesses were called, and Marie-Antoinette or her two counsel were allowed to cross-examine them. One of her counsel, Claude François Chauveau-Lagarde, defended Marie-Antoinette's foreign policy, the other, Tronchon, her home policy. Herman and the jurors chipped in whenever they felt like it, but Fouquier-Tinville held his fire for a closing statement. Marie-Antoinette's closing statement was: 'Yesterday I did not know the witnesses. I had no idea of the evidence they were going to present. Eh bien! Not one of them has adduced a single positive fact against me.' Indeed, not a single piece of writing had been produced. To supplement this deficiency, Fouquier had been hoping to recycle the evidence used at the king's trial. But this had been held by the Commission of Twenty-Four. This had been dissolved and its head, Charles-Elionor Dufriche-Valazé, had been arrested as a leading Girondin. He would leave his cell as a witness at Marie-Antoinette's trial before appearing at his own. His was the only corpse, apart from Oliver Cromwell's, to have been decapitated, as he had committed suicide in the reasonable expectation of avoiding a public beheading. The papers of his commission were thought to have been transferred to the CSG, but they did not arrive in time.

Marie-Antoinette added, 'I conclude by saying that I was only the wife of Louis XVI and that I obviously had to conform to his wishes.'[35] She had, however, said earlier, unprompted, 'my husband had a great deal of confidence in me', an admission to which Herman frequently returned. She had said this à propos of the king's speech of 23 June 1789 at the *séance royale*, which everyone now (including Marie-Antoinette) called a *lit de justice*. Herman had put it to her that the king's speech had been written by 'Desprémesnil and Thouret, assisted by Barentin'. (It had been drafted by Barentin and Vidaud de la Tour.) When the accused pleaded ignorance, Herman said that was strange given that the articles had been drafted in her apartments. 'It was in the Conseil d'état that the matter was settled,' she replied. 'Did the king not read you his speech half an hour before the *séance*?' he asked. 'Yes,' she replied, 'because he had a great deal of confidence in me.'

Herman then produced an interesting variant on the exile of Artois after the fall of the Bastille. 'Had you any knowledge of the ci-devant comte d'Artois' plan to blow up the chamber of the National Assembly?'[36] 'As this plan seemed too violent was he not persuaded to go on his travels' because his 'recklessness' would have ruined the plan of 'dissimulation' then adopted? Marie-Antoinette replied that Artois had 'decided to travel of his own free will'. Another 'traveller' had been la Polignac, as the court termed her. Herman asked the accused why 'she had stuffed the Polignac family, and several others had, with gold'. Marie-Antoinette's answer – 'they had court offices that made them rich' – was only partly true: the bulk of their wealth had come from straight gifts.

The most interesting witness to the October Days was Admiral d'Estaing, who was second-in-command of the Versailles National Guard. It will be remembered that D'Estaing's incompetence had rendered the campaign of 1778 largely fruitless. Nevertheless, he declared that he had 'much to complain of [regarding the accused] because, ignoring advice, she had prevented him from receiving the recompense he merited . . . of being made a marshal of France'. In short, he declared, 'I detest her.' However, he added that on 5 October the queen, having been advised to leave alone because 'the Parisians were coming to kill her', nevertheless 'had replied with great character: "If the Parisians are coming here to kill me, it will be at the feet of my husband, for I will not flee."' Marie-Antoinette was pleased to be able to reply: 'That is correct; they wanted to get me to leave on my own because they said I was the only one in any danger. I made the reply the witness cited.' As we have seen, Saint-Priest thought it was the other way round: the plan had been for the king to leave alone to confront the Parisians. Never mind, the queen came out well from the re-telling.

The pretext for the Parisians' march had been the banquet given for the Flanders regiment, and Herman sought to catch the accused out for 'claiming that she had not led her son by the hand' to the banquet. 'No,' she retorted, 'I did not say that, just that I don't remember hearing the [royalist] aria: Oh Richard, Oh mon Roi.'

It can be seen from these exchanges that Marie-Antoinette was prepared to bend the truth, exploit an opening, and trip Herman up. She continued in this vein when in their desperation to link Marie-Antoinette with the Girondins the prosecution made a silly mistake. They put it to her that 'despite the lively objections of Duranthon, at the time minister of justice, she had determined Louis Capet to veto' the decrees against the émigrés and refractory priests. Marie-Antoinette replied: 'that in the month of November, Duranthon was not a minister; that besides, she had no need to put pressure on her husband to do what he believed to be his duty. That she did not sit in Council where these sorts of matters were discussed and decided.'[37] Technically true.

Duranthon, the Girondin minister of justice, had been appointed the following April. Marie-Antoinette missed a trick here. For Robespierre, Herman and the CPS the trial of Marie-Antoinette was merely the warm-up act for the big trial, that of the captured Girondin leaders: Roland had committed suicide; Buzot's remains were discovered eaten by wolves or dogs. She could easily have shown that both she and Robespierre hated the Girondins. It wouldn't have saved her but at least it would have gained her points for style. She would then, however, have had to reveal that the minister of justice in question was Duport du Tertre, the conduit for the policy she and Barnave thrashed out, and that she didn't need to sit in the Council because decisions had already been taken in the committee.

Still on the theme of the Girondins, Herman accused her of bringing about the war. He traced this back to the Declaration of Pillnitz. She didn't reply that when she had seen the signatures of the king's brothers appended to that document she had exclaimed: 'Cain!' Instead, she pointed out that there was quite a time lag between this Declaration and that of war, and 'that it was not the Foreign Powers who had attacked France'. True, Herman said, but 'the accused cannot be unaware that this declaration was the result of the intrigues of a liberticidal faction whose authors will soon receive the punishment they deserve'. Marie-Antoinette was not sufficiently au fait with Revolution-speak to get the allusion to the Girondins, as she replied that 'she didn't know what he was referring to'. Marie-Antoinette clearly did not know that the Girondins were now the enemy and that Herman was trying to tar them by association with the accused. She had been cut off from political developments for over a year and there was a limit to the amount of information that could be conveyed in a screwed-up bit of paper serving as a decanter stopper. She did, however, add that the king had 'only acceded to the declaration of war on the unanimous advice of his council'.

Herman also tried to haul in Marie-Antoinette's association with earlier generations of villains: not just the 'execrable' Calonne but Lafayette and Bailly, whom Robespierre, speaking through Herman, blamed for facilitating the Flight to Varennes. The irony was that these people – maybe not Bailly – were her deadly enemies. She said, truthfully, that 'these two were the last people she would have employed'. Lafayette (whom Herman called the queen's 'favourite') was languishing in an imperial prison, Calonne was in London, but Bailly, who had been arrested in September, was both a witness in Marie-Antoinette's trial and coming up for his own.

There were moments of farce such as when La Tour du Pin was accused of participating in the banquet given for the Flanders Regiment. He replied that this was impossible since he was in Burgundy at the time. What was the minister of war doing in Burgundy? La Tour du Pin said he had never been a minister nor had any desire to be. He had been mistaken for his cousin La Tour du Pin

Gouvernet. It scarcely mattered, both were guillotined. Gouvernet was also called as a witness. He stepped forward and before and after giving his evidence bowed to the woman he still regarded as queen.

But comedy sat side by side with tragedy – an episode many consider to have been the darkest moment in the French Revolution. Certainly it was the cruellest in Marie-Antoinette's life. Several attempts were made to get the dauphin Louis-Charles to inform on his mother. The concierge at the Temple asked the boy whether he remembered the Flight to Varennes. Yes, he remembered being 'woken from his bed, dressed as a girl and told, "come to Montmédy"'. Incidentally, it is mainly later historians not contemporaries who have doubted that this was the destination. But they also got the boy (and they claimed his sister) to say that Bailly and Lafayette, 'great favourites' of the accused, 'were present during the escape and furthered it with all their power'. Herman tried to trick the accused by asking her whether she persisted in her claim that Bailly and Lafayette had no part in the escape. 'Yes,' she replied. 'I would point out,' he continued, 'that . . . you find yourself in contradiction with the statement of your son.' 'It is very easy to make a child of eight say what you want,' she said.[38]

Marie-Antoinette should have saved this splendid riposte to answer the worst of her son's induced accusations. There was no conclusive evidence to convict Marie-Antoinette, so it was thought necessary to blacken her character by accusing her and Madame Elizabeth of incest with the eight-year-old dauphin. Jacques Hébert organized this and visited the Temple where the boy signed a statement to the effect that his mother had taught him how to masturbate, that he did it so vigorously that one of his testicles had swelled and needed bandaging and that the three of them had lain together. His sister was interrogated and replied that she didn't fully understand the accusation but she had seen nothing. Madame Elizabeth likewise refuted the charge. Marie-Antoinette's character-sketch of the dauphin when aged four has relevance here. She told Madame de Tourzel: 'He has a tendency to repeat what he has heard and, without exactly lying he often embroiders it with what his imagination suggests.'[39]

Hébert's intervention had been orchestrated by Fouquier-Tinville, who concluded his preliminary observations:

That finally the widow Capet, immoral in every respect, the new Agrippina, is so perverse and so familiar with every crime that, forgetting her quality of mother and the limits placed by the laws of nature, she did not blush to give herself over (with Louis Charles Capet and by his own admission) to indecencies whose very name makes one shudder.[40]

When Hébert produced his evidence in court Marie-Antoinette disdained to answer the charge. But one juror would not let the matter rest: 'Citizen President I respectfully invite you to remind the accused that she has not replied to the matter raised by Citizen Hébert concerning what passed between her and her son.' Herman, perhaps with some distaste, put it to the queen, who replied: 'If I did not respond, it was because it would be against nature for a mother to reply to such an accusation. On this I appeal to all the mothers who may be here.' The *Anti-Fédéraliste*,[41] edited by Robespierre's volcanic associate Claude Payan, noted the 'theatrical tone' of the accused's apostrophe. The minutes of the trial record Marie-Antoinette's deep emotion as she uttered these words, but say nothing of their effect on her auditors. She had not planned to play the card of mother, as Madame de Staël had suggested. Her reply was one of spontaneous indignation, and all the more effective for that. Of this episode, de Staël wrote to the comte de Narbonne, 'Hell stalks the earth.'[42]

When the juror Vilate related the scene to Robespierre over dinner, he was so angry he broke his plate: 'That imbecile Hébert! Isn't it enough that she really is a Messalina without making her out to be an Agrippina and enlivening her last moments with a public relations triumph!'[43] For those less familiar with the genealogy of the Julio-Claudian dynasty than Robespierre, who won second prizes for Latin at university: Messalina, the wife of Claudius, was known for her promiscuity whereas Agrippina (the younger) was the mother of Nero with whom she was supposed to have had an incestuous relationship. She was accused of murdering Claudius to make way for her son Nero, who in turn poisoned her (Tacitus, *Annals*, XIV). Fouquier-Tinville, the CSG and Hébert were behind the introduction of the Agrippina comparison, whereas for Herman, Robespierre and the CPS, Messalina was quite sufficient.

This symbolized deeper tensions. Hébert's faction could not be ignored. It had captured the popular movement and the Cordelier Club and controlled the war ministry, easily the largest. The *journée* of 5 September was its high-water mark: the Convention was surrounded and forced to pass popular legislation: the law of suspects, price controls and the creation of the *armée révolutionnaire*. Two radicals were added to the CPS.

Four of the jurors were Hébertistes. Robespierre would exclude them from the juries that sat during the Grand Terror of the summer of 1794, which operated under the law of 22 prairial.[44] Curiously, on 27 September, a scant fortnight before Marie-Antoinette's trial, Hébert had proposed in the Jacobin Club that the ex-queen be moved back from the Conciergerie to the Temple, a proposal not taken up by the CPS. So much is fact, but Hébert's motives have not been established. It was suggested that he was involved in a plan to rescue the queen and had said, 'If I can't save her I will see to it that she perishes.'[45]

After the last witness had appeared, Fouquier-Tinville summed up the case for the prosecution. Most of his presentation concerned Marie-Antoinette's links with the Girondins and a list of the cities that had been in revolt against the Convention. That was the government's present preoccupation but it had nothing to do with Marie-Antoinette, who detested the Girondins and had been in prison during the whole of the civil war. Herman spoke at greater length. For form's sake, the jury stayed out for an hour before delivering their inevitable sentence. Herman pronounced sentence of death and since there was no appeal from the tribunal to the Cour de Cassation, that was it.

There are various accounts of how she greeted her sentence. The official account said, 'the accused did not show the slightest reaction.'[46] Her counsel Chauveau-Lagarde noted, 'She did not give the slightest sign of fear, indignation or weakness.' Payan wrote: 'the habit of crime gave her serenity or rather an effrontery which showed all over her face.'[47]

The sitting had continued through the night and Marie-Antoinette was returned to the Conciergerie at about 4.30 on the morning of 16 October.[48] She ate the wing of a chicken, asked for pen and paper, and wrote a lengthy testament addressed to Elizabeth by the light of two candles. 'I have just been condemned not to a shameful death, that's only for criminals, but to join your brother, innocent like him.' Then she turns to her children, and in particular her son. Elizabeth was to remind him of Louis XVI's last words to them, 'let him never seek to avenge our death'. Then she alluded to the boy's accusation of incest, 'a matter very heavy on my heart'. 'Pardon him, dear sister; think how easy it is at that age to make a child say whatever you want.' The letter never reached Elizabeth: it travelled via Robespierre to Edmé Courtois, who sifted and edited his papers until by a tortuous route it reached Provence, now restored as Louis XVIII.

Marie-Antoinette lay on her pallet weeping; then as dawn broke she asked for a drink of chocolate; it was procured from a nearby hostelry. She was also given a biscuit (*mignon*). It was so small that it was not tested for poison or there would have been little left to sustain her on her journey. She was pale, less as a result of fear than of illness: she had suffered repeated haemorrhages including one that night. She asked for a new dress. She had worn black for mourning throughout the trial, but for her last journey she was dressed in white.

At 10 a.m. the officers of the Tribunal read out her sentence. She said she had already heard it, but they said they had to follow regulations. Henri Sanson, the executioner, cut her hair, which was white and disordered. A strong man, like his biblical namesake, his strength was not needed in the new automated age. Perhaps not knowing his own strength he bound Marie-Antoinette's hands behind her back too tightly. Like many of his calling, he was not cruel, just professional and, by turns, philosophical. He was a sixth-generation executioner, first royal now republican – you had to be a Vicar of Bray in that line of work. His father had executed the king, reluctantly. Henri Sanson would execute not just Marie-Antoinette but her enemies, first Hébert then Robespierre. Not in revenge but in line of duty. His grandfather had broken Robert-François Damiens on the wheel for attempting to assassinate Louis XV with a fruit knife, though he would have left it to his assistants to pour the molten lead into his broken joints.

The queen's hands were loosened not because she complained but because the shock of seeing the tumbrel arrive produced a need to relieve herself. Her hands were unbound and she found a secluded corner. She had asked to be taken to the guillotine in a carriage like her husband, but this was refused. She had wanted to face the horse, but she was made to look out of the back. She was accompanied by a priest, but since he was a constitutional priest she refused to make her confession to him. It is sometimes said that she had had access to a refractory priest in prison and had already confessed, but her testament makes it clear that she did not know where to find one and would not have wanted to endanger him.

Jacques-Louis David sketched her on the way to her execution. He was not just a painter. Indeed, he was wont to say, never mind about my art, what I will be remembered for is the fortnight when I presided over the National Convention. He was a fervent supporter of Robespierre (though he deserted him in his hour of need) and a member of the CSG. In this capacity he had accompanied Hébert when he interrogated the dauphin over his supposed incest with his mother. Even in David's hostile sketch, however, ravaged by illness and suffering, Marie-Antoinette (to paraphrase Milton) 'appeared not less than queen ruin'd and th' excess of glory obscur'd'.

After its abusive covering of the trial the semi-official report of Marie-Antoinette's journey to the scaffold is surprisingly dispassionate:

Antoinette looked at the 30,000 men forming a double hedge along the entire route with an air of indifference; she displayed neither dejection nor pride. She seemed calm and oblivious to the cries of Vive la République . . . She spoke little to her confessor and looked at those at the windows with a certain insouciance . . . In the Rue Saint-Honoré she was seen to cast her eyes over the inscriptions placed on the front of the buildings; nor did that on the Palais de l'Égalité [former Palais Royal] escape her notice. At noon, being arrived at the Place de la Révolution ... she changed colour and became much paler than she had been heretofore. She mounted the scaffold with some courage.[49]

She did not address the crowd but lay straight down, glad to get it over. However, the arrangements took an interminable four minutes before the blade fell at 11.45. One (lying) witness said that after her head had been shown to the crowd – Vive la République – and put in its basket a locket was found in her pockets with two portraits, one of her husband, the other of 'her favourite Lafayette'. She was never really understood. Her body, as Louis XVI's had been, was taken to the Madeleine cemetery. However, her corpse was not just thrown into quicklime like the king's. On 1 November she was buried in a coffin. The Commune was charged: 'Coffin: 6 livres; grave and grave diggers: 15 livres 35 sols'.

'The king's death,' wrote the princesse de Tarente shortly afterwards, 'was gentle in comparison with hers. She had been tormented by the horror of prison, by illness, by lengthy questioning, and she did not have the consolation of seeing her children, nor the words of Malesherbes, nor the consolations of religion, nor even a vast crowd which sustains the courage of those of great character.'[50]

CONCLUSION

*I*n a famous passage Madame Campan writes: 'One day when I was helping [the queen] to organize the memoranda and reports which the ministers had asked her to give to the king, she sighed, and said *there has been no more happiness for me since they turned me into an intriguer*.'[1] These words were uttered as the Brienne ministry was beginning to unravel. But who or what turned her into an intriguer? Who sucked Marie-Antoinette into politics – Madame de Polignac, her Austrian relatives and agents, or the king's nervous collapse? Or is she merely being self-indulgent? The comte de Provence thought that the Brienne ministry was the only time Marie-Antoinette had a major influence on policy. Madame Campan sees a rather more gradual build-up over a six-year period, 1781–7, though both agree that 1787–8 was that of the queen's ascendancy: 'Marie-Antoinette . . . had no direct influence on matters of state until the death of M. de Maurepas, that of M. de Vergennes and the dismissal of M. de Calonne.'

Madame Campan should perhaps have gone back to the year before Maurepas' death, 1780, when the queen acquired two ministers, Castries and Ségur, who looked to her for protection. By the time of the 1787 Assembly of Notables she had somewhat fortuitously acquired a collection of ministers, often disciples of Choiseul, who regarded her as their *patronne*: Castries, Breteuil and Ségur. She also had the once-and-future minister Necker and the archbishop of Toulouse waiting in the wings. At the same time the king's minister and her enemy Calonne, who was also backed by the faction of her favourite Madame de Polignac, was fighting for his ministerial life and that of the regime in trying to force his ambitious reform package through the Assembly. Although Calonne was supported by the king, Louis would not allow him to stuff the Assembly with members of the Polignac faction. The Polignacs had dual loyalties: they were the queen's social set but the king's political party.

The case of the Polignacs shows that Marie-Antoinette's wish to 'deploy just enough influence to set up . . . [her] friends and a few zealous servitors' was ultimately incompatible with that of avoiding political engagement. For in order to preserve their position, turn it into more than a smash-and-grab raid, Madame de Polignac and her entourage needed ministers of their own independent of a queen who was waking up to the extent of their ambitions and cupidity. Madame de Polignac's position was vulnerable because Marie-Antoinette detested her lover, the sinister if cultivated comte de Vaudreuil. The decisive clash between Marie-Antoinette and her *société* came with the Assembly of Notables when the queen played a part in the downfall of Calonne, after which Yolande endured a spell of exile in England. She returned but by now Marie-Antoinette, without openly quarrelling with the favourite, deserted her salon in favour of that of the comtesse d'Ossun.

The suddenly deteriorating political situation after Calonne's fall gave Marie-Antoinette the opportunity and (in view of the king's nervous collapse) the duty to bring in her men to save the monarchy: the archbishop of Toulouse and Necker ideally together, actually in sequence – the king refused to appoint Necker because he had resigned in the middle of a war and been the focal point of the Notables' opposition. She said that in entering the political arena she was 'yielding to necessity and my unfortunate fate'. However, she had been working for Brienne and Necker's appointment for some years. Moreover, 'Louis XVI's long-contracted habit of telling her nothing about affairs of state' meant that she 'lacked knowledge about things it was important for her to know'.[2] She had to begin her political apprenticeship in the midst of a crisis, to learn on the job.

Judgement of her role in this period of her ascendancy depends on one's judgement of Brienne's premiership. Jean Egret, the historian of his period in office, considered that Brienne's reforms were what was needed to save the regime and that he was only brought down by a banal treasury crisis engineered by a closet Calonne supporter in the treasury. We have also noted the part played by Madame de Polignac and Artois in Brienne's fall. Marie-Antoinette was responsible for bringing Necker back and for nine months she supported him: over doubling the representation of the Third Estate and in thwarting the attempt by Artois and the Polignacs to topple him in April 1789. This faction returned to the breach and Marie-Antoinette persuaded the king to reject Necker's draft proposals for the *séance royale* of 23 June. Nevertheless she persuaded Necker not to resign and 'the union of the Orders was brought about by her moderating influence'. Then she turned against the Genevan and, after the fall of the Bastille, the Polignacs paid the price of their disastrous advice.

For me the most interesting of Marie-Antoinette's political interventions was her partnership with Barnave in the closing months of 1791. Their correspondence, published in 1913, shows how they thrashed out policy, whilst the La Marck–Pellenc correspondence demonstrates the mechanism by which these policies were implemented. And whereas she simply supported Brienne and Necker without, as far as we know, seeking to influence their policies, Barnave and the queen discussed everything, from whether the king should deploy his veto to the personnel of the general staff of the bodyguard that Barnave had been instrumental in getting for the king. But for the wrecking tactics of the Girondins, this experiment in epistolary government could have resulted in a strong constitutional monarchy at peace with Europe. Barnave's whole enterprise was predicated on peace with Austria. He wanted to transform Marie-Antoinette's nationality from being a liability into an asset and revivify the moribund alliance that had brought her to France. But the Girondins (who favoured a Prussian alliance) put paid to that.

Turning Marie-Antoinette's Austrian nationality into an asset required an alchemy beyond Barnave or probably anyone. Likewise his conceit that it would actually be easier for the queen to recapture her popularity 'because she has always been regarded as an enemy, she made open war, so to speak'. Therefore, if she embarked on a 'pronounced' popular policy she would be believed. 'The French people will soon get tired of hating.'[3]

The Austrian alliance had never been loved and Maria-Theresa, who thought a French marriage would save it, in fact undermined it and her daughter with short-sighted and callous interventions. And her pressure on her daughter and that of Joseph, Mercy and Vermond gained Austria nothing but the 4 million florins to settle the quarrel between France's two allies, Austria and the Dutch Republic. This spawned a legend that was brought up at the queen's trial.

Mercy, to maintain his credit, had strung Maria-Theresa and Joseph along by arguing that Marie-Antoinette was about to intervene on their behalf and was only prevented by a range of excuses: she would not apply herself (true); the king was about to obey her but was diverted by his ministers (false). In fact, Louis and Vergennes played hard cop and soft cop with Marie-Antoinette until Vergennes' death. The Habsburgs, who had been trying to have Vergennes dismissed for years, saw his death as the great opportunity. Maria-Theresa had blamed Marie-Antoinette for not bothering to influence the succession to d'Aiguillon; now surely she could place the Austrian candidate, Saint-Priest. In fact, the episode revealed what Marie-Antoinette had probably thought all along. She told an uncomprehending Mercy that it was wrong for Vienna to nominate ministers for Versailles. By trying to make her act against her conscience, the Austrians had achieved nothing but her unpopularity. All the vast correspondence between Vienna and Versailles, which has been available since 1866 and has formed the basis of all assessments of Marie-Antoinette, comes down to that.

When the Revolution came the boot was on the other foot. France was in no position to help Austria, while Joseph and Leopold had no intention of putting themselves out for their sister even if they could understand exactly what she wanted. Was it troops on the Luxembourg border to justify Bouillé's actions at the time of the Flight to Varennes? What did this mean, even if Mercy had actually transmitted Marie-Antoinette's request to Leopold? The troops never materialized. And what was a congress, 'not war but the threat of war', all about? Leopold did not know the full extent of Marie-Antoinette's involvement with Barnave but, at least in theory, he thought constitutional monarchy a good thing. He changed systems in December 1791 for the reasons given, but there remains doubt whether he would ever have gone to war if he had lived.

The Austrian correspondence, of course, contains much about Marie-Antoinette's personal life as well as her unrealized diplomatic potential, hence its abiding popularity. As a possessive mother never letting go, Maria-Theresa wanted to keep a motherly eye on her youngest daughter. She is constantly reminding her to wear a corset because one shoulder was fractionally higher than the other. She and Joseph share an obsession both prurient and dynastic with Marie-Antoinette's sex life and with her confinements and deliveries. When it is rumoured that Louis XVI has taken a mistress, Maria-Theresa tells her it is a woman's lot to accept these things – as she had done.

However, there is one striking omission from Mercy's reports and the queen-empress's enquiries. Although he dwells lovingly if disapprovingly on Marie-Antoinette's male admirers and their unescorted visits to the Trianon, on her midnight peregrinations, on her gambling for high stakes (which he exaggerates), Mercy never once mentions Fersen, though many speculated on his relationship to the queen. This omission may be suggestive – too serious to mention? Or an admission that he is not keeping a proper eye on her?

When R. M. Baron Klinckowström published a redacted version of his great-uncle Fersen's letters to Marie-Antoinette, the presence of asterisks raised suspicions that were not allayed by the editor's protestation that the redacted passages related only to sensitive political and financial matters, especially as the asterisks occurred at the beginning and end of the letters where expressions of endearment are usually placed. This indeed proved to be the case when some of the correspondence turned up at Sotheby's in 1982, was acquired by the Archives Nationales, and subjected to modern imaging techniques. But in a sense this coup was an anticlimax: before the restorations, the imagination could run riot; after them what we had was proof that Marie-Antoinette wrote such things as 'I love you madly' – the actual title of Evelyn Farr's work publishing her restorations (London, 2016) – but no hint of a sexual relationship. Yet why should there be? But for the suspicions raised by Klinckowström's Victorian coyness no one would ever have expected that eighteenth-century women of Marie-Antoinette's status would have put such things in a letter. There had been a triple distortion: twentieth-century mores applied to a nineteenth-century censorship of an eighteenth-century source.

That of course does not mean that Marie-Antoinette and Fersen were not lovers – just that we are no further forward in the quest. We will never know but I have hazarded a guess that they did become lovers after 1786 when Marie-Antoinette, having given birth to the fourth of her children by Louis XVI including two male heirs, told her brother Joseph that she did not want to bear any more children and, by implication, continue sexual relations with her husband.

Jeanne Arnaud-Bouteloup considers that Marie-Antoinette simply could not comprehend why she was 'detested', citing her famous rhetorical question to Madame Campan: 'What have I done to them then?' When she was not applauded at the opera in 1782 (having at last produced a dauphin), she responded: 'Well . . . too bad for the people of Paris. It's not my fault.'[4] Still less would she have understood why she would be credited with 'let them eat cake' or even the less rebarbative 'qu'ils mangent de la brioche' without the harsh double 'k' in 'cake'. Arnaud-Bouteloup sympathizes with the queen's failure to grasp the causes of her unpopularity because it was out of all proportion to its object[5] – after all what *had* she done to them? She was the scapegoat of an irrational age suffering a nervous collapse, the so-called rationality of the Enlightenment shot through with the charlatanism of a Mesmer, a Cagliostro and, for that matter, a Necker.

Of the above quotes, the cake/brioche one is apocryphal and the other two recorded much later. But there are others recorded at the time and some of these suggest that she did know why she was 'detested'. There are her letters to Joseph lamenting the canard of her sending millions of livres into Germany; but above all this: on 25 August 1788 she confided to Mercy: 'I tremble (forgive my weakness) that I am bringing him [Necker] back. My fate is to bring misfortune. And if diabolical plots should cause him to fail again [as in 1781] or if he should surrender some of the royal authority, I will be detested even more.'[6] This is a locus classicus for Marie-Antoinette because she is aware not only that she is 'detested' but why: because of her perceived and actual involvement in politics. The month before, walking in the Trianon gardens, she complained to Madame de Polignac:

How unfortunate she was to have chosen as principal minister [Brienne] a man who had enjoyed the reputation of eminent merit but who has rendered himself odious to the nation; how cruel it was to see herself hated when all she had wanted was the good of France; and at the same time to see her eldest son in such a parlous state and her brother humiliated in all his projects. And she concluded: Do you know a woman more to be pitied than me?

Although he did pity her, Bombelles, whose diary recounts these words, probably supplied by Madame de Polignac herself, thought Marie-Antoinette had only herself to blame because 'instead of remaining satisfied with the fine role of Queen of France, she wanted to be its king as well. Blinded by amour-propre and believing herself to be superior to the king her husband, she thought that this superiority would extend to events and the conduct of a machine too strong for her.' The abbé de Véri went as far as to say that 'people habitually referred to the queen's authority more than the king's'.[7] But note that all these quotes come from the short period of her ascendancy.

Bombelles was an old-school Austrophobe so he had a double reason to complain of a woman seeking to play a man's role in a bad cause. But is Marie-Antoinette's (greatly magnified) political involvement enough to explain such 'detestation'? Courtiers were disgruntled by the favours she bestowed on the 'parvenu' Polignacs – but there are 'ins' and 'outs' at any court. Her extravagance was no greater than that of many a queen or royal mistress, but it was ostentatious. She had only herself to blame for Rohan's believing that she had ordered expensive diamonds without telling the king because she had 'form'.

But none of these things – political involvement, extravagance, exclusive friendships – connotes the kind of unpleasant character that generally leads to detestation. The only unpleasant trait in Marie-Antoinette's character was a thirst for vengeance. This was satisfied early on with the disgrace of Madame du Barry, d'Aiguillon and Turgot (though her role in all three has been exaggerated). But it continued with her persecution of Cardinal Rohan. All but Turgot were unpopular, but the public (however defined) sympathized with them rather than the queen because vengeance is not a likeable quality, especially when exercised by those in a position to satisfy it. In the Revolution, Marie-Antoinette was not able to satisfy her vengeance but she displayed it nonetheless, thereby getting the worst of both worlds, as Mercy observed à propos of her attempts to get the king to dismiss Vergennes: in 1786 he told Kaunitz: 'The queen, in showing . . . [Vergennes] a marked malevolence has inured him to it . . . such an approach diminishes a great princess who should never display her hatred without being able to follow it up.'[8]

In the Revolution two instances of vengeance unsatisfied are worth considering. The first was the programme the queen outlined for a restoration of royal authority before the Flight to Varennes: 'pardon those who have merely been led astray, flatter them with expressions of love; except from the pardon the revolutionary leaders [*les chefs des factieux*], the City of Paris unless it returns to the old dispensation, and everyone who has not laid down his arms by a certain date; . . . Religion will be one of the great points to bring to the fore.' The king's manifesto does not mention punishments. Similarly, Lafayette was to be court-martialled. And in this context Soulavie's apothegm is appropriate: 'the queen could never understand that one needed the friendship of enemies,'[9] for on two key occasions she spurned the offer of Lafayette to save the monarchy.

It must, however, be said that Marie-Antoinette exhibited none of the qualities connoted by the cake/brioche trope: heartlessness and being out of touch with her people. Indeed, I have only found one instance of what we would call snobbery. When Barnave suggested that Cahier de Gerville be made minister of the interior, the queen, thinking that he lacked 'the required qualities', called him 'a small-time lawyer earning only 700 livres a year'.[10]

Marie-Antoinette was miserable as dauphine; sought revenge for her (imagined) humiliations as soon as she became queen; and with her manic rounds of pleasure desperately sought to throw scraps of meat to the wolf at the door. She inspired loyalty in strangers who were ready to risk their lives for her even when the chances of success were slight. But what did she get from those who were closest to her? Fersen had a string of mistresses – did she know? Madame de Polignac repaid her munificence by seeking to bring down 'her' premier, Brienne. Louis, rightly, excluded her from foreign affairs before the Revolution, but during it, when he turned to her in his distress, he made her feel like 'the second fiddle', to use her own words, without giving her a proper rehearsal. But shortly after her death Alexandre de Lameth said 'a great number of individuals were passionately devoted to her'.[11] However, it was repentant radicals like him who offered her undivided loyalty: Dumouriez, who asked her to let him save her and risked his life in the attempt; Mirabeau: 'I will save this unfortunate queen from her butchers or die in the attempt';[12] and Barnave, but with this difference, as Lamartine remarked, that whereas 'Mirabeau sold himself, Barnave gave himself'.[13] Repentant radicals; but Lamartine also said (of Barnave) that 'in a Revolution you don't repent, you expiate'.[14] Eliza Bradby, Barnave's biographer, thought that the Marie-Antoinette-Barnave correspondence 'evidently written to glorify Marie-Antoinette' was a forgery because it contradicted the received opinion concerning her. Bradby writes: 'The best part in the "Correspondance" belongs to Marie-Antoinette; she writes better and she seldom boasts. Occasionally she holds her ground and imposes her good sense on her advisers.'[15] The correspondence is genuine; Marie-Antoinette's reputation has been forged.

EPILOGUE: *UBI SUNT?*

fter the Varennes debacle Fersen toured the German-speaking lands in the vain hope of drumming up support for some form of intervention in France. At Coblenz he encountered the duc de Polignac and noted sourly, 'he has lost everything but he still maintains his silver service and his chef'.[1] Was Fersen gloating or shocked? He went on to Vienna and his diary records a long and fruitless conversation with Leopold. He was informed that Madame de Polignac had just arrived in the capital and notes 'went to see Madame de Polignac. She wept at seeing me. I felt pleasure and pain at seeing her.' Was it jealousy of Marie-Antoinette's feelings for the favourite that piqued him? Or was it more like the fallen angels, remembering former bliss in hell? His next diary entry may provide a clue. 'Went to see the duchesse de Polignac. She talks more of public affairs than of the queen.' A week later he accentuated the impression of callousness by substituting 'her friend' for 'the queen': she 'still rabbits on about public affairs and little of her friend'.[2] To my knowledge no one else considered that Yolande was indifferent to the fate of 'her friend'.

Two years later, on 20 October 1793, Fersen learned of Marie-Antoinette's death four days earlier. She had been, he wrote, 'the model of queens and of women'. He told his sister Sophie that there was no question of his marrying Eleanor Sullivan. Marie-Antoinette was irreplaceable.[3] On 19 March 1795, Madame de Korff gave Fersen the end of a note in Marie-Antoinette's hand. It said, 'Adieu, my heart is all yours.' Fersen did not know when it had been written, smuggled out of prison perhaps. But, as he told his sister, 'It seemed to me to be a final adieu and I was deeply moved.'[4] On 9 December 1793, Madame de Polignac died, whether of tuberculosis, cancer or a broken heart. She had always been sickly. Madame Vigée-Lebrun, who knew her, painted this picture of her final months:

> . . . the Duchess de Polignac, lived permanently at a place near Vienna. It was there that she heard of the death of Louis XVI, which affected her health

very seriously, but when she heard the dreadful news of the Queen's death she succumbed altogether. Her grief changed her to such an extent that her pretty face became unrecognizable, and everyone foresaw that she had not much longer to live. She did, in fact, die in a little while, leaving her family and some friends who would not leave her disconsolate at their loss.[5]

Ten days before, on 29 November, Barnave was guillotined. Fersen wrote: 'Barnave died like a coward.'[6] No one else, friend or foe, said he had died so and Fersen's quip was the product of jealousy. Marie-Antoinette had disposed of every bit of evidence concerning her political association with Barnave. Unfortunately the king, who was well aware of the risks Barnave was running, had not been quite so thorough. Just one brief note was discovered – the 'Plan for a ministerial committee arranged with MM. Barnave and Lameth' cited above. It was found in one of the king's bureaux straight after the fall of the Tuileries.

On 15 August 1792 it was read out to the Legislative Assembly. The 'ministerial committee' (now dubbed a 'counter-revolutionary committee') planned that the justice minister, du Tertre, should bring to the Assembly the decree against the émigrés marked 'le roi examinera', the formula for the veto, and that all the other ministers should then read statements of what measures they had taken to bring the émigrés to book. We know that they had all met at Duport du Tertre's house and that Duport had drunk two large glasses of water to stop his blood boiling if the Assembly insulted him – as a constitutional monarchist he was as hated on the left as on the right.

Cambon immediately proposed the arrest of Barnave and Lameth, which was decreed. But Fauchet thought the Assembly would be inconsistent if they didn't arrest all the members of this 'counter-revolutionary committee' – the ministers du Tertre, Duportail, Montmorin, Tarbé and Bertrand de Molleville. Their arrest was also decreed to maintain the Assembly's impartiality. Lameth was saved by Lafayette, who escorted him to the Army of the North. He later went on to write his *Histoire de l'Assemblée Constituante* in exile.

Barnave wrote his *Introduction à la Révolution française* in prison. He had plenty of time for his was a long captivity. Before his arrest, Barnave, who rode his horse every day, could easily have nipped over the Swiss border. But having blamed the émigrés, he scorned to be one himself. In prison his captors turned a blind eye to let him escape, but he spurned this too. However, after fifteen months in prison in Grenoble, just when his friends hoped he had been forgotten, he was transferred to Paris, where Robespierre decided all political trials should be held. Barnave was at first put in the Abbaye prison; then the

Conciergerie, the ante-chamber to the guillotine. He appeared before the Revolutionary Tribunal on 28 November – a month after Marie-Antoinette's appearance – together with Duport du Tertre. Du Tertre, having twice nearly been murdered after 10 August, went into hiding but was arrested a year later in the town of Versailles. Both he and Barnave ended up in the Conciergerie and were tried together, which was appropriate.

The *interrogatoire* and the trial latched on to this appropriateness. Barnave was asked whether, during the Legislative Assembly, 'he had had relations with various ministers'. Only for matters relating to his home *départements*, he lied. He added, 'I attest on my own head that never, absolutely never, have I had any correspondence with the Palace; that never, absolutely never, have I set foot in the Palace.' When Barnave's first English biographer, Eliza Bradby, was about to go to print, O. G. Heidenstam published the correspondence between Marie-Antoinette and Barnave, which is the basis of our contention that the two directed the government for a few crucial months. Bradby was disturbed, not that she had been unable to use this evidence, but because it cast doubt on her hero's revolutionary purity. So, faced with this evidence, and Barnave's denial at his trial, she pronounced the correspondence to be a forgery!

The Revolutionary Tribunal was under the same Robespierrist influence as for Marie-Antoinette's trial. Still Herman presiding; still Lanne his deputy. So they came up with Robespierre's analysis of the Flight to Varennes:

Q: Whether the escape of Capet was not a plot which had for its object the revision of the Constitution and whether he [Barnave] did not participate in this plot?
A: No. That he only knew the reasons for Capet's escape.[7]

(To add a personal note: As an undergraduate I read an essay to Richard Cobb, turning this accusation on its head with a simple Wildean inversion by arguing that Robespierre was right, but so what? The Constitution did need revising and the escape achieved some of its purpose with Barnave's help. I still hold to this view.)

Barnave put up a fine defence and the inevitable death sentence was greeted with total silence. His eye travelled over the judges, the jurors and the public with a mixture of 'irony and indignation'. Those who were expecting a show of Barnave's famous eloquence were not disappointed, but the spectators booed so loudly that Barnave's words were lost. In any case it was his co-defendant du Tertre who held the stage when he told the Revolutionary Tribunal: 'You are going to kill me, Posterity will try me.' There is no better indictment of the 'second revolution' he and Barnave had striven to prevent. On the way back to the Conciergerie, Barnave spotted Camille Desmoulins, who through his *Vieux Cordelier* was at that moment himself trying to stop the Revolution before its final descent into barbarism. Censorship being strict, Desmoulins had to write about life under Nero. No one missed the allegory; none more than Desmoulins' school friend Robespierre, who sent him to the guillotine in the spring. Desmoulins and Barnave, who had been bitter political opponents, shook hands.

Before his death, Barnave wrote to his sister:

> I am still young, and yet I have known, yet I have suffered, all the good and all the ill of which human life is composed. Gifted with a lively imagination, I have long believed in illusions. I am undeceived, and at the moment of leaving this life the only thing I regret is friendship. None could flatter himself more than I on having tasted its sweetness. And also the cultivation of my mind, a practice that often filled my days with delight.

Shall we end with that or this, also to his sister: 'What an immense space we have covered in these three years! We have stirred the earth very deeply; we found a fruitful soil. But how many corrupt exhalations arose from it. Back amid my hearth and home, I ask myself, had it been better never to have left it.'[8] All political careers end in failure and certainly did in the Revolution. Those who died of natural causes, like Mirabeau, or were assassinated, like Le Pelletier or Marat, would have been guillotined otherwise. Only second-raters like Barère not only survived but lived to a great age.

As he mounted the tumbrel, two men jeered, 'How now, Barnave, is the blood that is about to be shed so pure?' In the tumbrel Barnave and du Tertre chatted; reminisced about what could have been; what nearly was. On the scaffold Barnave was reported to have 'lifted his gaze heavenwards and cried out: "That is all the thanks I get for all I have done for liberty."' He was thirty-two, Duport du Tertre was thirty-eight, the same age as Marie-Antoinette.[9]

Du Tertre had talked, callously, of having Marie-Antoinette tried or assassinated. Barnave had talked of tainted blood. But men matured fast in the Revolution. Marie-Antoinette also had travelled a long way. She came to realize that men of talent could be found outside the ranks of the nobility and that the career open to talent, which had been excised from the *séance royale* of 23 June 1789, was a legitimate aspiration for them. All three subsequently worked together in a unique experiment in politics: epistolary government. Now all three had died within a month of each other and been interred in the same common ground.

I have suggested that Barnave, by returning to Grenoble in January 1792, deserted the queen in her hour of need. But there is evidence that he planned to return. He wrote in a draft letter 'I am going to spend some time in Dauphiné. I will return to Paris shortly.' The unknown correspondent may even have been the queen: 'Adieu,' he writes, 'I am the one whom you sought out through your attraction to men of talent.' She decided to continue the relationship with Barnave after the return from Varennes. Nor did she abandon the constitutional monarchy. With the final attack on the Tuileries imminent she told Fersen: 'whatever happens the king and the men of honour will not allow any infraction of the constitution and if it is overturned they will die with it'. Symbolically, Adrien Duport in National Guard uniform was at her side ready to fight to the end.[10]

Barnave and Marie-Antoinette had a marble resurrection: under the Consulate, Napoleon Bonaparte placed statues of Barnave and Vergniaud in the Senate because they were both great orators. The fact that Vergniaud's advocacy of war and virulent denunciation of Marie-Antoinette had sealed the fate of Barnave's peace policy was lost on Napoleon, who was not known for a sense of irony. After Napoleon's fall, kneeling statues of Louis and Marie-Antoinette were placed by Provence ('Cain'), now Louis XVIII, in the desecrated but clumsily restored chapel of the kings at Saint-Denis. Beneath them were placed the remains of the king and queen.

Marie-Antoinette's remains were identified by her Habsburg jaw and by two garters she had worn to her execution. Those of the king were more conjectural and perhaps jostled in the sarcophagus with a bone of Saint-Just or the shattered jaw of Robespierre. Madame Elizabeth was guillotined, rather pointlessly Robespierre considered, on 10 May 1794. The dauphin, prince royal or Louis XVII – take your pick – died from the studied neglect of his jailors on 8 June 1795. Madame de Staël had predicted that 'the young heir to so many misfortunes would die if deprived of the tender attentions of his mother'.[11] Several pretenders came forward posing as the boy, but DNA tests compared with those of his preserved heart have shown them to have been impostors.[12] His sister was freed on 18 December 1795 in an exchange with captured French prisoners and she later married Artois' elder son, the duc d'Angoulême. Their union was childless and she died on 19 October 1851.

NOTES

PREFACE

1. D. Hume, *The History of England*, London, 1754–61.
2. Pellenc, who had been Mirabeau's secretary, and La Marck, a confidant of the queen's.
3. H. Fleischmann, *Madame de Polignac et la cour galante de Marie-Antoinette*, Paris, 1910, *passim*.
4. Marquis de Bombelles, *Journal*, ed. J. Grassion, F. Durif and J. Charon-Bordas, 4 vols, Geneva, 1978–98, II, 77.
5. E. Farr, *Marie-Antoinette and Count Fersen*, London, 2013, 87.

1 FROM ARCHDUCHESS TO DAUPHINE

1. S. Zweig, *Marie Antoinette*, trans. E. and C. Paul, New York, 1933, 9.
2. P. and P. Girault de Coursac, *Louis XVI et Marie Antoinette. Vie conjugale, vie politique*, Paris, 1990, 10.
3. Mercy-Argenteau, *Correspondance secrète . . . avec l'Empereur Joseph II et le Prince de Kaunitz*, ed. A. d'Arneth and J. Flammermont, Paris, 1891, 2 vols [hereafter A & F], II, 85.
4. E. Lever, *Marie Antoinette*, trans. C. Temerson, New York, 2000, 11.
5. Coursac, *Louis XVI et Marie Antoinette*, 10.
6. P. de Ségur, *Marie Antoinette*, London, 2015, 9.
7. These have been published *in toto* by A. von Arneth, *Maria-Theresia und Marie-Antoinette ihr Briefwechsel*, Vienna, 1866, 353–86, and, unless otherwise stated, the following pages are based on them.
8. Ibid., 20,
9. Letter of 22 September 1784.
10. Coursac, *Louis XVI et Marie-Antoinette*, 10.
11. Ibid., 22.
12. Ibid., 24–5.
13. Ibid., 14.
14. Ibid., 44.
15. Ibid., 47.
16. Ibid., 115.
17. Ibid., 61.
18. A. C. Morris ed., *The Diary and Letters of Gouverneur Morris*, New York, 1888, 2 vols, I, 431 entry for 14 July 1791.
19. Duc de Lévis, *Portraits et souvenirs*, Paris, 1813, 17.
20. Madame de Flahaut, ibid., 431–2.
21. D'Ormesson, *Journal*, A.N. 144 A.P. 130, section 58.
22. Archives de la Marine, *Journal de Castries,* MS 182/7964, II, 371.
23. Prince de Ligne, *Fragments de ma vie*, Paris, 1928, 2 vols, I, 152.

24. P. de Nolhac, *Marie-Antoinette dauphine*, Paris, 1929, 80.
25. Ibid., 73.
26. Ibid., 78.
27. Ibid., 83.
28. Duc de Croÿ, *Journal, 1718–1784*, ed. vicomte de Grouchy and P. Cottin, Paris, 1906–7, 4 vols, III, 135, 134.
29. Marie-Antoinette to Maria-Theresa, 16 April 1771, Marie-Antoinette, *Correspondance de Marie-Antoinette*, ed. E. Lever, Paris, 2005, 72–3.
30. A. Geoffroy, *Gustave III et la cour de France*, Paris, 1866–7, 2 vols, I, 293, cited in E. Farr, *Marie-Antoinette and Count Fersen*, London, 2013, 43.
31. Coursac, *Louis XVI et Marie-Antoinette*, 33.
32. Ibid., 189.
33. Nolhac, *Marie-Antoinette dauphine*, 109–11.
34. Mercy to Maria-Theresa, 18 February 1778, in *Correspondance secrète entre Marie-Thérèse et le comte de Mercy-Argenteau*, ed. A. d'Arneth and M. Geffroy, 2nd edn, Paris, 1875, 3 vols [hereafter A & G], III, 168–9.
35. Coursac, *Louis XVI et Marie-Antoinette*, 203.
36. Ibid., 324.
37. Cited in M. Antoine, *Louis XV*, Paris, 1989, 990.
38. Ibid., 991–2.
39. Cited in Joël Felix, *Louis XVI et Marie-Antoinette*, Paris, 2006, 99.
40. Marie-Antoinette to Maria-Theresa, 14 May 1774, in *Correspondance*, ed. Lever, 168.
41. A. J. Barnave, *Oeuvres*, Paris, 1843, 4 vols, I, 83.

2 THE COURT UNDER LOUIS XVI AND MARIE-ANTOINETTE

1. P. and P. Girault de Coursac, *Louis XVI et Marie-Antoinette. Vie conjugale, vie politique*, Paris, 1990, 316. By 'protocol' she meant how to address foreign rulers, though Louis was already well versed in this.
2. Ibid., 322.
3. C. A. de Calonne (attrib.), *Lettre du Marquis de Caraccioli à M. d'Alembert*, Paris, 1781, 15.
4. Louis XVIII, 'Réflexions historiques sur Marie-Antoinette', *Revue des Deux Mondes* (1904), 7.
5. E. Farr, *Marie-Antoinette and Count Fersen*, London, 2013, 63.
6. The word is Soulavie's.
7. On this see D. Wick, 'The Court Nobility and the French Revolution: The Example of the Society of Thirty', *Eighteenth Century Studies*, 1980, XIII, 263–84; also G. Maugras, *La fin d'un société. Le duc de Lauzun et la cour de Marie-Antoinette*, 2nd edn, Paris, 1909.
8. A & G, II, 486.
9. The maréchal de Soubise lingered on in the Conseil d'état, a hangover from the previous reign, until Louis XVI told him to stop attending after the Diamond Necklace Affair.
10. A coadjutor was a bishop's auxiliary with the right to succeed him.
11. Louis XVIII, 'Réflexions historiques', 4.
12. *Mémoires du baron de Besenval*, ed. F. Barrière, Paris, 1846, 266.
13. Abbé de Véri, Archives Départementales de La Drôme (Valence), MSS Journal (unclassified), Cahiers 157 and 109
14. G. Maugras, *Lauzun*, Paris, 1907, 126.
15. For the fall of the Rohan-Guéméné see ibid., 256–8 and 293–9.
16. A.N.A.P. 144. 131, 14th and 15th meeting of the Comité des finances; see also M. Price, *Preserving the Monarchy: The Comte de Vergennes, 1774–1787*, Cambridge, 1995, 172–3.
17. J.-L. Soulavie, *Mémoires historiques et politiques du règne de Louis XVI*, Paris, 1801, 6 vols, VI, 27. Soulavie was given privileged access to Louis XVI's papers on the fall the monarchy.
18. H. Fleischmann, *Madame de Polignac et la cour galante de Marie-Antoinette*, Paris, 1910, 10, 17.

19. A & G, II, 367.
20. Soulavie, *Mémoires historiques*, VI, 31.
21. Ibid.
22. Ibid., 27–8.
23. Louis XVIII, 'Réflexions historiques', 8.
24. A & G, II, 165 and 495. Maurepas' aunt was the marquise de Mailly-Nesle, whilst the comte de Polignac's grandmother, the vicomtesse de Polignac, was born Françoise de Mailly. The mother of Maurepas' wife, of the same ministerial family, the Phélypeaux, was a Mailly and the Mailly intermarried with the Polignac. Indeed at the precise date, 1775, when Diane de Polignac secured her place as a lady-in-waiting, there was another Mailly/Polignac wedding. L. Boisnard, *Les Phélypeaux*, Paris, 1986, 111 and 178.
25. Mercy to Maria-Theresa, 13 April 1775.
26. A & G, III, 140.
27. From Chavaray's catalogue of 1909, item 65146, 15 francs, cited in Fleischmann, *Madame de Polignac*, 40.
28. Cited by P. de Nolhac, *La Reine Marie-Antoinette*, Paris, 1905, 190–1.
29. Louis XVIII, 'Réflexions historiques', 8.
30. Marquis de Bombelles, *Journal*, ed. J. Grassion, F. Durif and J. Charon-Bordas, 4 vols, Geneva, 1978–98, I, 313.
31. Soulavie, *Mémoires historiques*, VI, 29–30.
32. Louis XVIII, 'Réflexions historiques', 8.
33. Marie-Antoinette to Maria-Theresa, 14 September 1776, A & G, II, 486.
34. Mercy to Maria-Theresa, 17 August 1775, A & G, II, 475–6.
35. Mercy to Maria-Theresa, 18 April 1777, ibid., III, 45.
36. Abbé de Véri, *Journal, 1774–1780*, ed. J. de Witte, Paris, 1928–30, 2 vols, I, 131. Cited in A. Spawforth, *Versailles*, New York, 2008, 96.
37. Soulavie, *Mémoires historiques*, VI, 32–3.
38. M. Price, 'Lafayette, the Lameths and "republican monarchy", 1789–1791', forthcoming article, 5.
39. A. J. Barnave, *Oeuvres*, Paris, 1843, 4 vols, I, 85.
40. Bombelles, *Journal*, II, 77.
41. Coursac, *Louis XVI et Marie-Antoinette*, 718 ff.
42. Bombelles, *Journal*, I, 236.
43. Nolhac, *La Reine Marie-Antoinette*, 240.
44. A & G, III, 114, 12 September 1777.
45. Comte de Saint-Priest, *Mémoires*, ed. baron de Barante, Paris, 1929, 2 vols, II, 72–3.
46. Farr, *Marie-Antoinette and Count Fersen*, 58.
47. The title of Michael Roberts' classic is *Sweden as a Great Power, 1611–1697*, London, 1968.
48. Farr, *Marie-Antoinette and Count Fersen*, 109.
49. Joseph II to Marie-Antoinette, undated but probably 1775, *Marie-Antoinette, Joseph II und Leopold II ihr Briefwechsel*, ed. A. von Arneth, 2nd edn, Vienna, 1866, 12.
50. Saint-Priest, *Mémoires*, II, 67.
51. M. Klinckowström, *Le Comte de Fersen et la cour de France*, Paris, 1878, 2 vols 1, XXXV.
52. Coursac, *Louis XVI et Marie-Antoinette*, 695.
53. Farr, *Marie-Antoinette and Count Fersen*, 89.
54. A & G, III, 387 and 409.
55. Farr, *Marie-Antoinette and Count Fersen*, 91.
56. Ibid., 127.

3 A QUEEN IN SEARCH OF A ROLE, 1774–1781

1. A & F, II, 195.
2. A & G, II, 147.
3. Abbé de Véri, *Journal, 1774–1780*, ed. J. de Witte, Paris, 1928–30, 2 vols, I, 93.

4. A & G II, 356.
5. Since Anne of Austria, regent for the young Louis XIV.
6. Viry to the King of Sardinia, 20 May 1774, cited in J. Arnaud-Bouteloup, *Le rôle politique de Marie-Antoinette*, Paris, 1924, 61.
7. See J. Hardman and M. Price, eds, *Louis XVI and the comte de Vergennes: Correspondence, 1774–1787*, Oxford, 1998.
8. Maria-Theresa to Mercy, 2 August 1773.
9. Baron de Besenval, *Mémoires*, Paris, 1846, 169.
10. Véri, *Journal*, I, 388.
11. P. and P. Girault de Coursac, *Louis XVI et Marie-Antoinette. Vie conjugale, vie politique*, Paris, 1990, 303–4.
12. A *lettre de cachet* was an executive order under the king's signet seal or cachet to imprison or exile an individual. It had no other control than the counter-signature of the secretary of state, usually for the Maison du Roi, unless he himself was being exiled.
13. The king to La Vrillière, 11 May 1774, in *Louis XVI, Marie-Antoinette et Mme Elizabeth, lettres et documents inédits*, ed. F. Feuillet de Conches, Paris, 1864–9, 6 vols, I, 32–3.
14. Véri, *Journal*, I, 99.
15. Coursac, *Louis XVI et Marie-Antoinette*, 320.
16. Louis XVI to Vergennes, 5 March 1775, *Louis XVI and Vergennes: Correspondence*, 189.
17. Vergennes to the king, 12 April 1775, ibid., 195–6.
18. A & G, II, 366 n. 1.
19. Besenval, *Mémoires*, 1846, 163.
20. A & G, II, 362.
21. Joseph II to Marie-Antoinette, undated draft, ibid., 364.
22. Besenval, *Mémoires*, 1846, 165.
23. Marie-Antoinette to Maria-Theresa, 22 June 1775 A & G, II, 342–5.
24. Ibid., 13 July 1775, 362.
25. Coursac, *Louis XVI et Marie-Antoinette*, 399.
26. William Shakespeare, *Richard II*, Act I, line 280.
27. A & G, II, 356.
28. A & F, II, 454.
29. Coursac, *Louis XVI et Marie-Antoinette*, 475.
30. Véri, *Journal*, I, 299.
31. Duc de Croÿ, *Journal, 1718–1784*, ed. vicomte de Grouchy and P. Coffin, Paris, 1906–7, 4 vols, II, 457 and 461.
32. A & G, II, 362.
33. Cour de Aides, concerned mainly with taxes on alcoholic drinks.
34. Véri, *Journal*, I, 314.
35. Ibid., 316.
36. Joseph II to Marie-Antoinette, draft letter, July 1775, Marie-Antoinette, *Correspondance de Marie-Antoinette*, ed. E. Lever, Paris, 2005, 221–3.
37. Coursac, *Louis XVI et Marie-Antoinette*, 329–31.
38. S. Padover, *The Life and Death of Louis XVI*, London, 1965, 90.
39. A & G, II, 366 n. 1; Véri, *Journal*, I, 448.
40. Véri, *Journal*, I, 389–90. A letter from Vergennes to the king also makes it clear that it was not he, Vergennes, who had demanded Guines' recall. They both knew it was Turgot.
41. *Louis XVI and Vergennes: Correspondence*, no. 74.
42. Ibid., no. 78, draft.
43. Marie-Antoinette to Maria-Theresa, 15 May 1776, A & G, II, 441.
44. Ibid., III, 381–2 and 391.
45. Ibid., III, 449.
46. Joseph II to Marie-Antoinette, 29 May 1777, *Marie-Antoinette, Joseph II and Leopold II ihr Briefwechsel*, ed. A. von Arneth, 2nd edn, Vienna, 1866, 6.
47. Quoted by D. Beales, *Joseph II*, vol. 1, Cambridge, 1987.
48. A. Fraser, *Marie-Antoinette*, London, 2001, 149.

49. Padover, *Louis XVI*, 112.

50. J. Félix, *Louis XVI et Marie-Antoinette*, Paris, 2006, 236.

51. A & G, III, 476.

52. Véri, *Journal*, II, 94 and 97.

53. A.N. K164 no. 3, 1778 no. 7, 22 July.

54. Marie-Antoinette to Maria-Theresa, 12 June 1778, A & G, III, 213.

55. Mercy to Maria-Theresa, 18 February 1778, ibid., 168–9.

56. Coursac, *Louis XVI et Marie Antoinette*, 547.

57. Ibid., 548.

58. Ibid., 558.

59. Ibid., 560.

60. Coursac, *Louis XVI et Marie-Antoinette*, 578.

61. Maria-Theresa to Marie-Antoinette, 29 June 1777, A & G, III, 86.

62. Comte d'Angiviller, *Mémoires*, Copenhagen, 1933, 64.

63. Cited in J. L. H. Campan, *Mémoires sur la vie privée de Marie-Antoinette*, Paris, 1823, 2 vols, I, 200 n. 1.

64. Ibid., 200.

65. A & G, III, 340; Coursac, *Louis XVI et Marie-Antoinette*, 514.

66. Véri, *Journal*, II, 178.

67. Coursac, *Louis XVI et Marie-Antoinette*, 543–4.

68. Mercy to Maria-Theresa, 17 June 1779, A & G, III, 325.

69. As a Protestant he could not be called Controller-General.

70. Letter of 5 December 1778, *Louis XVI and Vergennes: Correspondence*, no. 137.

71. Véri, *Journal*, II, 345.

72. Véri, Mss Cahier, 106.

73. A & F, I, 25 n. For a fuller discussion of the 1780 crisis, see *Louis XVI and Vergennes: Correspondence*, 95–101.

74. A & G, III, 488–9.

75. Coursac, *Louis XVI et Marie-Antoinette*, 667.

76. Véri, *Journal*, II, 392.

77. A & G, III, 486 *et seq.*

78. Marie-Antoinette to Joseph II, 20 December 1780, in Marie-Antoinette, *Lettres*, ed. M. de La Rocheterie et le marquis de Beaucourt, Paris, 1895–6, 2 vols, I, 239.

79. Prince de Montbarey, *Mémoires du Prince de Montbarey*, Paris, 1826–7, 3 vols, II, 250, 197 and 327–8, and III, 25. My italics.

80. A & G, III, 405–96, 422.

81. A. J. Barnave, *Oeuvres*, Paris, 1843, 4 vols, I, 84.

82. Marie-Antoinette, *Lettres*, ed. La Rocheterie et de Beaucourt, I, 235 and 238.

83. Barnave, *Oeuvres*, I, 87.

84. Marie-Antoinette to Mercy, 25 August 1788, A & F, II, 211.

85. Arch. de la Marine, *Journal de Castries*, MS 182/7964, 1–2, I, fos 68 and 72–5.

86. Ibid., fos 76–7.

87. J.-L. Soulavie, *Historical and Political Memoirs of the Reign of Louis XVI from his Marriage to his Death*, London, 1802, 6 vols, IV, 204.

88. Joseph II to Mercy, 12 June 1781, A & F, I, 43.

89. Campan, *Mémoires*, I, 263–4.

90. Castries, *Journal*, I, 144.

91. A.N. K163 No. 13.12, cited In Padover, *Louis XVI*, 103 n.

92. Swedish dispatch to Gustavus, cited in Farr, *Marie-Antoinette and Count Fersen*, 98.

93. A & F, I, 71.

4 GROWING UNPOPULARITY, 1781–1785

1. Lenoir Papers, Ms 1423, mélanges, 39.

2. P. and P. Girault de Coursac, *Louis XVI et Marie-Antoinette. Vie conjugale, vie politique*, Paris, 1990, 674.
3. L. Petit de Bachaumont, *Mémoires secrets pour servir à l'histoire de la République des Lettres*, London, 1777–89, 36 vols, XXVII, 16 January 1784.
4. B. N. fonds Joly de Fleury n.a.f. 1438 ff. 217–23.
5. J. M. Augeard, *Mémoires secrets*, ed. E. Bavoux, 1866, 114.
6. D'Ormesson, Mss Journal, A.N. 144 A.P. 130 sections 55 and 56.
7. Louis XVIII, 'Réflections historiques sur Marie-Antoinette', *Revue des Deux Mondes* (1904), 9.
8. These went up to 1 January 1787.
9. D'Ormesson, Mss Journal, sections 64–5.
10. This was a technical crisis resulting from a faulty ratio between what the Bank paid for gold and for silver, resulting in a dearth of gold coins: piastres had to be hurriedly and expensively imported from Spain.
11. Archives des Affaires étrangères, MDF 1395 fo. 158 cited in M. Price, 'The Comte de Vergennes and the Baron de Breteuil: French Politics and Reform in the Reign of Louis XVI', PhD thesis, Cambridge University, 1988, 250–1.
12. E. Farr, *Marie-Antoinette and Count Fersen*, London, 2013, 119, deduces this from a letter Marie-Antoinette wrote to Maria-Christina on 16 November.
13. Castries, *Journal*, I, 205; marquis de Bombelles, *Journal*, ed. J. Grassion, F. Durif and J. Charon-Bordas, 4 vols, Geneva, 1978–98, I, 280.
14. Farr, *Marie-Antoinette and Count Fersen*, 110.
15. The comte de Saint-Priest, *Mémoires*, ed. baron de Barante, Paris, 1929, II, 72–3.
16. Coursac, *Louis XVI et Marie-Antoinette*, 606.
17. Ibid.
18. F. U. Wrangel, *Lettres de Axel Fersen à son père pendant la guerre d'Amérique*, Paris, 1929, 176, cited and translated by Farr, *Marie-Antoinette and Count Fersen*, 105.
19. A. Spawforth, *Versailles*, New York, 2008, 185–6.
20. P. Huisman and M. Jallut, *Marie-Antoinette*, New York, 1971, 158, cited by Spawforth, *Versailles*, 187.
21. Farr, *Marie-Antoinette and Count Fersen*, 112.
22. J. Hardman, *French Politics 1774–1789*, London, 1995, Appendix III.
23. Farr, *Marie-Antoinette and Count Fersen*, 111.
24. Bombelles, *Journal*, I, 271.
25. Farr, *Marie-Antoinette and Count Fersen*, 116.
26. The king to Vergennes, 23 May 1785, published by J.-L. Soulavie, *Mémoires historiques et politiques du règne de Louis XVI*, Paris, 1801, 6 vols, VI, 291.
27. Castries, *Journal*, I, 205.
28. Bombelles, *Journal*, I, 271.
29. Louis XVI to Vergennes, 1 November 1783, in *Louis XVI and the comte de Vergennes: Correspondence, 1774–1787*, ed. John Hardman and Munro Price, Oxford, 1998, 325.
30. Augeard, *Mémoires secrets*, 121; G. Maugras, *Lauzun*, Paris, 1907, 356–7.
31. Castries, *Journal*, I, 204; Castries transcribes the letter that his friend d'Ormesson shows him in oratio obliqua.
32. Ibid.
33. A.N. 144 A.P. 131 dossier 4.4.
34. A. J. Barnave, *Oeuvres*, Paris, 1843, 4 vols, I, 87.
35. C. A. de Calonne, *Réponse à l'écrit de M. Necker, publié en avril 1787*, London, 1788, 183 note.
36. *Correspondance intime du comte de Vaudreuil et du comte d'Artois*, ed. L. Pingaud, Paris, 1889, xiii–xiv.
37. Castries, *Journal*, I, 256.
38. H. Lüthy, *La Banque Protestante en France*, Paris, 1959–61, 2 vols, II, 686–711; L. Blanc, *Histoire de la Révolution française*, Paris, 1847–63, 12 vols, II, 151; P. Mansel, *Louis XVIII*, Stroud, 1981, 26–7; Augeard, *Mémoires secrets*, 136.

39. Castries, *Journal*, I, 256.

40. P. de Nolhac, *Marie-Antoinette dauphine*, Paris, 1929, 80; BN naf 10830, cited in M. Price, *Preserving the Monarchy: The comte de Vergennes*, 1774–1787, Cambridge, 1995, 147.

41. Augeard, *Mémoires secrets*, 137.

42. J. L. H. Campan, *Mémoires sur la vie privée de Marie-Antoinette*, Paris, 1823, 2 vols, I, 274.

43. Soulavie, *Mémoires historiques et politiques*, VI, 38–40.

44. J. Arnaud-Bouteloup, *Le rôle politique de Marie-Antoinette*, Paris, 1924, 184–5.

45. A. N. K164 no. 3, memorandum of Breteuil, 11 November 1784.

46. Castries, *Journal*, II, 258; *Louis XVI and the comte de Vergennes: correspondence, 1774–1787*, ed. John Hardman and Munro Price, Oxford, 1998, 353–4.

47. P. de Ségur, *Marie-Antoinette*, London, 2015, 257.

48. Farr, *Marie-Antoinette and Count Fersen*, 129.

49. Marie Antoinette to Vergennes, 30 January 1785, *Louis XVI and Vergennes: Correspondence*, 358.

50. Price, *Preserving the Monarchy*, 196.

51. Marie-Antoinette to Joseph II, 26 November 1784, cited in Arnaud-Bouteloup, *Role politique*, 139.

52. These anecdotes have been collected by Ségur, *Marie-Antoinette*, 238–9.

53. Talleyrand, *Mémoires*, 123.

54. Bombelles, *Journal*, I, 137.

55. Marie-Antoinette, *Correspondance de Marie-Antoinette*, ed. E. Lever, Paris, 2005, 491.

56. Bombelles, *Journal*, I, 169.

57. Ibid., 166.

58. Ibid., 208–9 and 156–7.

59. Fraser, *Marie-Antoinette*, 197.

60. Bombelles, *Journal*, I, 214.

61. Bombelles, *Journal*, II, 91.

62. Lever, *Correspondance*, 488–90.

63. A. Fraser, *Marie-Antoinette*, London, 2001, 207–8.

64. Marie-Antoinette to Madame de Tourzel, 24 July 1789, *Correspondance*, ed. Lever, 489.

65. Marie-Antoinette, *Lettres*, ed. M. La Rocheterie et le marquis de Beaucourt, Paris, 1895–6, 2 vols, II, 158.

5 THE DIAMOND NECKLACE AFFAIR, 1785–1786

1. P. and P. Girault de Coursac, *Louis XVI et Marie-Antoinette. Vie conjugale, vie politique*, Paris, 1990, 433–8.

2. Ibid., 811–14.

3. The term was originally applied by D. van Kley, *The Damiens Affair and the Unraveling of the Ancien Regime, 1750–1770*, Princeton, NJ, 1984.

4. Marquis de Bombelles, *Journal*, ed. J. Grassion, F. Derive and J. Charon-Bordas, 4 vols, Geneva, 1978–98, I, 193–4.

5. Ibid., 194.

6. R. Browne, 'The Diamond Necklace Affair Revisited', *Renaissance and Modern Studies*, 33 (1989).

7. F. Funck-Brentano, *L'affaire du collier*, Paris, 1903, 184.

8. J. L. H. Campan, *Mémoires sur la vie privée de Marie-Antoinette*, Paris, 1823, 2 vols, II, 9–10.

9. Bibliothèque de la ville de Paris, ms de la réserve, cited in Funck-Brentano, *Collier*, 238.

10. E. Farr, *Marie-Antoinette and Count Fersen*, London, 2013, 135.

11. The king to Vergennes, 16 August 1785, in *Louis XVI and the comte de Vergennes: Correspondence, 1774–1787*, ed. John Hardman and Munro Price, Oxford, 1998, 376.

12. Abbé de Véri, Archives Départementales de La Drôme (Valence), MSS Journal (unclassi-fied); Mss Cahier 140.

13. Published in J. Peuchet, *Archives de police de Paris*, Paris, 1838, 158–61.

14. Baron de Besenval, *Mémoires du baron de Besenval*, ed. F. de Barrière, Paris, 1846, 267.

15. The main source I have used for Rohan's interrogation is Castries' eye-witness account: Duc de Castries, *Papiers de famille*, Paris, 1978, 388 ff.

16. The king to Vergennes, 16 August 1785, *Louis XVI and Vergennes: Correspondence*, 376.

17. Miromesnil told Véri that Castries and Vergennes supported this proposal, Véri, Mss Cahier, 136.

18. Vergennes to Noailles, 10 October 1785, AAE C.P. Austria, 350 f. 228, cited in J.F. Labourdette, *Vergennes, ministre principal de Louis XVI*, Paris, 1990, 295–6; duc de Castries, *Papiers de famille*, Paris, 1978, 394–5.

19. Cited In Funck-Brentano, *Collier*, 261.

20. J.-L. Soulavie, *Mémoires historiques et politiques du règne de Louis XVI*, Paris, 1801, 6 vols, VI, 72.

21. Marie-Antoinette, *Correspondance de Marie-Antoinette*, ed. E. Lever, Paris, 2005, 444.

22. Lenoir Ms 1423, mélanges, 31–9, Bibliothèque municipal d'Orléans, MS 1421–3 (frag-mentary memoirs).

23. Louis XVIII, 'Réflexions historique sur Marie-Antoinette', *Revue des Deux Mondes* (1904), 7.

24. A & F, II, 32–6.

25. AAE CP Angleterre 556 ff. 282–83 cited in Labourdette, *Vergennes*, 299.

26. Mercy to Joseph II, 10 March 1786, A & F, II, 10.

27. Funck-Brentano, *Collier*, 302–4.

28. Marie-Antoinette to Mercy, Friday 19 May 1786, Marie-Antoinette, *Correspondance de Marie-Antoinette*, ed. E. Lever, Paris, 2005, 451.

29. Technically this was an *amende honorable* rather than an *amende sèche*, which implied infamy. L. Petit de Bachaumont, Mémoires secrets pour servir à l'histoire de la République des Lettres, London, 1777–89, 36 vols, XXXII, 78–9.

30. Funck-Brentano, Collier, 305.

31. Duc de Castries, *Papiers de famille*, Paris, 1978, 396; B. Stone, *The Parlement of Paris 1774–1789*, Chapel Hill, NC, 1981, 74–5; J.-C. Petitfils, *Louis XVI*, Paris, 2005, 510–11.

32. Vergennes to Adhémar, 5 June, AAE CP Angleterre, 556, fo. 294, quoted in Labourdette, *Vergennes*, 299–300.

33. Labourdette, *Vergennes*, 300–1.

34. The seven were Presidents de Gilbert, Rosambo and Lamoignon, and Conseillers Oursin, Pasquier, Delpeche and Barillon.

35. Lepeletier de Saint-Fargeau, Saron and Glatigny; A & F, II, 32–6.

36. Lenoir Ms 1423, mélanges, 3–5.

37. His 'commensal', a hark back to the medieval household when the king's personal servants, such as his almoner, enjoyed his board and lodging. Besenval, *Mémoires*, 275–6; Castries, *Papiers de famille*, 396.

38. That is the cordon bleu, of the Saint-Esprit.

39. Castries, *Papiers de famille*, 397.

40. Louis XVIII, 'Réflexions historiques sur Marie-Antoinette', 6.

41. Bachaumont, *Mémoires secrets*, XXXII, 94–5.

42. M. Lescure, ed., *Correspondance secrète sur Louis XVI . . .*, Paris, 1866, 2 vols, II, 46.

43. Campan, *Mémoires*, II, 25.

44. Alexander Pope, 'The Rape of the Lock'.

45. J.-L. Soulavie, *Mémoires historiques et politiques*, VI, 72.

46. Castries, *Papiers de famille*, 396; Stone, *The Parlement of Paris*, 74–5; Petitfils, *Louis XVI*, 510–11.

47. Bombelles, *Journal*, I, 282–3.

48. Farr, *Marie-Antoinette and Count Fersen*, 121–2.

49. Bombelles, *Journal*, I, 158, entry for 10 October 1782.

50. Véri, Mss Cahier 123.

51. Farr, *Marie-Antoinette and Count Fersen*, 142.
52. Mercy to Maria-Theresa, 15 June 1777, A & G, III, 50.
53. Mercy to Joseph II, 1 April 1786, A & F, II, 12–13.
54. Farr, *Marie-Antoinette and Count Fersen*, 145–6.
55. P. Huisman and M. Jallut, *Marie-Antoinette*, New York, 1971, 160; A. Spawforth, *Versailles*, New York, 2008, 189–90.
56. E. Farr, *I Love You Madly: Marie-Antoinette and Count Fersen, the Secret Letters*, London, 2016, 90.
57. E. Bimbinet, *La fuite de Louis XVI à Varennes*, Paris, 1868, appendix.
58. Comte de Saint-Priest, *Mémoires*, ed. baron de Barante, Paris, 1929, 80 and 92.

6 THE ASCENDANCY OF MARIE-ANTOINETTE, 1787–1788

1. Le Tellier, Mayor of Harfleur, *Voyage de Louis XVI dans sa Province de Normandie*, Paris, 1787, 88.
2. Duc de Castries, *Papiers de famille*, Paris, 1978, 396.
3. E.g. J. Félix, 'The Financial Origins of the French Revolution', in *The Origins of the French Revolution*, ed. P. Campbell, London, 2005, 35–62, 59–60.
4. Marquis de Bombelles, *Journal*, ed. J. Grassion, F. Durif and J. Charon-Bordas, 4 vols, Geneva, 1978–98, II, 96.
5. The précis, annotated by Calonne 'présenté au roi le 20 août 1786', survives only as an appendix to Calonne's *Réponse*, appendix, 79–89, and is based on a conflation of two manuscript versions then among Calonne's papers. The 'Observations sur l'époque à fixer' are in A.N. K677 no. 104 and are published in H. Glagau, *Reformversuche und Sturz des Absolutismus in Frankreich (1774–1788)*, Munich, 1908, 343–52.
6. Provinces that had retained the right to negotiate the level of taxation.
7. Provinces where taxes were assessed by royal officials.
8. Necker had set up pilot systems of devolved government in two administrative areas.
9. As former German territories, Alsace and Lorraine had customs barriers with France but not Germany.
10. Brittany was virtually exempt.
11. Royal legislation had to be registered in thirteen separate parlements, that of Paris covering just less than half the country.
12. A. Goodwin, 'Calonne, the Assembly of French Notables of 1787 and the Origins of the "Révolte Nobiliaire"', *English Historical Review*, CCLX (May 1946), 202–34, and CCLXI (September 1946), 329–77, 209.
13. A.N. K 164 no. 4, 'Objections et réponses', published by Glagau, *Reformversuche und Sturz*, 352–70.
14. Mercy to Joseph II, 20 August 1786, A & F, II, 40–1.
15. Abbé de Véri, Mss Cahier 109.
16. R. Lacour-Gayet, *Calonne*, Paris, 1963, 176–7.
17. Castries, *Journal*, II, 337–8.
18. A.N. K677 no. 108.
19. Mercy to Kaunitz, 10 March 1786, A & F, II, 11–12.
20. E. Waresquiel, *Juger la Reine*, Paris, 2016, 91.
21. Mercy to Kaunitz, 1 March 1787, A & F, II, 80–1.
22. J. Arnaud-Bouteloup, *Le rôle politique de Marie-Antoinette*, Paris, 1924, 164.
23. Mercy to Joseph II, 10 August 1782, A & F, I, 121.
24. Castries, *Journal*, II, 337.
25. Calonne to d'Angiviller, July 1787, A.N. 297 AP 3 no. 19.
26. Arsenal, MS 3978, 212.
27. Ibid.
28. See, e.g., a speech by Angran d'Allerai, Arsenal MS 3978, 215–16.
29. Bombelles, *Journal*, II, 177 n.
30. P. Chevallier, comte de Brienne, and Loménie de Brienne, *Journal de l'Assemblée des Notables de 1787*, ed. P. Chevallier, Paris, 1960, 44 and 50.

31. Ibid., 60.
32. A.N. 297 A.P. no. 119.
33. Lacour-Gayet, *Calonne*, 239.
34. F. Funck-Brentano, *L'affaire du collier*, Paris, 1903, 113–16; J. L. H. Campan, *Mémoires sur la vie privée de Marie-Antoinette*, Paris, 1823, 2 vols, II, 109.
35. De Brienne, *Journal*, ed. Chevallier, 64–5.
36. Ibid., 66–9.
37. Castries, *Journal*, II, 359.
38. De Brienne, *Journal*, ed. Chevallier, 47.
39. Comte de Brienne's diary, in ibid., 34.
40. Ibid., 57.
41. Comte de Saint-Priest, *Mémoires*, ed. baron de Barante, Paris, 1929, II, 79.
42. De Brienne, *Journal*, ed. Chevallier, 59 and 63.
43. Calonne to d'Angiviller, A.N. 297 A.P. no. 119; Castries, *Journal*, II, 355.
44. Toulouse's diary entry for 10 April, de Brienne, *Journal*, ed. Chevallier, 59.
45. Castries, *Journal*, II, 339, entry for 28 December 1786.
46. De Brienne, *Journal*, ed. Chevallier, xxii–xxviii, 84–7,103–6.
47. L. Petit de Bachaumont, *Mémoires secrets pour servir à l'histoire de la République des Lettres*, London, 1777–89, 36 vols, XXXV, 355.
48. De Brienne, *Journal*, ed. Chevallier, 59, 61.
49. Ibid., 59.
50. M. Lescure, ed., *Correspondance secrète sur Louis XVI . . .*, Paris, 1866, 2 vols, II, 131.
51. Castries, *Journal*, II, 363–6.
52. Ibid., 363, 4 May.
53. Ibid., 371.
54. De Brienne, *Journal*, ed. Chevallier 107.
55. Véri, Mss diary, Cahier 158.
56. Mme de Staël, *Considérations sur . . . la Révolution française*, op. posth, Paris, 1843, 97.
57. J. M. Augeard, *Mémoires secrets*, ed. E. Bavoux, 1866, 157–8.
58. Letter to the comtesse de Gramont, ed. A. Cans, *Revue Historique*, 60 (1902), 301–2.
59. Louis asked Brienne to have one memorandum ready for 5 p.m. to give him time to digest it between returning from hunting and the evening committees that started at 7 o'clock.
60. Marie-Antoinette to Joseph II, 16 May 1785, Marie-Antoinette, *Correspondance de Marie-Antoinette*, ed. E. Lever, Paris, 2005, 439.
61. Lescure, ed., *Correspondance secrète*, II, 108.
62. B. A. Luckner, 'The Role of the French Bishops in the Aristocratic Revolt of 1787–88', Manchester MA thesis, 1969, 154.
63. Bachaumont, *Mémoires secrets*, xxxv, 104.
64. Castries, *Journal*, II, 368.
65. *Mémoires du baron de Besenval*, ed. F. de Barrière, Paris, 1846, 321–2, 344.
66. E. Farr, *Marie-Antoinette and Count Fersen*, London, 2013, 149.
67. A. Foreman, *Georgiana, Duchess of Devonshire*, London, 1999, 195.
68. J. Necker, *De la Révolution française*, Paris, 1797, 3 vols, II, 5.
69. *Correspondance intime du comte de Vaudreuil et du comte d'Artois*, ed. L. Pingaud, Paris, 1889, 2 vols, I, xxiv.
70. P. de Nolhac, *Marie-Antoinette dauphine*, Paris, 1929, 198–200.
71. Farr, *Marie-Antoinette and Count Fersen*, 133.
72. Besenval, *Mémoires*, 345.
73. Mercy to Joseph II, 15 September 1787, A & F, II, 123.
74. 4 A.N. 297 A.P. 3 no. 114.
75. P.R.O. P.C. 125 no. 103.
76. J.-L. Soulavie, *Mémoires historiques et politiques du règne de Louis XVI*, Paris, 1801, 6 vols, VI, 246.
77. A & F, II, 4.

78. Besenval, *Mémoires*, 306.
79. Ibid., 305–6.
80. Farr, *Marie-Antoinette and Count Fersen*, 147.
81. Mercy, Dépêche d'office, 13 July 1787, A & F, II, 114.
82. *Correspondance de Marie-Antoinette*, ed. Lever, 458.
83. F. X. Audoin, *Histoire de l'Administration de la Guerre*, Paris, 1811, 4 vols, IV, 255–6, cited in J. Egret, La Pré-Révolution française 1787–1788, Paris, 1962, 50.
84. Marquis de Bouillé, *Souvenirs*, ed. P.-L. Kermaingant, Paris, 1906, 87.
85. M. Price, 'Lafayette, the Lameths and "Republican Monarchy", 1789–1791', forthcoming article, 8.
86. B. Stone, *The Parlement of Paris*, 1774–89, Chapel Hill, NC, 1981, 156.
87. Ibid.
88. *Malesherbes à Louis XVI ou les Avertissements de Cassandra, Mémoires inédits 1787–1788*, ed. V. André, Paris, 2010, 106; A & F, II, 141.
89. Letter to Joseph of 23 November 1787.
90. G. Sallier-Chaumont de Laroche, *Annales françaises depuis le commencement du règne de Louis XVI jusqu'aux états-géneraux, 1774–1789*, Paris, 1813, 128–9.
91. Marie-Antoinette to Joseph II, 23 November 1787, in Marie-Antoinette, *Lettres*, ed. M. de La Rocheterie et le marquis de Beaucourt, Paris, 1895–6, 2 vols, II, 108–9.
92. J. Flammermont, *Remonstrances du Parlement de Paris au XVIIIe siècle*, Paris 1888–98, 3 vols, III, 708; *Correspondance de Marie-Antoinette*, ed. Lever, 459.
93. M. Marion, *Le garde des sceaux Lamoignon*, Paris, 1905, passim.
94. A.N. 0'354 no. 102.
95. J. F. X. Droz, *Histoire du règne de Louis XVI*, Brussels, 1839, 2 vols, II, 97.
96. The king to Boisgelin, 15 July 1788, published in *Louis XVI, Marie-Antoinette et Mme Elizabeth, lettres et documents inédits*, ed. F. Feuillet de Conches, Paris, 1864–9, 6 vols, I, 203.
97. Bombelles, *Journal*, II, 213.
98. L. Gottschalk, *Lafayette between the American and French Revolution, 1783–1789*, Chicago, IL, 1950, 392.
99. M. Price, 'The comte de Vergennes and the baron de Breteuil', unpublished PhD thesis, University of Cambridge, 1988, 360–70.
100. Bombelles, *Journal*, II, 209.
101. Ibid., 215.
102. Ibid.
103. E. Bradby, *The Life of Barnave*, Oxford, 1915, 2 vols, I, 55.
104. Bombelles, *Journal*, II, 207.
105. A.N. 297 A.P. 3 no. 126, undated but August/September 1788, two draft letters, one addressed 'Sire', the other in the third person.
106. Miromesnil in conversation with the abbé de Véri, Mss Cahier 170.
107. Bombelles, *Journal*, II, 201.
108. Ibid., 205.
109. Véri, Mss Cahier 158.
110. Bombelles, *Journal*, II, 215–16. See also Thomas E. Kaiser, 'Who's Afraid of Marie-Antoinette? Diplomacy, Austrophobia, and the Queen', *French History*, 14 (2000), 241–71; idem, 'From the Austrian Committee to the Foreign Plot: Marie Antoinette, Austrophobia, and the Terror', *French Historical Studies*, 26 (2003), 579–617.
111. Campan, *Mémoires*, II, 31.
112. Véri's manuscript diary, cited in Arnaud-Bouteloup, *Marie-Antoinette*, 163. This corresponds with the now missing Cahier 166 of Véri's diary.
113. Bombelles, *Journal*, II, 207 and 227.
114. Véri, Mss diary, Cahier 167.
115. A.N. 297 A.P. 3 no. 126.
116. Véri, Mss diary, Cahier 163.

117. Baron de Besenval, *Mémoires du baron de Besenval*, ed. F. de Barrière, Paris, 1846, 343; Soulavie, *Mémoires historiques et politiques*, VI, 247–9 (Brienne's memoirs).
118. The relevant documents have been published by Feuillet de Conches, *Louis XVI*, I, 204–19.
119. Véri, Mss diary, Cahier 163.
120. Necker to Mercy, midnight 24 August, A & F, II, 210.
121. Bombelles, *Journal*, II, 240–1.
122. Farr, *Marie-Antoinette and Count Fersen*, 154–5.
123. Feuillet de Conches, *Louis XVI*, I, 217–18.
124. E.g., when Bertrand de Molleville asked Montmorin to read out in Council a memorandum on dismissing the Estates, Montmorin refused on the grounds that 'Necker would stop me and desire to have it communicated to himself before it was read, on which the King would order it to be delivered to him.' A. F. Bertrand de Molleville, *Last Year of the Reign of Louis XVI*, Boston, MA, 1909, 2 vols, I, 164.
125. Sallier, *Annales*, 126.
126. Véri, Mss diary, Cahier 158.
127. Bombelles, *Journal*, II, 227.

7 THE LAST YEAR AT VERSAILLES

1. A & F, II, 211.
2. *Mémoires du comte Alexander de Tilly*, Paris, 1828, 2 vols, I, 129.
3. J. Arnaud-Bouteloup, *Le rôle politique de Marie-Antoinette*, Paris, 1924, 168.
4. M. Lescure, ed., *Correspondance secrète sur Louis XVI . . .*, Paris, 1866, 2 vols, II, 294.
5. *Mémoires du comte Alexander de Tilly*, I, 150ff.
6. Lescure, *Correspondance secrète*, II, 346.
7. Extract from the abbé de Véri's Mss Journal (Cahier 165), published by the duc de Castries in *Revue de Paris*, November 1953, 84–6.
8. Véri, Mss Cahier 170.
9. Published in J.-L. Soulavie, *Mémoires historiques et politiques du règne de Louis XVI*, Paris, 1801, 6 vols, VI, 240–4. 'My preference was for a double representation for the third Estate and voting by head – as I had established in the provincial assemblies and was doing in all the provincial Estates that were being set up . . . those for Dauphiné had agreed and after my time were set up along the lines I indicated . . . Part of the kingdom would have been divided among provincial assemblies, with double representation and voting by head, and they would have nominated their deputies to the Estates-General; elections by the *baillages* would not have taken place.'
10. *Malesherbes à Louis XVI ou les Avertissements de Cassandra*, Mémoires inédits 1787–1788, ed. V. André, Paris, 2010, 147.
11. Ibid.
12. Soulavie, *Mémoires historiques et politiques*, VI, 242.
13. J. Egret, 'La seconde Assemblée des Notables', in *Annales Historiques de la Révolution française*, 1949, 193–228, 209.
14. A. J. Barnave, *Oeuvres*, Paris, 1843, 4 vols, I, 102.
15. Lescure, ed., *Correspondance secrète*, II, 330.
16. Ibid., 335.
17. Ibid., 313, entry for 19 December 1788.
18. Marie-Antoinette to Joseph II, 22 September 1784, Marie-Antoinette, *Correspondance de Marie-Antoinette*, ed. E. Lever, Paris, 2005, 409.
19. A. Chérest, *La chute de l'Ancien Régime*, 1787–9, 1884–6, 3 vols, II, 221; the details of the discussion preceding the Résultat are to be found in Barentin, *Mémoire autographe sur les derniers Conseils du Roi Louis XVI*, ed. M. Champion, Paris, 1844; and J. Necker, *De la Révolution française*, Paris, 1797, 87ff.

20. *Gazette de Leyde*, 2 January 1789; Comte de Saint-Priest, *Mémoires*, ed. baron de Barante, Paris, 1929, II, 77.

21. Bibliothèque municipale d'Orléans, Lenoir MS 1423, résidues, 122.

22. P.-V. Malouet, *Mémoires*, Paris, 1874, 2 vols, I, 220–1.

23. Article on Necker by Lally-Tollendal in the *Biographie-Michaud*.

24. Lescure, ed., *Correspondance secrète*, II, 328.

25. Véri, Mss Cahier 167.

26. C.-A. de Calonne, *Lettre au Roi*, London, 1789, 54.

27. Mercy to Joseph II, 2 April 1789, A & F, II, 230.

28. Mercy to Joseph II, 6 January 1789, ibid., 218.

29. Mercy to Joseph II, 22 February 1789, ibid., 223–4.

30. Lescure, ed., *Correspondance secrète*, II, 326–7 and 329.

31. A. F. Bertrand de Molleville, *Mémoires secrets pour servir à l'histoire de la dernière année du règne de Louis XVI*, roi de France, London 1797, 3 vols, I, 157–9.

32. Marquis de Bombelles, *Journal*, ed. J. Grassion, F. Durif and J. Charon-Bordas, 4 vols, Geneva, 1978–98, II, 293, entry for 4 April.

33. Lescure, ed., *Correspondance secrète*, II, 344.

34. This at least was the aim of Artois' best friend Vaudreuil, in de Bombelles, *Journal*, II, 314, entry for 13 May 1789.

35. Bombelles, *Journal*, II, 297; Véri, Mss Cahier 170.

36. Bombelles, *Journal*, II, 284; he encountered the queen there on 26 March.

37. Ibid., 299 and 302–3.

38. Saint-Priest, *Mémoires*, II, 79.

39. Bombelles, *Journal*, II, 303.

40. Véri, Mss Cahier 170.

41. These have been published in *La Révolution française*, LVI (1909), 193–8 and 318–29.

42. Lescure, ed., *Correspondance secrète*, II, 348.

43. Bombelles, *Journal*, II, 306.

44. Louis XVI to Necker *c.* 1 May 1789, J. Hardman, ed., *The French Revolution Sourcebook*, London and New York, 1999, 91.

45. Mercy to Joseph II, 17 December 1788.

46. Arnaud-Bouteloup, *Marie-Antoinette*, 187.

47. Marie-Antoinette to Mercy, 27 (February 1789), in *Louis XVI, Marie-Antoinette et Mme Elizabeth, lettres et documents inédits*, ed. F. Feuillet de Conches, Paris, 1864–9, 6 vols, I, 221–2.

48. Etats-Généraux, G. Lefèbvre et al., eds, *Recueil de documents relatifs aux Etats-Généraux de 1789*, Paris, 1953–70, 4 vols, I (2), 94.

49. Mercy to Joseph II, 4 July 1789, A & F, 253.

50. Lescure, ed., *Correspondance secrète*, II, 361–2.

51. Bombelles, *Journal*, II, 331.

52. C. Chapman and J. Dormer, *Elizabeth and Georgiana*, London, 2002, 100.

53. E. Farr, *Marie-Antoinette and Count Fersen*, London, 2013, 160.

54. Comtesse d'Adhémar, *Souvenirs sur Marie Antoinette . . .*, Paris, 1836, 4 vols, quoted in N. Hampson, Prelude to Terror, Oxford, 1988, 43. These memoirs are ghosted and perhaps apocryphal but seem to summarize the situation.

55. Necker, *Révolution française*, I, 286; G. de Montjoie, *Seconde partie de la conspiration de L-P-J d'Orleans, surnommé Egalité*, Paris, 1834, 44.

56. Adhémar, *Mémoires*, III, 156–7.

57. Comte d'Angiviller, *Mémoires*, Copenhagen, 1939, 152.

58. Necker, *Révolution française*, I, 200.

59. *Les intrigues du cabinet de la duchesse de Polignac etc*, London, 1790, cited in H. Fleischmann, Madame de Polignac et la cour galante de Marie-Antoinette, Paris, 1910, 241.

60. Necker, *Révolution française*, I, 253.

61. Letter transcribed in Adhémar, *Mémoires*, III, 171–5.

62. Marie-Antoinette to Mercy, 3 February 1791.
63. D'Angiviller, *Mémoires*, 154–5.
64. Montmorin took a similar view; A.N. K 679 nos 86 and 87–8 for their memoranda for the king.
65. J. L. H. Campan, *Mémoires sur la vie privée de Marie-Antoinette*, Paris, 1823, 2 vols, II, 232.
66. Vaudreuil, *Correspondance intime du Comte de Vaudreuil et du Comte d'Artois*, ed. L. Pingaud, 1889, 2 vols, I, xxvii–xxviii.
67. Mercy to Joseph II, 4 July 1789.
68. Saint-Priest, *Mémoires*, II, 83.
69. P. Caron, 'La Tentative de contre-révolution de juin–juillet 1789', *Revue d'histoire moderne*, 8 (1906), 5–34 and 649–78. Caron draws a perverse conclusion from his own evidence.
70. E. Farr, *I Love You Madly: Marie-Antoinette and Count Fersen, the Secret Letters*, London, 2016, 103–4. Broglie succeeded Puységur as war minister on 12 July, so Fersen, presumably informed by Marie-Antoinette as to what was afoot, wrote to them both via Marie-Antoinette to be sure.
71. Malouet, *Mémoires*, I, 250.
72. Barnave, *Oeuvres*, I, 108–9.
73. Journal de Fersen, in M. Klinckowström, *Le comte de Fersen et la cour de France*, Paris, 1878, 2 vols, II, 6.
74. J. N. Moreau, *Mes souvenirs*, Paris, 1898–1901, 2 vols, II, 439–41.
75. Comte de Paroy, *Mémoires*, Paris, 1895, 42.
76. Diane de Polignac, *Journal d'Italie et de Suisse*, 1789 (Gallica download), 11–13.
77. Marquis de La Fayette, *Mémoires*, Paris, 1837, 6 vols, II, 362; comte d'Allonville, *Mémoires secrets de 1770 à 1830*, Paris, 1838–45, 6 vols, II, 68.
78. Soulavie, *Mémoires historiques et politiques*, VI, 32–3.
79. Lettre de M. Le duc de Polignac à M. De Cazalès, 14 March 1791, Paris, no date [1791], cited in Fleischmann, *Madame de Polignac*, 53.
80. Campan, *Mémoires*, II, 238.
81. J. F. X. Droz, *Histoire du règne de Louis XVI*, Brussels, 1839, 2 vols, II, 345.
82. Saint-Priest, *Mémoires*, II, 84.
83. E.g. *Le vrai caractère de Marie-Antoinette*, cited in Fleischmann, *Madame de Polignac*, 59.
84. Ibid., 61–6.
85. Louis XVI to Madame de Polignac, 29 July 1789, Noel Chavaray Catalogue no. 331, January 1904 no. 51214, 100 francs, cited in Fleischmann, *Madame de Polignac*, 91, who transcribes Choisy as Noisy.
86. Diane de Polignac, *Journal*, 14–15.
87. *Dialogue entre M. Necker et Mme. de Polignac*, London, 1789; *Entretien de M. Necker avec la comtesse de Polignac*, London, 1789.
88. Lafayette, *Mémoires*, II, 268.
89. Marie-Antoinette to Mercy, in *Lettres*, ed. M. de La Rocheterie et le marquis de Beaucourt, Paris, 1895–6, 2 vols, II, 143.
90. M. Price, 'Lafayette, the Lameths and "Republican Monarchy", 1789–1791', forthcoming article, 3.
91. Barnave, *Oeuvres*, I, 101–3.
92. See e.g. Saint-Priest, *Mémoires*, I, 229.
93. Malouet, *Mémoires*, I, 304–5.
94. Marie-Antoinette to Mercy, 3 February 1791.
95. Duchesse de Tourzel, *Mémoires*, ed. duc des Cars, Paris, 1904, 2 vols, I, 3.
96. *Procès de Marie-Antoinette*, Paris 1793, reissued 1865, 20.
97. Lafayette, *Mémoires*, II, 329 n.2.
98. We have based our account of the October Days on Saint-Priest, *Mémoires*, II, 8–23.
99. Ibid., 10–11.

100. Lafayette, *Mémoires*, II, 341.
101. Saint-Priest, *Mémoires*, II, 18–19.
102. Ibid., 90.
103. Farr, *Marie-Antoinette and Count Fersen*, 17, citing Lord Holland, Foreign Reminiscences, London, 1855.
104. Published in A. Mousset, *Un témoin ignoré de la Révolution, le comte de Fernan Nunez*, 1924, 228.

8 APPEASEMENT AND PLANS FOR RESISTANCE

1. La Marck to Mercy, 23 August 1791, in M. A. de Bacourt, ed., *Correspondance entre le comte de Mirabeau et le comte de la Marck*, Paris, 1851, 2 vols, II, 292.
2. The best book on the *monarchiens* is R. Griffiths, *Le centre perdu, Malouet et les 'monarchiens'*, Grenoble, 1988, esp. 55–80.
3. D. Wick, 'The Court Nobility and the French Revolution: The Example of the Society of Thirty', *Eighteenth Century Studies*, XIII (1980), 263–84.
4. J. Arnaud-Bouteloup, *Le rôle politique de Marie-Antoinette*, Paris, 1924, 213.
5. The first king of Louis' dynasty, Hugh, comte de Paris, elected king of the French in 987, was nicknamed Capet from his style of hat.
6. A. J. Barnave, *Oeuvres*, Paris, 1843, 4 vols, I, 174–6.
7. A reference to the *parlementaire théorie de classes*, which claimed that each parlement was a part of an original whole.
8. Ibid.
9. Marquis de Bouillé, *Mémoires*, ed. S. A. Berville and J. F. Barrière, Paris, 1821, 165–9 and 174.
10. Bacourt, *Mirabeau*, I, 127–8.
11. Cited in M. Price, 'Lafayette, the Lameths and "Republican monarchy", 1789–1791', forthcoming article, 16.
12. Comte de Saint-Priest, *Mémoires*, ed. baron de Barante, Paris, 1929, II, 91.
13. Marie-Antoinette to Madame de Polignac, in Marie-Antoinette, *Lettres*, ed. M. La Rocheterie et le marquis de Beaucourt, Paris, 1895–6, 2 vols, II, 157 ; A. Söderjhelm, *Fersen et Marie-Antoinette. Correspondance et journal intime du comte Axel von Fersen*, Paris, 1930, 158; E. Farr, *Marie-Antoinette and Count Fersen*, London, 2013, 173–4.
14. Marquis de La Fayette, *Memoires*, Paris, 1837, 6 vols, III, 155–7.
15. S. Padover, *The Life and Death of Louis XVI*, London, 1965, 193.
16. A. Spawforth, *Versailles*, New York, 2008, 140.
17. Marie-Antoinette, *Lettres*, ed., La Rocheterie and de Beaucourt, II, 147.
18. M. Price, *The Fall of the Monarchy: Louis XVI, Marie-Antoinette and the baron de Breteuil*, London, 2002, 121.
19. Marie-Antoinette, ed., *Lettres*, ed., La Rocheterie and de Beaucourt, II, 148.
20. Ibid., 159.
21. Ibid., 168, letter to Leopold II, 1 May 1790.
22. Ibid., 146.
23. Madame Elizabeth, *Correspondance*, ed. F. Feuillet de Conches, Paris, 1868, I, 145.
24. J. F. X. Droz, *Histoire du règne de Louis XVI*, Brussels, 1839, 2 vols, II, 121.
25. Bouillé, *Mémoires*, 104–5.
26. L. Gottschalk, *Lafayette in the French Revolution*, Chicago, IL, 1973, 231.
27. Ibid., 325–6; *Correspondance* de Louis XVI, ed. Feuillet de Conches, IV, 40–1, for Esterhazy's account.
28. Extract from Mirabeau's 9th Note for the Court, Bacourt, Mirabeau, II, 196.
29. See especially the 8th and 28th notes, Bacourt, *Mirabeau*, I, 355 and 424.
30. Marie-Antoinette *Lettres*, ed., La Rocheterie and de Beaucourt II, 193.
31. The queen to Mercy, 15 August 1790.
32. Mirabeau to La Marck, 4 June 1790, in Bacourt, *Mirabeau*, I, 331.
33. The King to Bouillé, 1 September 1790, published in A.P. LIV, 513–14.

34. This is the title of chapter 15 of Gottschalk's *Lafayette in the French Revolution*.
35. Bouillé, son of the general, *Souvenirs*, Paris, 1906, 180.
36. R. M. von Klinckowström, *Le comte de Fersen et la cour de France, 1877–8*, 2 vols, II, 236.
37. A receipt exists for furniture for Compiègne 'for the estates' dated December 1790, in I. Dunlop, *Marie-Antoinette*, London, 1993, 246.
38. Marie-Antoinette to Mercy, 12 June 1790, Marie-Antoinette, *Correspondance de Marie-Antoinette*, ed. E. Lever, Paris, 2005, 510.
39. J. M. Roberts, *French Revolution Documents*, Oxford, 1966, I, 291.
40. Price, *The Fall of the Monarchy*, 116.
41. Cited in P. and P. Girault de Coursac, *Enquête sur le procès du roi Louis XVI*, Paris, 1982, 302.
42. F. de Fontanges, *La Fuite du Roi* (Gallica online) 74–7.
43. Axel von Fersen, *Diary and Correspondence*, trans. K. Wormely, ed. G. Fortescue, Boston, MA, 1909, 90, editor's note.
44. Fersen to Taube in ibid., 91.
45. Ibid., 93.
46. Ibid., 474–5.
47. Duchesse de Tourzel, *Mémoires*, ed. duc des Cars, Paris, 1904, 2 vols, I, 302; Bacourt, *Mirabeau*, I, 390, and II, 311; Marie-Antoinette, *Lettres*, ed. La Rocheterie et Beaucourt, II, 23.
48. A. Caiani, *Louis XVI and the French Revolution 1789–1792*, Cambridge, 2012, 95.
49. Tourzel, *Mémoires*, ed. duc des Cars, II, 274.
50. Fersen, *Diary and Correspondence*, 94.
51. Marie-Antoinette to Mercy, 20 April 1791, in *Correspondance*, ed. Lever, 528.
52. La Marck to the queen, 10 p.m. 21 April; Fontanges to La Marck, also 21 April, Bacourt, *Mirabeau*, II, 273.
53. J. L. H. Campan, *Mémoires sur la vie privée de Marie-Antoinette*, Paris, 1823, 2 vols, II, 139.
54. Montmorin to La Marck, 23 April 1791, in Bacourt, *Mirabeau*, II, 277.
55. J. Félix, *Louis XVI et Marie-Antoinette*, Paris, 2006, 554–5.
56. Marie-Antoinette to Mercy, 20 April 1791, in *Correspondance*, ed., Lever, 528.
57. Bacourt, *Mirabeau*, II, 199, 49th note for the court.
58. 'The lower portion of the people see only that they are reckoned with,' Louis told his émigré brothers, 'the bourgeoisie sees nothing above them. Vanity is satisfied.' Louis XVI, *Correspondance*, ed. F. Feuillet de Conches, II, 365–75.
59. Barnave, *Oeuvres*, I, iv–ix.
60. La Marck's Introduction, in Bacourt, *Mirabeau*, I, 155.
61. Georges Michon, *Adrien Duport et le parti feuillant*, Paris, 1924, 181–296.
62. Bacourt, *Mirabeau*, II, 283.
63. La Marck, *Mirabeau*, king to the queen, December 1790, Bacourt, Mirabeau, II, 183.
64. Bacourt, *Mirabeau*, I, 162–3, and II, 100, La Marck to Mercy, 30 December 1790.

9 THE FLIGHT TO VARENNES

1. E. Farr, *Marie-Antoinette and Count Fersen*, London, 2013, 77 and 188.
2. F. de Fontanges, *La fuite du Roi* (Gallica download), 84.
3. Duchesse de Tourzel, *Mémoires*, ed. duc de Cars, Paris, 1904, 2 vols, I, 324–5; her eyewitness account forms the basis of this section.
4. M. Klinckowström, *Le comte de Fersen et la cour de France*, Paris, 1878, 2 vols, I, 132, cited in Farr, *Marie-Antoinette and Count Fersen*, 191–2.
5. Farr, *Marie-Antoinette and Count Fersen*, 192.
6. M. Price, *The Fall of the Monarchy: Louis XVI, Marie-Antoinette and the Baron de Breteuil*, London, 2002, 172.

7. Farr, *Marie-Antoinette and Count Fersen*, 189.
8. Fontanges, *Fuite*, 91.
9. From the minutes drawn up by the Municipality of Varennes and published as an appendix to E. Bimbenet, *La fuite de Louis XVI à Varennes*, Paris, 1868.
10. J. L. H. Campan, *Mémoires sur la vie privée de Marie-Antoinette*, Paris, 1823, 2 vols, II, 50.
11. Comtesse de Boigne, *Mémoires*, Paris, 1982, 2 vols, 1, 83.
12. Cited in Price, *Fall of the Monarchy*, 183.
13. The king to Bouillé, 3 July 1791, *Louis XVI, Marie Antoinette et Mme Elizabeth, lettres et documents inédits*, ed. F. Feuillet de Conches, 1864–9, 6 vols, IV, 459.
14. Théodore de Lameth, *Notes et souvenirs*, ed. E. Welvert, Paris, 1913, 224–5 and 388.
15. F. de Fontanges, *L'arrestation de la famille royale à Varennes* (Gallica download), 111.
16. Tourzel, *Mémoires*, 1, 327.
17. Klinckowström, *Fersen*, 8.
18. N. Hampson, *Prelude to Terror*, Oxford, 1988, 174.
19. Published in M. Mortimer-Ternaux, *Histoire de la Terreur*, Paris, 1862–81, 8 vols, I, 353–1.
20. G. Lenotre, *Le drame de Varennes*, 39th edn, Paris, 1924, 237.
21. A. J. Barnave, Oeuvres, Paris, 1843, 4 vols, I, *Introduction à la Révolution française*, 130.
22. Ibid., 130–1.
23. Barnave to Marie-Antoinette, 28 August 1791, Marie-Antoinette, *Correspondance de Marie-Antoinette*, ed. E. Lever, Paris, 2005, 589.
24. Lenotre, *Varennes*, 233–4.
25. Barnave, *Oeuvres*, I, Introduction, chapter 11, 98–109.
26. E. Burke, *Reflections on the Revolution in France*, ed. L. G. Mitchell, Oxford, 1993, 74 and 76.
27. Campan, *Mémoires*, II, 154.
28. *Correspondance de Marie-Antoinette*, ed. Lever, 611–12.
29. Barnave to Marie Antoinette, 25 July 1791, in ibid., 560–1.
30. For an excellent discussion of this see T. C. W. Blanning, *The Origins of the French Revolutionary Wars*, New York, 1986, 101–3.
31. Barnave, Oeuvres, I, 189–95.
32. M. A. de Bacourt, ed., *Correspondance entre le comte de Mirabeau et le comte de la Marck*, Paris, 1851, 2 vols, II, 205.
33. Barnave, *Oeuvres*, I, 194.
34. Ibid., 80.
35. Campan, *Mémoires*, II, 152.
36. Note by Marie-Antoinette, Marie-Antoinette, *Correspondance de Marie-Antoinette*, ed. E. Lever, Paris, 2005, 550.
37. A. Lamartine, *Histoire des Girondins*, Paris, 1847, 8 vols, I, 160.
38. A.N. KK 375.
39. A.N. 440 AP/1, decoded and translated by Farr, Marie-Antoinette and Count Fersen, 202.
40. Klinckowström, *Le comte de* Fersen, 5.
41. A. Söderjhelm, Fersen et Marie-Antoinette: *Correspondance et journal intime du comte Axel von Fersen*, Paris, 1930, 229.
42. Klinckowström, *Le comte de Fersen*, 1 (my italics).
43. Note by Marie-Antoinette, Marie-Antoinette, *Correspondance de Marie-Antoinette*, ed. E. Lever, Paris, 2005, 553.
44. A.N. 440/AP/1, translated by Farr, Marie-Antoinette and Count Fersen, 207, who correctly dates this as 1791 not 1792.
45. Marie-Antoinette, *Lettres*, ed. M. de La Rocheterie et le marquis de Beaucourt, Paris, 1895–6, 2 vols, II, 259–60.
46. Bacourt, *Correspondance*, II, 294.
47. *Biographie de Bruxelles*, cited by Mme Campan's editor, 155ff.

48. The view of G. Michon, *Adrien Duport et le parti feuillant, Paris*, 1924, the best account of the Revision despite Michon's hostility to the king and the triumvirs.
49. Marie-Antoinette to Barnave, 7 August, in *Correspondance de Marie-Antoinette*, ed. Lever, 574.
50. Barnave to Marie Antoinette, 28 August, in ibid., 587–92.
51. The queen to Barnave, 25 August, Marie-Antoinette, *Correspondance de Marie-Antoinette*, ed. E. Lever, Paris, 2005, 586.
52. Marie-Antoinette to Mercy, 26 August 1791.
53. Marie-Antoinette to Mercy, 12 September, in *Correspondance de Marie-Antoinette*, ed. Lever, 608.
54. J. Flammermont, 'La correspondance de Pellenc avec les comtes de La Marck et Mercy', *Revue de la Révolution française*, 16 (1889), 481–502.
55. J. Arnaud-Bouteloup, *Le rôle politique de Marie-Antoinette*, Paris, 1924, 280–1.
56. Marie-Antoinette to Mercy, *Lettres*, ed. La Rocheterie et de Beaucourt, II, 270–81, 16–26 August and 5 September 1791.
57. J. Roberts and J. Hardman eds, *French Revolution Documents*, Oxford, 1966–73, 2 vols, I, 347–66, for the text of the Constitution and Louis' speech.
58. Archives of Austria, Frankreich 15 Hoffcorrespondenz, 7, cited in P. and P. Girault de Coursac, eds, *Louis XVI a la parole*, Paris, 1989, 270.
59. Price, *Fall of the Monarchy*, 224–5.
60. Marie-Antoinette to Mercy, 12 June 1790, in *Correspondance de Marie-Antoinette*, ed. Lever, 510.
61. Blanning, *Origins of the French Revolutionary Wars*, 86–7.
62. P. de Ségur, *Marie-Antoinette*, London, 2015, 340.
63. Farr, *Marie-Antoinette and Count Fersen*, 209 (my italics).
64. See below, p. 260.
65. R. Griffiths, *Le centre perdu, Malouet et les 'monarchiens'*, Grenoble, 1988, 104.
66. Campan, *Mémoires*, II, 150.

10 'MARIE-ANTOINETTE WILL BECOME QUEEN OF FRANCE AGAIN'

1. Gustavus III to Marie-Antoinette, 22 December 1791, Axel von Fersen, *Diary and Correspondence*, trans. K. Wormely, ed. G. Fortescue, Boston, MA, 1909, 216–17.
2. *Marie-Antoinette, Fersen et Barnave*, ed. O.-G. Heidenstam, Paris, 1913, 149.
3. J. L. H. Campan, *Mémoires sur la vie privée de Marie-Antoinette*, Paris, 1823, 2 vols, II, 152.
4. M. Price, *The Fall of the Monarchy: Louis XVI, Marie-Antoinette and the Baron de Breteuil*, London, 2002, 197–9.
5. A. J. Barnave, *Oeuvres*, Paris, 1843, 4 vols, I, 141.
6. A. F. Bertrand de Molleville, *Mémoires secrets pour servir à l'histoire de la dernière année du règne de Louis XVI, roi de France*, London, 1797, 3 vols, I, 208. But Narbonne countered: 'Yes, but while I use every means of making the Constitution succeed, you endeavour to have it executed in such a manner as may prove to the nation that it can never work.'
7. Barnave to Marie-Antoinette, 30 October, Marie-Antoinette, *Correspondance de Marie-Antoinette*, ed. E. Lever, Paris, 2005, 656.
8. Barnave to Marie-Antoinette, 27 October, Marie-Antoinette, *Correspondance de Marie-Antoinette*, ed. E. Lever, Paris, 2005, 653.
9. Molleville, *Mémoires secrets*, I, 359.
10. Ibid., 346. This was due to his position as Keeper of the Seals – chancellor he could not be because through all the turmoil of the Revolution, Maupeou refused to resign his post.
11. J. Hardman, *French Politics 1774–1789*, London, 1995, 170–5.
12. Molleville, *Mémoires secrets*, I, 312.
13. Ibid., II, 20.
14. Archives Parlementaires, LIV, 362–3.

15. Molleville, *Mémoires secrets*, I, 218.
16. Barnave, *Oeuvres*, I, 151.
17. Pellenc to La Marck, 12 November 1791, in M. A. Bacourt ed., *Correspondance entre le comte de Mirabeau et le comte de la Marck*, Paris, 1851, 2 vols, II, 340.
18. Archives Parlementaires, XLVIII, 482–3.
19. Marie-Antoinette to Barnave, 14 November, Marie-Antoinette, *Correspondance de Marie-Antoinette*, ed. E. Lever, Paris, 2005, 673.
20. Molleville, *Mémoires secrets*, I, 251.
21. For the question of the uniform, see *Marie-Antoinette, Fersen et Barnave*, ed. Heidenstam, 185–201.
22. Barnave, *Oeuvres*, I, v.
23. M. Klinckowström, *Le comte de Fersen et la cour de France*, Paris, 1878, 2 vols, I, 269, Marie- Antoinette to Fersen, 7 December 1791.
24. A.N. C221 160 (148) pièce 19, quoted in P. and P. Girault de Coursac, eds, *Louis XVI a la parole*, Paris, 1989, 276.
25. Duchesse de Tourzel, *Mémoires*, ed. duc des Cars, Paris, 1904, 2 vols, II, 29.
26. Klinckowström, *Le comte de Fersen*, II, 7.
27. Barnave to Marie-Antoinette, 5 November, Marie-Antoinette, *Correspondance de Marie-Antoinette*, ed. E. Lever, Paris, 2005, 664–6.
28. Marie-Antoinette to Barnave, 4 December, Marie-Antoinette, *Correspondance de Marie-Antoinette*, ed. E. Lever, Paris, 2005, 718.
29. Molleville, *Mémoires secrets*, I, 227–8.
30. G. Michon, *Adrien Duport et le parti feuillant*, Paris, 1924, 349.
31. Ibid., 380.
32. P. L. Roederer, *Chronique de cinquante jours*, Paris, 1832, 79.
33. A.A.E., Autriche, 363ff 531 f. 34, cited in P. and P. Girault de Coursac, *Enquête sur le procès du roi Louis XVI*, Paris, 1982, 373.
34. J. Chaumié, *Le réseau d'Antraigues et la Contre-Révolution*, Paris, 1965, 147.
35. A.A.E., Trèves, Sup. 4, f. 22, cited in Coursac, *Enquête*, 338.
36. L. C. Bigot de Saint-Croix, *Histoire de la conspiration du 10 août 1792*, London, 1793, 80, 87, 88.
37. *Correspondance de Marie-Antoinette*, ed. E Lever, Paris, 2005, 737.
38. Ibid., 734 n. 1.
39. Marie-Antoinette to Mercy, 15 December 1791, in ibid., 735–6.
40. J. Flammermont, *Négotiations secrètes de Louis XVI et du baron de Breteuil avec la cour de Berlin* (décembre 1791–juillet 1792), Paris, 1885, 17 and n.
41. T. C. W. Blanning, *The Origins of the French Revolutionary Wars*, London, 1986, 89.
42. J. Hardman, ed., *The French Revolution Sourcebook*, London and New York, 1999, 141.
43. Comte de Fersen, *Journal*, in Klinckowström, Le comte de Fersen, II, 13; Fersen's diary entry for 13 March 1792.
44. Bacourt, *Correspondance* de Mirabeau, 338.
45. Molleville, *Mémoires secrets*, I, 348.
46. Michon, *Adrien Duport*, 486.
47. Campan, *Mémoires*, II, 204.
48. Ibid., 205.
49. Marie-Antoinette to Barnave, 3 January 1792, in *Correspondance de Marie-Antoinette*, ed. Lever, 751–2.
50. Ibid., 868.
51. Barnave to Marie-Antoinette, 5 January 1792, in ibid., 753–6.
52. Barnave, *Oeuvres*, I, 142.
53. Ibid., 212.
54. Barnave to Marie-Antoinette, 5 January 1792, in *Correspondance de Marie-Antoinette*, ed. Lever, 753–6.
55. Campan, *Mémoires*, II, 268–89; Molleville, *Mémoires secrets*, II, 20.
56. A. Söderjhelm, *Fersen et Marie-Antoinette. Correspondance et journal intime du comte Axel von Fersen*, Paris, 1930, 229.

57. E. Farr, *Marie-Antoinette and Count Fersen*, London, 2013, 219, and idem, *I Love You Madly: Marie-Antoinette and Count Fersen, the Secret Letters*, London, 2016, 238.
58. A. Fraser, *Marie-Antoinette*, London, 2001, 338.
59. Klinckowström, *Le comte de Fersen*, II, 7.
60. P. de Ségur, *Marie-Antoinette*, London, 2015, 335.
61. Campan, *Mémoires*, II, 221.
62. Cited in Ségur, *Marie-Antoinette*, 338.
63. Molleville, *Mémoires secrets*, I, 363.
64. [Alexandre] de Lameth to Pellenc, undated but c. 15 March, cited in H. Glagau, *Die französische Legislative . . . 1791–1792*, Berlin, 1896, 301.
65. Klinckowström, *Le comte de Fersen*, II, 12.
66. Mercy to Kaunitz, 7 January 1792, published in Glagau, *Die französische Legislative*, 279–83.
67. Barnave, *Oeuvres*, I, 104–95.
68. Price, *Fall* of the Monarchy, 238.
69. *Louis XVI, Marie Antoinette et Mme Elizabeth, lettres et documents inédits*, ed. F. Feuillet de Conches, Paris, 1864–9, 6 vols, IV, 296–303.
70. Pellenc to La Marck, 14 March 1792, appendix to Glagau, *Die französische Legislative*, 298.
71. Ibid., 296, 298, 318.
72. Pellenc to La Marck, 14 March 1792, in ibid., 297.
73. Campan, *Mémoires*, II, 202–3.
74. Pellenc to La Marck, 14 March 1792, in Glagau, *Die französische Legislative*, 298–9.
75. Michon, *Adrien Duport*, appendix: Correspondance inédite de Barnave, 493, letter to Duport, 4 March 1792, and to Théodore de Lameth, 12 May 1792, 497.
76. J. Flammermont, 'La correspondance de Pellenc avec les comtes de La Marck et Mercy', *Revue de la Révolution française*, 16 (1889), 481–502, 400.
77. M. Price, 'Lafayette, the Lameths and "Republican Monarchy", 1789–1791', forthcoming article, 14.
78. Pellenc to La Marck, 14 January 1792, in Glagau, *Die französische Legislative*, appendix, 286.
79. A.P. LIV, 488.
80. Pellenc to La Marck, 2 April 1792, in Glagau, *Die französische Legislative*, 300.
81. A.P. LV, 539.
82. Madame Roland, *Mémoires*, Paris, 2004, 230.
83. B.N. 40 Lb, 10536.
84. Glagau, *Die französische Legislative*, 312.
85. Bigot, *Histoire de la conspiration*, 95–6.
86. Campan, *Mémoires*, II, 192.
87. Blanning, *Origins* of the French Revolution, 118.
88. M. Lescure, ed., *Correspondance secrète sur Louis XVI . . .*, Paris, 1866, 2 vols, II, 546.

11 THE FALL OF THE MONARCHY

1. Duchesse de Tourzel, *Mémoires*, ed. duc des Cars, Paris, 1904, 2 vols, II, 46.
2. J. Michelet, *Histoire de la Révolution française*, ed. G. Walter, Paris, 1952, 2 vols, I, 881–2.
3. Alexandre de Lameth to Barnave, 13 April, in G. Michon, *Adrien Duport et le parti feuillant*, Paris, 1924, 494,
4. Published in H. Glagau, *Die franzosiche Legislative . . . 1791–1792*, Berlin, 1896, 313.
5. M. Klinckowström, *Le comte de Fersen et la cour de France*, Paris, 1878, 2 vols, II, 305.
6. E. de Waresquiel, *Juger la Reine*, Paris, 2016, 169.
7. Marie-Antoinette, *Correspondance de Marie-Antoinette*, ed. E. Lever, Paris, 2005, 760–1.
8. Pellenc to La Marck, 2 June 1792, in J. Flammermont, 'La correspondance de Pellenc avec les comtes de La Marck et Mercy', *Revue de la Révolution française*, 16 (1889), 481–502, 493.

9. J. L. H. Campan, *Mémoires sur la vie privée de Marie-Antoinette*, Paris, 1823, 2 vols, II, 208–9.

10. A. F. Bertrand de Molleville, *Mémoires secrets pour servir à l'histoire de la dernière année du règne de Louis XVI, roi de France*, London, 1797, 3 vols, II, 188.

11. Barnave to Dumas, undated but c. June 1792, in G. Michon, *Adrien Duport et le parti feuillant*, Paris, 1924, 501, appendix containing some of Barnave's correspondence.

12. Letters of 27 June and 31 July 1792, published in Glagau, *Die französische Legislative*, 339 and 361.

13. Mercy to Kaunitz, 27 June 1792, and abbé Louis to Mercy, 26 June, published in ibid., 339 and 342.

14. C. F. Dumouriez, *Mémoires*, Paris, 1822–3, 4 vols, II, 278–9 and 294–6.

15. F. Hue, *Dernières années de Louis XVI*, 3rd edn, Paris, 1860, 282; Mallet du Pan dates this note to 3 August; P. and P. Girault de Coursac, eds, *Louis XVI a la parole*, Paris, 1989, 302.

16. P. de Ségur, *Marie-Antoinette*, London, 2015, 361.

17. P. L. Roederer, *Chronique de cinquante jours*, Paris, 1832, 50–3 and 76–8; Dumouriez, *Mémoires*, II, 153.

18. A. Söderjhelm, *Fersen et Marie-Antoinette. Correspondance et journal intime du comte Axel von Fersen*, Paris, 1930, 261.

19. Fersen to Taube, 29 July 1792, in Klinckowström, *Le comte de Fersen*, II, 33.

20. J. Arnaud-Bouteloup, *Le rôle politique de Marie-Antoinette*, Paris, 1924, 338.

21. Tourzel, *Mémoires*, II, 110.

22. *Procès de Marie-Antoinette*, Paris, 1793, reissued 1865, 117.

23. Campan, *Mémoires*, II, 198.

24. Pellenc to La Marck, late May 1792, published in Glagau, *Die französische Legislative*, 333.

25. A. Spawforth, *Versailles*, New York, 2008, 169.

26. Campan, *Mémoires*, II, 266–8.

27. Ibid., 231–3.

28. Ibid., 219.

29. Ibid., 240.

30. Tourzel, *Mémoires*, II, 175.

31. Madame de Staël's account, cited in J.-C. Petitfils, *Louis XVI*, Paris, 2005, 860.

32. Marquis de La Fayette, *Mémoires*, Paris, 1837, 6 vols, III, 346.

33. Ibid., 357.

34. Molleville, *Mémoires*, III, 10; La Fayette, *Mémoires*, III, 344.

35. La Fayette, *Mémoires*, III, 348.

36. Théodore de Lameth, *Notes et souvenirs*, ed. E. Welvert, Paris, 1913, 126–8.

37. La Fayette, *Mémoires*, IV, 346–7.

38. Note of 10 July, Klinckowström, *Le comte de Fersen*, II, 323.

39. Michon, *Adrien Duport*, 421; see also Mercy to Kaunitz, 31 July 1792, in Glagau, *Die französische Legislative*, 360–2, where the king is to be given 'powers approaching those which the English have delegated to their monarch' (my italics).

40. M. Price, *The Fall of the Monarchy: Louis XVI, Marie-Antoinette and the Baron de Breteuil*, London, 2002, 289–91.

41. Mercy to Kaunitz, 30 May 1792, published in Glagau, *Die französische Legislative*, 321.

42. Flammermont, 'La correspondance de Pellenc', 481–502.

43. Molleville, *Mémoires*, II, 170–80.

44. A. J. Barnave, *Oeuvres*, Paris, 1843, 4 vols, I, 106.

45. S. Padover, *The Life and Death of Louis XVI*, London, 1965, 258–9 and 265.

46. *Annales Historiques de la Révolution française* (1951), 198–201. At Marie-Antoinette's trial, Boze was questioned about what he termed 'a project to reconcile the former king with the people', but mentioned Thierry's role rather than his own, in *Procès de Marie-Antoinette*, 115.

47. Pellenc to La Marck, 5 August 1792, published in Glagau, *Die französische Legislative*, 366.

48. Roederer, *Chronique*, 299.

49. The following account of the rising is based mainly on Roederer, Mme de Tourzel and M. Reinhard, *10 août 1792: la chute de la royauté*, Paris, 1969, and Bigot de Sainte-Croix, *Histoire de la conspiration du 10 août 1792*, London, 1793.

50. Bigot, *Conspiration*, 34–5. Bigot was Louis XVI's last ministerial appointment.

51. Ibid., 45.

52. *Procès de Marie-Antoinette*, 41.

53. Bigot, *Conspiration*, 38.

54. Ibid., 27–8.

55. Tourzel, *Mémoires*, II, 109.

56. Bigot, *Conspiration*, 47.

57. Barnave, *Oeuvres*, I, 218.

58. Journal of John Moore, *Revue de la Révolution*, V (1883), 149.

59. Tourzel, *Mémoires*, II, 228–9.

12 IMPRISONMENT IN A TOWER

1. Marquis de Beaucourt, *Captivité et derniers moments de Louis XVI*, Paris, 1892, 2 vols, I, 240; J.-B. Cléry, *Journal de ce qui s'est passé à la tour du Temple pendant la captivité de Louis XVI, roi de France*, London, 1798, 40 and 52.

2. Beaucourt, *Captivité*, I, 214 and 240.

3. F. Hue, *Dernières années du règne de Louis XVI*, 3rd edn, Paris, 1860, 360; Cléry, *Journal*, 97.

4. Madame de Staël, *Réflexions sur le procès de la reine par une femme (anon.)*, Paris, 1793, 33.

5. G. Le Notre, *La captivité et la morte de Marie-Antoinette*, Paris, 1908, 59–63.

6. Cléry, *Journal*, 28–33.

7. Ibid., 211–13.

8. Ibid., 115–17.

9. Beaucourt, *Captivité*, I, 291.

10. Ibid., I, 19–20.

11. Ibid., I, 328 and 345; H. Edgeworth, abbé, *Dernières heures de Louis XVI*, Paris, 1816, 220.

12. Beaucourt, *Captivité*, II, 172, the account of the Semaines Parisiennes.

13. Le Notre, *Captivité*, 113–15.

14. Ibid., 92–5.

15. *Procès des Bourbons*, Hamburg, 1798, 2 vols, II, 192.

16. Le Notre, *Captivité*, 66.

17. Ibid., 79.

18. De Staël, *Réflexions sur le procès*, M. Cottret, 2006 edition of the above with commentary; Jacques Guilhaumou, review of the last in *La Révolution Française*, May 2006.

19. N. Col, *Révolution Française*, 4 (1997), 929.

20. De Staël, *Réflexions sur le procès*, 11.

21. L. C. Bigot de Sainte-Croix, *Histoire de la conspiration du 10 août 1792*, London, 1793, 100.

22. AP, LX, 59–61, cited by E. de Waresquiel, *Juger la Reine*, Paris, 2016, 22.

23. *Procès de Marie-Antoinette*, Paris 1793, reissued 1865, 128.

24. On the personnel of the Revolutionary Tribunal see J. Hardman, *Robespierre*, London and New York, 1999, 105–10.

25. Waresquiel, *Juger la Reine*, 135.

26. Ibid., 30–2.

27. *Procès de Marie-Antoinette*, 130.

28. Ibid., 11, cited in Waresquiel, *Juger la Reine*, 146.

29. *Procès des Bourbons*, I, 66.

30. E. Campardon, *Le Tribunal révolutionnaire de Paris*, Paris, 1866, 2 vols, I, 136.

31. Cited in Waresquiel, *Juger la Reine*, 179.

32. *Procès de Marie-Antoinette*, 127.

33. Ibid., 96.

34. Ibid., 120.

35. Ibid., 122.

36. Curiously, Artois' enemy Necker toyed with this idea.

37. H. Wallon, *Histoire du tribunal révolutionnaire de Paris*, Paris, 1880–2, 8 vols, I, 320–2.

38. *Procès de Marie-Antoinette*, 22, 80, 105.

39. Marie-Antoinette to Madame de Tourzel, 24 July 1789, Marie-Antoinette, *Correspondance de Marie-Antoinette*, ed. E. Lever, Paris, 2005, 489.

40. *Procès de Marie-Antoinette*, 28.

41. Anti-Fédéraliste, 15 October 1793, cited in Waresquiel, *Juger la Reine*, 194.

42. Ibid., 195.

43. Wallon, *Histoire*, I, 331; J. Vilate, *Causes secrètes de la Révolution du 9 au 10 thermidor*, Paris, year III [1795], 13.

44. Waresquiel, *Juger la Reine*, 130.

45. Ibid., 191, following Mallet du Pan and A. Aulard, *La Société des Jacobins*, Paris, 1897, 6 vols, V, 428.

46. *Procès de Marie-Antoinette*, 134.

47. Cited by Waresquiel, *Juger la Reine*, 235–6.

48. The following account of Marie-Antoinette's last hours is based on Le Notre, *Captivité*, 355–79.

49. *Procès de Marie-Antoinette*, 133.

50. Cited in P. de Ségur, *Marie-Antoinette*, London, 2015, 411.

CONCLUSION

1. J. L. H. Campan, *Mémoires sur la vie privée de Marie-Antoinette*, Paris, 1823, 2 vols, II, 31.

2. Ibid., 32.

3. Barnave to Marie Antoinette, 25 July 1791, Marie-Antoinette, *Correspondance de Marie-Antoinette*, ed. E. Lever, Paris, 2005, 560–1.

4. *Mémoires du comte Alexandre de Tilly*, Paris, 1828, 2 vols, I, 129.

5. J. Arnaud-Bouteloup, *Le rôle politique de Marie-Antoinette*, Paris, 1924, 168.

6. A & F, II, 211.

7. Abbé de Véri, Mss Cahier 158.

8. Mercy to Kaunitz, 10 March 1786, A & F, II, 11–12.

9. J.-L. Soulavie, *Mémoires historiques et politiques du règne de Louis XVI*, Paris, 1801, 6 vols, VI, 32–3.

10. M. Klinckowström, *Le comte de Fersen et la cour de France*, Paris, 1878, 2 vols, II, 7.

11. Mallet du Pan, *Mémoires et correspondances pour servir à l'histoire de la Révolution française*, ed. A. Sayous, Paris, 1851, 2 vols, II, 95.

12. M. A. de Bacourt, ed., *Correspondance entre le comte de Mirabeau et le comte de la Marck*, Paris, 1851, 2 vols, I, 162–3, and II, 100, La Marck to Mercy, 30 December 1790.

13. A. Lamartine, *Histoire des Girondins*, Paris, 1847, 8 vols, I, 175, cited in P. de Ségur, *Marie Antoinette*, London, 2015, 332.

14. Lamartine, *Girondins*, IV, 263.

15. E. Bradby, 'Marie Antoinette and the Constitutionalists; the Heidenstam Letters', *English Historical Review*, April 1916, 238–55, at 250–2.

EPILOGUE: *UBI SUNT?*

1. M. Klinckowström, *Le comte de Fersen et la cour de France*, Paris, 1878, 2 vols, I, 25.

2. Ibid., 15 and 20.

3. A. Fraser, *Marie-Antoinette*, London, 2001, 415.

4. E. Farr, *Marie-Antoinette and Count Fersen*, London, 2013, 264.
5. *The Memoirs of Madame Vigée-Lebrun*, trans. L Strachey, New York, 1903, Chapter 6, unpaginated,
6. M. Price, *The Fall of the Monarchy: Louis XVI, Marie-Antoinette and the Baron de Breteuil*, London, 2002, 345.
7. Unless otherwise stated the material for Barnave's trial and death is from E. Bradby, *The Life of Barnave*, Oxford, 1915, 2 vols, I, 329–35.
8. Barnave, *Oeuvres*, II, 342 and I, 220.
9. *Biographie de Bruxelles*, cited by the editor of J. L. H. Campan, *Mémoires sur la vie privée de Marie-Antoinette*, Paris, 1823, 205 n.
10. F. Vermale, 'Barnave: fragments inédits', *Bulletin de la Société d'archéologie, d'histoire et de géographie de la Drôme*, LXV – No. 265 – January 1935, 45–9 at 49; Marie-Antoinette to Fersen, 5 August 1792, Marie-Antoinette, *Correspondance de Marie-Antoinette*, ed. E. Lever, Paris, 2005, 810.
11. Mme G. de Staël, *Réflexions sur le procès de la reine par une femme* (anon.), Paris, 1793, 25.
12. D. Cadbury, *The Lost King of France*, New York, 2002.

A BIBLIOGRAPHICAL ESSAY

1. C. Berly, *Marie-Antoinette et ses biographes*, Paris, 2006.
2. E. Lever, *Marie-Antoinette*, Paris, 1991, and *Marie-Antoinette, Last Queen of France*, trans. C. Temerson, New York, 2000.
3. Marie-Antoinette, *Correspondance de Marie-Antoinette*, ed. Lever, Paris, 2005.
4. E. and J. Goncourt, *Histoire de Marie-Antoinette*, Slatkine reprints, 1986; J. Chalon, *Chère Marie-Antoinette*, Paris, 1988.
5. S. Zweig, *Marie-Antoinette: The Portrait of an Average Woman*, trans. E. and C. Paul, New York, 1933.
6. A second by Louis XVIII was written shortly thereafter, Louis XVIII, 'Réflections historiques sur Marie-Antoinette', *Revue des Deux Mondes* (1904), 241–63.
7. Mme G. de Staël, *Réflexions sur le procès de la reine par une femme (anon.)*, Paris, 1793, 13.

❖

A BIBLIOGRAPHICAL ESSAY

Writing an academic biography of Marie-Antoinette – one of the most popular of all historical subjects – is no easy task and indeed it has only been attempted once before. The title of Jeanne Arnaud-Bouteloup's 1924 *Le rôle politique de Marie-Antoinette* contains an unintended paradox: a queen of France, as Marie-Antoinette conceded, was not meant to have a political role. She did in fact stumble almost accidentally into one but only for two periods amounting in total to less than five years (1787–8 and 1791–2). So, even for an academic historian, her political role is not all there is to say about the queen. But Cécile Berly in *Marie-Antoinette et ses biographes* seems to imply that an academic biography is a contradiction in terms, though she relents in her final paragraph, having admitted the validity of such internet sites as *Let them eat cake* and souvenir mugs and cufflinks.[1]

Her real target, however, is what one might term the sheep in wolf's clothing. That is, the biography which puts the full panoply of scholarly apparatus – copious footnotes and bibliography – at the service of sales figures. Her particular *bête noire* is Evelyn Lever, whose *Marie-Antoinette* is chosen as the archetype of the genre. Such works as Lever's are often published by Fayard and typically contain a minimum of 700 widely spaced pages (boiled down to 300 in the American edition), have a mountainous bibliography, and the picture on the cover everyone expects.[2] It received glowing praise from popular journals but was studiously ignored by academic ones such as the *AHRF*, the central journal of the French Revolution. And this despite its scholarly apparatus and the fact that Lever has published the most easily accessible, if slightly incomplete, collection of Marie-Antoinette's correspondence.[3]

Works such as Lever's are sometimes written by members of the Académie française, which presents the English reader with the paradox of a work by an Academician who is not considered 'academic'. The British Academy is full of academics but sometimes important books fall outside its remit. Antonia

Fraser's *Marie-Antoinette*, although not written by an academic, may be considered to be in the Académie française tradition and is an excellent work.

Is it better to be ignored by the academic establishment or castigated by it? The latter has been the fate of the husband and wife team Paul and Pierrette Girault de Coursac. They ignore all but archival material in order to avoid preconceptions. However, they have their own *parti pris* and it is, for avowed royalists, an unusual not to say eccentric one: uniquely in the royalist tradition Marie-Antoinette is presented as the villain for neutering and betraying Louis XVI. Nevertheless, the Coursacs do fulfil one requirement of an academic book absent from Lever's: there is an argument, however eccentric and unconvincing many have found it to be. However, they deliberately ignore another criterion for an academic study: by dismissing historiography they necessarily fail to engage with other scholars, living or dead. This has inevitably incensed the former. And although to my mind there is too much such engagement today and historiography can be the enemy of originality, a degree of it is necessary to anchor a study.

Two of the five biographies Berly discusses are the productions of the brothers Goncourt and Chalon's *Chère Marie-Antoinette*, and these need not detain us.[4] But a third, Stefan Zweig's *Marie-Antoinette*, cannot be ignored, though Berly also notes Freud's gentle admonition to his friend that psychoanalysing the dead is a risky procedure. As one would expect from a close friend of Freud, Zweig devotes much space to a Freudian analysis of the late consummation of the marriage between Marie-Antoinette and Louis XVI and to the accusations of child molestation made against the former at her trial. Zweig's central argument, however, is proclaimed in his subtitle: *Marie-Antoinette: The Portrait of an Average Woman*.[5] In other words, in his view it was the Revolution that made her exceptional. A similar point was made by Jaurès a propos of Louis XVI: he owed his indisputably fine death to the Revolution.

An outstanding biography of Marie-Antoinette, first published in 1912 and perhaps the 'overall winner', is by Philippe de Ségur, despite (or because of) its author being from the Académie française which presumably utilizes the papers of his ancestor, a war minister and protégé of Marie-Antoinette's. Ségur was the first to gain access to the abbé de Véri's diary and he makes effective use of the information he unearthed.

The first serious study of Marie-Antoinette was written during her lifetime, though only just.[6] It was rushed out in August 1793, while the queen was still alive but awaiting trial, in a vain attempt to influence its outcome. Its author was Madame de Staël, celebrated bluestocking, daughter of a finance minister, lover of a war minister, and wife of an ambassador. While denying 'a superstitious

345

awe of Royalty', de Staël nevertheless finds the fall of the king and queen more affecting than that of mere mortals due to the contrast with past glories, 'because grief is a relative sensation . . . I measure the fall and suffer from each degree of it'. Recalling Marie-Antoinette's past pleasures, de Staël calls to mind the tomb placed in the grounds of the Trianon, the pleasure villa in the vast grounds of Versailles that Louis XVI gave her shortly after his accession in May 1774 when he was twenty and she nineteen. The inscription on the tomb reads 'Et moi aussi je vivais en Arcadia'.[7] In its more familiar Latin version it reads 'Et in Arcadia ego' ('I [death] am present even in Arcadia').

A part of the fascination with Marie-Antoinette's story lies in the apparent contrast between the happy-go-lucky dauphine and frivolous queen before the Revolution and the tragic destiny that awaited her.

BIBLIOGRAPHY

MANUSCRIPT SOURCES

Archives des Affaires Étrangères (A.A.E.)
M.D. (France) 1375–1400 for Vergennes.
Bibliothèque de l'Arsenal, MS 3978, the verbatim debates of Artois' bureau in the 1787 Assembly of Notables.

Archives Nationales (A.N.)
A.N. O1 354 (Maison du roi).
A.N. C220–3 (Convention Nationale, Papiers des Tuileries); four boxes of letters from and to Louis XVI, mostly after 1789, captured after 10 August.
A.N. C183–5, papers found in the Armoire de fer; documents considered important by the Convention are printed in Archives Parlementaires (abbreviated A.P.), LIV, 428ff.; there is a detailed inventory of the remainder in vol. LV, 668ff.
A.N. KK375, *Registre de perte et gain des parties de billard faites par le Roi contre la Reine et Madame Elizabeth à commencer du trente juillet 1791.*
K161, 163 and 164, 'cartons des rois'; communications to the king vastly outnumber those from him; K164, no. 3, correspondence with Vergennes, has been published together with Louis' surviving replies from the Tugny-Vergennes archive in *Louis XVI and the comte de Vergennes: Correspondence, 1774–1787*, ed. John Hardman and Munro Price, Oxford, 1998.
LA PORTE, ARNAUD DE, A.N. C192.

Archives Nationales (Archives Privées)
BRIENNE A.N. 4 A.P. 188.
CALONNE, A.N. 297 A.P. (especially 297 A.P. 3 fos 1–137 relating to the 1787 Assembly of Notables); A.N. K677 nos 102–79, many items covered by Calonne's private papers but in a more finished state.
CASTRIES, A.N. A.P. 306, the Castries Papers, especially 306.18–24.
MALESHERBES, A.N. 154 A.P. 11.147.
MIROMESNIL, A.N. K163 no. 8, letters to Louis XVI.
D'ORMESSON, A.N. 144 A.P. 130–3; the minister's diary is in 130 and the minutes of the Comité des finances at 131 *dossier* 5. Useful for the financing of the Polignacs, Vaudreuil and the rise of Calonne.

Bibliothèque Nationale (B.N.)
Archives Départementales de La Drôme (Valence), MSS Journal (unclassified); the archives also contain de Witte's copy of this diary of which *cahiers* 100–2 are missing in the original. Useful for Malesherbes and Miromesnil's (ignored) advice in the Diamond Necklace Affair.

Archives de la Marine, *Journal de Castries*, MS 182/7964, I–II; this diary by the queen's protégé is the indispensable guide to the crucial years, 1780–7.

Bibliothèque Municipale d'Orléans, MS 1421–3 (fragmentary memoirs left by the lieutenant de police Lenoir). Lenoir was a determined enemy of Marie-Antoinette in a key role.

Fonds Joly de Fleury, B.N. 1432–44.

B.N. nouv. ac.franc. 22103–12, Lefèvre d'Amécourt, king's agent in the Parlement (of special interest is his *Journal du règne de Louis XVI*, 22111, and the section *Ministres de Louis XVI*, starting at folio 1).

Public Record Office, Calonne papers, P.C.1/125.

PRINTED PRIMARY SOURCES

Adhémar, comtesse d', *Souvenirs sur Marie-Antoinette . . .*, Paris, 1836, 4 vols.

Allonville, comte d', *Mémoires secrets de 1770 à 1830*, Paris, 1838–45, 6 vols.

D'Angiviller, comte de, *Mémoires*, Copenhagen, 1933.

D'Arneth, A., *Marie-Antoinette, Joseph II und Leopold II*, 1866.

Assemblée des Notables de 1787, Procès-verbal, Paris, 1788.

Augeard, J. M., *Mémoires secrets*, ed. E. Bavoux, 1866.

Bachaumont, L. Petit de, *Mémoires secrets pour servir à l'histoire de la République des Lettres*, London, 1777–89, 36 vols.

Bacourt, M. A. de (ed.), *Correspondance entre le comte de Mirabeau et le comte de la Marck*, Paris, 1851, 2 vols.

Bailly, *Mémoires*, ed. S. A. Berville et J. F. Barrière, Paris, 1821, 3 vols.

Barentin, *Mémoire autographe sur les derniers Conseils du Roi Louis XVI*, ed. M. Champion, Paris, 1844.

Barentin, *Lettres et Bulletins à Louis XVI*, ed. A. Aulard, Paris, 1915.

Barnave, A. J., *Oeuvres*, Paris, 1843, 4 vols.

Barnave, A. J., *Introduction à la Révolution française*, ed. G. Rudé, 1960.

Beaumarchais, P.-A. Caron de, *Correspondance*, ed. B. Morton and D. Spinelli, Paris, 1969–78, 4 vols.

Bertrand de Molleville, A. F., *Mémoires secrets pour servir à l'histoire de la dernière année du règne de Louis XVI, roi de France*, London, 1797, 3 vols.

Besenval, baron de, *Mémoires*, ed. S. A. Berville and J. F. Barrière, Paris, 1821, 2 vols.

Besenval, baron de, *Mémoires du baron de Besenval*, ed. F. de Barrière, Paris, 1846.

Bigot de Saint-Croix, L. C., *Histoire de la conspiration du 10 août 1792*, London, 1793.

Billaud de Varennes, J. N., *Despotisme des ministres de France*, Amsterdam, 1789.

Boigne, comtesse de, *Mémoires*, Paris, 1982, 2 vols.

Bombelles, marquis de, *Journal*, ed. J. Grassion, F. Durif and J. Charon-Bordas, 4 vols, Geneva, 1978–98.

Bouillé, marquis de, *Memoires*, ed. S. A. Berville and J. F. Barrière, Paris, 1821.

Bouillé marquis de, *Souvenirs*, ed. P.-L. Kermaingant, Paris, 1906.

Brienne, comte de and Brienne, Lomenie de, *Journal de l'Assemblée des Notables de 1787*, ed. P. Chevallier, Paris, 1960.

Burke, E., *Reflections on the Revolution in France*, ed. L. G. Mitchell, Oxford, 1993.

Calonne, C. A. de (attrib.), *Les Comments*, Paris, 1781.

Calonne, C. A. de (attrib.), *Lettre du Marquis de Caraccioli à M. d'Alembert*, Paris, 1781.

Calonne, C. A. de, *Réponse de M. de Calonne à l'écrit de M. Necker, publié en avril 1787*, London, 1788.

Calonne, C. A. de, *Lettre au Roi*, London, 1789.

Campan, J. L. H., *Mémoires sur la vie privée de Marie-Antoinette*, Paris, 1823, 2 vols.

Castries, duc de, *Papiers de famille*, Paris, 1978.

Choiseul, duc de, *Relation du départ de Louis XVI le 20 juin 1791*, Paris, 1822.

Cléry, J.-B., *Journal de ce qui s'est passé à la tour du Temple pendant la captivité de Louis XVI, roi de France*, London, 1798.

BIBLIOGRAPHY

Croÿ, duc de, *Journal, 1718-1784*, ed. vicomte de Grouchy and P. Coffin, Paris, 1906-7, 4 vols.

Dispatches from Paris 1784-1790, ed. O. Browning, London, 1909-10.

Dumouriez, C. F., *Mémoires*, Paris, 1822-3, 4 vols.

Duquesnoy, Adrien, *Journal*, Paris, 1894, 2 vols.

Edgeworth, abbé H., *Dernières heures de Louis XVI*, Paris, 1816.

Elizabeth, Madame, *Correspondance*, ed. F. Feuillet de Conches, Paris, 1868.

Etats-Généraux, Lefèbvre, G. et al. (eds), *Recueil de documents relatifs aux Etats-Généraux de 1789*, Paris, 1953-70, 4 vols.

Flammermont, J., *Remonstrances du Parlement de Paris au XVIIIe siècle*, Paris 1888-98, 3 vols.

Flammermont, J., 'La correspondance de Pellenc avec les comtes de La Marck et Mercy', *Revue de la Révolution française*, vol. 16 (1889), 481-502.

Flammermont, J. (ed.), *Rapport . . . sur les correspondances des agents diplomatiques étrangères en France avant la Révolution*, Paris, 1896.

Fontanges, F. de, *La fuite du Roi* (Gallica download).

Fontanges, F. de, *L'arrestation de la famille royale à Varennes* (Gallica download).

Fortescue, Sir John (ed.), *George III, Correspondence 1760-1782*, London, 1927-8, 2 vols.

Géorgel, J.-F., *Mémoires pour servir à l'histoire des événements de la fin du XVIIIe siècle*, Paris, 1820.

Hardman, J. (ed.), *The French Revolution Sourcebook*, London and New York, 1999.

Hardman, J. and J. M. Roberts (eds), *French Revolution Documents*, Oxford, 1966-73.

Hardman, J. and M. Price (eds), *Louis XVI and the comte de Vergennes: Correspondence, 1774-1787*, Oxford, 1998.

Hézecques, comte de, *Page à la cour de Louis XVI, Souvenirs*, Paris, 1987.

Holland, Richard, Lord, *Foreign Reminiscences*, London, 1850.

Hue, F., *Dernières années du règne de Louis XVI*, 3rd edn, Paris, 1860.

Klinckowström, M., *Le comte de Fersen et la cour de France*, Paris, 1878, 2 vols.

La Fayette, marquis de, *Mémoires*, Paris, 1837, 6 vols.

Lally-Tollendal, article on Necker in the *Biographie-Michaud*.

Lameth, Alexandre de, *Histoire de l'Assemblée Constituante*, Paris, 1828.

Lameth, Théodore de, *Notes et souvenirs*, ed. E. Welvert, Paris, 1913.

Lescure, M. (ed.), *Correspondance secrète sur Louis XVI . . .*, Paris, 1866, 2 vols.

Le Tellier, Mayor of Harfleur, *Voyage de Louis XVI dans sa Province de Normandie*, Paris, 1787.

Lévis, duc de, *Portraits et souvenirs*, Paris, 1813.

Louis XV, *Lettres a son petit-fils . . .*, ed. P. Amiguet, Paris, 1938.

Louis XV, *Correspondance secrète inédite*, ed. M. E. Boutaric, Paris, 1866, 2 vols.

Louis XVI, *Réflexions sur mes Entretiens avec M. le Duc de La Vauguyon*, ed. E. Falloux, Paris, 1851.

Louis XVI, *Louis XVI a la parole*, ed. P. and P. Girault de Coursac, Paris, 1989.

Louis XVI, *Marie-Antoinette et Mme Elizabeth, lettres et documents inédits*, ed. F. Feuillet de Conches, Paris, 1864-9, 6 vols.

Louis XVIII, 'Réflections historiques sur Marie-Antoinette', *Revue des Deux Mondes* (1904), 241-63.

Louis-Philippe, *Memoirs*, ed. and trans. John Hardman, New York, 1977.

Luynes, duc de, *Mémoires du duc de Luynes sur la cour de Louis XV, 1735-58*, ed. L. Dussieux and E. Soulié, Paris, 1860-5, 17 vols.

Malesherbes, *Nouveaux documents inédits*, ed. P. Grosclaude, Paris, 1964.

Malesherbes à Louis XVI ou les Avertissements de Cassandra, Mémoires inédits 1787-1788, ed. V. André, Paris, 2010.

Mallet du Pan, *Mémoires et correspondances pour servir à l'histoire de la Révolution française*, ed. A. Sayous, Paris, 1851, 2 vols.

Malouet, P.-V., *Mémoires*, Paris, 1874, 2 vols.

Maria-Theresia und Marie-Antoinette ihr Briefwechsel, ed. A. von Arneth, Vienna, 1866.

Marie-Antoinette, *Correspondance secrète entre Marie-Thérèse et le comte de Mercy-Argenteau*, ed. A. d'Arneth and M. Geffroy, 2nd edn, Paris, 1875, 3 vols.

Marie-Antoinette, *Lettres*, ed. M. de La Rocheterie et le marquis de Beaucourt, Paris, 1895–6, 2 vols.

Marie-Antoinette, *Correspondance de Marie-Antoinette*, ed. E. Lever, Paris, 2005.

Marie-Antoinette, Joseph II und Leopold II ihr Briefwechsel, ed. A von Arneth, 2nd edn, Vienna, 1866.

Marie-Antoinette et Barnave, *Correspondance secrète*, ed. Alma Söderjhelm, Paris, 1934.

Marie-Antoinette, Fersen et Barnave, ed. O.-G. Heidenstam, Paris, 1913.

Marie-Antoinette and Count Fersen, *'I Love You Madly': Marie-Antoinette and Count Fersen, the Secret Letters*, ed. E. Farr, London, 2016.

Marmontel, *Mémoires*, ed. M. Tourneux, Paris, 1891, 3 vols.

Marmontel, *Mémoires*, ed. J. Renwick, Paris, 1972, 2 vols.

Mercy-Argenteau, *Correspondance secrète . . . avec l'Empereur Joseph II et le Prince de Kaunitz*, ed. A. d'Arneth and J. Flammermont, Paris, 1891, 2 vols.

Montbarey, prince de, *Mémoires du Prince de Montbarey*, Paris, 1826–7, 3 vols.

Montjoie, *Éloge historique et funèbre de Louis XVI*, Paris, 1796.

Montmorency-Luxembourg, duc de, *Le duc de Montmorency-Luxembourg*, ed. Paul Filleul, Paris, 1939.

Montyon, Auget de, *Particularités sur les ministres des finances les plus célèbres*, Paris, 1812.

Moreau, J. N., *Mes souvenirs*, Paris, 1898–1901, 2 vols.

Morellet, abbé de, *Lettres à Lord Shelburne depuis 1772 jusqu'à 1803*, ed. E. Fitzmaurice, Paris, 1898.

Necker, J., *Mémoire*, Paris, 6 March 1787.

Necker, J., *Sur l'administration de M. Necker par lui-même*, Paris, 1791.

Necker, J., *De la Révolution française*, Paris, 1797, 3 vols.

Paine, Thomas, *The Rights of Man*, ed. George Jacob Holyoake, London, 1950.

Papon, abbé, *Histoire du Gouvernement français depuis l'Assemblée des Notables tenue le 22 février 1787, jusqu'à la fin de Décembre du même année*, London, 1788.

Paroy, comte de, *Mémoires*, Paris, 1895.

Peuchet, J., *Archives de police de Paris*, Paris, 1838.

Polignac, Diane de, *Journal d'Italie et de Suisse* (1789) (Gallica download).

Procès des Bourbons, Hamburg, 1798, 2 vols.

Procès de Marie-Antoinette, Paris 1793, reissued 1865.

Procès-Verbal de l'Assemblée Générale des électeurs de Paris, Paris, 1790.

Proyart, abbé, *Oeuvres complètes*, Paris, 1819, 6 vols.

Raigecourt-Bombelles, *Correspondance du Marquis et de la Marquise de Raigecourt avec le Marquis et la Marquise de Bombelles pendant l'émigration, 1790–1800*, ed. M. de la Rocheterie, Paris, 1892.

Robespierre, M., *Oeuvres*, ed. Société des études Robespierristes, Paris, 1912–67, 10 vols.

Roederer, P. L., *Chronique de cinquante jours*, Paris, 1832.

Roland, Madame, *Mémoires*, Paris, 2004.

Saint-Priest, comte de, *Mémoires*, ed. baron de barante, Paris, 1929.

Sallier-Chaumont de Laroche, G., *Annales françaises depuis le commencement du règne de Louis XVI jusqu'aux états-généraux, 1774–1789*, Paris, 1813.

Ségur, comte de, *Mémoires ou souvenirs et anecdotes*, Paris, 1827, 3 vols.

Sénac de Meilhan, *Du gouvernement, des moeurs et des conditions en France avant la Révolution, avec le caractère des principaux personnages du règne de Louis XVI*, London, 1795.

Soulavie, J.-L., *Mémoires historiques et politiques du règne de Louis XVI*, Paris, 1801, 6 vols.

Soulavie, J.-L., *Historical and Political Memoirs of the Reign of Louis XVI from his Marriage to his Death*, London, 1802, 6 vols.

Staël, Mme G. de, *Réflexions sur le procès de la reine par une femme (anon)*, Paris, 1793.

Staël, Mme G. de, *Considérations sur . . . la Révolution française*, op. posth., Paris, 1843.

Staël-Holstein, baron de, *Correspondance diplomatique*, ed. L. Leouzon Le Duc, Paris, 1881.

Target, G.-J.-B., *Observations sur le procès de Louis XVI*, Paris, 1793.

Tilly, comte de, *Mémoires du comte Alexandre de Tilly*, Paris, 1828, 2 vols.

Tourzel, duchesse de, *Mémoires*, ed. duc des Cars, Paris, 1904, 2 vols.

Turgot, A. J. R., *Oeuvres*, ed. G. Schelle, Paris, 1913–23, 5 vols.

Vaudreuil, *Correspondance intime du comte de Vaudreuil et du comte d'Artois*, ed. L. Pingaud, Paris, 1889, 2 vols.

Véri, abbé de, *Journal, 1774–1780*, ed. J. de Witte, Paris, 1928–30, 2 vols.

Vigée-Lebrun, Élisabeth, *The Memoirs of Madame Vigée-Lebrun*, trans. L. Strachey, New York, 1903.

Vilate, J., *Causes secrètes de la Révolution du 9 au 10 thermidor*, Paris, year III [1795].

Walpole, H., *Règne de Richard III, ou doutes historiques sur les crimes qui lui sont imputés*, trans. Louis XVI, ed. Roussel L'Epinal, Paris, 1800.

Weber, *Mémoires concernant Marie-Antoinette*, ed. S. A. Berville et J. F. Barrière, Paris, 1822, 2 vols.

SECONDARY SOURCES

Adamson, J., *The Noble Revolt*, London, 2007.

Antoine, M., *Louis XV*, Paris, 1989.

Arnaud-Bouteloup, J., *Le rôle politique de Marie-Antoinette*, Paris, 1924.

Arneth, A. von, *Maria-Theresia und Marie-Antoinette ihr Briefwechsel*, Vienna, 1866.

Aston, N., *The End of an Elite: The French Bishops and the Coming of the French Revolution, 1786–1790*, Oxford, 1992.

Beales, D., *Joseph II*, vol. 1, Cambridge, 1987.

Beaucourt, marquis de, *Captivité et derniers moments de Louis XVI*, Paris, 1892, 2 vols.

Berly, C., *Marie-Antoinette et ses biographes*, Paris, 2006.

Bimbenet, E., *La fuite de Louis XVI à Varennes*, 1868.

Blanc, L., *Histoire de la Révolution française*, 1847–63, 12 vols.

Blanning, T. C. W., *The Origins of the French Revolutionary Wars*, London, 1986.

Blanning, T. C. W., *Joseph II*, London and New York, 1994.

Blanning, T. C. W., *The French Revolution: Class War or Culture Clash*, 2nd ed., Basingstoke, 1998.

Boisnard, L., *Les Phélypeaux*, Paris, 1986.

Bosher, J., *French Public Finances 1770–95*, Cambridge, 1970.

Bradby, E., *The Life of Barnave*, Oxford, 1915, 2 vols.

Browne, R., 'The Diamond Necklace Affair Revisited', *Renaissance and Modern Studies*, 33 (1989).

Burley, P., 'Louis XVI and a New Monarchy', unpublished PhD thesis, University of London (1981).

Cadbury, D., *The Lost King of France*, New York, 2002.

Caiani, A., *Louis XVI and the French Revolution 1789–1792*, Cambridge, 2012.

Campardon, E., *Le Tribunal révolutionnaire de Paris*, Paris, 1866, 2 vols.

Campbell, P. R., *Power and Politics in Old Regime France 1720–1745*, London and New York, 1996.

Caron, P., 'La Tentative de contre-révolution de juin–juillet 1789', *Revue d'histoire moderne*, 8 (1906), 5–34 and 649–78.

Carrè, H., *Quelque mots sur la presse clandestine*, Paris, 1893.

Chapman, C. and J. Dormer, *Elizabeth and Georgiana*, London, 2002.

Chaumié, J., *Le réseau d'Antraigues et la Contre-Révolution*, Paris, 1965.

Chérest, A., *La chute de l'Ancien Régime, 1787–1789*, Paris, 1884–6, 3 vols.

Cobb, R., *The Police and the People: French Popular Protest 1789–1820*, Oxford, 1970.

Cochin, A., *Les sociétés de pensée et la Révolution en Bretagne (1788–1789)*, Paris, 1925, 2 vols.

Collins, J., *The State in Early Modern France*, Cambridge, 1995.

Corwin, E. S., 'The French Objective in the American Revolution', *American Historical Review*, 21 (1915–16), 33–61.

Darnton, R., *The Literary Underground of the Old Regime*, Cambridge, MA, 1982.

Doniol, H., *Histoire de la participation de la France à l'établissement des États-Unis d'Amérique*, Paris, 1886–9, 5 vols.

Droz, J. F. X., *Histoire du règne de Louis XVI*, Brussels, 1839, 2 vols.

Duindam, J., *Vienna and Versailles: The Courts of Europe's Dynastic Rivals, 1550–1780*, Cambridge, 2003.

Dull, J., *The French Navy and Independence: A Study of Arms and Diplomacy, 1774–1787*, Princeton, NJ, 1975.

Dunlop, I., *Marie-Antoinette*, London, 1993.

Dussieux, L., *Le Château de Versailles*, Versailles, 1881, 2 vols.

Echeverria, D., *The Maupeou Revolution*, Baton Rouge, LO, 1985.

Egret, J., 'La seconde Assemblée des Notables', *Annales Historiques de la Révolution française* (1949), 193–228.

Egret, J., *La Pré-Révolution française 1787–1788*, Paris, 1962.

Egret, J., *Necker*, Paris, 1975.

Farr, E., *Marie-Antoinette and Count Fersen*, London, 2013.

Félix, J., 'The Financial Origins of the French Revolution', in P. Campbell (ed.), *The Origins of the French Revolution*, Basingstoke, 2005, 35–62.

Félix, J., *Louis XVI et Marie-Antoinette*, Paris, 2006.

Fitzsimmons, M., 'Privilege and the Polity in France, 1786–1791', *American Historical Review*, 92 (1987), 269–95.

Fitzsimmons, M., 'The Committee of the Constitution and the Remaking of France, 1787–1791', *French History*, vol. 4, no. 1 (1990), 23–47.

Fitzsimmons, M., 'From the Estates-General to the National Assembly, May 5–August 4, 1789', in P. Campbell (ed.), *The Origins of the French Revolution*, Basingstoke, 2005, 268–89.

Flammermont, J., *Négotiations secrètes de Louis XVI et du baron de Breteuil avec la cour de Berlin (décembre 1791–juillet 1792)*, Paris, 1885.

Flammermont, J., 'La correspondance de Pellenc avec les comtes de La Marck et Mercy', *Revue de la Révolution française*, 16 (1889), 481–502.

Fleischmann, H., *Madame de Polignac et la cour galante de Marie-Antoinette*, Paris, 1910.

Foreman, A., *Georgiana, Duchess of Devonshire*, London, 1999.

Fraser, A., *Marie-Antoinette*, London, 2001.

Fréville, H., *L'Intendance de Bretagne, 1689–1790*, Rennes, 1953, 3 vols.

Funck-Brentano, F., *L'affaire du collier*, Paris, 1903.

Geoffroy, A., *Gustave III et la cour de France*, Paris, 1866–7, 2 vols.

Girault de Coursac, P., *L'éducation d'un roi, Louis XVI*, Paris, 1972.

Girault de Coursac, P. and P., *Enquête sur le procès du roi Louis XVI*, Paris, 1982.

Girault de Coursac, P. and P., *Sur la route de Varennes*, Paris, 1984.

Girault de Coursac, P. and P., *Louis XVI et Marie-Antoinette. Vie conjugale, vie politique*, Paris, 1990.

Glagau, H., *Die französische Legislative . . . 1791–92*, Berlin, 1896.

Glagau, H., *Reformversuche und Sturz des Absolutismus in Frankreich (1774–1788)*, Munich, 1908.

Goodwin, A., 'Calonne, the Assembly of French Notables of 1787 and the Origins of the "Révolte Nobiliaire"', *English Historical Review*, CCLX (May 1946), 202–34, and CCLXI (September 1946), 329–77.

Gottschalk, L., *Lafayette between the American and French Revolution, 1783–1789*, Chicago, IL, 1950.

Gottschalk, L., *Lafayette in the French Revolution*, Chicago, IL, 1973.

Granier de Cassignac, M. A., *Histoire des causes de la Révolution française*, Paris, 1850.

Griffiths, R., *Le centre perdu, Malouet et les 'monarchiens'*, Grenoble, 1988.

Grosclaude, P., *Malesherbes*, Paris, 1961.

Gruder, V., 'Les Notables à la fin de l'ancien régime: L'*Avertissement* de 1787', *DHS*, 14 (1982) 45–56.

Gruder, V., *The Notables and the Nation . . . 1787–1788*, Cambridge, MA, and London, 2007.

Habermas, J., *The Structural Transformation of the Public Sphere: An Enquiry into a Category of Bourgeois Society*, 1962, Cambridge, MA, 1989.

Hampson, N., *Prelude to Terror*, Oxford, 1988.

Hardman, J., *French Politics 1774–1789*, London, 1995.

Hardman, J., *Robespierre*, London and New York, 1999.

Hardman, J., *Louis XVI: The Silent King*, London, 2000.

Hardman, J., *Overture to Revolution: The 1787 Assembly of Notables and the Crisis of France's Old Regime*, Oxford and New York, 2010.

Hardman, J., *The Life of Louis XVI*, New Haven, CT, and London, 2016.

Harris, R. D., *Necker, Reform Statesman of the Ancien Régime*, Berkeley, CA, 1979.

Harris, R. D., *Necker in the Revolution of 1789*, London, 1986.

Henshall, N., *The Myth of Absolutism: Change and Continuity in Early Modern European Monarchy*, London, 1992.

Hudson, R., *The Minister from France, Conrad-Alexandre Gérard, 1729–1790*, Euclid, OH, 1994.

Ilovaisky, O., *La Disgrâce de Calonne*, Paris, 2008.

Jarrett, D., *The Begetters of Revolution. England's Involvement with France, 1759–1789*, London, 1973.

Jones, P.M., *Reform and Revolution in France: The Politics of Transition, 1774–1791*, Cambridge, 1995.

Jordan, D., *The King's Trial*, Berkeley, CA, and London, 1979.

Kaiser, T., 'Who's Afraid of Marie-Antoinette? Diplomacy, Austrophobia and the Queen', *French History*, 14 (2000), 241–71.

Kaiser, T., 'From the Austrian Committee to the Foreign Plot: Marie-Antoinette, Austrophobia and the Terror', *French Historical Studies*, 26 (2003) 579–617.

Kaplan, S., *Bread, Politics and Political Economy in the Reign of Louis XV*, The Hague, 1976, 2 vols.

Kennedy, M., *The Jacobin Clubs in the French Revolution: The First Years*, Princeton, NJ, 1982.

van Kley, D., *The Religious Origins of the French Revolution . . . 1560–1791*, New Haven, CT, and London, 1996.

Kwass, M. D., *Privilege and the Politics of Taxation in Eighteenth-Century France: Liberté, egalité, fiscalité*, Cambridge, 2000.

Labourdette, J. F., *Vergennes, ministre principal de Louis XVI*, Paris, 1990.

Lacour-Gayet, R., *Calonne*, Paris, 1963.

Lamartine, A., *Histoire des Girondins*, Paris, 1847, 8 vols.

Laugier, L., *Turgot*, Paris, 1979.

Lenotre, G., *Le drame de Varennes*, 39th edn, Paris, 1924.

Lenotre, G., *La captivité et la mort de Marie-Antoinette*, Paris, 1908.

Lever, E., *Louis XVI*, Paris, 1985.

Lever, E., *Marie Antoinette*, trans. C. Temerson, New York, 2000.

Luçay, comte de, *Les secrétaires d'Etat en France depuis les origines jusqu'à 1774*, Paris, 1881.

Luckner, B. A., 'The Role of the French Bishops in the Aristocratic Revolt of 1787–88', University of Manchester MA thesis, 1969.

Lüthy, H., *La Banque Protestante en France*, Paris, 1959–61, 2 vols.

Mansel, P., *Louis XVIII*, London, 1981.

Mansel, P., *The Court of France, 1789–1830*, Cambridge, 1988.

Marion, M., *Dictionnaire des institutions de la France xviie–xviiie siècles*, Paris, 1989.

Mathews, G. T., *The Royal General Farms*, New York, 1958.

Mathiez, A., 'Les Girondins et la Cour à la veille du 10 août', *Annales historiques de la Révolution française* (1931), 193–212.

Maugras, G., *Lauzun*, Paris, 1907.

de Maupeou, J., *Le Chancelier Maupeou*, Paris, 1942.

Melton, J. van H., *The Rise of the Public in Enlightenment Europe*, Cambridge, 2000.

Michelet, J., *Histoire de la Révolution française*, ed. G. Walter, Paris, 1952, 2 vols.

Michelet, J., *History of the French Revolution*, trans. C. Cocks, Chicago, IL, 1967.

Michon, G., *Adrien Duport et le parti feuillant*, Paris, 1924. The appendix has some of Barnave's correspondence.

Morineau, M., 'Budgets de l'Etat et gestion des finances royales en France au dix-huitième siècle', *Revue Historique*, CCLXIV, no. 2 (1980), 289–335.

Morris, R., *The Peacemakers: The Great Powers and American Independence*, New York, 1965.

Mortimer-Ternaux, M., *Histoire de la Terreur*, Paris, 1862–81, 8 vols.

Mousnier, R., *Les institutions de la France sous la monarchie absolue*, vol. II, Paris, 1974.

Mousset, A., *Un témoin ignoré de la Révolution. Le comte de Fernan Nunez*, Paris, 1924.

de Nolhac, P., *Marie-Antoinette dauphine*, Paris, 1929.

Padover, S., *The Life and Death of Louis XVI*, London, 1965.

Patterson, A. T., *The Other Armada: The Franco-Spanish Attempt to Invade Britain in 1779*, Manchester, 1960.

Petitfils, J.-C., *Louis XVI*, Paris, 2005.

Pimodan, comte de, *Le comte de Mercy-Argenteau*, Paris, 1911.

Price, M., 'The "Ministry of the Hundred Hours": A Reappraisal', *French History*, 4, no. 3 (1990), 318–39.

Price, M., *Preserving the Monarchy: The comte de Vergennes, 1774–1787*, Cambridge, 1995.

Price, M., *The Fall of the Monarchy: Louis XVI, Marie-Antoinette and the Baron de Breteuil*, London, 2002.

Price, M., 'Mirabeau and the Court: Some New Evidence', *French Historical Studies*, 29, no. 1 (2006), 37–76.

Pugh, W., 'Calonne's New Deal', *Journal of Modern History*, vol. 11 (September 1939), 289–312.

Ranke, A. von, *Über Die Versammlung der französischen Notabeln im Jahre 1787*, Berlin, 1846.

Reinhard, M., *10 août 1792: la chute de la royauté*, Paris, 1969.

Renouvin, P., *Les Assemblées Provinciales de 1787*, Paris, 1921.

Schama, S., *Citizens*, London, 1989.

Schelle, G., *Du Pont de Nemours et l'école physiocratique*, Paris, 1888.

Scott, H., *British Foreign Policy in the Age of the American Revolution*, London, 1990.

Scott, S. F., *The Response of the Royal Army to the French Revolution . . . 1787–93*, Oxford, 1973.

de Ségur, P., *Marie-Antoinette*, London, 2015.

Shapiro, B., 'Revolutionary Justice in 1789–1790: The Comité des Recherches, the Châtelet, and the Fayettist Coalition', *French Historical Studies*, vol. 17, no. 3 (Spring 1992), 656–69.

Shapiro, B. M., *Revolutionary Justice in Paris, 1789–1790*, Cambridge, 1993.

Shapiro, B. M., *Traumatic Politics: The Deputies and the King in the Early French Revolution*, University Park, PA, 2009.

Skocpol, T., *States and Social Revolutions: A Comparative Analysis of France, Russia and China*, Cambridge, 1979.

Söderjhelm, A., *Fersen et Marie-Antoinette. Correspondance et journal intime du comte Axel von Fersen*, Paris, 1930.

Sonenscher, M., *Sans-Culottes*, Princeton, NJ, 2008.

Sorel, A., *L'Europe et la Révolution française, vol. II, La chute de la royauté*, Paris, 1908.

Sorel, A., *Europe and the French Revolution: The Political Traditions of the Old Regime*, trans. and ed. A. Cobban and J. W. Hunt, London, 1969.

Spawforth, A., *Versailles*, New York, 2008.

Stone, B., *The Parlement of Paris 1774–1789*, Chapel Hill, NC, 1981.

Stone, B., *The Genesis of the French Revolution: A Global-Historical Interpretation*, Cambridge, 1994.

Suzanne, G., *La tactique financière de Calonne*, Paris, 1901.

Swann, J., *Politics and the Parlement of Paris under Louis XV, 1754–1774*, Cambridge, 1995.

Tackett, T., *Becoming a Revolutionary*, University Park, PA, 2006.

Thiers, A., *Histoire de la Révolution française*, Brussels, 1844, 2 vols.

de Tocqueville, A., *Coup d'oeil sur le règne de Louis XVI*, Paris, 1850.

de Tocqueville, A., *The Ancien Régime and the French Revolution*, ed. H. Brogan, London, 1966.

Wahl, W. A., *Die Notabelnversammlung von 1787*, Freiburg im Breisgau, 1899.

Wallon, H., *Histoire du tribunal révolutionnaire de Paris*, Paris, 1880–2, 8 vols.

Walzer, M., *Regicide and Revolution*, Cambridge, 1974.

de Waresquiel, E., *Juger la Reine*, Paris, 2016.

Welshinger, H., *La mission secrète de Mirabeau à Berlin (1786–1787)*, Paris, 1900.

Wick, D., 'The Court Nobility and the French Revolution: The Example of the Society of Thirty', *Eighteenth Century Studies*, XIII (1980), 263–84.

Wick, D., *A Conspiracy of Well-Intentioned Men: The Society of Thirty and the French Revolution*, New York, 1987.

Zweig, S., *Marie Antoinette: The Portrait of an Average Woman*, trans. E. and C. Paul, New York, 1933.

INDEX